《中国贸易外经统计年鉴－2018》编辑委员会

2018 CHINA TRADE AND EXTERNAL ECONOMIC STATISTICAL YEARBOOK

Editorial Staff

Editor-in-Chief: Meng Qingxin Lin Tao

Associate Editor-in-Chief: Ye Jingyi Lu Shan

Editorial Staff: (in order of the number of strokes of the Chinese character of the surname)

Wan Ping Wang Yuexiang Shen Junli Fu Yuan

Fu Jiaqi Liu Yang Liu Xuling Liu Xiaoyan

Tang Weiwei Yan Xianpu Du Yan Li Dan

Li Min Zhang Min Chen Qunlin Luo Weihua

Hu Chunlin Yao Hu Yuan Yan Xia Huan

Executive Editor: Xu Lifang Ding Xiaoshan

English Translator: She Jingxiong

编者说明

一、《中国贸易外经统计年鉴—2018》是一部全面反映中国国内贸易、对外经济贸易和旅游业发展情况的资料性年刊。本年鉴收录了2017年中国国内消费品市场、批发和零售业、住宿和餐饮业、国际收支、对外贸易、利用外资、对外投资与经济合作和国内、国际旅游的主要统计数据，以及分省、自治区、直辖市和一些重要历史年份的相关统计数据。

二、本年鉴正文内容分为9个部分：1.综合篇；2.消费品市场篇；3.批发和零售业篇；4.住宿和餐饮业篇；5.国际收支篇；6.对外贸易篇；7.利用外资篇；8对外投资与经济合作篇；9.旅游篇。为便于读者使用，本年鉴对所用略语和主要统计指标的含义、统计范围和统计方法作了简要说明。

三、本年鉴中所涉及的全国性统计数据，均未包括香港、澳门特别行政区和台湾省数据。

四、本年鉴所列对外经济贸易和旅游统计资料由国家统计局贸易外经司根据商务部、海关总署、国家外汇管理局、公安部、文化和旅游部、国家市场监督管理总局等部门的资料加工整理，由于各部门职能不同，统计口径、范围和方法亦有所不同，因此书中有些数据可能不一致，使用统计数据时请参看附录。

五、本年鉴表中所使用的度量衡单位，均为国际统一标准计量单位。

六、年鉴表中的“空格”表示该项统计指标数据不足本表最小单位数、不详或无该项数据；“#”表示其中的主要项；“*”或“①”表示本表下有注释。

七、年鉴中没有标明年份的表均为2017年的数据。

PREFACE

I.*2018 China Trade and External Economic Statistical Yearbook* reflects the situation of China in the development of the domestic and foreign trade, the external economic transactions and the tourism synthetically. The yearbook covers the main data of the domestic trade, balance of payments, foreign trade, utilization of foreign capital, overseas direct investment and economic cooperation, and tourism of China in 2017, and embodies the data from national level and all the provinces, autonomous regions and municipalities. It also lists the time series relative data of important indicators by years.

II.The yearbook contains the following 9 chapters: 1.Integration; 2.Consumer Goods Market; 3.Wholsale and Retail Trades; 4.Hotels and Catering Services; 5. Balance of Payments; 6. Foreign Trade; 7. Utilization of Foreign Capital; 8.Overseas Direct Investment and Economic Cooperation; 9.Tourism. In addition, Explanatory Notes on Main Statistical Indicators are provided at the end of book.

III.The national data in the book do not include that of Hongkong Special Administrative Region, Macao Special Administrative Region and Taiwan Province.

IV.The major sources of data except these in the domestic trade are the regular statistical reporting forms provided by the relevant departments such as the Ministry of Commerce, the General Administration of Customs, the State Administration of Foreign Exchange ,the Ministry of Public Security, the Ministry of Culture and Tourism, the State Administration for Market Regulation. The book is edited by the Department of Trade and External Economic Relation Statistics of the National Bureau of Statistics. Since the functions of departments mentioned above are different, the requirement, the scope, the calculating specification and the method of statistics are not in the same, and some of the figures may not be in conformity. Readers who want to use the data please consult the explanatory note.

V.The units of measurement used in this yearbook are internationally standard measurement units.

VI.Notations used in the yearbook: (blank space) indicates that the figure is not large enough to be measured with the smallest unit in the table, or data are unknown or are not available; "#" indicates a major breakdown of the total; and "*" or "①" indicates footnotes at the end of the table.

VII.The data belong to 2017 in the table of without year in the yearbook.

目　　录

CONTENTS

第 1 篇　综合

Integration

第 2 篇　消费品市场

Consumer Goods Market

第3篇 批发和零售业
Wholesale and Retail Trades

第 4 篇 住宿和餐饮业
Hotels and Catering Services

第 5 篇　国际收支
Balance of Payments

第 6 篇　对外贸易
Foreign Trade

第 7 篇 利用外资

Utilization of Foreign Capital

第 8 篇 对外投资与经济合作

Overseas Direct Investment and Economic Cooperation

第 9 篇 旅游

Tourism

附 录

APPENDIX

综　合

INTEGRATION

第1篇

1-1 国内生产总值指数
Indices of Gross Domestic Product

(不变价，上年=100；Constant Price, Preceding Year=100)

年 份 Year	国民总收入 Gross National Income	国内生产总值 Gross Domestic Product	第一产业 Primary Industry	第二产业 Secondary Industry	第三产业 Tertiary Industry	#批发与零售业 Wholesale and Retail Trades	人均国内生产总值 Per Capita GDP
1978	111.7	111.7	104.1	115.0	113.8	123.1	110.2
1979	107.6	107.6	106.1	108.2	107.9	108.7	106.1
1980	107.8	107.8	98.5	113.6	106.0	98.1	106.5
1981	105.2	105.2	107.0	101.9	110.4	129.5	103.9
1982	109.2	109.1	111.5	105.6	113.0	99.3	107.5
1983	111.1	110.9	108.3	110.4	115.2	121.2	109.3
1984	115.3	115.2	112.9	114.5	119.3	124.7	113.7
1985	113.2	113.5	101.8	118.6	118.2	133.5	111.9
1986	108.5	108.8	103.3	110.2	112.0	109.4	107.2
1987	111.5	111.6	104.7	113.7	114.4	114.7	109.8
1988	111.3	111.3	102.5	114.5	113.2	111.8	109.5
1989	104.2	104.1	103.1	103.8	105.4	89.3	102.5
1990	104.1	103.8	107.3	103.2	102.3	94.7	102.3
1991	109.1	109.2	102.4	113.9	108.9	105.2	107.7
1992	114.1	114.2	104.7	121.2	112.4	110.5	112.8
1993	113.7	114.0	104.7	119.9	112.2	108.6	112.7
1994	113.1	113.1	104.0	118.4	111.1	108.2	111.8
1995	109.3	110.9	105.0	113.9	109.8	108.2	109.7
1996	110.1	110.0	105.0	112.1	109.2	107.6	108.8
1997	109.6	109.2	103.4	110.5	110.4	108.8	108.1
1998	107.3	107.8	103.4	108.9	108.4	106.5	106.8
1999	107.9	107.6	102.7	108.2	109.2	108.7	106.7
2000	108.6	108.4	102.3	109.4	109.7	109.4	107.6
2001	108.1	108.3	102.6	108.4	110.2	109.1	107.5
2002	109.5	109.1	102.7	109.8	110.5	108.8	108.4
2003	110.5	110.0	102.4	112.7	109.5	109.9	109.3
2004	110.5	110.1	106.1	111.1	110.1	106.6	109.4
2005	110.9	111.3	105.1	112.1	112.3	113.0	110.7
2006	113.3	112.7	104.8	113.4	114.1	119.5	112.1
2007	114.7	114.2	103.5	115.0	116.1	120.2	113.6
2008	110.1	109.6	105.2	109.8	110.5	115.9	109.1
2009	108.4	109.2	104.0	110.1	109.5	111.9	108.7
2010	110.3	110.6	104.3	112.7	109.7	114.6	110.1
2011	108.9	109.5	104.2	110.6	109.5	112.5	109.0
2012	108.5	107.7	104.5	108.2	108.0	110.3	107.2
2013	107.1	107.7	103.8	107.9	108.3	110.5	107.2
2014	108.3	107.3	104.1	107.3	107.8	109.7	106.7
2015	106.4	106.9	103.9	106.2	108.2	106.1	106.4
2016	106.7	106.7	103.3	106.1	107.8	106.7	106.1
2017	107.0	106.9	103.9	106.1	108.0	107.1	106.3

1-2 国内生产总值构成

Composition of Gross Domestic Product

（当年价，Current Price）

年 份 Year	国内生产总值 Gross Domestic Product (%)	第一产业 Primary Industry	第二产业 Secondary Industry	第三产业 Tertiary Industry	#批发与零售业 Wholesale and Retail Trades
1978	100	27.9	47.6	24.5	6.6
1979	100	30.9	46.8	22.3	4.9
1980	100	29.9	47.9	22.2	4.3
1981	100	31.6	45.8	22.6	4.7
1982	100	33.0	44.5	22.5	3.2
1983	100	32.8	44.1	23.1	3.3
1984	100	31.8	42.8	25.5	5.0
1985	100	28.1	42.6	29.3	8.9
1986	100	26.8	43.4	29.8	8.3
1987	100	26.5	43.2	30.3	8.8
1988	100	25.4	43.4	31.2	9.8
1989	100	24.7	42.4	32.9	9.0
1990	100	26.7	40.9	32.4	6.8
1991	100	24.2	41.4	34.5	8.4
1992	100	21.4	43.0	35.6	8.9
1993	100	19.4	46.1	34.5	7.9
1994	100	19.5	46.1	34.4	7.8
1995	100	19.7	46.7	33.7	7.8
1996	100	19.4	47.0	33.6	7.8
1997	100	18.0	47.0	35.0	8.0
1998	100	17.2	45.7	37.1	8.1
1999	100	16.1	45.3	38.6	8.3
2000	100	14.7	45.4	39.8	8.2
2001	100	14.1	44.7	41.3	8.3
2002	100	13.4	44.3	42.3	8.3
2003	100	12.4	45.5	42.1	8.2
2004	100	13.0	45.8	41.2	7.7
2005	100	11.7	46.9	41.4	7.5
2006	100	10.7	47.4	41.9	7.6
2007	100	10.4	46.7	42.9	7.8
2008	100	9.9	46.8	42.9	8.3
2009	100	9.9	45.7	44.4	8.4
2010	100	9.6	46.2	44.2	8.8
2011	100	9.4	46.4	44.2	8.9
2012	100	9.4	45.3	45.3	9.2
2013	100	9.3	44.0	46.7	9.5
2014	100	9.1	43.1	47.8	9.7
2015	100	8.8	40.9	50.2	9.6
2016	100	8.6	39.8	51.6	9.6
2017	100	7.9	40.5	51.6	9.4

1-3 三次产业贡献率

Share of the Contributions of the Three Strata of Industry to the Increase of GDP

(按不变价格计算，Data in this table are calculated at constant prices)

年 份 Year	国内生产总值 Gross Domestic Product (%)	第一产业 Primary Industry	第二产业 Secondary Industry	第三产业 Tertiary Industry
1990	100	40.5	39.6	19.9
1991	100	6.8	61.1	32.2
1992	100	8.2	63.2	28.7
1993	100	7.6	64.4	28.0
1994	100	6.3	66.3	27.4
1995	100	8.7	62.8	28.5
1996	100	9.3	62.2	28.5
1997	100	6.5	59.0	34.5
1998	100	7.2	59.7	33.0
1999	100	5.7	56.8	37.5
2000	100	4.2	59.5	36.3
2001	100	4.7	46.2	49.1
2002	100	4.2	49.2	46.6
2003	100	3.1	57.9	39.0
2004	100	7.4	51.7	40.9
2005	100	5.3	50.3	44.4
2006	100	4.4	49.5	46.1
2007	100	2.7	49.9	47.4
2008	100	5.3	48.4	46.3
2009	100	4.1	51.9	44.0
2010	100	3.6	57.2	39.2
2011	100	4.2	52.0	43.8
2012	100	5.2	49.9	44.9
2013	100	4.3	48.5	47.2
2014	100	4.7	47.8	47.5
2015	100	4.6	42.4	52.9
2016	100	4.3	38.2	57.5
2017	100	4.9	36.3	58.8

注：产业贡献率指各产业增加值增量与GDP增量之比。
Note: Share of the three industries refers to the proportion of the increment of every industrial value added to the increment of GDP.

1-4 三大需求对国内生产总值增长的贡献率和拉动
Share and Contribution of the Three Components of GDP by Expenditure Approach to the Growth of GDP

(按不变价格计算，Data in value terms in this table are calculated at constant prices)

年 份 Year	最终消费支出 Final Consumption Expenditure		资本形成总额 Gross Capital Formation		货物和服务净出口 Net Exports of Goods and Services	
	贡献率 Share (%)	拉动(百分点) Contribution (percentage points)	贡献率 Share (%)	拉动(百分点) Contribution (percentage points)	贡献率 Share (%)	拉动(百分点) Contribution (percentage points)
1978	39.4	4.6	66.0	7.6	-5.4	-0.6
1979	85.1	6.4	18.1	1.4	-3.2	-0.2
1980	77.5	6.1	20.7	1.6	1.8	0.2
1981	88.7	4.6	-1.1	-0.1	12.4	0.6
1982	56.4	5.1	23.0	2.1	20.6	1.8
1983	75.6	8.1	32.4	3.5	-8.0	-0.8
1984	69.4	10.6	41.2	6.3	-10.6	-1.7
1985	71.1	9.6	79.9	10.8	-51.0	-6.9
1986	50.4	4.5	15.5	1.4	34.1	3.0
1987	41.0	4.8	26.4	3.1	32.6	3.8
1988	43.2	4.9	55.9	6.3	0.9	0.1
1989	94.4	4.0	-19.0	-0.8	24.6	1.0
1990	81.0	3.2	-54.2	-2.1	73.2	2.8
1991	60.9	5.7	37.4	3.5	1.7	0.1
1992	56.4	8.0	52.7	7.5	-9.1	-1.2
1993	59.4	8.3	54.1	7.5	-13.5	-1.9
1994	33.8	4.4	36.1	4.7	30.1	4.0
1995	46.1	5.1	46.7	5.1	7.2	
1996	62.0	6.2	34.2	3.4	3.8	0.8
1997	42.8	3.9	14.5	1.3	42.7	0.3
1998	64.9	5.1	28.5	2.2	6.6	4.0
1999	89.0	6.8	20.8	1.6	-9.8	0.5
2000	78.9	6.6	21.6	1.8	-0.5	-0.8
2001	48.6	4.0	64.3	5.3	-12.9	
2002	57.3	5.2	37.9	3.4	4.8	-1.0
2003	35.8	3.6	69.6	7.0	-5.4	0.5
2004	43.0	4.3	61.3	6.2	-4.3	-0.6
2005	55.0	6.2	32.3	3.7	12.7	-0.4
2006	42.4	5.4	42.3	5.4	15.3	1.4
2007	45.8	6.5	43.4	6.2	10.8	1.9
2008	45.0	4.3	52.3	5.0	2.7	1.5
2009	56.8	5.2	86.0	7.9	-42.8	0.3
2010	46.3	4.9	65.2	6.9	-11.5	-3.9
2011	61.9	5.9	46.2	4.4	-8.1	-0.8
2012	54.9	4.3	43.4	3.4	1.7	0.2
2013	47.0	3.6	55.3	4.3	-2.3	-0.1
2014	48.8	3.6	46.9	3.4	4.3	0.3
2015	59.7	4.1	41.6	2.9	-1.3	-0.1
2016	66.5	4.5	43.1	2.9	-9.6	-0.7
2017	58.8	4.1	32.1	2.2	9.1	0.6

注：1.三大需求指支出法国内生产总值的三大构成项目，即最终消费支出、资本形成总额、货物和服务净出口。
2.贡献率指三大需求增量与支出法国内生产总值增量之比。
3.拉动指国内生产总值增长速度与三大需求贡献率的乘积。

Note: a) Three components of GDP by expenditure approach are final consumption expenditure, gross capital formation and net exports of goods and services.
b) Contribution share of the three components refers to the proportion of the increment of the each component of GDP to the increment of GDP.
c) Contribution of the three components refers to the growth rate of GDP multiplies the constribution share of the three components.

1–5 人口数及构成
Population and Its Composition

单位：万人
Unit: 10000 persons

年 份 Year	年底人口数 Total Population (year-end)	按性别分 by Sex				按城乡分 by Residence			
		男 Male		女 Female		城 镇 Urban		乡 村 Rural	
		人口数 Population	比重(%) Structure	人口数 Population	比重(%) Structure	人口数 Population	比重(%) Structure	人口数 Population	比重(%) Structure
1978	96259	49567	51.49	46692	48.51	17245	17.92	79014	82.08
1980	98705	50785	51.45	47920	48.55	19140	19.39	79565	80.61
1985	105851	54725	51.7	51126	48.3	25094	23.71	80757	76.29
1989	112704	58099	51.55	54605	48.45	29540	26.21	83164	73.79
1990	114333	58904	51.52	55429	48.48	30195	26.41	84138	73.59
1991	115823	59466	51.34	56357	48.66	31203	26.94	84620	73.06
1992	117171	59811	51.05	57360	48.95	32175	27.46	84996	72.54
1993	118517	60472	51.02	58045	48.98	33173	27.99	85344	72.01
1994	119850	61246	51.1	58604	48.9	34169	28.51	85681	71.49
1995	121121	61808	51.03	59313	48.97	35174	29.04	85947	70.96
1996	122389	62200	50.82	60189	49.18	37304	30.48	85085	69.52
1997	123626	63131	51.07	60495	48.93	39449	31.91	84177	68.09
1998	124761	63940	51.25	60821	48.75	41608	33.35	83153	66.65
1999	125786	64692	51.43	61094	48.57	43748	34.78	82038	65.22
2000	126743	65437	51.63	61306	48.37	45906	36.22	80837	63.78
2001	127627	65672	51.46	61955	48.54	48064	37.66	79563	62.34
2002	128453	66115	51.47	62338	48.53	50212	39.09	78241	60.91
2003	129227	66556	51.50	62671	48.50	52376	40.53	76851	59.47
2004	129988	66976	51.52	63012	48.48	54283	41.76	75705	58.24
2005	130756	67375	51.53	63381	48.47	56212	42.99	74544	57.01
2006	131448	67728	51.52	63720	48.48	58288	44.34	73160	55.66
2007	132129	68048	51.50	64081	48.50	60633	45.89	71496	54.11
2008	132802	68357	51.47	64445	48.53	62403	46.99	70339	53.01
2009	133450	68647	51.44	64803	48.56	64512	48.34	68938	51.66
2010	134091	68748	51.30	65343	48.70	66978	49.90	67113	50.10
2011	134735	69068	51.30	65667	48.70	69079	51.30	65656	48.70
2012	135404	69395	51.30	66009	48.70	71182	52.60	64222	47.40
2013	136072	69728	51.24	66344	48.76	73111	53.70	62961	46.30
2014	136782	70079	51.23	66703	48.77	74916	54.77	61866	45.23
2015	137462	70414	51.22	67048	48.78	77116	56.10	60346	43.90
2016	138271	70815	51.21	67456	48.79	79298	57.35	58973	42.65
2017	139008	71137	51.17	67871	48.83	81347	58.52	57661	41.48

1-6 居民消费价格指数和商品零售价格指数
Consumer Price Indices and Retail Price Indices

（上年价格=100，Preceding Year=100）

年 份 Year	居民消费价格指数 Consumer Price Index	城 市 Urban Areas	农 村 Rural Areas	商品零售价格指数 Retail Price Index
1978	100.7	100.7		100.7
1979	101.9	101.9		102.0
1980	107.5	107.5		106.0
1981	102.5	102.5		102.4
1982	102.0	102.0		101.9
1983	102.0	102.0		101.5
1984	102.7	102.7		102.8
1985	109.3	111.9	107.6	108.8
1986	106.5	107.0	106.1	106.0
1987	107.3	108.8	106.2	107.3
1988	118.8	120.7	117.5	118.5
1989	118.0	116.3	119.3	117.8
1990	103.1	101.3	104.5	102.1
1991	103.4	105.1	102.3	102.9
1992	106.4	108.6	104.7	105.4
1993	114.7	116.1	113.7	113.2
1994	124.1	125.0	123.4	121.7
1995	117.1	116.8	117.5	114.8
1996	108.3	108.8	107.9	106.1
1997	102.8	103.1	102.5	100.8
1998	99.2	99.4	99.0	97.4
1999	98.6	98.7	98.5	97.0
2000	100.4	100.8	99.9	98.5
2001	100.7	100.7	100.8	99.2
2002	99.2	99.0	99.6	98.7
2003	101.2	100.9	101.6	99.9
2004	103.9	103.3	104.8	102.8
2005	101.8	101.6	102.2	100.8
2006	101.5	101.5	101.5	101.0
2007	104.8	104.5	105.4	103.8
2008	105.9	105.6	106.5	105.9
2009	99.3	99.1	99.7	98.8
2010	103.3	103.2	103.6	103.1
2011	105.4	105.3	105.8	104.9
2012	102.6	102.7	102.5	102.0
2013	102.6	102.6	102.8	101.4
2014	102.0	102.1	101.8	101.0
2015	101.4	102.1	101.5	100.1
2016	102.0	102.1	101.9	100.7
2017	101.6	101.7	101.3	101.1

1-7 居民人均可支配收入与支出
National Average Disposable Income and Expenditure

单位：元
unit：yuan

项　　目	Item	2015年	2016年	2017年
全年可支配收入	**Annual Disposable Income**	**21966.2**	**23821.0**	**25973.8**
工资性收入	Income of Wages and Salaries	12459.0	13455.2	14620.3
经营净收入	Net Business Income	3955.6	4217.7	4501.8
财产净收入	Income from Properties	1739.6	1889.0	2107.4
转移性收入	Income from Transfer	3811.9	4259.1	4744.3
消费支出	**Consumption Expenditure**	**15712.4**	**17110.7**	**18322.1**
食品烟酒	Food,Tobacco and Liquor	4814.0	5151.0	5373.6
衣着	Clothing	1164.1	1202.7	1237.6
居住	Residence	3419.2	3746.4	4106.9
生活用品及服务	Household Facilities, Articles and Services	951.4	1043.7	1120.7
交通通信	Transport and Communications	2086.9	2337.8	2498.9
教育文化娱乐	Education, Cultural and Recreation	1723.1	1915.3	2086.2
医疗保健	Health Care and Medical Services	1164.5	1307.5	1451.2
其他用品及服务	Miscellaneous Goods and Services	389.2	406.3	447.0

1-8 城镇居民人均可支配收入与支出
Average Disposable Income and Expenditure of Urban

单位：元
unit：yuan

项　　目	Item	2015年	2016年	2017年
全年可支配收入	**Annual Disposable Income**	**31194.8**	**33616.2**	**36396.2**
工资性收入	Income of Wages and Salaries	19337.1	20665.0	22200.9
经营净收入	Net Business Income	3476.1	3770.1	4064.7
财产净收入	Income from Properties	3041.9	3271.3	3606.9
转移性收入	Income from Transfer	5339.7	5909.8	6523.6
消费支出	**Consumption Expenditure**	**21392.4**	**23078.9**	**24445.0**
食品烟酒	Food,Tobacco and Liquor	6359.7	6762.4	7001.0
衣着	Clothing	1701.1	1739.0	1757.9
居住	Residence	4726.0	5113.7	5564.0
生活用品及服务	Household Facilities, Articles and Services	1306.5	1426.8	1525.0
交通通信	Transport and Communications	2895.4	3173.9	3321.5
教育文化娱乐	Education, Cultural and Recreation	2382.8	2637.6	2846.6
医疗保健	Health Care and Medical Services	1443.4	1630.8	1777.4
其他用品及服务	Miscellaneous Goods and Services	577.5	594.7	651.5

1-9　农村居民人均可支配收入与支出
Average Disposable Income and Expenditure of Rural

单位：元
unit：yuan

项　目	Item	2015	2016	2017
全年可支配收入	**Annual Disposable Income**	**11421.7**	**12363.4**	**13432.4**
工资性收入	Income of Wages and Salaries	4600.3	5021.8	5498.4
经营净收入	Net Business Income	4503.6	4741.3	5027.8
财产净收入	Net Income from Property	251.5	272.1	303.0
转移净收入	Net Income from Transfers	2066.3	2328.2	2603.2
消费支出	**Expendses on Consumption**	**9222.6**	**101290.8**	**10954.5**
食品烟酒	Food ,Tobacco and Liquor	3048.0	3266.1	3415.4
衣着	Clothing	550.5	575.4	611.6
居住	Residence	1926.2	2147.1	2353.5
生活用品及服务	Household Facilities, Articles and Services	545.6	595.7	634.0
交通通信	Transport and Communications	1163.1	1359.9	1509.1
教育文化娱乐	Education, Cultural and Recreation	969.3	1070.3	1171.3
医疗保健	Health Care and Medical Services	846.0	929.2	1058.7
其他用品及服务	Miscellaneous Goods and Services	174.0	186.0	200.9

消费品市场

CONSUMER GOODS MARKET

第2篇

2-1 历年社会消费品零售总额
Total Retail Sales of Consumer Goods

年 份 Year	社会消费品零售总额(亿元) Total Retail Sales of Consumer Goods (100 million yuan)	比上年增长(%) Increase Over the Previous Year (%)
1952	276.8	
1963	604.5	0.1
1964	638.2	5.6
1965	670.3	5.0
1966	732.8	9.3
1967	770.5	5.1
1968	737.3	-4.3
1969	801.5	8.7
1970	858.0	7.0
1971	929.2	8.3
1972	1023.3	10.1
1973	1106.7	8.2
1974	1163.6	5.1
1975	1271.1	9.2
1976	1339.4	5.4
1977	1432.8	7.0
1978	1558.6	8.8
1979	1800.0	15.5
1980	2140.0	18.9
1981	2350.0	9.8
1982	2570.0	9.4
1983	2849.4	10.9
1984	3376.4	18.5
1985	4305.0	27.5
1986	4950.0	15.0
1987	5820.0	17.6
1988	7440.0	27.8
1989	8101.4	8.9
1990	8300.1	2.5
1991	9415.6	13.4
1992	10993.7	16.8
1993	14270.4	29.8
1994	18622.9	30.5
1995	23613.8	26.8
1996	28360.2	20.1
1997	31252.9	10.2
1998	33378.1	6.8
1999	35647.9	6.8
2000	39105.7	9.7
2001	43055.4	10.1
2002	48135.9	11.8
2003	52516.3	9.1
2004	59501.0	13.3
2005	68352.6	14.9
2006	79145.2	15.8
2007	93571.6	18.2
2008	114830.1	22.7
2009	133048.2	15.9
2010	158008.0	18.8
2011	187205.8	18.5
2012	214432.7	14.5
2013	242842.8	13.2
2014	271896.1	12.0
2015	300930.8	10.7
2016	332316.3	10.4
2017	366261.6	10.2

2-2 各地区社会消费品零售总额
Total Retail Sales of Consumer Goods by Region

单位：亿元
Unit：100 million yuan

地　区	Region	2012	2013	2014	2015	2016	2017
北　京	Beijing	8123.5	8872.1	9638.0	10338.0	11005.1	11575.4
天　津	Tianjin	3921.4	4470.4	4738.7	5257.3	5635.8	5729.7
河　北	Hebei	9254.0	10516.7	11820.5	12990.7	14364.7	15907.6
山　西	Shanxi	4506.8	5139.3	5717.9	6033.7	6480.5	6918.1
内蒙古	Inner Mongolia	4572.5	5114.2	5657.6	6107.7	6700.8	7160.2
辽　宁	Liaoning	9304.2	10581.4	11857.0	12787.2	13414.1	13807.2
吉　林	Jilin	4772.9	5426.4	6080.9	6651.9	7310.4	7855.8
黑龙江	Heilongjiang	5491.0	6251.2	7015.3	7640.2	8402.5	9099.2
上　海	Shanghai	7840.4	8557.0	9303.5	10131.5	10946.6	11830.3
江　苏	Jiangsu	18411.1	20878.2	23458.1	25876.8	28707.1	31737.4
浙　江	Zhejiang	14199.6	15970.8	17835.3	19784.7	21970.8	24308.5
安　徽	Anhui	6142.8	7044.7	7957.0	8908.0	10000.2	11192.6
福　建	Fujian	7256.5	8275.3	9346.7	10505.9	11674.5	13013.0
江　西	Jiangxi	4123.3	4696.1	5292.6	5925.5	6634.6	7448.1
山　东	Shandong	19651.9	22294.8	25111.5	27761.4	30645.8	33649.0
河　南	Henan	10915.6	12426.6	14005.0	15740.4	17618.4	19666.8
湖　北	Hubei	9682.4	11035.9	12449.3	14003.2	15649.2	17394.1
湖　南	Hunan	8318.7	9509.5	10723.5	12024.0	13436.5	14854.9
广　东	Guangdong	22677.1	25453.9	28471.1	31517.6	34739.1	38200.1
广　西	Guangxi	4516.6	5133.1	5772.8	6348.1	7027.3	7813.0
海　南	Hainan	950.2	1090.9	1224.5	1325.1	1453.7	1618.8
重　庆	Chongqing	4403.0	5055.8	5710.7	6424.0	7271.4	8067.7
四　川	Sichuan	9622.0	11001.0	12393.0	13877.7	15601.9	17480.5
贵　州	Guizhou	2266.3	2601.2	2936.9	3283.0	3709.0	4154.0
云　南	Yunnan	3597.9	4112.6	4632.9	5103.2	5722.9	6423.1
西　藏	Tibet	277.9	322.2	364.5	408.5	459.4	523.3
陕　西	Shaanxi	4581.6	5245.0	5918.7	6578.1	7367.6	8236.4
甘　肃	Gansu	2064.4	2368.8	2668.3	2907.2	3184.4	3426.6
青　海	Qinghai	480.3	549.6	620.8	691.0	767.3	839.0
宁　夏	Ningxia	590.5	668.5	737.2	789.6	850.1	930.4
新　疆	Xinjiang	1916.1	2179.5	2436.5	2606.0	2825.9	3044.6

2-3 各地区社会消费品零售总额构成
Total Retail Sales of Consumer Goods by Region

单位：亿元
Unit：100 million yuan

地区	Region	社会消费品零售总额 Total Retail Sales of Consumer Goods	城市 City	城区 Urban	镇区 Town	乡村 Village
全国	**National Total**	**366261.6**	**314289.7**	**242031.9**	**72257.7**	**51971.9**
北京	Beijing	11575.4	11288.6	10462.1	826.4	286.9
天津	Tianjin	5729.7	5508.8	4551.6	957.1	220.9
河北	Hebei	15907.6	12324.4	7652.4	4672.0	3583.3
山西	Shanxi	6918.1	5643.6	3787.9	1855.7	1274.5
内蒙古	Inner Mongolia	7160.2	6454.6	5087.9	1366.7	705.6
辽宁	Liaoning	13807.2	12412.8	10943.5	1469.3	1394.4
吉林	Jilin	7855.8	7043.8	5840.7	1203.0	812.0
黑龙江	Heilongjiang	9099.2	7959.0	6651.4	1307.6	1140.2
上海	Shanghai	11830.3	11320.7	11056.0	264.7	509.6
江苏	Jiangsu	31737.4	28385.3	21953.3	6432.1	3352.1
浙江	Zhejiang	24308.5	20168.1	14991.4	5176.7	4140.4
安徽	Anhui	11192.6	9009.4	6181.4	2828.1	2183.2
福建	Fujian	13013.0	11745.0	8441.9	3303.1	1268.0
江西	Jiangxi	7448.1	6167.3	4028.2	2139.1	1280.8
山东	Shandong	33649.0	26814.5	20682.5	6132.0	6834.6
河南	Henan	19666.8	16044.5	11222.4	4822.1	3622.3
湖北	Hubei	17394.1	14603.9	11665.5	2938.4	2790.2
湖南	Hunan	14854.9	13411.4	8522.8	4888.7	1443.4
广东	Guangdong	38200.1	33423.7	29566.9	3856.9	4776.3
广西	Guangxi	7813.0	6874.2	4464.8	2409.4	938.8
海南	Hainan	1618.8	1363.1	1088.3	274.9	255.6
重庆	Chongqing	8067.7	7651.2	5352.5	2298.7	416.5
四川	Sichuan	17480.5	14044.1	10125.6	3918.5	3436.4
贵州	Guizhou	4154.0	3388.5	2645.8	742.8	765.5
云南	Yunnan	6423.1	5534.1	3977.0	1557.1	889.0
西藏	Tibet	523.3	438.0	317.4	120.6	85.3
陕西	Shaanxi	8236.4	7270.5	5330.4	1940.1	965.8
甘肃	Gansu	3426.6	2729.9	2041.1	688.8	696.7
青海	Qinghai	839.0	728.1	427.2	300.9	110.9
宁夏	Ningxia	930.4	854.3	555.6	298.7	76.2
新疆	Xinjiang	3044.6	2760.6	2243.1	517.6	283.9

2-4　各地区网上零售额(2017年)
Online Retail Sales by Region (2017)

地区	Region	网上零售额 (亿元) Online Retail Sales (100 million yuan)	增长 (%) Growth Rate (%)	其中：实物商品网上零售额 (亿元) Online Retail Sales in Goods (100 million yuan)	增长 (%) Growth Rate (%)
全　国	**National Total**	**71750.7**	**32.2**	**54805.6**	**28.0**
北　京	Beijing	6823.6	15.9	5149.2	11.9
天　津	Tianjin	1061.8	37.1	830.2	31.1
河　北	Hebei	1352.2	33.4	1104.4	29.8
山　西	Shanxi	330.8	65.5	158.3	61.3
内蒙古	Inner Mongolia	242.1	54.2	98.2	26.5
辽　宁	Liaoning	819.8	32.6	554.4	33.6
吉　林	Jilin	286.0	26.4	122.3	22.4
黑龙江	Heilongjiang	321.7	48.6	155.0	25.8
上　海	Shanghai	6787.1	25.7	5817.9	23.9
江　苏	Jiangsu	7006.9	39.0	5545.3	34.8
浙　江	Zhejiang	12297.9	29.4	8503.2	27.7
安　徽	Anhui	1411.9	48.2	1107.0	46.2
福　建	Fujian	3147.2	36.7	2642.8	34.8
江　西	Jiangxi	686.3	49.3	529.4	39.1
山　东	Shandong	2539.3	37.5	2084.5	32.3
河　南	Henan	1735.7	51.5	977.5	44.2
湖　北	Hubei	1716.6	37.2	1131.8	30.0
湖　南	Hunan	1107.5	41.8	720.1	32.0
广　东	Guangdong	15683.3	34.2	13605.7	31.3
广　西	Guangxi	458.3	56.0	209.4	43.9
海　南	Hainan	213.4	38.9	33.0	25.5
重　庆	Chongqing	794.6	45.2	473.9	44.1
四　川	Sichuan	2013.4	22.5	1474.2	20.2
贵　州	Guizhou	352.5	78.5	188.1	60.7
云　南	Yunnan	388.6	38.5	211.8	26.4
西　藏	Tibet	26.5	393.6	9.5	121.3
陕　西	Shaanxi	1171.8	9.6	951.7	0.7
甘　肃	Gansu	235.6	85.0	44.6	39.4
青　海	Qinghai	32.3	212.2	10.4	15.1
宁　夏	Ningxia	45.2	147.8	20.1	42.5
新　疆	Xinjiang	76.7	53.4	52.6	20.0
不分地区	Not Classified by Region	584.1	-	289.2	-

2-5 亿元以上商品交易市场基本情况
Basic Statistics on Commodity Exchange Markets of Transaction Value over 100 Million Yuan

市　　场	Market	市场数量(个) Number of Markets (unit)	摊位数(个) Number of Booths (unit)	营业面积(万平方米) Operational Area (10000 sq.m)	成交额(亿元) Turnover (100 million yuan)	批　发 Wholesale Value	零　售 Retail Value
总　　计	**Total**	**4617**	**3347936**	**29691.8**	**108247.6**	**93996.9**	**14250.7**
综合市场	**Integrated Markets**	**1309**	**1254329**	**8166.8**	**25834.3**	**21612.0**	**4222.4**
生产资料综合市场	Production Comprehensive Markets	47	54861	787.6	1299.1	1293.1	6.0
工业消费品综合市场	Industrial Consumable Comprehensive Markets	267	462256	2700.3	8705.7	7376.3	1329.5
农产品综合市场	Farm Produce Comprehensive Markets	661	393923	2449.1	10681.7	8802.6	1879.1
其他综合市场	Other Comprehensive Markets	334	343289	2229.7	5147.8	4140.0	1007.7
专业市场	**Special Markets**	**3308**	**2093607**	**21525.0**	**82413.3**	**72384.9**	**10028.4**
生产资料市场	Production Markets	607	271210	6094.2	29330.6	29054.8	275.8
农业生产用具市场	Agricultural Production Equipment Markets	17	5038	174.9	255.9	255.9	
农用生产资料市场	Agricultural Production Markets	25	5107	99.2	132.0	132.0	
煤炭市场	Coal and Charcoal Markets	4	3346	198.3	264.0	264.0	
木材市场	Wood Markets	40	13414	501.3	690.5	690.5	
建材市场	Building Material Markets	214	111218	2331.1	1961.7	1685.8	275.8
化工材料及制品市场	Chemical Materials and Products Markets	31	17507	209.0	3846.2	3846.2	
金属材料市场	Metal Materials Markets	195	75558	2068.1	19771.0	19771.0	
机械设备市场	Mechanical Equipments Markets	45	24317	270.2	679.4	679.4	
其他生产资料市场	Others	36	15705	242.1	1730.0	1730.0	
农产品市场	Farm Produce Markets	937	507207	4207.8	19346.7	18365.7	981.0
粮油市场	Grain and Oil Markets	100	28544	358.1	1628.0	1578.5	49.5
肉禽蛋市场	Meat, Poultry and Eggs Markets	108	41729	282.9	1473.3	1266.3	207.0
水产品市场	Aquatic Products Markets	139	69077	451.9	3661.3	3487.6	173.7
蔬菜市场	Vegetables Markets	274	182064	1631.0	4262.2	4137.0	125.2
干鲜果品市场	Dried and Fresh Melons and Fruits Markets	124	67448	734.4	4588.7	4582.9	5.8
棉麻土畜、烟叶市场	Cotton, Local & Livestock Products, and Tobacco Markets	15	17270	139.3	465.4	457.5	7.9
其他农产品市场	Others	177	101075	610.2	3267.8	2855.8	412.0
食品、饮料及烟酒市场	Food, Beverages, Tobacco and Liquor Markets	117	61089	386.3	1206.8	1075.5	131.3
食品饮料市场	Food and Beverages Markets	34	21936	110.4	309.2	238.1	71.1
茶叶市场	Tea Markets	29	12418	107.0	254.9	240.4	14.5
烟酒市场	Tobacco and Liquor Markets	10	2872	28.0	104.6	101.4	3.3
其他食品饮料及烟酒市场	Others	44	23863	140.9	538.1	495.6	42.5

2-5 续表 Continued

市　　场	Market	市场数量(个) Number of Markets (unit)	摊位数(个) Number of Booths (unit)	营业面积(万平方米) Operational Area (10000 sq.m)	成交额(亿元) Turnover (100 million yuan)	批　发 Wholesale Value	零　售 Retail Value
纺织、服装、鞋帽市场	Textiles, Clothing, Shoes and Hats Markets	511	659568	3458.0	15169.3	14052.9	1116.4
布料及纺织品市场	Cloth and Textiles Markets	67	107392	990.6	6587.4	6568.4	19.1
服装市场	Clothing Markets	327	404441	1955.0	5826.2	4974.7	851.5
鞋帽市场	Shoes and Hats Markets	38	25170	132.6	633.3	627.8	5.6
其他纺织服装鞋帽市场	Others	79	122565	379.8	2122.3	1882.1	240.2
日用品及文化用品市场	Daily Use Articles and Cultural Goods Markets	79	51774	292.7	1202.8	1105.2	97.5
小商品市场	Merchandise Markets	32	26994	102.2	454.5	440.7	13.9
箱包市场	Luggage Markets	5	4986	59.1	185.5	185.5	
玩具市场	Toys Markets	4	1699	37.0	25.1	25.1	
文具市场	Stationary Markets	4	987	11.7	17.5	17.5	
图书、报刊杂志市场	Books, Newspapers and Magazines Markets	6	1174	6.9	35.7	19.5	16.2
音像制品及电子出版物市场	Video Products and E-journal Markets	3	609	2.1	15.8		15.8
体育用品市场	Sports Markets	1	260	1.3	1.8	1.8	
其他日用品及文化用品市场	Others	24	15065	72.3	466.7	415.1	51.6
黄金、珠宝、玉器等首饰市场	Gold, Jeweller, Jade Markets	25	15038	255.6	694.5	641.0	53.5
电器、通讯器材、电子设备市场	Electrical Appliances, Communication Appliances and Electronical Appliances Markets	121	51019	319.0	789.1	406.4	382.7
家电市场	Household Appliances Markets	32	10781	147.8	304.0	257.4	46.6
通讯器材市场	Communication Appliances Markets	20	10026	40.7	110.6	75.3	35.4
照相、摄像器材市场	Cameras and Video Equipments Markets	3	972	5.6	9.1	3.2	5.9
计算机及辅助设备市场	Computer and Auxillary Equipments Markets	56	24275	107.7	307.4	28.5	278.9
其他电器、通讯器材、电子设备市场	Others	10	4965	17.2	58.0	42.1	15.9
医药、医疗用品及器材市场	Medicine, Medical Materials and Medical Instruments Markets	22	42416	263.1	1314.7	1295.0	19.8
中药材市场	Chinese Medicine Markets	22	42416	263.1	1314.7	1295.0	19.8
其他医药、医疗用品及器材市场	Others						
家具、五金及装饰材料市场	Furniture, Hardware and Decoration Materials Markets	555	294399	4315.9	5442.6	3547.1	1895.5
家具市场	Furniture Markets	174	85677	1680.6	1777.7	1065.0	712.7
装饰材料市场	Decoration Materials Markets	221	108397	1567.8	1855.4	1061.4	794.0
灯具市场	Lamps Markets	16	6899	120.3	231.3	203.2	28.1
厨具、盥洗设备市场	Kitchen Utensils, Washing Equipments Markets	6	2997	34.6	27.4	24.7	2.7
五金材料市场	Hardware Materials Markets	77	49582	417.0	1048.6	978.3	70.4
其他装修市场	Others	61	40847	495.6	502.2	214.5	287.7
汽车、摩托车及零配件市场	Cars, Motorcycles and Spare Parts Markets	250	77339	1452.8	6621.2	1883.1	4738.1
汽车市场	Cars Markets	178	45263	1130.2	5637.0	1000.4	4636.5
摩托车市场	Motocycles Markets	10	3489	27.7	52.6	40.2	12.3
机动车零配件市场	Vehicle Spare Parts Markts	62	28587	294.9	931.7	842.4	89.3
花、鸟、鱼、虫市场	Flower, Bird, Fish and Insects Markets	28	22236	146.9	475.5	421.5	54.1
花卉市场	Flower Markets	23	20716	140.7	453.3	417.8	35.5
鸟市场	Bird Markets						
观赏鱼市场	Fish Markets						
其他花鸟鱼虫市场	Others	5	1520	6.2	22.3	3.7	18.6
旧货市场	Second Hand Markets	12	6461	23.5	31.8	7.3	24.6
古玩、古董、字画市场	Antiques,Calligraphy and Painting Markets	2	690	2.8	2.0		2.0
邮票、硬币市场	Stamps and Coins Markets						
其他旧货市场	Others	10	5771	20.7	29.8	7.3	22.5
其他专业市场	Others	44	33851	309.3	787.6	529.5	258.1

2-6 亿元以上商品交易市场摊位分类情况
Classification of Booths of Commodity Exchange Markets of Transaction Value over 100 Million Yuan

单位：亿元
Unit: 100 million yuan

类别	Classification	摊位数（个）Number of Booths (unit)	成交额（亿元）Turnover (100 million yuan)	批发 Wholesale Value	零售 Retail Value
总计	**Total**	**3347936**	**108247.6**	**93996.9**	**14250.7**
粮油、食品类		942363	30952.5	27679.4	3273.1
#粮油类	Grain and Oil	85077	3893.1	3534.4	358.7
肉禽蛋类	Meat, Poultry and Eggs	127461	3969.6	3082.3	887.3
水产品类	Aquatic Products	133079	6121.7	5354.9	766.8
蔬菜类	Vegetables	341709	7720.0	7064.7	655.3
干鲜果品类	Dried and Fresh Melons and Fruits	159471	7364.4	7075.8	288.7
饮料类	Beverages	45631	981.5	865.1	116.5
烟酒类	Tobacco and Liquor	40215	1088.9	926.0	162.9
服装鞋帽、针、纺织品类	Clothing, Shoes, Hats and Textiles	913180	17894.4	16177.3	1717.0
服装类	Clothing	556944	7637.4	6425.1	1212.3
鞋帽类	Footwear and Hats	133530	1864.3	1587.5	276.8
针、纺织品类	Knitwear and Textiles	222706	8392.6	8164.8	227.9
化妆品类	Cosmetics	23805	325.9	258.8	67.1
金银珠宝类	Gold, Silver and Jewellery	26383	954.4	861.7	92.8
日用品类	Articles for Daily Use	175612	3138.4	2696.0	442.4
#儿童玩具类	Children Toys	23960	327.8	263.9	63.8
五金、电料类	Hardware & Electrical Materials	119282	2520.7	2291.2	229.6
体育、娱乐用品类	Sports & Recreational Articles	12809	223.8	201.4	22.4
#照相器材类		1022	9.8	3.5	6.2
书报杂志类	Newspapers and Magazines	4299	78.6	58.6	20.0
电子出版物及音像制品类	E-journal and Video Products	7794	209.8	180.0	29.9
家用电器和音像器材类	Household Appliances and Video Equipments	31669	722.7	586.3	136.4
中西药品类	Traditional Chinese and Western Medicine	27589	1314.1	1280.4	33.7
#西药类	Western Medicine	1018	40.8	34.5	6.3
中草药及中成药类	Traditional Chinese	25236	1249.1	1226.7	22.4
文化办公用品类	Cultural and Official Goods	58894	1041.5	699.8	341.7
#计算机及其配套产品		26447	373.8	124.8	249.0
家具类	Furniture	119056	2410.4	1525.8	884.6
通讯器材类	Communication Appliances	19712	298.9	206.9	92.0
煤炭及制品类	Coal and Related Products	3379	374.9	373.2	1.8
木材及制品类	Wood and Wooden Products	24955	900.8	866.9	33.9
石油及制品类	Petroleum and Related Products	2004	1577.1	1575.7	1.4
化工材料及制品类	Raw Chemical Materials and Related Products	41521	4205.1	4195.9	9.1
#化肥类	Fertilizer	1762	77.9	75.3	2.5
金属材料类	Metal Materials	86638	20006.4	19965.9	40.5
建筑及装潢材料类	Building and Decoration Materials	276870	4891.1	3658.3	1232.8
机电产品及设备类	Mechanical & Electrical Products	51085	1533.4	1499.3	34.1
#农机类	Agricultural Machinery	6098	288.7	283.3	5.4
汽车类	Automobile	76488	6830.6	2111.9	4718.7
种子饲料类	Seed and Feedstuff	7681	92.7	86.6	6.1
棉麻类	Cotton and Hemp	3435	335.2	326.9	8.2
其他类	Others	205587	3343.9	2841.8	502.1

2-7 各地区亿元以上商品交易市场基本情况
Basic Statistics on Commodity Exchange Markets of Transaction Value over 100 Million Yuan by Region

年 份 Year	地 区 Region	市场数量(个) Number of Markets (unit)	摊位数(个) Number of Booths (unit)	营业面积(万平方米) Operational Area (10000 sq.m)	成交额(亿元) Turnover (100 million yuan)	批 发 Wholesale Value	零 售 Retail Value
	2000	3087	2115115	8261.6	16358.9	11648.0	4710.9
	2001	3273	2200662	9397.3	17719.1	12562.5	5156.5
	2002	3258	2190814	10313.2	19840.0	15450.9	4389.2
	2003	3265	2148866	10984.0	21514.5	16832.6	4681.9
	2004	3365	2229818	12477.5	26102.7	21116.9	4985.8
	2005	3323	2248803	13140.8	30020.9	24544.2	5476.7
	2006	3876	2527987	18072.3	37137.5	29679.9	7457.5
	2007	4121	2681630	19814.6	44085.1	35871.5	8213.6
	2008	4567	2839070	21225.2	52458.0	43120.0	9337.9
	2009	4687	2994781	23230.3	57963.8	48308.2	9655.5
	2010	4940	3193365	24832.3	72703.5	60954.9	11748.6
	2011	5075	3334787	26234.5	82017.3	69390.8	12626.5
	2012	5194	3494122	27899.4	93023.8	80141.8	12882.0
	2013	5089	3488170	28868.3	98365.1	84628.3	13736.8
	2014	5023	3534757	29567.9	100309.9	86323.7	13986.2
	2015	4952	3468638	30065.7	100133.8	85836.9	14296.8
	2016	4861	3457899	30023.4	102139.7	87859.3	14280.4
	2017	4617	3347936	29691.8	108247.6	93996.9	14250.7
北 京	Beijing	114	83672	660.2	3922.1	2629.5	1292.6
天 津	Tianjin	44	30655	316.3	1315.4	1256.9	58.5
河 北	Hebei	217	282964	2644.7	5918.0	5628.4	289.7
山 西	Shanxi	32	25059	250.4	639.6	613.8	25.7
内蒙古	Inner Mongolia	69	39726	559.7	693.5	490.7	202.8
辽 宁	Liaoning	200	172439	874.8	4044.0	3343.4	700.6
吉 林	Jilin	53	45168	301.1	550.5	337.3	213.2
黑龙江	Heilongjiang	78	48146	361.1	1061.3	740.1	321.2
上 海	Shanghai	134	54616	421.6	8947.9	8388.3	559.5
江 苏	Jiangsu	487	341024	3510.1	19796.6	18034.0	1762.6
浙 江	Zhejiang	725	442959	3185.7	17279.8	14572.9	2706.9
安 徽	Anhui	129	123276	1246.3	3037.7	2684.9	352.8
福 建	Fujian	118	45531	330.9	1498.3	1204.2	294.1
江 西	Jiangxi	97	89465	658.2	1979.5	1788.0	191.5
山 东	Shandong	498	355642	3645.8	9362.8	8495.9	866.9
河 南	Henan	154	122514	1336.5	3623.9	3161.2	462.7
湖 北	Hubei	143	78164	664.0	2252.3	1577.5	674.8
湖 南	Hunan	326	180645	1130.3	3940.0	3094.6	845.4
广 东	Guangdong	317	193707	1759.4	5462.9	4746.4	716.5
广 西	Guangxi	86	77230	399.5	1052.7	864.8	187.9
海 南	Hainan	5	2680	70.3	42.5	31.5	11.0
重 庆	Chongqing	146	96939	774.4	3532.5	3074.5	458.0
四 川	Sichuan	127	133589	1314.9	2825.0	2608.2	216.8
贵 州	Guizhou	54	48918	596.4	1097.5	879.1	218.3
云 南	Yunnan	37	46976	239.7	575.3	470.1	105.2
西 藏	Tibet	3	2781	3.5	23.9	18.3	5.6
陕 西	Shaanxi	51	33945	330.3	878.0	687.8	190.3
甘 肃	Gansu	27	23092	176.6	278.4	243.7	34.7
青 海	Qinghai	9	7443	55.5	63.7	46.3	17.4
宁 夏	Ningxia	37	25672	442.3	347.2	303.8	43.4
新 疆	Xinjiang	100	93299	1431.3	2205.0	1980.8	224.2

批发和零售业

WHOLESALE AND RETAIL TRADES

第3篇

3-1-1 限额以上批发和零售业企业基本情况
Basic Conditions of Enterprises above Designated Size of Wholesale and Retail Trades

项 目	Item	法人单位数（个）Number of Corporation Enterprises (unit)	年末从业人数（人）Engaged Persons at Year-end (person)
总 计	**Total**	**200170**	**11837989**
一、批发业	**Wholesale Trade**	**100988**	**5063213**
#国有控股	State-controlled Enterprises	8056	1127921
(一)按登记注册类型分	**by Type of Registration**		
1.内资企业	**Domestic Funded Enterprises**	**96000**	**4331273**
国有企业	State-owned Enterprises	1887	310232
集体企业	Collective-owned Enterprises	431	21651
股份合作企业	Cooperative Enterprises	105	3096
联营企业	Joint Ownership Enterprises	17	1088
国有联营企业	State Joint Ownership Enterprises	5	457
集体联营企业	Collective Joint Ownership Enterprises	6	125
国有与集体联营企业	Joint State-collective Enterprises	NA	467
其他联营企业	Other Joint Ownership Enterprises	NA	39
有限责任公司	Limited Liability Corporations	29638	1680898
国有独资公司	State Sole Funded Corporations	1548	163037
其他有限责任公司	Other Limited Liability Corporations	28090	1517861
股份有限公司	Share-holding Corporations Ltd.	2106	446659
私营企业	Private Enterprises	61032	1834929
私营独资企业	Private-funded Enterprises	472	10149
私营合伙企业	Private Partnership Enterprises	50	1124
私营有限责任公司	Private Limited Liability Corporations	59176	1753848
私营股份有限公司	Private Share-holding Corporations Ltd.	1334	69808
其他企业	Other Enterprises	784	32720
2.港、澳、台商投资企业	**Enterprises with Funds from Hongkong, Macao and Taiwan**	**2299**	**320168**
合资经营企业	Joint-venture Enterprises	328	27619
合作经营企业	Cooperative Enterprises	17	1962
独资经营企业	Enterprises with Sole Investment	1843	275351
投资股份有限公司	Share-holding Corporations Ltd. with Investment	54	7101
其他港澳台商投资企业	Other Enterprises with Funds from Hongkong, Macao and Taiwan	57	8135
3.外商投资企业	**Foreign Funded Enterprises**	**2689**	**411772**
中外合资经营企业	Joint-venture Enterprises	380	49368
中外合作经营企业	Cooperative Enterprises	18	1359
外资企业	Enterprises with Sole Foreign Investment	2175	338180
外商投资股份有限公司	Share-holding Corporations Ltd. with Foreign Investment	49	9461
其他外商投资企业	Other Foreign Funded Enterprises	67	13404

注：NA表示小于或等于3(下表同)。
Note:NA refers to less than or equal to three.The same applies to the tables following.

项目	Item	法人单位数（个） Number of Corporation Enterprises (unit)	年末从业人数（人） Engaged Persons at the Year-end (person)
(二)按国民经济行业分	**by Sector**		
农、林、牧产品批发	Wholesale of Agricultural, Forestry and Livestock Products	4946	200839
食品、饮料及烟草制品批发	Wholesale of Food, Beverages and Tobaccos	10983	1021175
米、面制品及食用油批发	Wholesale of Rice, Flour and Edible Oil	1754	106758
肉、禽、蛋、奶及水产品批发	Wholesale of Meal, Fowls, Eggs, Milk and Aquatic Products	1744	108839
酒、饮料及茶叶批发	Wholesale of Wine, Beverages and Teas	2259	232209
烟草制品批发	Wholesale of Tobaccos	510	249264
纺织、服装及家庭用品批发	Wholesale of Textiles, Wearing Apparel and Household Articles	13316	833329
服装批发	Wholesale of Garments	2820	253350
鞋帽批发	Wholesale of Shoes and Hats	974	65672
家用电器批发	Wholesale of Household Electrical Appliances	1802	172043
文化、体育用品及器材批发	Wholesale of Culture, Sports Appliances and Equipments	3203	209118
文具用品批发	Wholesale of Stationeries	1027	33830
体育用品及器材批发	Wholesale of Sports Appliances and Equipments	201	13650
图书批发	Wholesale of Books	298	42997
医药及医疗器材批发	Wholesale of Medicines and Medical Appliances	8008	704476
西药批发	Wholesale of Western Medicine	3612	386129
中药批发	Wholesale of Chinese Traditional Medicine	1834	175238
矿产品、建材及化工产品批发	Wholesale of Mineral Products, Building Materials and Chemical Products	39971	1181318
煤炭及制品批发	Wholesale of Coal and Related Products	4538	143938
石油及制品批发	Wholesale of Petroleum and Related Products	4452	355263
金属及金属矿批发	Wholesale of Metal Materials	12553	236333
建材批发	Wholesale of Building Materials	5949	153732
化肥批发	Wholesale of Chemical Fertilizer	1608	59088
农药批发	Wholesale of Pesticides	277	13526
机械设备、五金产品及电子产品批发	Wholesale of Machinery, Hardware and Electronic Products	16568	782269
汽车批发	Wholesale of Motor Vehicles	1711	93422
计算机、软件及辅助设备批发	Wholesale of Computer, Software and Assistant Appliances	1368	65332
通讯及广播电视设备批发	Wholesale of Communication, Radios and Televisions Equipments	1109	104130
贸易经纪与代理	Trade Broker and Agency	1291	38955
其他批发业	Other Wholesale not Classified Elsewhere	2702	91734

项　目	Item	法人单位数(个) Number of Corporation Enterprises (unit)	年末从业人数(人) Engaged Persons at the Year-end (person)	年末零售营业面积(平方米) Business Area of Retail Trade at the Year-end (m²)
二、零售业	**Retail Trade**	**99182**	**6774776**	**332501879**
#国有控股	State-controlled Enterprises	5171	841316	60722314
(一)按登记注册类型分	**by Type of Registration**			
1.内资企业	**Domestic Funded Enterprises**	**96810**	**5884853**	**294119708**
国有企业	State-owned Enterprises	1119	79540	3368057
集体企业	Collective-owned Enterprises	1241	54650	2865389
股份合作企业	Cooperative Enterprises	267	14075	495996
联营企业	Joint Ownership Enterprises	102	4308	196703
国有联营企业	State Joint Ownership Enterprises	18	1514	24143
集体联营企业	Collective Joint Ownership Enterprises	30	1159	46075
国有与集体联营企业	Joint State-collective Enterprises	27	736	67611
其他联营企业	Other Joint Ownership Enterprises	27	899	58874
有限责任公司	Limited Liability Corporations	32572	2554643	124536734
国有独资公司	State Sole Funded Corporations	797	77884	4327761
其他有限责任公司	Other Limited Liability Corporations	31775	2476759	120208973
股份有限公司	Share-holding Corporations Ltd.	2337	598487	48886892
私营企业	Private Enterprises	58217	2545480	112779189
私营独资企业	Private-funded Enterprises	4875	94906	5630697
私营合伙企业	Private Partnership Enterprises	473	12201	748182
私营有限责任公司	Private Limited Liability Corporations	51205	2312163	101372029
私营股份有限公司	Private Share-holding Corporations Ltd.	1664	126210	5028281
其他企业	Other Enterprises	955	33670	990748
2.港、澳、台商投资企业	**Enterprises with Funds from Hongkong, Macao and Taiwan**	**1448**	**469350**	**19123686**
合资经营企业	Joint-venture Enterprises	336	112097	5427968
合作经营企业	Cooperative Enterprises	31	5507	209133
独资经营企业	Enterprises with Sole Investment	978	332515	12645757
投资股份有限公司	Share-holding Corporations Ltd. with Investment	50	10782	367399
其他港澳台商投资企业	Other Enterprises with Funds from Hongkong, Macao and Taiwan	53	8449	473429
3.外商投资企业	**Foreign Funded Enterprises**	**924**	**420573**	**19258485**
中外合资经营企业	Joint-venture Enterprises	242	141053	7888737
中外合作经营企业	Cooperative Enterprises	21	8313	336645
外资企业	Enterprises with Sole Foreign Investment	570	236213	10173262
外商投资股份有限公司	Share-holding Corporations Ltd. with Foreign Investment	43	14376	473684
其他外商投资企业	Other Foreign Funded Enterprises	48	20618	386157

项 目	Item	法人单位数(个) Number of Corporation Enterprises (unit)	年末从业人数(人) Engaged Persons at the Year-end (person)	年末零售营业面积(平方米) Business Area of Retail Trade at the Year-end (㎡)
(二)按国民经济行业分	**by Sector**			
综合零售	Integrated Retail	12998	2314872	138950211
百货零售	Retail of General Merchandise	6311	1002203	79911457
超级市场零售	Retail of Supermarkets	5335	1195278	55172598
食品、饮料及烟草制品专门零售	Special Retail of Food, Beverages and Tobaccos	9319	378631	10004910
粮油零售	Retail of Cereal and Oil	1075	35419	1640383
肉、禽、蛋、奶及水产品零售	Retail of Meat, Poultry, Eggs, Milk and Aquatic Products	1494	68906	1895411
酒、饮料及茶叶零售	Retail of Wine, Beverages and Teas	2836	76341	1675707
烟草制品零售	Retail of Tobaccos	330	15010	283427
纺织、服装及日用品专门零售	Special Retail of Textiles, Garments and Daily Consumer Articles	5443	563332	15264671
服装零售	Retail of Garments	2657	364940	11438510
文化、体育用品及器材专门零售	Special Retail of Culture, Sports Appliances and Equipments	4475	246230	7209075
体育用品及器材零售	Retail of Sports Appliances and Equipments	204	20384	460967
图书、报刊零售	Retail of Books, Newspapers and Magazines	1323	109756	3453631
医药及医疗器材专门零售	Special Retail of Medicines and Medical Appliances	4958	566911	10314041
药品零售	Retail of Medicines	4372	549182	10058670
汽车、摩托车、燃料及零配件专门零售	Special Retail of Motor Vehicles, Motorcycles, Fuel and Parts	37496	1725171	108706241
汽车零售	Retail of Motor Vehicles	27493	1322300	67470885
机动车燃料零售	Retail of Fuel of Motor Vehicles	7732	352433	39111802
家用电器及电子产品专门零售	Special Retail of Household Electric Appliances and Electronic Products	11352	475706	19718154
日用家电设备零售	Retail of Household Electric Appliances	4120	177258	11563725
计算机、软件及辅助设备零售	Retail of Computer, Software and Assistant Appliances	2999	102586	1161273
通信设备零售	Retail of Communication Equipments	1309	78374	1225008
五金、家具及室内装饰材料专门零售	Special Retail of Hardware, Furniture and Interior Decoration Materials	6203	189519	14916961
货摊、无店铺及其他零售	Stalls, Non-shop and Other Retails	6938	314404	7417615
互联网零售	Retail on the Internet	4061	214639	2357372
(三)按零售业态分	**by Mode of Business Operation**			
有店铺零售	Store-based Retailing	91859	6382632	326676931
超市	Supermarket	7046	490478	14284701
大型超市	Hypermarket	2293	1083355	61372646
百货店	Department Store	5751	833617	67474276
专业店	Speciality Store	40294	1956598	94406819
专卖店	Exclusive Shop	29798	1600538	65740537
无店铺零售	Non-Store Selling	7323	392144	5824948

3-1-2 各地区限额以上批发业企业基本情况

Basic Conditions of Enterprises above Designated Size of Wholesale Trade by Region

地区	Region	批发业 Wholesale Trade		#国有控股 State-controlled Enterprises	
		法人单位数（个）Number of Corporation Enterprises (unit)	年末从业人数（人）Engaged Persons at the Year-end (person)	法人单位数（个）Number of Corporation Enterprises (unit)	年末从业人数（人）Engaged Persons at the Year-end (person)
全　国	**National Total**	**100988**	**5063213**	**8056**	**1127921**
北　京	Beijing	4469	399967	798	108921
天　津	Tianjin	3806	108335	430	23859
河　北	Hebei	1573	101494	153	25964
山　西	Shanxi	962	67943	259	30801
内蒙古	Inner Mongolia	640	31357	93	13055
辽　宁	Liaoning	2412	82901	221	29297
吉　林	Jilin	823	42251	88	15480
黑龙江	Heilongjiang	573	38726	129	24991
上　海	Shanghai	4567	466284	510	56351
江　苏	Jiangsu	11193	414877	573	57940
浙　江	Zhejiang	12600	402936	466	48132
安　徽	Anhui	2327	122346	207	37064
福　建	Fujian	6285	199977	359	38897
江　西	Jiangxi	1121	95833	132	41702
山　东	Shandong	7846	344720	325	77968
河　南	Henan	4174	245475	309	55525
湖　北	Hubei	2731	188037	216	50857
湖　南	Hunan	2119	113009	182	32131
广　东	Guangdong	18803	886133	909	122133
广　西	Guangxi	1328	74119	185	24453
海　南	Hainan	162	16461	18	2126
重　庆	Chongqing	2406	107858	229	19446
四　川	Sichuan	2307	150494	233	33240
贵　州	Guizhou	1067	62036	166	29590
云　南	Yunnan	1100	78607	143	29735
西　藏	Tibet	24	3491	13	1066
陕　西	Shaanxi	1184	91787	206	42714
甘　肃	Gansu	630	32028	76	9840
青　海	Qinghai	145	11598	34	6678
宁　夏	Ningxia	175	10951	32	5963
新　疆	Xinjiang	1436	71182	362	32002

3-1-3 各地区限额以上批发业企业基本情况(按登记注册类型分)

Basic Conditions of Enterprises above Designated Size of Wholesale Trade by Region and Type of Registration

地区	Region	内资企业 Domestic Funded Enterprises		国有企业 State-owned Enterprises	
		法人单位数(个) Number of Corporation Enterprises (unit)	年末从业人数(人) Engaged Persons at the Year-end (person)	法人单位数(个) Number of Corporation Enterprises (unit)	年末从业人数(人) Engaged Persons at the Year-end (person)
全 国	**National Total**	**96000**	**4331273**	**1887**	**310232**
北 京	Beijing	4063	268155	132	11199
天 津	Tianjin	3563	90405	46	2994
河 北	Hebei	1563	100135	45	10273
山 西	Shanxi	957	66050	53	9635
内蒙古	Inner Mongolia	639	31351	38	6898
辽 宁	Liaoning	2333	78318	57	11783
吉 林	Jilin	817	41833	39	7679
黑龙江	Heilongjiang	570	38324	44	6410
上 海	Shanghai	2973	169879	32	1629
江 苏	Jiangsu	10798	357367	209	19167
浙 江	Zhejiang	12320	382213	34	9490
安 徽	Anhui	2308	114724	39	10272
福 建	Fujian	6093	190127	68	12839
江 西	Jiangxi	1112	94734	50	12737
山 东	Shandong	7738	338553	85	6835
河 南	Henan	4159	244523	97	27662
湖 北	Hubei	2689	170790	68	12564
湖 南	Hunan	2103	110522	58	18391
广 东	Guangdong	17354	751477	244	16058
广 西	Guangxi	1318	73894	50	9060
海 南	Hainan	152	15079	8	1356
重 庆	Chongqing	2380	102661	52	6178
四 川	Sichuan	2285	147787	71	15521
贵 州	Guizhou	1061	61470	40	20630
云 南	Yunnan	1091	77404	31	15529
西 藏	Tibet	23	2728	8	743
陕 西	Shaanxi	1167	87192	69	13464
甘 肃	Gansu	627	31730	24	4324
青 海	Qinghai	141	10883	11	1132
宁 夏	Ningxia	175	10951	12	1610
新 疆	Xinjiang	1428	70014	73	6170

地区	Region	集体企业 Collective-owned Enterprises 法人单位数(个) Number of Corporation Enterprises (unit)	集体企业 Collective-owned Enterprises 年末从业人数(人) Engaged Persons at the Year-end (person)	股份合作企业 Cooperative Enterprises 法人单位数(个) Number of Corporation Enterprises (unit)	股份合作企业 Cooperative Enterprises 年末从业人数(人) Engaged Persons at the Year-end (person)
全　国	**National Total**	**431**	**21651**	**105**	**3096**
北　京	Beijing	16	444	17	280
天　津	Tianjin	13	199	5	123
河　北	Hebei	9	792	NA	49
山　西	Shanxi	23	2823	NA	16
内蒙古	Inner Mongolia	NA	60		
辽　宁	Liaoning	8	424	5	96
吉　林	Jilin	NA	11		
黑龙江	Heilongjiang	6	373		
上　海	Shanghai	4	127	NA	58
江　苏	Jiangsu	43	1272	NA	183
浙　江	Zhejiang	12	514	13	270
安　徽	Anhui	7	428	NA	223
福　建	Fujian	30	716	NA	42
江　西	Jiangxi	7	131	NA	28
山　东	Shandong	51	3464	6	148
河　南	Henan	25	1592	NA	151
湖　北	Hubei	13	685	5	203
湖　南	Hunan	5	215		
广　东	Guangdong	59	2093	20	479
广　西	Guangxi	20	1454	NA	29
海　南	Hainan				
重　庆	Chongqing	6	326	9	317
四　川	Sichuan	13	1186	NA	159
贵　州	Guizhou	16	381		
云　南	Yunnan	11	760	NA	60
西　藏	Tibet				
陕　西	Shaanxi	13	413	NA	92
甘　肃	Gansu	6	129	NA	61
青　海	Qinghai	NA	28	NA	5
宁　夏	Ningxia				
新　疆	Xinjiang	10	611	NA	24

地 区	Region	联营企业 Joint Ownership Enterprises		有限责任公司 Limited Liability Corporations	
		法人单位数 (个) Number of Corporation Enterprises (unit)	年末从业人数 (人) Engaged Persons at the Year-end (person)	法人单位数 (个) Number of Corporation Enterprises (unit)	年末从业人数 (人) Engaged Persons at the Year-end (person)
全 国	**National Total**	**17**	**1088**	**29638**	**1680898**
北 京	Beijing	NA	26	1513	145650
天 津	Tianjin			1095	43410
河 北	Hebei			354	27109
山 西	Shanxi	NA	11	280	28639
内 蒙 古	Inner Mongolia			258	13761
辽 宁	Liaoning	NA	12	758	27608
吉 林	Jilin			321	16532
黑 龙 江	Heilongjiang			243	13052
上 海	Shanghai	NA	462	923	71873
江 苏	Jiangsu			2142	122742
浙 江	Zhejiang			2174	102338
安 徽	Anhui	NA	17	847	43208
福 建	Fujian			2125	71300
江 西	Jiangxi			550	54808
山 东	Shandong	NA	50	1752	113584
河 南	Henan			2250	128068
湖 北	Hubei			1089	65145
湖 南	Hunan			470	29520
广 东	Guangdong	8	482	6250	286671
广 西	Guangxi			355	26179
海 南	Hainan			100	10535
重 庆	Chongqing			853	41194
四 川	Sichuan			791	63366
贵 州	Guizhou			360	21822
云 南	Yunnan			362	23251
西 藏	Tibet			11	1607
陕 西	Shaanxi			608	41669
甘 肃	Gansu			201	10599
青 海	Qinghai			50	2853
宁 夏	Ningxia			49	1944
新 疆	Xinjiang	NA	28	504	30861

地区	Region	股份有限公司 Share-holding Corporations Ltd. 法人单位数(个) Number of Corporation Enterprises (unit)	股份有限公司 Share-holding Corporations Ltd. 年末从业人数(人) Engaged Persons at the Year-end (person)	私营企业 Private Enterprises 法人单位数(个) Number of Corporation Enterprises (unit)	私营企业 Private Enterprises 年末从业人数(人) Engaged Persons at the Year-end (person)
全国	**National Total**	**2106**	**446659**	**61032**	**1834929**
北京	Beijing	103	19465	2280	91091
天津	Tianjin	53	1900	2351	41779
河北	Hebei	32	18340	1104	42772
山西	Shanxi	17	3102	577	21640
内蒙古	Inner Mongolia	22	1570	317	9049
辽宁	Liaoning	70	8455	1424	29735
吉林	Jilin	34	3222	421	14365
黑龙江	Heilongjiang	40	12435	233	5998
上海	Shanghai	97	20471	1910	75220
江苏	Jiangsu	160	26415	7999	175322
浙江	Zhejiang	183	34845	9859	234033
安徽	Anhui	57	16444	1339	43362
福建	Fujian	94	16242	3771	88858
江西	Jiangxi	46	9479	454	17425
山东	Shandong	123	39521	5565	170423
河南	Henan	134	21248	1626	64793
湖北	Hubei	77	44742	1388	44110
湖南	Hunan	53	5926	1503	55898
广东	Guangdong	347	76590	10375	367626
广西	Guangxi	39	7188	843	29218
海南	Hainan	8	816	36	2372
重庆	Chongqing	62	5230	1384	48874
四川	Sichuan	55	9609	1325	56464
贵州	Guizhou	22	1356	621	17262
云南	Yunnan	54	8097	619	29463
西藏	Tibet			4	378
陕西	Shaanxi	38	14362	402	15766
甘肃	Gansu	23	3330	369	13267
青海	Qinghai	7	4390	71	2475
宁夏	Ningxia	12	3805	102	3592
新疆	Xinjiang	44	8064	760	22299

地 区	Region	港、澳、台商投资企业 Enterprises with Funds from Hongkong, Macao and Taiwan		外商投资企业 Foreign Funded Enterprises	
		法人单位数 (个) Number of Corporation Enterprises (unit)	年末从业人数 (人) Engaged Persons at the Year-end (person)	法人单位数 (个) Number of Corporation Enterprises (unit)	年末从业人数 (人) Engaged Persons at the Year-end (person)
全 国	**National Total**	**2299**	**320168**	**2689**	**411772**
北 京	Beijing	138	49106	268	82706
天 津	Tianjin	92	7159	151	10771
河 北	Hebei	5	259	5	1100
山 西	Shanxi	4	1698	NA	195
内蒙古	Inner Mongolia	NA	6		
辽 宁	Liaoning	19	1957	60	2626
吉 林	Jilin	NA	92	NA	326
黑龙江	Heilongjiang	NA	402	NA	
上 海	Shanghai	509	109587	1085	186818
江 苏	Jiangsu	176	19216	219	38294
浙 江	Zhejiang	136	11626	144	9097
安 徽	Anhui	6	317	13	7305
福 建	Fujian	129	6381	63	3469
江 西	Jiangxi	6	341	NA	758
山 东	Shandong	37	3649	71	2518
河 南	Henan	10	299	5	653
湖 北	Hubei	24	4207	18	13040
湖 南	Hunan	7	1375	9	1112
广 东	Guangdong	944	90346	505	44310
广 西	Guangxi	4	72	6	153
海 南	Hainan	5	707	5	675
重 庆	Chongqing	12	3431	14	1766
四 川	Sichuan	9	1104	13	1603
贵 州	Guizhou	NA	126	NA	440
云 南	Yunnan	5	691	4	512
西 藏	Tibet	NA	763		
陕 西	Shaanxi	4	3870	13	725
甘 肃	Gansu	NA	162	NA	136
青 海	Qinghai	NA	662	NA	53
宁 夏	Ningxia				
新 疆	Xinjiang	4	557	4	611

3-1-4 各地区限额以上批发业企业基本情况(按国民经济行业分)

Basic Conditions of Enterprises above Designated Size of Wholesale Trade by Region and Sector

地区	Region	农、林、牧产品批发 Wholesale of Agricultural, Forestry and Livestock Products		食品、饮料及烟草制品批发 Wholesale of Food, Beverages and Tobaccos	
		法人单位数(个) Number of Corporation Enterprises (unit)	年末从业人数(人) Engaged Persons at the Year-end (person)	法人单位数(个) Number of Corporation Enterprises (unit)	年末从业人数(人) Engaged Persons at the Year-end (person)
全国	**National Total**	**4946**	**200839**	**10983**	**1021175**
北京	Beijing	103	5224	439	58567
天津	Tianjin	100	1926	241	12988
河北	Hebei	120	3861	171	17744
山西	Shanxi	34	1653	111	14014
内蒙古	Inner Mongolia	90	3353	61	8301
辽宁	Liaoning	182	3789	232	17175
吉林	Jilin	184	10484	95	7845
黑龙江	Heilongjiang	106	7739	75	8052
上海	Shanghai	69	2331	356	63498
江苏	Jiangsu	603	22116	836	60375
浙江	Zhejiang	176	4474	691	61863
安徽	Anhui	197	7768	438	34373
福建	Fujian	226	5435	776	50461
江西	Jiangxi	61	5895	169	18651
山东	Shandong	585	19196	950	66718
河南	Henan	542	27791	523	58178
湖北	Hubei	250	9478	492	50169
湖南	Hunan	143	7914	316	38662
广东	Guangdong	373	17407	1762	165976
广西	Guangxi	86	2686	204	19412
海南	Hainan	NA	43	21	2535
重庆	Chongqing	76	2600	425	27045
四川	Sichuan	91	4126	566	48602
贵州	Guizhou	24	673	174	28089
云南	Yunnan	88	3095	209	29198
西藏	Tibet	NA	37	8	785
陕西	Shaanxi	58	1829	277	22776
甘肃	Gansu	35	831	139	11064
青海	Qinghai	4	332	27	2145
宁夏	Ningxia	11	275	23	2519
新疆	Xinjiang	326	16478	176	13395

3-1-4 续表 1 Continued 1

地 区	Region	纺织、服装及家庭用品批发 Wholesale of Textiles, Wearing Apparel and Household Articles		文化、体育用品及器材批发 Wholesale of Culture, Sports Appliances and Equipments	
		法人单位数（个） Number of Corporation Enterprises (unit)	年末从业人数（人） Engaged Persons at the Year-end (person)	法人单位数（个） Number of Corporation Enterprises (unit)	年末从业人数（人） Engaged Persons at the Year-end (person)
全 国	**National Total**	**13316**	**833329**	**3203**	**209118**
北 京	Beijing	408	81058	224	30761
天 津	Tianjin	189	21584	92	2887
河 北	Hebei	86	4890	27	1807
山 西	Shanxi	29	5406	16	1012
内蒙古	Inner Mongolia	12	784	6	406
辽 宁	Liaoning	158	8378	51	2439
吉 林	Jilin	45	1214	15	1002
黑龙江	Heilongjiang	24	1235	9	273
上 海	Shanghai	611	124869	157	18477
江 苏	Jiangsu	1684	101630	296	14846
浙 江	Zhejiang	3881	132445	528	14980
安 徽	Anhui	197	16986	61	2701
福 建	Fujian	1546	45289	229	5864
江 西	Jiangxi	89	3293	16	622
山 东	Shandong	513	31930	182	15577
河 南	Henan	247	20248	115	8275
湖 北	Hubei	165	12429	51	6135
湖 南	Hunan	161	9545	102	4016
广 东	Guangdong	2722	166425	840	60056
广 西	Guangxi	98	5963	23	736
海 南	Hainan	10	952	NA	370
重 庆	Chongqing	105	8453	35	6089
四 川	Sichuan	142	8735	33	2135
贵 州	Guizhou	30	1741	12	1004
云 南	Yunnan	50	1865	24	3007
西 藏	Tibet			NA	92
陕 西	Shaanxi	35	11248	31	1592
甘 肃	Gansu	20	1627	16	869
青 海	Qinghai	4	122	NA	265
宁 夏	Ningxia	NA	137	NA	119
新 疆	Xinjiang	52	2848	6	704

地区	Region	医药及医疗器材批发 Wholesale of Medicines and Medical Appliances		矿产品、建材及化工产品批发 Wholesale of Mineral Products, Building Material and Chemical Products	
		法人单位数（个）Number of Corporation Enterprises (unit)	年末从业人数（人）Engaged Persons at the Year-end (person)	法人单位数（个）Number of Corporation Enterprises (unit)	年末从业人数（人）Engaged Persons at the Year-end (person)
全国	**National Total**	**8008**	**704476**	**39971**	**1181318**
北京	Beijing	588	49869	1315	61649
天津	Tianjin	137	8825	2143	35886
河北	Hebei	222	20255	720	31625
山西	Shanxi	108	11044	540	29926
内蒙古	Inner Mongolia	61	4543	349	11428
辽宁	Liaoning	232	12471	1061	25914
吉林	Jilin	169	9654	164	7405
黑龙江	Heilongjiang	83	3688	170	14235
上海	Shanghai	229	60584	1809	61202
江苏	Jiangsu	440	58709	5225	94543
浙江	Zhejiang	434	36104	4810	90163
安徽	Anhui	296	21494	663	22858
福建	Fujian	288	14466	2288	50577
江西	Jiangxi	236	29624	332	28397
山东	Shandong	420	39237	3768	119387
河南	Henan	331	35274	1715	65644
湖北	Hubei	427	46453	853	47219
湖南	Hunan	239	18918	746	19646
广东	Guangdong	1442	92948	6439	163352
广西	Guangxi	147	11658	553	24860
海南	Hainan	55	9739	56	2171
重庆	Chongqing	288	18516	1034	27400
四川	Sichuan	479	35728	711	30281
贵州	Guizhou	142	9376	579	14927
云南	Yunnan	141	15595	459	19649
西藏	Tibet	8	2117	NA	127
陕西	Shaanxi	146	11711	478	35741
甘肃	Gansu	94	6788	251	7853
青海	Qinghai	17	1324	75	6797
宁夏	Ningxia	19	1642	86	5233
新疆	Xinjiang	90	6122	578	25223

地区	Region	机械设备、五金产品及电子产品批发 Wholesale of Machinery, Hardware and Electronic Products 法人单位数(个) Number of Corporation Enterprises (unit)	年末从业人数(人) Engaged Persons at the Year-end (person)	贸易经纪与代理 Trade Broker and Agency 法人单位数(个) Number of Corporation Enterprises (unit)	年末从业人数(人) Engaged Persons at the Year-end (person)	其他批发业 Other Wholesale not Classified Elsewhere 法人单位数(个) Number of Corporation Enterprises (unit)	年末从业人数(人) Engaged Persons at the Year-end (person)
全　国	**National Total**	**16568**	**782269**	**1291**	**38955**	**2702**	**91734**
北　京	Beijing	1259	103299	56	4030	77	5510
天　津	Tianjin	690	18233	52	1936	162	4070
河　北	Hebei	201	20352	8	217	18	743
山　西	Shanxi	107	4330			17	558
内蒙古	Inner Mongolia	55	2337	NA	17	4	188
辽　宁	Liaoning	423	10119	16	1704	57	912
吉　林	Jilin	131	3752	NA	102	18	793
黑龙江	Heilongjiang	89	3008	9	120	8	376
上　海	Shanghai	1111	120878	93	4002	132	10443
江　苏	Jiangsu	1624	51861	150	2783	335	8014
浙　江	Zhejiang	1797	57095	70	1086	213	4726
安　徽	Anhui	359	12135	14	171	102	3860
福　建	Fujian	749	22389	38	1933	145	3563
江　西	Jiangxi	145	7753	22	420	51	1178
山　东	Shandong	1185	44051	48	2309	195	6315
河　南	Henan	582	25886	7	175	112	4004
湖　北	Hubei	422	14193	7	95	64	1866
湖　南	Hunan	330	11734	5	62	77	2512
广　东	Guangdong	3898	183953	664	17063	663	18953
广　西	Guangxi	184	8282	5	47	28	475
海　南	Hainan	15	651				
重　庆	Chongqing	352	14928	5	115	86	2712
四　川	Sichuan	239	15764	NA	115	44	5008
贵　州	Guizhou	87	5316	NA	5	17	905
云　南	Yunnan	104	4037	4	219	21	1942
西　藏	Tibet	4	312			NA	21
陕　西	Shaanxi	136	5813	NA	139	20	938
甘　肃	Gansu	66	2786			9	210
青　海	Qinghai	14	516			NA	97
宁　夏	Ningxia	25	744			7	282
新　疆	Xinjiang	185	5762	7	90	16	560

3-1-5 各地区限额以上零售业企业基本情况

Basic Conditions of Enterprises above Designated Size of Retail Trade by Region

地区	Region	零售业 Retail Trade		#国有控股 State-controlled Enterprises	
		法人单位数 (个) Number of Corporation Enterprises (unit)	年末从业人数 (人) Engaged Persons at the Year-end (person)	法人单位数 (个) Number of Corporation Enterprises (unit)	年末从业人数 (人) Engaged Persons at the Year-end (person)
全国	**National Total**	**99182**	**6774776**	**5171**	**841316**
北京	Beijing	1875	320822	335	64997
天津	Tianjin	955	86781	157	19907
河北	Hebei	2526	255101	109	28419
山西	Shanxi	2051	150391	186	29684
内蒙古	Inner Mongolia	1235	81718	72	16145
辽宁	Liaoning	2289	184960	146	32116
吉林	Jilin	1861	97276	76	12773
黑龙江	Heilongjiang	1168	92631	120	10588
上海	Shanghai	1870	356647	372	56601
江苏	Jiangsu	8411	522277	301	37947
浙江	Zhejiang	5791	379812	441	36432
安徽	Anhui	4875	251095	136	25144
福建	Fujian	6069	276191	189	23547
江西	Jiangxi	2894	146993	67	12119
山东	Shandong	8007	544063	208	50021
河南	Henan	7381	434003	311	33847
湖北	Hubei	4459	321044	228	67678
湖南	Hunan	5180	264196	146	26257
广东	Guangdong	8954	697034	464	88191
广西	Guangxi	2288	130957	169	12588
海南	Hainan	206	27299	20	7044
重庆	Chongqing	3483	208586	133	46631
四川	Sichuan	4346	300873	141	30305
贵州	Guizhou	2416	101540	123	11198
云南	Yunnan	2241	138256	107	15496
西藏	Tibet	86	6101	13	2022
陕西	Shaanxi	3687	223275	214	23177
甘肃	Gansu	1092	70342	85	9571
青海	Qinghai	231	16426	12	1271
宁夏	Ningxia	273	27582	17	866
新疆	Xinjiang	982	60504	73	8734

3-1-6 各地区限额以上零售业企业基本情况(按登记注册类型分)

Basic Conditions of Enterprises above Designated Size of Retail Trade by Region and Type of Registration

地区	Region	内资企业 Domestic Funded Enterprises		国有企业 State-owned Enterprises	
		法人单位数(个) Number of Corporation Enterprises (unit)	年末从业人数(人) Engaged Persons at the Year-end (person)	法人单位数(个) Number of Corporation Enterprises (unit)	年末从业人数(人) Engaged Persons at the Year-end (person)
全国	**National Total**	**96810**	**5884853**	**1119**	**79540**
北京	Beijing	1759	262357	65	6535
天津	Tianjin	894	67634	24	3550
河北	Hebei	2510	249244	27	1019
山西	Shanxi	2027	146328	57	2433
内蒙古	Inner Mongolia	1226	80474	10	350
辽宁	Liaoning	2208	162404	61	2708
吉林	Jilin	1838	93241	4	124
黑龙江	Heilongjiang	1134	85325	53	2943
上海	Shanghai	1569	190134	36	1747
江苏	Jiangsu	8179	416206	49	2988
浙江	Zhejiang	5600	335993	29	1225
安徽	Anhui	4816	232465	10	1777
福建	Fujian	5929	223381	18	841
江西	Jiangxi	2860	138401	20	1060
山东	Shandong	7896	510127	45	6567
河南	Henan	7334	419324	122	9487
湖北	Hubei	4407	298983	79	3502
湖南	Hunan	5135	250031	50	5518
广东	Guangdong	8527	527886	102	6798
广西	Guangxi	2236	120367	32	1946
海南	Hainan	197	24673	NA	135
重庆	Chongqing	3431	194513	11	1436
四川	Sichuan	4257	266496	38	2174
贵州	Guizhou	2379	94859	31	716
云南	Yunnan	2206	122988	21	895
西藏	Tibet	84	6043	5	468
陕西	Shaanxi	3624	194725	64	7306
甘肃	Gansu	1084	68582	20	955
青海	Qinghai	228	16021		
宁夏	Ningxia	269	27038	12	239
新疆	Xinjiang	967	58610	21	2098

3-1-6 续表 1 Continued 1

地 区	Region	集体企业 Collective-owned Enterprises 法人单位数（个） Number of Corporation Enterprises (unit)	集体企业 Collective-owned Enterprises 年末从业人数（人） Engaged Persons at the Year-end (person)	股份合作企业 Cooperative Enterprises 法人单位数（个） Number of Corporation Enterprises (unit)	股份合作企业 Cooperative Enterprises 年末从业人数（人） Engaged Persons at the Year-end (person)
全 国	**National Total**	**1241**	**54650**	**267**	**14075**
北 京	Beijing	40	1408	23	807
天 津	Tianjin	27	616	5	148
河 北	Hebei	69	3222	14	4594
山 西	Shanxi	66	2731	NA	35
内蒙古	Inner Mongolia	5	144	NA	17
辽 宁	Liaoning	27	1212	6	89
吉 林	Jilin	12	229	4	2024
黑龙江	Heilongjiang	20	1306	11	443
上 海	Shanghai	19	1280	10	193
江 苏	Jiangsu	100	3014	12	214
浙 江	Zhejiang	33	1303	40	982
安 徽	Anhui	21	580	7	210
福 建	Fujian	66	1882	NA	30
江 西	Jiangxi	7	265	4	98
山 东	Shandong	114	5914	19	989
河 南	Henan	91	3967	4	119
湖 北	Hubei	74	9089	7	298
湖 南	Hunan	41	3219	4	191
广 东	Guangdong	184	5193	32	388
广 西	Guangxi	33	1426	NA	30
海 南	Hainan	NA	31		
重 庆	Chongqing	12	893	12	453
四 川	Sichuan	24	454	12	254
贵 州	Guizhou	11	106	NA	173
云 南	Yunnan	33	1718	29	987
西 藏	Tibet				
陕 西	Shaanxi	89	2754	NA	181
甘 肃	Gansu	19	642	NA	79
青 海	Qinghai				
宁 夏	Ningxia	NA	14		
新 疆	Xinjiang	NA	38	NA	49

3-1-6 续表 2 Continued 2

地区	Region	联营企业 Joint Ownership Enterprises 法人单位数(个) Number of Corporation Enterprises (unit)	联营企业 年末从业人数(人) Engaged Persons at the Year-end (person)	有限责任公司 Limited Liability Corporations 法人单位数(个) Number of Corporation Enterprises (unit)	有限责任公司 年末从业人数(人) Engaged Persons at the Year-end (person)
全　国	**National Total**	**102**	**4308**	**32572**	**2554643**
北　京	Beijing	NA	21	830	160103
天　津	Tianjin	4	65	382	37201
河　北	Hebei			643	80063
山　西	Shanxi			337	36201
内蒙古	Inner Mongolia			478	35989
辽　宁	Liaoning	NA	70	784	77096
吉　林	Jilin			717	40327
黑龙江	Heilongjiang	NA	169	489	41302
上　海	Shanghai	19	289	662	97385
江　苏	Jiangsu	6	143	1830	145310
浙　江	Zhejiang	10	164	1460	123018
安　徽	Anhui	NA	61	1441	94721
福　建	Fujian	NA	14	2261	98508
江　西	Jiangxi			1145	63130
山　东	Shandong	9	654	2042	202919
河　南	Henan	5	125	3630	231635
湖　北	Hubei	NA	89	1619	132673
湖　南	Hunan	NA	283	836	65666
广　东	Guangdong	25	1989	3835	269745
广　西	Guangxi			620	45613
海　南	Hainan			155	19968
重　庆	Chongqing	NA	28	963	59960
四　川	Sichuan	6	115	1373	117815
贵　州	Guizhou	NA	16	655	38921
云　南	Yunnan			706	48971
西　藏	Tibet			35	2700
陕　西	Shaanxi	NA	5	1707	114562
甘　肃	Gansu	NA	8	449	35364
青　海	Qinghai			88	8630
宁　夏	Ningxia			85	11212
新　疆	Xinjiang			315	17935

地区	Region	股份有限公司 Share-holding Corporations Ltd. 法人单位数(个) Number of Corporation Enterprises (unit)	股份有限公司 Share-holding Corporations Ltd. 年末从业人数(人) Engaged Persons at the Year-end (person)	私营企业 Private Enterprises 法人单位数(个) Number of Corporation Enterprises (unit)	私营企业 Private Enterprises 年末从业人数(人) Engaged Persons at the Year-end (person)
全　国	**National Total**	**2337**	**598487**	**58217**	**2545480**
北　京	Beijing	43	36182	756	57294
天　津	Tianjin	21	7329	429	18707
河　北	Hebei	48	20825	1698	139371
山　西	Shanxi	41	10686	1515	94043
内蒙古	Inner Mongolia	49	11984	673	31663
辽　宁	Liaoning	64	22838	1246	58082
吉　林	Jilin	65	15639	1020	34453
黑龙江	Heilongjiang	66	11022	479	27970
上　海	Shanghai	59	18564	761	70605
江　苏	Jiangsu	207	32197	5718	220676
浙　江	Zhejiang	122	27858	3838	180469
安　徽	Anhui	100	20143	3208	114218
福　建	Fujian	85	11115	3468	108703
江　西	Jiangxi	75	13448	1592	60032
山　东	Shandong	194	61137	5366	228184
河　南	Henan	219	34594	3203	138028
湖　北	Hubei	101	53981	2475	97468
湖　南	Hunan	108	30986	4065	142936
广　东	Guangdong	193	40038	4085	201089
广　西	Guangxi	45	8705	1503	62585
海　南	Hainan	8	2630	30	1909
重　庆	Chongqing	75	31852	2339	99562
四　川	Sichuan	103	33777	2670	110554
贵　州	Guizhou	36	5981	1632	48765
云　南	Yunnan	55	5284	1330	64293
西　藏	Tibet	8	653	35	2146
陕　西	Shaanxi	78	8448	1638	59873
甘　肃	Gansu	37	6150	542	24934
青　海	Qinghai	8	992	131	6386
宁　夏	Ningxia	7	2465	164	13108
新　疆	Xinjiang	17	10984	608	27374

地 区	Region	港、澳、台商投资企业 Enterprises with Funds from Hongkong, Macao and Taiwan		外商投资企业 Foreign Funded Enterprises	
		法人单位数 (个) Number of Corporation Enterprises (unit)	年末从业人数 (人) Engaged Persons at the Year-end (person)	法人单位数 (个) Number of Corporation Enterprises (unit)	年末从业人数 (人) Engaged Persons at the Year-end (person)
全 国	**National Total**	**1448**	**469350**	**924**	**420573**
北 京	Beijing	57	19008	59	39457
天 津	Tianjin	35	11513	26	7634
河 北	Hebei	9	1518	7	4339
山 西	Shanxi	17	2893	7	1170
内蒙古	Inner Mongolia	8	1049	NA	195
辽 宁	Liaoning	49	11775	32	10781
吉 林	Jilin	14	2964	9	1071
黑龙江	Heilongjiang	25	5098	9	2208
上 海	Shanghai	183	81174	118	85339
江 苏	Jiangsu	139	65887	93	40184
浙 江	Zhejiang	112	25995	79	17824
安 徽	Anhui	47	15037	12	3593
福 建	Fujian	78	27377	62	25433
江 西	Jiangxi	22	4927	12	3665
山 东	Shandong	69	25618	42	8318
河 南	Henan	32	12522	15	2157
湖 北	Hubei	36	10956	16	11105
湖 南	Hunan	27	8328	18	5837
广 东	Guangdong	255	75492	172	93656
广 西	Guangxi	42	8727	10	1863
海 南	Hainan	5	1023	4	1603
重 庆	Chongqing	35	8129	17	5944
四 川	Sichuan	48	14988	41	19389
贵 州	Guizhou	23	3251	14	3430
云 南	Yunnan	22	5636	13	9632
西 藏	Tibet	NA	47	NA	11
陕 西	Shaanxi	37	15874	26	12676
甘 肃	Gansu	7	1100	NA	660
青 海	Qinghai	NA	405		
宁 夏	Ningxia	NA	459	NA	85
新 疆	Xinjiang	8	580	7	1314

3-1-7 各地区限额以上零售业企业基本情况(按国民经济行业分)

Basic Conditions of Enterprises above Designated Size of Retail Trade by Region and Sector

地区	Region	综合零售 Integrated Retail		食品、饮料及烟草制品专门零售 Special Retail of Food, Beverages and Tobaccos	
		法人单位数(个) Number of Corporation Enterprises (unit)	年末从业人数(人) Engaged Persons at the Year-end (person)	法人单位数(个) Number of Corporation Enterprises (unit)	年末从业人数(人) Engaged Persons at the Year-end (person)
全国	**National Total**	**12998**	**2314872**	**9319**	**378631**
北京	Beijing	189	107156	89	16250
天津	Tianjin	93	22946	72	5606
河北	Hebei	448	130487	98	3410
山西	Shanxi	355	46530	160	7750
内蒙古	Inner Mongolia	138	24535	73	2398
辽宁	Liaoning	282	86248	116	3683
吉林	Jilin	222	32930	172	4721
黑龙江	Heilongjiang	221	38912	45	2002
上海	Shanghai	235	106047	117	20028
江苏	Jiangsu	797	176716	1010	40681
浙江	Zhejiang	473	102511	377	13600
安徽	Anhui	848	98154	580	17168
福建	Fujian	585	74572	1132	35212
江西	Jiangxi	310	48426	326	13497
山东	Shandong	991	207603	761	26398
河南	Henan	1178	151868	515	22554
湖北	Hubei	779	141527	462	21699
湖南	Hunan	673	83292	435	20566
广东	Guangdong	806	182995	563	28418
广西	Guangxi	338	44843	164	4859
海南	Hainan	62	11580	7	405
重庆	Chongqing	427	75123	425	14536
四川	Sichuan	619	105154	380	15536
贵州	Guizhou	327	29027	258	5602
云南	Yunnan	405	39140	351	12214
西藏	Tibet	20	2173	4	172
陕西	Shaanxi	775	87979	460	13665
甘肃	Gansu	219	23229	105	3914
青海	Qinghai	40	5243	22	499
宁夏	Ningxia	38	12459	16	663
新疆	Xinjiang	105	15467	24	925

地区	Region	纺织、服装及日用品专门零售 Special Retail of Textiles, Garments and Daily Consumer Articles 法人单位数(个) Number of Corporation Enterprises (unit)	年末从业人数(人) Engaged Persons at the Year-end (person)	文化、体育用品及器材专门零售 Special Retail of Culture, Sports Appliances and Equipments 法人单位数(个) Number of Corporation Enterprises (unit)	年末从业人数(人) Engaged Persons at the Year-end (person)
全国	**National Total**	**5443**	**563332**	**4475**	**246230**
北京	Beijing	166	34016	126	15374
天津	Tianjin	59	7561	60	4140
河北	Hebei	103	8980	68	8486
山西	Shanxi	121	11928	91	3998
内蒙古	Inner Mongolia	54	3247	49	2249
辽宁	Liaoning	146	7907	121	6197
吉林	Jilin	96	4497	88	3045
黑龙江	Heilongjiang	84	10735	78	3846
上海	Shanghai	299	125067	109	12969
江苏	Jiangsu	542	35686	586	21447
浙江	Zhejiang	305	33173	227	12857
安徽	Anhui	208	9166	181	5905
福建	Fujian	442	25387	258	8993
江西	Jiangxi	144	6196	63	7432
山东	Shandong	430	34070	313	18156
河南	Henan	352	17116	387	22405
湖北	Hubei	243	17894	185	7936
湖南	Hunan	218	12201	222	11449
广东	Guangdong	641	89157	387	20848
广西	Guangxi	67	2488	129	5073
海南	Hainan	5	889	15	683
重庆	Chongqing	201	17911	95	6628
四川	Sichuan	159	18416	131	12864
贵州	Guizhou	36	3198	79	2597
云南	Yunnan	66	4855	113	6280
西藏	Tibet	NA	32	4	93
陕西	Shaanxi	162	12043	181	7972
甘肃	Gansu	38	3075	68	2594
青海	Qinghai	8	1211	7	466
宁夏	Ningxia	8	1682	18	667
新疆	Xinjiang	38	3548	36	2581

地 区	Region	医药及医疗器材专门零售 Special Retail of Medicines and Medical Appliances 法人单位数(个) Number of Corporation Enterprises (unit)	医药及医疗器材专门零售 年末从业人数(人) Engaged Persons at the Year-end (person)	汽车、摩托车、燃料及零配件专门零售 Special Retail of Motor Vehicles, Motorcycles, Fuel and Parts 法人单位数(个) Number of Corporation Enterprises (unit)	汽车、摩托车、燃料及零配件专门零售 年末从业人数(人) Engaged Persons at the Year-end (person)
全 国	**National Total**	**4958**	**566911**	**37496**	**1725171**
北 京	Beijing	95	10777	776	61531
天 津	Tianjin	38	3265	486	30367
河 北	Hebei	132	20443	1176	60131
山 西	Shanxi	116	16522	820	46326
内 蒙 古	Inner Mongolia	86	7488	625	33712
辽 宁	Liaoning	163	24838	1039	41658
吉 林	Jilin	143	13032	679	27793
黑 龙 江	Heilongjiang	114	12102	437	16721
上 海	Shanghai	120	12992	724	44514
江 苏	Jiangsu	421	38708	2974	131750
浙 江	Zhejiang	309	29262	2490	123532
安 徽	Anhui	213	21995	1391	58057
福 建	Fujian	171	13410	1399	63253
江 西	Jiangxi	116	11996	1069	36148
山 东	Shandong	432	50458	3200	133986
河 南	Henan	317	33419	2531	109136
湖 北	Hubei	236	21340	1307	64815
湖 南	Hunan	210	28892	2135	72848
广 东	Guangdong	418	59869	3869	207206
广 西	Guangxi	124	18024	925	37210
海 南	Hainan	5	1661	75	9363
重 庆	Chongqing	146	14981	1107	47144
四 川	Sichuan	227	23354	1921	84746
贵 州	Guizhou	115	11122	1222	40524
云 南	Yunnan	100	24152	854	40706
西 藏	Tibet	NA	85	45	2813
陕 西	Shaanxi	212	20320	1048	47193
甘 肃	Gansu	74	9825	378	18205
青 海	Qinghai	16	1458	112	6148
宁 夏	Ningxia	32	2821	129	6811
新 疆	Xinjiang	55	8300	553	20824

3-1-7 续表 3 Continued 3

地 区	Region	家用电器及电子产品专门零售 Special Retail of Household Electric Appliances and Electronic Products		五金、家具及室内装饰材料专门零售 Special Retail of Hardware, Furniture and Interior Decoration Materials		货摊、无店铺及其他零售业 Stall, Non-shop and Other Retails	
		法人单位数（个） Number of Corporation Enterprises (unit)	年末从业人数（人） Engaged Persons at the Year-end (person)	法人单位数（个） Number of Corporation Enterprises (unit)	年末从业人数（人） Engaged Persons at the Year-end (person)	法人单位数（个） Number of Corporation Enterprises (unit)	年末从业人数（人） Engaged Persons at the Year-end (person)
全 国	**National Total**	**11352**	**475706**	**6203**	**189519**	**6938**	**314404**
北 京	Beijing	245	51106	56	9094	133	15518
天 津	Tianjin	58	4579	50	1564	39	6753
河 北	Hebei	364	17503	67	3055	70	2606
山 西	Shanxi	197	5995	88	2796	103	8546
内蒙古	Inner Mongolia	116	5250	46	1284	48	1555
辽 宁	Liaoning	269	8729	70	2029	83	3671
吉 林	Jilin	193	6097	157	2595	111	2566
黑龙江	Heilongjiang	100	5454	32	1479	57	1380
上 海	Shanghai	91	11694	71	5944	104	17392
江 苏	Jiangsu	964	41549	597	13015	520	22725
浙 江	Zhejiang	572	25533	211	5087	827	34257
安 徽	Anhui	627	17203	304	7039	523	16408
福 建	Fujian	583	17228	530	11758	969	26378
江 西	Jiangxi	379	11676	190	4224	297	7398
山 东	Shandong	853	35515	656	22856	371	15021
河 南	Henan	1042	34914	550	20160	509	22431
湖 北	Hubei	661	22645	320	9278	266	13910
湖 南	Hunan	582	17082	306	7085	399	10781
广 东	Guangdong	1003	47061	659	16038	608	45442
广 西	Guangxi	362	12367	80	1449	99	4644
海 南	Hainan	26	2161	6	270	5	287
重 庆	Chongqing	451	15895	447	10471	184	5897
四 川	Sichuan	539	20914	199	5745	171	14144
贵 州	Guizhou	241	5882	78	922	60	2666
云 南	Yunnan	207	7192	83	2238	62	1479
西 藏	Tibet	7	667			NA	66
陕 西	Shaanxi	357	14212	272	12565	220	7326
甘 肃	Gansu	103	3244	51	4754	56	1502
青 海	Qinghai	14	878	NA	141	9	382
宁 夏	Ningxia	25	2072	4	159	NA	248
新 疆	Xinjiang	121	3409	20	4425	30	1025

3-2-1 限额以上批发和零售业企业商品购、销、存情况

项　目	Item	商品购进额 Total Purchases Value	#进 口 Imports
总　计	**Total**	**5722878090**	**437438066**
一、批发业	**Wholesale Trade**	**4681653902**	**407540039**
#国有控股	State-controlled Enterprises	1774083168	127912599
(一)按登记注册类型分	**by Type of Registration**		
1.内资企业	**Domestic Funded Enterprises**	**4030110643**	**242084100**
国有企业	State-owned Enterprises	169553648	9309460
集体企业	Collective-owned Enterprises	7507122	492387
股份合作企业	Cooperative Enterprises	2446958	148459
联营企业	Joint Ownership Enterprises	276820	6871
国有联营企业	State Joint Ownership Enterprises	44057	1184
集体联营企业	Collective Joint Ownership Enterprises	53500	
国有与集体联营企业	Joint State-collective Enterprises	167060	5687
其他联营企业	Other Joint Ownership Enterprises	12205	
有限责任公司	Limited Liability Corporations	2111138395	141067859
国有独资公司	State Sole Funded Corporations	417164150	16547933
其他有限责任公司	Other Limited Liability Corporations	1693974242	124519923
股份有限公司	Share-holding Corporations Ltd.	412905089	29662709
私营企业	Private Enterprises	1319560607	61384410
私营独资企业	Private-funded Enterprises	3757054	23837
私营合伙企业	Private Partnership Enterprises	296815	6335
私营有限责任公司	Private Limited Liability Corporations	1284973769	60455127
私营股份有限公司	Private Share-holding Corporations Ltd.	30532972	899111
其他企业	Other Enterprises	6722015	11939
2.港、澳、台商投资企业	**Enterprises with Funds from Hongkong, Macao and Taiwan**	**219673892**	**30262310**
合资经营企业	Joint-venture Enterprises	39493463	1720774
合作经营企业	Cooperative Enterprises	1158864	55234
独资经营企业	Enterprises with Sole Investment	175017240	27901759
投资股份有限公司	Share-holding Corporations Ltd. with Investment	1382217	118382
其他港澳台商投资企业	Other Enterprises with Funds from Hongkong, Macao and Taiwan	2622112	466160
3.外商投资企业	**Foreign Funded Enterprises**	**431869369**	**135193635**
中外合资经营企业	Joint-venture Enterprises	143541276	6405390
中外合作经营企业	Cooperative Enterprises	440120	100548
外资企业	Enterprises with Sole Foreign Investment	277347235	126038804
外商投资股份有限公司	Share-holding Corporations Ltd. with Foreign Investment	3844778	289134
其他外商投资企业	Other Foreign Funded Enterprises	6695962	2359759

注：部分数据合计数由于单位取舍不同而产生的计算误差，未做机械调整(下表同)。
Note: Statistical discrepancies on totals figures due to rounding are not adjusted. The same applies to the tables following.

Total Purchases, Sales and Inventory of Enterprises above Designated Size of Wholesale and Retail Trades

单位：万元

Unit: 10000 yuan

商品销售额 Total Sales Value	#出 口 Exports	期末商品库存额 Inventory (year-end)
6301812537	**236170982**	**433970049**
5070959768	**235446007**	**316090047**
1914372716	58275018	111471475
4317933255	**194290874**	**258292866**
220348067	5188050	23760638
8353745	121473	460428
2522846	12760	90436
306081	9738	45831
60216		5158
57167		14740
174913	9738	23531
13786		2402
2243559042	82246883	122848964
437161220	8939482	20288850
1806397824	73307403	102560113
422054195	20791712	40293524
1413043768	85908616	70561495
4201773	15006	206178
431664		18637
1374569944	84423310	68029935
33840386	1470299	2306751
7745519	11644	231555
249464475	**6757371**	**22568083**
41687654	304429	2612113
1445703	106328	27455
201628956	6230995	19684481
1745999	50998	126132
2956165	64619	117901
503562040	**34397759**	**35229103**
157517497	1882843	6136943
520629	287	35862
332664251	31611392	28142403
5010447	51150	286052
7849222	852090	627847

项 目	Item	商品购进额 Total Purchases Value	#进 口 Imports
(二)按国民经济行业分	**by Sector**		
农、林、牧产品批发	holesale of Agricultural, Forestry and Livestock Products	88170280	8851015
食品、饮料及烟草制品批发	Wholesale of Food, Beverages and Tobaccos	357392341	19027770
米、面制品及食用油批发	Wholesale of Rice, Flour and Edible Oil	63390592	9543346
肉、禽、蛋、奶及水产品批发	Wholesale of Meal, Fowls, Eggs and Aquatic Products	24660810	2691844
酒、饮料及茶叶批发	Wholesale of Wine, Beverages and Teas	61326822	1487041
烟草制品批发	Wholesales of Tobaccos	120390807	462080
纺织、服装及家庭用品批发	Wholesale of Textiles, Wearing Apparel and Household Articles	371225406	19454952
服装批发	Wholesale of Garments	66453620	3975840
鞋帽批发	Wholesale of Shoes and Hats	18270336	869944
家用电器批发	Wholesale of Household Electrical Appliances	140402299	3609583
文化、体育用品及器材批发	Wholesale of Culture, Sports Appliances and Equipments	91898998	5333933
文具用品批发	Wholesale of Stationeries	23614944	1441444
体育用品及器材批发	Wholesale of Sports Appliances and Equipments	9297253	155316
图书批发	Wholesale of Books	9077911	317702
医药及医疗器材批发	Wholesale of Medicines and Medical Appliances	246331868	30711243
西药批发	Wholesale of Western Medicine	150219460	6514084
中药批发	Wholesale of Chinese Traditional Medicine	45172420	1524441
矿产品、建材及化工产品批发	Wholesale of Mineral Products, Building Materials and Chemical Products	2694575863	166819772
煤炭及制品批发	Wholesale of Coal and Related Products	279950399	6936015
石油及制品批发	Wholesale of Petroleum and Related Products	671272856	45941793
金属及金属矿批发	Wholesale of Metal Materials	1139608128	69439256
建材批发	Wholesale of Building Materials	133782427	7659379
化肥批发	Wholesale of Chemical Fertilizer	43385762	1870039
农药批发	Wholesale of Pesticides	3432296	70056
机械设备、五金产品及电子产品批发	Wholesale of Machinery, Hardware and Electronic Products	699937125	140267871
汽车批发	Wholesale of Motor Vehicles	252147094	42926452
计算机、软件及辅助设备批发	Wholesale of Computer, Software and Assistant Appliances	57683654	9429084
通讯及广播电视设备批发	Wholesale of Communication, Radios and Televisions Equipments	118802564	30952802
贸易经纪与代理	Trade Broker and Agency	53518178	11036515
其他批发	Other Wholesale not Classified Elsewhere	78603849	6036976

单位：万元
Unit: 10000 yuan

商品销售额 Total Sales Value	#出 口 Exports	期末商品库存额 Inventory (year-end)
93725201	1621867	22810266
453568737	8916602	35893333
67020292	2192515	9834643
28740793	1592780	2613002
77895670	401129	5895161
175300980	947737	10643121
408214196	73132905	49383052
80861326	25885656	7948944
21038034	7055533	1721121
136172222	5359383	28962422
99581335	5896076	13596513
25440419	1131725	1450482
10380073	879306	808527
9904582	33637	1710305
271333168	2915414	26403048
167895596	1585386	15504052
53606471	390567	5021178
2824172720	52353976	107992400
298551547	1286678	9124805
698326508	10859532	27891098
1184909873	14849609	43869914
143474551	4991669	5683382
46050776	1307617	4065452
4007101	911517	420113
778027873	69730600	51698322
285038902	4354118	16811576
63453566	8739550	4872926
122260125	4505049	7410674
57898348	15718854	2365674
84438192	5159719	5947446

项 目	Item	商品购进额 Total Purchases Value	#进 口 Imports
二、零售业	**Retail Trade**	**1041224189**	**29898028**
#国有控股	State-controlled Enterprises	178548460	2636118
(一)按登记注册类型分	**by Type of Registration**		
1.内资企业	**Domestic Funded Enterprises**	**917008899**	**21757031**
国有企业	State-owned Enterprises	9592784	287360
集体企业	Collective-owned Enterprises	8122331	5807
股份合作企业	Cooperative Enterprises	1567002	390
联营企业	Joint Ownership Enterprises	778713	
国有联营企业	State Joint Ownership Enterprises	88108	
集体联营企业	Collective Joint Ownership Enterprises	248936	
国有与集体联营企业	Joint State-collective Enterprises	237139	
其他联营企业	Other Joint Ownership Enterprises	204531	
有限责任公司	Limited Liability Corporations	430571529	11432245
国有独资公司	State Sole Funded Corporations	18459754	583064
其他有限责任公司	Other Limited Liability Corporations	412111778	10849185
股份有限公司	Share-holding Corporations Ltd.	114337811	459267
私营企业	Private Enterprises	349732299	9566106
私营独资企业	Private-funded Enterprises	10524567	22661
私营合伙企业	Private Partnership Enterprises	1310632	21900
私营有限责任公司	Private Limited Liability Corporations	325138779	9351615
私营股份有限公司	Private Share-holding Corporations Ltd.	12758327	169930
其他企业	Other Enterprises	2306434	5860
2.港、澳、台商投资企业	**Enterprises with Funds from Hongkong, Macao and Taiwan**	**58801704**	**4307932**
合资经营企业	Joint-venture Enterprises	16391694	810034
合作经营企业	Cooperative Enterprises	695694	1842
独资经营企业	Enterprises with Sole Investment	39463872	3425570
投资股份有限公司	Share-holding Corporations Ltd. with Investment	1386401	27823
其他港澳台商投资企业	Other Enterprises with Funds from Hongkong, Macao and Taiwan	864046	42664
3.外商投资企业	**Foreign Funded Enterprises**	**65413589**	**3833067**
中外合资经营企业	Joint-venture Enterprises	24762094	1513069
中外合作经营企业	Cooperative Enterprises	1072148	6660
外资企业	Enterprises with Sole Foreign Investment	30295644	2276659
外商投资股份有限公司	Share-holding Corporations Ltd. with Foreign Investment	1487504	
其他外商投资企业	Other Foreign Funded Enterprises	7796199	36679

单位：万元
Unit: 10000 yuan

商品销售额 Total Sales Value	#出口 Exports	期末商品库存额 Inventory (year-end)
1230852765	**724979**	**117880000**
233612753	107156	15828635
1073963170	**655313**	**102445774**
11229476	10115	1066257
8957461		450681
1717967		129847
931816		17836
127878		2599
269876		5046
284571		2494
249493		7696
497444758	293761	42334378
23839239	57351	1802846
473605518	236411	40531530
153169921	6471	16309065
397687885	344945	42011673
11816561	2409	677813
1460089		78567
369280298	337812	39623253
15130938	4724	1632042
2823888	21	126042
74220388	**52605**	**8829913**
20436090	8573	2352152
855503		44842
50113219	38181	6135593
1728274		236999
1087306	5851	60325
82669207	**17064**	**6604317**
32468213	1365	2511174
1203597		112678
39041653	14810	3484941
2203890		213618
7751861	890	281910

项 目	Item	商品购进额 Total Purchases Value	#进 口 Imports
(二)按国民经济行业分	**by Sector**		
综合零售	Integrated Retail	194575867	1874482
百货零售	Retail of General Merchandise	96560614	1304260
超级市场零售	Retail of Supermarkets	88660121	390715
食品、饮料及烟草制品专门零售	Special Retail of Food, Beverages and Tobaccos	33456696	267619
粮油零售	Retail of Cereal and Oil	4121534	6656
肉、禽、蛋、奶及水产品零售	Retail of Meat, Poultry, Eggs, Milk and Aquatic Products	5928852	10271
酒、饮料及茶叶零售	Retail of Wine, Beverages and Teas	8371958	35951
烟草制品零售	Retail of Tobaccos	1811907	108071
纺织、服装及日用品专门零售	Special Retail of Textiles, Garments and Daily Consumer Articles	40013175	2947801
服装零售	Retail of Garments	24467668	2214695
文化、体育用品及器材专门零售	Special Retail of Culture, Sports Appliances and Equipments	28038742	1062080
体育用品及器材零售	Retail of Sports Appliances and Equipments	1815075	9057
图书、报刊零售	Retail of Books, Newspaper and Magazines	10137090	547315
医药及医疗器材专门零售	Special Retail of Medicines and Medical Appliances	49018085	163101
药品零售	Retail of Medicines	46857373	47330
汽车、摩托车、燃料及零配件专门零售	Special Retail of Motor Vehicles, Motorcycles Fuel and Parts	501332246	22066217
汽车零售	Retail of Motor Vehicles	385181322	21762660
机动车燃料零售	Retail of Fuel of Motor Vehicles	107095697	179995
家用电器及电子产品专门零售	Special Retail of Household Electric Appliances and Electronic Products	88940575	473169
日用家电设备零售	Retail of Household Electric Appliances	35545642	71438
计算机、软件及辅助设备零售	Retail of Computer, Software and Assistant Appliances	23605321	229256
通信设备零售	Retail of Communication Equipments	10072948	57341
五金、家具及室内装饰材料专门零售	Special Retail of Hardware, Furniture and Interior Decoration Materials	27652211	282397
货摊、无店铺及其他零售	Stall, Non-shop and Other Retails	78196589	761170
互联网零售	Retail on the Internet	65296087	600727
(三)按零售业态分	**by Mode of Business Operation**		
有店铺零售	Store-based Retailing	935231623	28763479
超市	Supermarket	29129272	87219
大型超市	Hypermarket	84733301	137235
百货店	Department Store	87517978	1524830
专业店	Speciality Store	351520704	8226275
专卖店	Exclusive Shop	330219569	17734669
无店铺零售	Non-Store Selling	105992566	1134549

3-2-1 Continued 3

单位：万元
Unit: 10000 yuan

商品销售额 Total Sales Value	#出口 Exports	期末商品库存额 Inventory (year-end)
242519167	30620	28863132
130257881	7778	12338239
101024337	22737	15754820
42091499	34046	3254996
5338078	6	480215
6950940	12703	303962
10151471	6006	1132555
2173684		389088
58235024	78851	9797242
36295198	44918	6389062
33803140	157580	6660019
2763892	3340	447480
11118446	16663	2068288
56486009	5263	6623616
53643398	2020	6376204
572450397	138200	47069851
412185343	79057	41387994
149001792	48839	4654221
100468288	24676	9163140
39910194	39	4676265
25836886	3183	1619304
11925554	1064	1223163
33352324	103510	2276552
91446918	152235	4171460
75881209	86163	3291881
1107222905	404346	110502010
33295437	4325	9441462
98118367	20615	9423933
120545868	8306	11471022
417800810	151783	35584953
373757712	108017	39921622
123629860	320633	7377990

3-2-2 各地区限额以上批发业企业商品购、销、存情况

Total Purchases, Sales and Inventory of Enterprises above Designated Size of Wholesale Trade by Region

单位：万元

Unit: 10000 yuan

地区	Region	商品购进额 Total Purchases Value	#进口 Imports	商品销售额 Total Sales Value	#出口 Exports	期末商品库存额 Inventory (year-end)
全国	**National Total**	**4681653902**	**407540039**	**5070959768**	**235446007**	**316090047**
北京	Beijing	494177241	89692353	529998758	24179698	47222995
天津	Tianjin	267600106	14886689	279116405	4960906	14591339
河北	Hebei	64711206	905694	72113686	1019461	3239177
山西	Shanxi	67711967	229357	73423460	477794	2650836
内蒙古	Inner Mongolia	24807628	1911298	28485857	495172	4263334
辽宁	Liaoning	125197572	1295306	133702954	2164985	6556333
吉林	Jilin	19512350	338832	20209525	138339	3621611
黑龙江	Heilongjiang	26657258	5324578	30128137	601698	4135011
上海	Shanghai	796260464	130984406	879030166	39589711	49017385
江苏	Jiangsu	408341349	14326183	433340598	24777475	37208749
浙江	Zhejiang	452012198	26180954	482031936	45568843	20398539
安徽	Anhui	66705697	2538005	73870499	2214571	6011447
福建	Fujian	208914880	20398792	227840392	15766714	11412410
江西	Jiangxi	22662105	111955	30752876	657323	1955990
山东	Shandong	218284349	7959875	240252192	10395113	11568920
河南	Henan	89842035	1131368	101268265	1029692	6720227
湖北	Hubei	106560170	610718	119011756	3850132	8054137
湖南	Hunan	50929878	482598	54916814	559834	4451816
广东	Guangdong	668486557	64710994	695014421	45154617	40818450
广西	Guangxi	49463848	1645628	55011286	3208673	2836379
海南	Hainan	15936613	341660	17658512	204491	560223
重庆	Chongqing	72754959	3485617	81434378	1834235	3680646
四川	Sichuan	73449988	1133083	82115244	1186429	4732689
贵州	Guizhou	30314729	83534	38082638	1055063	2256804
云南	Yunnan	59770146	3085556	68532388	2527111	5226655
西藏	Tibet	779194	6005	1086938		106004
陕西	Shaanxi	77664589	256850	91292050	917079	2666598
甘肃	Gansu	33464793	174139	35252131	196390	1968890
青海	Qinghai	7636645	27000	10120880	53657	405190
宁夏	Ningxia	12006532	43768	12103948	27527	718141
新疆	Xinjiang	69036856	13237243	73760678	633274	7033122

3-2-2 续表 Continued

国有控股 单位：万元

State-controlled Enterprises Unit: 10000 yuan

地 区	Region	商品购进额 Total Purchases Value	#进口 Imports	商品销售额 Total Sales Value	#出口 Exports	期末商品库存额 Inventory (year-end)
全 国	**National Total**	**1774083168**	**127912599**	**1914372716**	**58275018**	**111471475**
北 京	Beijing	277284561	45025636	286022727	19944531	24168486
天 津	Tianjin	141422999	7499157	143774177	2265414	7497746
河 北	Hebei	21309357	696422	24854886	91494	1000418
山 西	Shanxi	49992138	216276	52976757	17037	1214019
内蒙古	Inner Mongolia	15920665	1039578	17719079	408309	3447276
辽 宁	Liaoning	68121627	130376	72895509	463073	3453741
吉 林	Jilin	12912969	162523	12209614	48153	2919559
黑龙江	Heilongjiang	17573831	4792575	20175040	353019	3551644
上 海	Shanghai	242574423	9924580	262858441	7724157	9553943
江 苏	Jiangsu	72184912	2473285	85424996	5943824	4213727
浙 江	Zhejiang	105134388	7399857	114714321	5451241	5311934
安 徽	Anhui	28240318	1630360	30918333	938525	2417419
福 建	Fujian	83863204	14893293	91091578	3215601	5425853
江 西	Jiangxi	10251390	36933	15582014	25307	1008520
山 东	Shandong	51117814	957353	57694055	733192	2239484
河 南	Henan	33387743	476680	38016076	218265	4119296
湖 北	Hubei	51169206	137813	55704482	523411	3703405
湖 南	Hunan	21185133	136688	20737188	165751	2542817
广 东	Guangdong	197665693	11437292	200377162	6355709	7765208
广 西	Guangxi	25075542	796278	28287482	26035	1289509
海 南	Hainan	2860855	184	3385275	2078	270327
重 庆	Chongqing	21168710	2284593	24989267	934839	1002853
四 川	Sichuan	31733965	275266	37069531	220639	1774629
贵 州	Guizhou	14645605	40188	19632302	551761	1146659
云 南	Yunnan	43520410	2197706	50617069	909777	3658209
西 藏	Tibet	544221	84	714835		82319
陕 西	Shaanxi	45168095	127869	52779120	548314	1233606
甘 肃	Gansu	24897463	868	25841905	4006	1109423
青 海	Qinghai	5811712	27000	6355485		185734
宁 夏	Ningxia	5845955	2703	5699270	775	534706
新 疆	Xinjiang	51498263	13093183	55254740	190781	3629006

3-2-3 各地区限额以上批发业企业商品购、销、存情况（按登记注册类型分）

Total Purchases, Sales and Inventory of Enterprises above Designated Size of Wholesale Trade by Region and Type of Registration

内资企业　　　　单位：万元

Domestic Funded Enterprises　　　　Unit: 10000 yuan

地区	Region	商品购进额 Total Purchases Value	#进口 Imports	商品销售额 Total Sales Value	#出口 Exports	期末商品库存额 Inventory (year-end)
全国	**National Total**	**4030110643**	**242084100**	**4317933255**	**194290874**	**258292866**
北京	Beijing	369763382	55064080	385723568	22207858	32584486
天津	Tianjin	243531764	10623718	252097108	3795351	11940112
河北	Hebei	62622183	905656	69791064	1019423	3222088
山西	Shanxi	66229056	51138	71908878	477794	2612301
内蒙古	Inner Mongolia	24733739	1911298	28412065	495172	4263237
辽宁	Liaoning	123587840	1058193	131689494	2021023	6403513
吉林	Jilin	17810450	338832	18316868	138339	3604539
黑龙江	Heilongjiang	24687556	5324578	28140564	601698	4134266
上海	Shanghai	496948816	24205229	525793042	12957295	23155270
江苏	Jiangsu	369026996	7681758	387596113	19994692	34603687
浙江	Zhejiang	422451674	24288526	451381036	44681905	19139050
安徽	Anhui	61962228	2147521	68397847	2205713	4609946
福建	Fujian	198071604	19565016	215184344	15425369	10675884
江西	Jiangxi	22219564	103285	30278615	414321	1943768
山东	Shandong	212371864	7653216	232969128	9128610	11029009
河南	Henan	86681314	1131331	97985931	953990	6710974
湖北	Hubei	93523953	463404	104745067	3783313	6819944
湖南	Hunan	49143032	330236	52574333	549683	4412208
广东	Guangdong	601308810	56609058	619438582	41983653	35052894
广西	Guangxi	49175701	1600660	54700855	3171814	2823915
海南	Hainan	14795542	204499	16453724	70854	546991
重庆	Chongqing	67531737	2877813	75632049	1617884	3405823
四川	Sichuan	68187904	1066896	76709844	1186429	4482921
贵州	Guizhou	30029659	83534	37745884	1055063	2246569
云南	Yunnan	59103589	3073051	67785005	2526611	5150853
西藏	Tibet	660753	6005	916543		104430
陕西	Shaanxi	72170733	233419	85474554	917079	2574892
甘肃	Gansu	33438813	174139	35220535	196390	1968284
青海	Qinghai	7442441	27000	9164846	53657	341560
宁夏	Ningxia	12006532	43768	12103948	27527	718141
新疆	Xinjiang	68891414	13237243	73601821	632364	7011311

3-2-3 续表 1 Continued 1

国有企业 单位：万元

State-owned Enterprises Unit: 10000 yuan

地 区	Region	商品购进额 Total Purchases Value	#进口 Imports	商品销售额 Total Sales Value	#出口 Exports	期末商品库存额 Inventory (year-end)
全 国	**National Total**	**169553648**	**9309460**	**220348067**	**5188050**	**23760638**
北 京	Beijing	30609832	8018949	32553014	1409177	2201719
天 津	Tianjin	9219501	650109	9527335	241163	554775
河 北	Hebei	4355390	130	5937954	34756	406571
山 西	Shanxi	2642400	50	3657160		349029
内蒙古	Inner Mongolia	2129425	46	3377782		2508965
辽 宁	Liaoning	7499179	26152	8898501	116944	530022
吉 林	Jilin	1913132	2399	2664055		2448623
黑龙江	Heilongjiang	4326576	1405	5177731	2200	577837
上 海	Shanghai	3067662	90173	3421255	278465	163649
江 苏	Jiangsu	12350164	69335	15631972	1427616	851109
浙 江	Zhejiang	6768887	4307	10364912	102572	467266
安 徽	Anhui	3818215	38205	5867580	167697	478557
福 建	Fujian	6517766	98713	8526682	1001916	423876
江 西	Jiangxi	2941590	8611	4741218	13049	415309
山 东	Shandong	2018135	43437	2227464	6377	194945
河 南	Henan	7352927	8304	10322379		2234464
湖 北	Hubei	5063217	7341	7595648		866424
湖 南	Hunan	5609636	6129	8597386	5640	1227738
广 东	Guangdong	5630953	149876	6436889	255479	885965
广 西	Guangxi	3270938	1311	4755670	572	336313
海 南	Hainan	2318177		2795048		209763
重 庆	Chongqing	5076000	1042	7971846	69	196918
四 川	Sichuan	5817080	2723	9243277	73368	791730
贵 州	Guizhou	5026623		7823996		771999
云 南	Yunnan	7646297	45	12190331	21163	2257065
西 藏	Tibet	477980		630056		67570
陕 西	Shaanxi	6052504	642	8011581	25551	225487
甘 肃	Gansu	1947778	868	2619939	4006	208023
青 海	Qinghai	906935		1095333		30926
宁 夏	Ningxia	1083222		1270752		78006
新 疆	Xinjiang	6095527	79158	6413321	270	799995

3-2-3 续表 2 Continued 2

集体企业 | 单位：万元

Collective-owned Enterprises | Unit: 10000 yuan

地 区	Region	商品购进额 Total Purchases Value	#进口 Imports	商品销售额 Total Sales Value	#出口 Exports	期末商品库存额 Inventory (year-end)
全 国	**National Total**	**7507122**	**492387**	**8353745**	**121473**	**460428**
北 京	Beijing	664876	478622	682526		16333
天 津	Tianjin	81866		90392		11575
河 北	Hebei	139879		156507		11370
山 西	Shanxi	525416		628990		52150
内蒙古	Inner Mongolia	141574		149350		2800
辽 宁	Liaoning	146221		183128		8723
吉 林	Jilin	1914		2084		73
黑龙江	Heilongjiang	45553		46186		365
上 海	Shanghai	60767	187	64754		10128
江 苏	Jiangsu	511935		563675	28959	25778
浙 江	Zhejiang	79867		85636	3166	8985
安 徽	Anhui	55477		57324		2034
福 建	Fujian	291980	1290	293778	48262	40895
江 西	Jiangxi	37523		38857		3982
山 东	Shandong	1030441		1100152		25773
河 南	Henan	1020905		1158368		11137
湖 北	Hubei	157026		170423		4381
湖 南	Hunan	105443		134287		11849
广 东	Guangdong	375742		412881	30251	32469
广 西	Guangxi	676937	220	736220		16371
海 南	Hainan					
重 庆	Chongqing	172013		180544		9283
四 川	Sichuan	639590		861726	5727	51792
贵 州	Guizhou	82298		79942		8704
云 南	Yunnan	146953	12068	169220	5108	14697
西 藏	Tibet					
陕 西	Shaanxi	121764		136695		3584
甘 肃	Gansu	44027		49290		4657
青 海	Qinghai	6776		6723		98
宁 夏	Ningxia					
新 疆	Xinjiang	142359		114087		70442

3-2-3 续表 3 Continued 3

股份合作企业 单位：万元

Cooperative Enterprises Unit: 10000 yuan

地 区	Region	商品购进额 Total Purchases Value	#进口 Imports	商品销售额 Total Sales Value	#出口 Exports	期末商品库存额 Inventory (year-end)
全 国	**National Total**	**2446958**	**148459**	**2522846**	**12760**	**90436**
北 京	Beijing	140968	1062	152031		17893
天 津	Tianjin	17272		18763		1163
河 北	Hebei	8234		11059		65
山 西	Shanxi	398		602		11
内蒙古	Inner Mongolia					
辽 宁	Liaoning	27871		27087		3150
吉 林	Jilin					
黑龙江	Heilongjiang					
上 海	Shanghai	21597	5600	22876		549
江 苏	Jiangsu	1356586	130424	1370027	698	9321
浙 江	Zhejiang	78810		90802		7249
安 徽	Anhui	87707		87629		1445
福 建	Fujian	11837		12063	12062	260
江 西	Jiangxi	4107		3391		1350
山 东	Shandong	40270	3100	40542		2644
河 南	Henan	6270		6239		107
湖 北	Hubei	24969		25958		1299
湖 南	Hunan					
广 东	Guangdong	131432	8273	140813		7815
广 西	Guangxi	3748		3750		108
海 南	Hainan					
重 庆	Chongqing	394604		410132		18777
四 川	Sichuan	18331		20334		1140
贵 州	Guizhou					
云 南	Yunnan	6372		12751		1555
西 藏	Tibet					
陕 西	Shaanxi	22540		24265		236
甘 肃	Gansu	27554		29794		4867
青 海	Qinghai	1562		1436		125
宁 夏	Ningxia					
新 疆	Xinjiang	13919		10502		9307

3-2-3 续表 4 Continued 4

联营企业 单位：万元

Joint Ownership Enterprises Unit: 10000 yuan

地区	Region	商品购进额 Total Purchases Value	#进口 Imports	商品销售额 Total Sales Value	#出口 Exports	期末商品库存额 Inventory (year-end)
全国	**National Total**	**276820**	**6871**	**306081**	**9738**	**45831**
北京	Beijing	23378	6871	24869	9738	2240
天津	Tianjin					
河北	Hebei					
山西	Shanxi	5990		6109		15
内蒙古	Inner Mongolia					
辽宁	Liaoning	1957		2350		1766
吉林	Jilin					
黑龙江	Heilongjiang					
上海	Shanghai	151828		159108		21452
江苏	Jiangsu					
浙江	Zhejiang					
安徽	Anhui	6090		6098		172
福建	Fujian					
江西	Jiangxi					
山东	Shandong	8633		9686		12208
河南	Henan					
湖北	Hubei					
湖南	Hunan					
广东	Guangdong	73743		92669		7914
广西	Guangxi					
海南	Hainan					
重庆	Chongqing					
四川	Sichuan					
贵州	Guizhou					
云南	Yunnan					
西藏	Tibet					
陕西	Shaanxi					
甘肃	Gansu					
青海	Qinghai					
宁夏	Ningxia					
新疆	Xinjiang	5201		5192		64

3-2-3 续表 5 Continued 5

有限责任公司
Limited Liability Corporations

单位：万元
Unit: 10000 yuan

地 区	Region	商品购进额 Total Purchases Value	#进 口 Imports	商品销售额 Total Sales Value	#出 口 Exports	期末商品库存额 Inventory (year-end)
全 国	**National Total**	**2111138395**	**141067859**	**2243559042**	**82246883**	**122848964**
北 京	Beijing	259795833	37834224	269849408	15315007	23887644
天 津	Tianjin	170131151	8327027	174045898	1499318	8046364
河 北	Hebei	32242859	766793	35092201	267780	1213372
山 西	Shanxi	47589250	38028	50174367	27104	1049338
内蒙古	Inner Mongolia	13853084	1167983	15495838	468567	1192624
辽 宁	Liaoning	43787069	566414	46771582	942981	3264239
吉 林	Jilin	8901685	263100	7900409	89838	686531
黑龙江	Heilongjiang	13992474	4951402	14766369	505179	2994376
上 海	Shanghai	249801722	9978863	267644512	7754332	15044808
江 苏	Jiangsu	135823374	4225351	150968807	9258177	7573697
浙 江	Zhejiang	169508831	11832480	179876791	13386071	7670287
安 徽	Anhui	33769392	1437773	36604021	547413	2319747
福 建	Fujian	84097541	6300197	92513373	4865919	4885482
江 西	Jiangxi	13681706	55122	15277938	245833	935164
山 东	Shandong	101302629	3862056	113611493	4597087	4850395
河 南	Henan	53263566	992987	59000202	581490	2254538
湖 北	Hubei	51747933	354769	56439890	825725	3589297
湖 南	Hunan	21684821	144071	19114911	282764	1744136
广 东	Guangdong	336788074	31172576	346514421	16060972	16424398
广 西	Guangxi	29987042	854483	32028011	489124	1378950
海 南	Hainan	11003487	148262	11991791	24854	271805
重 庆	Chongqing	37871811	2729330	40840353	1072954	2000192
四 川	Sichuan	39132657	878168	41477654	926535	1740191
贵 州	Guizhou	17668939	17496	21869547	326370	1048759
云 南	Yunnan	35278732	2233587	37823051	1079625	1476858
西 藏	Tibet	152799	6005	238591		32204
陕 西	Shaanxi	46134004	142293	52003577	570554	1425418
甘 肃	Gansu	10469873	3552	10836851	35278	495871
青 海	Qinghai	4371225	27000	4796018	21591	125874
宁 夏	Ningxia	1569901	4133	1615877	775	70181
新 疆	Xinjiang	35734931	9752334	36375290	177666	3156224

3-2-3 续表 6 Continued 6

股份有限公司

Share-holding Corporations Ltd.

单位：万元

Unit: 10000 yuan

地 区	Region	商品购进额 Total Purchases Value	#进 口 Imports	商品销售额 Total Sales Value	#出 口 Exports	期末商品库存额 Inventory (year-end)
全 国	**National Total**	**412905089**	**29662709**	**422054195**	**20791712**	**40293524**
北 京	Beijing	26922918	5903371	27804591	4671274	2079668
天 津	Tianjin	5010118	189424	5798111	964679	162019
河 北	Hebei	2336072	52543	2503827	64244	142046
山 西	Shanxi	2670935		3203787	353385	133392
内 蒙 古	Inner Mongolia	4299008	39830	4305062		203478
辽 宁	Liaoning	44585949	26747	46459084	129319	1029547
吉 林	Jilin	4084969	9513	4124824		97333
黑 龙 江	Heilongjiang	3340461	4365	4858855	8584	277646
上 海	Shanghai	24577948	1025442	26217156	1134770	1550599
江 苏	Jiangsu	52556009	886530	38353018	1426473	19630056
浙 江	Zhejiang	36433606	2465852	40020648	2861217	1432260
安 徽	Anhui	9408092	505140	9432792	1034907	752418
福 建	Fujian	34855481	10242284	35757852	1631570	2630320
江 西	Jiangxi	1453450		4738083		227074
山 东	Shandong	10930801	1042083	11783448	182850	681057
河 南	Henan	9338639		9762260	83966	1322832
湖 北	Hubei	19594196	12910	21613498	39637	1300315
湖 南	Hunan	1600301	2884	2237930	43058	238773
广 东	Guangdong	52402007	3867974	46634181	5548128	2663351
广 西	Guangxi	2138606	1723	2758547	31572	106505
海 南	Hainan	414445	13907	498011	16278	25617
重 庆	Chongqing	3754494		3926123	21	171336
四 川	Sichuan	3629014	8245	4261695	26433	230273
贵 州	Guizhou	1541903	28111	1657563	225391	43768
云 南	Yunnan	6202153	5170	6930285	48252	380892
西 藏	Tibet					
陕 西	Shaanxi	12244819		16752109	220682	437663
甘 肃	Gansu	15288699		15481160		817461
青 海	Qinghai	1022003		1390445		145185
宁 夏	Ningxia	4320456		3959910		442214
新 疆	Xinjiang	15947536	3328662	18829340	45022	938426

3-2-3 续表 7 Continued 7

私营企业 单位：万元

Private Enterprises Unit: 10000 yuan

地 区	Region	商品购进额 Total Purchases Value	#进口 Imports	商品销售额 Total Sales Value	#出口 Exports	期末商品库存额 Inventory (year-end)
全 国	**National Total**	**1319560607**	**61384410**	**1413043768**	**85908616**	**70561495**
北 京	Beijing	51605577	2820981	54657130	802661	4378989
天 津	Tianjin	59071855	1457157	62616608	1090191	3164217
河 北	Hebei	23481371	86190	26022269	652642	1438975
山 西	Shanxi	12731583	13061	14163115	95407	1018954
内蒙古	Inner Mongolia	4306144	703438	5079403	26605	354497
辽 宁	Liaoning	27500922	438879	29305675	831779	1564226
吉 林	Jilin	2908750	63820	3625496	48502	371978
黑龙江	Heilongjiang	2922693	367407	3232519	85735	282494
上 海	Shanghai	217891939	13104963	226855904	3789728	6345878
江 苏	Jiangsu	164462514	2370118	178436290	7848548	6447775
浙 江	Zhejiang	209235051	9985887	220576351	28328761	9535829
安 徽	Anhui	14687110	166402	16198479	455697	1053972
福 建	Fujian	72249249	2915325	78027649	7865640	2692468
江 西	Jiangxi	4088507	39552	5462359	155439	360667
山 东	Shandong	96146497	2702475	103230373	4342246	5230806
河 南	Henan	15541640	130040	17530320	288534	883342
湖 北	Hubei	16511049	88384	18291744	2917951	1043866
湖 南	Hunan	20080467	177151	22418326	218220	1185711
广 东	Guangdong	205534959	21406546	218737860	20086302	15024805
广 西	Guangxi	13059846	742068	14377118	2650547	985354
海 南	Hainan	1059434	42330	1168874	29723	39807
重 庆	Chongqing	20187103	147440	22148113	544840	1007281
四 川	Sichuan	18862094	177761	20742672	154366	1660144
贵 州	Guizhou	5702807	37927	6305457	503302	373321
云 南	Yunnan	9726454	822181	10544827	1372463	1019224
西 藏	Tibet	29974		47896		4655
陕 西	Shaanxi	7430533	90484	8351056	97455	465243
甘 肃	Gansu	5657433	169719	6199797	157107	437005
青 海	Qinghai	1133941		1874891	32066	39352
宁 夏	Ningxia	5032954	39635	5257410	26753	127741
新 疆	Xinjiang	10720157	77089	11557786	409406	2022919

3-2-3 续表 8 Continued 8

其他企业 单位：万元

Other Enterprises Unit: 10000 yuan

地　区	Region	商品购进额 Total Purchases Value	#进口 Imports	商品销售额 Total Sales Value	#出口 Exports	期末商品库存额 Inventory (year-end)
全　国	**National Total**	**6722015**	**11939**	**7745519**	**11644**	**231555**
北　京	Beijing					
天　津	Tianjin					
河　北	Hebei	58378		67247		9688
山　西	Shanxi	63084		74747	1898	9411
内蒙古	Inner Mongolia	4506		4631		873
辽　宁	Liaoning	38673		42087		1840
吉　林	Jilin					
黑龙江	Heilongjiang	59799		58905		1547
上　海	Shanghai	1375353		1407477		18208
江　苏	Jiangsu	1966414		2272324	4221	65952
浙　江	Zhejiang	346621		365896	118	17174
安　徽	Anhui	130147		143924		1600
福　建	Fujian	47751	7206	52948		2583
江　西	Jiangxi	12681		16771		221
山　东	Shandong	894459	65	965971	50	31182
河　南	Henan	157368		206163		4554
湖　北	Hubei	425563		607905		14363
湖　南	Hunan	62364		71494		4001
广　东	Guangdong	371901	3813	468868	2520	6178
广　西	Guangxi	38583	855	41539		314
海　南	Hainan					
重　庆	Chongqing	75712		154938		2036
四　川	Sichuan	89139		102486		7652
贵　州	Guizhou	7090		9380		18
云　南	Yunnan	96629		114539		563
西　藏	Tibet					
陕　西	Shaanxi	164569		195271	2837	17261
甘　肃	Gansu	3447		3704		401
青　海	Qinghai					
宁　夏	Ningxia					
新　疆	Xinjiang	231784		296303		13935

港、澳、台商投资企业　　　　单位：万元

Enterprises with Funds from Hongkong, Macao and Taiwan　　　　Unit: 10000 yuan

地　区	Region	商品购进额 Total Purchases Value	#进口 Imports	商品销售额 Total Sales Value	#出口 Exports	期末商品库存额 Inventory (year-end)
全　国	**National Total**	**219673892**	**30262310**	**249464475**	**6757371**	**22568083**
北　京	Beijing	51835686	3208613	54529363	152398	5320834
天　津	Tianjin	13304715	919543	14567049	793321	1932098
河　北	Hebei	334095		377694		685
山　西	Shanxi	1473283	178219	1505001		38417
内蒙古	Inner Mongolia	73889		73792		97
辽　宁	Liaoning	525424	17890	636254	7259	64529
吉　林	Jilin	93458		96956		548
黑龙江	Heilongjiang	142037		159650		745
上　海	Shanghai	73213160	18647763	87616805	2713979	7199490
江　苏	Jiangsu	11803811	545055	14180740	200498	780818
浙　江	Zhejiang	7684441	863091	8508497	417512	407234
安　徽	Anhui	2488040	390484	2447810		1236702
福　建	Fujian	5917823	578572	6544370	175722	470119
江　西	Jiangxi	121448		125479	10178	12037
山　东	Shandong	3664416	61183	4837083	907959	414679
河　南	Henan	2848916		2872492	66515	1462
湖　北	Hubei	2787147	30158	3244479		937945
湖　南	Hunan	215471	98258	291927		15745
广　东	Guangdong	30410958	4096834	34580667	1145055	3246928
广　西	Guangxi	161061	36350	168704	32835	1770
海　南	Hainan	1076174	133654	1107155	133637	2582
重　庆	Chongqing	3927134	386738	4389429	3	165621
四　川	Sichuan	4331004	64450	4432794		186240
贵　州	Guizhou	240412		274909		7546
云　南	Yunnan	419806	5455	443510	500	5788
西　藏	Tibet	118441		170395		1574
陕　西	Shaanxi	134305		184813		32737
甘　肃	Gansu	16261		19529		1
青　海	Qinghai	191085		951850		63158
宁　夏	Ningxia					
新　疆	Xinjiang	119991		125279		19954

3-2-3 续表 10 Continued 10

外商投资企业 单位：万元

Foreign Funded Enterprises Unit: 10000 yuan

地区	Region	商品购进额 Total Purchases Value	#进口 Imports	商品销售额 Total Sales Value	#出口 Exports	期末商品库存额 Inventory (year-end)
全国	**National Total**	**431869369**	**135193635**	**503562040**	**34397759**	**35229103**
北京	Beijing	72578173	31419660	89745827	1819441	9317675
天津	Tianjin	10763627	3343429	12452248	372234	719129
河北	Hebei	1754929	39	1944928	38	16405
山西	Shanxi	9628		9582		119
内蒙古	Inner Mongolia					
辽宁	Liaoning	1084308	219222	1377206	136703	88291
吉林	Jilin	1608442		1795701		16525
黑龙江	Heilongjiang	1827665		1827924		
上海	Shanghai	226098488	88131414	265620320	23918437	18662625
江苏	Jiangsu	27510542	6099371	31563745	4582285	1824244
浙江	Zhejiang	21876083	1029337	22142403	469426	852255
安徽	Anhui	2255429		3024842	8858	164800
福建	Fujian	4925453	255205	6111677	165623	266408
江西	Jiangxi	321093	8671	348782	232823	185
山东	Shandong	2248068	245475	2445981	358544	125232
河南	Henan	311804	37	409842	9186	7791
湖北	Hubei	10249070	117156	11022210	66819	296248
湖南	Hunan	1571376	54105	2050554	10151	23862
广东	Guangdong	36766790	4005102	40995172	2025909	2518627
广西	Guangxi	127086	8618	141726	4024	10694
海南	Hainan	64896	3508	97633		10650
重庆	Chongqing	1296088	221067	1412900	216348	109203
四川	Sichuan	931081	1737	972606		63527
贵州	Guizhou	44658		61846		2689
云南	Yunnan	246751	7050	303873		70015
西藏	Tibet					
陕西	Shaanxi	5359551	23432	5632683		58969
甘肃	Gansu	9719		12068		605
青海	Qinghai	3119		4183		473
宁夏	Ningxia					
新疆	Xinjiang	25452		33578	910	1857

3-2-4 各地区限额以上批发业企业商品购、销、存情况（按国民经济行业分）

Total Purchases, Sales and Inventory of Enterprises above Designated Size of Wholesale Trade by Region and Sector

农、林、牧产品批发　　　　单位：万元

Wholesale of Agricultural, Forestry and Livestock Products　　　　Unit: 10000 yuan

地区	Region	商品购进额 Total Purchases Value	#进口 Imports	商品销售额 Total Sales Value	#出口 Exports	期末商品库存额 Inventory (year-end)
全国	**National Total**	**88170280**	**8851015**	**93725201**	**1621867**	**22810266**
北京	Beijing	12565035	4678417	12340190	46878	1426712
天津	Tianjin	2260143	71425	2254537	24406	709318
河北	Hebei	1449154	2930	1550581	25	182895
山西	Shanxi	251690	211	261034	7707	131799
内蒙古	Inner Mongolia	649282	3561	1319868	49077	2309774
辽宁	Liaoning	4202472	30273	3879646	48499	1401238
吉林	Jilin	1762751		2276815	31795	2442181
黑龙江	Heilongjiang	2589337	91	2510563	1950	2487324
上海	Shanghai	7756005	1190037	7954796	24873	546831
江苏	Jiangsu	7251045	98089	8173699	41035	600561
浙江	Zhejiang	2340329	127045	2495879	185474	351569
安徽	Anhui	1279915	11098	1339861	13245	437834
福建	Fujian	3070345	325323	3136662	374206	480550
江西	Jiangxi	344583		435869	25619	204928
山东	Shandong	5872509	243392	6189350	231320	566026
河南	Henan	4610061	372196	4742742	73520	2691318
湖北	Hubei	2937596	34799	4616535	28742	730281
湖南	Hunan	1297073	38604	1654347	9924	193035
广东	Guangdong	10571163	1344820	11394471	291807	1031009
广西	Guangxi	1275497	59137	1369056	45111	204042
海南	Hainan	14917		15131		77
重庆	Chongqing	860985	9644	980725	6889	76396
四川	Sichuan	1157948		1274650	176	133360
贵州	Guizhou	106600	6337	119432		17936
云南	Yunnan	373609	23751	454530	18510	81528
西藏	Tibet	627		802		262
陕西	Shaanxi	490632		544290	13759	37122
甘肃	Gansu	219461	3302	237615	13837	28918
青海	Qinghai	92383		100081		5234
宁夏	Ningxia	83062		89656	640	15937
新疆	Xinjiang	10434071	176533	10011788	12843	3284271

食品、饮料及烟草制品批发 单位：万元
Wholesale of Food, Beverages and Tobaccos Unit: 10000 yuan

地区	Region	商品购进额 Total Purchases Value	#进口 Imports	商品销售额 Total Sales Value	#出口 Exports	期末商品库存额 Inventory (year-end)
全国	**National Total**	**357392341**	**19027770**	**453568737**	**8916602**	**35893333**
北京	Beijing	24982047	4073039	28690150	317933	1867874
天津	Tianjin	9057434	979698	11482365	680595	899716
河北	Hebei	5391202	5537	7322740	33912	519940
山西	Shanxi	3984408		5390863		492399
内蒙古	Inner Mongolia	2393785	46	3222377	10103	385976
辽宁	Liaoning	5387995	103374	6897352	87985	614900
吉林	Jilin	2352474	3701	3305836		360446
黑龙江	Heilongjiang	3633556	14370	4574446	34607	600688
上海	Shanghai	44761060	7198567	52909398	1699886	4022611
江苏	Jiangsu	21242901	271641	27404353	285288	1303900
浙江	Zhejiang	21979200	473400	28086773	490503	1919368
安徽	Anhui	8930374	736648	12153871	276263	1145755
福建	Fujian	20035045	1128821	23673758	1478537	1479044
江西	Jiangxi	4034357	5467	6020584	64769	576298
山东	Shandong	19323889	499565	24438548	632299	1468840
河南	Henan	12309894	21280	16634286	78000	1042544
湖北	Hubei	14150450	13086	18462808	27483	1737926
湖南	Hunan	9077171	111444	13272708	51879	1850236
广东	Guangdong	47278579	2551674	57452380	1310806	4812576
广西	Guangxi	10064894	333955	12357618	357990	675996
海南	Hainan	2478808	388	2986806	163	216244
重庆	Chongqing	11031441	33023	14544073	92	503650
四川	Sichuan	12700891	28078	17199436	51812	1831540
贵州	Guizhou	13166491	150	17791078	62210	1406082
云南	Yunnan	10871353	412765	15948489	705629	2673510
西藏	Tibet	516868	84	695337		75881
陕西	Shaanxi	6216786	13288	8434675	16904	423029
甘肃	Gansu	2580467	3014	3519046	38770	294067
青海	Qinghai	1073961		1328426	2172	44327
宁夏	Ningxia	1285396		1480043		78981
新疆	Xinjiang	5099164	11667	5888114	120012	568989

纺织、服装及家庭用品批发　　　　单位：万元
Wholesale of Textiles, Wearing Apparel and Household Articles　　　　Unit: 10000 yuan

地区	Region	商品购进额 Total Purchases Value	#进口 Imports	商品销售额 Total Sales Value	#出口 Exports	期末商品库存额 Inventory (year-end)
全国	**National Total**	**371225406**	**19454952**	**408214196**	**73132905**	**49383052**
北京	Beijing	51655274	3686184	55017746	646165	6306721
天津	Tianjin	7929533	195018	9126180	709908	518342
河北	Hebei	2188424	14381	2545940	197190	261242
山西	Shanxi	861679		965338	362578	110406
内蒙古	Inner Mongolia	284076		326473		81204
辽宁	Liaoning	2144029	309340	2489318	748353	216856
吉林	Jilin	346915		407608	8823	27982
黑龙江	Heilongjiang	338571	49194	396841	115578	25846
上海	Shanghai	36707923	6804789	52522319	7733447	5915332
江苏	Jiangsu	84749416	1336683	74361871	10116488	22632435
浙江	Zhejiang	57981266	2836394	63991020	24758528	3396577
安徽	Anhui	9377249	303544	10714944	976487	583087
福建	Fujian	29079637	1034740	33193371	8479172	1512264
江西	Jiangxi	1144797	10099	1205439	111957	90160
山东	Shandong	12598140	705307	17382930	4401812	833376
河南	Henan	5446036	59666	6110990	196371	370584
湖北	Hubei	3488263	111502	4070380	241846	258983
湖南	Hunan	2184740	59160	2542819	57856	310437
广东	Guangdong	42872971	1414146	49338526	11304262	4187986
广西	Guangxi	2018453	142108	2114501	974143	206929
海南	Hainan	244181	5576	256571	11737	34891
重庆	Chongqing	9138039	366570	9666575	5251	826362
四川	Sichuan	2224450	9291	2465257	381551	227074
贵州	Guizhou	320816		352350		40434
云南	Yunnan	992497	921	1422410	308783	94978
西藏	Tibet					
陕西	Shaanxi	3959871		4093712	164339	158611
甘肃	Gansu	209010		231313	3099	36719
青海	Qinghai	29634		34920	29895	3093
宁夏	Ningxia	45576		110765	1378	11219
新疆	Xinjiang	663940	339	755769	85908	102922

3-2-4 续表 3 Continued 3

文化、体育用品及器材批发
Wholesale of Culture, Sports Appliances and Equipments

单位：万元
Unit: 10000 yuan

地区	Region	商品购进额 Total Purchases Value	#进口 Imports	商品销售额 Total Sales Value	#出口 Exports	期末商品库存额 Inventory (year-end)
全国	**National Total**	**91898998**	**5333933**	**99581335**	**5896076**	**13596513**
北京	Beijing	15185448	656231	16142384	118980	2157410
天津	Tianjin	1806134	26027	2075261	306960	429348
河北	Hebei	713973		924997	24401	68442
山西	Shanxi	494260		532966	17899	86627
内蒙古	Inner Mongolia	117307		124145		3990
辽宁	Liaoning	645659		774354	25124	114563
吉林	Jilin	119414		114457		25771
黑龙江	Heilongjiang	79322		94200		3548
上海	Shanghai	12562984	2269517	14737297	282263	1698068
江苏	Jiangsu	6186959	79801	6579915	500211	481630
浙江	Zhejiang	9001368	445393	9685171	2129081	876251
安徽	Anhui	3096220	244794	3296496	361813	482202
福建	Fujian	3478867	146724	3968975	730766	171280
江西	Jiangxi	243482		260096	158	7027
山东	Shandong	5497828	89953	5683892	152889	438210
河南	Henan	2022170	16114	2106348	23549	173153
湖北	Hubei	1779156	4860	2139597	2160	161736
湖南	Hunan	1396708	85	1572520	73787	173038
广东	Guangdong	21813701	922604	23584931	739429	5205393
广西	Guangxi	443547		496370	11987	36887
海南	Hainan	60330		60671	3243	7960
重庆	Chongqing	892560		1060806	13213	160458
四川	Sichuan	1605027	361838	1169526	370407	98466
贵州	Guizhou	178135		199347		16670
云南	Yunnan	1108562	4644	911654		341016
西藏	Tibet	17135		13179		3957
陕西	Shaanxi	498161		575196	7756	53058
甘肃	Gansu	327711	65348	361388		54689
青海	Qinghai	20031		23812		7942
宁夏	Ningxia	27445		25968		5557
新疆	Xinjiang	479394		285417		52165

医药及医疗器材批发
Wholesale of Medicines and Medical Appliances

单位：万元
Unit: 10000 yuan

地　区	Region	商品购进额 Total Purchases Value	#进　口 Imports	商品销售额 Total Sales Value	#出　口 Exports	期末商品库存额 Inventory (year-end)
全　国	**National Total**	**246331868**	**30711243**	**271333168**	**2915414**	**26403048**
北　京	Beijing	21414635	4094681	24201912	406743	3305096
天　津	Tianjin	4562390	93830	5145488	56871	344849
河　北	Hebei	7415039	24213	8129476	37764	862727
山　西	Shanxi	2443243	3797	2790253		261402
内蒙古	Inner Mongolia	1055019	4251	1421534		130865
辽　宁	Liaoning	5384386	202269	6058869	9532	579932
吉　林	Jilin	2257249	13794	2834300	4882	261122
黑龙江	Heilongjiang	1545976	5361	1755430		103564
上　海	Shanghai	24829140	9108224	31812982	692747	4430443
江　苏	Jiangsu	18407800	1243951	22109272	305148	2208850
浙　江	Zhejiang	15555415	578384	17459714	662218	1541274
安　徽	Anhui	9677853	27804	10800659	79956	656057
福　建	Fujian	4577965	45803	5026900		444780
江　西	Jiangxi	4679391	29132	6366990	51801	399133
山　东	Shandong	13511816	43606	15357903	22376	1197555
河　南	Henan	11758192	53283	13235225	886	802033
湖　北	Hubei	14442262	59995	16202099	50764	1480370
湖　南	Hunan	5125092	19249	5837276	3813	535702
广　东	Guangdong	43847512	14560608	35622618	419345	3111637
广　西	Guangxi	2126258	29647	2628230	10492	314805
海　南	Hainan	1102985	111555	1728031	2994	147695
重　庆	Chongqing	6182048	76198	6785005	49418	573566
四　川	Sichuan	9221599	201760	10536500	17671	944731
贵　州	Guizhou	2674940	4485	3160718		234212
云　南	Yunnan	4776022	1566	5067838	25871	450929
西　藏	Tibet	199047	5920	336259		16270
陕　西	Shaanxi	3880414	11741	4794529	3733	370542
甘　肃	Gansu	1486373	250	1692353		368240
青　海	Qinghai	250723	27000	286453		57962
宁　夏	Ningxia	460021	27922	500387	389	43718
新　疆	Xinjiang	1481063	964	1647965		222986

矿产品、建材及化工产品批发　　单位：万元

Wholesale of Mineral Products, Building Materials and Chemical Products　　Unit: 10000 yuan

地　区	Region	商品购进额 Total Purchases Value	#进 口 Imports	商品销售额 Total Sales Value	#出 口 Exports	期末商品库存额 Inventory (year-end)
全　国	**National Total**	**2694575863**	**166819772**	**2824172720**	**52353976**	**107992400**
北　京	Beijing	240467386	36938142	246102327	14098814	17348123
天　津	Tianjin	208779119	6246015	213933170	1577160	8886230
河　北	Hebei	32835570	843043	36182763	189140	1057322
山　西	Shanxi	56154082	220067	59732501	56894	1406576
内蒙古	Inner Mongolia	19464090	1846797	21147355	404413	1251230
辽　宁	Liaoning	101448380	235563	106652258	772756	3076896
吉　林	Jilin	10004904	277561	8237654	70812	380104
黑龙江	Heilongjiang	15300413	5143799	17375858	401425	786462
上　海	Shanghai	469532465	30630631	488257887	5902818	17696658
江　苏	Jiangsu	220875366	5483901	239926346	4906317	7382439
浙　江	Zhejiang	282101195	19936520	294527895	8319066	8782081
安　徽	Anhui	23141860	743176	23577901	230973	887401
福　建	Fujian	122807105	15071782	130836412	2370323	5401034
江　西	Jiangxi	7268910	36496	11079411	54699	475973
山　东	Shandong	141612431	4848558	148349800	2196536	5429271
河　南	Henan	41081107	459451	44779363	183223	1218617
湖　北	Hubei	52823605	208827	55789417	212973	3005795
湖　南	Hunan	22146245	186742	18982403	276735	1027907
广　东	Guangdong	324323842	18835266	327515198	7374090	11968727
广　西	Guangxi	29746070	1069059	31956599	304101	1144041
海　南	Hainan	11746937	219934	12264821	176483	132612
重　庆	Chongqing	29241531	1842397	31590703	749590	974657
四　川	Sichuan	37057072	425556	39325358	166528	849828
贵　州	Guizhou	11921465	66588	14362304	490952	438128
云　南	Yunnan	34543840	2164084	37135856	430184	1152846
西　藏	Tibet	11695		10533		1163
陕　西	Shaanxi	58367535	144821	68363006	184232	1460944
甘　肃	Gansu	26932993	14672	27446588	16265	1109078
青　海	Qinghai	5517219		7625126	21591	273308
宁　夏	Ningxia	9584315	3130	9308649	25120	519889
新　疆	Xinjiang	47737116	12677193	51797258	189763	2467061

机械设备、五金产品及电子产品批发　　　　单位：万元

Wholesale of Machinery, Hardware and Electronic Products　　　　Unit: 10000 yuan

地　区	Region	商品购进额 Total Purchases Value	#进 口 Imports	商品销售额 Total Sales Value	#出 口 Exports	期末商品库存额 Inventory (year-end)
全　国	**National Total**	**699937125**	**140267871**	**778027873**	**69730600**	**51698322**
北　京	Beijing	117962107	32796032	136798190	5550437	12836755
天　津	Tianjin	23808891	6864546	24977652	569379	2276655
河　北	Hebei	11327371	13837	11989792	390949	276917
山　西	Shanxi	3408123	1242	3617753	32716	129757
内 蒙 古	Inner Mongolia	755786	56643	825798	26982	98112
辽　宁	Liaoning	4900518	341276	5727153	447173	460229
吉　林	Jilin	2466068	41732	2812757	17211	109397
黑 龙 江	Heilongjiang	2915861	20796	3119385	10461	104165
上　海	Shanghai	189240772	71676118	217776463	21668110	13838924
江　苏	Jiangsu	40209433	5461186	44489031	6890878	2210832
浙　江	Zhejiang	52470367	1507143	54752156	7841720	3316014
安　徽	Anhui	8381224	76754	8960778	229951	1727044
福　建	Fujian	11282143	916434	12769511	1111774	1106051
江　西	Jiangxi	4063558	19689	4362050	254700	163142
山　东	Shandong	14647481	1314383	17514723	2604773	953044
河　南	Henan	10945413	127111	11812633	446375	364678
湖　北	Hubei	15875084	177649	16493122	3259663	637277
湖　南	Hunan	8793665	55788	9998055	52388	311141
广　东	Guangdong	136720312	16985387	146497836	14239842	8583642
广　西	Guangxi	3010134	6125	3258125	1137625	234160
海　南	Hainan	288456	4206	346482	9870	20744
重　庆	Chongqing	14199910	1136240	15465836	988691	530623
四　川	Sichuan	8945022	87322	9561186	175422	612396
贵　州	Guizhou	1763518	5974	1882342	483206	87747
云　南	Yunnan	1931271	34423	2034800	473300	108253
西　藏	Tibet	27901		24679		8441
陕　西	Shaanxi	4065756	86354	4282973	500805	153599
甘　肃	Gansu	1670932	87553	1715142	117485	75112
青　海	Qinghai	649469		717847		13220
宁　夏	Ningxia	254056	1431	270745		34475
新　疆	Xinjiang	2956522	364498	3172878	198714	315776

贸易经纪与代理 单位：万元

Trade Broker and Agency Unit: 10000 yuan

地 区	Region	商品购进额 Total Purchases Value	#进 口 Imports	商品销售额 Total Sales Value	#出 口 Exports	期末商品库存额 Inventory (year-end)
全 国	**National Total**	**53518178**	**11036515**	**57898348**	**15718854**	**2365674**
北 京	Beijing	5182469	1717910	5704359	1919484	191615
天 津	Tianjin	2100318	208758	2498617	707816	100396
河 北	Hebei	140664	1755	151632	146079	288
山 西	Shanxi					
内蒙古	Inner Mongolia	76089		77439		986
辽 宁	Liaoning	285224	35889	356553	14327	51716
吉 林	Jilin	4816		4781		806
黑龙江	Heilongjiang	61468	20804	82297	33710	14306
上 海	Shanghai	2901818	856524	3399797	874545	351960
江 苏	Jiangsu	3843024	184140	4171596	1535530	83020
浙 江	Zhejiang	794796	7349	966423	837999	13945
安 徽	Anhui	435374	393230	418365	40269	24446
福 建	Fujian	1213661	5236	1518262	615039	55266
江 西	Jiangxi	435924	11062	439236	54512	5024
山 东	Shandong	652337	62537	862363	140864	77439
河 南	Henan	53227		64428	13113	879
湖 北	Hubei	529205		555810	18930	9088
湖 南	Hunan	37593	2689	48213	16990	296
广 东	Guangdong	31435775	7067917	33063388	8293937	1182837
广 西	Guangxi	15689	38	18208	15164	2190
海 南	Hainan					
重 庆	Chongqing	83192	29	106952	21090	1952
四 川	Sichuan	37485	17839	43407	17433	4828
贵 州	Guizhou	5127		18792	18694	160
云 南	Yunnan	3098021	440066	3224563	340233	180800
西 藏	Tibet					
陕 西	Shaanxi	58597	642	65280	25551	5679
甘 肃	Gansu					
青 海	Qinghai					
宁 夏	Ningxia					
新 疆	Xinjiang	36285	2101	37587	17545	5752

3-2-4 续表 8 Continued 8

其他批发业
Other Wholesale not Classified Elsewhere

单位：万元
Unit: 10000 yuan

地区	Region	商品购进额 Total Purchases Value	#进口 Imports	商品销售额 Total Sales Value	#出口 Exports	期末商品库存额 Inventory (year-end)
全国	**National Total**	**78603849**	**6036976**	**84438192**	**5159719**	**5947446**
北京	Beijing	4762838	1051718	5001501	1074264	1782689
天津	Tianjin	7296145	201372	7623136	327812	426484
河北	Hebei	3249809		3315764		9403
山西	Shanxi	114481	4040	132752		31871
内蒙古	Inner Mongolia	12195		20868	4597	1197
辽宁	Liaoning	798908	37321	867449	11236	40002
吉林	Jilin	197759	2044	215318	4816	13802
黑龙江	Heilongjiang	192754	70164	219117	3969	9108
上海	Shanghai	7968296	1249999	9659227	711022	516559
江苏	Jiangsu	5575404	166791	6124515	196580	305082
浙江	Zhejiang	9788263	269326	10066904	344255	201460
安徽	Anhui	2385629	957	2607625	5615	67620
福建	Fujian	13370113	1723930	13716542	606897	762141
江西	Jiangxi	447103	11	583201	39108	34304
山东	Shandong	4567918	152575	4472683	12244	605159
河南	Henan	1615936	22267	1782250	14656	56422
湖北	Hubei	534549		681988	7570	32683
湖南	Hunan	871591	8837	1008473	16463	50023
广东	Guangdong	9622702	1028573	10545074	1181099	734641
广西	Guangxi	763307	5558	812579	352061	17331
海南	Hainan					
重庆	Chongqing	1125253	21518	1233704		32983
四川	Sichuan	500496	1400	539923	5429	30466
贵州	Guizhou	177637		196274		15436
云南	Yunnan	2074972	3336	2332248	224603	142797
西藏	Tibet	5920		6150		30
陕西	Shaanxi	126837	5	138388		4013
甘肃	Gansu	37846		48686	6934	2066
青海	Qinghai	3225		4215		106
宁夏	Ningxia	266662	11286	317736		8368
新疆	Xinjiang	149302	3948	163902	8489	13200

3-2-5 各地区限额以上零售业企业商品购、销、存情况

Total Purchases, Sales and Inventory of Enterprises above Designated Size of Retail Trade by Region

单位：万元

Unit: 10000 yuan

地 区	Region	商品购进额 Total Purchases Value	#进口 Imports	商品销售额 Total Sales Value	#出口 Exports	期末商品库存额 Inventory (year-end)
全 国	**National Total**	**1041224189**	**29898028**	**1230852765**	**724979**	**117880000**
北 京	Beijing	74686254	2123578	81134498	15565	6978897
天 津	Tianjin	18646599	1279277	22917062	2957	1625050
河 北	Hebei	27026641	611954	31017937	972	5341224
山 西	Shanxi	18990673	356235	22475052	5064	3199524
内蒙古	Inner Mongolia	11843880	192118	13509448	1049	1298873
辽 宁	Liaoning	26476721	764810	31847851	16356	2770262
吉 林	Jilin	15148752	240201	19721963	4602	1745219
黑龙江	Heilongjiang	13549972	224129	16584896		1434834
上 海	Shanghai	59113405	4440773	74373054	7565	8934018
江 苏	Jiangsu	92377316	2412929	112008174	48904	14382728
浙 江	Zhejiang	69366195	3480966	83989069	40098	7712955
安 徽	Anhui	35021247	509607	41045186	6245	3468729
福 建	Fujian	46911252	1371120	57728924	143676	3684334
江 西	Jiangxi	15571253	255188	17847796	21677	2263909
山 东	Shandong	79843510	765849	89188151	28545	7465948
河 南	Henan	44041262	628696	51572820	20379	4142424
湖 北	Hubei	51527807	749789	58978146	10941	4932719
湖 南	Hunan	41398328	877059	49653278	24102	4121179
广 东	Guangdong	107459478	4088742	129343668	129247	13790916
广 西	Guangxi	16843329	264682	19296345	16973	1681755
海 南	Hainan	5101505	288310	5875479		646460
重 庆	Chongqing	29653112	840414	35345348	27102	2330760
四 川	Sichuan	48734863	1528394	54913483	52214	4124034
贵 州	Guizhou	17319941	335785	20927995		1610152
云 南	Yunnan	19789648	321735	24725422	22729	2201704
西 藏	Tibet	1324896	20077	1399583	2	158053
陕 西	Shaanxi	30964819	625667	37269305	77739	3048135
甘 肃	Gansu	7667143	109574	9130758	88	933670
青 海	Qinghai	1823124	1197	2330320		214362
宁 夏	Ningxia	3074914	59727	3300261		441346
新 疆	Xinjiang	9926350	129446	11401493	188	1195827

国有控股
State-controlled Enterprises

单位：万元
Unit: 10000 yuan

地区	Region	商品购进额 Total Purchases Value	#进口 Imports	商品销售额 Total Sales Value	#出口 Exports	期末商品库存额 Inventory (year-end)
全国	**National Total**	**178548460**	**2636118**	**233612753**	**107156**	**15828635**
北京	Beijing	18212245	1012977	20333058	12747	1713857
天津	Tianjin	5121875	23803	5641222		448815
河北	Hebei	5385329	134952	6470619		423650
山西	Shanxi	4744767	1225	5753296		731985
内蒙古	Inner Mongolia	3985638	215	4501874		206959
辽宁	Liaoning	4703499	39912	5985454		241187
吉林	Jilin	3742174		6122588		541156
黑龙江	Heilongjiang	1692349	2297	2126139		170795
上海	Shanghai	11135356	131266	12639876	3073	1796554
江苏	Jiangsu	11286654	16396	16038591	5378	780905
浙江	Zhejiang	7523725	159880	14990074	328	610251
安徽	Anhui	6440962	4748	7922630		357787
福建	Fujian	5987641	267104	9316729	2700	566856
江西	Jiangxi	1717555	24079	1889494	4351	521455
山东	Shandong	9058807		11120126		760423
河南	Henan	4382440	44426	5150595	15	356675
湖北	Hubei	13573770	7472	16474513		958646
湖南	Hunan	6754331	54772	10624838		277174
广东	Guangdong	14666335	422159	22226310		1702226
广西	Guangxi	1538236	14089	1795444		115584
海南	Hainan	2301368	132794	2691457		283005
重庆	Chongqing	6107302	71915	8759014		515668
四川	Sichuan	9387958	2477	10807138	49651	562662
贵州	Guizhou	3749621	5788	5729511		212528
云南	Yunnan	5105219	8001	6901138		198341
西藏	Tibet	892343	75	873902		28873
陕西	Shaanxi	3818808	34627	4600838	28913	379640
甘肃	Gansu	2665481	16641	2931866		100097
青海	Qinghai	307650	389	355966		17779
宁夏	Ningxia	61238	1639	68180		7250
新疆	Xinjiang	2497784		2770272		239852

3-2-6 各地区限额以上零售业企业商品购、销、存情况 (按登记注册类型分)

Total Purchases, Sales and Inventory of Enterprises above Designated Size of Retail Trade by Region and Type of Registration

内资企业
Domestic Funded Enterprises

单位：万元
Unit: 10000 yuan

地 区	Region	商品购进额 Total Purchases Value	#进口 Imports	商品销售额 Total Sales Value	#出口 Exports	期末商品库存额 Inventory (year-end)
全 国	**National Total**	**917008899**	**21757031**	**1073963170**	**655313**	**102445774**
北 京	Beijing	63006615	1479350	66119411	15558	5476315
天 津	Tianjin	15996532	1210114	19271649	1221	1350530
河 北	Hebei	25911052	560089	29871600	972	5247173
山 西	Shanxi	18563987	295062	21945346	5064	3117400
内蒙古	Inner Mongolia	11660476	192067	13301877	1049	1277216
辽 宁	Liaoning	23980094	633145	28699808	16355	2547469
吉 林	Jilin	14746924	202769	18994977	4602	1701282
黑龙江	Heilongjiang	12942628	222283	15767011		1377096
上 海	Shanghai	40012911	883871	45740941	3121	4690155
江 苏	Jiangsu	78841001	1904217	95628413	48904	12981309
浙 江	Zhejiang	60923447	2727078	73828253	39900	6776104
安 徽	Anhui	32978939	479698	38420294	6245	3318515
福 建	Fujian	40283928	1201976	48082383	141481	3284163
江 西	Jiangxi	14581687	179526	16696407	20787	2136624
山 东	Shandong	76118610	644734	84756470	17990	6980042
河 南	Henan	42431877	576096	48995863	20379	3990632
湖 北	Hubei	48671833	702229	55598705	8757	4651286
湖 南	Hunan	39948387	689391	47990911	24102	4005323
广 东	Guangdong	81038402	3209749	99494761	90221	10680070
广 西	Guangxi	15460602	173002	17749458	10147	1580052
海 南	Hainan	4803431	269316	5479523		626574
重 庆	Chongqing	27501989	654944	32876220	27102	2154066
四 川	Sichuan	44373389	1397731	49722250	52214	3728895
贵 州	Guizhou	16404105	235510	19882365		1501003
云 南	Yunnan	17521137	283239	22103176	22034	1783464
西 藏	Tibet	1312359	20077	1386119	2	153153
陕 西	Shaanxi	25260380	444652	30330791	76830	2611869
甘 肃	Gansu	7475689	109574	8892104	88	916428
青 海	Qinghai	1763916	1197	2262654		210149
宁 夏	Ningxia	2979061	59727	3195956		430948
新 疆	Xinjiang	9513511	114618	10877473	188	1160469

国有企业
State-owned Enterprises

单位：万元
Unit: 10000 yuan

地区	Region	商品购进额 Total Purchases Value	#进口 Imports	商品销售额 Total Sales Value	#出口 Exports	期末商品库存额 Inventory (year-end)
全国	**National Total**	**9592784**	**287360**	**11229476**	**10115**	**1066257**
北京	Beijing	925085	192894	1077918	4775	111260
天津	Tianjin	772962		857769		88321
河北	Hebei	72579		83257		6050
山西	Shanxi	256716	414	288983		24442
内蒙古	Inner Mongolia	35981		38753		4155
辽宁	Liaoning	158475		181515		26908
吉林	Jilin	24795		25918		3299
黑龙江	Heilongjiang	308263		340266		21179
上海	Shanghai	265546	36225	316528	989	65750
江苏	Jiangsu	306264	1449	356491		44582
浙江	Zhejiang	142796		157336		15252
安徽	Anhui	120983		130912		3095
福建	Fujian	111028		117375		8590
江西	Jiangxi	63653		77250	4351	11946
山东	Shandong	701556		735254		36303
河南	Henan	555591		632807		33008
湖北	Hubei	637425	6902	733714		41434
湖南	Hunan	907004	45621	1060588		37049
广东	Guangdong	784420		821913		129229
广西	Guangxi	142263		166054		11025
海南	Hainan	9769		10353		1662
重庆	Chongqing	139093		449764		8922
四川	Sichuan	186355		451413		16185
贵州	Guizhou	88865	1868	94989		12832
云南	Yunnan	148233	273	160894		16975
西藏	Tibet	184113	75	225511		17156
陕西	Shaanxi	1211650		1302250		171699
甘肃	Gansu	69450		78599		8671
青海	Qinghai					
宁夏	Ningxia	16032	1639	17768		1643
新疆	Xinjiang	245839		237333		87635

3-2-6 续表 2 Continued 2

集体企业 单位：万元
Collective-owned Enterprises Unit: 10000 yuan

地 区	Region	商品购进额 Total Purchases Value	#进 口 Imports	商品销售额 Total Sales Value	#出 口 Exports	期末商品库存额 Inventory (year-end)
全 国	**National Total**	**8122331**	**5807**	**8957461**		**450681**
北 京	Beijing	236290	5717	263065		22620
天 津	Tianjin	97856		125195		5891
河 北	Hebei	343558		376587		17575
山 西	Shanxi	277636		319240		19489
内 蒙 古	Inner Mongolia	114835		131295		6403
辽 宁	Liaoning	80259		87081		4926
吉 林	Jilin	27511		29038		2155
黑 龙 江	Heilongjiang	179538		187518		13544
上 海	Shanghai	66131		80701		27059
江 苏	Jiangsu	731618		793044		22591
浙 江	Zhejiang	142703		160665		10330
安 徽	Anhui	41288		45569		1201
福 建	Fujian	291674		316243		10520
江 西	Jiangxi	37657		41493		7683
山 东	Shandong	895698		944351		34595
河 南	Henan	550572		605449		23721
湖 北	Hubei	1580315		1697815		93845
湖 南	Hunan	305975		349541		10334
广 东	Guangdong	768034	90	880081		48781
广 西	Guangxi	290677		324376		13844
海 南	Hainan	3552		3473		107
重 庆	Chongqing	41516		46969		1107
四 川	Sichuan	71954		82102		1859
贵 州	Guizhou	67917		95161		3835
云 南	Yunnan	356239		399554		11490
西 藏	Tibet					
陕 西	Shaanxi	448595		500852		25109
甘 肃	Gansu	63043		62963		7271
青 海	Qinghai					
宁 夏	Ningxia	585		986		36
新 疆	Xinjiang	9105		7055		2760

股份合作企业　　单位：万元
Cooperative Enterprises　　Unit: 10000 yuan

地区	Region	商品购进额 Total Purchases Value	#进口 Imports	商品销售额 Total Sales Value	#出口 Exports	期末商品库存额 Inventory (year-end)
全国	**National Total**	**1567002**	**390**	**1717967**		**129847**
北京	Beijing	316647		328546		16189
天津	Tianjin	15301		21035		1055
河北	Hebei	142959		122131		31628
山西	Shanxi	7037		8679		155
内蒙古	Inner Mongolia	1901		2256		51
辽宁	Liaoning	14796	390	19048		543
吉林	Jilin	43766		65462		3620
黑龙江	Heilongjiang	26891		41229		7275
上海	Shanghai	22605		27939		594
江苏	Jiangsu	21254		32230		1197
浙江	Zhejiang	142427		167029		10898
安徽	Anhui	9037		10321		2731
福建	Fujian	2192		2636		159
江西	Jiangxi	19889		19982		732
山东	Shandong	128508		136269		13490
河南	Henan	9633		10244		164
湖北	Hubei	32218		40282		1072
湖南	Hunan	17339		17458		676
广东	Guangdong	54674		62117		4023
广西	Guangxi	1185		1588		5
海南	Hainan					
重庆	Chongqing	54840		59163		2583
四川	Sichuan	38682		44206		1688
贵州	Guizhou	20948		20346		742
云南	Yunnan	320945		353858		26889
西藏	Tibet					
陕西	Shaanxi	98764		100918		801
甘肃	Gansu	2426		2368		887
青海	Qinghai					
宁夏	Ningxia					
新疆	Xinjiang	138		626		

3-2-6 续表 4 Continued 4

联营企业 单位：万元
Joint Ownership Enterprises Unit: 10000 yuan

地 区	Region	商品购进额 Total Purchases Value	#进 口 Imports	商品销售额 Total Sales Value	#出 口 Exports	期末商品库存额 Inventory (year-end)
全 国	**National Total**	**778713**		**931816**		**17836**
北 京	Beijing	11528		12357		83
天 津	Tianjin	11495		18416		449
河 北	Hebei					
山 西	Shanxi					
内蒙古	Inner Mongolia					
辽 宁	Liaoning	11317		13342		453
吉 林	Jilin					
黑龙江	Heilongjiang	55240		63124		1027
上 海	Shanghai	111350		140969		1029
江 苏	Jiangsu	20667		22741		363
浙 江	Zhejiang	61358		77146		976
安 徽	Anhui	8805		10218		77
福 建	Fujian	1012		1382		51
江 西	Jiangxi					
山 东	Shandong	135734		158348		2717
河 南	Henan	6769		7768		478
湖 北	Hubei	23854		23860		41
湖 南	Hunan	60279		65555		2198
广 东	Guangdong	206199		253961		6460
广 西	Guangxi					
海 南	Hainan					
重 庆	Chongqing	6449		7171		32
四 川	Sichuan	13917		15679		535
贵 州	Guizhou	28353		35441		821
云 南	Yunnan					
西 藏	Tibet					
陕 西	Shaanxi	1267		1250		15
甘 肃	Gansu	3119		3088		31
青 海	Qinghai					
宁 夏	Ningxia					
新 疆	Xinjiang					

3-2-6 续表 5 Continued 5

有限责任公司
Limited Liability Corporations

单位：万元
Unit: 10000 yuan

地 区	Region	商品购进额 Total Purchases Value	#进口 Imports	商品销售额 Total Sales Value	#出口 Exports	期末商品库存额 Inventory (year-end)
全 国	**National Total**	**430571529**	**11432245**	**497444758**	**293761**	**42334378**
北 京	Beijing	41678044	829630	43936670	7828	3311485
天 津	Tianjin	8486972	540388	10897211		630264
河 北	Hebei	10691530	360990	12211861	470	1041795
山 西	Shanxi	4154457	58230	4931877		593666
内蒙古	Inner Mongolia	5034653	121473	5742100	286	531000
辽 宁	Liaoning	11215715	404981	13269677	595	1131299
吉 林	Jilin	6307028	93786	7393157	2429	551709
黑龙江	Heilongjiang	6237627	101558	7783238		706094
上 海	Shanghai	21009258	474770	23884669	1486	2252516
江 苏	Jiangsu	29331295	793113	35730893	36507	2137535
浙 江	Zhejiang	26389324	1177856	30640168	12587	2426187
安 徽	Anhui	14153366	283647	16630751	1989	1580855
福 建	Fujian	18129428	512285	21340921	23902	1490646
江 西	Jiangxi	7577189	113004	8680891	3573	904547
山 东	Shandong	31734970	341873	34722932	3998	3447872
河 南	Henan	24230219	400351	28056829	13016	2393803
湖 北	Hubei	23769469	229104	26617885	898	2636166
湖 南	Hunan	11825822	293619	13344055	1	894003
广 东	Guangdong	45941889	2187614	53691309	31301	5684366
广 西	Guangxi	7065734	41131	8186148	2900	667772
海 南	Hainan	3219686	210457	3741693		553546
重 庆	Chongqing	11024518	358411	12376918	2363	995591
四 川	Sichuan	21571152	805990	24435972	49651	1634341
贵 州	Guizhou	6972746	147597	8697753		730912
云 南	Yunnan	8396239	181318	11027950	21101	699141
西 藏	Tibet	591590	12655	670764		90011
陕 西	Shaanxi	14558763	262773	18104665	76604	1616310
甘 肃	Gansu	3124789	43535	3919778	88	385713
青 海	Qinghai	885145	1112	1219820		105833
宁 夏	Ningxia	1284422	11344	1367543		145912
新 疆	Xinjiang	3978490	37650	4188659	188	363488

3-2-6 续表 6 Continued 6

股份有限公司
Share-holding Corporations Ltd.

单位：万元
Unit: 10000 yuan

地区	Region	商品购进额 Total Purchases Value	#进口 Imports	商品销售额 Total Sales Value	#出口 Exports	期末商品库存额 Inventory (year-end)
全国	**National Total**	**114337811**	**459267**	**153169921**	**6471**	**16309065**
北京	Beijing	8409511	1756	8559980	187	579606
天津	Tianjin	1991850		2166584		159006
河北	Hebei	3232802	19941	4083355		257098
山西	Shanxi	2646362		3216805		413640
内蒙古	Inner Mongolia	2531872	51	3008752		103620
辽宁	Liaoning	4105660	2121	5294554	34	150941
吉林	Jilin	3681944	1602	5953702	638	595104
黑龙江	Heilongjiang	2188668	15457	3018859		188210
上海	Shanghai	5081856	2228	5407437		753810
江苏	Jiangsu	9570267	56788	13966167		6961245
浙江	Zhejiang	3824947	69093	9087984		498281
安徽	Anhui	4687475	29495	5956589		268707
福建	Fujian	2202392	74248	2813045	2957	150279
江西	Jiangxi	1215926		1341033		501593
山东	Shandong	11083958	22408	13279047	1858	588382
河南	Henan	3880185	33327	4720321		360967
湖北	Hubei	10223340		12234515		676963
湖南	Hunan	6072206		9687376		407469
广东	Guangdong	4554335	19394	11252289	797	1196927
广西	Guangxi	1789984	70	1978410		146076
海南	Hainan	1356048	3110	1476206		44697
重庆	Chongqing	3162924	50	5150078		148959
四川	Sichuan	7822373	10594	8393913		554466
贵州	Guizhou	2230790		3237349		95895
云南	Yunnan	1625510	7745	1726075		61667
西藏	Tibet	349537		279742		7170
陕西	Shaanxi	1166091	32454	1374210		75844
甘肃	Gansu	1997511	22540	2087795		186087
青海	Qinghai	166018		185020		7284
宁夏	Ningxia	273532	10	292709		15565
新疆	Xinjiang	1211938	34785	1940020		153507

私营企业
Private Enterprises

单位：万元
Unit: 10000 yuan

地 区	Region	商品购进额 Total Purchases Value	#进口 Imports	商品销售额 Total Sales Value	#出口 Exports	期末商品库存额 Inventory (year-end)
全 国	**National Total**	**349732299**	**9566106**	**397687885**	**344945**	**42011673**
北 京	Beijing	11428330	449353	11939431	2767	1435072
天 津	Tianjin	4620097	669726	5184425	1221	465527
河 北	Hebei	11415126	179159	12980099	502	3892440
山 西	Shanxi	11210006	236418	13166083	5064	2065276
内蒙古	Inner Mongolia	3925195	70393	4360706	763	629827
辽 宁	Liaoning	8369295	225653	9807577	15725	1231472
吉 林	Jilin	4599412	107381	5459116	1535	541948
黑龙江	Heilongjiang	3906359	105269	4277583		437102
上 海	Shanghai	13450226	370648	15876165	645	1588932
江 苏	Jiangsu	38203548	1052859	43840960	12398	3792395
浙 江	Zhejiang	30157912	1480129	33464313	27313	3811499
安 徽	Anhui	13910633	166556	15568437	4236	1457354
福 建	Fujian	19436244	615444	23348969	114623	1610724
江 西	Jiangxi	5652184	66522	6515903	12863	708591
山 东	Shandong	31187524	279813	34486351	12134	2837967
河 南	Henan	13119795	142418	14873039	7362	1173583
湖 北	Hubei	12265061	466223	14084274	7859	1196876
湖 南	Hunan	20664461	350152	23359570	24101	2647571
广 东	Guangdong	28548607	1002651	32327498	58123	3601128
广 西	Guangxi	6169403	131801	7090691	7247	740372
海 南	Hainan	214377	55749	247799		26562
重 庆	Chongqing	12970558	295879	14683584	24739	991214
四 川	Sichuan	14507396	581147	16108355	2564	1515239
贵 州	Guizhou	6981643	86046	7686523		654652
云 南	Yunnan	6579665	93903	8328360	933	964084
西 藏	Tibet	185475	7347	208459	2	38581
陕 西	Shaanxi	7677720	144967	8824829	226	717484
甘 肃	Gansu	2199606	43499	2720644		320864
青 海	Qinghai	710488	85	855603		96978
宁 夏	Ningxia	1404490	46733	1516950		267793
新 疆	Xinjiang	4061462	42183	4495589		552566

其他企业
Other Enterprises

单位：万元
Unit: 10000 yuan

地　区	Region	商品购进额 Total Purchases Value	#进口 Imports	商品销售额 Total Sales Value	#出口 Exports	期末商品库存额 Inventory (year-end)
全　国	**National Total**	**2306434**	**5860**	**2823888**	**21**	**126042**
北　京	Beijing	**1180**		**1445**		
天　津	Tianjin			1015		16
河　北	Hebei	12497		14311		587
山　西	Shanxi	11772		13679		733
内蒙古	Inner Mongolia	16038	149	18015		2160
辽　宁	Liaoning	24576		27014		927
吉　林	Jilin	62469		68583		3445
黑龙江	Heilongjiang	40042		55193		2665
上　海	Shanghai	5938		6533		464
江　苏	Jiangsu	656090	7	885887		21403
浙　江	Zhejiang	61979		73613		2680
安　徽	Anhui	47351		67496	21	4495
福　建	Fujian	109958		141812		13194
江　西	Jiangxi	15190		19855		1533
山　东	Shandong	250664	641	293918		18717
河　南	Henan	79113		89405		4907
湖　北	Hubei	140152		166359		4888
湖　南	Hunan	95301		106769		6023
广　东	Guangdong	180244		205595		9158
广　西	Guangxi	1356		2192		958
海　南	Hainan					
重　庆	Chongqing	102091	604	102573		5659
四　川	Sichuan	161560		190610		4582
贵　州	Guizhou	12842		14804		1314
云　南	Yunnan	94306		106484		3218
西　藏	Tibet	1644		1643		235
陕　西	Shaanxi	97531	4459	121815		4606
甘　肃	Gansu	15745		16869		6905
青　海	Qinghai	2265		2211		55
宁　夏	Ningxia					
新　疆	Xinjiang	6540		8190		515

港、澳、台商投资企业
Enterprises with Funds from Hong Kong, Macao and Taiwan

单位：万元
Unit: 10000 yuan

地区	Region	商品购进额 Total Purchases Value	#进口 Imports	商品销售额 Total Sales Value	#出口 Exports	期末商品库存额 Inventory (year-end)
全　国	**National Total**	**58801704**	**4307932**	**74220388**	**52605**	**8829913**
北　京	Beijing	3606067	285227	4159639		616177
天　津	Tianjin	1519638	67425	2005647	1197	121613
河　北	Hebei	197850	15463	212257		19641
山　西	Shanxi	351094	61173	443948		59132
内蒙古	Inner Mongolia	174162	52	197565		20307
辽　宁	Liaoning	1288531	76794	1833911	1	124289
吉　林	Jilin	207441		480425		20521
黑龙江	Heilongjiang	363875	1846	561634		33396
上　海	Shanghai	9399016	1677766	13771757	3212	1977324
江　苏	Jiangsu	7696124	351329	9564373		913159
浙　江	Zhejiang	4929508	287690	5916949		630364
安　徽	Anhui	1834533	28783	2326830		108473
福　建	Fujian	2829832	71690	3161929	2195	202673
江　西	Jiangxi	570840	75662	635687		73671
山　东	Shandong	2577685	8756	2973044	550	367234
河　南	Henan	1261523	52600	2191429		113437
湖　北	Hubei	1756129	32378	2075064	1635	192080
湖　南	Hunan	793442	149561	995762		62516
广　东	Guangdong	9094716	623999	10545760	36359	2076151
广　西	Guangxi	1220336	60709	1365499	5851	79951
海　南	Hainan	135643	18994	200973		6883
重　庆	Chongqing	804208	81040	937902		88428
四　川	Sichuan	1677558	20876	2096647		206473
贵　州	Guizhou	380450	32688	487190		24822
云　南	Yunnan	1413810	38077	1662606	696	289243
西　藏	Tibet	9072		10264		1435
陕　西	Shaanxi	2145921	173830	2759247	909	344331
甘　肃	Gansu	181729		227817		16942
青　海	Qinghai	59208		67666		4213
宁　夏	Ningxia	91119		97217		10397
新　疆	Xinjiang	230644	13524	253750		24638

3-2-6 续表 10 Continued 10

外商投资企业 单位：万元
Foreign Funded Enterprises Unit: 10000 yuan

地区	Region	商品购进额 Total Purchases Value	#进口 Imports	商品销售额 Total Sales Value	#出口 Exports	期末商品库存额 Inventory (year-end)
全国	**National Total**	**65413589**	**3833067**	**82669207**	**17064**	**6604317**
北京	Beijing	8073573	359002	10855448	7	886404
天津	Tianjin	1130429	1738	1639765	540	152907
河北	Hebei	917740	36401	934080		74410
山西	Shanxi	75593		85759		22991
内蒙古	Inner Mongolia	9242		10006		1351
辽宁	Liaoning	1208096	54872	1314132		98504
吉林	Jilin	194387	37432	246561		23416
黑龙江	Heilongjiang	243469		256251		24343
上海	Shanghai	9701478	1879137	14860355	1232	2266540
江苏	Jiangsu	5840191	157383	6815389		488261
浙江	Zhejiang	3513240	466197	4243867	198	306487
安徽	Anhui	207775	1127	298062		41741
福建	Fujian	3797492	97454	6484612		197498
江西	Jiangxi	418726		515702	890	53614
山东	Shandong	1147214	112360	1458638	10005	118672
河南	Henan	347861		385528		38355
湖北	Hubei	1099845	15182	1304378	549	89354
湖南	Hunan	656500	38106	666605		53341
广东	Guangdong	17326359	254994	19303147	2667	1034694
广西	Guangxi	162391	30971	181388	976	21752
海南	Hainan	162431		194982		13003
重庆	Chongqing	1346915	104430	1531226		88266
四川	Sichuan	2683916	109787	3094585		188666
贵州	Guizhou	535386	67586	558440		84328
云南	Yunnan	854701	419	959640		128998
西藏	Tibet	3465		3200		3465
陕西	Shaanxi	3558517	7185	4179266		91935
甘肃	Gansu	9725		10837		300
青海	Qinghai					
宁夏	Ningxia	4735		7088		1
新疆	Xinjiang	182196	1304	270270		10720

3-2-7 各地区限额以上零售业企业商品购、销、存情况（按国民经济行业分）

Total Purchases, Sales and Inventory of Enterprises above Designated Size of Retail Trade by Region and Sector

综合零售
Integrated Retail

单位：万元
Unit: 10000 yuan

地区	Region	商品购进额 Total Purchases Value	#进口 Imports	商品销售额 Total Sales Value	#出口 Exports	期末商品库存额 Inventory (year-end)
全国	**National Total**	**194575867**	**1874482**	**242519167**	**30620**	**28863132**
北京	Beijing	12796178	339166	14292569		708080
天津	Tianjin	1606050	3707	2342447		204277
河北	Hebei	7149525	955	8433535	378	2685507
山西	Shanxi	2659794	129293	3713849		357653
内蒙古	Inner Mongolia	1244430	337	1753525	251	177968
辽宁	Liaoning	4918399	5823	8078054	35	422123
吉林	Jilin	4395997	4463	7090902	200	596115
黑龙江	Heilongjiang	3754969	2637	5675831		282943
上海	Shanghai	11628066	792543	14981639	1547	1967529
江苏	Jiangsu	17962281	53466	22828593	9	7874932
浙江	Zhejiang	10474307	28921	12633399	971	1180497
安徽	Anhui	8345856	22496	9784403		1002222
福建	Fujian	6498232	73684	7605955	281	397954
江西	Jiangxi	2574574	1084	3139118	3	400668
山东	Shandong	17422133	24882	20518747	2193	1515062
河南	Henan	7667496	15948	10146259	851	710402
湖北	Hubei	14948884	2480	18127974		1424035
湖南	Hunan	9595397	52244	10848608	127	1617421
广东	Guangdong	16778498	97134	18850677	67	1992284
广西	Guangxi	2738627	5731	3616956	4537	303252
海南	Hainan	1203739	132934	1604609		306288
重庆	Chongqing	5180772	12877	7758696	20	445942
四川	Sichuan	7510708	14778	9026781		673338
贵州	Guizhou	1961903	38554	2381741		185368
云南	Yunnan	3145485	3157	3678613	19060	414647
西藏	Tibet	74547	22	125014	2	46026
陕西	Shaanxi	6614643	9029	8469911		563746
甘肃	Gansu	1099012	6077	1506852	88	181288
青海	Qinghai	302421	20	516498		29927
宁夏	Ningxia	909224		992855		81321
新疆	Xinjiang	1413720	40	1994557		114317

食品、饮料及烟草制品专门零售
Special Retail of Food, Beverages and Tobaccos

单位：万元
Unit: 10000 yuan

地区	Region	商品购进额 Total Purchases Value	#进口 Imports	商品销售额 Total Sales Value	#出口 Exports	期末商品库存额 Inventory (year-end)
全国	**National Total**	**33456696**	**267619**	**42091499**	**34046**	**3254996**
北京	Beijing	709294		1032225		104536
天津	Tianjin	305801	1738	411169	80	42291
河北	Hebei	169311	1272	220238		38775
山西	Shanxi	563024		672492	2570	68638
内蒙古	Inner Mongolia	245150	37	316788		31956
辽宁	Liaoning	327564	13047	516328	3224	73523
吉林	Jilin	403560	1768	538437	1430	60301
黑龙江	Heilongjiang	134530		149375		14557
上海	Shanghai	978127	7146	1265902		77863
江苏	Jiangsu	3825136	12024	4568342	5378	306802
浙江	Zhejiang	894800	9813	1086094		108852
安徽	Anhui	1661757	2198	1915639	2673	138525
福建	Fujian	3902384	39300	4633695	1056	270626
江西	Jiangxi	777322	1444	1002501	985	90296
山东	Shandong	2724948	8523	3106561	5402	194924
河南	Henan	1596889	3021	1913872		124716
湖北	Hubei	2952885	1787	3515338		167213
湖南	Hunan	1661941	7721	1989139	114	118843
广东	Guangdong	2823819	111793	4396903	9110	479212
广西	Guangxi	298996	1527	353027	40	50606
海南	Hainan	29015	277	31992		7603
重庆	Chongqing	1357837	3062	1638904		86931
四川	Sichuan	1432484	2558	1706995		203241
贵州	Guizhou	728646	5353	927688		71618
云南	Yunnan	1450790	4781	2372304	1075	137180
西藏	Tibet	44551	75	59520		7124
陕西	Shaanxi	1166948	27208	1393218	909	119934
甘肃	Gansu	187678		233789		35795
青海	Qinghai	22532		24597		3322
宁夏	Ningxia	38452	146	47096		8163
新疆	Xinjiang	40525		51331		11030

纺织、服装及日用品专门零售 单位：万元

Special Retail of Textiles, Garments and Daily Consumer Articles Unit: 10000 yuan

地区	Region	商品购进额 Total Purchases Value	#进口 Imports	商品销售额 Total Sales Value	#出口 Exports	期末商品库存额 Inventory (year-end)
全国	**National Total**	**40013175**	**2947801**	**58235024**	**78851**	**9797242**
北京	Beijing	2514981	137333	3695132	14	854538
天津	Tianjin	790374		1107148		122530
河北	Hebei	493370	1050	587800	570	93980
山西	Shanxi	793331	3212	1103149		143962
内蒙古	Inner Mongolia	264224		358716	94	47874
辽宁	Liaoning	666481	61126	960258	865	196236
吉林	Jilin	425742	53	479479		67695
黑龙江	Heilongjiang	877514	21904	1057814		69009
上海	Shanghai	9189435	2336637	16398337	3357	2997610
江苏	Jiangsu	3608133	3844	4435319	7119	535271
浙江	Zhejiang	2628138	117101	3734973	6734	753399
安徽	Anhui	776373	36	956748	1184	136066
福建	Fujian	2938509	6442	4057822	7585	208616
江西	Jiangxi	365892	491	551670	7434	62790
山东	Shandong	2345747	19071	2821202	5197	449238
河南	Henan	1071815	491	1293350	1713	97199
湖北	Hubei	1247980	21236	1603358	1896	246778
湖南	Hunan	965062	3083	1234111	23	289993
广东	Guangdong	4093343	140070	6303042	34031	1562121
广西	Guangxi	205591	1719	237301		35581
海南	Hainan	27702		37085		11192
重庆	Chongqing	986125	28547	1294112	160	183905
四川	Sichuan	877720		1244841		240285
贵州	Guizhou	139098	187	184525		45531
云南	Yunnan	288755	7617	395281	696	76946
西藏	Tibet	39065		25921		16344
陕西	Shaanxi	910509	36551	1427366		176139
甘肃	Gansu	92572		137097		30254
青海	Qinghai	53474		70544		8623
宁夏	Ningxia	30097		38405		13116
新疆	Xinjiang	306023		403118	179	24421

文化、体育用品及器材专门零售
Special Retail of Culture, Sports Appliances and Equipments

单位：万元
Unit: 10000 yuan

地区	Region	商品购进额 Total Purchases Value	#进口 Imports	商品销售额 Total Sales Value	#出口 Exports	期末商品库存额 Inventory (year-end)
全国	**National Total**	**28038742**	**1062080**	**33803140**	**157580**	**6660019**
北京	Beijing	3396425	478785	4204031	12157	1098896
天津	Tianjin	560105	1210	666447		90083
河北	Hebei	415817	43984	527658		71062
山西	Shanxi	339695	1530	373163	1276	156580
内蒙古	Inner Mongolia	114225	149	130185		46823
辽宁	Liaoning	605705		759599		136625
吉林	Jilin	231045	39	249909	646	61772
黑龙江	Heilongjiang	275169	4241	389514		72493
上海	Shanghai	1440302	454445	2270549	1526	652512
江苏	Jiangsu	3298268	10008	3803907	3862	1027565
浙江	Zhejiang	1262099	1394	1402651	587	458513
安徽	Anhui	850346	271	918630		156672
福建	Fujian	1986591	12741	2793560	107211	251319
江西	Jiangxi	994418	225	999537	350	139280
山东	Shandong	1768624	1390	2011625	2352	299657
河南	Henan	1442868	10	1811750	2581	164139
湖北	Hubei	719699	8185	856862		129381
湖南	Hunan	1035113	1047	1196195	17335	130665
广东	Guangdong	1549628	5112	1886612	5797	428794
广西	Guangxi	315862		403156		49659
海南	Hainan	27742		32966		4292
重庆	Chongqing	741288	123	912638		95010
四川	Sichuan	1098766	30002	1188983		218823
贵州	Guizhou	238006		257680		29114
云南	Yunnan	1609734	1916	1754303	1625	112386
西藏	Tibet	4584		5389		761
陕西	Shaanxi	1071945	5268	1378535	275	255701
甘肃	Gansu	300304		275666		163554
青海	Qinghai	8579		10047		3080
宁夏	Ningxia	49581	5	53180		27417
新疆	Xinjiang	286209		278212		127391

3-2-7 续表 4 Continued 4

医药及医疗器材专门零售

Special Retail of Medicines and Medical Appliances

单位：万元

Unit: 10000 yuan

地区	Region	商品购进额 Total Purchases Value	#进口 Imports	商品销售额 Total Sales Value	#出口 Exports	期末商品库存额 Inventory (year-end)
全国	**National Total**	**49018085**	**163101**	**56486009**	**5263**	**6623616**
北京	Beijing	3186046	60941	3341801		285463
天津	Tianjin	271511		313733	1657	41330
河北	Hebei	863192	19231	1044697		159247
山西	Shanxi	1880241		2173115		347116
内蒙古	Inner Mongolia	329674	775	421733		74739
辽宁	Liaoning	1987904	3739	2233484		336117
吉林	Jilin	994878	2243	1165102	1037	143408
黑龙江	Heilongjiang	1445864	2381	1695107		194129
上海	Shanghai	2217952	2278	2542418		222995
江苏	Jiangsu	3207074	7478	3711973		372228
浙江	Zhejiang	2565236	1027	2904657		396180
安徽	Anhui	1670508		1925974		217453
福建	Fujian	1444158	438	1627692		178006
江西	Jiangxi	562928	226	608833		295989
山东	Shandong	6362390	11960	6854714	29	647927
河南	Henan	1690496	6286	2032683	15	189407
湖北	Hubei	2127266	17972	2684091	2525	224055
湖南	Hunan	2275808	214	2656802		229120
广东	Guangdong	3927204	7530	4730619		740299
广西	Guangxi	2928704	929	3273665		263815
海南	Hainan	41865		61031		15147
重庆	Chongqing	1197147	1891	1445996		130011
四川	Sichuan	1289057	6405	1479881		218071
贵州	Guizhou	537276	4175	658935		76761
云南	Yunnan	936390	3233	1302088		158114
西藏	Tibet	4375		12231		1206
陕西	Shaanxi	1097922		1253421		130942
甘肃	Gansu	458743	100	608289		84790
青海	Qinghai	57411		69301		17637
宁夏	Ningxia	179223	1649	208112		31963
新疆	Xinjiang	1279642		1443831		199950

汽车、摩托车、燃料及零配件专门零售

Special Retail of Motor Vehicles, Motorcycles, Fuel and Parts

单位：万元

Unit: 10000 yuan

地区	Region	商品购进额 Total Purchases Value	#进口 Imports	商品销售额 Total Sales Value	#出口 Exports	期末商品库存额 Inventory (year-end)
全国	**National Total**	**501332246**	**22066217**	**572450397**	**138200**	**47069851**
北京	Beijing	27513870	929879	27908260	439	2350476
天津	Tianjin	11482829	1263354	12154347		985627
河北	Hebei	15677547	538537	17460955		2003477
山西	Shanxi	10495067	221630	11834399	1217	1914766
内蒙古	Inner Mongolia	8587302	190718	9278491		752384
辽宁	Liaoning	13539511	675279	14787171	3925	1249606
吉林	Jilin	7612717	223527	8650271		670415
黑龙江	Heilongjiang	5310410	191323	5799468		538704
上海	Shanghai	19584451	772749	20930512	490	2362145
江苏	Jiangsu	43087061	2263780	51568134	949	3423569
浙江	Zhejiang	40343489	3060813	49177737	23057	3320145
安徽	Anhui	15666044	441762	18542491		1331475
福建	Fujian	18421547	1045614	23247202		1345839
江西	Jiangxi	7776802	240374	8554063		824786
山东	Shandong	35679907	693000	38695591	1461	3493606
河南	Henan	23285361	566069	25540244		2194513
湖北	Hubei	19393587	671944	21262080		1722486
湖南	Hunan	20869412	801229	25789692		1416309
广东	Guangdong	54544085	3395162	66416341	51540	6006943
广西	Guangxi	8449849	238354	9171854	774	746997
海南	Hainan	3444992	150843	3757429		213767
重庆	Chongqing	13108896	633164	14455668	4153	1050963
四川	Sichuan	27646134	1459915	29981871	2564	2206076
贵州	Guizhou	11989226	285650	14451496		1067465
云南	Yunnan	10933027	297874	13503477		1146755
西藏	Tibet	1098525	19980	1106746		73122
陕西	Shaanxi	12145086	537913	13700021	47622	1386906
甘肃	Gansu	4891111	103397	5453714		354368
青海	Qinghai	1228778	1177	1395308		143396
宁夏	Ningxia	1553944	57927	1646949		235135
新疆	Xinjiang	5971679	93280	6228415	9	537629

3-2-7 续表 6 Continued 6

家用电器及电子产品专门零售 单位：万元

Special Retail of Household Electric Appliances and Electronic Products Unit: 10000 yuan

地区	Region	商品购进额 Total Purchases Value	#进口 Imports	商品销售额 Total Sales Value	#出口 Exports	期末商品库存额 Inventory (year-end)
全国	**National Total**	**88940575**	**473169**	**100468288**	**24676**	**9163140**
北京	Beijing	19495535	37616	21061078		1175647
天津	Tianjin	1001064	3	1484936		97670
河北	Hebei	1401888	5960	1764107		247388
山西	Shanxi	825919		981557		134613
内蒙古	Inner Mongolia	754196	102	827072		114924
辽宁	Liaoning	1914222	4769	1976806		305310
吉林	Jilin	504237	4744	844632		63599
黑龙江	Heilongjiang	1159964		1157738		236165
上海	Shanghai	3625220	1973	4450279		245837
江苏	Jiangsu	7481374	14995	8697197	518	527645
浙江	Zhejiang	3713938	215167	4192495	18	466083
安徽	Anhui	2719437	8051	2975261		266567
福建	Fujian	2972886	9387	3423907	2195	228479
江西	Jiangxi	1356761	100	1520967		132662
山东	Shandong	7151254	5761	7833342	10122	578436
河南	Henan	4025682	28	4681839		410957
湖北	Hubei	4202428	16597	4143357	898	746446
湖南	Hunan	2833748	8140	3231585	3554	179705
广东	Guangdong	8019371	68240	8935311	544	1646843
广西	Guangxi	1430312	12677	1686018	6827	197486
海南	Hainan	293317	4257	309502		81190
重庆	Chongqing	2894686	32073	3207383		183483
四川	Sichuan	3441127	14114	3825530		260113
贵州	Guizhou	879233	1868	950042		73748
云南	Yunnan	759314	2154	984740		102660
西藏	Tibet	48643		52846		8086
陕西	Shaanxi	2979022	2852	3917157		288903
甘肃	Gansu	295510		422960		43012
青海	Qinghai	72401		122267		7585
宁夏	Ningxia	306729		299797		41911
新疆	Xinjiang	381157	1541	506580		69987

五金、家具及室内装饰材料专门零售 单位：万元

Special Retail of Hardware, Furniture and Interior Decoration Materials Unit: 10000 yuan

地 区	Region	商品购进额 Total Purchases Value	#进 口 Imports	商品销售额 Total Sales Value	#出 口 Exports	期末商品库存额 Inventory (year-end)
全 国	**National Total**	**27652211**	**282397**	**33352324**	**103510**	**2276552**
北 京	Beijing	682353	24667	1006312	144	150543
天 津	Tianjin	441038	2616	615961	1221	18095
河 北	Hebei	197136	965	238784	24	30727
山 西	Shanxi	592186		663053		37793
内 蒙 古	Inner Mongolia	123618		151961		15436
辽 宁	Liaoning	235447	1	303913	6963	33143
吉 林	Jilin	265762	3320	336463	1183	36276
黑 龙 江	Heilongjiang	185737		210641		13571
上 海	Shanghai	737426	32863	1030251	645	99842
江 苏	Jiangsu	2756727	44444	3640855	30180	115023
浙 江	Zhejiang	453667	3900	632882	1066	61751
安 徽	Anhui	1073089	439	1235244	4	67230
福 建	Fujian	3009685	88750	3484794	7116	377166
江 西	Jiangxi	412182	3020	499685		40826
山 东	Shandong	2757590	924	3043340	1790	179792
河 南	Henan	1755548	382	2012644	7369	158238
湖 北	Hubei	1295643	930	1659711	5623	86223
湖 南	Hunan	1024887	2227	1218731		63259
广 东	Guangdong	2403297	27573	2884297	4386	269202
广 西	Guangxi	277431	2841	295908	4795	24515
海 南	Hainan	12305		15266		5410
重 庆	Chongqing	2805909	2342	3099653	2363	87145
四 川	Sichuan	852348	10	966446		45564
贵 州	Guizhou	121046		136930		13582
云 南	Yunnan	492205	451	516769		44236
西 藏	Tibet					
陕 西	Shaanxi	2384686	5147	2788390	28638	84209
甘 肃	Gansu	79250		171219		11243
青 海	Qinghai	48221		77746		1
宁 夏	Ningxia	5035		8092		1395
新 疆	Xinjiang	170757	34585	406383		105117

货摊、无店铺及其他零售业
Stalls,Non-shop and Other Retails

单位：万元
Unit: 10000 yuan

地 区	Region	商品购进额 Total Purchases Value	#进口 Imports	商品销售额 Total Sales Value	#出口 Exports	期末商品库存额 Inventory (year-end)
全 国	**National Total**	**78196589**	**761170**	**91446918**	**152235**	**4171460**
北 京	Beijing	4391570	115191	4593089	2811	250717
天 津	Tianjin	2187827	6649	3820873		23148
河 北	Hebei	658855		740163		11060
山 西	Shanxi	841415	571	960275		38404
内蒙古	Inner Mongolia	181059		270977	704	36770
辽 宁	Liaoning	2281486	1026	2232238	1343	17579
吉 林	Jilin	314814	45	366767	105	45639
黑龙江	Heilongjiang	405815	1643	449408		13263
上 海	Shanghai	9712424	40138	10503168		307685
江 苏	Jiangsu	7151262	2889	8753854	890	199694
浙 江	Zhejiang	7030521	42830	8224182	7664	967535
安 徽	Anhui	2257837	34355	2790796	2384	152519
福 建	Fujian	5737260	94764	6854298	18232	426329
江 西	Jiangxi	750373	8225	971422	12905	276613
山 东	Shandong	3630918	338	4303029		107306
河 南	Henan	1505107	36461	2140179	7850	92853
湖 北	Hubei	4639435	8657	5125374		186101
湖 南	Hunan	1136960	1155	1488416	2949	75864
广 东	Guangdong	13320233	236128	14939867	23772	665218
广 西	Guangxi	197957	905	258459		9844
海 南	Hainan	20830		25599		1571
重 庆	Chongqing	1380452	126336	1532298	20407	67371
四 川	Sichuan	4586519	611	5492155	49651	58523
贵 州	Guizhou	725506		978958		46965
云 南	Yunnan	173946	552	217847	274	8780
西 藏	Tibet	10607		11917		5385
陕 西	Shaanxi	2594058	1701	2941284	294	41656
甘 肃	Gansu	262964		321173		29366
青 海	Qinghai	29309		44012		791
宁 夏	Ningxia	2631		5774		925
新 疆	Xinjiang	76639		89066		5986

3-2-8 限额以上批发和零售业商品销售类值

项　目	Item	合　计 Total Sale Value	
		2016	2017
1.粮油、食品、饮料、烟酒类	Grain and Oil, Food, Beverages, Tobacco and Liquor	695775032	722877430
(1)粮油、食品类	Grain and Oil, foods	394777375	405092299
#粮油类	Grain and Oil	137570851	144166302
肉禽蛋类	Meat, Poultry and Eggs	46736827	45740332
(2)饮料类	Beverages	49160711	52672674
(3)烟酒类	Tobacco and Liquor	251836947	265112456
2.服装、鞋帽、针纺织品类	Clothing, Shoes, Hats and Textiles	341489282	332165967
(1)服装类	Clothing	195175799	183776915
(2)鞋帽类	Shoes and Hats	52960453	55590341
(3)针、纺织品类	Knitwear and Textiles	93353031	92798711
3.化妆品类	Cosmetics	35860237	40738351
4.金银珠宝类	Gold, Silver and Jewellery	70708777	73102189
5.日用品类	Articles for Daily Use	116876548	124072623
儿童玩具类	Children Toys	5649476	6318671
6.五金、电料类	Hardware and Electrical Materials	46391277	48115445
7.体育、娱乐用品类	Sports and Recreation Articles	17291992	21430132
8.书报杂志类	Newspapers and Magazines	20221045	20912411
9.电子出版物及音像制品类	E-journals and Video Products	1902868	1807330
10.家用电器和音像器材类	Household Appliances and Video Appliances	178676753	199958180
11.中西药品类	Traditional Chinese and Western Medicines	267916293	288250623
#西药类	Western Medicines	189119709	202925190
中草药及中成药类	Traditional Chinese Medicines	41190137	42324675
12.文化办公用品类	Cultural and Offices Appliances	138453167	157477693
13.家具类	Furniture	37393454	36829070
14.通讯器材类	Communication Appliances	170204307	198913933
15.煤炭及制品类	Coal and Related Products	225446176	273822196
16.木材及制品类	Wood and Wooden Products	21845371	25904233
17.石油及制品类	Petroleum and Related Products	714060735	857181374
18.化工材料及制品类	Chemical Materials and Related Products	381263494	460854048
#化肥类	Fertilizers	47350632	47942755
19.金属材料类	Metal Materials	954361935	1176138420
20.建筑及装潢材料类	Building and Decoration Materials	96147570	102333115
21.机电产品及设备类	Mechanical and Electrical Products	174354305	194212826
#农机类	Agricultural Machineries	7386158	7520155
22.汽车类	Automobiles	702977485	750713059
23.种子饲料类	Seeds and Feedstuff	16427657	18372389
24.棉麻类	Cotton, Hemp	19952070	23478987
25.其他类	Others	260498449	269343183

Sale Values of Enterprises above Designated Size of Wholesale and Retail Trades by Category of Commodities

单位：万元

Unit: 10000 yuan

批发额 Wholesale Value		零售额 Retail Value	
2016	2017	2016	2017
480477830	502524036	215297202	220353394
244223518	251770772	150553857	153321527
101287817	108626458	36283034	35539844
24412313	24062888	22324514	21677444
27412757	29937375	21747954	22735299
208841556	220815888	42995391	44296568
197159734	186600406	144329548	145565561
93000012	80213290	102175787	103563625
25894149	27574684	27066304	28015657
78265574	78812433	15087457	13986278
13641510	15601729	22218727	25136622
40751660	43407160	29957117	29695029
62203586	68956088	54672962	55116535
1999290	2413871	3650186	3904800
32656881	34553783	13734396	13561662
10943587	13998825	6348405	7431307
9327428	9345839	10893617	11566572
670709	588344	1232159	1218986
88637131	105419108	90039622	94539072
183312631	193435558	84603662	94815065
129704150	136360489	59415559	66564701
27897494	27573571	13292643	14751104
105392520	120864515	33060647	36613178
9583871	8740091	27809583	28088979
131264990	155612385	38939317	43301548
215404259	266546203	10041917	7275993
21845371	25904233		
527091600	659747733	186969135	197433641
381263494	460854048		
47350632	47942755		
954361935	1176138420		
62425227	70121245	33722343	32211870
163147130	183675623	11207175	10537203
7386158	7520155		
299262241	328494205	403715244	422218854
16427657	18372389		
19530822	23158625	421248	320362
228980868	237731171	31517581	31612012

3-2-9 各地区限额以上批发和零售业商品销售类值

Sale Values of Enterprises above Designated Size of Wholesale and Retail Trades by Category of Commodities and Region

粮油、食品、饮料、烟酒类

Grain and Oil, Food, Beverages, Tobacco and Liquor

单位：万元

Unit: 10000 yuan

地区	Region	合计 Total Sale Value		批发额 Wholesale Value		零售额 Retail Value	
		2016	2017	2016	2017	2016	2017
全国	**National Total**	**695775032**	**722877430**	**480477830**	**502524036**	**215297202**	**220353394**
北京	Beijing	38054190	41605066	29627955	32650048	8426235	8955018
天津	Tianjin	19787753	17215149	15649949	13834905	4137804	3380244
河北	Hebei	12086637	13237768	7865488	8484560	4221149	4753208
山西	Shanxi	8207572	8587985	4947199	5190187	3260373	3397798
内蒙古	Inner Mongolia	7945918	6258146	5095399	4484465	2850519	1773681
辽宁	Liaoning	13624547	13464866	9422317	9672654	4202230	3792212
吉林	Jilin	8775956	9711898	4455330	5391195	4320626	4320703
黑龙江	Heilongjiang	13815401	13966265	9625960	9649047	4189441	4317218
上海	Shanghai	52172259	63617011	42483885	52888357	9688374	10728654
江苏	Jiangsu	51104494	54661837	31596787	34425706	19507707	20236131
浙江	Zhejiang	39728839	38096600	30114647	29484307	9614192	8612293
安徽	Anhui	22936671	24104075	13161254	13552428	9775417	10551647
福建	Fujian	33028727	37343502	23214334	25414674	9814393	11928828
江西	Jiangxi	9129380	10515613	5941165	6599811	3188215	3915802
山东	Shandong	58525585	53964927	34905770	33275835	23619815	20689092
河南	Henan	38671163	34234106	27419639	21578595	11251524	12655511
湖北	Hubei	38661253	38698654	19552960	19848933	19108293	18849721
湖南	Hunan	21991047	23063627	13144187	14068902	8846860	8994725
广东	Guangdong	73666672	77278690	59489692	63212746	14176980	14065944
广西	Guangxi	9411077	11802969	7552200	9579961	1858877	2223008
海南	Hainan	3199993	3351763	2857767	2982265	342226	369498
重庆	Chongqing	24808177	24688956	17634686	16855436	7173491	7833520
四川	Sichuan	30243834	31448275	17283356	18064067	12960478	13384208
贵州	Guizhou	17218194	18417914	14152546	14769503	3065648	3648411
云南	Yunnan	16298180	19259600	11159659	13734379	5138521	5525221
西藏	Tibet	799838	866017	633176	692494	166662	173523
陕西	Shaanxi	13054925	15192978	7277951	8262713	5776974	6930265
甘肃	Gansu	8454575	7153150	5593429	4770254	2861146	2382896
青海	Qinghai	1594119	1688597	1282301	1343877	311818	344721
宁夏	Ningxia	1809387	2034655	1344778	1489878	464609	544777
新疆	Xinjiang	6968670	7346771	5992065	6271857	976605	1074914

3-2-9 续表 1 Continued 1

粮油、食品类

Grain and Oil, Food

单位：万元

Unit: 10000 yuan

地区	Region	合计 Total Sale Value		批发额 Wholesale Value		零售额 Retail Value	
		2016	2017	2016	2017	2016	2017
全国	**National Total**	**394777375**	**405092299**	**244223518**	**251770772**	**150553857**	**153321527**
北京	Beijing	23291016	25943787	17281552	19774050	6009464	6169737
天津	Tianjin	15561004	13287890	12363810	10529755	3197194	2758135
河北	Hebei	4746894	5516258	1897737	2214948	2849157	3301310
山西	Shanxi	3698145	3729152	1404425	1342536	2293720	2386616
内蒙古	Inner Mongolia	4572430	3005573	2324986	1617781	2247444	1387793
辽宁	Liaoning	8046789	8015415	4869505	5156386	3177284	2859029
吉林	Jilin	5681720	6704251	2369601	3294288	3312119	3409963
黑龙江	Heilongjiang	9381967	9496830	6327215	6364838	3054752	3131992
上海	Shanghai	37195190	46218631	30385276	38420127	6809914	7798504
江苏	Jiangsu	30998826	33090505	16883541	18712437	14115285	14378068
浙江	Zhejiang	20515968	17967792	13153490	11412915	7362478	6554877
安徽	Anhui	11682637	12080685	5053528	5062367	6629109	7018318
福建	Fujian	18752234	21437695	12067873	13328835	6684361	8108860
江西	Jiangxi	3645504	4494190	1356271	1627505	2289233	2866685
山东	Shandong	39780023	36117456	23054020	21464907	16726003	14652549
河南	Henan	23180875	17671307	16105805	9655446	7075070	8015861
湖北	Hubei	21013017	20850103	7991189	7973026	13021828	12877077
湖南	Hunan	9461351	10293763	3700624	4179997	5760727	6113766
广东	Guangdong	45421041	47664769	35314290	37682981	10106751	9981788
广西	Guangxi	4531799	6557595	3096214	4808562	1435585	1749033
海南	Hainan	461146	440585	240812	221317	220334	219267
重庆	Chongqing	14404426	13403034	8891987	7331879	5512439	6071155
四川	Sichuan	12835714	11706192	5158138	4355156	7677576	7351036
贵州	Guizhou	2047427	2236806	731800	733979	1315627	1502827
云南	Yunnan	7763704	10593995	3840833	6248355	3922871	4345640
西藏	Tibet	106113	114239	2475	6173	103638	108066
陕西	Shaanxi	6202859	7774200	2260794	2951388	3942065	4822812
甘肃	Gansu	5700880	4359838	3295157	2440322	2405723	1919517
青海	Qinghai	267139	304060	33786	44673	233353	259388
宁夏	Ningxia	551860	631308	191602	204462	360258	426846
新疆	Xinjiang	3277677	3384399	2575182	2609385	702495	775014

3-2-9 续表 2 Continued 2

粮油类
Grain and Oil

单位：万元
Unit: 10000 yuan

地 区	Region	合 计 Total Sale Value		批发额 Wholesale Value		零售额 Retail Value	
		2016	2017	2016	2017	2016	2017
全 国	**National Total**	**137570851**	**144166302**	**101287817**	**96767881**	**36283034**	**35539844**
北 京	Beijing	9776174	10537058	8923169	9082492	853005	819803
天 津	Tianjin	5310881	6023799	4636372	5193700	674510	292946
河 北	Hebei	1747237	1744345	1085506	1443376	661731	703380
山 西	Shanxi	1277026	1271584	542774	535746	734252	763818
内蒙古	Inner Mongolia	1098611	1528061	698647	670277	399964	435369
辽 宁	Liaoning	4221295	4255879	3405028	4480747	816267	650360
吉 林	Jilin	3019710	3770323	1834883	1422113	1184827	1231304
黑龙江	Heilongjiang	4965257	5059864	4123147	4304086	842110	867759
上 海	Shanghai	19998405	21860921	18104625	15470428	1893780	1822617
江 苏	Jiangsu	11048406	11285357	7436328	7677366	3612079	3286503
浙 江	Zhejiang	6885522	6042367	5535446	3881109	1350076	1144639
安 徽	Anhui	3476347	3884636	1822828	1988104	1653519	1784735
福 建	Fujian	6499572	7344575	5363166	5929493	1136406	1410464
江 西	Jiangxi	1121193	1361787	535397	477066	585797	718836
山 东	Shandong	11225433	10944068	7632465	9335543	3592969	3033710
河 南	Henan	6571935	6436540	4416088	2938871	2155847	2409964
湖 北	Hubei	5174037	5441907	2429020	2492157	2745017	2833828
湖 南	Hunan	3597972	3759852	1867926	1834411	1730046	1627095
广 东	Guangdong	14348519	13375451	11958736	9355371	2389782	2046248
广 西	Guangxi	1140250	1474600	795957	711499	344293	443641
海 南	Hainan	178954	147712	74949	111705	104006	73299
重 庆	Chongqing	4501456	3932407	3117972	2691688	1383483	1401839
四 川	Sichuan	3675693	3946204	1546710	1415181	2128983	2220473
贵 州	Guizhou	806226	859795	340062	269023	466164	534601
云 南	Yunnan	2246793	4067952	1090765	1302887	1156028	1133446
西 藏	Tibet	24662	24050	939	1549	23723	23174
陕 西	Shaanxi	1617671	1846138	525079	475485	1092592	1226531
甘 肃	Gansu	581750	556066	316361	277439	265389	265911
青 海	Qinghai	50715	62087	4093	3017	46622	48472
宁 夏	Ningxia	143784	171853	82548	66815	61236	74612
新 疆	Xinjiang	1239367	1149066	1040833	929139	198535	210471

3-2-9 续表 3 Continued 3

肉禽蛋类
Meat, Poultry and Eggs

单位：万元
Unit: 10000 yuan

地　区	Region	合　计 Total Sale Value		批发额 Wholesale Value		零售额 Retail Value	
		2016	2017	2016	2017	2016	2017
全　国	**National Total**	**46736827**	**45740332**	**24412313**	**24062888**	**22324514**	**21677444**
北　京	Beijing	2438370	2877523	1552676	1922416	885694	955107
天　津	Tianjin	585992	519221	356689	392998	229303	126223
河　北	Hebei	450106	517954	52037	86550	398069	431404
山　西	Shanxi	432826	416287	109204	88470	323622	327817
内蒙古	Inner Mongolia	549333	233286	235558	32061	313775	201225
辽　宁	Liaoning	610879	620455	196501	214883	414378	405572
吉　林	Jilin	708072	706041	222963	236429	485109	469612
黑龙江	Heilongjiang	464632	468852	115439	113736	349193	355117
上　海	Shanghai	2828769	3087705	1959788	2307250	868981	780456
江　苏	Jiangsu	3232788	3342987	1652255	1644946	1580533	1698041
浙　江	Zhejiang	1936979	1869684	1038206	1036861	898773	832823
安　徽	Anhui	1834156	1871050	726666	878558	1107490	992492
福　建	Fujian	1769392	1709849	953074	811531	816318	898317
江　西	Jiangxi	614946	772478	247003	335607	367943	436871
山　东	Shandong	4143675	3965634	1619545	1635302	2524130	2330332
河　南	Henan	2495145	2591033	1364661	1397896	1130484	1193137
湖　北	Hubei	3670932	2558382	1422365	707852	2248567	1850530
湖　南	Hunan	1563783	1828104	624129	789845	939654	1038259
广　东	Guangdong	8286184	8467584	6361470	6712001	1924714	1755583
广　西	Guangxi	447133	547163	259197	308742	187936	238420
海　南	Hainan	20149	17387	3180	87	16969	17300
重　庆	Chongqing	2316560	2273131	1553678	1378202	762882	894929
四　川	Sichuan	2362835	1730188	850214	353543	1512621	1376645
贵　州	Guizhou	353169	443699	112724	144564	240445	299135
云　南	Yunnan	970957	1060121	164932	166148	806025	893973
西　藏	Tibet	29991	36228	496	5228	29495	31000
陕　西	Shaanxi	489084	644189	94523	133029	394561	511160
甘　肃	Gansu	771456	156781	426904	56149	344552	100632
青　海	Qinghai	42183	42685	10452	8722	31731	33963
宁　夏	Ningxia	60472	66128	9384	12938	51088	53190
新　疆	Xinjiang	255878	298524	116398	150344	139480	148180

3-2-9 续表 4 Continued 4

饮料类
Beverages

单位：万元
Unit: 10000 yuan

地 区	Region	合 计 Total Sale Value		批发额 Wholesale Value		零售额 Retail Value	
		2016	2017	2016	2017	2016	2017
全 国	**National Total**	**49160711**	**52672674**	**27412757**	**29937375**	**21747954**	**22735299**
北 京	Beijing	4379241	4471594	3539380	3345335	839861	1126259
天 津	Tianjin	475619	294924	254269	142376	221350	152548
河 北	Hebei	609706	623102	78877	68933	530829	554169
山 西	Shanxi	346441	344651	80764	71672	265677	272979
内蒙古	Inner Mongolia	313737	173028	89808	30195	223929	142833
辽 宁	Liaoning	801873	585648	402500	224176	399373	361472
吉 林	Jilin	344309	358463	55074	73746	289235	284717
黑龙江	Heilongjiang	711619	837619	288902	385391	422717	452228
上 海	Shanghai	2968803	3476376	2382240	2900896	586563	575480
江 苏	Jiangsu	2593833	2925423	1060349	1177237	1533484	1748186
浙 江	Zhejiang	6478668	7011218	5548568	6113028	930100	898190
安 徽	Anhui	1484185	1467350	399722	326763	1084463	1140587
福 建	Fujian	2970462	3890575	990761	1536218	1979701	2354357
江 西	Jiangxi	495467	592546	146009	178068	349458	414478
山 东	Shandong	2676650	2343761	707750	625912	1968900	1717849
河 南	Henan	2519800	2782291	960456	1010219	1559344	1772071
湖 北	Hubei	2349710	2351387	415600	483483	1934110	1867904
湖 南	Hunan	1897213	1996979	712209	818282	1185004	1178697
广 东	Guangdong	7841703	8327315	6285788	6765757	1555915	1561558
广 西	Guangxi	620128	653770	403852	431811	216276	221959
海 南	Hainan	42650	52246	11633	11343	31017	40903
重 庆	Chongqing	744672	1242922	278058	732387	466614	510535
四 川	Sichuan	2049152	2185659	806683	863094	1242469	1322565
贵 州	Guizhou	579985	656114	294514	312031	285471	344083
云 南	Yunnan	1282874	1350894	652741	749578	630133	601316
西 藏	Tibet	8266	8345	1219	755	7047	7591
陕 西	Shaanxi	1018190	1058248	257590	222079	760600	836169
甘 肃	Gansu	192986	182705	87365	75500	105621	107205
青 海	Qinghai	62594	65842	45319	45727	17275	20115
宁 夏	Ningxia	98004	108034	59716	61217	38288	46817
新 疆	Xinjiang	202170	253646	115042	154167	87128	99479

烟酒类
Tobacco and Liquor

单位：万元
Unit: 10000 yuan

地区	Region	合计 Total Sale Value		批发额 Wholesale Value		零售额 Retail Value	
		2016	2017	2016	2017	2016	2017
全国	**National Total**	**251836947**	**265112456**	**208841556**	**220815888**	**42995391**	**44296568**
北京	Beijing	10383933	11189685	8807023	9530663	1576910	1659022
天津	Tianjin	3751129	3632336	3031870	3162774	719259	469562
河北	Hebei	6730037	7098409	5888874	6200680	841163	897729
山西	Shanxi	4162986	4514182	3462010	3775978	700976	738203
内蒙古	Inner Mongolia	3059751	3079544	2680605	2836489	379146	243055
辽宁	Liaoning	4775885	4863803	4150312	4292091	625573	571712
吉林	Jilin	2749928	2649184	2030656	2023161	719272	626023
黑龙江	Heilongjiang	3721814	3631816	3009843	2898819	711971	732997
上海	Shanghai	12008266	13922005	9716369	11567336	2291897	2354669
江苏	Jiangsu	17511835	18645909	13652897	14536032	3858938	4109877
浙江	Zhejiang	12734204	13117590	11412590	11958364	1321614	1159227
安徽	Anhui	9769849	10556041	7708005	8163298	2061844	2392743
福建	Fujian	11306031	12015233	10155700	10549621	1150331	1465612
江西	Jiangxi	4988408	5428877	4438884	4794238	549524	634639
山东	Shandong	16068913	15503710	11144000	11185016	4924913	4318694
河南	Henan	12970489	13780508	10353379	10912930	2617110	2867578
湖北	Hubei	15298527	15497164	11146172	11392424	4152355	4104740
湖南	Hunan	10632483	10772885	8731354	9070622	1901129	1702263
广东	Guangdong	20403929	21286606	17889615	18764008	2514314	2522598
广西	Guangxi	4259150	4591604	4052134	4339588	207016	252016
海南	Hainan	2696197	2858932	2605322	2749605	90875	109328
重庆	Chongqing	9659079	10043000	8464641	8791170	1194438	1251830
四川	Sichuan	15358967	17556425	11318534	12845818	4040433	4710607
贵州	Guizhou	14590782	15524995	13126232	13723494	1464550	1801502
云南	Yunnan	7251601	7314712	6666084	6736446	585517	578266
西藏	Tibet	685459	743433	629482	685567	55977	57867
陕西	Shaanxi	5833877	6360530	4759569	5089247	1074308	1271284
甘肃	Gansu	2560709	2610607	2210907	2254432	349802	356175
青海	Qinghai	1264386	1318695	1203196	1253476	61190	65218
宁夏	Ningxia	1159523	1295312	1093461	1224199	66062	71114
新疆	Xinjiang	3488822	3708726	3301839	3508306	186983	200420

服装、鞋帽、针纺织品类 单位：万元

Clothing, Shoes, Hats and Textiles Unit: 10000 yuan

地 区	Region	合 计 Total Sale Value		批发额 Wholesale Value		零售额 Retail Value	
		2016	2017	2016	2017	2016	2017
全 国	**National Total**	**341489282**	**332165967**	**197159734**	**186600406**	**144329548**	**145565561**
北 京	Beijing	10940233	11256596	4733637	4790953	6206596	6465643
天 津	Tianjin	10793199	6060538	7108881	3213013	3684318	2847525
河 北	Hebei	4622299	4885934	330284	432464	4292015	4453470
山 西	Shanxi	2957346	3533918	127505	661804	2829841	2872114
内蒙古	Inner Mongolia	2659787	1558291	305098	237118	2354689	1321173
辽 宁	Liaoning	9106262	5315326	3842796	1100311	5263466	4215015
吉 林	Jilin	4035780	3907075	76097	177688	3959683	3729388
黑龙江	Heilongjiang	4917760	4864765	165694	179950	4752066	4684815
上 海	Shanghai	38827517	41985982	25899232	26262984	12928285	15722998
江 苏	Jiangsu	51763777	56900855	39007770	43201852	12756007	13699003
浙 江	Zhejiang	44931724	41648436	35428703	33169039	9503021	8479397
安 徽	Anhui	5196171	5225775	1793084	1610077	3403087	3615698
福 建	Fujian	30178810	33909292	23528880	26307677	6649930	7601615
江 西	Jiangxi	1851058	2159872	402885	472636	1448173	1687236
山 东	Shandong	17213408	14878742	5959144	4989074	11254264	9889668
河 南	Henan	7841072	8420038	1351723	1551596	6489349	6868442
湖 北	Hubei	9529567	9841207	1236766	1418753	8292801	8422454
湖 南	Hunan	5392415	5283795	982374	780251	4410041	4503544
广 东	Guangdong	51285757	40026410	38335675	27931204	12950082	12095206
广 西	Guangxi	1730270	2435898	596148	1195674	1134122	1240224
海 南	Hainan	336908	377798	13427	11793	323481	366006
重 庆	Chongqing	6508091	7396496	2605934	3276770	3902157	4119726
四 川	Sichuan	6208416	6494097	852022	876075	5356394	5618022
贵 州	Guizhou	929043	906957	81085	70772	847958	836184
云 南	Yunnan	1488777	1450524	348821	360918	1139956	1089606
西 藏	Tibet	41064	59409	749	31	40315	59377
陕 西	Shaanxi	7603265	8668962	1731143	1893044	5872122	6775918
甘 肃	Gansu	770873	782532	48472	69469	722401	713063
青 海	Qinghai	245349	251869	37516	31228	207833	220641
宁 夏	Ningxia	341704	406326	2602	67568	339102	338759
新 疆	Xinjiang	1241581	1272253	225585	258621	1015996	1013632

3-2-9 续表 7 Continued 7

服装类 单位：万元

Clothing Unit: 10000 yuan

地区	Region	合计 Total Sale Value		批发额 Wholesale Value		零售额 Retail Value	
		2016	2017	2016	2017	2016	2017
全国	**National Total**	**195175799**	**183776915**	**93000012**	**80213290**	**102175787**	**103563625**
北京	Beijing	7147302	7369325	2329994	2343972	4817308	5025353
天津	Tianjin	8939682	4525307	5976361	2272741	2963321	2252566
河北	Hebei	2962462	3128156	98523	132211	2863939	2995945
山西	Shanxi	2328917	2894693	98729	649836	2230188	2244857
内蒙古	Inner Mongolia	1886920	1069451	241270	163099	1645650	906353
辽宁	Liaoning	7483673	4016460	3500324	798905	3983349	3217555
吉林	Jilin	2571892	2485579	40144	52370	2531748	2433209
黑龙江	Heilongjiang	3533603	3495590	80380	78166	3453223	3417424
上海	Shanghai	25567687	27495390	15169062	15118548	10398625	12376842
江苏	Jiangsu	22163902	25161196	13089583	15316609	9074319	9844587
浙江	Zhejiang	19262653	16682295	11853031	9900662	7409622	6781633
安徽	Anhui	3147985	3227686	840638	740380	2307347	2487306
福建	Fujian	10212913	10746116	7008445	6880216	3204468	3865900
江西	Jiangxi	1187735	1445198	205098	289844	982637	1155354
山东	Shandong	10552295	8971383	3208366	2429485	7343929	6541898
河南	Henan	5402645	5732519	767619	841422	4635026	4891098
湖北	Hubei	6419148	6700400	614990	737480	5804158	5962920
湖南	Hunan	3600210	3547861	721667	511037	2878543	3036824
广东	Guangdong	31894800	24328882	23111904	16152706	8782896	8176176
广西	Guangxi	914965	1041501	103864	142884	811101	898617
海南	Hainan	252651	279158	8041	6360	244610	272799
重庆	Chongqing	4647058	5317847	1698251	2201008	2948807	3116839
四川	Sichuan	3637025	3763160	341790	340507	3295235	3422653
贵州	Guizhou	632106	597127	50397	40105	581709	557023
云南	Yunnan	819738	784902	93809	104556	725929	680347
西藏	Tibet	28009	50898	315	7	27694	50891
陕西	Shaanxi	6152472	7042431	1604746	1783266	4547726	5259165
甘肃	Gansu	541881	570362	13375	39163	528506	531199
青海	Qinghai	144656	155383	675	705	143981	154678
宁夏	Ningxia	237966	258120	1759	25198	236207	232921
新疆	Xinjiang	900849	892538	126861	119842	773988	772695

3-2-9 续表 8 Continued 8

鞋帽类
Shoes and Hats

单位：万元
Unit: 10000 yuan

地区	Region	合计 Total Sale Value		批发额 Wholesale Value		零售额 Retail Value	
		2016	2017	2016	2017	2016	2017
全国	**National Total**	**52960453**	**55590341**	**25894149**	**27574684**	**27066304**	**28015657**
北京	Beijing	2303941	2365144	1220500	1228556	1083441	1136588
天津	Tianjin	803177	699355	215442	178061	587735	521294
河北	Hebei	934537	949505	31332	28778	903205	920727
山西	Shanxi	408284	396393	17952	4197	390332	392196
内蒙古	Inner Mongolia	495675	271683	19055	1171	476620	270512
辽宁	Liaoning	976155	810561	139792	109624	836363	700937
吉林	Jilin	797659	772357	44	44422	797615	727935
黑龙江	Heilongjiang	995929	1003502	58154	78905	937775	924597
上海	Shanghai	6273374	7118062	4222584	4270180	2050790	2847882
江苏	Jiangsu	5826112	6447264	3804307	4339266	2021805	2107998
浙江	Zhejiang	4251206	4116829	3060357	3056064	1190849	1060765
安徽	Anhui	963461	904175	325340	264668	638121	639507
福建	Fujian	8774305	10128164	6426072	7276015	2348233	2852149
江西	Jiangxi	292333	340973	26718	27460	265615	313513
山东	Shandong	2766694	2349020	471113	402871	2295581	1946149
河南	Henan	1348529	1484726	198179	239413	1150350	1245313
湖北	Hubei	1846563	1932987	387258	424283	1459305	1508703
湖南	Hunan	943754	875249	74243	60041	869511	815208
广东	Guangdong	6967489	7154673	4198803	4368356	2768686	2786318
广西	Guangxi	267392	263948	47301	33512	220091	230436
海南	Hainan	60936	76278	3249	3145	57687	73133
重庆	Chongqing	1149035	1348149	481959	644251	667076	703898
四川	Sichuan	1616701	1743597	235256	271271	1381445	1472327
贵州	Guizhou	191799	201951	29216	19874	162583	182077
云南	Yunnan	337308	338905	58369	57784	278939	281121
西藏	Tibet	9549	4931	191	6	9358	4925
陕西	Shaanxi	893915	1036415	77466	81576	816449	954839
甘肃	Gansu	146845	141104	30041	27554	116804	113551
青海	Qinghai	49449	49905	238	251	49211	49654
宁夏	Ningxia	64741	61066	838	710	63903	60356
新疆	Xinjiang	203611	203471	32784	32421	170827	171051

3-2-9 续表 9 Continued 9

针、纺织品类
Knitwear and Textiles

单位：万元
Unit: 10000 yuan

地区	Region	合计 Total Sale Value		批发额 Wholesale Value		零售额 Retail Value	
		2016	2017	2016	2017	2016	2017
全国	**National Total**	**93353031**	**92798711**	**78265574**	**78812433**	**15087457**	**13986278**
北京	Beijing	1488990	1522126	1183142	1218424	305848	303702
天津	Tianjin	1050340	835876	917078	762210	133262	73666
河北	Hebei	725301	808273	200430	271476	524871	536797
山西	Shanxi	220144	242832	10823	7771	209321	235061
内蒙古	Inner Mongolia	277193	217157	44774	72849	232419	144309
辽宁	Liaoning	646435	488305	202682	191782	443753	296523
吉林	Jilin	666229	649139	35909	80896	630320	568243
黑龙江	Heilongjiang	388228	365673	27160	22878	361068	342794
上海	Shanghai	6986455	7372530	6507585	6874256	478870	498274
江苏	Jiangsu	23773764	25292396	22113882	23545977	1659882	1746419
浙江	Zhejiang	21417866	20849313	20515316	20212314	902550	636999
安徽	Anhui	1084725	1093914	627106	605030	457619	488885
福建	Fujian	11191593	13035012	10094364	12151446	1097229	883566
江西	Jiangxi	370989	373701	171068	155332	199921	218369
山东	Shandong	3894420	3558340	2279666	2156720	1614754	1401620
河南	Henan	1089898	1202792	385924	470761	703974	732031
湖北	Hubei	1263856	1207820	234518	256990	1029338	950831
湖南	Hunan	848452	860686	186465	209173	661987	651513
广东	Guangdong	12423469	8542855	11024969	7410143	1398500	1132712
广西	Guangxi	547913	1130449	444983	1019278	102930	111171
海南	Hainan	23321	22362	2137	2288	21184	20074
重庆	Chongqing	711999	730500	425725	431511	286274	298989
四川	Sichuan	954690	987339	274976	264297	679714	723042
贵州	Guizhou	105138	107878	1472	10794	103666	97085
云南	Yunnan	331731	326716	196642	198578	135089	128138
西藏	Tibet	3506	3579	243	18	3263	3562
陕西	Shaanxi	556878	590117	48931	28203	507947	561914
甘肃	Gansu	82148	71066	5057	2752	77091	68314
青海	Qinghai	51244	46581	36602	30272	14642	16309
宁夏	Ningxia	38997	87141	5	41660	38992	45481
新疆	Xinjiang	137121	176244	65940	106358	71181	69886

3-2-9 续表 10 Continued 10

化妆品类　　　　　　　　　　　　　　　　　　　　　　　　单位：万元

Cosmetics　　　　　　　　　　　　　　　　　　　　　　　Unit: 10000 yuan

地　区	Region	合　计 Total Sale Value		批发额 Wholesale Value		零售额 Retail Value	
		2016	2017	2016	2017	2016	2017
全　国	**National Total**	**35860237**	**40738351**	**13641510**	**15601729**	**22218727**	**25136622**
北　京	Beijing	2908160	3193389	1027969	1180149	1880191	2013239
天　津	Tianjin	796397	873082	164376	179412	632021	693670
河　北	Hebei	662790	679451	94462	82915	568328	596536
山　西	Shanxi	262293	277343	1361	1160	260932	276183
内蒙古	Inner Mongolia	305868	257371	1925	1954	303943	255417
辽　宁	Liaoning	672731	671615	88384	57984	584347	613631
吉　林	Jilin	355725	321694	4528	10728	351197	310966
黑龙江	Heilongjiang	422167	422125	92260	88507	329907	333618
上　海	Shanghai	9796019	11613714	6771168	7724792	3024851	3888922
江　苏	Jiangsu	2026663	2485392	337005	428178	1689658	2057215
浙　江	Zhejiang	1688208	1894203	589229	774094	1098979	1120109
安　徽	Anhui	966690	1058431	350875	390517	615815	667914
福　建	Fujian	765141	917008	242227	201741	522914	715267
江　西	Jiangxi	203738	240312	10547	10634	193191	229678
山　东	Shandong	1720090	1516920	340124	260370	1379966	1256550
河　南	Henan	1212776	1683149	102563	87186	1110213	1595963
湖　北	Hubei	2035805	2288033	128227	235486	1907578	2052547
湖　南	Hunan	620573	627968	80809	110041	539764	517927
广　东	Guangdong	4105738	4484455	2266993	2559592	1838745	1924863
广　西	Guangxi	214733	364009	20305	127574	194428	236435
海　南	Hainan	291600	429545	1921	576	289679	428969
重　庆	Chongqing	997293	1194914	597598	778552	399695	416363
四　川	Sichuan	1181315	1304630	174506	161413	1006809	1143217
贵　州	Guizhou	172326	197484	4183	5117	168143	192366
云　南	Yunnan	302174	338748	22915	13280	279259	325468
西　藏	Tibet	13362	10756	818	32	12544	10724
陕　西	Shaanxi	701824	863374	52224	48953	649600	814421
甘　肃	Gansu	162723	189438	29174	38234	133549	151205
青　海	Qinghai	43328	63369	868	4107	42460	59262
宁　夏	Ningxia	54965	64644	17	27	54948	64617
新　疆	Xinjiang	197024	211787	41950	38426	155074	173360

3-2-9 续表 11 Continued 11

金银珠宝类 单位：万元

Gold, Silver and Jewellery Unit: 10000 yuan

地 区	Region	合 计 Total Sale Value		批发额 Wholesale Value		零售额 Retail Value	
		2016	2017	2016	2017	2016	2017
全 国	**National Total**	**70708777**	**73102189**	**40751660**	**43407160**	**29957117**	**29695029**
北 京	Beijing	12468188	13078356	9846217	10708499	2621971	2369857
天 津	Tianjin	2251147	2494095	1650577	2015654	600570	478442
河 北	Hebei	855238	916893	32636	39791	822602	877101
山 西	Shanxi	447815	529769	98980	146325	348835	383445
内 蒙 古	Inner Mongolia	453471	363622	33128	41400	420343	322221
辽 宁	Liaoning	1386822	1401880	301233	271003	1085589	1130877
吉 林	Jilin	714550	772611	1593	53414	712957	719196
黑 龙 江	Heilongjiang	515767	475969	12176	7416	503591	468553
上 海	Shanghai	7191654	7710498	5135532	5600905	2056122	2109593
江 苏	Jiangsu	5317501	5759716	2069465	2196046	3248036	3563670
浙 江	Zhejiang	4010271	2882724	2084532	1453115	1925739	1429609
安 徽	Anhui	951055	1066820	178840	208324	772215	858496
福 建	Fujian	2256543	3367673	651557	1505780	1604986	1861893
江 西	Jiangxi	369115	484658	4106	5909	365009	478749
山 东	Shandong	3002328	2811974	701926	794557	2300402	2017418
河 南	Henan	1913717	1922810	523019	476170	1390698	1446640
湖 北	Hubei	1865374	1733224	293439	225123	1571935	1508101
湖 南	Hunan	1104412	1238034	168150	243978	936262	994055
广 东	Guangdong	15043420	16721569	12462346	13943748	2581074	2777821
广 西	Guangxi	232034	251974	8242	5262	223792	246712
海 南	Hainan	98622	115296		2892	98622	112403
重 庆	Chongqing	1172775	1297584	744992	735442	427783	562142
四 川	Sichuan	2179052	1510258	1433189	781465	745863	728793
贵 州	Guizhou	218682	134138	89055	48	129627	134090
云 南	Yunnan	2957274	2149093	1861170	1467447	1096104	681647
西 藏	Tibet	8858	6918			8858	6918
陕 西	Shaanxi	943739	1046470	179722	215869	764017	830601
甘 肃	Gansu	381386	457053	176572	250793	204814	206260
青 海	Qinghai	37816	39040			37816	39040
宁 夏	Ningxia	119786	117101	9	25	119777	117076
新 疆	Xinjiang	240369	244369	9260	10758	231109	233612

日用品类 单位：万元
Articles for Daily Use Unit: 10000 yuan

地 区	Region	合 计 Total Sale Value		批发额 Wholesale Value		零售额 Retail Value	
		2016	2017	2016	2017	2016	2017
全 国	**National Total**	**116876548**	**124072623**	**62203586**	**68956088**	**54672962**	**55116535**
北 京	Beijing	9960431	9239889	5412960	6076849	4547471	3163040
天 津	Tianjin	2982957	2333308	1866190	1443033	1116767	890276
河 北	Hebei	1368733	1372139	169366	181653	1199367	1190486
山 西	Shanxi	467396	490110	54671	46507	412725	443603
内蒙古	Inner Mongolia	465153	338886	46801	24233	418352	314654
辽 宁	Liaoning	2773338	2316628	1053251	1217909	1720087	1098719
吉 林	Jilin	902874	856950	58718	71116	844156	785834
黑龙江	Heilongjiang	827078	798402	136463	104175	690615	694227
上 海	Shanghai	17739671	22003040	13912347	17778526	3827324	4224514
江 苏	Jiangsu	7407220	7937331	2659046	2726242	4748174	5211089
浙 江	Zhejiang	11186172	11461985	7941908	8585607	3244264	2876378
安 徽	Anhui	2929043	3160864	1523790	1540009	1405253	1620854
福 建	Fujian	3972959	4902212	1829023	2237790	2143936	2664422
江 西	Jiangxi	688755	810901	78310	92966	610445	717936
山 东	Shandong	6205247	5576689	1541178	1423975	4664069	4152714
河 南	Henan	3254866	3699039	437406	587413	2817460	3111626
湖 北	Hubei	3818118	4042953	626846	634682	3191272	3408271
湖 南	Hunan	2299319	2386851	399590	505060	1899729	1881791
广 东	Guangdong	26241990	27464539	19556788	20371250	6685202	7093289
广 西	Guangxi	859328	981215	290061	345172	569267	636044
海 南	Hainan	405557	455267	57700	60571	347857	394696
重 庆	Chongqing	2778657	3401982	1094822	1474510	1683835	1927472
四 川	Sichuan	3033336	3387503	570712	554848	2462624	2832655
贵 州	Guizhou	543045	610329	48964	74611	494081	535718
云 南	Yunnan	1698889	1677670	628348	552273	1070541	1125397
西 藏	Tibet	5840	7006	661	32	5179	6974
陕 西	Shaanxi	1382951	1636014	147751	167968	1235200	1468046
甘 肃	Gansu	230393	236929	21000	19597	209393	217332
青 海	Qinghai	66917	68817	4527	3373	62390	65444
宁 夏	Ningxia	115968	116861	5747	5623	110221	111238
新 疆	Xinjiang	264348	300312	28642	48514	235706	251798

3-2-9 续表 13 Continued 13

儿童玩具类
Children Toys

单位：万元
Unit: 10000 yuan

地 区	Region	合 计 Total Sale Value 2016	2017	批发额 Wholesale Value 2016	2017	零售额 Retail Value 2016	2017
全 国	**National Total**	**5649476**	**6318671**	**1999290**	**2413871**	**3650186**	**3904800**
北 京	Beijing	216000	750959	95030	199707	120970	551252
天 津	Tianjin	65329	43003	15608	2314	49721	40689
河 北	Hebei	116501	99408	281	439	116220	98969
山 西	Shanxi	85706	79643	29729	19595	55977	60048
内蒙古	Inner Mongolia	25967	20972	2977	2304	22990	18668
辽 宁	Liaoning	57732	57343	419	1926	57313	55418
吉 林	Jilin	51141	40902	203	272	50938	40630
黑龙江	Heilongjiang	64056	34866	1449	230	62607	34636
上 海	Shanghai	638513	848009	294351	547731	344162	300278
江 苏	Jiangsu	922877	932802	401744	450358	521133	482444
浙 江	Zhejiang	525449	461742	354886	319265	170563	142477
安 徽	Anhui	181913	236199	21908	21426	160005	214773
福 建	Fujian	181494	224006	61858	70022	119636	153984
江 西	Jiangxi	47742	45833	8227	8860	39515	36973
山 东	Shandong	441459	309968	53972	29905	387487	280064
河 南	Henan	143801	172088	5228	26145	138573	145943
湖 北	Hubei	264785	257494	3639	9127	261146	248368
湖 南	Hunan	133664	126922	5436	3918	128228	123004
广 东	Guangdong	913561	946789	604152	664828	309409	281961
广 西	Guangxi	21562	27472	147	220	21415	27253
海 南	Hainan	8169	9450	5	57	8164	9393
重 庆	Chongqing	88605	101797	12906	10217	75699	91580
四 川	Sichuan	147521	152750	3853	3648	143668	149102
贵 州	Guizhou	38037	39691	190	79	37847	39612
云 南	Yunnan	55327	56702	5159	5349	50168	51353
西 藏	Tibet	1391	292	273	9	1118	283
陕 西	Shaanxi	163262	197995	8793	11139	154469	186856
甘 肃	Gansu	22771	17806	866	539	21905	17267
青 海	Qinghai	939	1162			939	1162
宁 夏	Ningxia	2154	2281		1	2154	2280
新 疆	Xinjiang	22046	22324	5999	4243	16047	18081

3-2-9 续表 14 Continued 14

五金、电料类 单位：万元

Hardware and Electrical Materials Unit: 10000 yuan

地　区	Region	合　计 Total Sale Value		批发额 Wholesale Value		零售额 Retail Value	
		2016	2017	2016	2017	2016	2017
全　国	**National Total**	**46391277**	**48115445**	**32656881**	**34553783**	**13734396**	**13561662**
北　京	Beijing	1092745	1169706	967558	1027969	125187	141737
天　津	Tianjin	4041832	1828972	3711980	1662097	329852	166875
河　北	Hebei	351213	365707	210458	210174	140755	155533
山　西	Shanxi	269102	329888	58706	54105	210396	275782
内蒙古	Inner Mongolia	169876	145431	15119	18869	154757	126563
辽　宁	Liaoning	693650	399534	348763	273346	344887	126188
吉　林	Jilin	231856	280636	20463	56115	211393	224521
黑龙江	Heilongjiang	215220	261186	26493	39556	188727	221631
上　海	Shanghai	7138930	8397811	7010471	8269930	128459	127881
江　苏	Jiangsu	6105786	6748242	3306418	3769710	2799368	2978532
浙　江	Zhejiang	4565493	4954369	4170444	4674312	395049	280057
安　徽	Anhui	589010	704449	353691	414583	235319	289867
福　建	Fujian	1428057	1814165	850224	1044121	577833	770044
江　西	Jiangxi	148023	226981	23506	55284	124517	171697
山　东	Shandong	3851815	3621150	1752090	1732656	2099725	1888494
河　南	Henan	1747856	1956700	753803	962015	994053	994685
湖　北	Hubei	1198304	1078424	349335	300100	848969	778324
湖　南	Hunan	1115704	1107397	307544	321090	808160	786306
广　东	Guangdong	8534869	9565862	7053508	8198112	1481361	1367750
广　西	Guangxi	620381	707196	582999	656664	37382	50532
海　南	Hainan	14268	15923	10131	11097	4137	4826
重　庆	Chongqing	748135	812493	311126	339335	437009	473158
四　川	Sichuan	414448	425301	113993	112748	300455	312553
贵　州	Guizhou	129887	90594	65869	30861	64018	59733
云　南	Yunnan	125272	138683	53752	69867	71520	68816
西　藏	Tibet	802	1069	2	3	800	1067
陕　西	Shaanxi	478134	547640	114852	117610	363282	430031
甘　肃	Gansu	229080	246736	24987	25561	204093	221175
青　海	Qinghai	1397	1558	103	477	1294	1081
宁　夏	Ningxia	2319	2243	1		2318	2243
新　疆	Xinjiang	137814	169400	88493	105418	49321	63982

体育、娱乐用品类
Sports and Recreation Articles

单位：万元
Unit: 10000 yuan

地区	Region	合计 Total Sale Value		批发额 Wholesale Value		零售额 Retail Value	
		2016	2017	2016	2017	2016	2017
全国	**National Total**	**17291992**	**21430132**	**10943587**	**13998825**	**6348405**	**7431307**
北京	Beijing	7214638	9003682	6101978	7758436	1112660	1245246
天津	Tianjin	213881	554356	54532	307336	159349	247020
河北	Hebei	138098	171570	18512	32944	119586	138626
山西	Shanxi	75009	76844	18734	19318	56275	57527
内蒙古	Inner Mongolia	62786	58959	22	5343	62764	53616
辽宁	Liaoning	164717	131476	22362	15628	142355	115848
吉林	Jilin	155829	151442	274	296	155555	151146
黑龙江	Heilongjiang	95697	97542	4337	10	91360	97533
上海	Shanghai	1848391	2747499	1554065	2279576	294326	467923
江苏	Jiangsu	1474239	1666465	854933	948014	619306	718452
浙江	Zhejiang	537464	565197	322631	329794	214833	235403
安徽	Anhui	230739	281618	51236	57594	179503	224024
福建	Fujian	427789	616783	250338	366158	177451	250625
江西	Jiangxi	75176	77957	20185	12079	54991	65878
山东	Shandong	392753	359106	71906	67517	320847	291590
河南	Henan	393322	444749	84342	105619	308980	339130
湖北	Hubei	288059	297614	17697	6527	270362	291087
湖南	Hunan	188008	215848	52069	70258	135939	145590
广东	Guangdong	2090528	2155712	1224482	1216227	866046	939485
广西	Guangxi	95401	109999	15781	14939	79620	95060
海南	Hainan	16258	16335		26	16258	16310
重庆	Chongqing	128275	146977	74129	97235	54146	49741
四川	Sichuan	258945	311566	9316	7401	249629	304165
贵州	Guizhou	55539	74990	5927	14739	49612	60251
云南	Yunnan	70483	65270	11675	13861	58808	51408
西藏	Tibet	102	134			102	134
陕西	Shaanxi	534806	960837	100925	251170	433881	709667
甘肃	Gansu	34669	35156	205	100	34464	35056
青海	Qinghai	1366	1406		12	1366	1394
宁夏	Ningxia	12113	15854	510	181	11603	15673
新疆	Xinjiang	16915	17191	485	489	16430	16702

书报杂志类
Newspapers and Magazines

单位：万元
Unit: 10000 yuan

地 区	Region	合 计 Total Sale Value		批发额 Wholesale Value		零售额 Retail Value	
		2016	2017	2016	2017	2016	2017
全 国	**National Total**	**20221045**	**20912411**	**9327428**	**9345839**	**10893617**	**11566572**
北 京	Beijing	2062495	2154834	1203191	1315479	859304	839355
天 津	Tianjin	419089	427638	124382	136931	294707	290707
河 北	Hebei	857886	769909	429253	390577	428633	379332
山 西	Shanxi	485114	409814	255796	199341	229318	210473
内 蒙 古	Inner Mongolia	149491	143830	92203	75725	57288	68105
辽 宁	Liaoning	185964	181890	54207	64170	131757	117720
吉 林	Jilin	173080	180770	52335	59302	120745	121468
黑 龙 江	Heilongjiang	244047	289965	68224	87664	175823	202301
上 海	Shanghai	518660	559118	243609	268580	275051	290538
江 苏	Jiangsu	1969833	2254206	567722	586804	1402111	1667402
浙 江	Zhejiang	1072321	1109895	448515	451676	623806	658219
安 徽	Anhui	1060349	1061133	466897	460483	593452	600650
福 建	Fujian	522703	619400	229841	276440	292862	342960
江 西	Jiangxi	653271	684175	272559	271607	380712	412567
山 东	Shandong	1109488	1279294	577408	677390	532080	601904
河 南	Henan	943591	1031826	405706	453080	537885	578745
湖 北	Hubei	1260474	1169491	644451	573815	616023	595676
湖 南	Hunan	967516	955455	530784	506189	436732	449266
广 东	Guangdong	1747061	1352232	1223829	842436	523232	509796
广 西	Guangxi	399777	463455	186994	186944	212783	276511
海 南	Hainan	74941	83525	45307	48030	29634	35495
重 庆	Chongqing	416260	426147	175838	176493	240422	249654
四 川	Sichuan	761889	879282	113334	192205	648555	687077
贵 州	Guizhou	288530	327460	146444	166869	142086	160591
云 南	Yunnan	541481	615255	253670	306909	287811	308346
西 藏	Tibet	14892	17172	9714	10379	5178	6793
陕 西	Shaanxi	569599	679948	146844	169013	422755	510936
甘 肃	Gansu	252764	256209	118941	128786	133823	127423
青 海	Qinghai	32718	35292	21610	23636	11108	11656
宁 夏	Ningxia	45366	44817	25648	25968	19718	18849
新 疆	Xinjiang	420400	448974	192175	212918	228225	236056

3-2-9 续表 17 Continued 17

电子出版物及音像制品类
E-journals and Video Products

单位：万元
Unit: 10000 yuan

地 区	Region	合 计 Total Sale Value		批发额 Wholesale Value		零售额 Retail Value	
		2016	2017	2016	2017	2016	2017
全 国	**National Total**	**1902868**	**1807330**	**670709**	**588344**	**1232159**	**1218986**
北 京	Beijing	497114	478609	220795	181565	276319	297044
天 津	Tianjin	13758	12805	3584	5587	10174	7218
河 北	Hebei	29178	37906	355	638	28823	37268
山 西	Shanxi	21168	20989	10095	10074	11073	10916
内 蒙 古	Inner Mongolia	10932	5430	3030		7902	5430
辽 宁	Liaoning	23216	11372	7874	5294	15342	6078
吉 林	Jilin	30326	23541	856	9	29470	23531
黑 龙 江	Heilongjiang	16688	16053	8927	7624	7761	8430
上 海	Shanghai	22540	21824	13527	14976	9013	6848
江 苏	Jiangsu	166258	171184	58482	67659	107776	103525
浙 江	Zhejiang	78958	78857	57558	58428	21400	20429
安 徽	Anhui	28072	31786	2859	2370	25213	29416
福 建	Fujian	25038	47165	6637	6587	18401	40578
江 西	Jiangxi	102294	113013	14794	13506	87500	99507
山 东	Shandong	98202	78524	11406	6463	86796	72061
河 南	Henan	67772	90681	10878	21250	56894	69431
湖 北	Hubei	52376	53124	2209	3923	50167	49201
湖 南	Hunan	61702	67192	18030	20075	43672	47117
广 东	Guangdong	320033	256988	170202	128484	149831	128504
广 西	Guangxi	8322	6139	733	442	7589	5697
海 南	Hainan	3692	1507	103	16	3589	1491
重 庆	Chongqing	29851	28600	9933	9343	19918	19257
四 川	Sichuan	22530	18599	7042	111	15488	18488
贵 州	Guizhou	9439	9268	1175	1228	8264	8041
云 南	Yunnan	44976	24204	21392	13810	23584	10394
西 藏	Tibet	11	10			11	10
陕 西	Shaanxi	101174	86823	7876	8488	93298	78335
甘 肃	Gansu	3121	2963	28	34	3093	2929
青 海	Qinghai	7098	3989	329	360	6769	3629
宁 夏	Ningxia	2455	3244			2455	3244
新 疆	Xinjiang	4574	4943		3	4574	4940

家用电器和音像器材类 单位：万元

Household Appliances and Video Appliances Unit: 10000 yuan

地区	Region	合计 Total Sale Value		批发额 Wholesale Value		零售额 Retail Value	
		2016	2017	2016	2017	2016	2017
全国	**National Total**	**178676753**	**199958180**	**88637131**	**105419108**	**90039622**	**94539072**
北京	Beijing	19909558	24013489	14934327	17960989	4975231	6052500
天津	Tianjin	3940406	3437519	2350379	2085611	1590027	1351907
河北	Hebei	3413062	4124333	922480	1471357	2490582	2652976
山西	Shanxi	1319995	1695302	233252	544538	1086743	1150765
内蒙古	Inner Mongolia	998030	888780	157108	192866	840922	695914
辽宁	Liaoning	3388025	3315036	824084	828519	2563941	2486517
吉林	Jilin	1538628	1521187	110262	139421	1428366	1381766
黑龙江	Heilongjiang	1341043	1316907	232284	185138	1108759	1131769
上海	Shanghai	10169101	8813423	5080173	5380304	5088928	3433119
江苏	Jiangsu	22524882	26849691	14055114	17092706	8469768	9756985
浙江	Zhejiang	11446313	13048490	7345293	8718052	4101020	4330438
安徽	Anhui	7265618	8392031	3614145	4200767	3651473	4191264
福建	Fujian	4719738	5569133	2127762	2288179	2591976	3280954
江西	Jiangxi	2380636	2780442	776646	943672	1603990	1836769
山东	Shandong	19908999	20939618	9176281	11044667	10732718	9894951
河南	Henan	6943865	8560660	2672537	3690797	4271328	4869863
湖北	Hubei	7074178	7524077	1513569	1763620	5560609	5760457
湖南	Hunan	5501209	5841190	1249919	1397923	4251290	4443267
广东	Guangdong	22049387	26298583	14329764	17777023	7719623	8521560
广西	Guangxi	2474777	2568806	1006203	1021303	1468574	1547503
海南	Hainan	367289	408849	169425	189218	197864	219631
重庆	Chongqing	5843951	6712076	2439227	3075200	3404724	3636876
四川	Sichuan	6552452	7306539	959920	1086020	5592532	6220519
贵州	Guizhou	1173804	1253617	454967	470329	718837	783288
云南	Yunnan	1531979	1561427	638056	708111	893923	853317
西藏	Tibet	21793	12339			21793	12339
陕西	Shaanxi	3407332	3812918	784647	741341	2622685	3071578
甘肃	Gansu	436769	384696	126865	96600	309904	288096
青海	Qinghai	142809	154376	29831	33267	112978	121109
宁夏	Ningxia	200070	206223	27046	28956	173024	177267
新疆	Xinjiang	691055	646424	295563	262616	395492	383807

3-2-9 续表 19 Continued 19

中西药品类　　单位：万元

Traditional Chinese and Western Medicines　　Unit: 10000 yuan

地 区	Region	合 计 Total Sale Value		批发额 Wholesale Value		零售额 Retail Value	
		2016	2017	2016	2017	2016	2017
全 国	**National Total**	**267916293**	**288250623**	**183312631**	**193435558**	**84603662**	**94815065**
北 京	Beijing	19146059	19337916	14932070	12614091	4213989	6723825
天 津	Tianjin	6944193	5537308	6511339	5253270	432854	284038
河 北	Hebei	7790099	8793243	5246514	5860433	2543585	2932810
山 西	Shanxi	3498629	3992888	2346975	2626605	1151654	1366283
内蒙古	Inner Mongolia	1225662	1319575	831461	838551	394201	481025
辽 宁	Liaoning	7210897	7320009	3290167	3372990	3920730	3947019
吉 林	Jilin	3050695	3859130	1905334	2496067	1145361	1363063
黑龙江	Heilongjiang	4500642	3525727	2564487	1781280	1936155	1744447
上 海	Shanghai	17391362	19079598	13131446	14500006	4259916	4579592
江 苏	Jiangsu	23343824	26044109	13580597	15447106	9763227	10597003
浙 江	Zhejiang	16487926	17352851	8977536	9378091	7510390	7974760
安 徽	Anhui	12317196	11747969	7647343	6557693	4669853	5190276
福 建	Fujian	5602528	5579947	3548460	3388742	2054068	2191206
江 西	Jiangxi	5832652	7275776	4017042	4983367	1815610	2292409
山 东	Shandong	18760332	20751206	11889689	13305761	6870643	7445445
河 南	Henan	12951658	15764306	10341992	12714266	2609666	3050041
湖 北	Hubei	15933501	17978000	10313704	11734274	5619797	6243726
湖 南	Hunan	8752319	9422437	5284963	5923647	3467356	3498790
广 东	Guangdong	33313514	35302256	26384102	27574702	6929412	7727554
广 西	Guangxi	4426456	5368703	2427317	3010298	1999139	2358405
海 南	Hainan	1756287	1679592	1704078	1617309	52209	62283
重 庆	Chongqing	9044007	9792406	5802487	6091328	3241520	3701078
四 川	Sichuan	9592353	10232700	7325876	7905301	2266477	2327399
贵 州	Guizhou	2968833	3478093	2091064	2366740	877769	1111353
云 南	Yunnan	5993411	6209411	4467101	4480599	1526310	1728812
西 藏	Tibet	360694	349145	344442	334326	16252	14819
陕 西	Shaanxi	4303616	5245732	3056669	3746191	1246947	1499541
甘 肃	Gansu	1954838	2132349	1492429	1476394	462409	655955
青 海	Qinghai	293905	309637	195256	223875	98649	85762
宁 夏	Ningxia	587440	673840	165026	208699	422414	465141
新 疆	Xinjiang	2580768	2794766	1495668	1623557	1085100	1171209

3-2-9 续表 20 Continued 20

西药类 单位：万元

Western Medicines Unit: 10000 yuan

地区	Region	合计 Total Sale Value		批发额 Wholesale Value		零售额 Retail Value	
		2016	2017	2016	2017	2016	2017
全国	**National Total**	**189119709**	**202925190**	**129704150**	**136360489**	**59415559**	**66564701**
北京	Beijing	13033046	13446747	10048708	8655785	2984338	4790962
天津	Tianjin	3615213	2549286	3405627	2433743	209586	115542
河北	Hebei	5343310	6318167	3532072	4173059	1811238	2145108
山西	Shanxi	2473880	2719364	1697692	1786493	776188	932871
内蒙古	Inner Mongolia	648619	669861	498878	481872	149741	187989
辽宁	Liaoning	5236802	5421998	2370010	2506249	2866792	2915749
吉林	Jilin	1574934	1827775	1161852	1356652	413082	471124
黑龙江	Heilongjiang	2336897	1926433	993776	754439	1343121	1171994
上海	Shanghai	14648541	15384686	11260356	11709760	3388185	3674927
江苏	Jiangsu	18891701	21116176	11140932	12828325	7750769	8287851
浙江	Zhejiang	12183142	12600983	6728526	6741269	5454616	5859714
安徽	Anhui	9128718	8537590	5893687	4908313	3235031	3629277
福建	Fujian	4111503	3863110	2527058	2206033	1584445	1657078
江西	Jiangxi	3630850	4743903	2350694	3185910	1280156	1557994
山东	Shandong	9949798	10273881	6407331	6444520	3542467	3829361
河南	Henan	7972192	10155082	6590380	8478834	1381812	1676249
湖北	Hubei	13288031	15285465	8732020	10138614	4556011	5146851
湖南	Hunan	5593634	5935575	3514060	4018670	2079574	1916905
广东	Guangdong	22119530	23436963	17383445	18131835	4736085	5305128
广西	Guangxi	3299231	4011439	1700227	2135616	1599004	1875823
海南	Hainan	1495568	1439833	1449765	1387246	45803	52587
重庆	Chongqing	6576760	7188693	4239246	4499370	2337514	2689324
四川	Sichuan	7194425	7682236	5642036	6027013	1552389	1655223
贵州	Guizhou	2088218	2509237	1456408	1705652	631810	803585
云南	Yunnan	4884924	5035349	3715369	3760599	1169555	1274750
西藏	Tibet	17114	47826	13675	41596	3439	6230
陕西	Shaanxi	3392246	3899161	2502756	2912532	889490	986629
甘肃	Gansu	1560620	1769768	1205038	1222741	355582	547027
青海	Qinghai	217954	242860	151586	188973	66368	53887
宁夏	Ningxia	456534	527911	112678	148971	343856	378940
新疆	Xinjiang	2155773	2357833	1278260	1389810	877513	968023

中草药及中成药类
Traditional Chinese Medicines

单位：万元
Unit: 10000 yuan

地 区	Region	合 计 Total Sale Value		批发额 Wholesale Value		零售额 Retail Value	
		2016	2017	2016	2017	2016	2017
全 国	**National Total**	**41190137**	**42324675**	**27897494**	**27573571**	**13292643**	**14751104**
北 京	Beijing	3422866	3445917	2306093	1814177	1116773	1631740
天 津	Tianjin	1998926	1148451	1898053	1116365	100873	32087
河 北	Hebei	1281625	1414013	807331	892551	474294	521462
山 西	Shanxi	558991	614590	362191	390478	196800	224112
内蒙古	Inner Mongolia	113431	119789	81675	77657	31756	42132
辽 宁	Liaoning	974457	1012013	438643	472554	535814	539459
吉 林	Jilin	557155	843470	329885	615989	227270	227480
黑龙江	Heilongjiang	733386	696894	528979	498828	204407	198066
上 海	Shanghai	1913818	2032839	1120680	1213968	793138	818872
江 苏	Jiangsu	3165522	3298591	1714390	1762605	1451132	1535986
浙 江	Zhejiang	2870466	2911364	1492332	1520935	1378134	1390429
安 徽	Anhui	1707234	1747761	1035739	1015522	671495	732240
福 建	Fujian	497204	515809	267421	273043	229783	242767
江 西	Jiangxi	1623870	1622875	1224093	1157329	399777	465546
山 东	Shandong	2863329	2942956	1554269	1591406	1309060	1351550
河 南	Henan	1600145	1952846	1162915	1422044	437230	530802
湖 北	Hubei	1488428	1309142	981449	762307	506979	546834
湖 南	Hunan	1047421	1111934	615186	662708	432235	449226
广 东	Guangdong	6811322	7130659	5963890	6156289	847432	974370
广 西	Guangxi	772385	935558	468332	546012	304053	389546
海 南	Hainan	153147	131357	146741	124618	6406	6738
重 庆	Chongqing	961531	1076918	583713	628495	377818	448423
四 川	Sichuan	1176194	1285063	840250	931579	335944	353484
贵 州	Guizhou	632338	660988	507893	494855	124445	166133
云 南	Yunnan	911095	920928	674500	619149	236595	301779
西 藏	Tibet	192910	173696	190070	170656	2840	3040
陕 西	Shaanxi	472577	563044	219386	228986	253191	334058
甘 肃	Gansu	258012	259295	193331	199375	64681	59920
青 海	Qinghai	25362	23350	8057	7162	17305	16189
宁 夏	Ningxia	110399	124374	39963	53416	70436	70959
新 疆	Xinjiang	294591	298192	140041	152515	154550	145677

文化办公用品类
Cultural and Offices Appliances

单位：万元
Unit: 10000 yuan

地 区	Region	合 计 Total Sale Value		批发额 Wholesale Value		零售额 Retail Value	
		2016	2017	2016	2017	2016	2017
全 国	**National Total**	**138453167**	**157477693**	**105392520**	**120864515**	**33060647**	**36613178**
北 京	Beijing	29318239	35436352	23742132	28093830	5576107	7342522
天 津	Tianjin	1351438	734238	947149	532742	404289	201496
河 北	Hebei	751145	637580	384692	313061	366453	324519
山 西	Shanxi	264182	302218	151558	175822	112624	126396
内蒙古	Inner Mongolia	221891	164036	41119	21766	180772	142269
辽 宁	Liaoning	1113284	1016794	385532	397307	727752	619487
吉 林	Jilin	387849	412196	35941	61959	351908	350238
黑龙江	Heilongjiang	500759	551678	82618	106655	418141	445023
上 海	Shanghai	21623401	24176078	18880582	21285458	2742819	2890620
江 苏	Jiangsu	12025329	13038781	8160219	8934975	3865110	4103806
浙 江	Zhejiang	6035675	6305887	4640434	4917136	1395241	1388751
安 徽	Anhui	2389223	4266129	1662705	3413979	726518	852150
福 建	Fujian	2439630	3462701	1422745	2250517	1016885	1212185
江 西	Jiangxi	358779	385318	88474	84072	270305	301246
山 东	Shandong	5987163	6705806	3313475	3905633	2673688	2800173
河 南	Henan	1720443	1958804	617731	707270	1102712	1251534
湖 北	Hubei	4170701	4327499	2484544	2448050	1686157	1879449
湖 南	Hunan	1278865	1497130	477522	586807	801343	910323
广 东	Guangdong	35805219	40394006	31776633	35644363	4028586	4749643
广 西	Guangxi	373462	518694	129572	225538	243890	293156
海 南	Hainan	64683	60413	34714	31470	29969	28944
重 庆	Chongqing	2578381	2492851	1276458	1278254	1301923	1214597
四 川	Sichuan	5147227	5984198	3685898	4604158	1461329	1380040
贵 州	Guizhou	252613	278209	93731	65570	158882	212639
云 南	Yunnan	558677	508344	336758	275781	221919	232563
西 藏	Tibet	1451	5338		4	1451	5334
陕 西	Shaanxi	1157091	1235211	293670	231190	863421	1004021
甘 肃	Gansu	196296	187733	53037	46823	143259	140910
青 海	Qinghai	12976	7355	5588	21	7388	7333
宁 夏	Ningxia	67355	58764	15472	9667	51883	49097
新 疆	Xinjiang	299739	367355	171816	214637	127923	152718

家具类 Furniture

单位：万元 Unit: 10000 yuan

地 区	Region	合 计 Total Sale Value		批发额 Wholesale Value		零售额 Retail Value	
		2016	2017	2016	2017	2016	2017
全 国	**National Total**	**37393454**	**36829070**	**9583871**	**8740091**	**27809583**	**28088979**
北 京	Beijing	1202493	1497729	186908	143539	1015585	1354190
天 津	Tianjin	582240	987570	282545	702476	299695	285094
河 北	Hebei	802235	819540	39065	60936	763170	758604
山 西	Shanxi	412181	431549	2516	2658	409665	428891
内 蒙 古	Inner Mongolia	554505	278620	335	147	554170	278473
辽 宁	Liaoning	492791	269811	37184	16267	455607	253544
吉 林	Jilin	582687	624893	2	28	582685	624865
黑 龙 江	Heilongjiang	381060	455776	2959	45741	378101	410035
上 海	Shanghai	1506677	1773951	792636	966177	714041	807774
江 苏	Jiangsu	2585128	3041510	446094	589530	2139034	2451980
浙 江	Zhejiang	2214085	1616812	1293485	1061267	920600	555545
安 徽	Anhui	1111311	1190712	34458	46905	1076853	1143807
福 建	Fujian	2312506	2352760	787458	601748	1525048	1751012
江 西	Jiangxi	523887	654005	5715	14386	518172	639619
山 东	Shandong	4307344	3502632	387382	267486	3919962	3235146
河 南	Henan	2110746	2257484	228407	265793	1882339	1991691
湖 北	Hubei	1567530	1656415	34554	48370	1532976	1608045
湖 南	Hunan	1046904	1118001	90622	82711	956282	1035290
广 东	Guangdong	5968415	5155174	4154052	3226483	1814363	1928691
广 西	Guangxi	65989	83260	9692	6632	56297	76628
海 南	Hainan	12441	11918		7	12441	11911
重 庆	Chongqing	3069848	2732884	670883	458207	2398965	2274677
四 川	Sichuan	1418691	1431344	5646	18776	1413045	1412567
贵 州	Guizhou	79191	98721	1273	1690	77918	97031
云 南	Yunnan	256927	290599	11844	23066	245083	267533
西 藏	Tibet						
陕 西	Shaanxi	1510264	1646195	2497	2982	1507767	1643213
甘 肃	Gansu	248529	246939	15425	14701	233104	232238
青 海	Qinghai	68236	71017	1867		66369	71017
宁 夏	Ningxia	7719	8488		5	7719	8483
新 疆	Xinjiang	390895	522761	58366	71377	332529	451385

3-2-9 续表 24 Continued 24

通讯器材类 单位：万元

Communication Appliances Unit: 10000 yuan

地 区	Region	合 计 Total Sale Value		批发额 Wholesale Value		零售额 Retail Value	
		2016	2017	2016	2017	2016	2017
全 国	**National Total**	**170204307**	**198913933**	**131264990**	**155612385**	**38939317**	**43301548**
北 京	Beijing	54861504	58580511	42675530	47402196	12185974	11178315
天 津	Tianjin	2197390	1394947	1847978	1070932	349412	324015
河 北	Hebei	762912	1113718	310221	447134	452691	666584
山 西	Shanxi	88149	127691	6385	43140	81764	84550
内蒙古	Inner Mongolia	316361	296400	194660	185415	121701	110985
辽 宁	Liaoning	1475869	2052761	330036	367577	1145833	1685184
吉 林	Jilin	381053	446821	45374	94341	335679	352480
黑龙江	Heilongjiang	828324	871950	294539	307962	533785	563988
上 海	Shanghai	30057011	30319650	27672696	26713212	2384315	3606439
江 苏	Jiangsu	10482478	15440601	7496516	12101534	2985962	3339067
浙 江	Zhejiang	6261194	7661491	4553208	5654774	1707986	2006717
安 徽	Anhui	739980	1178307	249294	632704	490686	545603
福 建	Fujian	2806602	3230243	1579728	1394110	1226874	1836133
江 西	Jiangxi	568122	805930	231667	478969	336455	326961
山 东	Shandong	3121857	3110619	954700	1151648	2167157	1958972
河 南	Henan	1259468	2779623	441164	1802934	818304	976690
湖 北	Hubei	3520430	5132915	2157685	3283111	1362745	1849803
湖 南	Hunan	976447	1606739	373203	912750	603244	693989
广 东	Guangdong	38646120	50361817	33539707	44192225	5106413	6169592
广 西	Guangxi	365370	412823	118979	144083	246391	268740
海 南	Hainan	61613	73132	40283	50162	21330	22970
重 庆	Chongqing	4812710	4518125	3554080	3395033	1258630	1123092
四 川	Sichuan	2679442	3045209	1443084	1539053	1236358	1506156
贵 州	Guizhou	450245	981880	324805	813011	125440	168869
云 南	Yunnan	405375	621810	167582	358346	237793	263464
西 藏	Tibet	32430	30786			32430	30786
陕 西	Shaanxi	1276139	1556965	222316	258203	1053823	1298762
甘 肃	Gansu	257714	418572	121324	283261	136390	135311
青 海	Qinghai	251580	120791	226812	97366	24768	23425
宁 夏	Ningxia	58884	55727	9815	12554	49069	43173
新 疆	Xinjiang	201534	565379	81617	424645	119917	140734

煤炭及制品类
Coal and Related Products

单位：万元
Unit: 10000 yuan

地 区	Region	合 计 Total Sale Value		批发额 Wholesale Value		零售额 Retail Value	
		2016	2017	2016	2017	2016	2017
全 国	**National Total**	**225446176**	**273822196**	**215404259**	**266546203**	**10041917**	**7275993**
北 京	Beijing	24543894	35124614	24512343	35095563	31551	29051
天 津	Tianjin	27920176	20286152	27282120	20195751	638056	90401
河 北	Hebei	9651155	10830284	9539495	10720213	111660	110071
山 西	Shanxi	17918773	21993324	17745489	21870046	173284	123278
内蒙古	Inner Mongolia	9425214	12240737	8883352	12088109	541862	152629
辽 宁	Liaoning	3310883	4564218	3233031	4539057	77852	25161
吉 林	Jilin	295261	352513	126720	181625	168541	170887
黑龙江	Heilongjiang	1749122	2253497	1616296	2097324	132826	156173
上 海	Shanghai	10363112	15356863	10361522	15356518	1590	345
江 苏	Jiangsu	18634756	21990565	17904552	21282280	730204	708285
浙 江	Zhejiang	14281964	20278197	14241927	20266499	40037	11698
安 徽	Anhui	4788490	6297087	4667487	6159927	121003	137160
福 建	Fujian	6127719	9842380	5955131	9697237	172588	145143
江 西	Jiangxi	808029	823481	735159	769352	72870	54129
山 东	Shandong	25078873	22637925	22170147	20795167	2908726	1842758
河 南	Henan	9170187	12501870	8436761	11845820	733426	656050
湖 北	Hubei	1873507	2611600	1531082	2398451	342425	213149
湖 南	Hunan	1798804	1886489	1119467	1415835	679337	470655
广 东	Guangdong	10029848	13543752	9734988	13491891	294860	51861
广 西	Guangxi	2222429	2273807	2185427	2234501	37002	39307
海 南	Hainan	31198	29122	31198	29122		
重 庆	Chongqing	4477030	3782100	4341327	3669275	135703	112825
四 川	Sichuan	1444590	1658014	1226334	1503902	218256	154112
贵 州	Guizhou	3565696	3365810	3502386	3292595	63310	73215
云 南	Yunnan	2688180	3163364	2585484	3087276	102696	76088
西 藏	Tibet						
陕 西	Shaanxi	11541577	21084331	10099571	19508073	1442006	1576258
甘 肃	Gansu	242107	330137	201599	262695	40508	67442
青 海	Qinghai	407116	380488	393179	364185	13937	16303
宁 夏	Ningxia	134487	350874	134477	350874	10	
新 疆	Xinjiang	921999	1988601	906206	1977039	15793	11562

3-2-9 续表 26 Continued 26

木材及制品类 单位：万元

Wood and Wooden Products Unit: 10000 yuan

地 区	Region	合 计 Total Sale Value 2016	合 计 Total Sale Value 2017	批发额 Wholesale Value 2016	批发额 Wholesale Value 2017	零售额 Retail Value 2016	零售额 Retail Value 2017
全 国	**National Total**	**21845371**	**25904233**	**21845371**	**25904233**		
北 京	Beijing	3360802	3731982	3360802	3731982		
天 津	Tianjin	805175	610821	805175	610821		
河 北	Hebei	107488	71268	107488	71268		
山 西	Shanxi	31921	13840	31921	13840		
内蒙古	Inner Mongolia	523289	513693	523289	513693		
辽 宁	Liaoning	38129	29149	38129	29149		
吉 林	Jilin	28	855	28	855		
黑龙江	Heilongjiang	555850	1153419	555850	1153419		
上 海	Shanghai	2209531	3431872	2209531	3431872		
江 苏	Jiangsu	1739781	2972680	1739781	2972680		
浙 江	Zhejiang	4721124	4546286	4721124	4546286		
安 徽	Anhui	148798	184509	148798	184509		
福 建	Fujian	2247233	2445957	2247233	2445957		
江 西	Jiangxi	80957	128238	80957	128238		
山 东	Shandong	2228728	2497872	2228728	2497872		
河 南	Henan	88986	80670	88986	80670		
湖 北	Hubei	64873	131528	64873	131528		
湖 南	Hunan	82993	93200	82993	93200		
广 东	Guangdong	2014712	2414468	2014712	2414468		
广 西	Guangxi	50053	92932	50053	92932		
海 南	Hainan		2692		2692		
重 庆	Chongqing	299890	255925	299890	255925		
四 川	Sichuan	138368	126788	138368	126788		
贵 州	Guizhou	5158	8091	5158	8091		
云 南	Yunnan	242866	223307	242866	223307		
西 藏	Tibet						
陕 西	Shaanxi	3462	57801	3462	57801		
甘 肃	Gansu	22070	25501	22070	25501		
青 海	Qinghai						
宁 夏	Ningxia	243	111	243	111		
新 疆	Xinjiang	32864	58778	32864	58778		

石油及制品类
Petroleum and Related Products

单位：万元
Unit: 10000 yuan

地 区	Region	合 计 Total Sale Value		批发额 Wholesale Value		零售额 Retail Value	
		2016	2017	2016	2017	2016	2017
全 国	**National Total**	**714060735**	**857181374**	**527091600**	**659747733**	**186969135**	**197433641**
北 京	Beijing	50441888	58966161	45698595	54079876	4743293	4886285
天 津	Tianjin	42934972	46006401	39025124	42150386	3909848	3856015
河 北	Hebei	11225464	17136619	7008469	12041520	4216995	5095099
山 西	Shanxi	4718037	5757393	1068928	2109764	3649109	3647629
内蒙古	Inner Mongolia	8276472	8924413	3030105	4621228	5246367	4303185
辽 宁	Liaoning	47197823	61869221	42031052	56390487	5166771	5478734
吉 林	Jilin	8052390	8148256	3512180	3297613	4540210	4850643
黑龙江	Heilongjiang	10058812	12333164	6765428	8899100	3293384	3434064
上 海	Shanghai	80585108	86369942	76469906	81076577	4115202	5293365
江 苏	Jiangsu	38433677	46869675	24356373	32319437	14077304	14550238
浙 江	Zhejiang	47060582	60921628	34808152	47610778	12252430	13310850
安 徽	Anhui	10659572	12321879	4526979	5347800	6132593	6974079
福 建	Fujian	26346009	28373896	20174512	21754093	6171497	6619803
江 西	Jiangxi	6022735	6567404	789932	1161803	5232803	5405601
山 东	Shandong	35866359	51638925	22212419	37575557	13653940	14063368
河 南	Henan	16003668	17706212	8563174	9139301	7440494	8566911
湖 北	Hubei	33780343	38225852	26969021	31821697	6811322	6404155
湖 南	Hunan	10673044	12749036	2763551	3969400	7909493	8779636
广 东	Guangdong	87496067	115997713	67941526	95122823	19554541	20874890
广 西	Guangxi	9383795	11011194	5015220	6340876	4368575	4670319
海 南	Hainan	3393651	3940138	2352986	2784485	1040665	1155653
重 庆	Chongqing	12935328	13140952	7903574	8601217	5031754	4539735
四 川	Sichuan	23493061	27032200	12206854	14946275	11286207	12085925
贵 州	Guizhou	7489863	6828121	1337230	1517744	6152633	5310377
云 南	Yunnan	10210860	12996530	3678007	5805145	6532853	7191385
西 藏	Tibet	616924	789413	17167	48558	599757	740855
陕 西	Shaanxi	16860329	21218969	10475728	14101193	6384601	7117776
甘 肃	Gansu	20165556	19695859	16933297	16287708	3232259	3408151
青 海	Qinghai	2301960	2519200	1018535	1100953	1283425	1418247
宁 夏	Ningxia	4040378	4809523	3367718	4003786	672660	805737
新 疆	Xinjiang	27336008	36315485	25069858	33720552	2266150	2594933

3-2-9 续表 28 Continued 28

化工材料及制品类 单位：万元

Chemical Materials and Related Products Unit: 10000 yuan

地区	Region	合计 Total Sale Value		批发额 Wholesale Value		零售额 Retail Value	
		2016	2017	2016	2017	2016	2017
全国	**National Total**	**381263494**	**460854048**	**381263494**	**460854048**		
北京	Beijing	52416595	64908213	52416595	64908213		
天津	Tianjin	19735069	22751898	19735069	22751898		
河北	Hebei	3228853	4135986	3228853	4135986		
山西	Shanxi	3143493	3582756	3143493	3582756		
内蒙古	Inner Mongolia	1437750	1809134	1437750	1809134		
辽宁	Liaoning	6282712	7456768	6282712	7456768		
吉林	Jilin	1042468	1325475	1042468	1325475		
黑龙江	Heilongjiang	3502950	2880100	3502950	2880100		
上海	Shanghai	48394168	61391893	48394168	61391893		
江苏	Jiangsu	38992141	47827619	38992141	47827619		
浙江	Zhejiang	53280015	70012950	53280015	70012950		
安徽	Anhui	3051619	3810005	3051619	3810005		
福建	Fujian	21875680	30146664	21875680	30146664		
江西	Jiangxi	466506	633798	466506	633798		
山东	Shandong	19802423	21523095	19802423	21523095		
河南	Henan	5442428	5942614	5442428	5942614		
湖北	Hubei	5087048	4651867	5087048	4651867		
湖南	Hunan	1910898	2504755	1910898	2504755		
广东	Guangdong	41177622	51910984	41177622	51910984		
广西	Guangxi	1621372	2765478	1621372	2765478		
海南	Hainan	14407185	10707250	14407185	10707250		
重庆	Chongqing	8240101	8207853	8240101	8207853		
四川	Sichuan	5067930	7766572	5067930	7766572		
贵州	Guizhou	5008702	2879846	5008702	2879846		
云南	Yunnan	6926267	7631924	6926267	7631924		
西藏	Tibet	14673	16783	14673	16783		
陕西	Shaanxi	2513418	4106215	2513418	4106215		
甘肃	Gansu	2321457	1582917	2321457	1582917		
青海	Qinghai	239377	211871	239377	211871		
宁夏	Ningxia	82887	232881	82887	232881		
新疆	Xinjiang	4549692	5537885	4549692	5537885		

化肥类
Fertilizers

单位：万元
Unit: 10000 yuan

地 区	Region	合 计 Total Sale Value 2016	合 计 Total Sale Value 2017	批发额 Wholesale Value 2016	批发额 Wholesale Value 2017	零售额 Retail Value 2016	零售额 Retail Value 2017
全 国	**National Total**	**47350632**	**47942755**	**47350632**	**47942755**		
北 京	Beijing	7149504	7733362	7149504	7733362		
天 津	Tianjin	284051	219269	284051	219269		
河 北	Hebei	1255203	941662	1255203	941662		
山 西	Shanxi	686022	715230	686022	715230		
内蒙古	Inner Mongolia	338086	290487	338086	290487		
辽 宁	Liaoning	724681	661326	724681	661326		
吉 林	Jilin	526862	693736	526862	693736		
黑龙江	Heilongjiang	2461359	2486947	2461359	2486947		
上 海	Shanghai	2100404	2918186	2100404	2918186		
江 苏	Jiangsu	1599770	1599684	1599770	1599684		
浙 江	Zhejiang	1120957	1191148	1120957	1191148		
安 徽	Anhui	1260759	1637640	1260759	1637640		
福 建	Fujian	953984	1327567	953984	1327567		
江 西	Jiangxi	201381	243215	201381	243215		
山 东	Shandong	6236121	5275464	6236121	5275464		
河 南	Henan	2317228	2517366	2317228	2517366		
湖 北	Hubei	2477226	2477544	2477226	2477544		
湖 南	Hunan	476711	697455	476711	697455		
广 东	Guangdong	1668357	1689317	1668357	1689317		
广 西	Guangxi	582154	603753	582154	603753		
海 南	Hainan	100876	124854	100876	124854		
重 庆	Chongqing	1980773	1850928	1980773	1850928		
四 川	Sichuan	1607573	2066092	1607573	2066092		
贵 州	Guizhou	2835781	1328779	2835781	1328779		
云 南	Yunnan	3339998	4033904	3339998	4033904		
西 藏	Tibet	14673	16783	14673	16783		
陕 西	Shaanxi	263640	285822	263640	285822		
甘 肃	Gansu	504964	324989	504964	324989		
青 海	Qinghai	194825	175285	194825	175285		
宁 夏	Ningxia	40518	29987	40518	29987		
新 疆	Xinjiang	2046194	1784980	2046194	1784980		

3-2-9 续表 30 Continued 30

金属材料类 单位：万元

Metal Materials Unit: 10000 yuan

地区	Region	合计 Total Sale Value		批发额 Wholesale Value		零售额 Retail Value	
		2016	2017	2016	2017	2016	2017
全国	**National Total**	**954361935**	**1176138420**	**954361935**	**1176138420**		
北京	Beijing	62387373	79972741	62387373	79972741		
天津	Tianjin	132268978	123099987	132268978	123099987		
河北	Hebei	22898116	25117666	22898116	25117666		
山西	Shanxi	28695747	22363980	28695747	22363980		
内蒙古	Inner Mongolia	1957271	2246985	1957271	2246985		
辽宁	Liaoning	18910024	26309249	18910024	26309249		
吉林	Jilin	1751064	2050394	1751064	2050394		
黑龙江	Heilongjiang	1523876	1921917	1523876	1921917		
上海	Shanghai	225704136	279600182	225704136	279600182		
江苏	Jiangsu	76807891	109244843	76807891	109244843		
浙江	Zhejiang	94137165	118926809	94137165	118926809		
安徽	Anhui	6398378	9135013	6398378	9135013		
福建	Fujian	33999534	47774309	33999534	47774309		
江西	Jiangxi	2855407	3485965	2855407	3485965		
山东	Shandong	36613924	47057186	36613924	47057186		
河南	Henan	12686132	16943243	12686132	16943243		
湖北	Hubei	14382739	16199200	14382739	16199200		
湖南	Hunan	10469705	9184476	10469705	9184476		
广东	Guangdong	92386975	131107689	92386975	131107689		
广西	Guangxi	15517163	16424465	15517163	16424465		
海南	Hainan	1087302	235717	1087302	235717		
重庆	Chongqing	13230068	14501815	13230068	14501815		
四川	Sichuan	9199247	12741413	9199247	12741413		
贵州	Guizhou	4006739	4619934	4006739	4619934		
云南	Yunnan	11814775	16814064	11814775	16814064		
西藏	Tibet						
陕西	Shaanxi	4176704	11425794	4176704	11425794		
甘肃	Gansu	4287158	7869272	4287158	7869272		
青海	Qinghai	4802728	5959901	4802728	5959901		
宁夏	Ningxia	1741900	4006033	1741900	4006033		
新疆	Xinjiang	7663721	9798180	7663721	9798180		

建筑及装潢材料类
Building and Decoration Materials

单位：万元
Unit: 10000 yuan

地 区	Region	合 计 Total Sale Value		批发额 Wholesale Value		零售额 Retail Value	
		2016	2017	2016	2017	2016	2017
全 国	**National Total**	**96147570**	**102333115**	**62425227**	**70121245**	**33722343**	**32211870**
北 京	Beijing	2857219	3488176	2572932	3102753	284287	385423
天 津	Tianjin	4028596	1810694	3084349	1508413	944247	302281
河 北	Hebei	732960	920107	380019	507746	352941	412361
山 西	Shanxi	720793	741359	270238	214616	450555	526743
内蒙古	Inner Mongolia	603345	833232	286371	632278	316974	200954
辽 宁	Liaoning	1319937	595323	761711	433179	558226	162144
吉 林	Jilin	960424	1165793	128210	305617	832214	860176
黑龙江	Heilongjiang	2279126	2257625	889399	723662	1389727	1533963
上 海	Shanghai	4792418	3666125	4126687	3273449	665731	392676
江 苏	Jiangsu	13321505	15769322	7001047	8984086	6320458	6785236
浙 江	Zhejiang	6890039	6506848	5462533	5929424	1427506	577424
安 徽	Anhui	1907808	1855173	911144	980805	996664	874368
福 建	Fujian	8275648	10233651	6301233	7646051	1974415	2587600
江 西	Jiangxi	711464	1038966	321050	532187	390414	506780
山 东	Shandong	10139054	9013611	5994601	5787044	4144453	3226567
河 南	Henan	3410320	5951304	2418045	4813332	992275	1137973
湖 北	Hubei	3593211	3707795	1080262	1364399	2512949	2343396
湖 南	Hunan	2115913	2182266	777492	782791	1338421	1399474
广 东	Guangdong	12933448	15304882	11229672	13563706	1703776	1741176
广 西	Guangxi	735429	1187109	634115	1068069	101314	119040
海 南	Hainan	10704	44509	8316	43460	2388	1049
重 庆	Chongqing	4234323	4293485	2397346	2585749	1836977	1707736
四 川	Sichuan	3589380	3185678	1867152	1675059	1722228	1510619
贵 州	Guizhou	687373	951262	580042	824958	107331	126303
云 南	Yunnan	2765805	2782568	2108259	1859925	657546	922643
西 藏	Tibet						
陕 西	Shaanxi	1785453	2050096	327670	483504	1457783	1566591
甘 肃	Gansu	357530	385257	201516	200988	156014	184270
青 海	Qinghai	5041	532	4267	46	774	486
宁 夏	Ningxia	5002	14644	4598	3328	404	11316
新 疆	Xinjiang	378301	395727	294951	290623	83350	105104

机电产品及设备类
Mechanical and Electrical Products

单位：万元
Unit: 10000 yuan

地　区	Region	合计 Total Sale Value 2016	合计 Total Sale Value 2017	批发额 Wholesale Value 2016	批发额 Wholesale Value 2017	零售额 Retail Value 2016	零售额 Retail Value 2017
全　国	**National Total**	**174354305**	**194212826**	**163147130**	**183675623**	**11207175**	**10537203**
北　京	Beijing	22454826	25229807	21997023	24801699	457803	428108
天　津	Tianjin	4038409	3429512	3918591	3362964	119818	66548
河　北	Hebei	893576	741395	783069	697650	110507	43745
山　西	Shanxi	5065931	1631910	5003726	1585998	62205	45912
内蒙古	Inner Mongolia	369782	272197	221584	211188	148198	61008
辽　宁	Liaoning	3708565	2149227	3593410	2066954	115155	82273
吉　林	Jilin	352660	456128	242618	353163	110042	102965
黑龙江	Heilongjiang	751769	691281	635660	554604	116109	136677
上　海	Shanghai	42242655	52466829	42160608	52393107	82047	73722
江　苏	Jiangsu	14921933	16831612	13447596	15642333	1474337	1189279
浙　江	Zhejiang	9855006	12200520	9653464	12048208	201542	152312
安　徽	Anhui	2127509	2596380	1941099	2366819	186410	229561
福　建	Fujian	4919841	5719114	4241011	4942137	678830	776977
江　西	Jiangxi	551362	560968	436502	403550	114860	157418
山　东	Shandong	11571197	10438159	9592672	8730178	1978525	1707981
河　南	Henan	3991296	4607489	3292929	3905867	698367	701622
湖　北	Hubei	2522799	2762738	1911429	2199736	611370	563001
湖　南	Hunan	1666260	2170298	1093965	1529283	572295	641015
广　东	Guangdong	31648260	37922167	30131546	36460526	1516714	1461641
广　西	Guangxi	887670	1445360	787429	1335643	100241	109717
海　南	Hainan	47481	51980	38484	33355	8997	18625
重　庆	Chongqing	3545539	3073595	2815566	2352507	729973	721088
四　川	Sichuan	2420830	2530952	1824712	1920992	596118	609961
贵　州	Guizhou	255846	281306	197233	227725	58613	53581
云　南	Yunnan	718132	849942	563940	699126	154192	150816
西　藏	Tibet	27552	17225	26809	16446	743	778
陕　西	Shaanxi	936888	1032446	808463	866693	128425	165753
甘　肃	Gansu	814468	789604	765549	735049	48919	54555
青　海	Qinghai	333886	294099	333420	293303	466	796
宁　夏	Ningxia	45418	53694	44129	53327	1289	366
新　疆	Xinjiang	666960	914896	642893	885493	24067	29403

农机类
Agricultural Machineries

单位：万元
Unit: 10000 yuan

地区	Region	合计 Total Sale Value 2016	合计 Total Sale Value 2017	批发额 Wholesale Value 2016	批发额 Wholesale Value 2017	零售额 Retail Value 2016	零售额 Retail Value 2017
全　国	**National Total**	**7386158**	**7520155**	**7386158**	**7520155**		
北　京	Beijing	183575	248393	183575	248393		
天　津	Tianjin	63725	25201	63725	25201		
河　北	Hebei	141866	121960	141866	121960		
山　西	Shanxi	23953	35225	23953	35225		
内蒙古	Inner Mongolia	114476	72439	114476	72439		
辽　宁	Liaoning	114124	63316	114124	63316		
吉　林	Jilin	47996	81434	47996	81434		
黑龙江	Heilongjiang	249641	247970	249641	247970		
上　海	Shanghai	418284	508541	418284	508541		
江　苏	Jiangsu	914202	1124941	914202	1124941		
浙　江	Zhejiang	88934	95350	88934	95350		
安　徽	Anhui	270838	287762	270838	287762		
福　建	Fujian	131176	143293	131176	143293		
江　西	Jiangxi	25615	29703	25615	29703		
山　东	Shandong	1582643	1308641	1582643	1308641		
河　南	Henan	1099676	1136332	1099676	1136332		
湖　北	Hubei	320054	323379	320054	323379		
湖　南	Hunan	338217	388431	338217	388431		
广　东	Guangdong	60942	68088	60942	68088		
广　西	Guangxi	96101	223045	96101	223045		
海　南	Hainan	46	141	46	141		
重　庆	Chongqing	138166	134195	138166	134195		
四　川	Sichuan	592939	412802	592939	412802		
贵　州	Guizhou	22273	22085	22273	22085		
云　南	Yunnan	38179	90191	38179	90191		
西　藏	Tibet	22220	11049	22220	11049		
陕　西	Shaanxi	61073	52375	61073	52375		
甘　肃	Gansu	33962	24722	33962	24722		
青　海	Qinghai	33677	32924	33677	32924		
宁　夏	Ningxia	22851	21415	22851	21415		
新　疆	Xinjiang	134737	184812	134737	184812		

3-2-9 续表 34 Continued 34

汽车类
Automobiles

单位：万元
Unit: 10000 yuan

地 区	Region	合 计 Total Sale Value		批发额 Wholesale Value		零售额 Retail Value	
		2016	2017	2016	2017	2016	2017
全 国	**National Total**	**702977485**	**750713059**	**299262241**	**328494205**	**403715244**	**422218854**
北 京	Beijing	77587305	82553774	58260929	62316184	19326376	20237590
天 津	Tianjin	35971688	23710366	26453997	15691367	9517691	8018999
河 北	Hebei	24404052	25366581	11450195	11175802	12953857	14190779
山 西	Shanxi	7434477	8141498	331761	800401	7102716	7341097
内蒙古	Inner Mongolia	5231706	4986321	89338	240603	5142368	4745718
辽 宁	Liaoning	11583623	12442692	1710429	2203242	9873194	10239450
吉 林	Jilin	6487028	7908987	1304536	2032709	5182492	5876278
黑龙江	Heilongjiang	6160229	6683602	1725202	2063862	4435027	4619740
上 海	Shanghai	106370665	120604763	88074540	101708627	18296125	18896136
江 苏	Jiangsu	45864198	48509231	8066053	9107673	37798145	39401558
浙 江	Zhejiang	50659962	60930384	17147392	26193435	33512570	34736949
安 徽	Anhui	13939309	15957328	1492954	2100642	12446355	13856686
福 建	Fujian	16737947	19088608	2133255	2516950	14604692	16571658
江 西	Jiangxi	10026852	12075592	1771451	2242343	8255401	9833249
山 东	Shandong	37169039	36098648	4986453	5515192	32182586	30583456
河 南	Henan	24787635	26321741	2629090	2490457	22158545	23831284
湖 北	Hubei	27964138	26133476	10883459	8794153	17080679	17339323
湖 南	Hunan	20032297	22564218	4009404	5589567	16022893	16974651
广 东	Guangdong	86511248	97769366	43381591	51643949	43129657	46125417
广 西	Guangxi	7928827	9212647	691617	737391	7237210	8475256
海 南	Hainan	2024125	1972438	540141	296004	1483984	1676435
重 庆	Chongqing	19952637	18310795	7893966	6826051	12058671	11484744
四 川	Sichuan	20565035	21851523	1153909	1326195	19411126	20525328
贵 州	Guizhou	7368668	7909967	459086	567968	6909582	7341999
云 南	Yunnan	7829654	8062441	286037	330034	7543617	7732407
西 藏	Tibet	250717	272650	3482	37024	247235	235626
陕 西	Shaanxi	11168550	14084734	1132013	2757208	10036537	11327526
甘 肃	Gansu	3263886	3236687	172628	174476	3091258	3062211
青 海	Qinghai	1180735	1336790	14150	33928	1166585	1302861
宁 夏	Ningxia	1542488	1652084	129839	226730	1412649	1425354
新 疆	Xinjiang	4978768	4963130	883345	754038	4095423	4209092

种子饲料类
Seeds and Feedstuff

单位：万元
Unit: 10000 yuan

地 区	Region	合 计 Total Sale Value		批发额 Wholesale Value		零售额 Retail Value	
		2016	2017	2016	2017	2016	2017
全 国	**National Total**	**16427657**	**18372389**	**16427657**	**18372389**		
北 京	Beijing	1564072	1858301	1564072	1858301		
天 津	Tianjin	546684	729836	546684	729836		
河 北	Hebei	96669	117664	96669	117664		
山 西	Shanxi	55478	49725	55478	49725		
内蒙古	Inner Mongolia	86831	61233	86831	61233		
辽 宁	Liaoning	519358	538332	519358	538332		
吉 林	Jilin	99857	117010	99857	117010		
黑龙江	Heilongjiang	248822	203797	248822	203797		
上 海	Shanghai	1923016	1824581	1923016	1824581		
江 苏	Jiangsu	841644	1057912	841644	1057912		
浙 江	Zhejiang	455838	616794	455838	616794		
安 徽	Anhui	551545	571912	551545	571912		
福 建	Fujian	1462726	1661274	1462726	1661274		
江 西	Jiangxi	37518	72088	37518	72088		
山 东	Shandong	2199218	2073677	2199218	2073677		
河 南	Henan	1063287	1092482	1063287	1092482		
湖 北	Hubei	187078	202641	187078	202641		
湖 南	Hunan	251352	285924	251352	285924		
广 东	Guangdong	2791565	3438693	2791565	3438693		
广 西	Guangxi	91340	212597	91340	212597		
海 南	Hainan	811	18971	811	18971		
重 庆	Chongqing	331179	337203	331179	337203		
四 川	Sichuan	314021	357527	314021	357527		
贵 州	Guizhou	40439	36236	40439	36236		
云 南	Yunnan	78731	103552	78731	103552		
西 藏	Tibet						
陕 西	Shaanxi	45465	67180	45465	67180		
甘 肃	Gansu	85520	84405	85520	84405		
青 海	Qinghai	790	2595	790	2595		
宁 夏	Ningxia	2923	3614	2923	3614		
新 疆	Xinjiang	453880	574632	453880	574632		

3-2-9 续表 36 Continued 36

棉麻类
Cotton, Hemp

单位：万元
Unit: 10000 yuan

地 区	Region	合 计 Total Sale Value		批发额 Wholesale Value		零售额 Retail Value	
		2016	2017	2016	2017	2016	2017
全 国	**National Total**	**19952070**	**23478987**	**19530822**	**23158625**	**421248**	**320362**
北 京	Beijing	1849094	2618702	1849094	2618702		
天 津	Tianjin	440719	292646	440719	292646		
河 北	Hebei	541476	654049	526851	634145	14625	19904
山 西	Shanxi	1342	1952	4	787	1338	1165
内蒙古	Inner Mongolia	16	2			16	2
辽 宁	Liaoning	14918	10070	14110	9637	808	433
吉 林	Jilin	725	137	1	1	724	136
黑龙江	Heilongjiang	196	280		1	196	279
上 海	Shanghai	431715	381617	431565	381450	150	168
江 苏	Jiangsu	2203229	2710470	2157726	2650034	45503	60436
浙 江	Zhejiang	720517	1047544	717805	1047167	2712	377
安 徽	Anhui	177787	149125	162971	145705	14816	3420
福 建	Fujian	503074	714667	459527	667124	43547	47543
江 西	Jiangxi	92823	145135	88471	136585	4352	8550
山 东	Shandong	1218941	1451669	1153267	1439485	65674	12184
河 南	Henan	729360	942346	701332	935417	28028	6929
湖 北	Hubei	2316972	2325540	2191263	2236831	125709	88709
湖 南	Hunan	235659	259660	187559	215395	48100	44266
广 东	Guangdong	511255	735949	510185	735206	1070	743
广 西	Guangxi	15206	15686	15194	15398	12	288
海 南	Hainan						
重 庆	Chongqing	91097	225231	87384	220623	3713	4608
四 川	Sichuan	264387	271102	249221	263437	15166	7665
贵 州	Guizhou	1363	1486		33	1363	1453
云 南	Yunnan	16426	23980	15031	20237	1395	3743
西 藏	Tibet						
陕 西	Shaanxi	50428	32071	49902	25781	526	6290
甘 肃	Gansu	3364	1433	2765	820	599	613
青 海	Qinghai						
宁 夏	Ningxia						
新 疆	Xinjiang	7519985	8466439	7518877	8465981	1108	458

其他类
Others

单位：万元
Unit: 10000 yuan

地区	Region	合计 Total Sale Value		批发额 Wholesale Value		零售额 Retail Value	
		2016	2017	2016	2017	2016	2017
全国	**National Total**	**260498449**	**269343183**	**228980868**	**237731171**	**31517581**	**31612012**
北京	Beijing	19245226	21638308	17875961	20460691	1369265	1177617
天津	Tianjin	21397180	16337923	20005031	15639029	1392149	698894
河北	Hebei	634119	722310	513770	522448	120349	199862
山西	Shanxi	3413596	3863229	2765432	3145785	648164	717444
内蒙古	Inner Mongolia	1182216	964684	420961	530878	761255	433806
辽宁	Liaoning	3249104	3021534	2283626	1968890	965478	1052644
吉林	Jilin	945890	1096477	353589	387278	592301	709200
黑龙江	Heilongjiang	873076	1049235	349746	513214	523330	536021
上海	Shanghai	44737840	45903704	43872170	44799336	865670	1104368
江苏	Jiangsu	8238608	9313195	7002576	8023370	1236032	1289825
浙江	Zhejiang	23522799	24169600	21695901	22460504	1826898	1709096
安徽	Anhui	6305108	5048630	5657054	4151049	648054	897581
福建	Fujian	14933627	18034900	12923627	15928281	2010000	2106619
江西	Jiangxi	1729323	2238914	1105285	1420843	624038	818071
山东	Shandong	11261265	11005617	8755782	8976001	2505483	2029616
河南	Henan	7310045	8601304	5749344	6615507	1560701	1985797
湖北	Hubei	3274525	3589323	1478476	1673660	1796049	1915663
湖南	Hunan	4533843	4046215	3163815	2652304	1370028	1393912
广东	Guangdong	53285355	59166359	47545994	52896419	5739361	6269940
广西	Guangxi	3632692	4483711	3206459	4063559	426233	420152
海南	Hainan	138063	121452	73943	86205	64120	35247
重庆	Chongqing	4320920	4213981	3324125	3309862	996795	904119
四川	Sichuan	3424604	3388554	2646551	2720345	778053	668209
贵州	Guizhou	3781480	2516499	3037668	1959015	743812	557485
云南	Yunnan	10831165	10150470	10320843	9727022	510322	423448
西藏	Tibet	55842	76891	24165	39097	31677	37794
陕西	Shaanxi	1371524	2257017	346864	1185471	1024660	1071546
甘肃	Gansu	394726	490594	240615	280214	154111	210380
青海	Qinghai	1439571	212892	1324441	133551	115130	79341
宁夏	Ningxia	122244	182901	116046	160511	6198	22390
新疆	Xinjiang	912878	1436763	801013	1300834	111865	135929

3-3-1 限额以上批发和零售业企业年末资产负债

项　目	Item	流动资产合计 Total Working Capitals	#存货 Stock	固定资产原价 Original Value of Fixed Assets
总　计	**Total**	**2170942589**	**357999894**	**252614541**
一、批发业	**Wholesale Trade**	**1753755784**	**269180461**	**134216920**
#国有控股	State-controlled Enterprises	598983775	110161417	64440415
(一)按登记注册类型分	**by Type of Registration**			
1.内资企业	**Domestic Funded Enterprises**	**1463796384**	**219141422**	**119567199**
国有企业	State-owned Enterprises	92708530	25371300	15055842
集体企业	Collective-owned Enterprises	2820986	446810	560140
股份合作企业	Cooperative Enterprises	580887	88321	108635
联营企业	Joint Ownership Enterprises	217260	100036	15576
国有联营企业	State Joint Ownership Enterprises	24038	5929	4419
集体联营企业	Collective Joint Ownership Enterprises	40511	3824	10601
国有与集体联营企业	Joint State-collective Enterprises	144288	87074	409
其他联营企业	Other Joint Ownership Enterprises	8424	3209	146
有限责任公司	Limited Liability Corporations	758345396	110027853	51833302
国有独资公司	State Sole Funded Corporations	121575309	22142215	14861516
其他有限责任公司	Other Limited Liability Corporations	636770090	87885637	36971785
股份有限公司	Share-holding Corporations Ltd.	152222586	21972410	20384300
私营企业	Private Enterprises	455723798	60948868	31156810
私营独资企业	Private-funded Enterprises	1386485	331868	289817
私营合伙企业	Private Partnership Enterprises	85192	19470	12764
私营有限责任公司	Private Limited Liability Corporations	441785119	58219616	29477793
私营股份有限公司	Private Share-holding Corporations Ltd.	12467008	2377917	1376440
其他企业	Other Enterprises	1176935	185826	452602
2.港、澳、台商投资企业	**Enterprises with Funds from Hongkong, Macao and Taiwan**	**124182494**	**19602346**	**6039815**
合资经营企业	Joint-venture Enterprises	17887555	2833007	948890
合作经营企业	Cooperative Enterprises	600505	33808	56563
独资经营企业	Enterprises with Sole Investment	102072434	16459304	4721054
投资股份有限公司	Share-holding Corporations Ltd. with Investment	1954354	157325	183484
其他港澳台商投资企业	Other Enterprises with Funds from Hongkong, Macao and Taiwan	1667644	118908	129829
3.外商投资企业	**Foreign Funded Enterprises**	**165776909**	**30436697**	**8609909**
中外合资经营企业	Joint-venture Enterprises	30752736	5470880	1629422
中外合作经营企业	Cooperative Enterprises	232904	26137	37027
外资企业	Enterprises with Sole Foreign Investment	131199819	24132117	6508066
外商投资股份有限公司	Share-holding Corporations Ltd. with Foreign Investment	1217270	268413	257201
其他外商投资企业	Other Foreign Funded Enterprises	2374182	539154	178195

注：限额以上批发和零售业企业中，因包含了部分视同法人单位，财务指标数据存在资产≠负债+所有者权益的问题(下表同)。

Note: Of enterprises above designated size of wholesale and retail trades, the financial data have the problem of total assets≠liabilities+total owners' equities, because some of them are regarded as legal entities. The same applies to the tables following.

Assets and Liabilities of Enterprises above Designated Size of Wholesale and Retail Trades at the Year-end

单位：万元
Unit:10000 yuan

累计折旧 Accumulated Depreciation	#本年折旧 Current Year Depreciation	资产总计 Total Assets	负债合计 Total Liabilities	所有者权益合计 Total Owners' Equities	实收资本 Paicl-up Capitals	#国家资本 State-owned Capitals	#港澳台资本 Capitals from Hongkong, Macao and Taiwan	#外商资本 Foreign Capitals
92604914	**14628601**	**2832103978**	**2030996479**	**801277574**	**545864458**	**88025738**	**40618544**	**30158535**
50366232	**7701675**	**2220045020**	**1615967656**	**604497991**	**382832538**	**74028849**	**18174653**	**23611755**
25655975	3422719	820224801	561668954	258992189	116833024	72017212	165385	918464
43468906	**6628983**	**1867768024**	**1365602902**	**502569413**	**334072634**	**72672347**	**191629**	**746730**
7203802	773613	116466498	57373091	59093407	10228969	5543859	1	1
242146	17447	3961733	2947579	1014157	379056	1590	1	1
46192	5617	696460	563283	133176	86348	699		
4582	614	246235	192655	53579	26745	612		
2865	307	25806	6232	19573	3055	605		
1279	297	67530	53751	13779	10076	7		
347	10	144421	127690	16731	10605			
93		8477	4981	3496	3009			
17286650	2930448	962509422	730769370	232216047	155006902	54854704	27719	244848
4911969	897496	178257839	127137409	51593943	25688118	18832890		
12374681	2032955	784251585	603631961	180622107	129318786	36021813	27719	244848
8426007	1012717	236505797	147439138	89029479	32708089	12129484	116709	462127
10148150	1865723	545638194	425345868	120257797	135268997	139301	47202	39756
51582	9152	1722678	1258016	464665	182784			
3963	440	103619	65219	38400	35307	2392		
9666469	1777883	527706817	414102862	113569429	126140458	125671	47182	39605
426139	78254	16105081	9919776	6185305	8910448	11238	20	151
111390	22804	1743692	971917	771773	367534	2100		
2627270	**431343**	**150586115**	**112904425**	**37694806**	**22098354**	**711863**	**17932089**	**122385**
388993	46702	23005054	16763741	6241315	3501262	687197	1481339	79381
12955	955	754667	613454	141214	80674		14449	64
2129819	367959	121582377	92311457	29284032	17245327	24666	15679100	22692
36417	9351	3023554	1804682	1218874	724109		625147	
59093	6381	2220465	1411091	809376	546982		132056	20249
4270054	**641348**	**201690881**	**137460333**	**64233770**	**26661552**	**644638**	**50933**	**22742641**
716227	86656	38048234	30845811	7205652	4427304	468967	40757	2392909
23484	1406	257125	217833	39292	40294	3558	97	25376
3283820	505473	158727404	104076845	54650566	21258137	82831	6187	19979487
138066	36704	1834308	940481	893830	424864	88771	1772	245476
108459	11110	2823806	1379369	1444437	510956	510	2120	99394

项　　目	Item	流动资产合计 Total Working Capitals	#存货 Stock	固定资产原价 Original Value of Fixed Assets
(二)按国民经济行业分	**by Sector**			
农、林、牧产品批发	Wholesale of Agricultural, Forestry and Livestock Products	58867297	21645781	8249548
食品、饮料及烟草制品批发	Wholesale of Food, Beverages and Tobaccos	178381727	35900064	26490945
米、面制品及食用油批发	Wholesale of Rice, Flour and Edible Oil	32502158	11357848	3728960
肉、禽、蛋、奶及水产品批发	Wholesale of Meal, Fowls, Eggs, Milk and Aquatic Products	8840588	1616275	2187363
酒、饮料及茶叶批发	Wholesale of Wine, Beverages and Teas	45509558	6574574	2731738
烟草制品批发	Wholesale of Tobaccos	54445317	10731819	11978902
纺织、服装及家庭用品批发	Wholesale of Textiles, Wearing Apparel and Household Articles	183673649	30074608	9280022
服装批发	Wholesale of Garments	35699100	6512781	2719546
鞋帽批发	Wholesale of Shoes and Hats	8937563	1489749	734953
家用电器批发	Wholesale of Household Electrical Appliances	77797493	11336069	1148140
文化、体育用品及器材批发	Wholesale of Culture, Sports Appliances and Equipments	49851085	11930254	2965214
文具用品批发	Wholesale of Stationeries	9557319	1317983	486541
体育用品及器材批发	Wholesale of Sports Appliances and Equipments	3958654	804507	241374
图书批发	Wholesale of Books	9572284	1540327	1103947
医药及医疗器材批发	Wholesale of Medicines and Medical Appliances	129170421	23451729	9157299
西药批发	Wholesale of Western Medicine	78263845	14008072	4523413
中药批发	Wholesale of Chinese Traditional Medicine	24632891	4314214	1493500
矿产品、建材及化工产品批发	Wholesale of Mineral Products, Building Materials and Chemical Products	779970838	94509927	62127899
煤炭及制品批发	Wholesale of Coal and Related Products	110153567	9481769	10587216
石油及制品批发	Wholesale of Petroleum and Related Products	145553697	25771722	32307295
金属及金属矿批发	Wholesale of Metal Materials	313036823	35078908	8841562
建材批发	Wholesale of Building Materials	65569441	6313872	3164451
化肥批发	Wholesale of Chemical Fertilizer	22458789	3664344	1636621
农药批发	Wholesale of Pesticides	2363469	404606	96120
机械设备、五金产品及电子产品批发	Wholesale of Machinery, Hardware and Electronic Products	297428410	44394103	12685462
汽车批发	Wholesale of Motor Vehicles	81746329	14215072	2142339
计算机、软件及辅助设备批发	Wholesale of Computer, Software and Assistant Appliances	23783589	3494240	605678
通讯及广播电视设备批发	Wholesale of Communication, Radios and Televisions Equipments	37217096	6408013	934582
贸易经纪与代理	Trade Broker and Agency	42875314	2037396	991451
其他批发业	Other Wholesale not Classified Elsewhere	33537050	5236594	2269085

3-3-1 Continued 1

单位：万元
Unit:10000 yuan

累计折旧 Accumulated Depreciation	#本年折旧 Current Year Depreciation	资产总计 Total Assets	负债合计 Total Liabilities	所有者权益合计 Total Owners' Equities	实收资本 Paicl-up Capitals	#国家资本 State-owned Capitals	#港澳台资本 Capitals from Hongkong, Macao and Taiwan	#外商资本 Foreign Capitals
2442937	337631	84475900	58312175	26157739	20795772	3832212	472277	487450
10721231	1367675	227522520	124266379	103256696	24914255	6695861	1555370	1868876
1013983	150436	41488431	34030457	7457975	3991426	916452	276528	113505
658766	110625	12517011	8208248	4308755	2258129	224475	40056	54900
1031048	160842	53150903	32848362	20302541	5131013	390469	522883	682286
6273120	638621	66803606	14048716	52754888	2609028	1843718		
3959223	662165	217971133	167578369	50392768	24442000	1271480	3417458	3043872
1216747	199688	48539325	31316207	17223122	6591699	281694	1103957	358384
326091	52851	10395437	6646241	3749197	1461332	94687	247962	33209
429826	102164	85160358	75406504	9753851	5346917	127746	1000704	1479998
1167046	177909	63303457	43415319	19888139	11435223	2408987	2311376	852019
186274	29605	10758869	8329533	2429338	1429737	150496	172488	313221
86479	17211	4425606	3488385	937219	512276	15855	196135	41490
416318	59304	14892615	9450206	5442412	3125771	1238145	448025	18810
3630886	678899	152555321	111294932	41235497	26382053	3437254	322325	1200878
1529328	296430	92422628	67568564	24853566	17871655	2552458	139465	806732
460044	96533	28803934	22419093	6384841	4529097	281381	44323	9314
22728731	3480745	1022784067	773797397	249424881	205187515	48844485	5874847	6298846
2940010	693254	160097937	118767172	41330200	29411966	8916712	409713	559479
13046834	1715655	208668461	149211342	59895494	47555799	19137060	1883572	618841
3074148	486179	384609620	308111209	76498305	54964126	12912322	857990	1477769
962827	179624	84585355	63625046	20957389	31133040	2518019	1547652	253139
449703	66553	28640078	22294690	6345390	4897404	471660	71861	1084795
37616	9721	3096160	2095946	1000215	981256	95562	166	3311
4723280	834535	356141166	262200705	93953244	58703021	4862237	3614431	9435145
642165	160724	97723962	76441166	21282796	19494192	1403241	1001989	2839604
219028	35363	26182295	20598917	5583379	3334816	56936	287087	343469
509415	80972	41575133	33065587	8509545	6829027	182283	635818	300438
323403	53420	50722892	40632107	10090828	4830164	1654865	178002	303189
669508	108701	44568553	34470275	10098206	6142539	1021478	428572	121488

项　　目	Item	流动资产合　计 Total Current Assets	#存　货 Stock	固定资产原　价 Original Value of Fixed Assets
二、零售业	**Retail Trade**	**417186809**	**88819437**	**118397624**
#国有控股	State-controlled Enterprises	79272258	11789342	29713746
(一)按登记注册类型分	**by Type of Registration**			
1.内资企业	**Domestic Funded Enterprises**	**358303866**	**77232909**	**100827055**
国有企业	State-owned Enterprises	4069093	924168	2076425
集体企业	Collective-owned Enterprises	1332581	292753	801404
股份合作企业	Cooperative Enterprises	360050	85238	216925
联营企业	Joint Ownership Enterprises	163896	22219	79965
国有联营企业	State Joint Ownership Enterprises	31287	2329	8215
集体联营企业	Collective Joint Ownership Enterprises	34713	10673	12251
国有与集体联营企业	Joint State-collective Enterprises	44086	2820	47160
其他联营企业	Other Joint Ownership Enterprises	53806	6398	12342
有限责任公司	Limited Liability Corporations	166715954	34520495	41985621
国有独资公司	State Sole Funded Corporations	8974071	1307715	3308859
其他有限责任公司	Other Limited Liability Corporations	157741884	33212784	38676765
股份有限公司	Share-holding Corporations Ltd.	58231807	7646152	24044147
私营企业	Private Enterprises	126955578	33617942	31215861
私营独资企业	Private-funded Enterprises	1837033	552172	1263875
私营合伙企业	Private Partnership Enterprises	258987	70902	153831
私营有限责任公司	Private Limited Liability Corporations	118882502	31604964	28421260
私营股份有限公司	Private Share-holding Corporations Ltd.	5977057	1389908	1376891
其他企业	Other Enterprises	474914	123947	406714
2.港、澳、台商投资企业	**Enterprises with Funds from Hongkong, Macao and Taiwan**	**29700886**	**6588670**	**9241021**
合资经营企业	Joint-venture Enterprises	10018725	1568289	2478714
合作经营企业	Cooperative Enterprises	294579	41511	196017
独资经营企业	Enterprises with Sole Investment	18222452	4736250	6095759
投资股份有限公司	Share-holding Corporations Ltd. with Investment	808721	201521	266631
其他港澳台商投资企业	Other Enterprises with Funds from Hongkong, Macao and Taiwan	356414	41106	203905
3.外商投资企业	**Foreign Funded Enterprises**	**29182056**	**4997859**	**8329545**
中外合资经营企业	Joint-venture Enterprises	7066736	1593813	2811649
中外合作经营企业	Cooperative Enterprises	557165	79939	265891
外资企业	Enterprises with Sole Foreign Investment	18844994	2925229	4486788
外商投资股份有限公司	Share-holding Corporations Ltd. with Foreign Investment	701344	155886	466367
其他外商投资企业	Other Foreign Funded Enterprises	2011825	242993	298853

单位：万元
Unit:10000 yuan

累计折旧 Accumulated Depreciation	#本年折旧 Current Year Depreciation	资产总计 Total Assets	负债合计 Total Liabilities	所有者权益合计 Total Owners' Equities	实收资本 Paicl-up Capitals	#国家资本 State-owned Capitals	#港澳台资本 Capitals from Hongkong, Macao and Taiwan	#外商资本 Foreign Capitals
42238677	**6926930**	**612058956**	**415028821**	**196779581**	**163031922**	**13996891**	**22443892**	**6546781**
11124205	1328116	126626999	77033255	49097454	19193654	11983474	71862	286732
34256660	**5674515**	**512619662**	**359022167**	**153346939**	**119107662**	**13186733**	**251039**	**295120**
734802	82128	6518261	3678439	2839818	692799	537874	31	59
313804	33531	2194021	1272582	921443	392721	4490	10	10
57294	5956	589517	391209	198313	174726	1205		
25962	3622	300677	94770	205910	78047	14792		
5352	737	34333	25914	8421	5897	667		
4156	633	46364	18395	27968	10842	501		
11503	1975	97604	22487	75116	46903	13538		
4951	276	122377	27973	94405	14407	86		
14709484	2431638	230299869	170748795	59551021	53440488	8381968	169977	203519
1090621	120648	14548840	10144175	4404665	2513698	2078694		
13618868	2310988	215751026	160604619	55146354	50926786	6303276	169977	203519
8724570	1180892	101102683	57664258	43184723	12892039	4150226	64360	73939
9597469	1915131	170662751	124813825	45852122	51109220	94959	16627	17561
298191	59348	3210188	1294555	1915636	1084975	3498	106	96
48267	8157	447786	231478	218310	157760	637	26	
8818612	1764793	158466217	117897576	40569837	48233312	89605	16496	17465
432404	82832	8538558	5390218	3148339	1633173	1222		
93276	21621	951886	358299	593588	327628	1222	33	33
3965003	**672109**	**58841505**	**27645707**	**31195797**	**24937908**	**60191**	**21954871**	**195098**
963135	154956	15791678	7499621	8292056	3231614	53632	1112700	153809
104319	6934	451900	173794	278107	159377	6399	99057	3007
2708041	481097	40707048	18729897	21977152	21168370	160	20426610	28661
100297	15143	1265868	824904	440961	267375		229075	2144
89220	13972	625025	417502	207523	111177		87431	7477
4017022	**580314**	**40597795**	**28360947**	**12236850**	**18986358**	**749967**	**237986**	**6056564**
1396180	132054	10904879	6516975	4387903	2698442	722745	12638	1043941
194963	7909	928395	546764	381630	377137	3845	188824	94421
2169973	376643	24787680	18008036	6779646	15295549		16099	4606070
135270	23463	1660571	1206766	453805	394313		4035	223475
120640	40246	2316274	2082405	233869	220920	23378	16390	88660

3-3-1 续表 3

项目	Item	流动资产合计 Total Current Assets	#存货 Stock	固定资产原价 Original Value of Fixed Assets
(二)按国民经济行业分	**by Sector**			
综合零售	Integrated Retail	86934901	14408183	46504484
百货零售	Retail of General Merchandise	54268221	6328055	30538708
超级市场零售	Retail of Supermarkets	30380546	7518426	14974317
食品、饮料及烟草制品专门零售	Special Retail of Food, Beverages and Tobaccos	14881938	3427135	4860855
粮油零售	Retail of Cereal and Oil	1813669	628288	784414
肉、禽、蛋、奶及水产品零售	Retail of Meat, Poultry, Eggs, Milk and Aquatic Products	1416578	319748	906617
酒、饮料及茶叶零售	Retail of Wine, Beverages and Teas	4167381	1071684	952017
烟草制品零售	Retail of Tobaccos	1076438	345020	171987
纺织、服装及日用品专门零售	Special Retail of Textiles, Garments and Daily Consumer Articles	26460830	9178870	5245946
服装零售	Retail of Garments	17601805	5829332	3470732
文化、体育用品及器材专门零售	Special Retail of Culture, Sports Appliances and Equipments	18368314	5780605	4642569
体育用品及器材零售	Retail of Sports Appliances and Equipments	980654	323345	353869
图书、报刊零售	Retail of Books, Newspapers and Magazines	7751957	1601023	2680315
医药及医疗器材专门零售	Special Retail of Medicines and Medical Appliances	27012714	5750223	2705763
药品零售	Retail of Medicines	25484832	5511906	2506479
汽车、摩托车、燃料及零配件专门零售	Special Retail of Motor Vehicles, Motorcycles, Fuel and Parts	166614787	37934639	41612729
汽车零售	Retail of Motor Vehicles	123202570	33397601	24899910
机动车燃料零售	Retail of Automotive Fuels	39248971	3629951	16014958
家用电器及电子产品专门零售	Special Retail of Household Electric Appliances and Electronic Products	39314287	6561756	4416724
日用家电设备零售	Retail of Household Electric Appliances	22204160	2705700	2301421
计算机、软件及辅助设备零售	Retail of Computer, Software and Assistant Appliances	6320606	1461406	524974
通信设备零售	Retail of Communication Equipments	3748765	933548	369076
五金、家具及室内装饰材料专门零售	Special Retail of Hardware, Furniture and Interior Decoration Materials	9802104	2024356	3682273
货摊、无店铺及其他零售	Stalls, Non-shop and Other Retails	27796932	3753671	4726282
互联网零售	Retail on the Internet	21720390	3023418	1363007
(三)按零售业态分	**by Mode of Business Operation**			
有店铺零售	Store-based Retailing	378582193	82025841	115279864
超市	Supermarket	10314880	2859365	3867466
大型超市	Hypermarket	28944245	6954618	16039993
百货店	Department Store	53324167	6070977	27973585
专业店	Speciality Store	146603276	28788107	35228277
专卖店	Exclusive Shop	119943037	33127827	24448335
无店铺零售	Non-Store Selling	38604615	6793596	3117759

3-3-1 Continued 3

单位：万元
Unit:10000 yuan

累计折旧 Accumulated Depreciation	#本年折旧 Current Year Depreciation	资产总计 Total Assets	负债合计 Total Liabilities	所有者权益合计 Total Owners' Equities	实收资本 Paicl-up Capitals	#国家资本 State-owned Capitals	#港澳台资本 Capitals from Hongkong, Macao and Taiwan	#外商资本 Foreign Capitals
17010086	2376852	167092443	107352516	59739925	52881712	2313235	17538275	3084865
10139452	1380788	114364659	66459717	47904944	39712638	1574852	15961323	1240127
6516408	938827	49035201	37944743	11090462	11857914	671579	1437228	1615556
1384580	262341	22038855	12025268	10013587	5351668	597835	221783	60755
208150	30356	2901564	1741137	1160428	608185	143291	29941	9
256978	51519	2512051	1331784	1180269	729223	36700	11590	2582
280709	52581	5672935	3140386	2532549	1249300	100490	65574	2076
71854	9229	1497046	538080	958966	332862	226305		
2030534	386825	35394190	23947122	11447068	8755996	306526	2204318	1098958
1351433	260043	23813761	16272247	7541518	6072622	221412	1541598	831801
1686308	262805	26245215	14914237	11332214	5932019	1653122	202211	423842
97213	33301	1386114	835506	550610	458071	3124	67403	175873
1053489	140827	12184039	6297980	5886061	2066174	1506224	1917	73337
945795	188186	34018872	24377664	9642095	5771747	596167	69752	15391
887518	169986	31794891	23006146	8788616	5402279	587844	62468	3953
15354304	2697137	226991698	161242407	65497862	62946966	6897907	1495558	916400
8748414	1840628	158306777	121794767	36514279	50307154	910304	1439856	514115
6360496	815153	63624182	35867983	27502500	11523789	5970608	49114	387190
1352268	223264	50654116	33260751	17393465	10461750	60232	149736	226749
655822	89067	29283053	19263936	10019189	3692293	17147	136331	144612
211111	49348	7437943	4394983	3042982	1937266	17593	9260	31143
140176	26050	4644934	3278424	1366513	874510	15283	243	41471
988367	217951	14835216	9360063	5473809	3970232	92771	83186	607367
1486437	311586	34788359	28548798	6239564	6959839	1479103	479080	112460
399487	134385	24705476	22321624	2383850	4482460	1062825	379644	61628
41268962	6671961	565749788	377614328	187884910	154618385	12631227	21822196	6342781
1307801	247874	30133126	11183207	18949918	19553210	147594	14454732	112911
6810669	961081	48158635	37784763	10375021	9647307	718749	1491931	2167914
9348042	1248562	96884560	63639638	33244924	25081236	1572663	2067458	990290
12353914	1922609	204426952	132985980	71164063	49736752	7421680	1366879	834418
9075448	1860859	155540557	111336480	44208956	43814226	1948596	2173421	1615746
969715	254969	46309169	37414493	8894670	8413536	1365663	621696	204000

3-3-2 各地区限额以上批发业企业年末资产负债
Assets and Liabilities of Enterprises above Designated Size of Wholesale Trade by Region at the Year-end

单位：万元
Unit: 10000 yuan

地区	Region	资产总计 Total Assets	#流动资产合计 Total Working Capitals	#固定资产合计 Total Fixed Assets	负债合计 Total Liabilities	所有者权益合计 Total Owners' Equities
全国	**National Total**	**2220045020**	**1753755784**	**91654201**	**1615967656**	**604497991**
北京	Beijing	387376709	283745507	6989870	273534806	113841902
天津	Tianjin	130899214	110559972	2389570	108085512	22810147
河北	Hebei	34710338	28976762	3450604	26694028	8016310
山西	Shanxi	41466716	28885358	3839792	30936309	10530407
内蒙古	Inner Mongolia	17410314	13131841	1415790	13282670	4127644
辽宁	Liaoning	41406123	34577066	2513926	32700175	8621105
吉林	Jilin	13163775	11425229	994764	10708346	2455429
黑龙江	Heilongjiang	17381127	14347202	1367032	14337080	3011173
上海	Shanghai	283707583	224195803	5793961	201224624	82488183
江苏	Jiangsu	164208851	137121205	6994737	123984748	40196500
浙江	Zhejiang	189433862	148970111	5939531	142500196	46933166
安徽	Anhui	35333613	28489303	1768985	25073577	10260036
福建	Fujian	96834563	73769417	3651753	62462157	34372406
江西	Jiangxi	14871300	11654161	1794087	10528500	4342800
山东	Shandong	93296673	73630716	7708664	70240755	23055918
河南	Henan	40189429	31498603	4209773	27223692	13439250
湖北	Hubei	41990920	32718276	4280372	28722250	13268670
湖南	Hunan	21772720	15872954	2192983	14625492	7147228
广东	Guangdong	290967887	240431238	10299238	220572411	70405641
广西	Guangxi	26026384	19886270	1254783	18543962	7482422
海南	Hainan	12922120	9862919	336580	7581569	5340551
重庆	Chongqing	32690547	27335333	1736985	22600112	10090435
四川	Sichuan	35291321	29392071	1953228	26186910	9104410
贵州	Guizhou	28916351	25085960	1130755	16728177	12188174
云南	Yunnan	32727493	25306585	1753475	19319782	13407711
西藏	Tibet	935575	763050	107485	521296	414278
陕西	Shaanxi	26467002	20163541	1463818	17951516	8524429
甘肃	Gansu	10452917	6626201	1183031	5466079	4986838
青海	Qinghai	13329001	12006995	368079	10918637	2410364
宁夏	Ningxia	7368140	6172146	442539	5476880	1963420
新疆	Xinjiang	36496452	27153989	2328011	27235408	9261044

3-3-2 续表 Continued

国有控股 单位：万元

State-controlled Enterprises Unit: 10000 yuan

地　区	Region	资产总计 Total Assets	#流动资产合计 Total Working Capitals	#固定资产合计 Total Fixed Assets	负债合计 Total Liabilities	所有者权益合计 Total Owners' Equities
全　国	**National Total**	**820224801**	**598983775**	**41932059**	**561668954**	**258992189**
北　京	Beijing	211439729	141312341	4491110	143620641	67819089
天　津	Tianjin	68649282	55659126	1255952	56141164	12508118
河　北	Hebei	12705261	11055124	918755	9392486	3312775
山　西	Shanxi	25813232	18218317	3085941	20901156	4912076
内蒙古	Inner Mongolia	9299076	6997790	705655	7113096	2185981
辽　宁	Liaoning	13790877	11197201	1572364	9736866	3969168
吉　林	Jilin	7986761	7091628	575156	6699030	1287731
黑龙江	Heilongjiang	13098296	10776586	1054995	10800418	2264444
上　海	Shanghai	71204964	50380199	1793736	50259996	20944968
江　苏	Jiangsu	43923280	33582971	2393843	30161548	13761732
浙　江	Zhejiang	35494779	27583027	1583097	23572771	11922008
安　徽	Anhui	16660224	12865661	707956	10391525	6268698
福　建	Fujian	36091732	25110070	1419357	20481840	15609892
江　西	Jiangxi	8020807	5770893	1393988	5514317	2506490
山　东	Shandong	18948706	14432027	1969480	13112485	5836221
河　南	Henan	14811912	11653011	1011604	10423605	4861820
湖　北	Hubei	14564255	9525070	2427672	9429651	5134605
湖　南	Hunan	10072839	6922908	1053670	6104173	3968666
广　东	Guangdong	65664485	48134868	4440494	43008295	22656190
广　西	Guangxi	13055184	9071225	863736	8134299	4920885
海　南	Hainan	1127840	969010	70328	377915	749925
重　庆	Chongqing	12808505	9884332	786399	7707173	5101332
四　川	Sichuan	13200098	10406720	1053206	8725536	4474563
贵　州	Guizhou	14807339	11938342	821337	8698255	6109084
云　南	Yunnan	22552575	17704209	990589	11623985	10928590
西　藏	Tibet	459262	346809	94172	129290	329972
陕　西	Shaanxi	14756687	10582864	915864	9849543	4916087
甘　肃	Gansu	5015945	2485964	630821	1606340	3409604
青　海	Qinghai	2674676	2202197	255882	1349218	1325458
宁　夏	Ningxia	1367293	612462	317036	850769	588684
新　疆	Xinjiang	20158901	14510823	1277864	15751568	4407333

3-3-3 各地区限额以上批发业企业年末资产负债(按登记注册类型分)
Assets and Liabilities of Enterprises above Designated Size of Wholesale Trade by Region and Type of Registration at the Year-end

内资企业 单位：万元
Domestic Funded Enterprises Unit: 10000 yuan

地区	Region	资产总计 Total Assets	#流动资产合计 Total Working Capitals	#固定资产合计 Total Fixed Assets	负债合计 Total Liabilities	所有者权益合计 Total Owners' Equities
全国	**National Total**	**1867768024**	**1463796384**	**83575134**	**1365602902**	**502569413**
北京	Beijing	286209697	201845878	5790103	201870043	84339654
天津	Tianjin	111941650	93262900	2211905	92269331	19668764
河北	Hebei	33738601	28229685	3402975	25897258	7841343
山西	Shanxi	41225400	28688521	3826813	30870213	10355188
内蒙古	Inner Mongolia	17398927	13120454	1415790	13277656	4121271
辽宁	Liaoning	37638589	32034332	2488352	30163741	7390006
吉林	Jilin	12879250	11149380	994040	10461748	2417502
黑龙江	Heilongjiang	17241521	14208762	1366503	14201453	3007194
上海	Shanghai	155361565	114741822	3229616	111451153	43912412
江苏	Jiangsu	143435127	120449785	6150554	111033109	32374415
浙江	Zhejiang	179084779	140840744	5683006	134403413	44680866
安徽	Anhui	33390062	26640648	1698478	22883320	10506742
福建	Fujian	89472663	68467962	2913567	57979444	31493218
江西	Jiangxi	14628703	11443289	1772607	10349287	4279416
山东	Shandong	89571417	70413507	7543733	67528685	22042733
河南	Henan	39408488	30785048	4180074	26610790	13271210
湖北	Hubei	37358290	28711621	4134413	24724757	12633534
湖南	Hunan	21131261	15339340	2173498	14092313	7038947
广东	Guangdong	252084792	209807250	9134092	193390628	58691216
广西	Guangxi	25718940	19687312	1250759	18328297	7390643
海南	Hainan	11625831	8992592	159887	6851387	4774443
重庆	Chongqing	30572727	25602791	1623816	21208063	9364664
四川	Sichuan	34080159	28406055	1902476	24901049	9179109
贵州	Guizhou	28266716	24969051	986554	16359415	11907301
云南	Yunnan	32323629	25019363	1745260	19113000	13210629
西藏	Tibet	868268	735016	107246	477647	390621
陕西	Shaanxi	25234727	19334694	1444559	16968976	8274694
甘肃	Gansu	10445581	6618971	1182961	5459929	4985652
青海	Qinghai	12461000	11425356	336322	10188961	2272039
宁夏	Ningxia	7368140	6172146	442539	5476880	1963420
新疆	Xinjiang	35601523	26652109	2282636	26810956	8790567

国有企业
State-owned Enterprises

单位：万元
Unit: 10000 yuan

地区	Region	资产总计 Total Assets	#流动资产合计 Total Working Capitals	#固定资产合计 Total Fixed Assets	负债合计 Total Liabilities	所有者权益合计 Total Owners' Equities
全国	**National Total**	**116466498**	**92708530**	**8771783**	**57373091**	**59093407**
北京	Beijing	29415167	21201661	612708	19590202	9824965
天津	Tianjin	3133338	2781497	125552	2145163	988175
河北	Hebei	1673727	1481438	139052	455639	1218088
山西	Shanxi	1643523	1322419	252903	694701	948822
内蒙古	Inner Mongolia	3976259	3686667	206137	3085806	890453
辽宁	Liaoning	4342344	3443909	662222	1963815	2378529
吉林	Jilin	4567712	4210636	297484	3833204	734508
黑龙江	Heilongjiang	1787177	1534082	197248	821997	965183
上海	Shanghai	1481005	1113508	79991	1138382	342624
江苏	Jiangsu	7833935	6839484	582624	2098420	5735514
浙江	Zhejiang	4226240	3796185	273766	897934	3328306
安徽	Anhui	3298032	2497415	245443	1203290	2094741
福建	Fujian	3436677	2842641	397688	943448	2493229
江西	Jiangxi	1919201	1507561	300622	549762	1369439
山东	Shandong	902442	636681	176559	618179	284263
河南	Henan	4925324	4317421	431007	2857181	2068143
湖北	Hubei	3060780	2567592	336111	1770382	1290398
湖南	Hunan	3587397	2520323	536666	1187982	2399415
广东	Guangdong	4514218	2618537	274736	2392578	2121641
广西	Guangxi	1458516	1091451	232742	489078	969438
海南	Hainan	788774	700423	38152	189657	599117
重庆	Chongqing	2312383	1828543	233252	808843	1503540
四川	Sichuan	3498089	2878445	464341	768836	2729253
贵州	Guizhou	3316535	2580529	418642	1148549	2167986
云南	Yunnan	7755931	6782423	494230	2044003	5711928
西藏	Tibet	379692	290136	79060	99599	280093
陕西	Shaanxi	2567475	1879748	274663	1138624	1428851
甘肃	Gansu	714820	498317	75639	132799	582021
青海	Qinghai	369183	329043	18246	59727	309456
宁夏	Ningxia	448315	303785	58846	81454	366860
新疆	Xinjiang	3132286	2626030	255451	2163858	968428

3-3-3 续表 2 Continued 2

集体企业 单位：万元
Collective-owned Enterprises Unit: 10000 yuan

地 区	Region	资产总计 Total Assets	#流动资产合计 Total Working Capitals	#固定资产合计 Total Fixed Assets	负债合计 Total Liabilities	所有者权益合计 Total Owners' Equities
全 国	**National Total**	**3961733**	**2820986**	**375845**	**2947579**	**1014157**
北 京	Beijing	869856	475664	29382	632945	236910
天 津	Tianjin	99221	83439	6808	68964	30257
河 北	Hebei	201467	130521	23064	132814	68653
山 西	Shanxi	334513	249483	40690	247554	86959
内蒙古	Inner Mongolia	25780	22388	1960	8651	17129
辽 宁	Liaoning	139739	106290	3013	132321	7418
吉 林	Jilin	249	129	120	205	44
黑龙江	Heilongjiang	17699	12822	3013	10286	7413
上 海	Shanghai	39852	38542	514	33908	5944
江 苏	Jiangsu	265585	159564	65706	179750	85836
浙 江	Zhejiang	81698	67506	8189	55786	25912
安 徽	Anhui	13384	7795	4977	5311	8074
福 建	Fujian	101995	89742	7863	81507	20489
江 西	Jiangxi	9657	8262	1206	5915	3742
山 东	Shandong	366027	295318	49481	303288	62738
河 南	Henan	101690	83305	11966	68844	32846
湖 北	Hubei	92048	77948	8409	89236	2812
湖 南	Hunan	7193	2191	4444	3396	3798
广 东	Guangdong	164334	121565	18214	95827	68507
广 西	Guangxi	141759	122473	7940	119730	22029
海 南	Hainan					
重 庆	Chongqing	24342	21462	1564	17836	6506
四 川	Sichuan	590847	430280	41386	452499	138348
贵 州	Guizhou	46125	30542	8924	33946	12179
云 南	Yunnan	36569	25042	5940	29279	7291
西 藏	Tibet					
陕 西	Shaanxi	31530	26777	4316	28034	3496
甘 肃	Gansu	15237	10818	3101	12175	3062
青 海	Qinghai	4327	2512	1784	2219	2108
宁 夏	Ningxia					
新 疆	Xinjiang	139010	118606	11871	95353	43657

股份合作企业 单位：万元

Cooperative Enterprises Unit: 10000 yuan

地区	Region	资产总计 Total Assets	#流动资产合计 Total Working Capitals	#固定资产合计 Total Fixed Assets	负债合计 Total Liabilities	所有者权益合计 Total Owners' Equities
全国	**National Total**	**696460**	**580887**	**67696**	**563283**	**133176**
北京	Beijing	119372	73384	29034	109319	10053
天津	Tianjin	21749	20155	1594	18859	2890
河北	Hebei	2539	2288	251	1943	596
山西	Shanxi	2687	2536	140	675	2012
内蒙古	Inner Mongolia					
辽宁	Liaoning	8500	8196	268	6795	1705
吉林	Jilin					
黑龙江	Heilongjiang					
上海	Shanghai	13310	12862	448	7667	5643
江苏	Jiangsu	130794	122129	1308	121698	9096
浙江	Zhejiang	52342	49576	1793	39474	12868
安徽	Anhui	58736	42593	2816	38253	20483
福建	Fujian	1231	650	581	439	792
江西	Jiangxi	3015	2938	77	2828	187
山东	Shandong	8777	7241	514	5696	3081
河南	Henan	921	556	84	1464	-543
湖北	Hubei	5655	4716	906	3775	1880
湖南	Hunan					
广东	Guangdong	60914	54234	3740	41657	19257
广西	Guangxi	436	80	126	433	3
海南	Hainan					
重庆	Chongqing	132279	110839	20211	109183	23096
四川	Sichuan	12812	11966	365	12376	436
贵州	Guizhou					
云南	Yunnan	7728	4610	1777	4921	2807
西藏	Tibet					
陕西	Shaanxi	12836	12649	120	11346	1489
甘肃	Gansu	23621	22240	376	13031	10590
青海	Qinghai	1858	1657		1637	221
宁夏	Ningxia					
新疆	Xinjiang	14348	12792	1167	9814	4534

联营企业
Joint Ownership Enterprises

单位：万元
Unit: 10000 yuan

地 区	Region	资产总计 Total Assets	#流动资产合计 Total Working Capitals	#固定资产合计 Total Fixed Assets	负债合计 Total Liabilities	所有者权益合计 Total Owners' Equities
全 国	**National Total**	**246235**	**217260**	**11239**	**192655**	**53579**
北 京	Beijing	7113	7007	106	6416	697
天 津	Tianjin					
河 北	Hebei					
山 西	Shanxi	619	228	273	549	69
内蒙古	Inner Mongolia					
辽 宁	Liaoning	7580	6255	1325	1868	5712
吉 林	Jilin					
黑龙江	Heilongjiang					
上 海	Shanghai	139651	139363	217	122967	16684
江 苏	Jiangsu					
浙 江	Zhejiang					
安 徽	Anhui	1361	934	427	150	1211
福 建	Fujian					
江 西	Jiangxi					
山 东	Shandong	53269	29311	7177	47899	5370
河 南	Henan					
湖 北	Hubei					
湖 南	Hunan					
广 东	Guangdong	34887	32818	1414	12426	22461
广 西	Guangxi					
海 南	Hainan					
重 庆	Chongqing					
四 川	Sichuan					
贵 州	Guizhou					
云 南	Yunnan					
西 藏	Tibet					
陕 西	Shaanxi					
甘 肃	Gansu					
青 海	Qinghai					
宁 夏	Ningxia					
新 疆	Xinjiang	1755	1344	300	380	1375

3-3-3 续表 5 Continued 5

有限责任公司
Limited Liability Corporations

单位：万元
Unit: 10000 yuan

地 区	Region	资产总计 Total Assets	#流动资产合计 Total Working Capitals	#固定资产合计 Total Fixed Assets	负债合计 Total Liabilities	所有者权益合计 Total Owners' Equities
全 国	**National Total**	**962509422**	**758345396**	**37299500**	**730769370**	**232216047**
北 京	Beijing	189488887	138159360	4172841	138941072	50547815
天 津	Tianjin	81123217	65156492	1609415	66487178	14636039
河 北	Hebei	14784736	12941413	918858	11976606	2808130
山 西	Shanxi	22350772	15315069	2958473	18705323	3645448
内蒙古	Inner Mongolia	8071066	5366725	822527	6080666	1990400
辽 宁	Liaoning	17405000	15160979	882569	14590394	2814605
吉 林	Jilin	5084467	4366549	345382	4282941	801526
黑龙江	Heilongjiang	11961238	9933400	711191	10856942	1104856
上 海	Shanghai	77532766	57676201	1677302	54507239	23027526
江 苏	Jiangsu	61530711	49711120	2505778	49184834	12345769
浙 江	Zhejiang	63015088	50155181	1798463	49688636	13326452
安 徽	Anhui	15726050	13342589	631962	11897938	3828112
福 建	Fujian	38013208	28401395	961923	25695141	12318067
江 西	Jiangxi	7366554	6134325	729141	5906079	1460475
山 东	Shandong	39870360	33850363	2492235	31703104	8167256
河 南	Henan	23062692	18297972	1971567	16406863	7129341
湖 北	Hubei	18601287	14827370	1682476	12895310	5705978
湖 南	Hunan	9044119	6768638	731998	7240414	1803706
广 东	Guangdong	121654683	102873580	4103307	96512433	25142281
广 西	Guangxi	15477975	11648578	609238	11330592	4147382
海 南	Hainan	8757204	6882948	73910	5705586	3051618
重 庆	Chongqing	18827654	16085681	721761	14038456	4789199
四 川	Sichuan	18255662	14928694	740334	14873721	3381941
贵 州	Guizhou	19653816	17733268	374908	11128965	8524851
云 南	Yunnan	16563027	12579329	490012	11113819	5449208
西 藏	Tibet	433265	404905	19458	355052	78213
陕 西	Shaanxi	15380702	11786004	802809	10759534	4621168
甘 肃	Gansu	3968393	2054648	519961	2143424	1824969
青 海	Qinghai	1085051	763776	74683	740366	344685
宁 夏	Ningxia	1655087	1497842	85199	1538916	116172
新 疆	Xinjiang	16764685	13541001	1079819	13481826	3282859

3-3-3 续表 6 Continued 6

股份有限公司
Share-holding Corporations Ltd.

单位：万元
Unit: 10000 yuan

地　区	Region	资产总计 Total Assets	#流动资产合计 Total Working Capitals	#固定资产合计 Total Fixed Assets	负债合计 Total Liabilities	所有者权益合计 Total Owners' Equities
全　国	**National Total**	**236505797**	**152222586**	**13737257**	**147439138**	**89029479**
北　京	Beijing	35063017	15917230	321956	18977150	16085866
天　津	Tianjin	1782558	1650021	34821	1414710	367848
河　北	Hebei	5871116	4320246	1352979	4574125	1296990
山　西	Shanxi	8011907	4567539	129771	4011196	4000711
内蒙古	Inner Mongolia	1114087	743656	109835	703002	411085
辽　宁	Liaoning	3248981	2497668	429220	2988991	175147
吉　林	Jilin	985406	747594	113830	657011	328395
黑龙江	Heilongjiang	2100537	1513871	354432	1384639	682460
上　海	Shanghai	13445424	8226644	500990	6858880	6586544
江　苏	Jiangsu	27182669	23892149	428444	23882463	3300205
浙　江	Zhejiang	23953876	13921644	931010	13674466	10279410
安　徽	Anhui	7177422	5121198	250217	4674268	2503154
福　建	Fujian	18362923	12401673	536172	9744780	8618143
江　西	Jiangxi	3055530	1881212	581468	2253817	801714
山　东	Shandong	10147503	6692076	1149484	6366078	3781425
河　南	Henan	4441337	2991501	614914	2927304	1514033
湖　北	Hubei	8046562	4938996	1460380	4499992	3546570
湖　南	Hunan	1590957	838779	83895	931131	659826
广　东	Guangdong	33019816	21847089	2219098	19223622	13796194
广　西	Guangxi	1610548	649999	172530	539484	1071064
海　南	Hainan	1179221	527310	33717	641772	537449
重　庆	Chongqing	1806563	1203601	166984	1061408	745154
四　川	Sichuan	2443543	1928572	185500	1893809	549734
贵　州	Guizhou	1639326	1447957	68007	1224309	415017
云　南	Yunnan	2140912	1441501	287128	1435909	705003
西　藏	Tibet					
陕　西	Shaanxi	4300250	3123965	156042	3183375	1125818
甘　肃	Gansu	2145329	1336176	240487	680735	1464593
青　海	Qinghai	1774441	1502960	207086	907405	867036
宁　夏	Ningxia	681888	136053	199412	572222	181827
新　疆	Xinjiang	8182149	4213706	417448	5551085	2631064

3-3-3 续表 7 Continued 7

私营企业 单位：万元

Private Enterprises Unit: 10000 yuan

地区	Region	资产总计 Total Assets	#流动资产合计 Total Working Capitals	#固定资产合计 Total Fixed Assets	负债合计 Total Liabilities	所有者权益合计 Total Owners' Equities
全国	**National Total**	**545638194**	**455723798**	**22939158**	**425345868**	**120257797**
北京	Beijing	31246285	26011572	624077	23612938	7633347
天津	Tianjin	25781567	23571295	433716	22134458	3643555
河北	Hebei	11183827	9339661	962198	8746213	2437613
山西	Shanxi	8859642	7212549	441546	7193239	1666403
内蒙古	Inner Mongolia	4210240	3299813	275040	3398568	811673
辽宁	Liaoning	12468973	10801604	503043	10470480	1998494
吉林	Jilin	2239389	1824023	236377	1687514	551875
黑龙江	Heilongjiang	1368892	1210483	99074	1123153	245738
上海	Shanghai	62586746	47461933	970146	48690334	13896412
江苏	Jiangsu	45779678	39127636	2472570	35035801	10716382
浙江	Zhejiang	87701184	72805587	2662272	70011358	17689326
安徽	Anhui	7099956	5619800	555975	5059539	2040417
福建	Fujian	29551136	24729763	1006182	21512633	8038502
江西	Jiangxi	2272244	1907463	159119	1629490	642754
山东	Shandong	38014203	28800333	3582606	28416199	9598004
河南	Henan	6809256	5060422	1134222	4329247	2480010
湖北	Hubei	7444792	6246281	602292	5430542	2014250
湖南	Hunan	6880802	5197877	812508	4721477	2159325
广东	Guangdong	92529683	82202637	2495899	75072877	17453828
广西	Guangxi	7022024	6171859	225853	5845416	1176608
海南	Hainan	900631	881911	14108	314372	586259
重庆	Chongqing	7446486	6339083	474311	5168025	2278460
四川	Sichuan	9231801	8199674	460944	6888424	2343377
贵州	Guizhou	3609867	3176386	116073	2823624	786242
云南	Yunnan	5805910	4182581	462116	4482087	1323823
西藏	Tibet	55311	39975	8728	22996	32315
陕西	Shaanxi	2886975	2475159	185290	1827483	1059492
甘肃	Gansu	3576473	2696037	342449	2476600	1099873
青海	Qinghai	9226141	8825408	34523	8477608	748533
宁夏	Ningxia	4582850	4234466	99082	3284289	1298561
新疆	Xinjiang	7265230	6070527	486819	5458884	1806346

3-3-3 续表 8 Continued 8

其他企业
Other Enterprises

单位：万元
Unit: 10000 yuan

地 区	Region	资产总计 Total Assets	#流动资产合计 Total Working Capitals	#固定资产合计 Total Fixed Assets	负债合计 Total Liabilities	所有者权益合计 Total Owners' Equities
全 国	**National Total**	**1743692**	**1176935**	**372661**	**971917**	**771773**
北 京	Beijing					
天 津	Tianjin					
河 北	Hebei	21189	14117	6573	9917	11272
山 西	Shanxi	21738	18699	3017	16975	4763
内 蒙 古	Inner Mongolia	1494	1203	291	963	531
辽 宁	Liaoning	17473	9433	6691	9076	8396
吉 林	Jilin	2027	449	846	873	1154
黑 龙 江	Heilongjiang	5980	4104	1545	4435	1544
上 海	Shanghai	122812	72769	8	91777	31036
江 苏	Jiangsu	711756	597704	94124	530143	181612
浙 江	Zhejiang	54351	45065	7512	35759	18592
安 徽	Anhui	15122	8324	6660	4571	10550
福 建	Fujian	5493	2097	3159	1497	3996
江 西	Jiangxi	2503	1528	975	1397	1106
山 东	Shandong	208837	102183	85677	68241	140596
河 南	Henan	67267	33871	16315	19887	47380
湖 北	Hubei	107167	48717	43841	35522	71646
湖 南	Hunan	20793	11531	3988	7914	12879
广 东	Guangdong	106257	56790	17683	39209	67048
广 西	Guangxi	7683	2871	2330	3565	4118
海 南	Hainan					
重 庆	Chongqing	23020	13580	5733	4311	18709
四 川	Sichuan	47404	28424	9606	11384	36020
贵 州	Guizhou	1047	369		20	1027
云 南	Yunnan	13552	3877	4056	2981	10570
西 藏	Tibet					
陕 西	Shaanxi	54958	30392	21319	20579	34380
甘 肃	Gansu	1709	735	950	1165	544
青 海	Qinghai					
宁 夏	Ningxia					
新 疆	Xinjiang	102060	68103	29762	49756	52304

港、澳、台商投资企业
Enterprises with Funds from Hong Kong,Macao and Taiwan

单位：万元
Unit: 10000 yuan

地区	Region	资产总计 Total Assets	#流动资产合计 Total Working Capitals	#固定资产合计 Total Fixed Assets	负债合计 Total Liabilities	所有者权益合计 Total Owners' Equities
全国	**National Total**	**150586115**	**124182494**	**3525652**	**112904425**	**37694806**
北京	Beijing	43902324	36597905	559481	38319360	5582964
天津	Tianjin	14812017	13568571	90123	12647947	2164070
河北	Hebei	370250	302239	25562	385859	-15609
山西	Shanxi	240705	196334	12872	63751	176954
内蒙古	Inner Mongolia	11386	11386		5013	6373
辽宁	Liaoning	2494785	1501773	14498	1839184	655601
吉林	Jilin	11377	11369	8	8805	2572
黑龙江	Heilongjiang	7232	6066	529	3435	3797
上海	Shanghai	38521375	31792584	842599	24876839	13644537
江苏	Jiangsu	7289631	6162642	360863	4448871	2840760
浙江	Zhejiang	4384629	3440522	149147	3098046	1286583
安徽	Anhui	914989	897510	5222	844451	70539
福建	Fujian	4319719	3456592	205021	2743123	1576596
江西	Jiangxi	68946	58470	9482	36984	31962
山东	Shandong	2789613	2364197	125214	2196143	593470
河南	Henan	702684	674450	2232	569966	132718
湖北	Hubei	2328694	1996447	63165	1942971	385723
湖南	Hunan	171575	121097	1881	106865	64710
广东	Guangdong	21971778	17556878	561675	15342469	6642421
广西	Guangxi	51925	49736	2186	37140	14786
海南	Hainan	432894	138460	176297	139000	293895
重庆	Chongqing	1373762	1227485	71796	969960	403802
四川	Sichuan	714800	680664	16547	570817	143983
贵州	Guizhou	629698	100590	140957	357473	272225
云南	Yunnan	176849	98382	5401	107191	69658
西藏	Tibet	67307	28035	239	43649	23657
陕西	Shaanxi	80646	73305	6829	63110	17536
甘肃	Gansu	4227	4202	18	2655	1573
青海	Qinghai	866434	580135	31699	727489	138945
宁夏	Ningxia					
新疆	Xinjiang	873864	484468	44109	405859	468005

外商投资企业
Foreign Funded Enterprises

单位：万元
Unit: 10000 yuan

地区	Region	资产总计 Total Assets	#流动资产合计 Total Working Capitals	#固定资产合计 Total Fixed Assets	负债合计 Total Liabilities	所有者权益合计 Total Owners' Equities
全　国	**National Total**	**201690881**	**165776909**	**4553414**	**137460333**	**64233770**
北　京	Beijing	57264688	45301725	640286	33345404	23919284
天　津	Tianjin	4145547	3728502	87542	3168234	977312
河　北	Hebei	601487	444838	22067	410912	190575
山　西	Shanxi	610	503	108	2345	-1735
内蒙古	Inner Mongolia					
辽　宁	Liaoning	1272748	1040961	11076	697250	575498
吉　林	Jilin	273148	264480	716	237794	35355
黑龙江	Heilongjiang	132374	132374		132193	181
上　海	Shanghai	89824643	77661396	1721747	64896633	24931234
江　苏	Jiangsu	13484094	10508777	483320	8502769	4981325
浙　江	Zhejiang	5964454	4688844	107378	4998737	965717
安　徽	Anhui	1028561	951145	65286	1345806	-317245
福　建	Fujian	3042181	1844863	533165	1739589	1302591
江　西	Jiangxi	173651	152403	11998	142229	31422
山　东	Shandong	935643	853013	39717	515927	419716
河　南	Henan	78258	39105	27467	42936	35322
湖　北	Hubei	2303936	2010208	82793	2054523	249413
湖　南	Hunan	469884	412517	17604	426314	43571
广　东	Guangdong	16911318	13067110	603471	11839314	5072004
广　西	Guangxi	255518	149222	1838	178525	76993
海　南	Hainan	863395	731867	396	591182	272213
重　庆	Chongqing	744058	505057	41373	422089	321968
四　川	Sichuan	496362	305353	34204	715044	-218682
贵　州	Guizhou	19937	16319	3244	11289	8647
云　南	Yunnan	227016	188841	2814	99591	127425
西　藏	Tibet					
陕　西	Shaanxi	1151629	755541	12430	919430	232199
甘　肃	Gansu	3109	3028	52	3495	-386
青　海	Qinghai	1566	1504	57	2186	-620
宁　夏	Ningxia					
新　疆	Xinjiang	21066	17412	1265	18593	2473

3-3-4 各地区限额以上批发业企业年末资产负债(按国民经济行业分)

Assets and Liabilities of Enterprises above Designated Size of Wholesale Trade by Region and Sector at the Year-end

农、林、牧产品批发　　　　单位：万元

Wholesale of Agricultural, Forestry and Livestock Products　　　　Unit: 10000 yuan

地　区	Region	资产总计 Total Assets	#流动资产合计 Total Working Capitals	#固定资产合计 Total Fixed Assets	负债合计 Total Liabilities	所有者权益合计 Total Owners' Equities
全　国	**National Total**	**84475900**	**58867297**	**6244515**	**58312175**	**26157739**
北　京	Beijing	19320453	9537257	230664	11738957	7581497
天　津	Tianjin	1704976	1463206	47612	1363657	341319
河　北	Hebei	888562	598741	147996	540139	348423
山　西	Shanxi	303671	211298	76029	183806	119865
内蒙古	Inner Mongolia	3638821	3283229	248614	3223420	415402
辽　宁	Liaoning	2512411	2043076	186383	2025158	487254
吉　林	Jilin	5188114	4693530	340567	4801308	386806
黑龙江	Heilongjiang	4645073	3725308	308739	4000981	644092
上　海	Shanghai	5453108	3658204	189055	3465197	1987911
江　苏	Jiangsu	4097700	3131950	590341	2902319	1195381
浙　江	Zhejiang	2037558	1446528	147141	1600377	437181
安　徽	Anhui	1238162	792446	235355	694071	544091
福　建	Fujian	1674986	1398803	115800	1210690	464296
江　西	Jiangxi	336097	186578	100513	220566	115531
山　东	Shandong	3814029	2593053	691604	2318016	1496013
河　南	Henan	4819014	3543239	681908	2919110	1899904
湖　北	Hubei	2278334	1790078	316220	1344921	933413
湖　南	Hunan	921000	568575	179009	464342	456658
广　东	Guangdong	6448339	3536957	403371	2882053	3560298
广　西	Guangxi	1025231	776717	59050	830449	194782
海　南	Hainan	2023	1957	66	1560	463
重　庆	Chongqing	392374	205284	73485	207577	184798
四　川	Sichuan	1022041	765411	88329	654939	367102
贵　州	Guizhou	82487	60627	9115	52078	30409
云　南	Yunnan	374032	247023	74194	200097	173935
西　藏	Tibet	5996	1291	3593	2013	3982
陕　西	Shaanxi	322673	188710	80131	198088	124584
甘　肃	Gansu	202081	150621	32860	102918	99163
青　海	Xinjiang	61205	49723	7761	44798	16407
宁　夏	Ningxia	54287	37081	7817	24987	29300
新　疆	Xinjiang	9611063	8180796	571193	8093583	1517479

3-3-4 续表 1 Continued 1

食品、饮料及烟草制品批发 单位：万元
Wholesale of Food, Beverages and Tobaccos Unit: 10000 yuan

地区	Region	资产总计 Total Assets	#流动资产合计 Total Working Capitals	#固定资产合计 Total Fixed Assets	负债合计 Total Liabilities	所有者权益合计 Total Owners' Equities
全国	**National Total**	**227522520**	**178381727**	**16983667**	**124266379**	**103256696**
北京	Beijing	19460608	15368103	640635	14149306	5311302
天津	Tianjin	5168980	4731676	168458	3878578	1290402
河北	Hebei	2735029	2230728	270953	1160032	1574997
山西	Shanxi	2040670	1583375	270537	915056	1125614
内蒙古	Inner Mongolia	1486518	1253742	150096	635978	850539
辽宁	Liaoning	5016957	4403977	320886	2528544	2488413
吉林	Jilin	1552262	1326748	173943	918281	633980
黑龙江	Heilongjiang	4330734	3744372	273286	3099823	1231471
上海	Shanghai	24924087	17408203	751812	15599360	9324727
江苏	Jiangsu	14858280	12643156	1067518	8039115	6819164
浙江	Zhejiang	15327812	12058404	940221	8196947	7130865
安徽	Anhui	6475853	5090516	456522	3188787	3287066
福建	Fujian	10630824	7833190	794979	4889441	5741383
江西	Jiangxi	2714823	2160548	377114	1058883	1655940
山东	Shandong	9277551	6898510	1493597	5297284	3980267
河南	Henan	5697531	4014502	1104891	2313368	3384162
湖北	Hubei	7973969	6383615	859507	4258318	3715651
湖南	Hunan	6881983	4431080	1123769	3500637	3381346
广东	Guangdong	25944500	19847010	1433484	16220213	9724287
广西	Guangxi	5960958	4787718	248984	4305280	1655678
海南	Hainan	979582	882545	39266	369181	610401
重庆	Chongqing	4618492	3189576	640113	1982252	2636240
四川	Sichuan	9636686	8326554	737155	5229092	4407594
贵州	Guizhou	14024864	13022999	527096	5727868	8296996
云南	Yunnan	10260159	8110910	790892	3334986	6925172
西藏	Tibet	388572	300292	79410	90316	298256
陕西	Shaanxi	3047775	2438888	358786	977202	2070573
甘肃	Gansu	1675102	988952	372678	592415	1082687
青海	Xinjiang	490623	416143	25461	133239	357383
宁夏	Ningxia	597255	377406	109408	132757	464499
新疆	Xinjiang	3343481	2128289	382210	1543841	1799640

3-3-4 续表 2 Continued 2

纺织、服装及家庭用品批发　　　　单位：万元

Wholesale of Textiles, Wearing Apparel and Household Articles　　　　Unit: 10000 yuan

地　区	Region	资产总计 Total Assets	#流动资产合计 Total Working Capitals	#固定资产合计 Total Fixed Assets	负债合计 Total Liabilities	所有者权益合计 Total Owners' Equities
全　国	**National Total**	**217971133**	**183673649**	**5764776**	**167578369**	**50392768**
北　京	Beijing	42028349	36272471	460541	36115904	5912445
天　津	Tianjin	3947657	3508227	163838	3195102	752556
河　北	Hebei	1370493	1331749	19466	1178447	192047
山　西	Shanxi	3238258	1234190	8469	763660	2474598
内蒙古	Inner Mongolia	214287	184812	1463	192767	21520
辽　宁	Liaoning	1021772	832025	106319	805055	216717
吉　林	Jilin	141789	102675	7779	106514	35275
黑龙江	Heilongjiang	159826	88225	41692	154917	4909
上　海	Shanghai	30179806	24126632	1113749	20172415	10007391
江　苏	Jiangsu	40560771	35147600	862499	31671836	8888935
浙　江	Zhejiang	28615284	23655575	980984	22319842	6295442
安　徽	Anhui	4105149	3634854	155489	3921212	183938
福　建	Fujian	12790099	10617010	542640	8064182	4725917
江　西	Jiangxi	720841	681633	18077	595804	125037
山　东	Shandong	7935620	7127231	212734	6810478	1125141
河　南	Henan	2423544	2033066	132928	1700261	723284
湖　北	Hubei	1452467	1305604	61933	1300708	151759
湖　南	Hunan	1066973	936329	64389	867156	199817
广　东	Guangdong	26527474	22107603	629021	20106418	6421056
广　西	Guangxi	1043763	812348	31152	808750	235013
海　南	Hainan	156156	154955	790	128048	28108
重　庆	Chongqing	3965982	3839758	29659	3209796	756187
四　川	Sichuan	945233	782658	47502	623057	322176
贵　州	Guizhou	682084	670960	1687	661620	20464
云　南	Yunnan	1351722	1321430	3873	1042748	308974
西　藏	Tibet					
陕　西	Shaanxi	641582	584206	30720	549577	92005
甘　肃	Gansu	85736	68609	13388	60429	25307
青　海	Xinjiang	27254	24131	1180	9073	18181
宁　夏	Ningxia	89377	78257	9104	70643	18734
新　疆	Xinjiang	481785	408826	11711	371950	109835

文化、体育用品及器材批发
Wholesale of Culture, Sports Appliances and Equipments

单位：万元
Unit: 10000 yuan

地 区	Region	资产总计 Total Assets	#流动资产合计 Total Working Capitals	#固定资产合计 Total Fixed Assets	负债合计 Total Liabilities	所有者权益合计 Total Owners' Equities
全 国	**National Total**	**63303457**	**49851085**	**2006480**	**43415319**	**19888139**
北 京	Beijing	13591043	9226822	385739	9448782	4142261
天 津	Tianjin	1329091	951435	23306	671970	657121
河 北	Hebei	527045	343326	38531	326453	200591
山 西	Shanxi	420660	315977	22779	273328	147333
内蒙古	Inner Mongolia	270613	203521	2537	146240	124373
辽 宁	Liaoning	397479	359268	6862	285958	111521
吉 林	Jilin	141414	102199	29130	94216	47198
黑龙江	Heilongjiang	108531	49461	44543	79011	29520
上 海	Shanghai	6389403	5662047	105482	3980362	2409041
江 苏	Jiangsu	4312439	2928063	221785	2215051	2097389
浙 江	Zhejiang	4745360	4265495	116792	3753429	991931
安 徽	Anhui	2581756	1937473	18906	1521804	1059953
福 建	Fujian	1955732	1427391	59932	1311728	644004
江 西	Jiangxi	81107	79359	859	35993	45114
山 东	Shandong	2991602	2580596	215541	2363111	628492
河 南	Henan	959324	625635	65532	502063	457261
湖 北	Hubei	1256226	1092298	66967	880839	375388
湖 南	Hunan	1629992	982000	56651	1143810	486182
广 东	Guangdong	14096803	12194422	374359	10214438	3882365
广 西	Guangxi	623726	366942	15680	379713	244013
海 南	Hainan	107672	57482	17252	37198	70474
重 庆	Chongqing	692010	669322	10926	411257	280753
四 川	Sichuan	2088376	1876464	17198	1929905	158471
贵 州	Guizhou	342100	309207	5929	271788	70312
云 南	Yunnan	688833	548430	9922	489254	199578
西 藏	Tibet	14179	10824	2104	7475	6705
陕 西	Shaanxi	305356	231004	13844	192792	112564
甘 肃	Gansu	305365	218067	18884	195740	109625
青 海	Xinjiang	44251	30442	4859	35371	8880
宁 夏	Ningxia	34305	23190	2588	18979	15326
新 疆	Xinjiang	271663	182923	31061	197263	74400

3-3-4 续表 4 Continued 4

医药及医疗器材批发 单位：万元
Wholesale of Medicines and Medical Appliances Unit: 10000 yuan

地 区	Region	资产总计 Total Assets	#流动资产合计 Total Working Capitals	#固定资产合计 Total Fixed Assets	负债合计 Total Liabilities	所有者权益合计 Total Owners' Equities
全 国	**National Total**	**152555321**	**129170421**	**5911878**	**111294932**	**41235497**
北 京	Beijing	18165311	14064233	317533	12169597	5995715
天 津	Tianjin	2951319	2720816	51624	2227150	724169
河 北	Hebei	3958730	3627836	155842	3294940	663790
山 西	Shanxi	1587338	1408359	68504	1319046	268292
内蒙古	Inner Mongolia	809719	749899	37951	611610	198109
辽 宁	Liaoning	3464079	3092705	135003	2658566	805513
吉 林	Jilin	1970034	1749859	92199	1595527	374507
黑龙江	Heilongjiang	805605	731878	19336	647426	158179
上 海	Shanghai	16516382	13336699	876347	10992902	5523480
江 苏	Jiangsu	10805575	9646211	431605	8635743	2145437
浙 江	Zhejiang	8509620	6942349	325075	5638085	2871035
安 徽	Anhui	5085956	4361500	305101	3865138	1220819
福 建	Fujian	2226442	1784295	79544	1538434	688008
江 西	Jiangxi	3300938	2835159	150156	2544378	756561
山 东	Shandong	10500958	9034187	476508	8211835	2289123
河 南	Henan	7517711	6826615	254963	6322164	1195548
湖 北	Hubei	9614481	8202916	509769	6586340	3028141
湖 南	Hunan	2922670	2538540	182292	2232292	690377
广 东	Guangdong	18237489	15402054	500492	12784985	5452504
广 西	Guangxi	1424530	1259279	81427	1130606	293923
海 南	Hainan	2609913	1826473	25378	1729389	880524
重 庆	Chongqing	3732588	3024061	180773	2487498	1245090
四 川	Sichuan	5165117	4618921	202363	3904492	1260626
贵 州	Guizhou	2034050	1749470	97987	1525116	508934
云 南	Yunnan	2782224	2449599	128849	1989698	792526
西 藏	Tibet	444214	394125	9247	383015	61199
陕 西	Shaanxi	2654905	2516137	52876	2309066	345839
甘 肃	Gansu	1252109	957365	59277	851884	400225
青 海	Xinjiang	189259	168086	5264	144245	45014
宁 夏	Ningxia	293519	256053	19908	230669	62850
新 疆	Xinjiang	1022536	894743	78685	733096	289440

3-3-4 续表 5 Continued 5

矿产品、建材及化工产品批发

Wholesale of Mineral Products, Building Materials and Chemical Products

单位：万元

Unit: 10000 yuan

地区	Region	资产总计 Total Assets	#流动资产合计 Total Working Capitals	#固定资产合计 Total Fixed Assets	负债合计 Total Liabilities	所有者权益合计 Total Owners' Equities
全国	**National Total**	**1022784067**	**779970838**	**42913128**	**773797397**	**249424881**
北京	Beijing	149085339	103207410	3187981	105677179	43408160
天津	Tianjin	96806556	80955178	1441060	81182142	15624414
河北	Hebei	15848455	12992867	1480817	12873388	2975068
山西	Shanxi	32165649	22540844	3336524	26011946	6153703
内蒙古	Inner Mongolia	10047441	6626155	950657	7659115	2388326
辽宁	Liaoning	21535673	18245439	1574536	18288453	3162377
吉林	Jilin	3319057	2687803	293291	2566420	752636
黑龙江	Heilongjiang	6477325	5319935	619146	5665616	778275
上海	Shanghai	120739336	91716079	1650246	89777627	30963709
江苏	Jiangsu	64702223	53346970	3051511	52520452	12178641
浙江	Zhejiang	104970670	79519878	2842732	80773619	24197051
安徽	Anhui	10598368	7906870	424665	7460456	3137912
福建	Fujian	55614068	40955709	1421156	37145494	18468575
江西	Jiangxi	5994661	4128221	1078081	4507351	1487310
山东	Shandong	48074733	36869820	3582141	37498198	10576535
河南	Henan	15127846	11617162	1492639	10936426	4664933
湖北	Hubei	12825550	8134588	2275204	8512332	4313218
湖南	Hunan	5839270	4310895	445193	4205031	1634239
广东	Guangdong	107931571	87405583	5187717	83162712	24771857
广西	Guangxi	14395575	10484404	772760	9892756	4502820
海南	Hainan	8989403	6867341	253334	5254319	3735085
重庆	Chongqing	12192675	10020224	579757	8750979	3441696
四川	Sichuan	12718926	9667936	713305	10532358	2186568
贵州	Guizhou	10732738	8403407	454484	7696487	3036252
云南	Yunnan	14632081	10290010	673760	10502929	4129152
西藏	Tibet	45387	31900	6817	20010	25376
陕西	Shaanxi	17956599	12821260	843049	12449431	5516111
甘肃	Gansu	6308812	3728383	602414	3130677	3178135
青海	Xinjiang	12295742	11142275	314462	10394905	1900836
宁夏	Ningxia	5800508	5026814	279748	4604434	1268235
新疆	Xinjiang	19011831	12999478	1083941	14144154	4867676

机械设备、五金产品及电子产品批发 单位：万元
Wholesale of Machinery, Hardware and Electronic Products Unit: 10000 yuan

地 区	Region	资产总计 Total Assets	#流动资产合计 Total Working Capitals	#固定资产合计 Total Fixed Assets	负债合计 Total Liabilities	所有者权益合计 Total Owners' Equities
全 国	**National Total**	**356141166**	**297428410**	**9409631**	**262200705**	**93953244**
北 京	Beijing	94609359	74743430	1530468	60366648	34242711
天 津	Tianjin	14680870	12407590	396131	11984994	2692322
河 北	Hebei	6147257	4751045	1277182	4859693	1287565
山 西	Shanxi	1625715	1520484	48106	1409641	216074
内 蒙 古	Inner Mongolia	875125	766142	22564	755750	119375
辽 宁	Liaoning	6035927	4405283	130746	4868882	1167045
吉 林	Jilin	680116	614681	36370	500582	179534
黑 龙 江	Heilongjiang	717831	610875	55446	550449	167382
上 海	Shanghai	73121422	62771937	964133	52589860	20534786
江 苏	Jiangsu	21758887	17637598	566406	15737855	6021032
浙 江	Zhejiang	22511693	18845313	479917	18028089	4483604
安 徽	Anhui	4217229	3897378	92334	3620382	596847
福 建	Fujian	6366858	5368956	546148	4334170	2032688
江 西	Jiangxi	1492265	1385012	51229	1423130	69134
山 东	Shandong	8325999	6652677	744409	6024471	2301528
河 南	Henan	2976269	2440258	277713	2075839	900429
湖 北	Hubei	6196832	5502729	152712	5559808	637024
湖 南	Hunan	2206139	1867689	106011	2011399	194740
广 东	Guangdong	62941153	54482334	1283771	50267552	12686714
广 西	Guangxi	1449697	1303458	41588	1115400	334297
海 南	Hainan	77370	72167	493	61875	15496
重 庆	Chongqing	6697452	6124952	136750	5296347	1401104
四 川	Sichuan	3440562	3140857	101946	3118420	322143
贵 州	Guizhou	911249	797980	29877	730045	181204
云 南	Yunnan	1079643	946626	22236	851636	228007
西 藏	Tibet	26505	18473	6315	11138	15368
陕 西	Shaanxi	1459086	1316767	78638	1225746	233340
甘 肃	Gansu	586864	479843	82083	514542	72322
青 海	Xinjiang	203066	169309	6701	147972	55094
宁 夏	Ningxia	151139	138141	7853	138723	12416
新 疆	Xinjiang	2571586	2248426	133355	2019667	551919

贸易经纪与代理
Trade Broker and Agency

单位：万元
Unit: 10000 yuan

地 区	Region	资产总计 Total Assets	#流动资产合计 Total Working Capitals	#固定资产合计 Total Fixed Assets	负债合计 Total Liabilities	所有者权益合计 Total Owners' Equities
全 国	**National Total**	**50722892**	**42875314**	**693699**	**40632107**	**10090828**
北 京	Beijing	20458162	15778158	134998	14575694	5882468
天 津	Tianjin	1127662	962688	26625	1010644	117019
河 北	Hebei	26466	26095	101	25031	1435
山 西	Shanxi					
内蒙古	Inner Mongolia	2105	1597	508	1453	652
辽 宁	Liaoning	281683	244004	31767	188770	92913
吉 林	Jilin	1852	1277	474	2372	-519
黑龙江	Heilongjiang	37678	34049	2580	31351	6327
上 海	Shanghai	2027963	1739702	49570	1461122	566841
江 苏	Jiangsu	1129511	1018856	30485	883358	246153
浙 江	Zhejiang	309047	282982	10211	273864	35183
安 徽	Anhui	73301	68334	4393	54108	19193
福 建	Fujian	690576	564902	30338	529548	161028
江 西	Jiangxi	74469	65096	2178	51607	22861
山 东	Shandong	541881	483143	30420	446869	95013
河 南	Henan	9799	8984	494	5380	4418
湖 北	Hubei	104658	103851	523	81838	22820
湖 南	Hunan	5569	5016	552	4503	1066
广 东	Guangdong	23037151	20762125	313714	20316884	2720308
广 西	Guangxi	4533	4463	28	3720	813
海 南	Hainan					
重 庆	Chongqing	13907	10618	2081	9312	4595
四 川	Sichuan	34447	30279	4068	25514	8934
贵 州	Guizhou	10328	7185	292	9195	1133
云 南	Yunnan	640572	613781	807	581182	59391
西 藏	Tibet					
陕 西	Shaanxi	31146	30344	492	24314	6832
甘 肃	Gansu					
青 海	Xinjiang					
宁 夏	Ningxia					
新 疆	Xinjiang	48425	27785	16000	34474	13951

其他批发业
Other Wholesale not Classified Elsewhere

单位：万元
Unit: 10000 yuan

地　区	Region	资产总计 Total Assets	#流动资产合计 Total Working Capitals	#固定资产合计 Total Fixed Assets	负债合计 Total Liabilities	所有者权益合计 Total Owners' Equities
全　国	**National Total**	**44568553**	**33537050**	**1726428**	**34470275**	**10098206**
北　京	Beijing	10658083	5547623	101311	9292739	1365343
天　津	Tianjin	3182102	2859157	70915	2571276	610826
河　北	Hebei	3208299	3074374	59717	2435906	772394
山　西	Shanxi	84753	70832	8846	59825	24928
内蒙古	Inner Mongolia	65685	62744	1400	56337	9348
辽　宁	Liaoning	1140141	951289	21424	1050789	89352
吉　林	Jilin	169138	146457	21010	123126	46012
黑龙江	Heilongjiang	98525	43099	2264	107507	-8982
上　海	Shanghai	4356076	3776301	93567	3185779	1170297
江　苏	Jiangsu	1983464	1620800	172587	1379018	604369
浙　江	Zhejiang	2406817	1953587	96457	1915943	490874
安　徽	Anhui	957837	799931	76220	747620	210217
福　建	Fujian	4884977	3819162	61216	3438470	1446507
江　西	Jiangxi	156100	132556	15881	90787	65312
山　东	Shandong	1834300	1391499	261710	1270493	563808
河　南	Henan	658391	389142	198706	449081	209311
湖　北	Hubei	288403	202596	37537	197147	91257
湖　南	Hunan	299124	232830	35116	196321	102804
广　东	Guangdong	5803408	4693151	173308	4617156	1186253
广　西	Guangxi	98371	90942	4115	77288	21083
海　南	Hainan					
重　庆	Chongqing	385066	251537	83441	245095	139971
四　川	Sichuan	239933	182991	41362	169136	70797
贵　州	Guizhou	96450	64125	4288	53981	42469
云　南	Yunnan	918228	778776	48941	327253	590976
西　藏	Tibet	10722	6146		7330	3392
陕　西	Shaanxi	47879	36225	5282	25298	22581
甘　肃	Gansu	36848	34362	1447	17473	19375
青　海	Xinjiang	17601	6888	2390	9033	8568
宁　夏	Ningxia	347749	235205	6114	255688	92061
新　疆	Xinjiang	134083	82723	19856	97380	36703

3-3-5 各地区限额以上零售业企业年末资产负债

Assets and Liabilities of Enterprises above Designated Size of Retail Trade by Region at the Year-end

单位：万元

Unit: 10000 yuan

地区	Region	资产总计 Total Assets	#流动资产合计 Total Working Capitals	#固定资产合计 Total Fixed Assets	负债合计 Total Liabilities	所有者权益合计 Total Owners' Equities
全国	**National Total**	**612058956**	**417186809**	**81805686**	**415028821**	**196779581**
北京	Beijing	46415306	35092217	2955918	35363426	11051881
天津	Tianjin	12754442	7553198	1600452	9344087	3410356
河北	Hebei	16406186	10861671	3119058	11902840	4503346
山西	Shanxi	11874324	8246277	2164425	9366823	2507500
内蒙古	Inner Mongolia	7045010	4718619	1429186	5720246	1324764
辽宁	Liaoning	17226678	11847374	2587925	14018264	3169689
吉林	Jilin	10987353	6601689	2914967	7988526	2895914
黑龙江	Heilongjiang	8355073	5051048	1804943	6430538	1924535
上海	Shanghai	36522855	27283273	4132480	26040654	10484201
江苏	Jiangsu	60093074	38186833	8426460	39254925	20839321
浙江	Zhejiang	37554719	26387063	4684032	28486734	9068058
安徽	Anhui	19206724	13456351	3104019	12682245	6524479
福建	Fujian	19416731	13874301	2200484	10708156	8708575
江西	Jiangxi	10081300	6951509	1420367	6361973	3719328
山东	Shandong	41421735	28611320	7048786	30545266	11244990
河南	Henan	21866326	15398166	3845967	14338070	7528256
湖北	Hubei	25651639	16616071	4744448	17948600	7703039
湖南	Hunan	35964163	12960627	4346354	13403303	22560860
广东	Guangdong	67678372	54717132	4419158	43895604	23782993
广西	Guangxi	9779481	7692147	964699	6840549	2938932
海南	Hainan	2955541	1987181	450572	1893519	1062022
重庆	Chongqing	13587169	9098069	2001598	9440828	4149266
四川	Sichuan	22844257	15250367	3204654	15175202	7669055
贵州	Guizhou	11779299	8823823	1473265	8554438	3224860
云南	Yunnan	11256611	7606505	1631256	7598955	3657656
西藏	Tibet	669337	420243	131551	376508	292829
陕西	Shaanxi	16745992	11312573	2501398	10817243	5928749
甘肃	Gansu	5474553	3411461	840937	3426670	2023554
青海	Qinghai	1234444	843520	293231	881164	353280
宁夏	Ningxia	2329603	1608080	275547	1535499	794105
新疆	Xinjiang	6880660	4718100	1087549	4687966	1733188

3-3-5 续表 Continued

国有控股 单位：万元

State-controlled Enterprises Unit: 10000 yuan

地区	Region	资产总计 Total Assets	#流动资产合计 Total Working Capitals	#固定资产合计 Total Fixed Assets	负债合计 Total Liabilities	所有者权益合计 Total Owners' Equities
全国	**National Total**	**126626999**	**79272258**	**20180533**	**77033255**	**49097454**
北京	Beijing	14890058	9274230	1097207	8908818	5981239
天津	Tianjin	2808259	1371302	666712	1503864	1304394
河北	Hebei	3368002	2182179	665880	2033042	1334959
山西	Shanxi	3290794	1911887	864495	2511574	779221
内蒙古	Inner Mongolia	1215855	498413	475754	1138853	77002
辽宁	Liaoning	2933960	1684009	578117	1588474	1308103
吉林	Jilin	3274603	1401809	1335928	2496885	761428
黑龙江	Heilongjiang	1339742	772011	467173	1070682	269060
上海	Shanghai	8098482	4894728	1710422	4861647	3236835
江苏	Jiangsu	9955802	7241202	1214228	6488033	3467769
浙江	Zhejiang	4169097	2231138	672948	2729131	1439965
安徽	Anhui	5144422	3551067	560675	3007299	2137123
福建	Fujian	2610069	1606879	313881	1280866	1329202
江西	Jiangxi	1725909	982008	145722	683803	1042107
山东	Shandong	6465452	4413216	852671	4604617	1895484
河南	Henan	1955615	1171697	338765	1212174	743441
湖北	Hubei	6363619	2867975	1916437	4115271	2248348
湖南	Hunan	4545976	2459368	1019239	2657658	1888317
广东	Guangdong	19351411	15444167	1063671	9728172	9623239
广西	Guangxi	1178668	673273	254129	647520	531148
海南	Hainan	960361	624097	171873	393548	566812
重庆	Chongqing	3646588	1849038	695360	2710319	939194
四川	Sichuan	4981522	2589888	937382	2552744	2428778
贵州	Guizhou	5505915	4048781	721163	3998723	1507192
云南	Yunnan	2355660	950504	481660	1452229	903430
西藏	Tibet	224349	87323	73741	136010	88339
陕西	Shaanxi	1980514	1172234	350939	1226104	754410
甘肃	Gansu	686953	268210	227580	399030	267241
青海	Qinghai	116146	73673	34947	69679	46467
宁夏	Ningxia	69087	41885	16743	40109	28978
新疆	Xinjiang	1414111	934067	255091	786376	168229

3-3-6 各地区限额以上零售业企业年末资产负债(按登记注册类型分)

Assets and Liabilities of Enterprises above Designated Size of Retail Trade by Region and Type of Registration at the Year-end

内资企业 单位：万元
Domestic Funded Enterprises Unit: 10000 yuan

地　区	Region	资产总计 Total Assets	#流动资产合计 Total Working Capitals	#固定资产合计 Total Fixed Assets	负债合计 Total Liabilities	所有者权益合计 Total Owners' Equities
全　国	**National Total**	**512619662**	**358303866**	**71806805**	**359022167**	**153346939**
北　京	Beijing	34192412	24465774	2495435	26650813	7541599
天　津	Tianjin	9919877	6408872	1279137	7593936	2325942
河　北	Hebei	16028848	10626320	3050872	11660547	4368302
山　西	Shanxi	11583309	8059858	2076422	9167070	2416239
内蒙古	Inner Mongolia	6730349	4532788	1384806	5423447	1306901
辽　宁	Liaoning	15390665	10928231	2154036	12504385	2847555
吉　林	Jilin	10242493	6061107	2806058	7378688	2760893
黑龙江	Heilongjiang	7770962	4788380	1583585	5874557	1896406
上　海	Shanghai	21578030	16043712	2517392	16008933	5571097
江　苏	Jiangsu	51695431	33521384	7086848	33701997	17994606
浙　江	Zhejiang	31823053	22544496	3753651	24913510	6909616
安　徽	Anhui	18389175	12930097	2917653	12008505	6380670
福　建	Fujian	15545873	11340962	1938303	9349339	6196534
江　西	Jiangxi	9629360	6693874	1338128	5972336	3657023
山　东	Shandong	39458372	27372179	6628189	29222298	10604596
河　南	Henan	19981352	14152885	3270955	12794110	7187241
湖　北	Hubei	23942133	15371742	4518519	16664694	7277439
湖　南	Hunan	20573259	12351034	4187286	12889573	7683685
广　东	Guangdong	53089793	44044591	3401267	34596359	18493659
广　西	Guangxi	9059977	7265682	798196	6419946	2640032
海　南	Hainan	2596946	1856638	427161	1629427	967519
重　庆	Chongqing	12415884	8337332	1740935	8694138	3724671
四　川	Sichuan	20547856	13836367	2826231	13723602	6824254
贵　州	Guizhou	11203574	8411833	1366441	8166178	3037396
云　南	Yunnan	9709701	6517415	1447173	6782130	2927571
西　藏	Tibet	659689	418049	127196	372025	287664
陕　西	Shaanxi	13263322	9073401	2241275	8493368	4769953
甘　肃	Gansu	5396017	3353433	825730	3386755	1984933
青　海	Qinghai	1216078	831623	287348	870716	345361
宁　夏	Ningxia	2296228	1591060	263336	1519179	777049
新　疆	Xinjiang	6689644	4572747	1067241	4589606	1640533

国有企业
State-owned Enterprises

单位：万元
Unit: 10000 yuan

地 区	Region	资产总计 Total Assets	#流动资产合计 Total Working Capitals	#固定资产合计 Total Fixed Assets	负债合计 Total Liabilities	所有者权益合计 Total Owners' Equities
全 国	**National Total**	**6518261**	**4069093**	**1497355**	**3678439**	**2839818**
北 京	Beijing	889123	525100	131398	395952	493171
天 津	Tianjin	381528	162763	167633	109316	272212
河 北	Hebei	36983	20772	14689	41175	-4192
山 西	Shanxi	123243	70211	38163	105667	17575
内蒙古	Inner Mongolia	23642	15526	7207	18308	5333
辽 宁	Liaoning	109323	87877	17454	96181	13142
吉 林	Jilin	9735	8302	931	8771	965
黑龙江	Heilongjiang	398742	68929	326750	349387	49354
上 海	Shanghai	188921	153996	17014	94513	94408
江 苏	Jiangsu	251632	181123	32332	198100	53532
浙 江	Zhejiang	94562	69398	22484	51296	43266
安 徽	Anhui	26587	18446	7359	22419	4168
福 建	Fujian	32344	17078	9216	21688	10656
江 西	Jiangxi	44459	25176	8053	32845	11614
山 东	Shandong	297235	192938	61710	282834	14400
河 南	Henan	182287	109156	50837	128349	53937
湖 北	Hubei	334903	209563	116257	86189	248714
湖 南	Hunan	274278	92774	91206	96395	177883
广 东	Guangdong	1341299	1015955	110159	592187	749112
广 西	Guangxi	114643	82226	12882	86527	28115
海 南	Hainan	7960	6034	1836	6504	1456
重 庆	Chongqing	75317	31300	28372	33973	41344
四 川	Sichuan	191128	127087	21335	113615	77513
贵 州	Guizhou	106993	85615	7517	82157	24836
云 南	Yunnan	98183	59137	22296	61675	36509
西 藏	Tibet	49511	26238	13078	24178	25332
陕 西	Shaanxi	496427	421580	65258	379893	116534
甘 肃	Gansu	47507	34452	8018	29441	18066
青 海	Qinghai					
宁 夏	Ningxia	15258	11815	2281	6636	8622
新 疆	Xinjiang	274508	138525	83630	122267	152241

3-3-6 续表 2 Continued 2

集体企业

Collective-owned Enterprises

单位：万元

Unit: 10000 yuan

地 区	Region	资产总计 Total Assets	#流动资产合计 Total Working Capitals	#固定资产合计 Total Fixed Assets	负债合计 Total Liabilities	所有者权益合计 Total Owners' Equities
全 国	**National Total**	**2194021**	**1332581**	**517501**	**1272582**	**921443**
北 京	Beijing	160843	119625	17739	152180	8663
天 津	Tianjin	73680	48154	4221	27589	46092
河 北	Hebei	91989	66278	18995	54369	37620
山 西	Shanxi	88405	54984	23806	59035	29370
内蒙古	Inner Mongolia	21307	10204	11088	9348	11959
辽 宁	Liaoning	42683	33757	8278	27968	14714
吉 林	Jilin	6869	3360	2528	3868	3002
黑龙江	Heilongjiang	23723	13487	5891	22194	1530
上 海	Shanghai	123343	82015	8095	64408	58935
江 苏	Jiangsu	247508	97293	72492	77210	170298
浙 江	Zhejiang	85969	59493	19898	54619	31350
安 徽	Anhui	6947	4102	1217	3777	3171
福 建	Fujian	41064	20466	17292	17417	23647
江 西	Jiangxi	9653	7195	1241	6536	3117
山 东	Shandong	242646	125799	74238	130705	111941
河 南	Henan	96477	63340	20493	55686	40791
湖 北	Hubei	234674	125696	83159	164093	70581
湖 南	Hunan	61880	26314	28013	34839	27041
广 东	Guangdong	226642	180821	27331	125511	101131
广 西	Guangxi	47968	28715	9055	34486	13481
海 南	Hainan	762	637	75	336	427
重 庆	Chongqing	13309	10360	2183	8314	4995
四 川	Sichuan	19103	13600	3435	7214	11889
贵 州	Guizhou	40429	34520	2404	11933	28496
云 南	Yunnan	61519	38087	18673	50060	11459
西 藏	Tibet					
陕 西	Shaanxi	90426	46628	22741	44460	45966
甘 肃	Gansu	22873	10681	10503	15587	7286
青 海	Qinghai					
宁 夏	Ningxia	130	102	28	52	78
新 疆	Xinjiang	11200	6867	2389	8788	2413

3-3-6 续表 3 Continued 3

股份合作企业
Cooperative Enterprises

单位：万元
Unit: 10000 yuan

地 区	Region	资产总计 Total Assets	#流动资产合计 Total Working Capitals	#固定资产合计 Total Fixed Assets	负债合计 Total Liabilities	所有者权益合计 Total Owners' Equities
全 国	**National Total**	**589517**	**360050**	**171410**	**391209**	**198313**
北 京	Beijing	113662	105834	5958	92244	21418
天 津	Tianjin	13604	10670	2562	6836	6768
河 北	Hebei	145451	29912	92497	85673	59778
山 西	Shanxi	1192	1023	129	850	342
内 蒙 古	Inner Mongolia	748	284	245	224	525
辽 宁	Liaoning	8285	6745	980	5717	2568
吉 林	Jilin	14222	7878	6157	11016	3207
黑 龙 江	Heilongjiang	23357	18172	4629	19128	4229
上 海	Shanghai	17441	16273	651	7473	9969
江 苏	Jiangsu	16102	12261	1839	5830	10273
浙 江	Zhejiang	55435	40370	7253	39154	16281
安 徽	Anhui	6780	5107	1545	2712	4068
福 建	Fujian	475	225	200	86	389
江 西	Jiangxi	5269	3973	1296	2507	2762
山 东	Shandong	52867	32751	16733	48955	3912
河 南	Henan	1959	1057	423	1714	245
湖 北	Hubei	10488	5804	2922	3991	6498
湖 南	Hunan	2783	1645	980	1600	1183
广 东	Guangdong	18574	16505	1716	9814	8761
广 西	Guangxi	441	435	6	188	253
海 南	Hainan					
重 庆	Chongqing	10334	6214	3590	4751	5583
四 川	Sichuan	9423	5000	2350	5089	4334
贵 州	Guizhou	17860	10472	6090	11896	5964
云 南	Yunnan	31509	16556	7656	22034	9474
西 藏	Tibet					
陕 西	Shaanxi	8330	2805	2472	81	8249
甘 肃	Gansu	1632	1549	83	915	717
青 海	Qinghai					
宁 夏	Ningxia					
新 疆	Xinjiang	1294	530	448	732	563

3-3-6 续表 4 Continued 4

联营企业
Joint Ownership Enterprises

单位：万元
Unit: 10000 yuan

地区	Region	资产总计 Total Assets	#流动资产合计 Total Working Capitals	#固定资产合计 Total Fixed Assets	负债合计 Total Liabilities	所有者权益合计 Total Owners' Equities
全国	**National Total**	**300677**	**163896**	**55867**	**94770**	**205910**
北京	Beijing	1075	309	766	542	532
天津	Tianjin	10331	7839	233	1455	8876
河北	Hebei					
山西	Shanxi					
内蒙古	Inner Mongolia					
辽宁	Liaoning	2196	2060	136	359	1837
吉林	Jilin					
黑龙江	Heilongjiang	16432	10502	5855	10954	5478
上海	Shanghai	27874	24681	2091	5048	22826
江苏	Jiangsu	3932	2533	632	751	3181
浙江	Zhejiang	13322	11121	1402	4781	8541
安徽	Anhui	2064	1948	87	1803	262
福建	Fujian	863	771	92	145	719
江西	Jiangxi					
山东	Shandong	56910	7933	34222	12633	44276
河南	Henan	1214	534	567	142	1072
湖北	Hubei	836	686	140	206	631
湖南	Hunan	75355	17559	1013	1885	73470
广东	Guangdong	73465	67985	3225	49183	24283
广西	Guangxi					
海南	Hainan					
重庆	Chongqing	1862	1347	189	502	1361
四川	Sichuan	4042	2177	1668	1100	2942
贵州	Guizhou	6887	2245	3544	2531	4356
云南	Yunnan					
西藏	Tibet					
陕西	Shaanxi	62	53	5	9	53
甘肃	Gansu	1955	1613		741	1214
青海	Qinghai					
宁夏	Ningxia					
新疆	Xinjiang					

3-3-6 续表 5 Continued 5

有限责任公司 单位：万元

Limited Liability Corporations Unit: 10000 yuan

地区	Region	资产总计 Total Assets	#流动资产合计 Total Working Capitals	#固定资产合计 Total Fixed Assets	负债合计 Total Liabilities	所有者权益合计 Total Owners' Equities
全国	**National Total**	**230299869**	**166715954**	**29609740**	**170748795**	**59551021**
北京	Beijing	19635138	14828449	1140364	16469157	3165981
天津	Tianjin	5317378	3700049	465229	4355784	961596
河北	Hebei	6349293	4020891	1445207	4849701	1499592
山西	Shanxi	3156777	2052995	659766	2596687	560090
内蒙古	Inner Mongolia	3483777	2316008	733556	2729584	754193
辽宁	Liaoning	6771739	5009922	855575	6101972	668425
吉林	Jilin	4269182	2784747	907121	3298500	970682
黑龙江	Heilongjiang	3856201	2302263	739905	3076436	779765
上海	Shanghai	10260324	7048740	1603065	7915670	2344654
江苏	Jiangsu	16034116	11390276	2297304	11924410	4110856
浙江	Zhejiang	13035894	9430341	1532727	10161946	2873948
安徽	Anhui	7382247	5207584	956218	4816013	2566234
福建	Fujian	6745133	4933084	864912	4249839	2495294
江西	Jiangxi	4925106	3425746	550894	2883590	2041516
山东	Shandong	16829839	12081253	2454663	12988343	3841497
河南	Henan	12030154	8670573	1838300	8102168	3927986
湖北	Hubei	13355059	9473276	1850720	9750534	3604525
湖南	Hunan	6080794	4524722	784701	4299669	1781125
广东	Guangdong	25599242	21158668	1772158	17978156	7621226
广西	Guangxi	4341111	3597413	254570	3090904	1250207
海南	Hainan	2133903	1620440	283011	1344103	789800
重庆	Chongqing	4795791	3237525	590164	3735961	1059830
四川	Sichuan	9457425	7278059	948650	7187062	2270363
贵州	Guizhou	5938306	4541779	700764	4545815	1392490
云南	Yunnan	4091226	2438329	725138	2777682	1313544
西藏	Tibet	332813	186224	67762	223234	109579
陕西	Shaanxi	8161049	5432520	1512633	5362289	2798760
甘肃	Gansu	2022677	1246210	412248	1369628	653048
青海	Qinghai	716132	473781	195642	542125	174007
宁夏	Ningxia	905914	624846	96909	563995	341919
新疆	Xinjiang	2286128	1679241	369864	1457838	828290

股份有限公司　　　　　　　　　　　　　　　　单位：万元
Share-holding Corporations Ltd.　　　　　　　　Unit: 10000 yuan

地　区	Region	资产总计 Total Assets	#流动资产合计 Total Working Capitals	#固定资产合计 Total Fixed Assets	负债合计 Total Liabilities	所有者权益合计 Total Owners' Equities
全　国	**National Total**	**101102683**	**58231807**	**16575765**	**57664258**	**43184723**
北　京	Beijing	7514526	4140720	612814	4068349	3446177
天　津	Tianjin	1380470	477680	374546	756425	624045
河　北	Hebei	2853145	1856601	468469	1661975	1191170
山　西	Shanxi	1471246	870122	385817	1032252	438994
内蒙古	Inner Mongolia	705154	276284	288149	703626	1528
辽　宁	Liaoning	2771053	1474022	567794	1484041	1249629
吉　林	Jilin	3005884	1164694	1366907	2107424	795547
黑龙江	Heilongjiang	1676637	1071170	206670	982222	694415
上　海	Shanghai	4120623	2813470	568961	1951925	2168698
江　苏	Jiangsu	16986434	9525382	1570695	9144708	7841725
浙　江	Zhejiang	3034418	1144741	343697	1952665	1081752
安　徽	Anhui	4656621	2960559	1025766	3026229	1630391
福　建	Fujian	1737503	952749	214948	733960	1003542
江　西	Jiangxi	1184716	737580	214426	712748	471968
山　东	Shandong	8575186	5694624	1405306	6395179	2547514
河　南	Henan	1597988	1018939	227292	1030464	567524
湖　北	Hubei	4409337	1633530	1493852	2876164	1533173
湖　南	Hunan	6348671	2820628	1699653	3639322	2709349
广　东	Guangdong	11565479	9522216	569259	5003803	6561675
广　西	Guangxi	1291337	870229	235708	714189	577148
海　南	Hainan	332469	138800	127355	173939	158530
重　庆	Chongqing	1968306	1054093	450226	1194124	777108
四　川	Sichuan	4503204	1704716	1089385	2136469	2366734
贵　州	Guizhou	2037296	1514000	259687	1350845	686451
云　南	Yunnan	884189	515162	138526	574208	309981
西　藏	Tibet	46092	15204	26542	25984	20108
陕　西	Shaanxi	845687	527749	86535	370859	474828
甘　肃	Gansu	1527268	726359	155377	731638	771302
青　海	Qinghai	99935	30096	45171	69390	30545
宁　夏	Ningxia	332524	163458	23896	138941	193583
新　疆	Xinjiang	1639285	816230	332336	920191	259589

3-3-6 续表 7 Continued 7

私营企业 单位：万元

Private Enterprises Unit: 10000 yuan

地 区	Region	资产总计 Total Assets	#流动资产合计 Total Working Capitals	#固定资产合计 Total Fixed Assets	负债合计 Total Liabilities	所有者权益合计 Total Owners' Equities
全 国	**National Total**	**170662751**	**126955578**	**23046577**	**124813825**	**45852122**
北 京	Beijing	5876983	4745259	586019	5472280	404703
天 津	Tianjin	2741701	2001451	264670	2335641	406060
河 北	Hebei	6546932	4629675	1009943	4965957	1580975
山 西	Shanxi	6730505	5006420	967350	5369333	1361172
内 蒙 古	Inner Mongolia	2479702	1903985	342835	1950364	529338
辽 宁	Liaoning	5668421	4304836	699833	4777068	891353
吉 林	Jilin	2912251	2087161	503817	1945065	967186
黑 龙 江	Heilongjiang	1767790	1301832	289301	1413566	354224
上 海	Shanghai	6834865	5902697	314900	5966329	870536
江 苏	Jiangsu	17894744	12197371	3003072	12274130	5620637
浙 江	Zhejiang	15458838	11769737	1811792	12629886	2829025
安 徽	Anhui	6273852	4714903	915661	4123853	2149999
福 建	Fujian	6919644	5373665	823103	4295294	2624350
江 西	Jiangxi	3450059	2487855	559109	2332590	1117469
山 东	Shandong	13289245	9184226	2528939	9316514	3973746
河 南	Henan	6025983	4264421	1120650	3459067	2566916
湖 北	Hubei	5528951	3893683	939310	3754065	1774886
湖 南	Hunan	7704045	4852991	1577381	4809138	2894907
广 东	Guangdong	14226974	12057499	909757	10820949	3406110
广 西	Guangxi	3262381	2685476	285543	2493250	769131
海 南	Hainan	121851	90728	14884	104545	17306
重 庆	Chongqing	5520894	3971703	662794	3696186	1824708
四 川	Sichuan	6328185	4684764	749705	4258931	2069254
贵 州	Guizhou	3050169	2219233	385185	2159021	891147
云 南	Yunnan	4513893	3434368	523067	3286431	1227462
西 藏	Tibet	231193	190342	19775	98627	132565
陕 西	Shaanxi	3626397	2623832	540349	2323257	1303140
甘 肃	Gansu	1761422	1328708	233948	1236849	524574
青 海	Qinghai	398789	326983	46169	258080	140710
宁 夏	Ningxia	1042401	790839	140222	809554	232847
新 疆	Xinjiang	2473690	1928935	277494	2078004	395686

3-3-6 续表 8 Continued 8

其他企业
Other Enterprises

单位：万元
Unit: 10000 yuan

地 区	Region	资产总计 Total Assets	#流动资产合计 Total Working Capitals	#固定资产合计 Total Fixed Assets	负债合计 Total Liabilities	所有者权益合计 Total Owners' Equities
全 国	**National Total**	**951886**	**474914**	**332595**	**358299**	**593588**
北 京	Beijing	1063	477	376	110	953
天 津	Tianjin	1184	266	43	891	294
河 北	Hebei	5054	2190	1072	1696	3358
山 西	Shanxi	11941	4103	1391	3245	8695
内蒙古	Inner Mongolia	16020	10497	1727	11993	4026
辽 宁	Liaoning	16965	9013	3986	11079	5887
吉 林	Jilin	24351	4966	18597	4045	20306
黑龙江	Heilongjiang	8081	2026	4585	670	7411
上 海	Shanghai	4639	1842	2615	3568	1071
江 苏	Jiangsu	260963	115143	108481	76859	184105
浙 江	Zhejiang	44615	19295	14398	19163	25452
安 徽	Anhui	34078	17449	9801	11701	22376
福 建	Fujian	68848	42923	8542	30912	37936
江 西	Jiangxi	10097	6349	3108	1521	8577
山 东	Shandong	114443	52656	52378	47133	67310
河 南	Henan	45290	24865	12394	16521	28769
湖 北	Hubei	67885	29504	32159	29453	38432
湖 南	Hunan	25452	14402	4339	6725	18728
广 东	Guangdong	38118	24943	7662	16757	21361
广 西	Guangxi	2098	1189	432	401	1697
海 南	Hainan					
重 庆	Chongqing	30071	24790	3417	20328	9743
四 川	Sichuan	35346	20964	9704	14123	21223
贵 州	Guizhou	5634	3968	1250	1979	3654
云 南	Yunnan	29182	15775	11817	10041	19141
西 藏	Tibet	81	42	39	1	80
陕 西	Shaanxi	34943	18234	11282	12519	22424
甘 肃	Gansu	10683	3860	5553	1956	8727
青 海	Qinghai	1222	763	367	1122	100
宁 夏	Ningxia					
新 疆	Xinjiang	3539	2419	1080	1787	1752

港、澳、台商投资企业
Enterprises with Funds from Hong Kong, Macao and Taiwan

单位：万元
Unit: 10000 yuan

地区	Region	资产总计 Total Assets	#流动资产合计 Total Working Capitals	#固定资产合计 Total Fixed Assets	负债合计 Total Liabilities	所有者权益合计 Total Owners' Equities
全 国	**National Total**	**58841505**	**29700886**	**5652198**	**27645707**	**31195797**
北 京	Beijing	2442167	2089067	98575	1486501	955666
天 津	Tianjin	1384891	759150	113379	853625	531266
河 北	Hebei	72516	50644	15937	53996	18520
山 西	Shanxi	254064	168768	69919	142495	111569
内蒙古	Inner Mongolia	309734	183109	43484	281404	28330
辽 宁	Liaoning	994406	504294	284006	722176	272230
吉 林	Jilin	654561	481292	89871	545129	109432
黑龙江	Heilongjiang	374232	167324	153460	326683	47549
上 海	Shanghai	7672938	5948649	637994	4938533	2734406
江 苏	Jiangsu	5012069	2895176	902612	3556433	1455636
浙 江	Zhejiang	3053351	1925718	582163	1786603	1266748
安 徽	Anhui	716021	453396	166100	475335	240686
福 建	Fujian	2807728	1662595	165425	636018	2171710
江 西	Jiangxi	305255	133206	62297	253360	51894
山 东	Shandong	1202172	825138	260074	807569	394602
河 南	Henan	1753855	1141069	562049	1389877	363978
湖 北	Hubei	777849	636753	104527	601702	176148
湖 南	Hunan	15063673	369216	103007	345550	14718123
广 东	Guangdong	8088964	5598852	466834	4767153	3321812
广 西	Guangxi	580400	321453	152746	345786	234614
海 南	Hainan	183984	50018	7120	153300	30684
重 庆	Chongqing	500647	314619	133906	299790	200857
四 川	Sichuan	1084008	705506	164370	739164	344844
贵 州	Guizhou	324219	217736	78987	200792	123426
云 南	Yunnan	970872	693606	64528	511452	459420
西 藏	Tibet	9388	1969	4333	4272	5115
陕 西	Shaanxi	2035701	1258485	126187	1305940	729761
甘 肃	Gansu	76089	55732	15057	38111	37979
青 海	Qinghai	18366	11897	5884	10447	7919
宁 夏	Ningxia	29078	13870	11180	15986	13093
新 疆	Xinjiang	88306	62579	6187	50525	37781

外商投资企业 单位：万元
Foreign Funded Enterprises Unit: 10000 yuan

地 区	Region	资产总计 Total Assets	#流动资产合计 Total Working Capitals	#固定资产合计 Total Fixed Assets	负债合计 Total Liabilities	所有者权益合计 Total Owners' Equities
全 国	**National Total**	**40597795**	**29182056**	**4346684**	**28360947**	**12236850**
北 京	Beijing	9780727	8537377	361907	7226112	2554616
天 津	Tianjin	1449674	385176	207936	896526	553148
河 北	Hebei	304822	184707	52249	188297	116525
山 西	Shanxi	36951	17651	18084	57258	-20307
内 蒙 古	Inner Mongolia	4928	2722	897	15395	-10467
辽 宁	Liaoning	841607	414849	149883	791703	49904
吉 林	Jilin	90298	59291	19038	64709	25590
黑 龙 江	Heilongjiang	209878	95344	67898	229298	-19420
上 海	Shanghai	7271886	5290912	977095	5093188	2178699
江 苏	Jiangsu	3385574	1770273	437001	1996495	1389079
浙 江	Zhejiang	2678315	1916848	348218	1786621	891694
安 徽	Anhui	101528	72858	20266	198405	-96877
福 建	Fujian	1063130	870744	96756	722799	340330
江 西	Jiangxi	146686	124429	19942	136276	10410
山 东	Shandong	761191	414003	160523	515399	245792
河 南	Henan	131120	104212	12963	154083	-22963
湖 北	Hubei	931657	607577	121402	682205	249452
湖 南	Hunan	327231	240377	56061	168180	159052
广 东	Guangdong	6499616	5073689	551056	4532093	1967523
广 西	Guangxi	139104	105012	13757	74817	64287
海 南	Hainan	174612	80525	16291	110792	63820
重 庆	Chongqing	670638	446118	126757	446900	223738
四 川	Sichuan	1212393	708493	214053	712436	499957
贵 州	Guizhou	251506	194254	27836	187468	64038
云 南	Yunnan	576038	395484	119554	305372	270666
西 藏	Tibet	261	225	23	211	50
陕 西	Shaanxi	1446969	980686	133936	1017935	429034
甘 肃	Gansu	2447	2297	150	1805	642
青 海	Qinghai					
宁 夏	Ningxia	4298	3149	1032	334	3963
新 疆	Xinjiang	102710	82774	14120	47835	54875

3-3-7 各地区限额以上零售业企业年末资产负债(按国民经济行业分)

Assets and Liabilities of Enterprises above Designated Size of Retail Trade by Region and Sector at the Year-end

综合零售 单位：万元

Integrated Retail Unit: 10000 yuan

地区	Region	资产总计 Total Assets	#流动资产合计 Total Working Capitals	#固定资产合计 Total Fixed Assets	负债合计 Total Liabilities	所有者权益合计 Total Owners' Equities
全国	**National Total**	**167092443**	**86934901**	**31186289**	**107352516**	**59739925**
北京	Beijing	11927231	6881711	1327949	8849254	3077977
天津	Tianjin	2227127	877106	378020	1897477	329652
河北	Hebei	5083963	2531321	1705617	4076166	1007797
山西	Shanxi	2460543	1555728	450909	2171729	288814
内蒙古	Inner Mongolia	1299012	840552	302296	1061702	237310
辽宁	Liaoning	6441949	3662572	1248711	5260953	1180996
吉林	Jilin	4595795	2078950	1854911	3468982	1126814
黑龙江	Heilongjiang	3007993	1247914	963920	2205263	802730
上海	Shanghai	9483051	5627101	2157384	6566898	2916153
江苏	Jiangsu	14960867	7414992	3147433	10071488	4889379
浙江	Zhejiang	9901931	5771712	1882825	7082268	2819664
安徽	Anhui	4629176	2732101	1006935	3231896	1397280
福建	Fujian	4669720	2850023	543387	2012029	2657692
江西	Jiangxi	2174400	1278770	516909	1653960	520440
山东	Shandong	13909052	9085730	2803493	10404982	3504070
河南	Henan	5097953	3237155	1278348	3714073	1383879
湖北	Hubei	7474038	3494967	2046658	5022999	2451038
湖南	Hunan	21457626	3680483	1869735	4625526	16832100
广东	Guangdong	11967980	7638874	1112226	7621522	4346458
广西	Guangxi	1809289	1012985	409900	1269682	539607
海南	Hainan	1600370	1030084	215892	968863	631507
重庆	Chongqing	3864982	2424096	641117	2775220	1089761
四川	Sichuan	4779695	2809014	916478	3354411	1425284
贵州	Guizhou	1266464	827590	238535	956438	310026
云南	Yunnan	1929671	1242791	353825	1177467	752203
西藏	Tibet	78328	44918	17826	65438	12890
陕西	Shaanxi	5443497	3196554	1006672	3262938	2180558
甘肃	Gansu	1214971	679948	207929	747610	467361
青海	Qinghai	295324	126678	138045	235780	59543
宁夏	Ningxia	631197	335758	83214	349943	281253
新疆	Xinjiang	1409248	716723	359190	1189559	219689

3-3-7 续表 1 Continued 1

食品、饮料及烟草制品专门零售 单位：万元

Special Retail of Food, Beverages and Tobaccos Unit: 10000 yuan

地区	Region	资产总计 Total Assets	#流动资产合计 Total Working Capitals	#固定资产合计 Total Fixed Assets	负债合计 Total Liabilities	所有者权益合计 Total Owners' Equities
全 国	**National Total**	**22038855**	**14881938**	**3744394**	**12025268**	**10013587**
北 京	Beijing	944249	703858	157880	470586	473663
天 津	Tianjin	324839	245770	19939	195593	129246
河 北	Hebei	172398	115040	30823	115312	57086
山 西	Shanxi	445576	250003	107077	284478	161097
内蒙古	Inner Mongolia	240089	161840	42843	133025	107064
辽 宁	Liaoning	222201	174683	22371	153574	68628
吉 林	Jilin	491243	311886	79147	321694	169549
黑龙江	Heilongjiang	65667	42447	17248	39497	26170
上 海	Shanghai	504483	352286	63799	390094	114389
江 苏	Jiangsu	2597686	1709947	453215	1605441	992245
浙 江	Zhejiang	644753	452924	108422	386374	258378
安 徽	Anhui	724863	493872	142757	394294	330568
福 建	Fujian	1193232	740519	270527	433700	759532
江 西	Jiangxi	659856	412689	128598	246824	413032
山 东	Shandong	1258320	685813	422107	706309	552011
河 南	Henan	734298	435344	209575	346701	387596
湖 北	Hubei	1470718	1091161	258266	541192	929526
湖 南	Hunan	671060	325896	189613	350231	320829
广 东	Guangdong	3247545	2455022	202640	1580017	1667529
广 西	Guangxi	305500	219455	22752	197784	107716
海 南	Hainan	20350	15989	4288	16710	3640
重 庆	Chongqing	590366	357928	109848	276943	313423
四 川	Sichuan	1649847	1394719	132179	1235106	414741
贵 州	Guizhou	753890	422833	89861	413538	340352
云 南	Yunnan	949010	630514	176873	571150	377860
西 藏	Tibet	24234	10395	8620	11875	12359
陕 西	Shaanxi	691396	413650	195975	333121	358275
甘 肃	Gansu	251538	156957	48932	158647	92892
青 海	Qinghai	41243	27015	6547	23953	17290
宁 夏	Ningxia	63768	36862	10694	46212	17556
新 疆	Xinjiang	84637	34621	10978	45293	39344

纺织、服装及日用品专门零售
Special Retail of Textiles, Garments and Daily Consumer Articles

单位：万元
Unit: 10000 yuan

地 区	Region	资产总计 Total Assets	#流动资产合计 Total Working Capitals	#固定资产合计 Total Fixed Assets	负债合计 Total Liabilities	所有者权益合计 Total Owners' Equities
全 国	**National Total**	**35394190**	**26460830**	**3366397**	**23947122**	**11447068**
北 京	Beijing	2089005	1779409	122962	1507579	581426
天 津	Tianjin	1435142	520728	234832	930555	504587
河 北	Hebei	616519	399766	85723	570228	46291
山 西	Shanxi	598276	472257	72375	500882	97395
内蒙古	Inner Mongolia	226161	183536	32040	188053	38108
辽 宁	Liaoning	737066	588149	73257	687279	49787
吉 林	Jilin	336918	198769	117839	242996	93922
黑龙江	Heilongjiang	722060	436909	189979	503103	218957
上 海	Shanghai	9443969	7394514	633950	6270991	3172977
江 苏	Jiangsu	3488765	2282790	309149	2423830	1064935
浙 江	Zhejiang	2463485	1994260	132236	1686533	776952
安 徽	Anhui	434129	343235	67239	305189	128940
福 建	Fujian	915099	777795	79893	491323	423777
江 西	Jiangxi	359524	213374	27319	149751	209773
山 东	Shandong	1344296	921002	181485	938943	405353
河 南	Henan	534561	341936	126066	307635	226926
湖 北	Hubei	848485	622747	141092	544969	303515
湖 南	Hunan	410096	305842	63473	283736	126360
广 东	Guangdong	4835886	4026378	215678	3098223	1737663
广 西	Guangxi	542015	408800	4904	345870	196145
海 南	Hainan	25045	21557	2573	23827	1218
重 庆	Chongqing	676476	507021	131162	459137	217339
四 川	Sichuan	630650	503555	73253	404863	225786
贵 州	Guizhou	102928	77773	13818	70730	32198
云 南	Yunnan	327341	196905	73030	221024	106317
西 藏	Tibet	116910	116824	23	28287	88624
陕 西	Shaanxi	565984	400454	58488	287169	278815
甘 肃	Gansu	114432	87978	13837	70920	43512
青 海	Qinghai	77246	39820	34966	73763	3483
宁 夏	Ningxia	42349	36515	5331	35661	6688
新 疆	Xinjiang	333372	260232	48425	294073	39299

3-3-7 续表 3 Continued 3

文化、体育用品及器材专门零售 单位：万元

Special Retail of Culture, Sports Appliances and Equipments Unit: 10000 yuan

地区	Region	资产总计 Total Assets	#流动资产合计 Total Working Capitals	#固定资产合计 Total Fixed Assets	负债合计 Total Liabilities	所有者权益合计 Total Owners' Equities
全国	**National Total**	**26245215**	**18368314**	**3159851**	**14914237**	**11332214**
北京	Beijing	3079123	2481546	186746	1935824	1143299
天津	Tianjin	782285	547170	136800	616364	165921
河北	Hebei	582968	400089	79100	288948	294020
山西	Shanxi	411843	298507	66321	223474	188370
内蒙古	Inner Mongolia	176409	132725	20402	120277	56132
辽宁	Liaoning	454676	295563	50890	340866	113809
吉林	Jilin	179503	134903	24807	123067	56436
黑龙江	Heilongjiang	408527	282726	100408	234310	174216
上海	Shanghai	1556553	1201014	210950	1025244	531309
江苏	Jiangsu	2409552	1659621	268485	1478479	932222
浙江	Zhejiang	1523461	1071582	234533	989174	534288
安徽	Anhui	684891	585830	47443	311632	373260
福建	Fujian	1290148	920430	104929	606152	683997
江西	Jiangxi	1504068	900464	126969	520682	983385
山东	Shandong	1014697	727307	192463	676318	338380
河南	Henan	885010	576735	168819	418328	466682
湖北	Hubei	679032	494240	98707	404947	274086
湖南	Hunan	787383	559614	119885	369473	417911
广东	Guangdong	1547558	1108670	156154	842038	705604
广西	Guangxi	312406	208112	41409	135385	177021
海南	Hainan	69258	47869	15180	80268	-11011
重庆	Chongqing	924724	420164	96941	486378	438346
四川	Sichuan	1597843	947743	160627	734589	863254
贵州	Guizhou	281783	259874	10179	212759	69025
云南	Yunnan	791776	596754	127789	539788	251988
西藏	Tibet	6352	3933	2412	3696	2656
陕西	Shaanxi	742322	498140	149906	428731	313591
甘肃	Gansu	1066253	701584	50986	492797	573456
青海	Qinghai	20763	14017	5218	10505	10258
宁夏	Ningxia	81902	50361	16290	49644	32258
新疆	Xinjiang	392146	241027	88103	214100	178046

医药及医疗器材专门零售 单位：万元

Special Retail of Medicines and Medical Appliances Unit: 10000 yuan

地 区	Region	资产总计 Total Assets	#流动资产合计 Total Working Capitals	#固定资产合计 Total Fixed Assets	负债合计 Total Liabilities	所有者权益合计 Total Owners' Equities
全 国	**National Total**	**34018872**	**27012714**	**1926250**	**24377664**	**9642095**
北 京	Beijing	4653596	2902247	42180	3322705	1330891
天 津	Tianjin	246438	164860	10373	112245	134193
河 北	Hebei	565946	425609	22256	326771	239175
山 西	Shanxi	1040843	920793	35603	781766	259076
内 蒙 古	Inner Mongolia	242174	208562	14254	187932	54242
辽 宁	Liaoning	1285741	1168505	58705	1035543	250198
吉 林	Jilin	861188	744752	49042	685205	175983
黑 龙 江	Heilongjiang	857817	758675	70005	644726	213091
上 海	Shanghai	1203270	1033133	52879	933827	269444
江 苏	Jiangsu	1654671	1327821	167335	1179146	475525
浙 江	Zhejiang	1892955	1275498	93666	1455904	437051
安 徽	Anhui	1223827	1052436	99918	923933	299894
福 建	Fujian	841421	628628	52919	492255	349165
江 西	Jiangxi	363758	282630	32111	281615	82144
山 东	Shandong	3844323	3252357	261025	3004276	841062
河 南	Henan	870681	680837	103415	627935	242746
湖 北	Hubei	1633869	1386267	93041	1279902	353967
湖 南	Hunan	1885192	1390512	100757	1000829	884363
广 东	Guangdong	2369903	2028246	124066	1594535	775238
广 西	Guangxi	1761428	1542927	118700	1199584	561844
海 南	Hainan	32069	29589	1052	16254	15815
重 庆	Chongqing	568654	445094	45219	424092	144562
四 川	Sichuan	724999	570374	52041	574256	150743
贵 州	Guizhou	390337	323892	25857	287555	102782
云 南	Yunnan	962121	702449	73293	547957	414164
西 藏	Tibet	7782	4060	3523	6340	1442
陕 西	Shaanxi	579800	493204	43985	436596	143204
甘 肃	Gansu	366899	309015	20907	273332	93568
青 海	Qinghai	84082	80102	2274	71207	12875
宁 夏	Ningxia	141977	114730	13385	106738	35239
新 疆	Xinjiang	861111	764910	42464	562703	298409

汽车、摩托车、燃料及零配件专门零售 单位：万元

Special Retail of Motor Vehicles, Motorcycles, Fuel and Parts Unit: 10000 yuan

地区	Region	资产总计 Total Assets	#流动资产合计 Total Working Capitals	#固定资产合计 Total Fixed Assets	负债合计 Total Liabilities	所有者权益合计 Total Owners' Equities
全国	**National Total**	**226991698**	**166614787**	**28856455**	**161242407**	**65497862**
北京	Beijing	9954155	7811775	874376	7709260	2244896
天津	Tianjin	5345569	3688264	671711	3504778	1840791
河北	Hebei	7747608	5776667	1041745	5436635	2310973
山西	Shanxi	5208997	3794846	924670	4027158	1181839
内蒙古	Inner Mongolia	3839040	2462119	822791	3280658	558382
辽宁	Liaoning	5944395	4296592	831624	4712437	1194575
吉林	Jilin	3681035	2511230	642284	2610748	967374
黑龙江	Heilongjiang	2497241	1818507	272755	2152233	345007
上海	Shanghai	7196259	5562150	546072	4945516	2252743
江苏	Jiangsu	20076127	14503465	2870574	13582610	6493518
浙江	Zhejiang	15123856	11080995	1754562	12347340	2776516
安徽	Anhui	8745830	6121290	1374934	5726265	3019565
福建	Fujian	6559584	4802484	756721	4254234	2305350
江西	Jiangxi	3644700	2798205	438762	2645656	999044
山东	Shandong	14907654	10354184	2191263	11383844	3891317
河南	Henan	10129906	7649791	1291694	7096447	3033459
湖北	Hubei	9171064	6246207	1454519	7009503	2161561
湖南	Hunan	8927166	5638044	1681557	5878362	3048804
广东	Guangdong	33126808	28228862	2002198	21130170	11996908
广西	Guangxi	3425564	2853183	276919	2425385	1000178
海南	Hainan	997352	661623	196445	600053	397298
重庆	Chongqing	4783704	3203239	719689	3711597	1075032
四川	Sichuan	10178825	6356269	1632591	6437594	3741232
贵州	Guizhou	7681302	5981485	1034307	5658065	2023236
云南	Yunnan	5656047	3708445	765988	4111332	1544715
西藏	Tibet	392643	211583	91699	239259	153384
陕西	Shaanxi	5771517	4157308	702368	4223733	1547784
甘肃	Gansu	1910285	1113038	389333	1337162	548794
青海	Qinghai	580551	464704	72040	391142	189409
宁夏	Ningxia	1171099	876436	116184	840194	330905
新疆	Xinjiang	2615815	1881797	414080	1833037	323273

3-3-7 续表 6 Continued 6

家用电器及电子产品专门零售 单位：万元

Special Retail of Household Electric Appliances and Electronic Products Unit: 10000 yuan

地区	Region	资产总计 Total Assets	#流动资产合计 Total Working Capitals	#固定资产合计 Total Fixed Assets	负债合计 Total Liabilities	所有者权益合计 Total Owners' Equities
全国	**National Total**	**50654116**	**39314287**	**3263675**	**33260751**	**17393465**
北京	Beijing	10841214	10068813	109055	7460229	3380986
天津	Tianjin	1240425	899676	8974	1104990	135436
河北	Hebei	1169579	892382	62840	758446	411133
山西	Shanxi	357298	307828	28575	259743	97556
内蒙古	Inner Mongolia	519040	386226	84114	346413	172627
辽宁	Liaoning	790756	609944	114261	576081	214675
吉林	Jilin	413538	313750	57048	276372	137166
黑龙江	Heilongjiang	423120	267564	88810	372995	50124
上海	Shanghai	1680629	1433874	40677	998052	682577
江苏	Jiangsu	11093103	6331299	631319	6083993	5009133
浙江	Zhejiang	1833586	1500318	119431	1365077	468581
安徽	Anhui	1212733	931893	161086	825582	387151
福建	Fujian	1087663	900531	77998	652217	435447
江西	Jiangxi	649330	550413	32042	450071	199259
山东	Shandong	2335224	1716952	382963	1765865	569359
河南	Henan	1895836	1440270	203708	1081310	814526
湖北	Hubei	1771315	1279755	351407	1044439	726876
湖南	Hunan	819752	546666	118238	439088	380665
广东	Guangdong	4212967	3657390	205988	3231285	981682
广西	Guangxi	1317624	1235174	36072	1087068	230556
海南	Hainan	167872	147407	13452	147350	20522
重庆	Chongqing	966342	824948	81968	613945	352397
四川	Sichuan	1437841	1126891	83214	936113	501728
贵州	Guizhou	303249	262002	16063	196610	106640
云南	Yunnan	363757	315586	23808	247561	116196
西藏	Tibet	27309	20246	3101	15337	11972
陕西	Shaanxi	1095148	787730	90408	526500	568648
甘肃	Gansu	172734	155153	8346	107353	65381
青海	Qinghai	45220	39785	4675	28436	16784
宁夏	Ningxia	163942	145417	9651	97254	66688
新疆	Xinjiang	245970	218405	14383	164976	80994

五金、家具及室内装饰材料专门零售 单位：万元

Special Retail of Hardware, Furniture and Interior Decoration Materials Unit: 10000 yuan

地区	Region	资产总计 Total Assets	#流动资产合计 Total Working Capitals	#固定资产合计 Total Fixed Assets	负债合计 Total Liabilities	所有者权益合计 Total Owners' Equities
全国	**National Total**	**14835216**	**9802104**	**2820850**	**9360063**	**5473809**
北京	Beijing	650286	460890	73715	503126	147160
天津	Tianjin	577797	400280	102086	457458	120338
河北	Hebei	124256	89746	18589	75755	48501
山西	Shanxi	332160	201464	83066	225229	106931
内蒙古	Inner Mongolia	120817	102511	16006	100542	20275
辽宁	Liaoning	212531	116200	65360	197994	13196
吉林	Jilin	219413	154887	46318	138902	80511
黑龙江	Heilongjiang	166547	42027	73231	117995	48552
上海	Shanghai	771874	341932	261018	612097	159776
江苏	Jiangsu	944592	590424	255482	592112	352480
浙江	Zhejiang	481645	303615	123993	364217	117428
安徽	Anhui	665852	504862	101305	465310	200542
福建	Fujian	1028919	789263	117120	629650	399269
江西	Jiangxi	247929	177034	34211	135891	112038
山东	Shandong	1293380	814332	309424	627520	665860
河南	Henan	702236	426750	177462	331909	370327
湖北	Hubei	930154	567346	141139	674776	255378
湖南	Hunan	305620	199425	67381	137337	168282
广东	Guangdong	1630626	1311841	158587	1174251	456375
广西	Guangxi	111268	97100	7268	75048	36220
海南	Hainan	15478	11706	1101	20349	-4871
重庆	Chongqing	744922	515583	140263	327228	417694
四川	Sichuan	421662	226574	101315	246003	175659
贵州	Guizhou	88395	72688	9070	57706	30689
云南	Yunnan	124881	106441	12387	80342	44539
西藏	Tibet					
陕西	Shaanxi	924575	574924	181178	567862	356713
甘肃	Gansu	174430	61150	72040	110986	63444
青海	Qinghai	3934	1045	449	3080	854
宁夏	Ningxia	19590	5309	13927	8183	11407
新疆	Xinjiang	799447	534755	56359	301205	498242

货摊、无店铺及其他零售 单位：万元

Stalls, Non-shop and Other Retails Unit: 10000 yuan

地 区	Region	资产总计 Total Assets	#流动资产合计 Total Working Capitals	#固定资产合计 Total Fixed Assets	负债合计 Total Liabilities	所有者权益合计 Total Owners' Equities
全 国	**National Total**	**34788359**	**27796932**	**3481528**	**28548798**	**6239564**
北 京	Beijing	2276448	2001968	61055	3604864	-1328416
天 津	Tianjin	574820	209345	37718	524629	50191
河 北	Hebei	342950	231052	72365	254579	88371
山 西	Shanxi	1018788	444851	395829	892366	126423
内蒙古	Inner Mongolia	382269	240548	94441	301645	80624
辽 宁	Liaoning	1137361	935165	122746	1053537	83824
吉 林	Jilin	208721	152562	43572	120561	88161
黑龙江	Heilongjiang	206103	154279	28586	160414	45688
上 海	Shanghai	4682767	4337270	165750	4297935	384832
江 苏	Jiangsu	2867711	2366475	323468	2237826	629885
浙 江	Zhejiang	3689046	2936158	234364	2809847	879199
安 徽	Anhui	885424	690832	102404	498144	387280
福 建	Fujian	1830944	1464628	196990	1136597	694347
江 西	Jiangxi	477734	337930	83446	277523	200211
山 东	Shandong	1514789	1053643	304564	1037210	477579
河 南	Henan	1015845	609348	286880	413730	602115
湖 北	Hubei	1672965	1433382	159619	1425872	247093
湖 南	Hunan	700267	314146	135714	318721	381547
广 东	Guangdong	4739100	4261848	241620	3623563	1115537
广 西	Guangxi	194387	114411	46775	104743	89644
海 南	Hainan	27748	21358	589	19844	7904
重 庆	Chongqing	466999	399995	35390	366288	100712
四 川	Sichuan	1422894	1315228	52957	1252267	170627
贵 州	Guizhou	910951	595686	35575	701039	209913
云 南	Yunnan	152009	106621	24262	102334	49675
西 藏	Tibet	15779	8283	4347	6276	9504
陕 西	Shaanxi	931753	790607	72417	750593	181160
甘 肃	Gansu	203012	146638	28627	127863	75148
青 海	Qinghai	86082	50354	29018	43297	42784
宁 夏	Ningxia	13779	6691	6872	1670	12109
新 疆	Xinjiang	138914	65630	53568	83021	55893

3-4-1 限额以上批发和零售业企业损益及分配

项 目	Item	主营业务收入 Revenue from Principal Business	主营业务成本 Cost of Principal Business
总 计	**Total**	**5528094784**	**5108271909**
一、批发业	**Wholesale Trade**	**4457936427**	**4169353313**
#国有控股	State-controlled Enterprises	1668783155	1567992810
(一)按登记注册类型分	**by Type of Registration**		
1.内资企业	**Domestic Funded Enterprises**	**3801572458**	**3589162854**
国有企业	State-owned Enterprises	194223383	156094767
集体企业	Collective-owned Enterprises	7536723	7005779
股份合作企业	Cooperative Enterprises	2198425	2111994
联营企业	Joint Ownership Enterprises	271158	241992
国有联营企业	State Joint Ownership Enterprises	51226	43461
集体联营企业	Collective Joint Ownership Enterprises	56560	51671
国有与集体联营企业	Joint State-collective Enterprises	150866	134693
其他联营企业	Other Joint Ownership Enterprises	12506	12168
有限责任公司	Limited Liability Corporations	1963132330	1872787454
国有独资公司	State Sole Funded Corporations	383856646	369395239
其他有限责任公司	Other Limited Liability Corporations	1579275681	1503392219
股份有限公司	Share-holding Corporations Ltd.	377367752	357847764
私营企业	Private Enterprises	1249638179	1186665738
私营独资企业	Private-funded Enterprises	3790268	3334436
私营合伙企业	Private Partnership Enterprises	388183	361059
私营有限责任公司	Private Limited Liability Corporations	1215086160	1155027024
私营股份有限公司	Private Share-holding Corporations Ltd.	30373574	27943223
其他企业	Other Enterprises	7204512	6407374
2.港、澳、台商投资企业	**Enterprises with Funds from Hongkong, Macao and Taiwan**	**219114056**	**196168028**
合资经营企业	Joint-venture Enterprises	36157608	34495769
合作经营企业	Cooperative Enterprises	1305559	1186502
独资经营企业	Enterprises with Sole Investment	177445577	156714901
投资股份有限公司	Share-holding Corporations Ltd. with Investment	1554875	1341320
其他港澳台商投资企业	Other Enterprises with Funds from Hongkong, Macao and Taiwan	2650437	2429532
3.外商投资企业	**Foreign Funded Enterprises**	**437249915**	**384022435**
中外合资经营企业	Joint-venture Enterprises	135212431	124603438
中外合作经营企业	Cooperative Enterprises	508625	475887
外资企业	Enterprises with Sole Foreign Investment	289818168	249080352
外商投资股份有限公司	Share-holding Corporations Ltd. with Foreign Investment	4430328	3478039
其他外商投资企业	Other Foreign Funded Enterprises	7280365	6384720

Income and Distribution of Enterprises above Designated Size of Wholesale and Retail Trades

单位：万元
Unit: 10000 yuan

主营业务税金及附加 Taxes and Other Charges on Principal Business	主营业务利润 Profits from Principal Business	其他业务利润 Profits from Other Business	销售费用 Selling Expenses	管理费用 Administrative Expenses
29468317	**390354558**	**19669321**	**193235701**	**90655079**
24533889	**264049225**	**9833671**	**120838728**	**57463816**
19426053	81364292	3054000	32347666	15108453
22980660	**189428944**	**6408462**	**77965254**	**41339682**
14747690	23380926	1143238	4619828	5577694
23871	507073	41557	203700	161536
3971	82460	3089	39939	21480
702	28464	1253	15436	3959
214	7551	51	1640	2215
360	4529	1180	834	763
124	16049	21	12828	800
3	335	1	134	182
5648354	84696522	2753660	36338424	16655367
1852610	12608797	485413	4768695	2736061
3795742	72087720	2268246	31569729	13919307
612953	18907035	827313	9982368	3567261
1892433	61080008	1636661	26593938	15232912
24113	431719	801	90112	80544
2996	24128		67102	7949
1784526	58274610	1572146	25373358	14565464
80793	2349558	63716	1063365	578954
50687	746451	1701	171627	119476
465144	**22480884**	**724044**	**12042802**	**6373732**
83051	1578788	108095	589546	576361
2401	116656	212	65307	21826
370021	20360655	609453	11175562	5659600
3950	209605	5014	107453	68189
5725	215180	1273	104936	47755
1088090	**52139390**	**2701163**	**30830671**	**9750408**
208092	10400901	157950	7423930	776300
738	32000	-642	19879	12289
859868	39877948	2523951	22259682	8676312
10233	942056	11565	688798	139943
9163	886482	8339	438382	145565

项　　目	Item	财务费用 Financial Expenses	#利息支出 Interest Expense
总　　计	**Total**	**24288509**	**21101240**
一、批发业	**Wholesale Trade**	**17662451**	**17409662**
#国有控股	State-controlled Enterprises	5471509	7793390
(一)按登记注册类型分	**by Type of Registration**		
1.内资企业	**Domestic Funded Enterprises**	**17015724**	**15809266**
国有企业	State-owned Enterprises	-272444	825651
集体企业	Collective-owned Enterprises	52683	37179
股份合作企业	Cooperative Enterprises	6386	4686
联营企业	Joint Ownership Enterprises	2110	773
国有联营企业	State Joint Ownership Enterprises	-52	40
集体联营企业	Collective Joint Ownership Enterprises	888	714
国有与集体联营企业	Joint State-collective Enterprises	1269	14
其他联营企业	Other Joint Ownership Enterprises	6	5
有限责任公司	Limited Liability Corporations	9088332	8742024
国有独资公司	State Sole Funded Corporations	1591499	2048477
其他有限责任公司	Other Limited Liability Corporations	7496835	6693546
股份有限公司	Share-holding Corporations Ltd.	1686818	1916938
私营企业	Private Enterprises	6421895	4272407
私营独资企业	Private-funded Enterprises	15186	4563
私营合伙企业	Private Partnership Enterprises	1031	315
私营有限责任公司	Private Limited Liability Corporations	6263445	4176851
私营股份有限公司	Private Share-holding Corporations Ltd.	142227	90678
其他企业	Other Enterprises	29948	9618
2.港、澳、台商投资企业	**Enterprises with Funds from Hongkong, Macao and Taiwan**	**356616**	**620382**
合资经营企业	Joint-venture Enterprises	187084	194580
合作经营企业	Cooperative Enterprises	1089	1740
独资经营企业	Enterprises with Sole Investment	139650	397494
投资股份有限公司	Share-holding Corporations Ltd. With Investment	7323	9236
其他港澳台商投资企业	Other Enterprises with Funds from Hongkong, Macao and Taiwan	21469	17334
3.外商投资企业	**Foreign Funded Enterprises**	**290111**	**980014**
中外合资经营企业	Joint-venture Enterprises	294131	280964
中外合作经营企业	Cooperative Enterprises	1988	468
外资企业	Enterprises with Sole Foreign Investment	-8932	691186
外商投资股份有限公司	Share-holding Corporations Ltd. With Foreign Investment	2901	3421
其他外商投资企业	Other Foreign Funded Enterprises	27	3973

3-4-1 Continued 1

单位：万元
Unit: 10000 yuan

营业利润 Operating Profits	利润总额 Total Profits	应交所得税 Income Tax Payable	应付职工薪酬 Payables to Employees	应交增值税 VAT Payable
116304822	**122880907**	**25000732**	**94716399**	**61377931**
87640284	**92322049**	**19691081**	**53897273**	**44127028**
33899903	36006147	8600613	18106270	18769452
66021761	**69470327**	**14500280**	**39030740**	**35845489**
14231477	15220005	3746547	6112998	6858539
127665	149397	17247	109678	80052
19801	20373	2563	15658	8255
5910	5651	1048	5480	5149
3870	3912	1046	3304	1463
918	622		377	2139
1110	1110		1675	1518
12	7	2	124	28
28335382	29972510	7007316	16285369	15887147
4844008	5547942	1216183	2722364	2527339
23491373	24424565	5791130	13563005	13359812
7210513	7506637	942715	4262988	3846374
15666664	16191257	2755680	12113083	9089952
223894	223235	19295	40597	60925
14132	27190	1261	4619	11852
14580525	15077929	2595566	11592328	8715587
848120	862902	139558	475541	301591
424346	404505	27175	125489	70026
5782596	**6410944**	**1482199**	**4791819**	**2503269**
799267	899270	125726	379623	342169
31721	36479	8271	45347	15322
4808946	5328924	1328952	4256721	2084539
54058	55510	9460	63162	34716
88604	90764	9793	46968	26525
15835927	**16440780**	**3708604**	**10074712**	**5778271**
2244780	2282169	514336	952210	1506647
596	-3680	2733	12000	3428
13121838	13683325	3057742	8824938	4170402
131666	136257	40812	146523	53887
337051	342709	92983	139043	43907

项　目	Item	主营业务收入 Revenue from Principal Business	主营业务成本 Cost of Principal Business
(二)按国民经济行业分	**by Sector**		
农、林、牧产品批发	Wholesale of Agricultural, Forestry and Livestock Products	86445990	82030858
食品、饮料及烟草制品批发	Wholesale of Food, Beverages and Tobaccos	396752286	321844719
米、面制品及食用油批发	Wholesale of Rice, Flour and Edible Oil	59928334	56193024
肉、禽、蛋、奶及水产品批发	Wholesale of Meal, Fowls, Eggs, Milk and Aquatic Products	26819107	23983988
酒、饮料及茶叶批发	Wholesale of Wine, Beverages and Teas	66523411	51084413
烟草制品批发	Wholesale of Tobaccos	151347565	109316169
纺织、服装及家庭用品批发	Wholesale of Textiles, Wearing Apparel and Household Articles	365902300	323697384
服装批发	Wholesale of Garments	73451925	62319301
鞋帽批发	Wholesale of Shoes and Hats	19146317	15968161
家用电器批发	Wholesale of Household Electrical Appliances	120011528	110753150
文化、体育用品及器材批发	Wholesale of Culture, Sports Appliances and Equipments	88891885	81071687
文具用品批发	Wholesale of Stationeries	22736694	21585762
体育用品及器材批发	Wholesale of Sports Appliances and Equipments	9165606	8337126
图书批发	Wholesale of Books	9028400	7471587
医药及医疗器材批发	Wholesale of Medicines and Medical Appliances	237913284	208422089
西药批发	Wholesale of Western Medicine	146785005	132312200
中药批发	Wholesale of Chinese Traditional Medicine	47299009	41193449
矿产品、建材及化工产品批发	Wholesale of Mineral Products, Building Materials and Chemical Products	2473762148	2404659133
煤炭及制品批发	Wholesale of Coal and Related Products	256144874	246170279
石油及制品批发	Wholesale of Petroleum and Related Products	616229207	596243962
金属及金属矿批发	Wholesale of Metal Materials	1032859600	1015923195
建材批发	Wholesale of Building Materials	127361703	121301557
化肥批发	Wholesale of Chemical Fertilizer	43206326	41336565
农药批发	Wholesale of Pesticides	3883663	3465787
机械设备、五金产品及电子产品批发	Wholesale of Machinery, Hardware and Electronic Products	679425841	625204240
汽车批发	Wholesale of Motor Vehicles	243780951	222855636
计算机、软件及辅助设备批发	Wholesale of Computer, Software and Assistant Appliances	56501290	54045907
通讯及广播电视设备批发	Wholesale of Communication, Radios and Televisions Equipments	99411352	93654661
贸易经纪与代理	Trade Broker and Agency	52968049	50914062
其他批发业	Other Wholesale not Classified Elsewhere	75874662	71509145

单位：万元
Unit: 10000 yuan

主营业务税金及附加 Taxes and Other Charges on Principal Business	主营业务利润 Profits from Principal Business	其他业务利润 Profits from Other Business	销售费用 Selling Expenses	管理费用 Administrative Expenses
194146	4220986	177841	1774752	1487610
18483628	56423939	2195136	20690959	11444794
95959	3639351	551186	2496571	948452
70065	2765054	48304	1226623	625078
455467	14983531	201745	7136780	1804981
17581232	24450164	934982	3826239	5545902
814433	41390483	895206	22906244	9729998
205051	10927573	332792	5286469	2895107
60287	3117869	13730	1117673	1144708
165893	9092485	209679	5751768	2151484
209068	7611130	706408	3797381	1970963
34203	1116729	30679	507515	330099
17582	810898	367320	683610	257629
15331	1541482	111904	685965	526222
645113	28846082	1376946	15619983	6501282
333604	14139201	704192	7490855	3103824
148009	5957551	194110	3676017	1152203
2449283	66653732	2062722	26947786	13404769
542913	9431682	357813	4234978	1801109
598852	19386393	585982	8473774	2742928
586980	16349425	542164	5610598	3545836
280056	5780090	186028	1936447	1445790
66923	1802838	37953	764742	428150
7001	410875	2978	202244	99083
1398790	52822811	2233141	26753825	11133329
700451	20224864	658035	13386285	1691554
53137	2402246	250258	1012237	787133
105326	5651365	461336	2746531	1475380
52883	2001104	115193	766424	631844
286552	4078965	71080	1581372	1159227

项　　目	Item	财务费用 Financial Expenses	#利息支出 Interest Expenses
(二)按国民经济行业分	**by Sector**		
农、林、牧产品批发	Wholesale of Agricultural, Forestry and Livestock Products	954480	1054083
食品、饮料及烟草制品批发	Wholesale of Food, Beverages and Tobaccos	93496	1048598
米、面制品及食用油批发	Wholesale of Rice, Flour and Edible Oil	392631	434373
肉、禽、蛋、奶及水产品批发	Wholesale of Meal, Fowls, Eggs, Milk and Aquatic Products	120236	93222
酒、饮料及茶叶批发	Wholesale of Wine, Beverages and Teas	96699	152496
烟草制品批发	Wholesale of Tobaccos	-977020	18684
纺织、服装及家庭用品批发	Wholesale of Textiles, Wearing Apparel and Household Articles	1113745	865416
服装批发	Wholesale of Garments	336272	269803
鞋帽批发	Wholesale of Shoes and Hats	61393	20104
家用电器批发	Wholesale of Household Electrical Appliances	88595	127175
文化、体育用品及器材批发	Wholesale of Culture, Sports Appliances and Equipments	309788	356099
文具用品批发	Wholesale of Stationeries	55970	43737
体育用品及器材批发	Wholesale of Sports Appliances and Equipments	9692	14857
图书批发	Wholesale of Books	-79272	56447
医药及医疗器材批发	Wholesale of Medicines and Medical Appliances	1295862	1442440
西药批发	Wholesale of Western Medicine	928624	774169
中药批发	Wholesale of Chinese Traditional Medicine	222521	147838
矿产品、建材及化工产品批发	Wholesale of Mineral Products, Building Materials and Chemical Products	11209243	9899455
煤炭及制品批发	Wholesale of Coal and Related Products	1815923	1635527
石油及制品批发	Wholesale of Petroleum and Related Products	1783125	1522840
金属及金属矿批发	Wholesale of Metal Materials	4712436	4268991
建材批发	Wholesale of Building Materials	918024	750253
化肥批发	Wholesale of Chemical Fertilizer	367084	336888
农药批发	Wholesale of Pesticides	50498	32164
机械设备、五金产品及电子产品批发	Wholesale of Machinery, Hardware and Electronic Products	1979832	2057171
汽车批发	Wholesale of Motor Vehicles	206241	527570
计算机、软件及辅助设备批发	Wholesale of Computer, Software and Assistant Appliances	206595	143427
通讯及广播电视设备批发	Wholesale of Communication, Radios and Televisions Equipments	336916	347278
贸易经纪与代理	Trade Broker and Agency	289461	344079
其他批发业	Other Wholesale not Classified Elsewhere	416538	342325

单位：万元
Unit: 10000 yuan

营业利润 Operating Profits	利润总额 Total Profits	应交所得税 Income Tax Payable	应付职工薪酬 Payables to Employees	应交增值税 VAT Payable
1489927	2305053	233174	1471162	310209
27055374	28065857	6236065	12115657	11394739
410257	761126	109589	777283	272867
760365	804744	79500	684666	231718
6776404	6813037	1557878	2051082	2093105
16401059	16865997	4079952	6209656	7644528
9957936	10617443	2118229	8015968	4477702
3058626	3150272	696148	2139286	1047746
884283	916756	206218	499986	328929
1763636	1809160	371538	1898949	961652
2564875	2719977	496744	2161836	776959
264952	268464	64210	285995	140576
223487	243847	59070	179543	81353
667514	701979	47765	540002	15678
7332730	7503268	1632931	6666687	4830627
3820348	3918977	833370	3098514	2698762
1132315	1185264	212818	1186591	976284
19122541	19918815	4315130	11911209	13178149
2625184	2666023	480410	1313265	1943468
6147172	6168688	1528221	3794331	4398475
3319984	3761240	1004350	2492816	2801871
1816622	1932891	319352	985466	995132
269081	270602	66084	376559	1306012
86564	100350	15140	104658	11335
18046110	18737049	4221005	10242966	7675618
6768131	7169710	1704472	1515803	3385466
519895	578572	151351	821020	301835
1377248	1328055	367684	1326576	1023764
799411	858655	135530	477235	240465
1271380	1595934	302279	834562	1242552

项　目	Item	主营业务收入 Revenue from Principal Business	主营业务成本 Cost of Principal Business
二、零售业	**Retail Trade**	**1070158359**	**938918600**
#国有控股	State-controlled Enterprises	187345991	166653600
(一)按登记注册类型分	**by Type of Registration**		
1.内资企业	**Domestic Funded Enterprises**	**935911416**	**831317728**
国有企业	State-owned Enterprises	9985357	8676325
集体企业	Collective-owned Enterprises	8096014	7103153
股份合作企业	Cooperative Enterprises	1558540	1344748
联营企业	Joint Ownership Enterprises	844878	738660
国有联营企业	State Joint Ownership Enterprises	112749	93494
集体联营企业	Collective Joint Ownership Enterprises	253863	226310
国有与集体联营企业	Joint State-collective Enterprises	245883	221998
其他联营企业	Other Joint Ownership Enterprises	232383	196860
有限责任公司	Limited Liability Corporations	436230529	388313910
国有独资公司	State Sole Funded Corporations	19520055	17421629
其他有限责任公司	Other Limited Liability Corporations	416710477	370892286
股份有限公司	Share-holding Corporations Ltd.	121654787	108461044
私营企业	Private Enterprises	354840480	314492784
私营独资企业	Private-funded Enterprises	10896221	9106000
私营合伙企业	Private Partnership Enterprises	1348872	1146734
私营有限责任公司	Private Limited Liability Corporations	329305370	292827144
私营股份有限公司	Private Share-holding Corporations Ltd.	13290018	11412911
其他企业	Other Enterprises	2700832	2187105
2.港、澳、台商投资企业	**Enterprises with Funds from Hongkong, Macao and Taiwan**	**64504762**	**51658784**
合资经营企业	Joint-venture Enterprises	16932388	13888920
合作经营企业	Cooperative Enterprises	762547	639108
独资经营企业	Enterprises with Sole Investment	44327361	35118480
投资股份有限公司	Share-holding Corporations Ltd. with Investment	1544427	1248227
其他港澳台商投资企业	Other Enterprises with Funds from Hongkong, Macao and Taiwan	938046	764058
3.外商投资企业	**Foreign Funded Enterprises**	**69742187**	**55942088**
中外合资经营企业	Joint-venture Enterprises	26217314	21198470
中外合作经营企业	Cooperative Enterprises	1067338	882390
外资企业	Enterprises with Sole Foreign Investment	33585446	26078942
外商投资股份有限公司	Share-holding Corporations Ltd. with Foreign Investment	1940026	1530550
其他外商投资企业	Other Foreign Funded Enterprises	6932067	6251730

单位：万元
Unit: 10000 yuan

主营业务税金及附加 Taxes and Other Charges on Principal Business	主营业务利润 Profits from Principal Business	其他业务利润 Profits from Other Business	销售费用 Selling Expenses	管理费用 Administrative Expenses
4934422	**126305337**	**9835654**	**72396977**	**33191264**
670662	20021729	1663464	11506916	4504386
4285145	**100308543**	**7655411**	**54422600**	**27293992**
63458	1245574	111162	594943	410489
63361	929500	23089	292890	254123
9520	204272	4400	58300	65853
4044	102174	231	30360	16392
426	18829	22	4666	1857
1536	26017	64	6536	5532
1033	22852	103	11385	4947
1049	34474	42	7776	4058
1736913	46179706	3942442	27118323	12035446
74948	2023478	148749	987211	525918
1661964	44156227	3793697	26131117	11509527
501107	12692636	1402524	8044347	3165442
1879087	38468609	2169706	18168496	11248710
141819	1648402	30927	395824	341582
13361	188777	823	55565	46150
1624109	34854117	2087540	16854192	10421295
99798	1777309	50420	862920	439684
27657	486070	1862	114949	97541
331865	**12514113**	**1137802**	**8874330**	**3050902**
84040	2959428	310085	1991390	724009
3104	120335	4703	58644	36549
232825	8976056	769463	6457035	2207339
6709	289491	35340	243998	52414
5186	168802	18217	123271	30595
317417	**13482682**	**1042439**	**9100047**	**2846368**
122355	4896489	336735	3138614	840021
6340	178608	69171	168873	35933
162519	7343985	586313	4945370	1768823
13561	395915	29615	260559	140403
12641	667696	20612	586634	61188

项　目	Item	财务费用 Financial Expenses	#利息支出 Interest Expenses
二、零售业	**Retail Trade**	**6626059**	**3691578**
#国有控股	State-controlled Enterprises	510765	457294
(一)按登记注册类型分	**by Type of Registration**		
1.内资企业	**Domestic Funded Enterprises**	**6182222**	**3256860**
国有企业	State-owned Enterprises	29825	15578
集体企业	Collective-owned Enterprises	40909	27711
股份合作企业	Cooperative Enterprises	15315	11179
联营企业	Joint Ownership Enterprises	1454	96
国有联营企业	State Joint Ownership Enterprises	67	22
集体联营企业	Collective Joint Ownership Enterprises	987	64
国有与集体联营企业	Joint State-collective Enterprises	-50	-37
其他联营企业	Other Joint Ownership Enterprises	451	46
有限责任公司	Limited Liability Corporations	2688421	1467527
国有独资公司	State Sole Funded Corporations	30032	34163
其他有限责任公司	Other Limited Liability Corporations	2658389	1433366
股份有限公司	Share-holding Corporations Ltd.	474019	416828
私营企业	Private Enterprises	2913374	1313803
私营独资企业	Private-funded Enterprises	90602	20613
私营合伙企业	Private Partnership Enterprises	9128	3797
私营有限责任公司	Private Limited Liability Corporations	2694489	1238743
私营股份有限公司	Private Share-holding Corporations Ltd.	119157	50650
其他企业	Other Enterprises	18898	4138
2.港、澳、台商投资企业	**Enterprises with Funds from Hongkong, Macao and Taiwan**	**223146**	**199727**
合资经营企业	Joint-venture Enterprises	52642	89936
合作经营企业	Cooperative Enterprises	1775	615
独资经营企业	Enterprises with Sole Investment	152772	98623
投资股份有限公司	Share-holding Corporations Ltd. with Investment	8487	5736
其他港澳台商投资企业	Other Enterprises with Funds from Hongkong, Macao and Taiwan	7472	4815
3.外商投资企业	**Foreign Funded Enterprises**	**220687**	**234997**
中外合资经营企业	Joint-venture Enterprises	30152	30868
中外合作经营企业	Cooperative Enterprises	-264	464
外资企业	Enterprises with Sole Foreign Investment	155087	176157
外商投资股份有限公司	Share-holding Corporations Ltd. with Foreign Investment	29562	20894
其他外商投资企业	Other Foreign Funded Enterprises	6152	6617

单位：万元
Unit: 10000 yuan

营业利润 Operating Profits	利润总额 Total Profits	应交所得税 Income Tax Payable	应付职工薪酬 Payables to Employees	应交增值税 VAT payable
28664536	**30558858**	**5309647**	**40819123**	**17250903**
6036804	6193598	1034606	6429463	3164170
23122957	**24681932**	**3870682**	**34559188**	**14491242**
357315	386130	53429	475049	170071
377046	375130	52635	200325	99774
50249	49344	8225	92132	29504
56657	57373	12206	29902	15355
12263	12295	3141	13839	4284
13052	12854	2166	5913	2942
8535	9290	3218	5785	3714
22812	22938	3683	4366	4419
9423542	9846273	1875280	15397854	6717386
675467	703754	106787	624445	452561
8748072	9142521	1768496	14773410	6264828
3567261	3542585	537461	5709158	2060780
9033197	10184308	1318885	12508925	5362888
816376	796671	58505	328099	195414
84101	78853	6013	96397	27455
7633715	8823509	1175479	11484147	4961544
499009	485275	78897	600283	178475
257690	240789	12564	145845	35481
2657860	**2792745**	**731366**	**3401307**	**1331523**
1064778	1081629	207739	881850	318001
42724	48656	13011	39299	14220
1478609	1540720	492198	2321537	945879
26791	30402	9008	121219	24952
44958	91340	9408	37402	28473
2883722	**3084183**	**707599**	**2858636**	**1428141**
1427756	1512308	317792	924370	575497
43133	51255	6377	58675	21606
1345698	1446793	370971	1654768	729597
27873	25087	5673	96692	37589
39259	48735	6788	124135	63854

项　目	Item	主营业务收入 Revenue from Principal Business	主营业务成本 Cost of Principal Business
(二)按国民经济行业分	**by Sector**		
综合零售	Integrated Retail	202959353	171753504
百货零售	Retail of General Merchandise	105269028	88597569
超级市场零售	Retail of Supermarkets	87795133	74902258
食品、饮料及烟草制品专门零售	Special Retail of Food, Beverages and Tobaccos	38209825	30728721
粮油零售	Retail of Cereal and Oil	5009012	4424046
肉、禽、蛋、奶及水产品零售	Retail of Meat, Poultry, Eggs, Milk and Aquatic Products	6506121	5531761
酒、饮料及茶叶零售	Retail of Wine, Beverages and Teas	9027836	7230483
烟草制品零售	Retail of Tobaccos	1948680	1609162
纺织、服装及日用品专门零售	Special Retail of Textiles, Garments and Daily Consumer Articles	50759752	35688134
服装零售	Retail of Garments	31190065	21125872
文化、体育用品及器材专门零售	Special Retail of Culture, Sports Appliances and Equipments	30563823	24647367
体育用品及器材零售	Retail of Sports Appliances and Equipments	2412273	1778783
图书、报刊零售	Retail of Books, Newspapers and Magazines	10732380	8282954
医药及医疗器材专门零售	Special Retail of Medicines and Medical Appliances	49797856	42075798
药品零售	Retail of Medicines	47287713	40195181
汽车、摩托车、燃料及零配件专门零售	Special Retail of Motor Vehicles, Motorcycles, Fuel and Parts	499417795	461655818
汽车零售	Retail of Motor Vehicles	369761346	344892528
机动车燃料零售	Retail of Fuel of Motor Vehicles	119635214	107730412
家用电器及电子产品专门零售	Special Retail of Household Electric Appliances and Electronic Products	88181745	78493745
日用家电设备零售	Retail of Household Electric Appliances	34595143	30697483
计算机、软件及辅助设备零售	Retail of Computer, Software and Assistant Appliances	22868671	20627257
通信设备零售	Retail of Communication Equipments	10529485	9432521
五金、家具及室内装饰材料专门零售	Special Retail of Hardware, Furniture and Interior Decoration Materials	29330258	24124884
货摊、无店铺及其他零售	Stalls, Non-shop and Other Retails	80937962	69750642
互联网零售	Retail on the Internet	66589253	57782144
(三)按零售业态分	**by Mode of Business Operation**		
有店铺零售	Store-based Retailing	962146678	844802035
超市	Supermarket	30358007	25744755
大型超市	Hypermarket	83997549	71849649
百货店	Department Store	96672648	80576070
专业店	Speciality Store	364770366	325250163
专卖店	Exclusive Shop	330290324	294351034
无店铺零售	Non-Store Selling	108011681	94116565

单位：万元
Unit: 10000 yuan

主营业务税金及附加 Taxes and Other Charges on Principal Business	主营业务利润 Profits from Principal Business	其他业务利润 Profits from Other Business	销售费用 Selling Expenses	管理费用 Administrative Expenses
1369588	29836261	5462749	21789475	9466073
946479	15724980	3033157	9303681	5844970
359482	12533393	2200506	11343115	3044792
295200	7185904	176178	3211251	1580110
25681	559285	22245	264684	145424
43026	931334	12797	348286	253624
85841	1711512	68427	621632	385969
20753	318765	7462	137190	94802
363774	14707844	373088	9075587	3377958
234649	9829544	253768	6268893	2307794
264592	5651864	293820	2628732	1744612
12041	621449	3948	427990	164159
35281	2414145	182540	1036076	827284
221141	7500917	226835	4294122	1781188
203458	6889074	218612	4057816	1614593
1397279	36364698	2467831	17069907	9190798
1027607	23841211	2203820	10978647	7461219
320240	11584562	239416	5679234	1474631
385802	9302198	438574	5334556	2466283
144778	3752882	209451	2328754	931970
83294	2158120	24343	1088215	482226
26721	1070243	139740	729935	313697
381737	4823637	48751	1658150	1337542
255320	10932000	347835	7335197	2246696
156635	8650474	215901	6409255	1580716
4672751	112671892	9523966	62852273	30210574
217130	4396122	313281	2426871	1205805
310793	11837107	2463061	11155868	2953253
950709	15145869	2563235	8593841	5642373
1455914	38064289	1718710	18272165	9001524
1261692	34677598	1993055	18354670	9023349
261671	13633445	311687	9544704	2980690

项 目	Item	财务费用 Financial Expense	#利息支出 Interest Expenses
(二)按国民经济行业分	**by Sector**		
综合零售	Integrated Retail	1537583	1039340
百货零售	Retail of General Merchandise	1060937	777206
超级市场零售	Retail of Supermarkets	425303	244829
食品、饮料及烟草制品专门零售	Special Retail of Food, Beverages and Tobaccos	236523	106955
粮油零售	Retail of Cereal and Oil	41741	20162
肉、禽、蛋、奶及水产品零售	Retail of Meat, Poultry, Eggs, Milk and Aquatic Products	43713	17960
酒、饮料及茶叶零售	Retail of Wine, Beverages and Teas	70862	27433
烟草制品零售	Retail of Tobaccos	2323	3614
纺织、服装及日用品专门零售	Special Retail of Textiles, Garments and Daily Consumer Articles	318483	165141
服装零售	Retail of Garments	235091	131580
文化、体育用品及器材专门零售	Special Retail of Culture, Sports Appliances and Equipments	195388	100148
体育用品及器材零售	Retail of Sports Appliances and Equipments	18225	4135
图书、报刊零售	Retail of Books, Newspapers and Magazines	3970	10210
医药及医疗器材专门零售	Special Retail of Medicines and Medical Appliances	349310	280021
药品零售	Retail of Medicines	328528	263869
汽车、摩托车、燃料及零配件专门零售	Special Retail of Motor Vehicles, Motorcycles, Fuel and Parts	3132478	1588056
汽车零售	Retail of Motor Vehicles	2849551	1445537
机动车燃料零售	Retail of Fuel of Motor Vehicles	231167	123477
家用电器及电子产品专门零售	Special Retail of Household Electric Appliances and Electronic Products	362144	217694
日用家电设备零售	Retail of Household Electric Appliances	136192	153205
计算机、软件及辅助设备零售	Retail of Computer, Software and Assistant Appliances	49606	16801
通信设备零售	Retail of Communication Equipments	59105	21075
五金、家具及室内装饰材料专门零售	Special Retail of Hardware, Furniture and Interior Decoration Materials	254727	83463
货摊、无店铺及其他零售	Stalls, Non-shop and Other Retails	239423	110772
互联网零售	Retail on the Internet	165423	78053
(三)按零售业态分	**by Mode of Business Operation**		
有店铺零售	Store-based Retailing	6321111	3547567
超市	Supermarket	247846	111576
大型超市	Hypermarket	350242	229535
百货店	Department Store	1074154	774204
专业店	Speciality Store	2060238	1142214
专卖店	Exclusive Shop	2224377	1138522
无店铺零售	Non-Store Selling	304948	144012

单位：万元
Unit: 10000 yuan

营业利润 Operating Profits	利润总额 Total Profits	应交所得税 Income Tax Payable	应付职工薪酬 Payables to Employees	应交增值税 VAT payable
5949488	6027660	1394675	12104819	3223715
4506544	4534384	1004309	6532242	1897197
1396263	1461888	363741	5072470	1112846
2464654	2510170	308225	1816952	774946
146869	196574	20748	172939	47142
317122	308950	28975	281108	70516
683496	659003	82521	376951	177993
160071	169291	29052	106374	45544
2499991	2516335	556301	3641023	1503642
1388516	1409281	333003	2426308	985742
1412872	1493771	168663	1806051	361261
24158	27548	7461	126229	37118
729542	816346	32088	1062351	62552
1583936	2901333	286181	2928766	1110382
1355440	2686029	245607	2806853	1011956
9873501	10037665	1861688	12688915	7600792
5745549	6002674	1225238	9583860	5163309
3878102	3788032	576494	2864876	2255265
1720928	1679874	209398	2533258	1173475
729467	745092	77525	896633	453522
569512	553154	101261	622839	284052
146154	154753	29198	398784	137389
1643576	1778906	205079	917151	527358
1515594	1613146	319445	2382198	975338
699355	785626	200233	1825535	705159
27498460	29270753	5041729	37686493	16032585
914423	902619	110111	1705394	403522
1277808	1305507	372107	6528894	1178996
4375398	4306079	960609	4316462	1816889
10981655	12394154	1595360	12015998	6070096
7979742	8158331	1627737	11112167	5390278
1166076	1288105	267918	3132630	1218318

3-4-2 各地区限额以上批发业企业损益及分配

地区	Region	主营业务收入 Revenue from Principal Business	主营业务成本 Cost of Principal Business	主营业务税金及附加 Taxes and Other Charges on Principal Business	主营业务利润 Profits from Principal Business	其他业务利润 Profits from Other Business	销售费用 Selling Expenses	管理费用 Administr-ative Expenses
全国	**National Total**	**4457936427**	**4169353313**	**24533889**	**264049225**	**9833671**	**120838728**	**57463816**
北京	Beijing	452381550	421566907	938429	29876214	2366827	15090959	7910669
天津	Tianjin	243093898	236116172	654354	6323372	954630	3170876	1304968
河北	Hebei	63401579	59369203	720427	3311949	81912	1317747	689389
山西	Shanxi	62894967	59606719	507815	2780433	149856	1334412	803006
内蒙古	Inner Mongolia	25261039	23206030	386245	1668764	103600	903614	365750
辽宁	Liaoning	117477977	113339623	573865	3564489	165807	1667824	874931
吉林	Jilin	18704983	17072298	291661	1341024	24879	925489	296956
黑龙江	Heilongjiang	27388756	25712977	351599	1324180	54123	644097	356096
上海	Shanghai	766686833	714158030	1163846	51364957	1800061	28513584	10036445
江苏	Jiangsu	384135208	358699490	1686926	23748792	647555	10157239	5045617
浙江	Zhejiang	423733750	404512705	1625076	17595969	594953	8154203	3948452
安徽	Anhui	64740242	58389611	844800	5505831	69610	2566069	940463
福建	Fujian	200189354	189432718	903287	9853349	204740	3607851	2115928
江西	Jiangxi	28109136	24449360	602170	3057606	34560	1348396	604587
山东	Shandong	217244605	203213307	1488573	12542725	309308	4764783	2703046
河南	Henan	90045600	80823976	1399441	7822183	130891	2267655	1631132
湖北	Hubei	103631797	94739518	936141	7956138	108882	3520244	1731351
湖南	Hunan	48549823	42555438	1161943	4832442	69814	1863865	1066396
广东	Guangdong	615556399	577542048	2392226	35622125	1362504	16734084	9272111
广西	Guangxi	48150918	45204740	571277	2374901	49990	987849	640571
海南	Hainan	16134506	14747872	192953	1193681	23103	551885	145080
重庆	Chongqing	72780684	66771323	1057798	4951563	125132	1749584	1036490
四川	Sichuan	71030079	64485724	1093251	5451104	137333	2340490	928533
贵州	Guizhou	33324035	26651482	743546	5929007	22264	1102275	647580
云南	Yunnan	60907345	55180231	711203	5015911	62149	1602648	696161
西藏	Tibet	962171	660054	81149	220968	62	121401	50325
陕西	Shaanxi	81467568	76932649	633499	3901420	60533	1728628	615326
甘肃	Gansu	34334893	32749086	275776	1310031	26870	528822	295756
青海	Qinghai	9871871	9150974	157780	563117	4511	192129	88763
宁夏	Ningxia	10473941	10025258	89702	358981	33764	184704	79644
新疆	Xinjiang	65270919	62287790	297131	2685998	53448	1195322	542293

Income and Distribution of Enterprises above Designated Size of Wholesale Trade by Region

单位：万元

Unit: 10000 yuan

财务费用 Financial Expenses	#利息支出 Interest Expenses	营业利润 Operating Profits	利润总额 Total Profits	应交所得税 Income Tax Payable	应付职工薪酬 Payables to Employees	应交增值税 VAT Payable
17662451	**17409662**	**87640284**	**92322049**	**19691081**	**53897273**	**44127028**
1857646	3718953	10193338	10640672	2582375	7714754	3954550
1642363	1442765	943169	1293414	501645	1105317	1886590
270660	212885	1217808	1242730	255815	1219057	672307
427634	376989	376743	519731	182407	800056	1664946
149080	224064	211281	307841	111981	258849	673395
385330	292855	864347	871561	229669	745401	589005
111235	160585	264388	470390	103023	371197	263205
138785	181035	335126	377105	90723	429438	416120
1450206	1782886	14833431	15804056	3625163	9546352	4723399
1478139	904422	8653021	8896551	1916783	3615817	3874611
2030608	1964340	6296809	6814369	1378084	3752193	4042066
167692	176913	1729769	1820670	314934	952626	951692
1042946	766445	3948795	4153620	643006	1706324	1079394
65258	76272	1004895	1105850	234107	663454	624849
1143081	545535	4473513	4609170	846503	2423644	2449312
529965	266563	3481697	3509128	575887	1396777	1202027
409797	297968	2365159	2487834	540441	1551318	1147446
196065	166027	1779289	1793986	336903	863921	962855
2066955	1719235	10183868	10669171	2188017	7864576	5472146
247974	281326	591738	635383	146629	554647	604166
161452	170396	394988	413896	97466	170311	137126
255392	187953	2203837	2324156	331816	966276	935628
285246	263346	1306174	1500862	407227	1269475	930188
79363	150084	4112285	4137005	992317	662150	1270666
270256	340297	2636613	2734211	595832	916093	832772
-3833	455	54446	65425	6547	61986	293451
261769	274676	1609012	1503833	206054	693197	856811
111595	89817	375252	379667	63751	517676	653833
5222	10596	309075	244702	15057	87632	94118
115194	51048	18304	24918	20546	97470	133976
309376	312931	872115	970143	150373	919289	734378

国有控股
State-controlled Enterprises

地 区	Region	主营业务收入 Revenue from Principal Business	主营业务成本 Cost of Principal Business	主营业务税金及附加 Taxes and Other Charges on Principal Business	主营业务利润 Profits from Principal Business	其他业务利润 Profits from Other Business	销售费用 Selling Expenses	管理费用 Administrative Expenses
全 国	**National Total**	**1668783155**	**1567992810**	**19426053**	**81364292**	**3054000**	**32347666**	**15108453**
北 京	Beijing	241965552	231173142	563398	10229012	860951	4572732	2292434
天 津	Tianjin	125381470	123202183	262650	1916637	881822	516478	394103
河 北	Hebei	21904271	19861928	670727	1371616	15677	345420	293552
山 西	Shanxi	45312278	43330705	475821	1505752	112523	521320	518126
内 蒙 古	Inner Mongolia	15493267	14518572	348510	626185	3730	207773	179175
辽 宁	Liaoning	63243347	61225059	519888	1498400	88003	601170	337287
吉 林	Jilin	11476352	10655718	267348	553286	16216	515825	135579
黑 龙 江	Heilongjiang	18661642	17486954	325071	849617	40342	457465	245949
上 海	Shanghai	226315331	216371330	537596	9406405	132373	5757909	878382
江 苏	Jiangsu	77368893	71041379	1232235	5095279	47180	1854497	855927
浙 江	Zhejiang	98560931	93274956	1355295	3930680	176195	1101712	806840
安 徽	Anhui	26697390	23482290	756114	2458986	23209	718011	404529
福 建	Fujian	78579141	74716878	700294	3161969	120851	1219519	537286
江 西	Jiangxi	13836256	11919708	545553	1370995	8069	418286	275137
山 东	Shandong	53159488	49269946	1021619	2867923	66000	1208552	812953
河 南	Henan	33343273	29792368	1103407	2447498	37159	739010	647567
湖 北	Hubei	47032703	43499501	729564	2803638	49194	1245261	612963
湖 南	Hunan	18466522	15163581	943267	2359674	18320	847723	515444
广 东	Guangdong	174757622	163967097	1777949	9012576	114810	3812776	1314877
广 西	Guangxi	24285145	22480178	536797	1268170	17397	408170	358968
海 南	Hainan	2902877	2475759	180608	246510	1611	40381	54721
重 庆	Chongqing	22122654	19653297	837905	1631452	58589	420483	407778
四 川	Sichuan	31170039	27885959	977031	2307049	33508	662775	434135
贵 州	Guizhou	17341575	13741411	645267	2954897	13692	695471	426134
云 南	Yunnan	44577837	40006149	683652	3888036	17643	1018060	423177
西 藏	Tibet	620397	455783	78310	86304		21154	44118
陕 西	Shaanxi	48313065	45187264	575981	2549820	41801	1196025	344628
甘 肃	Gansu	25686156	24706079	262389	717688	7456	273716	177281
青 海	Qinghai	6644363	6085752	154985	403626	3511	116252	60323
宁 夏	Ningxia	5020026	4741547	85974	192505	27889	102656	43701
新 疆	Xinjiang	48543293	46620337	270848	1652108	18279	731084	275379

单位：万元

Unit: 10000 yuan

财务费用 Financial Expenses	#利息支出 Interest Expenses	营业利润 Operating Profits	利润总额 Total Profits	应交所得税 Income Tax Payable	应付职工薪酬 Payables to Employees	应交增值税 VAT Payable
5471509	**7793390**	**33899903**	**36006147**	**8600613**	**18106270**	**18769452**
1377031	2188466	3763826	3787286	1130109	2824419	1424119
988681	1125522	309346	405028	175788	340524	351736
84331	45608	700498	713971	148538	308841	343179
279377	285799	184137	287359	142595	441499	1483435
38410	146951	121308	156002	85588	166580	549176
114055	143717	462776	516889	151600	415216	339470
51686	118335	76826	260015	63877	258794	190310
87499	164110	175571	212781	67889	372246	346577
407568	542460	3328543	3419664	762563	1081064	1231927
269701	291037	2572162	2726232	651458	819998	1057439
184270	307347	2713132	2937167	610163	837992	1099799
58300	112527	1073523	1104692	226619	440051	395464
248323	342589	1633925	1900920	332129	667164	454636
20317	45890	586916	658177	159039	360024	321705
89570	89566	795912	847361	224466	917439	624554
102447	135926	972071	1006842	263901	649110	552301
32723	78135	921751	981941	235237	691849	603315
28886	87860	1020608	1078505	250788	442675	563762
277332	468811	4208238	4369019	1018984	1795167	1756378
118856	181861	480301	504684	112502	336541	373642
-13824	3609	190196	195830	43374	56790	65511
85995	92898	773352	821237	155260	442520	421967
68887	131394	328957	605635	272817	531267	521665
66437	102423	1783718	1804316	424478	491831	631153
120525	223304	2456390	2531248	569603	692315	687482
-3836	191	26198	28113	3228	44205	271093
80407	67155	1223814	1116292	150278	466992	707540
33141	46901	244968	251413	45450	373831	594038
-4612	6006	262318	214605	13677	65782	86489
-1544	3344	81025	82524	18045	72125	121302
180570	213648	427598	480399	701419	598288	3145

3-4-3 各地区限额以上批发业企业损益及分配(按登记注册类型分)

内资企业

Domestic Funded Enterprises

地区	Region	主营业务收入 Revenue from Principal Business	主营业务成本 Cost of Principal Business	主营业务税金及附加 Taxes and Other Charges on Principal Business	主营业务利润 Profits from Principal Business	其他业务利润 Profits from Other Business	销售费用 Selling Expenses	管理费用 Administrative Expenses
全国	**National Total**	**3801572458**	**3589162854**	**22980660**	**189428944**	**6408462**	**77965254**	**41339682**
北京	Beijing	329889659	313343028	664622	15882009	1271034	7229601	4242847
天津	Tianjin	220552191	215547635	357287	4647269	920234	2086547	1007362
河北	Hebei	61353744	57405715	718300	3229729	81354	1292304	669782
山西	Shanxi	61599470	58338924	506827	2753719	149639	1319032	798455
内蒙古	Inner Mongolia	25197969	23144974	386094	1666901	103600	902648	365405
辽宁	Liaoning	115664466	111782319	569133	3313014	164263	1547555	816968
吉林	Jilin	16825498	15381873	287175	1156450	24784	778155	293242
黑龙江	Heilongjiang	25675305	24005004	350647	1319654	53999	641605	354450
上海	Shanghai	455325934	443443752	598424	11283758	479547	4928579	2586626
江苏	Jiangsu	344570431	325548359	1585761	17436311	513336	7287045	3345911
浙江	Zhejiang	397282889	379279950	1603965	16398974	515464	7300647	3738069
安徽	Anhui	59873464	54319054	829848	4724562	68336	1873064	867206
福建	Fujian	188709225	178957268	880355	8871602	179532	3188266	1886837
江西	Jiangxi	27662022	24042896	601208	3017918	24184	1320637	597722
山东	Shandong	210758218	197061341	1481389	12215488	271969	4625319	2592652
河南	Henan	87233838	78061621	1397049	7775168	130775	2250531	1623900
湖北	Hubei	91548695	84619070	897332	6032293	70771	2283683	1313400
湖南	Hunan	46513714	40823507	1147223	4542984	69814	1667715	1032204
广东	Guangdong	549623937	517407497	2235802	29980638	735719	13507721	7451266
广西	Guangxi	47879724	44941546	570967	2367211	49861	985414	637425
海南	Hainan	14949742	13606221	191683	1151838	18081	513740	130699
重庆	Chongqing	67800166	62069810	1053604	4676752	122282	1629210	1011520
四川	Sichuan	66325344	59963522	1088701	5273121	128825	2282644	1022450
贵州	Guizhou	32999881	26372188	735725	5891968	20151	1087853	630081
云南	Yunnan	60236062	54573415	709445	4953202	60658	1578017	683809
西藏	Tibet	816533	561106	80136	175291	62	85630	49376
陕西	Shaanxi	75853108	71420364	632330	3800414	60302	1691553	596353
甘肃	Gansu	34307254	32727222	275658	1304374	26870	524652	295212
青海	Qinghai	8943824	8228701	157452	557671	4511	184394	86767
宁夏	Ningxia	10473941	10025258	89702	358981	33764	184704	79644
新疆	Xinjiang	65126210	62159715	296816	2669679	54741	1186789	532042

Income and Distribution of Enterprises above Designated Size of Wholesale Trade by Region and Type of Registration

单位：万元

Unit: 10000 yuan

财务费用 Financial Expenses	#利息支出 Interest Expenses	营业利润 Operating Profits	利润总额 Total Profits	应交所得税 Income Tax Payable	应付职工薪酬 Payables to Employees	应交增值税 VAT Payable
17015724	**15809266**	**66021761**	**69470327**	**14500280**	**39030740**	**35845489**
2023160	3257410	4966541	5144761	1439913	4378557	2179452
1557591	1335897	601755	823670	372722	811038	1114675
258968	208143	1190765	1214167	254892	1201759	665226
428761	376169	363252	506325	179632	790848	1655673
149003	224064	210804	307342	111902	258781	672975
352100	264821	649667	658255	213497	681687	553742
111402	160585	231009	437554	91412	359397	238074
138778	181031	334728	376690	90219	427098	417687
1254647	1225509	3902851	4180295	876455	2198272	1328409
1387244	859676	6722097	6859178	1452317	2697803	3077426
1947283	1869890	6161419	6663656	1311605	3515761	3931011
178530	179808	1704697	1828488	315777	855848	869557
1021145	764640	3576677	3791247	550488	1559256	946090
63757	74639	992918	1092793	231233	652980	619482
1108043	533292	4403396	4543007	827934	2364745	2425642
505855	265107	3473547	3497308	574967	1389014	1195740
380297	276655	2075400	2168871	463748	1334480	946623
194807	165874	1719726	1744646	324721	846877	910968
1966529	1542580	8652988	9054211	1821980	5989143	4720788
244627	278259	592862	637206	146364	553223	603375
168323	160544	393744	412400	98910	156211	130217
240356	177981	2081702	2185569	312235	925333	913787
260196	240076	1098870	1371443	401860	1233049	906358
75221	146001	4103214	4127721	989776	617133	1258242
267439	337575	2586256	2680716	590092	900594	815840
-3662	455	45314	52577	5391	56544	285836
198307	242013	1611940	1490129	202868	667708	849342
111588	89808	374315	378890	63411	514776	652778
3754	10596	314828	250515	15057	84311	94100
115194	51048	18304	24918	20546	97470	133976
306481	309120	866175	965779	148356	911044	732398

国有企业
State-owned Enterprises

地　区	Region	主营业务收入 Revenue from Principal Business	主营业务成本 Cost of Principal Business	主营业务税金及附加 Taxes and Other Charges on Principal Business	主营业务利润 Profits from Principal Business	其他业务利润 Profits from Other Business	销售费用 Selling Expenses	管理费用 Administrative Expenses
全　国	**National Total**	**194223382**	**156094767**	**14747690**	**23380926**	**1143238**	**4619828**	**5577694**
北　京	Beijing	29368329	27720563	315485	1332281	174690	322898	327448
天　津	Tianjin	8218675	7909159	132328	177188	773263	48217	77917
河　北	Hebei	5148936	3819663	655774	673499	7464	105794	184508
山　西	Shanxi	3198216	2346308	403346	448562	6426	60448	143841
内蒙古	Inner Mongolia	2729388	2211041	321202	197145	2645	80459	119744
辽　宁	Liaoning	8302335	7116994	487600	697741	3275	162062	177996
吉　林	Jilin	2500140	2126120	253694	120326	4766	132227	97145
黑龙江	Heilongjiang	4864565	4171034	311547	381984	10930	116949	141963
上　海	Shanghai	2974953	2737110	7775	230068	5897	45248	32045
江　苏	Jiangsu	13727907	10806931	1154105	1766871	4294	279034	306529
浙　江	Zhejiang	8648688	6031311	1136360	1481017	9728	133239	254426
安　徽	Anhui	5108220	3690875	649508	767837	1037	90378	202291
福　建	Fujian	7291181	5650122	634648	1006411	12712	146811	238282
江　西	Jiangxi	4276102	2964933	519852	791317	1195	93145	166863
山　东	Shandong	2071706	1906742	41623	123341	3875	48896	57531
河　南	Henan	9190906	6575998	1069522	1545386	2890	344806	469807
湖　北	Hubei	6306857	4601350	682789	1022718	4399	171082	248330
湖　南	Hunan	7775246	5455004	916167	1404075	10948	245125	339225
广　东	Guangdong	5902777	5220493	286018	396266	11180	159758	166882
广　西	Guangxi	4140495	3045189	504687	590619	4909	106362	183022
海　南	Hainan	2396133	2007722	179995	208416	762	23124	47369
重　庆	Chongqing	6966717	5194912	820519	951286	40945	190192	285366
四　川	Sichuan	7980019	5676612	913903	1389504	6525	212381	322147
贵　州	Guizhou	6864187	5008427	595033	1260727	6749	369303	291854
云　南	Yunnan	10578741	7078093	649040	2851608	251	549256	264353
西　藏	Tibet	544868	391346	71798	81724		15913	39433
陕　西	Shaanxi	7051598	5822931	496257	732410	3067	211297	171103
甘　肃	Gansu	2401467	1864752	251978	284737	3318	54116	81722
青　海	Qinghai	982305	819827	75769	86709	137	12471	29403
宁　夏	Ningxia	1089442	908684	83670	97088	21393	12773	33272
新　疆	Xinjiang	5622283	5214522	125698	282063	3568	76064	75877

单位：万元
Unit: 10000 yuan

财务费用 Financial Expenses	#利息支出 Interest Expenses	营业利润 Operating Profits	利润总额 Total Profits	应交所得税 Income Tax Payable	应付职工薪酬 Payables to Employees	应交增值税 VAT Payable
-272444	**825651**	**14231477**	**15220005**	**3746547**	**6112998**	**6858539**
259607	307869	734688	788402	181999	381730	217494
-711	19551	59967	61754	39189	59940	76520
-28479	1982	418386	419841	105898	196730	206159
-24627	3221	277986	282677	72730	119680	140516
-7340	113009	214857	231837	59272	109368	240580
-24380	13679	394950	411530	104063	176752	178550
22002	85678	75209	151836	37919	139392	85959
-10056	9748	125367	131756	47040	184425	120864
-5271	8864	228650	233378	45301	30935	33285
-94153	12242	1294450	1344638	329375	319164	586196
-106491	497	1212269	1220528	305924	217791	451523
-36406	25344	532772	539294	150295	178277	189201
-8803	8012	649155	659444	165215	229464	250768
-23448	980	447654	512171	130769	143450	189681
7748	6023	16289	38297	8043	53180	21772
-4375	55189	749615	776334	199349	468083	416591
-27496	21352	568208	605179	144397	330082	282569
-22222	19202	862636	897370	230634	298253	423498
40645	39512	60407	141463	23133	150465	130931
-13449	5294	325337	341615	87033	189793	180609
-17589	302	179097	183862	40587	49025	62577
-22057	3272	536247	558224	125501	285077	321132
-31154	7673	653531	915431	238966	316013	436522
-845	11005	612479	633138	169003	350343	314587
-77795	13302	2157027	2242220	500634	519806	579430
-4041		31041	32826	3061	40432	255208
2388	5183	359326	373546	92912	206689	195004
-6004	512	159236	160402	38079	234364	84940
-8818	534	62425	61972	11420	24109	66003
-5435	18	83792	85732	14676	33966	53012
6611	26602	148424	183308	44131	76220	66858

集体企业
Collective-owned Enterprises

地 区	Region	主营业务收入 Revenue from Principal Business	主营业务成本 Cost of Principal Business	主营业务税金及附加 Taxes and Other Charges on Principal Business	主营业务利润 Profits from Principal Business	其他业务利润 Profits from Other Business	销售费用 Selling Expenses	管理费用 Administrative Expenses
全 国	**National Total**	**7536723**	**7005779**	**23871**	**507073**	**41557**	**203700**	**161536**
北 京	Beijing	601600	593110	166	8324	17228	3429	8050
天 津	Tianjin	76467	74858	106	1503	660	932	1778
河 北	Hebei	138534	130955	447	7132	8673	3563	4263
山 西	Shanxi	620318	526001	2344	91973	7996	74081	19649
内蒙古	Inner Mongolia	148652	136758	972	10922		4565	4112
辽 宁	Liaoning	156840	139027	443	17370	158	737	16584
吉 林	Jilin	2023	1914	66	43			43
黑龙江	Heilongjiang	50257	46491	62	3704		900	1142
上 海	Shanghai	55836	51988	119	3729	173	1313	1422
江 苏	Jiangsu	501206	437345	2574	61287	322	6786	8579
浙 江	Zhejiang	74169	68402	194	5573	342	2346	1638
安 徽	Anhui	53917	50705	52	3160		1040	720
福 建	Fujian	268718	253236	800	14682	780	9232	5193
江 西	Jiangxi	38641	34567	387	3687	464	2032	1125
山 东	Shandong	1042519	956360	7370	78789	308	16313	25567
河 南	Henan	1024976	976596	3734	44646		9193	7802
湖 北	Hubei	149776	142822	198	6756		1971	3420
湖 南	Hunan	108111	102881	219	5011		1399	1968
广 东	Guangdong	389763	357285	1056	31422	1104	11310	8394
广 西	Guangxi	630989	608993	1080	20916	2961	15038	7750
海 南	Hainan							
重 庆	Chongqing	166390	157874	320	8196	248	2898	3545
四 川	Sichuan	716375	675128	447	40800	9	10354	12885
贵 州	Guizhou	77956	66801	303	10852	2	4159	4739
云 南	Yunnan	152845	142834	73	9938		4357	3136
西 藏	Tibet							
陕 西	Shaanxi	129362	123391	248	5723		2090	2657
甘 肃	Gansu	45124	41587	28	3509		1957	831
青 海	Qinghai	4721	4118	5	598		205	363
宁 夏	Ningxia							
新 疆	Xinjiang	110638	103752	58	6828	129	11500	4181

3-4-3 Continued 2

单位：万元
Unit: 10000 yuan

财务费用 Financial Expenses	#利息支出 Interest Expenses	营业利润 Operating Profits	利润总额 Total Profits	应交所得税 Income Tax Payable	应付职工薪酬 Payables to Employees	应交增值税 VAT Payable
52683	**37179**	**127665**	**149397**	**17247**	**109678**	**80052**
11619	12525	5047	5457	320	6121	10414
196	75	-5619	-5657	170	1199	1070
5592	5832	11644	11418	194	1308	1048
1440	1167	-1322	3582	1219	20530	16904
185	120	2060	2060	424	323	748
2069	28	-1604	2140	8	4694	654
					40	
583	536	1227	1226	3	1017	55
384		1095	1135	284	1533	611
3739	1222	39097	37829	2800	5443	4191
537	606	1663	2005	341	1762	604
116	73	1284	1606	34	994	274
802	494	292	2253	179	3940	1291
52	39	480	511	43	2544	170
7783	5635	30494	30839	4605	17062	16487
1548	172	25451	25930	4044	5049	17248
1034	1187	1709	1730	26	3190	389
1025		619	562	69	1442	251
872	695	12677	12546	785	8168	2657
660	80	1892	3161	627	4459	1342
899	273	572	1185	258	1642	1097
7958	2810	15784	5448	597	8392	1441
1620	1431	390	267	39	1521	379
1378	1386	1224	1322	20	3585	159
173	266	429	131	144	1275	474
93	83	846	861		300	44
20		13	13	4	30	
306	444	-19779	-163	10	2115	50

股份合作企业
Cooperative Enterprises

地区	Region	主营业务收入 Revenue from Principal Business	主营业务成本 Cost of Principal Business	主营业务税金及附加 Taxes and Other Charges on Principal Business	主营业务利润 Profits from Principal Business	其他业务利润 Profits from Other Business	销售费用 Selling Expenses	管理费用 Administr-ative Expenses
全国	**National Total**	**2198425**	**2111994**	**3971**	**82460**	**3089**	**39939**	**21480**
北京	Beijing	131630	125925	117	5588	511	2706	3340
天津	Tianjin	16037	14764	25	1248		731	374
河北	Hebei	9452	9019	24	409	28	67	344
山西	Shanxi	573	472	1	100		55	35
内蒙古	Inner Mongolia							
辽宁	Liaoning	24992	22884	465	1643		1367	268
吉林	Jilin							
黑龙江	Heilongjiang							
上海	Shanghai	19146	18078	20	1048	13	362	517
江苏	Jiangsu	1171082	1159035	44	12003	1052	10088	2415
浙江	Zhejiang	80321	74662	146	5513	7	2031	1356
安徽	Anhui	81250	80030	119	1101		412	409
福建	Fujian	12037	11891	8	138		31	75
江西	Jiangxi	3055	2786	40	229		300	
山东	Shandong	37202	35181	100	1921		505	378
河南	Henan	5333	5010	5	318	64	243	169
湖北	Hubei	23720	19360	168	4192		1235	827
湖南	Hunan							
广东	Guangdong	124700	114953	364	9383	1234	3575	4310
广西	Guangxi	3637	3454	5	178		178	105
海南	Hainan							
重庆	Chongqing	364052	330784	2202	31066	180	13650	4615
四川	Sichuan	17780	15873	33	1874		1658	148
贵州	Guizhou							
云南	Yunnan	7641	6934	5	702		199	354
西藏	Tibet							
陕西	Shaanxi	24135	22104	61	1970		57	776
甘肃	Gansu	29694	28591	15	1088		371	434
青海	Qinghai	1409	1350		59		25	4
宁夏	Ningxia							
新疆	Xinjiang	9547	8854	4	689		93	227

3-4-3 Continued 3

单位：万元
Unit: 10000 yuan

财务费用 Financial Expenses		营业利润 Operating Profits	利润总额 Total Profits	应交所得税 Income Tax Payable	应付职工薪酬 Payables to Employees	应交增值税 VAT Payable
	#利息支出 Interest Expenses					
6386	**4686**	**19801**	**20373**	**2563**	**15658**	**8255**
1763	1542	-1579	-1545	55	1611	871
131	246	12	12	10	537	203
1		-2	26		160	10
		9	9	2	48	13
8		1	8	3	339	77
44	47	125	129	21	281	153
78	1023	2643	2624	705	1816	356
191	168	1934	1933	219	1406	737
129		164	274	99	798	130
26		5	5		114	
		-71	-31		139	
99	47	1231	1258	207	275	301
17	17	-47	-47		363	46
205	116	1544	2009	78	721	173
441	424	2031	2022	436	3765	1217
5	5	-2	-2		72	1
2469	552	10527	10304	644	1425	3004
31	9	38	-49		467	155
2	2	165	190		308	48
306	290	831	960	82	523	496
245	1	39	39	1	215	109
28	28		3	1	19	155
167	169	203	242		256	

联营企业
Joint Ownership Enterprises

地区	Region	主营业务收入 Revenue from Principal Business	主营业务成本 Cost of Principal Business	主营业务税金及附加 Taxes and Other Charges on Principal Business	主营业务利润 Profits from Principal Business	其他业务利润 Profits from Other Business	销售费用 Selling Expenses	管理费用 Administr-ative Expenses
全国	**National Total**	**271158**	**241992**	**702**	**28464**	**1253**	**15436**	**3959**
北京	Beijing	22623	21603	39	981	21	375	520
天津	Tianjin							
河北	Hebei							
山西	Shanxi	5221	5120	8	93		121	206
内蒙古	Inner Mongolia							
辽宁	Liaoning	2068	1891	12	165		21	22
吉林	Jilin							
黑龙江	Heilongjiang							
上海	Shanghai	135990	119729	110	16151		12909	742
江苏	Jiangsu							
浙江	Zhejiang							
安徽	Anhui	6038	5783	1	254		78	48
福建	Fujian							
江西	Jiangxi							
山东	Shandong	9528	8345	3	1180	1180	223	201
河南	Henan							
湖北	Hubei							
湖南	Hunan							
广东	Guangdong	84605	74826	527	9252	52	1660	2026
广西	Guangxi							
海南	Hainan							
重庆	Chongqing							
四川	Sichuan							
贵州	Guizhou							
云南	Yunnan							
西藏	Tibet							
陕西	Shaanxi							
甘肃	Gansu							
青海	Qinghai							
宁夏	Ningxia							
新疆	Xinjiang	5085	4695	2	388		49	194

3-4-3 Continued 4

单位：万元
Unit: 10000 yuan

财务费用 Financial Expenses	#利息支出 Interest Expenses	营业利润 Operating Profits	利润总额 Total Profits	应交所得税 Income Tax Payable	应付职工薪酬 Payables to Employees	应交增值税 VAT Payablc
2110	**773**	**5910**	**5651**	**1048**	**5480**	**5149**
30	53	23	16	8	500	858
	1	-233	-233		24	1
20	4	102	102		40	11
1224		1279	1279	45	1649	898
7		121	121		60	
721	706	36	36		143	1961
104	5	4441	4189	995	2980	1385
4	4	141	141		84	35

有限责任公司
Limited Liability Corporations

地区	Region	主营业务收入 Revenue from Principal Business	主营业务成本 Cost of Principal Business	主营业务税金及附加 Taxes and Other Charges on Principal Business	主营业务利润 Profits from Principal Business	其他业务利润 Profits from Other Business	销售费用 Selling Expenses	管理费用 Administr-ative Expenses
全国	**National Total**	**1963132330**	**1872787454**	**5648354**	**84696522**	**2753660**	**36338424**	**16655367**
北京	Beijing	226998808	216754195	254696	9989917	745895	4582329	2437727
天津	Tianjin	152180005	149059766	171508	2948731	120282	1060507	533458
河北	Hebei	30933859	29590963	30161	1312735	17662	576693	195476
山西	Shanxi	42726602	41371801	82283	1272518	105215	630219	407453
内蒙古	Inner Mongolia	14056112	13174924	43292	837896	79885	378180	150842
辽宁	Liaoning	41189543	39936252	40527	1212764	101903	589695	253363
吉林	Jilin	7135933	6602932	15852	517149	11996	338976	98855
黑龙江	Heilongjiang	13702129	13214588	17959	469582	7908	259137	132643
上海	Shanghai	232754941	227454303	486499	4814139	231661	2200245	1069022
江苏	Jiangsu	133764242	127448447	160510	6155285	240111	3042533	1082713
浙江	Zhejiang	158069099	152716414	273440	5079245	226575	2230524	1046692
安徽	Anhui	31870379	29815532	133317	1921530	27187	905935	303900
福建	Fujian	80118377	76796476	113356	3208545	58487	1181837	737560
江西	Jiangxi	14021419	12678512	50313	1292594	12426	696550	275663
山东	Shandong	98315875	92001124	1119616	5195135	92359	1899570	1168217
河南	Henan	52624080	48694033	186616	3743431	84344	1173407	719341
湖北	Hubei	48725897	46316501	91494	2317902	22273	930767	489942
湖南	Hunan	16614952	15372419	51079	1191454	16051	697967	267426
广东	Guangdong	305059206	286749071	1613496	16696639	349614	7554308	3193495
广西	Guangxi	27657662	26657550	42529	957583	22763	440448	241654
海南	Hainan	11095164	10254463	8675	832026	11977	446280	60548
重庆	Chongqing	36987861	34981158	144584	1862119	42649	754385	366080
四川	Sichuan	35342684	33438247	96266	1808171	53787	939267	326348
贵州	Guizhou	19022225	14888526	113544	4020155	8778	484381	227331
云南	Yunnan	33757453	32650375	36747	1070331	22342	498180	202643
西藏	Tibet	228980	146522	7946	74512	62	67009	8216
陕西	Shaanxi	47422928	45199649	99391	2123888	31357	969818	313892
甘肃	Gansu	12725206	12176275	11942	536989	3715	264171	78826
青海	Qinghai	4211935	4105685	4621	101629	3667	67371	21844
宁夏	Ningxia	1316514	1275192	1739	39583	3030	25116	11210
新疆	Xinjiang	32502261	31265559	144356	1092346	-2301	452619	232987

3-4-3 Continued 5

单位：万元
Unit: 10000 yuan

财务费用 Financial Expenses	#利息支出 Interest Expenses	营业利润 Operating Profits	利润总额 Total Profits	应交所得税 Income Tax Payable	应付职工薪酬 Payables to Employees	应交增值税 VAT Payable
9088332	**8742024**	**28335382**	**29972510**	**7007316**	**16285369**	**15887147**
1243594	1870816	3084706	3233413	1137236	2793400	1335550
1246182	1149168	527594	672230	261112	473608	632803
153270	74626	455819	455054	80526	175108	180319
333911	291151	-127788	4301	70674	358906	1365024
84747	58338	-52780	-41535	39493	97517	379640
196833	137738	206402	204459	65502	197192	183310
62406	55906	41876	156387	35061	118622	68643
129996	160704	92755	137809	25261	94198	32408
513310	684999	2017529	2135605	455139	1102049	504581
651386	465816	2106063	2195865	478245	1029479	1060705
814424	697938	1902585	2175663	491695	1178429	1709989
97930	86776	589196	642460	108174	334454	395916
477555	360039	1071882	1289110	156968	567849	306643
60224	62223	302635	337110	68750	336186	273798
381436	235109	1986923	2069078	433070	1048704	981905
342806	169042	1582000	1588036	249686	541175	501883
160458	120396	790665	785229	190597	454162	362354
77956	80181	185545	191915	33788	216933	210683
821602	757347	5728396	5790230	1315102	2661551	2841086
164447	202252	193152	209487	43306	188303	148983
185955	151187	165496	182449	51223	88162	53787
155965	118016	800373	883232	119476	293616	305853
194304	174120	-135521	-125697	70944	467227	222338
26062	102880	3319863	3322945	804173	169096	838120
215788	218458	244256	282089	69744	199999	108997
97	311	-42	5254	1086	13198	27798
113906	76204	1047880	938374	88988	280684	414555
28864	25246	163565	159618	14025	147974	75275
7436	6170	15392	14808	2756	19890	10102
18409	17342	-11767	-10994	1832	11899	5813
127073	131524	40731	88526	43683	625799	348286

股份有限公司
Share-holding Corporations Ltd.

地区	Region	主营业务收入 Revenue from Principal Business	主营业务成本 Cost of Principal Business	主营业务税金及附加 Taxes and Other Charges on Principal Business	主营业务利润 Profits from Principal Business	其他业务利润 Profits from Other Business	销售费用 Selling Expenses	管理费用 Administr-ative Expenses
全国	**National Total**	**377367752**	**357847764**	**612953**	**18907035**	**827313**	**9982368**	**3567261**
北京	Beijing	25260780	23975831	28422	1256527	170930	588883	321769
天津	Tianjin	5120544	5002472	2377	115695	1409	52705	21926
河北	Hebei	2088443	1984840	4967	98636	4397	73354	35868
山西	Shanxi	2759716	2547074	3056	209586	4477	161867	25258
内蒙古	Inner Mongolia	3536196	3382826	2260	151110	872	50890	17160
辽宁	Liaoning	39591507	39193882	16115	381510	4635	281672	75718
吉林	Jilin	3907547	3735781	4294	167472	3020	121366	14423
黑龙江	Heilongjiang	4068478	3811235	6872	250371	27806	191027	31442
上海	Shanghai	22051668	20733256	25891	1292521	31509	534782	355842
江苏	Jiangsu	37046401	34809041	49074	2188286	86701	1414824	338246
浙江	Zhejiang	34340822	32640452	35762	1664608	87194	922822	375752
安徽	Anhui	8258047	7361991	11351	884705	11960	264187	110636
福建	Fujian	31229552	30091918	33412	1104222	79696	654079	141417
江西	Jiangxi	4125366	3802128	6351	316887	4827	172603	45470
山东	Shandong	16156006	14959695	40096	1156215	106339	787613	227552
河南	Henan	8391290	7733036	27421	630833	10658	251145	111573
湖北	Hubei	18216322	16919842	34968	1261512	9851	702106	248714
湖南	Hunan	2015617	1770905	7929	236783	13853	86119	49201
广东	Guangdong	42311608	39593848	123384	2594376	47506	1057685	693991
广西	Guangxi	2339707	2155295	4899	179513	4006	110677	25298
海南	Hainan	439747	399164	1260	39323	508	12073	10311
重庆	Chongqing	3478727	3240717	11764	226246	15455	90379	37563
四川	Sichuan	3746680	3336414	7772	402494	22420	261180	30508
贵州	Guizhou	1567798	1388869	3617	175312	481	42774	12069
云南	Yunnan	5934937	5586121	8324	340492	10239	172469	46906
西藏	Tibet							
陕西	Shaanxi	13915638	13367737	20640	527261	16981	334647	23505
甘肃	Gansu	13443507	13321708	3628	118171	2880	58134	58563
青海	Qinghai	2276253	1911337	76086	288830	95	87715	22118
宁夏	Ningxia	3500727	3421803	1526	77398	6280	83536	6704
新疆	Xinjiang	16248121	15668546	9435	570140	40328	359055	51758

单位：万元
Unit: 10000 yuan

财务费用 Financial Expenses	#利息支出 Interest Expenses	营业利润 Operating Profits	利润总额 Total Profits	应交所得税 Income Tax Payable	应付职工薪酬 Payables to Employees	应交增值税 VAT Payable
1686818	**1916938**	**7210513**	**7506637**	**942715**	**4262988**	**3846374**
306691	519122	620716	583153	-3558	342318	185093
4511	2052	41397	47197	10546	21046	7162
1937	49705	39388	53235	3503	46428	59598
6960	3133	44523	47918	7796	10918	23933
11320	7964	83853	96356	4797	10788	3115
67318	64803	-64045	-57181	14535	138017	108390
8845	5988	32274	46812	4915	36229	48859
9931	3385	19967	8482	8808	124167	210795
83189	26597	788956	801840	156052	360406	98523
109899	88825	684444	706852	179238	294872	274633
166722	281881	1317241	1370248	119774	402596	205335
58693	40467	318634	331961	14787	126265	83787
118532	145522	593217	582548	88062	245871	96541
5539	3028	107140	97537	21392	73918	50373
59374	49849	112740	114999	47740	350643	663716
35974	6637	211914	208223	26536	119744	61313
80816	80311	243572	292507	72530	326051	121973
13733	12452	98148	101569	13036	45199	9860
254084	176102	919551	1181734	103762	676388	306197
9552	5325	21192	23859	850	44726	112720
-1243	6341	17856	18325	4408	6045	5035
12183	9320	104964	111138	5378	43974	52675
15353	4522	66310	67762	9092	72566	59346
19005	11931	60190	57099	673	9744	10532
22116	17335	101680	61854	7281	52476	28916
59942	146695	92900	67551	4308	103422	195002
34910	37382	-29261	-20795	3418	31903	464230
-451	867	194449	147872	180	30285	12366
1506	1094	-10606	-11320	1883	32069	63775
109877	108303	377209	367302	10993	83914	222580

私营企业
Private Enterprises

地 区	Region	主营业务收入 Revenue from Principal Business	主营业务成本 Cost of Principal Business	主营业务税金及附加 Taxes and Other Charges on Principal Business	主营业务利润 Profits from Principal Business	其他业务利润 Profits from Other Business	销售费用 Selling Expenses	管理费用 Administrative Expenses
全 国	**National Total**	**1249638179**	**1186665738**	**1892433**	**61080008**	**1636661**	**26593938**	**15232912**
北 京	Beijing	47505889	44151801	65698	3288390	161759	1728981	1143992
天 津	Tianjin	54940463	53486617	50944	1402902	24620	923455	371910
河 北	Hebei	22968177	21811680	26877	1129620	43131	529504	248196
山 西	Shanxi	12219315	11482626	15629	721060	25524	384739	200872
内蒙古	Inner Mongolia	4722990	4234646	18366	469978	20199	388554	73489
辽 宁	Liaoning	26356993	25335337	23961	997695	54239	511193	292120
吉 林	Jilin	3279854	2915126	13268	351460	5002	185405	82566
黑龙江	Heilongjiang	2928637	2704299	11900	212438	7355	73475	47193
上 海	Shanghai	196130429	191152267	77717	4900445	210294	2120182	1125934
江 苏	Jiangsu	156259658	149000956	210965	7047737	180703	2481617	1577002
浙 江	Zhejiang	195716354	187401040	157920	8157394	191618	4008808	2056291
安 徽	Anhui	14353568	13180992	35319	1137257	28152	609311	247676
福 建	Fujian	69741322	66113060	97661	3530601	27857	1193940	763022
江 西	Jiangxi	5180913	4544705	24123	612085	5273	355901	108466
山 东	Shandong	92204129	86418712	263999	5521418	67507	1849047	1094364
河 南	Henan	15801650	13918097	102797	1780756	32820	465491	309656
湖 北	Hubei	17554076	16120478	78800	1354798	34248	463145	308719
湖 南	Hunan	19928754	18060344	171151	1697259	28740	634589	372382
广 东	Guangdong	195283947	184936053	208292	10139602	325015	4702306	3361648
广 西	Guangxi	13066502	12434522	17687	614293	15223	311427	178733
海 南	Hainan	1018698	944872	1753	72073	4834	32263	12470
重 庆	Chongqing	19693500	18048527	66397	1578576	21988	574221	309458
四 川	Sichuan	18421451	16737366	69716	1614369	46083	855030	327994
贵 州	Guizhou	5460569	5012822	23222	424525	4141	187204	94041
云 南	Yunnan	9690323	9005961	15232	669130	27815	352142	165446
西 藏	Tibet	42686	23238	392	19056		2708	1728
陕 西	Shaanxi	7123313	6720403	13837	389073	8873	169679	79047
甘 肃	Gansu	5658592	5291072	8065	359455	16957	145849	74654
青 海	Qinghai	1467201	1386386	972	79843	612	16609	13036
宁 夏	Ningxia	4567259	4419578	2767	144914	3061	63279	28457
新 疆	Xinjiang	10350967	9672155	17006	661806	13018	273885	162350

单位：万元
Unit: 10000 yuan

财务费用 Financial Expenses	#利息支出 Interest Expenses	营业利润 Operating Profits	利润总额 Total Profits	应交所得税 Income Tax Payable	应付职工薪酬 Payables to Employees	应交增值税 VAT Payable
6421895	**4272407**	**15666664**	**16191257**	**2755680**	**12113083**	**9089952**
199855	545484	522939	535866	123853	852878	429172
307282	164806	-21596	48135	61695	254708	396918
126213	75586	262721	271864	64700	778926	216757
110980	77472	168989	166967	27090	279930	109197
60092	44634	-36979	18836	7917	40721	48892
109883	48570	111800	95244	29381	164315	82744
18149	13013	82041	82440	13518	65005	34612
8295	6658	94007	96013	9108	23122	52766
661223	504487	854795	996504	216999	700875	686569
708059	288946	2483379	2463833	451747	999909	1133474
1071462	888428	1723323	1890562	393566	1711219	1562003
57938	27136	257181	307600	41860	212615	200008
432643	250405	1259492	1256081	139983	511581	290812
21336	8333	134261	144675	10280	96309	105460
644294	233763	2166944	2202832	329434	879035	713256
126618	33680	890168	884815	94601	250318	196812
160362	50887	437233	449573	54386	208951	173824
123745	53988	569622	550844	47189	283635	266325
847591	568119	1855786	1852572	372690	2478776	1431538
83409	65303	49331	57568	14548	124106	159716
1201	2714	31294	27765	2692	12979	8818
90715	46539	618289	612831	60560	295736	226467
73268	50696	491384	501180	82168	364926	186259
29379	18754	109972	113952	15889	86373	94526
105911	87076	73346	84413	12274	122839	98238
282	144	14315	14497	1244	2914	2830
20495	12868	100742	100905	16125	71387	42367
53481	26584	79702	78578	7889	99944	28178
5539	2998	42550	25846	696	9978	5475
100714	32594	-43115	-38499	2155	19536	11376
61481	41742	282747	296965	49443	109537	94563

其他企业
Other Enterprises

地　区	Region	主营业务收　入 Revenue from Principal Business	主营业务成　本 Cost of Principal Business	主营业务税金及附加 Taxes and Other Charges on Principal Business	主营业务利　润 Profits from Principal Business	其他业务利　润 Profits from Other Business	销售费用 Selling Expenses	管理费用 Administr-ative Expenses
全　国	**National Total**	**7204512**	**6407374**	**50687**	**746451**	**1701**	**171627**	**119476**
北　京	Beijing							
天　津	Tianjin							
河　北	Hebei	66343	58596	50	7697		3329	1129
山　西	Shanxi	69508	59522	161	9825		7501	1139
内蒙古	Inner Mongolia	4631	4779	2	-150			59
辽　宁	Liaoning	40187	36053	11	4123	53	808	897
吉　林	Jilin						181	211
黑龙江	Heilongjiang	61238	57358	2308	1572		117	66
上　海	Shanghai	1202972	1177023	294	25655		13538	1103
江　苏	Jiangsu	2099935	1886604	8489	204842	154	52163	30427
浙　江	Zhejiang	353437	347668	143	5626	1	878	1913
安　徽	Anhui	142045	133146	181	8718		1724	1526
福　建	Fujian	48039	40564	470	7005		2336	1286
江　西	Jiangxi	16525	15265	142	1118		107	135
山　东	Shandong	921253	775181	8580	137492	402	23152	18843
河　南	Henan	195604	158853	6955	29796		6246	5552
湖　北	Hubei	572047	498717	8914	64416		13378	13449
湖　南	Hunan	71034	61954	679	8401	223	2516	2002
广　东	Guangdong	467332	360968	2663	103701	15	17119	20520
广　西	Guangxi	40732	36543	79	4110		1284	864
海　南	Hainan							
重　庆	Chongqing	142919	115837	7818	19264	818	3486	4893
四　川	Sichuan	100356	83883	564	15909		2774	2422
贵　州	Guizhou	7146	6743	7	396		30	46
云　南	Yunnan	114122	103097	24	11001	11	1415	970
西　藏	Tibet							
陕　西	Shaanxi	186135	164150	1895	20090	24	3966	5373
甘　肃	Gansu	3665	3237	1	427		56	183
青　海	Qinghai							
宁　夏	Ningxia							
新　疆	Xinjiang	277307	221632	257	55418		13524	4468

单位：万元
Unit: 10000 yuan

财务费用 Financial Expenses	#利息支出 Interest Expenses	营业利润 Operating Profits	利润总额 Total Profits	应交所得税 Income Tax Payable	应付职工薪酬 Payables to Employees	应交增值税 VAT Payable
29948	**9618**	**424346**	**404505**	**27175**	**125489**	**70026**
434	413	2808	2728	71	3099	1336
97	23	1088	1105	121	812	87
-1		-208	-212		63	
350		2062	1954	6	338	7
-1		-391	79		109	
28		1404	1404		169	799
544	515	10423	10426	2615	544	3787
8236	1602	112020	107537	10207	47121	17871
437	372	2404	2715	85	2559	818
125	12	5345	5172	527	2386	242
389	169	2633	1807	80	437	34
55	37	820	820		434	1
6588	2160	88739	85667	4836	15704	26244
3268	370	14447	14017	752	4282	1847
4919	2406	32468	32645	1734	11324	5341
570	51	3155	2386	5	1414	351
1190	376	69698	69456	5078	7050	5777
3	1	1958	1517		1764	5
181	9	10730	8657	419	3863	3559
435	246	7344	7369	93	3458	297
1		321	321		55	98
40	17	8559	8629	140	1581	52
1097	507	9831	8661	309	3728	1444
		188	188		77	3
963	332	36499	29457	96	13118	26

港、澳、台商投资企业
Enterprises with Funds from Hong Kong, Macao and Taiwan

地　区	Region	主营业务收入 Revenue from Principal Business	主营业务成本 Cost of Principal Business	主营业务税金及附加 Taxes and Other Charges on Principal Business	主营业务利润 Profits from Principal Business	其他业务利润 Profits from Other Business	销售费用 Selling Expenses	管理费用 Administrative Expenses
全　国	**National Total**	**219114056**	**196168028**	**465144**	**22480884**	**724044**	**12042802**	**6373732**
北　京	Beijing	48695098	44768516	59557	3867025	208449	2180678	1476502
天　津	Tianjin	12686547	11942813	36298	707436	14527	456043	106878
河　北	Hebei	322816	311069	932	10815	557	9049	8971
山　西	Shanxi	1287308	1260927	962	25419	35	13344	4330
内蒙古	Inner Mongolia	63070	61056	151	1863		966	345
辽　宁	Liaoning	562270	484903	1512	75855	33	26847	15827
吉　林	Jilin	84687	81360	361	2966		1600	84
黑龙江	Heilongjiang	151124	146625	44	4455	124	2492	1596
上　海	Shanghai	76198163	65789465	153147	10255551	305289	5792159	2505626
江　苏	Jiangsu	11886568	9760089	41410	2085069	36205	701666	817061
浙　江	Zhejiang	7416312	6871461	10997	533854	12964	292477	131886
安　徽	Anhui	2278587	2172953	2411	103223	6	71511	7647
福　建	Fujian	5752588	5341982	9893	400713	14090	173303	124561
江　西	Jiangxi	107676	95729	267	11680	9027	4423	3575
山　东	Shandong	4327675	4138244	3860	185571	33681	82313	69326
河　南	Henan	2467120	2439344	1705	26071	116	2016	4464
湖　北	Hubei	2893432	2559313	7939	326180	9958	134664	91007
湖　南	Hunan	269857	176932	7038	85887		42391	8274
广　东	Guangdong	30692193	27181525	111042	3399626	61548	1869159	926800
广　西	Guangxi	147780	146414	128	1238		1285	711
海　南	Hainan	1099064	1077025	814	21225	4960	26258	5067
重　庆	Chongqing	3856071	3703583	2450	150038	2813	43025	9916
四　川	Sichuan	3853752	3804481	1959	47312	6823	23404	11097
贵　州	Guizhou	271511	240062	7565	23884	2114	4584	16435
云　南	Yunnan	386503	362916	466	23121	724	9780	6849
西　藏	Tibet	145637	98948	1013	45676		35771	949
陕　西	Shaanxi	158143	119552	556	38035		24625	9484
甘　肃	Gansu	16691	13567	66	3058		2420	
青　海	Qinghai	923660	919074	303	4283		7190	1601
宁　夏	Ningxia							
新　疆	Xinjiang	112152	98100	298	13754		7359	6863

单位：万元
Unit: 10000 yuan

财务费用 Financial Expenses	#利息支出 Interest Expenses	营业利润 Operating Profits	利润总额 Total Profits	应交所得税 Income Tax Payable	应付职工薪酬 Payables to Employees	应交增值税 VAT Payable
356616	**620382**	**5782596**	**6410944**	**1482199**	**4791819**	**2503269**
29324	181118	630558	801147	201294	1013897	311972
84792	84960	84635	198264	77126	87660	265760
9950	2706	-16407	-14193	271	6258	-35
-1143	803	14288	14170	2774	8435	9066
76		477	499	79	68	420
29602	27637	174456	178192	2585	33329	14686
3		1280	1337	58	216	702
1	3	378	395	502	2340	262
-1236	132407	2966292	3214965	732146	1963813	893432
34926	29925	618602	672952	143669	249946	291600
24430	32028	69037	73031	38785	125857	59360
-6441	-5851	29591	29903	5909	3490	-3683
14703	-7389	153829	155366	37244	84667	51515
460	406	9380	9849	2355	2918	1976
28515	11449	20471	17254	4482	32542	8404
23920	1428	5507	9909	484	2684	3604
30407	18876	66473	69795	14451	35633	27820
-566	24	35788	25615	5726	6138	15279
18238	83446	770566	795938	192320	1003180	493172
646	578	-1399	-2092	61	376	447
2439	23	-10534	-10226	-2203	5311	2638
13872	9960	91696	96115	13733	26690	18263
8969	5413	11927	13074	2843	14315	8953
4115	4083	6845	7061	1082	42418	10495
2423	2542	32869	32974	582	7789	2200
-171		9132	12848	1156	5442	7615
16		4243	4272	549	17754	4804
-1	1	639	651	182	1782	590
1456		-5965	-6054		2910	18
2890	3806	7942	7934	1954	3961	1934

外商投资企业
Foreign Funded Enterprises

地　区	Region	主营业务收入 Revenue from Principal Business	主营业务成本 Cost of Principal Business	主营业务税金及附加 Taxes and Other Charges on Principal Business	主营业务利润 Profits from Principal Business	其他业务利润 Profits from Other Business	销售费用 Selling Expenses	管理费用 Administr-ative Expenses
全　国	**National Total**	**437249915**	**384022435**	**1088090**	**52139390**	**2701163**	**30830671**	**9750408**
北　京	Beijing	73796792	63455363	214249	10127180	887344	5680680	2191320
天　津	Tianjin	9855160	8625724	260769	968667	19869	628286	190728
河　北	Hebei	1725019	1652419	1194	71406		16394	10636
山　西	Shanxi	8189	6869	27	1293	182	2035	222
内蒙古	Inner Mongolia							
辽　宁	Liaoning	1251242	1072401	3221	175620	1511	93421	42136
吉　林	Jilin	1794798	1609065	4125	181608	95	145735	3631
黑龙江	Heilongjiang	1562328	1561348	908	72		1	50
上　海	Shanghai	235162736	204924813	412276	29825647	1015225	17792846	4944194
江　苏	Jiangsu	27678209	23391042	59755	4227412	98013	2168529	882646
浙　江	Zhejiang	19034549	18361295	10115	663139	66524	561079	78497
安　徽	Anhui	2588191	1897604	12541	678046	1268	621493	65610
福　建	Fujian	5727541	5133468	13040	581033	11118	246283	104531
江　西	Jiangxi	339438	310735	694	28009	1348	23336	3290
山　东	Shandong	2158711	2013722	3324	141665	3659	57152	41069
河　南	Henan	344642	323012	686	20944		15108	2769
湖　北	Hubei	9189670	7561134	30870	1597666	28153	1101898	326944
湖　南	Hunan	1766252	1555000	7682	203570		153758	25918
广　东	Guangdong	35240269	32953027	45383	2241859	565236	1357204	894046
广　西	Guangxi	123415	116780	183	6452	129	1150	2435
海　南	Hainan	85700	64626	456	20618	62	11886	9315
重　庆	Chongqing	1124447	997930	1744	124773	37	77350	15053
四　川	Sichuan	850982	717721	2591	130670	1686	34443	-105015
贵　州	Guizhou	52644	39233	256	13155	-1	9837	1064
云　南	Yunnan	284780	243900	1293	39587	767	14850	5504
西　藏	Tibet							
陕　西	Shaanxi	5456318	5392733	614	62971	231	12450	9489
甘　肃	Gansu	10948	8297	52	2599		1749	543
青　海	Qinghai	4388	3199	25	1164		544	395
宁　夏	Ningxia							
新　疆	Xinjiang	32557	29975	17	2565	-1293	1174	3388

单位：万元

Unit: 10000 yuan

财务费用 Financial Expenses	#利息支出 Interest Expenses	营业利润 Operating Profits	利润总额 Total Profits	应交所得税 Income Tax Payable	应付职工薪酬 Payables to Employees	应交增值税 VAT Payable
290111	**980014**	**15835927**	**16440780**	**3708604**	**10074712**	**5778271**
-194838	280425	4596240	4694764	941168	2322300	1463125
-20	21908	256779	271480	51797	206619	506155
1743	2035	43450	42755	652	11041	7116
17	17	-798	-764		773	206
3628	396	40224	35114	13586	30385	20577
-171		32098	31500	11553	11584	24429
6		20	20	2		-1830
196794	424971	7964288	8408797	2016562	5384267	2501559
55970	14821	1312321	1364421	320798	668067	505585
58895	62423	66353	77682	27694	110575	51695
-4398	2955	-4519	-37721	-6751	93288	85818
7099	9194	218289	207007	55274	62402	81789
1041	1227	2598	3208	519	7556	3392
6524	794	49646	48910	14087	26357	15266
189	28	2643	1911	436	5078	2682
-908	2438	223286	249169	62243	181204	173003
1824	130	23776	23725	6456	10906	36608
82188	93210	760314	819021	173717	872253	258186
2700	2488	275	270	205	1049	344
-9310	9829	11778	11722	759	8789	4271
1165	11	30439	42472	5848	14253	3578
16082	17858	195376	116345	2524	22111	14878
27	1	2226	2223	1459	2599	1930
393	180	17489	20521	5158	7709	14732
63446	32663	-7172	9432	2638	7735	2666
8	8	299	126	158	1118	465
12		212	241		410	
5	4	-2003	-3571	63	4284	46

3-4-4 各地区限额以上批发业企业损益及分配(按国民经济行业分)

农、林、牧产品批发

Wholesale of Agricultural, Forestry and Livestock Products

地区	Region	主营业务收入 Revenue from Principal Business	主营业务成本 Cost of Principal Business	主营业务税金及附加 Taxes and Other Charges on Principal Business	主营业务利润 Profits from Principal Business	其他业务利润 Profits from Other Business	销售费用 Selling Expenses	管理费用 Administr-ative Expenses
全国	**National Total**	**86445990**	**82030858**	**194146**	**4220986**	**177841**	**1774752**	**1487610**
北京	Beijing	11040200	10584288	8850	447062	70029	136238	221408
天津	Tianjin	2066296	2019937	1052	45307	262	51929	20148
河北	Hebei	1422241	1354864	1113	66264	5524	31552	22959
山西	Shanxi	247960	224445	128	23387	409	12585	8773
内蒙古	Inner Mongolia	1132229	1235485	7955	-111211	10980	69745	33874
辽宁	Liaoning	3671094	3484525	2632	183937	2082	118986	41897
吉林	Jilin	2191964	2299324	2661	-110021	7169	123444	42576
黑龙江	Heilongjiang	2384830	2268481	6288	110061	2091	99782	46716
上海	Shanghai	7094598	6998096	7989	88513	2129	51106	66409
江苏	Jiangsu	7714583	7130553	22500	561530	2226	147120	121832
浙江	Zhejiang	2336661	2261633	3211	71817	5903	44240	44613
安徽	Anhui	1286452	1183164	2386	100902	8747	44509	40545
福建	Fujian	2969996	2833183	6690	130123	1216	58586	48862
江西	Jiangxi	405083	383662	995	20426	1191	13990	17652
山东	Shandong	5851841	5365687	23353	462801	6117	138458	105385
河南	Henan	4418299	3801222	43713	573364	5339	119453	129572
湖北	Hubei	4227338	4024050	15873	187415	223	55329	49726
湖南	Hunan	1495064	1340101	11875	143088	14022	59458	49491
广东	Guangdong	10552571	9985637	6284	560650	7459	159423	150028
广西	Guangxi	1262013	1187111	3804	71098	2989	23395	16198
海南	Hainan	15086	14802	1	283		22	139
重庆	Chongqing	874917	792950	4561	77406	644	19213	18250
四川	Sichuan	1151951	1097529	2156	52266	6238	17246	23747
贵州	Guizhou	111846	101046	213	10587	-33	2756	3347
云南	Yunnan	438933	393138	1979	43816	2148	13091	18057
西藏	Tibet	819	754	2	63		10	469
陕西	Shaanxi	525208	490016	847	34345	721	8340	10175
甘肃	Gansu	229492	212444	91	16957		7131	4172
青海	Qinghai	91152	89702	4	1446	47	1893	1146
宁夏	Ningxia	88114	81096	71	6947	25	4195	2105
新疆	Xinjiang	9147159	8791932	4869	350358	11944	141527	127339

Income and Distribution of Enterprises above Designated Size of Wholesale Trade by Region and Sector

单位：万元
Unit: 10000 yuan

财务费用 Financial Expenses	#利息支出 Interest Expenses	营业利润 Operating Profits	利润总额 Total Profits	应交所得税 Income Tax Payable	应付职工薪酬 Payables to Employees	应交增值税 VAT Payable
954480	**1054083**	**1489927**	**2305053**	**233174**	**1471162**	**310209**
186179	245013	362589	416538	49204	148584	33889
43690	42957	-51324	2833	3046	14860	2555
8972	6229	12966	23331	1916	15327	-4842
1908	1246	5394	6261	422	5153	414
33938	112112	-47797	33918	2077	16750	-2713
36312	31230	7779	26051	3235	15721	-13888
61931	109938	-124213	41289	4766	43680	-5193
34973	78732	59087	99774	6123	37833	-395
54453	31725	48054	67066	12556	42644	-1086
42323	17311	215930	259110	32429	99919	51943
40450	32857	-7474	25959	2766	38419	4360
13518	7721	10069	30176	2197	33905	4029
29236	12921	-3785	37970	4858	27729	15840
3825	2644	-12926	6604	376	17791	775
52387	30116	303274	312186	20764	85556	60901
74934	83133	283160	318929	34817	99800	37231
27403	39055	72330	103498	4989	41400	12230
14509	5369	34661	45675	4429	32851	4696
63987	46169	194884	221060	20980	107668	30539
21492	19177	14302	24277	5025	11231	5946
		122	131		99	7
4353	2843	42223	35587	2111	32940	4912
14503	13029	1437	18084	1527	29941	3630
1471	1043	3323	5192	48	2129	-53
4254	3449	10317	16294	246	9560	-742
13		-430	-431		189	
2367	1402	14867	14989	347	6766	211
2885	2743	2998	4724	299	3201	237
221	237	-1442	-1274		1210	39
425	344	334	1026	96	859	-878
77568	73338	39219	108227	11526	447445	65616

食品、饮料及烟草制品批发
Wholesale of Food, Beverages and Tobaccos

地区	Region	主营业务收入 Revenue from Principal Business	主营业务成本 Cost of Principal Business	主营业务税金及附加 Taxes and Other Charges on Principal Business	主营业务利润 Profits from Principal Business	其他业务利润 Profits from Other Business	销售费用 Selling Expenses	管理费用 Administrative Expenses
全国	**National Total**	**396752286**	**321844719**	**18483628**	**56423939**	**2195136**	**20690959**	**11444794**
北京	Beijing	23803398	20497590	353141	2952667	351911	2090184	492369
天津	Tianjin	9108339	7711064	205123	1192152	777689	654126	152219
河北	Hebei	6323602	4777284	660060	886258	12798	237647	220387
山西	Shanxi	4525173	3374583	421242	729348	15010	199350	176566
内蒙古	Inner Mongolia	2746178	2032545	322148	391485	1800	99323	118419
辽宁	Liaoning	6149099	4945234	483021	720844	4920	189790	196712
吉林	Jilin	3082638	2455517	255422	371699	8428	150628	103746
黑龙江	Heilongjiang	4025610	3227782	316632	481196	11366	119899	158735
上海	Shanghai	46321051	40330098	442831	5548122	457361	3514820	1420055
江苏	Jiangsu	23969864	19191205	1192699	3585960	33783	1361958	497135
浙江	Zhejiang	24627646	20020643	1278889	3328114	66470	1331672	610468
安徽	Anhui	10562153	8134527	704914	1722712	8259	622821	306249
福建	Fujian	20327051	17509996	664780	2152275	20788	692274	502142
江西	Jiangxi	5544766	4029204	526675	988887	2816	191879	219457
山东	Shandong	22012407	18236004	1067523	2708880	118303	927639	714152
河南	Henan	15339660	11706282	1112033	2521345	14912	546537	605518
湖北	Hubei	15685881	11938590	751712	2995579	26631	1130798	572516
湖南	Hunan	12124856	9193508	941176	1990172	15598	520276	449889
广东	Guangdong	50528001	43138736	1652594	5736671	95073	2472182	1442006
广西	Guangxi	10745765	9465773	514300	765692	6900	183151	225057
海南	Hainan	2561621	2162012	180229	219380	1180	29330	51471
重庆	Chongqing	13010083	10585229	854937	1569917	50812	405391	400229
四川	Sichuan	15248446	11653505	1004178	2590763	35260	991572	480264
贵州	Guizhou	15336868	9978168	675894	4682806	9451	673101	406475
云南	Yunnan	14085666	10242859	653430	3189377	5110	692985	340892
西藏	Tibet	601680	436227	78320	87133		17176	41495
陕西	Shaanxi	7590267	6039101	503450	1047716	3723	301087	210516
甘肃	Gansu	3199951	2492622	253699	453630	12749	124638	115771
青海	Qinghai	1136654	930508	76581	129565	442	42474	33253
宁夏	Ningxia	1170700	957349	83988	129363	22084	24775	38097
新疆	Xinjiang	5257211	4450974	252007	554230	3509	151476	142534

单位：万元

Unit: 10000 yuan

财务费用 Financial Expenses	#利息支出 Interest Expenses	营业利润 Operating Profits	利润总额 Total Profits	应交所得税 Income Tax Payable	应付职工薪酬 Payables to Employees	应交增值税 VAT Payable
93496	**1048598**	**27055374**	**28065857**	**6236065**	**12115657**	**11394739**
57919	120816	1055395	1070699	221839	821875	512858
-19668	10577	320939	344144	93010	167308	189194
-14547	14038	471108	478871	118834	235137	236096
-19377	2275	378190	386065	99894	151176	179924
-22477	8423	226019	240242	62265	109669	245595
-12602	15605	370401	385431	101332	184268	179147
-8220	6659	148305	148416	38127	136370	94688
16612	32737	198291	203225	53693	188941	126497
7348	123587	1320734	1425548	294761	898973	459819
-62583	35917	1850616	1886343	443229	566345	865742
-42905	80781	1864986	1949313	422334	774313	725031
-24466	49364	905578	895428	212861	365556	416252
49800	42226	1024003	1045721	206725	472347	363468
-18467	6997	613563	672472	162124	170898	209266
48296	33911	1082289	1096613	232516	646386	496968
23733	9227	1355502	1354629	248655	594342	481413
25698	31486	1204036	1212263	276785	591514	409416
36354	72106	1023629	1043237	250031	415859	495038
105073	143918	2160479	2283174	425322	1606206	949840
53011	60832	329684	347868	89340	230841	256282
-17351	452	179943	184740	40805	54868	63810
2175	14019	793385	854000	150072	401419	407793
-2037	22334	1038898	1302928	307629	548699	568657
-61965	9182	3678269	3682999	932014	418576	907054
-20913	54000	2265292	2366299	512412	574653	589206
-4060	1	33043	34509	3149	43359	271030
11139	6834	512106	496855	111212	239762	235187
8917	10062	209660	209162	45151	305829	100417
-7942	678	70824	70569	11433	29126	66123
-3072	541	97352	100059	14613	39007	55250
10072	29013	272854	294035	53898	132035	237678

纺织、服装及家庭用品批发
Wholesale of Textiles, Wearing Apparel and Household Articles

地区	Region	主营业务收入 Revenue from Principal Business	主营业务成本 Cost of Principal Business	主营业务税金及附加 Taxes and Other Charges on Principal Business	主营业务利润 Profits from Principal Business	其他业务利润 Profits from Other Business	销售费用 Selling Expenses	管理费用 Administr-ative Expenses
全国	**National Total**	**365902300**	**323697384**	**814433**	**41390483**	**895206**	**22906244**	**9729998**
北京	Beijing	47050055	42263503	65894	4720658	155484	2933566	1512320
天津	Tianjin	8089713	7221531	17252	850930	8935	420721	127841
河北	Hebei	2217695	2112125	2106	103464	5772	46996	21700
山西	Shanxi	810102	666077	1134	142891	136	105989	14176
内蒙古	Inner Mongolia	281478	237895	471	43112	1404	17885	25690
辽宁	Liaoning	2264876	2060451	4120	200305	5630	115820	63298
吉林	Jilin	357671	327980	980	28711	202	14265	5679
黑龙江	Heilongjiang	334534	319672	451	14411	1483	12635	4342
上海	Shanghai	46134279	33761506	171661	12201112	266050	7758949	2188472
江苏	Jiangsu	67681103	60773705	109941	6797457	120171	2914504	1944227
浙江	Zhejiang	58943185	54556899	62989	4323297	135945	2318162	1048828
安徽	Anhui	9357421	8215772	21227	1120422	11602	941843	109251
福建	Fujian	30245503	27851829	41613	2352061	44938	821148	512674
江西	Jiangxi	1081799	1005593	2209	73997	6694	37991	14055
山东	Shandong	15762659	14821884	33858	906917	28311	468113	208783
河南	Henan	5440090	4980844	31218	428028	3840	124266	66974
湖北	Hubei	3593799	3126607	10847	456345	6201	256511	144843
湖南	Hunan	2226002	1988950	8809	228243	6002	133313	46939
广东	Guangdong	44661437	39253674	114435	5293328	58395	2889868	1434924
广西	Guangxi	1962997	1863501	2788	96708	3975	60846	32448
海南	Hainan	225461	210901	349	14211	2611	11732	1771
重庆	Chongqing	9112276	8637463	88794	386019	9947	176647	101213
四川	Sichuan	2188165	1986051	4716	197398	6351	105088	36190
贵州	Guizhou	306347	267204	680	38463	105	15557	4698
云南	Yunnan	1231982	1078056	2609	151317	89	90788	8809
西藏	Tibet							
陕西	Shaanxi	3343173	3200186	11489	131498	4161	64034	27584
甘肃	Gansu	207649	185507	456	21686	27	13936	4521
青海	Qinghai	34920	33553	4	1363		497	748
宁夏	Ningxia	96804	94594	386	1824	1	2503	461
新疆	Xinjiang	659126	593871	947	64308	744	32071	16540

单位：万元
Unit: 10000 yuan

财务费用 Financial Expenses	#利息支出 Interest Expenses	营业利润 Operating Profits	利润总额 Total Profits	应交所得税 Income Tax Payable	应付职工薪酬 Payables to Employees	应交增值税 VAT Payable
1113745	**865416**	**9957936**	**10617443**	**2118229**	**8015968**	**4477702**
-40730	58817	872715	914417	186862	1113912	377182
12488	12038	353277	387508	89865	161466	142082
10431	10119	42222	42445	7191	46872	8460
3071	1251	36858	36788	5347	17784	5772
907	1014	-1696	-1503	108	9776	2017
10862	1557	17067	14047	7820	69545	14231
612	13	8842	8187	843	6013	801
1900	1837	-3950	-808	76	4258	1524
62829	134251	2772106	2960328	642561	1971913	1113722
245834	118256	2082396	2156971	475287	945122	801817
402123	288694	776397	847878	209533	1122915	662578
7651	20308	80508	53392	-1970	172374	101944
132429	41497	978357	909308	105632	359455	120293
659	1824	28988	29404	5851	18564	8673
76342	48515	214486	242377	44608	204192	170954
19181	5850	228907	240947	40065	71995	54483
7707	1971	45870	52454	11039	86601	27314
6384	3326	43714	45849	5912	52525	40534
111226	88165	972955	1248759	208418	1348789	652025
9808	4461	-8640	-8255	1983	28588	13475
2768	1875	2556	2891	756	5366	2226
13410	9118	229762	245687	44422	41855	77153
6277	4005	61212	63567	8645	59399	32437
614	497	9095	9289	1771	9504	2965
1312	2022	58083	58481	8904	20241	21294
1330	480	42690	43024	5560	46633	12156
758	731	2523	2555	459	6741	2900
309	105	13	258	18	450	-82
255	2	-1831	-1790	128	657	429
4998	2817	12454	12988	535	12463	6344

文化、体育用品及器材批发
Wholesale of Culture, Sports Appliances and Equipments

地区	Region	主营业务收入 Revenue from Principal Business	主营业务成本 Cost of Principal Business	主营业务税金及附加 Taxes and Other Charges on Principal Business	主营业务利润 Profits from Principal Business	其他业务利润 Profits from Other Business	销售费用 Selling Expenses	管理费用 Administrative Expenses
全国	**National Total**	**88891885**	**81071687**	**209068**	**7611130**	**706408**	**3797381**	**1970963**
北京	Beijing	14844695	13548706	31048	1264941	179283	738144	397498
天津	Tianjin	1894571	1710615	1960	181996	2743	40506	31450
河北	Hebei	847899	683827	1425	162647		8049	18578
山西	Shanxi	433802	395718	598	37486	841	14438	13942
内蒙古	Inner Mongolia	101624	92453	89	9082	51	2954	5200
辽宁	Liaoning	660728	608015	1917	50796	2904	30042	15687
吉林	Jilin	106881	92853	377	13651	380	4376	10467
黑龙江	Heilongjiang	93087	69324	19	23744	45	1378	5386
上海	Shanghai	12866073	11398741	33699	1433633	17303	868324	273834
江苏	Jiangsu	5720988	5166236	15085	539667	89275	234385	131164
浙江	Zhejiang	8843146	8322968	7502	512676	9851	224602	129113
安徽	Anhui	2860784	2720983	1943	137858	1716	47422	24295
福建	Fujian	3566494	3302290	12907	251297	4515	71856	69868
江西	Jiangxi	236305	217858	270	18177		4829	4047
山东	Shandong	5492430	5089489	9647	393294	14251	152476	123758
河南	Henan	1795046	1613020	8756	173270	15612	51323	25849
湖北	Hubei	1747783	1580227	5146	162410	9974	58630	48874
湖南	Hunan	1425934	1253548	9259	163127	204	53868	37892
广东	Guangdong	20767100	19071886	60576	1634638	347618	991575	509513
广西	Guangxi	429002	393850	853	34299	912	19531	10111
海南	Hainan	49051	42660	16	6375	746	4599	2641
重庆	Chongqing	945980	787130	3043	155807	3161	67468	16311
四川	Sichuan	1104756	1051894	1157	51705	845	26111	12244
贵州	Guizhou	195827	160768	95	34964		7432	5148
云南	Yunnan	767420	705869	601	60950	1125	26565	7390
西藏	Tibet	13179	11464		1715		472	658
陕西	Shaanxi	522641	483106	639	38896	471	18869	12494
甘肃	Gansu	294068	267938	230	25900	4	8641	15268
青海	Qinghai	23812	14848	15	8949	1627	5501	4592
宁夏	Ningxia	21645	18612	1	3032	117	861	1678
新疆	Xinjiang	219134	194791	194	24149	834	12154	6013

3-4-4 Continued 3

单位：万元

Unit: 10000 yuan

财务费用 Financial Expenses	#利息支出 Interest Expenses	营业利润 Operating Profits	利润总额 Total Profits	应交所得税 Income Tax Payable	应付职工薪酬 Payables to Employees	应交增值税 VAT Payable
309788	**356099**	**2564875**	**2719977**	**496744**	**2161836**	**776959**
33020	127206	388858	393035	102736	482558	103284
3399	1184	39712	42749	13842	24879	9220
921	811	71876	71359	1376	14388	6331
-261	630	15305	15333	4897	4944	727
-721		4046	2812	3	2216	1457
1827	480	10944	10939	2206	21073	10387
-316	-309	4209	4763	1379	9274	297
129	76	540	802	21	1479	71
21696	28317	401503	492134	136607	410091	130249
30825	26181	235223	250074	29534	123560	70357
58870	35339	148827	152564	31694	113501	104786
25897	4750	166636	168521	938	20757	4715
19994	8392	114253	115966	16106	43426	25107
718	826	8574	8075	9	2978	204
3447	17923	112369	122239	9446	127714	15340
8974	3574	72982	75000	7779	27162	14377
2940	1540	74571	75665	5842	57297	16185
-11704	2153	92384	91750	4514	38844	17433
97320	70557	409315	426112	102435	513524	214420
1901	3549	1888	1628	633	8540	321
138	130	136	414		3758	10
492	-49	79502	83048	13692	38796	24778
9276	18499	26067	28139	3414	14834	4226
1101	2146	21459	20619	62	7896	488
-1100	580	49058	50794	4757	13933	1546
-21		607	593	81	356	
473	760	6675	6967	1030	10785	1677
918	502	800	1474	63	3287	-1698
-60	9	601	727	182	7728	85
-29		590	663		1268	8
-276	343	5365	5020	1466	10990	571

医药及医疗器材批发
Wholesale of Medicines and Medical Appliances

地 区	Region	主营业务收入 Revenue from Principal Business	主营业务成本 Cost of Principal Business	主营业务税金及附加 Taxes and Other Charges on Principal Business	主营业务利润 Profits from Principal Business	其他业务利润 Profits from Other Business	销售费用 Selling Expenses	管理费用 Administr-ative Expenses
全 国	**National Total**	**237913284**	**208422089**	**645113**	**28846082**	**1376946**	**15619983**	**6501282**
北 京	Beijing	20920493	17850651	63933	3005909	292662	1609764	741620
天 津	Tianjin	4448254	3961086	10816	476352	17106	236380	117071
河 北	Hebei	7112295	6601096	12255	498944	8886	200135	130550
山 西	Shanxi	2422229	2144137	6515	271577	8398	157002	106391
内蒙古	Inner Mongolia	1116582	963071	3749	149762	881	55110	29840
辽 宁	Liaoning	5292564	4801647	11523	479394	15592	189953	117261
吉 林	Jilin	2535415	2045196	10226	479993	2845	275178	62710
黑龙江	Heilongjiang	1566142	1414442	3566	148134	2358	58195	37685
上 海	Shanghai	28161170	22877787	59908	5223475	401710	3075345	1181038
江 苏	Jiangsu	19173287	16373705	59761	2739821	286840	2093439	436188
浙 江	Zhejiang	15169189	13632451	31064	1505674	72052	764510	331833
安 徽	Anhui	9375499	8576970	23050	775479	16389	380879	195963
福 建	Fujian	4421947	4086941	10151	324855	3052	112020	101352
江 西	Jiangxi	6033022	4988497	26096	1018429	7225	650797	173003
山 东	Shandong	13683446	11998683	44576	1640187	12256	837317	347557
河 南	Henan	11578969	10555204	33434	990331	47349	364144	222232
湖 北	Hubei	14034366	12660894	41682	1331790	8320	539629	330623
湖 南	Hunan	5077536	4554888	22877	499771	11978	202385	124211
广 东	Guangdong	31415491	27883998	75816	3455677	63387	1836628	883066
广 西	Guangxi	2337097	2034257	7346	295494	2750	157752	76027
海 南	Hainan	1529888	1021381	8235	500272	12713	420194	55710
重 庆	Chongqing	5881864	5325850	15770	540244	23972	220917	142847
四 川	Sichuan	9202480	8268385	24542	909553	23317	430270	220435
贵 州	Guizhou	2738720	2426112	6717	305891	2875	111232	68593
云 南	Yunnan	4393600	3918407	10964	464229	19038	280949	84267
西 藏	Tibet	306223	173260	2712	130251	62	98605	5568
陕 西	Shaanxi	4294419	3958011	8397	328011	3862	107334	76522
甘 肃	Gansu	1554098	1414260	3467	136371	6002	62216	40351
青 海	Qinghai	245908	222498	450	22960	6	8485	7369
宁 夏	Ningxia	432506	390052	922	41532	1935	19550	9903
新 疆	Xinjiang	1458585	1298272	4592	155721	1128	63669	43496

单位：万元
Unit: 10000 yuan

财务费用 Financial Expenses	#利息支出 Interest Expenses	营业利润 Operating Profits	利润总额 Total Profits	应交所得税 Income Tax Payable	应付职工薪酬 Payables to Employees	应交增值税 VAT Payable
1295862	**1442440**	**7332730**	**7503268**	**1632931**	**6666687**	**4830627**
100482	475012	1013043	992785	255361	882848	429752
40865	30820	99497	101609	29483	93487	65837
48782	35570	120789	109047	32292	148615	117944
22363	18232	32711	30120	9206	247660	45722
6456	4071	59590	60235	9228	21182	12242
37805	30251	149583	142863	32013	76630	65134
16634	4393	128507	146674	30790	50921	51028
7102	4306	50625	45360	5588	20612	17174
24719	51405	1295353	1341943	335271	1457026	460583
94548	81156	447599	449821	116195	677559	422054
79344	78754	424602	438467	103185	311933	301074
45827	37066	180718	192049	35531	95087	175003
31861	23978	91470	83146	18859	86240	39639
27922	18604	167013	179908	26624	193555	197085
99677	72855	401265	451011	85259	266780	735958
101990	48914	353323	340477	64818	143838	207032
137847	122422	333217	402299	90568	301776	209390
36425	23854	141006	144052	24001	93653	86523
151479	135060	936759	936041	174776	725406	536211
11950	6355	50278	43469	7800	49021	57825
-7011	20342	44041	44876	12613	77085	52819
34097	24061	174703	186625	23313	151756	92500
36710	22593	235010	227017	42343	176682	166556
20357	17523	109043	109828	24683	52684	58844
23449	11815	85981	87243	15126	95181	100860
-48	264	26307	35509	3213	16246	21699
33282	26912	92635	93352	9180	64994	42115
17246	6382	21708	20010	5127	31430	18799
1767	873	7415	6790	483	6424	3749
3872	2360	8561	8522	2425	9479	5462
8063	6237	50378	52120	7577	40898	34014

矿产品、建材及化工产品批发

Wholesale of Mineral Products, Building Materials and Chemical Products

地 区	Region	主营业务收入 Revenue from Principal Business	主营业务成本 Cost of Principal Business	主营业务税金及附加 Taxes and Other Charges on Principal Business	主营业务利润 Profits from Principal Business	其他业务利润 Profits from Other Business	销售费用 Selling Expenses	管理费用 Administr-ative Expenses
全 国	**National Total**	**2473762148**	**2404659133**	**2449283**	**66653732**	**2062722**	**26947786**	**13404769**
北 京	Beijing	213267905	207597033	144071	5526801	299749	2155289	1392831
天 津	Tianjin	186685187	184014904	107678	2562605	114657	1186367	485457
河 北	Hebei	31588448	30420805	28948	1138695	44911	520958	203535
山 西	Shanxi	51348258	49830047	75425	1442786	120291	796369	455913
内蒙古	Inner Mongolia	19035332	17865835	47963	1121534	82177	612763	133632
辽 宁	Liaoning	93284885	91726447	59611	1498827	127188	873877	307056
吉 林	Jilin	7515089	7231422	14887	268780	3579	176962	30431
黑龙江	Heilongjiang	15968156	15525249	12770	430137	31687	312623	69297
上 海	Shanghai	421828761	414028450	156237	7644074	238171	2785888	1829125
江 苏	Jiangsu	210606480	204268836	186791	6150853	63024	2107428	1286554
浙 江	Zhejiang	255576569	249970138	189429	5417002	246081	2158588	1177513
安 徽	Anhui	20652310	19430386	28879	1193045	10673	318676	137645
福 建	Fujian	113891988	110206252	122436	3563300	112639	1538425	591656
江 西	Jiangxi	9975879	9247081	37381	691417	9561	273577	107147
山 东	Shandong	133526409	128484452	236434	4805523	112346	1654645	852801
河 南	Henan	39448913	37060751	122332	2265830	40100	686820	433296
湖 北	Hubei	49185566	47370278	70829	1744459	22923	771026	297104
湖 南	Hunan	16641302	15599694	112992	928616	17800	309247	199269
广 东	Guangdong	287526278	279122350	232233	8171695	166970	3227432	1903709
广 西	Guangxi	27581984	26613820	36757	931407	27179	457312	239437
海 南	Hainan	11484883	11050295	3899	430689	5506	63520	26393
重 庆	Chongqing	28041005	26602691	53990	1384324	15469	438250	224344
四 川	Sichuan	33227150	32040849	43473	1142828	27629	505203	161481
贵 州	Guizhou	12739697	11921806	57684	760207	5118	250367	133173
云 南	Yunnan	33035032	32186722	34057	814253	28038	378886	181799
西 藏	Tibet	9480	12139	2	-2661		3121	1081
陕 西	Shaanxi	61245245	59002494	102201	2140550	43307	1154180	222718
甘 肃	Gansu	27259064	26669305	16309	573450	5738	267192	101154
青 海	Qinghai	7899590	7430269	80242	389079	859	127735	38328
宁 夏	Ningxia	8134612	7972307	3726	158579	7566	122920	19316
新 疆	Xinjiang	45550691	44156026	29617	1365048	31786	712140	161574

单位：万元
Unit: 10000 yuan

财务费用 Financial Expenses	#利息支出 Interest Expenses	营业利润 Operating Profits	利润总额 Total Profits	应交所得税 Income Tax Payable	应付职工薪酬 Payables to Employees	应交增值税 VAT Payable
11209243	**9899455**	**19122541**	**19918815**	**4315130**	**11911209**	**13178149**
1335358	1898303	409303	543600	366410	1278455	818728
1322041	1111327	118473	153254	189054	332334	506591
157821	95227	298855	295434	58162	690884	191434
414297	346888	-157609	-18876	44765	348222	1418245
113932	92175	-31050	-30100	37322	82292	397106
228897	164811	70058	57197	62664	292277	276118
35250	36736	35388	56431	8176	95588	82649
71872	59093	-12876	-17423	15743	159435	265319
1064227	1116910	2551588	2711454	661070	1410549	777380
828936	446341	2401303	2451787	537188	729274	997660
1267199	1290355	2602026	2854300	473733	876710	1232844
79236	53674	275116	320513	30528	147222	121177
655093	486655	1338503	1537967	215973	504340	341838
47763	40305	187143	190681	32523	199982	181339
730033	273985	1798842	1809443	354938	772164	688513
246592	103710	891664	880255	132563	319102	281649
114936	75022	586216	564868	110405	345160	294778
90129	51927	331390	317360	26964	111417	193516
868734	717576	2783579	2784083	599854	1580877	1693388
143845	181867	148482	165760	32849	178473	248188
182935	147520	174750	187339	42707	23440	17145
152520	100098	653292	604837	52055	182620	188481
174695	153304	-312694	-322023	21144	228209	83405
104356	107925	273972	290093	29054	134418	266333
219526	229219	53013	33538	28962	137080	84850
41		-6441	-6440		71	
201114	235684	905206	810282	69338	275318	546347
74122	64276	124763	129623	9487	154219	518605
7715	5792	229023	165350	2446	40013	22788
91521	25345	-65371	-64167	3040	40483	72084
184507	187404	466634	462396	66011	240581	369651

机械设备、五金产品及电子产品批发

Wholesale of Machinery, Hardware and Electronic Products

地　区	Region	主营业务收入 Revenue from Principal Business	主营业务成本 Cost of Principal Business	主营业务税金及附加 Taxes and Other Charges on Principal Business	主营业务利润 Profits from Principal Business	其他业务利润 Profits from Other Business	销售费用 Selling Expenses	管理费用 Administr-ative Expenses
全　国	**National Total**	**679425841**	**625204240**	**1398790**	**52822811**	**2233141**	**26753825**	**11133329**
北　京	Beijing	111181289	99980755	252108	10948426	928456	5167430	2862488
天　津	Tianjin	22047496	20854682	263650	929164	18571	447917	290812
河　北	Hebei	10461972	10055377	11939	394656	3643	265069	59183
山　西	Shanxi	2987723	2863793	2517	121413	4540	42584	22178
内蒙古	Inner Mongolia	755197	694321	1872	59004	6285	42501	16616
辽　宁	Liaoning	5090482	4705337	8387	376758	6933	129508	109344
吉　林	Jilin	2700283	2425108	6462	268713	1985	173978	37103
黑龙江	Heilongjiang	2720662	2610885	11574	98203	4596	31893	30022
上　海	Shanghai	192426849	174141378	271162	18014309	395278	9755498	2673442
江　苏	Jiangsu	40141903	37167261	66256	2908386	47569	1161107	522661
浙　江	Zhejiang	48363031	46146225	35270	2181536	57568	1234514	540917
安　徽	Anhui	7995636	7636716	9321	349599	11155	172874	85370
福　建	Fujian	11508913	10632714	27700	848499	8288	206755	237051
江　西	Jiangxi	3896982	3684311	4860	207811	6995	160054	60618
山　东	Shandong	15911593	14471683	55398	1384512	12719	509947	301628
河　南	Henan	10344394	9677395	33434	633565	3320	299915	116441
湖　北	Hubei	14061257	13002186	35999	1023072	33712	695125	273256
湖　南	Hunan	8594809	7795152	34442	765215	3871	554967	127528
广　东	Guangdong	130560614	121057507	206762	9296345	597844	4655725	2468030
广　西	Guangxi	3058062	2889886	4368	163808	5285	79403	37925
海　南	Hainan	268516	245821	224	22471	347	22488	6955
重　庆	Chongqing	13634074	12856025	26785	751264	19729	402826	115659
四　川	Sichuan	8365698	7887943	11259	466496	37462	248856	-15909
贵　州	Guizhou	1703835	1623403	1563	78869	2930	35823	19349
云　南	Yunnan	1842819	1721768	4759	116292	3699	57353	27346
西　藏	Tibet	24641	21000	89	3552		1332	1051
陕　西	Shaanxi	3750142	3587085	4169	158888	4287	66921	48464
甘　肃	Gansu	1545970	1469710	1450	74810	2351	41585	12323
青　海	Qinghai	435621	426016	469	9136	1531	4582	2929
宁　夏	Ningxia	247037	233592	362	13083	1189	8590	5675
新　疆	Xinjiang	2798341	2639205	4180	154956	1003	76705	36874

单位：万元
Unit: 10000 yuan

财务费用 Financial Expenses	#利息支出 Interest Expenses	营业利润 Operating Profits	利润总额 Total Profits	应交所得税 Income Tax Payable	应付职工薪酬 Payables to Employees	应交增值税 VAT Payable
1979832	**2057171**	**18046110**	**18737049**	**4221005**	**10242966**	**7675618**
176099	621562	5290513	5490242	1280294	2728028	1669935
220596	209851	131787	150042	61211	230214	623893
4891	50089	135429	156113	24226	62212	106285
5442	6234	65580	63664	17180	21870	11998
17151	6259	2156	2204	798	15377	17166
67373	46552	242192	237219	19036	70905	46990
5132	3077	54572	55904	16717	26522	34748
4723	3975	37812	40148	8274	14796	3819
215940	283148	6120452	6449284	1450332	3059943	1690437
234191	154302	1249335	1257256	249710	407377	480065
186713	133585	399043	424388	116418	475702	827824
14900	1624	82439	103118	21993	78820	21500
41363	25843	377192	377632	68486	161992	102877
794	3938	-6677	3300	5151	51152	18458
113733	63472	466132	474468	84947	279303	188964
33017	10384	197343	195344	36071	124131	77679
89092	25564	26348	53327	36481	118468	167134
8846	4345	76025	67446	19061	104287	112805
370023	281525	2526273	2538673	604599	1710236	1167961
5365	4955	49406	53577	8754	46018	19069
-26	77	-6560	-6494	584	5694	1109
44414	37006	184696	260257	42239	103508	120018
43667	27490	244184	170929	20342	196172	56015
11498	10471	12030	14327	3700	29927	33340
19474	17663	24549	27185	4024	26690	23742
161	191	1214	1538	105	1610	777
11412	2320	28099	31228	8764	43488	16795
6603	5121	11396	10692	2796	11945	13757
3213	2902	3247	2960	495	2245	1243
2159	2166	-1654	-304	92	4231	1541
21873	11480	21557	31383	8125	30103	17674

贸易经纪与代理

Trade Broker and Agency

地 区	Region	主营业务收入 Revenue from Principal Business	主营业务成本 Cost of Principal Business	主营业务税金及附加 Taxes and Other Charges on Principal Business	主营业务利润 Profits from Principal Business	其他业务利润 Profits from Other Business	销售费用 Selling Expenses	管理费用 Administrative Expenses
全 国	**National Total**	**52968049**	**50914062**	**52883**	**2001104**	**115193**	**766424**	**631844**
北 京	Beijing	5751803	5297580	13255	440968	74484	120143	126785
天 津	Tianjin	2065596	1979676	1566	84354	11105	88007	24147
河 北	Hebei	151128	145065	16	6047	11	5024	1039
山 西	Shanxi							
内蒙古	Inner Mongolia	74054	71815	1882	357	22	174	90
辽 宁	Liaoning	295026	272449	396	22181	1	9983	10264
吉 林	Jilin	4153	3534	8	611		766	51
黑龙江	Heilongjiang	83106	76334	51	6721	286	3315	1465
上 海	Shanghai	3086098	2843147	7905	235046	9161	120045	107782
江 苏	Jiangsu	3726944	3581632	2231	143081	1950	48373	31449
浙 江	Zhejiang	792535	760948	265	31322	3	17254	11484
安 徽	Anhui	380827	360674	284	19869		2451	1573
福 建	Fujian	1453855	1409087	2215	42553	2289	17440	10139
江 西	Jiangxi	392200	384710	118	7372		3348	2063
山 东	Shandong	771278	696170	3350	71758	1034	32301	6680
河 南	Henan	58535	52913	95	5527		908	2964
湖 北	Hubei	477264	474116	249	2899	53	886	1230
湖 南	Hunan	47051	35361	2102	9588		1772	2124
广 东	Guangdong	29997986	29193687	15293	789006	11889	257737	284402
广 西	Guangxi	16941	15838	13	1090		461	204
海 南	Hainan							
重 庆	Chongqing	106131	103080	959	2092		621	653
四 川	Sichuan	38925	35543	49	3333	131	2236	922
贵 州	Guizhou	18792	17296	112	1384	1466	796	175
云 南	Yunnan	3076005	3010186	372	65447		28199	1862
西 藏	Tibet							
陕 西	Shaanxi	65210	59194	10	6006		3022	1039
甘 肃	Gansu							
青 海	Qinghai							
宁 夏	Ningxia							
新 疆	Xinjiang	36606	34027	86	2493	1308	1162	1258

3-4-4 Continued 7

单位：万元
Unit: 10000 yuan

财务费用 Financial Expenses	#利息支出 Interest Expenses	营业利润 Operating Profits	利润总额 Total Profits	应交所得税 Income Tax Payable	应付职工薪酬 Payables to Employees	应交增值税 VAT Payable
289461	**344079**	**799411**	**858655**	**135530**	**477235**	**240465**
-50287	111702	509148	521091	56067	128796	41645
3583	6320	35345	38764	1292	39699	3472
799	81	-804	-625	7	780	19
1		94	103		34	3
1835	979	883	1722	621	9729	1605
58	58	-263	-263	9	370	17
	109	2226	2593	784	714	307
-1047	3015	75543	75553	22986	91972	13867
27248	8331	40714	43989	7729	19395	7964
3640	1340	-5064	-2134	769	5663	253
1301	343	13618	14011	2499	11807	-77
6197	2871	22388	23982	5531	10712	9088
551	508	1410	1649	411	1566	1014
10505	1783	21254	21308	5446	7906	15190
44	51	1585	1607	179	663	329
401	298	133	444	211	710	175
1673	29	4017	4139	3	238	465
258172	184931	49189	81040	23996	139759	139949
119		307	319	2	224	2
-38	-2	857	893	108	495	1106
-175	63	756	1064	267	1466	3342
266		148	184		300	
23578	20254	24447	25497	6413	3014	489
-75	23	2070	2176	196	800	123
1112	992	-590	-451	4	423	118

其他批发业

Other Wholesale not Classified Elsewhere

地　区	Region	主营业务收入 Revenue from Principal Business	主营业务成本 Cost of Principal Business	主营业务税金及附加 Taxes and Other Charges on Principal Business	主营业务利润 Profits from Principal Business	其他业务利润 Profits from Other Business	销售费用 Selling Expenses	管理费用 Administr-ative Expenses
全　国	**National Total**	**75874662**	**71509145**	**286552**	**4078965**	**71080**	**1581372**	**1159227**
北　京	Beijing	4521712	3946801	6129	568782	14769	140202	163348
天　津	Tianjin	6688446	6642677	45256	513	3563	44924	55824
河　北	Hebei	3276300	3218759	2564	54977	367	2315	11458
山　西	Shanxi	119721	107920	257	11544	231	6094	5066
内蒙古	Inner Mongolia	18366	12610	115	5641		3158	2390
辽　宁	Liaoning	769224	735519	2257	31448	558	9864	13412
吉　林	Jilin	210890	191364	637	18889	291	5892	4193
黑龙江	Heilongjiang	212630	200807	248	11575	211	4377	2447
上　海	Shanghai	8767953	7778827	12455	976671	12898	583609	296288
江　苏	Jiangsu	5400058	5046357	31662	322039	2717	88924	74408
浙　江	Zhejiang	9081789	8840800	16456	224533	1080	60663	53682
安　徽	Anhui	2269161	2130419	52795	85947	1068	34595	39571
福　建	Fujian	11803608	11600425	14796	188387	7015	89347	42184
江　西	Jiangxi	543100	508443	3566	31091	78	11932	6545
山　东	Shandong	4232541	4049255	14433	168853	3971	43887	42303
河　南	Henan	1621694	1376347	14427	230920	418	74290	28285
湖　北	Hubei	618544	562571	3804	52169	847	12310	13179
湖　南	Hunan	917270	794235	18412	104623	339	28578	29055
广　东	Guangdong	9546921	8834573	28234	684114	13869	243514	196433
广　西	Guangxi	757058	740704	1050	15304		5997	3165
海　南	Hainan							
重　庆	Chongqing	1174354	1080906	8960	84488	1397	18252	16984
四　川	Sichuan	502508	464026	1722	36760	101	13907	9159
贵　州	Guizhou	172103	155679	588	15836	351	5209	6622
云　南	Yunnan	2035890	1923227	2433	110230	2902	33831	25739
西　藏	Tibet	6150	5210	24	916		686	3
陕　西	Shaanxi	131264	113456	2297	15511	1	4840	5815
甘　肃	Gansu	44602	37300	74	7228		3483	2196
青　海	Qinghai	4215	3581	15	619		963	398
宁　夏	Ningxia	282525	277655	247	4623	848	1310	2410
新　疆	Xinjiang	144065	128692	639	14734	1190	4419	6666

单位：万元
Unit: 10000 yuan

财务费用 Financial Expenses	#利息支出 Interest Expenses	营业利润 Operating Profits	利润总额 Total Profits	应交所得税 Income Tax Payable	应付职工薪酬 Payables to Employees	应交增值税 VAT Payable
416538	**342325**	**1271380**	**1595934**	**302279**	**834562**	**1242552**
59607	60522	291774	298265	63601	129699	-32724
15369	17692	-104537	72511	20842	41070	343746
52588	721	65367	66755	11810	4843	10580
192	233	312	376	696	3248	2143
-107	9	-82	-70	181	1553	523
13020	1391	-4561	-3909	743	5254	9280
152	19	9040	8989	2216	2460	4171
1475	170	3370	3434	421	1371	1803
41	10528	248098	280747	69018	203242	78427
36817	16626	129905	141201	25483	47265	177009
35174	22636	93467	123634	17652	33036	183316
3827	2062	15086	43461	10359	27098	107149
76973	122062	6415	21927	837	40083	61245
1493	626	17808	13758	1038	6969	8035
8660	2975	73603	79526	8578	33642	76525
21501	1721	97232	101940	10941	15745	47833
3772	610	22437	23017	4121	8392	10823
13448	2919	32464	34480	1988	14247	11845
40940	51334	150436	150229	27637	132112	87812
482	130	6031	6739	243	1711	3058
3969	858	45418	53222	3804	12887	18887
2331	2030	11302	11158	1917	14073	11920
1665	1297	4947	4474	985	6716	1695
676	1294	65872	68881	14988	35741	11526
81		146	146		156	-55
727	261	4665	4961	428	4651	2200
145	1	1404	1427	370	1024	816
-2		-605	-679		436	174
20063	20290	-19677	-19091	151	1487	79
1459	1308	4243	4425	1231	4351	2711

3-4-5 各地区限额以上零售业企业损益及分配

地区	Region	主营业务收入 Revenue from Principal Business	主营业务成本 Cost of Principal Business	主营业务税金及附加 Taxes and Other Charges on Principal Business	主营业务利润 Profits from Principal Business	其他业务利润 Profits from Other Business	销售费用 Selling Expenses	管理费用 Administrative Expenses
全国	**National Total**	**1070158359**	**938918600**	**4934422**	**126305337**	**9835654**	**72396977**	**33191264**
北京	Beijing	71420057	62973559	259032	8187466	1493832	6228018	2273768
天津	Tianjin	20024349	17904603	65034	2054712	157997	1568769	688041
河北	Hebei	26785651	24191335	93937	2500379	286937	1536711	849049
山西	Shanxi	19373650	17728656	50282	1594712	122005	1046925	543510
内蒙古	Inner Mongolia	12018846	10879979	44064	1094803	79052	685952	313890
辽宁	Liaoning	27208251	24415857	107575	2684819	201561	1659556	1073511
吉林	Jilin	15090271	13430494	66576	1593201	169871	702320	662449
黑龙江	Heilongjiang	13948600	12383217	73902	1491481	161333	669866	447302
上海	Shanghai	65217952	52231674	299773	12686505	668018	8612621	3507675
江苏	Jiangsu	97958340	86755837	389517	10812986	912269	5807260	2863819
浙江	Zhejiang	68984780	61195569	222227	7566984	830708	4907795	2060483
安徽	Anhui	35813264	32031115	131292	3650857	183390	1926135	953610
福建	Fujian	47401928	41738300	214647	5448981	200208	2722319	1379274
江西	Jiangxi	16310274	14397143	91821	1821310	126303	886659	495360
山东	Shandong	79819613	70752029	438815	8628769	591008	3976495	2075839
河南	Henan	45149111	39202895	337554	5608662	403401	2182876	1406154
湖北	Hubei	48769655	42757579	303916	5708160	500593	3017868	1402258
湖南	Hunan	44957964	39581227	314595	5062142	207907	2463521	1220007
广东	Guangdong	114440373	98086986	431193	15922194	1165890	9748605	3493945
广西	Guangxi	16801467	15110974	56600	1633893	143050	944140	450852
海南	Hainan	5033272	4278971	34137	720164	50855	357792	164044
重庆	Chongqing	31345655	27260813	217866	3866976	322515	2000741	946209
四川	Sichuan	49143251	43720025	182326	5240900	328716	3165656	1224227
贵州	Guizhou	18519840	16520252	65240	1934348	104997	929407	373730
云南	Yunnan	21393086	19205927	55935	2131224	119547	1214405	471344
西藏	Tibet	1277730	1185125	8745	83860	1753	53915	32082
陕西	Shaanxi	32864499	28559958	277277	4027264	150198	1980711	1086784
甘肃	Gansu	8190216	7276656	32965	880595	41566	447026	190008
青海	Qinghai	2082578	1860420	6523	215635	21070	118958	67343
宁夏	Ningxia	2855479	2491955	10858	352666	30310	222477	89840
新疆	Xinjiang	9958357	8809470	50198	1098689	58793	611478	384857

Income and Distribution of Enterprises above Designated Size of Retail Trade by Region

单位：万元
Unit: 10000 yuan

财务费用 Financial Expenses	#利息支出 Interest Expenses	营业利润 Operating Profits	利润总额 Total Profits	应交所得税 Income Tax Payable	应付职工薪酬 Payables to Employees	应交增值税 VAT Payable
6626059	**3691578**	**28664536**	**30558858**	**5309647**	**40819123**	**17250903**
414027	461568	1217062	1267480	379638	3063092	983057
141812	66692	-282008	-209066	-3075	699704	329436
232460	111509	287705	328396	76669	1388412	426035
158709	94017	-7223	-423	40375	779648	255053
87122	30780	149508	193219	41676	519859	336575
283244	114109	269418	1380520	100321	1000577	518132
177080	111392	353537	317390	66403	659324	227082
121461	68900	472269	461478	63529	402132	176702
200498	121320	1741621	1933153	574116	2996511	1160245
604769	350507	3169937	3144061	570388	2769622	1799604
457391	381967	1255609	1345247	373610	3139019	1135076
192944	67695	834856	862789	102934	1133100	370593
197217	113138	1655634	1636730	163029	1519944	554437
109937	54524	453010	453586	41319	631649	210753
576352	257859	2462491	2485540	426763	2345694	1364968
397285	118329	2025079	2015581	270190	1493819	752193
323914	203210	1545764	1533715	281376	1729618	675436
295937	128344	1418648	1308293	130709	3033611	616335
476252	254024	4219169	4546140	741438	4449433	2321113
67737	42569	328618	428347	53364	576954	204657
36239	24906	245367	244257	69224	183902	63931
161291	85615	1024038	1050834	110803	940674	538721
259272	146664	1134883	1155872	191964	2026631	565303
108937	43729	568999	552434	93197	550553	333150
100680	72580	547712	558289	75582	757535	268680
1930	533	7650	13277	2381	41164	15000
171788	69226	1172702	1134474	176489	988621	460041
69970	31337	207568	212835	31351	354250	306976
77409	5508	35963	48132	9651	79575	34491
26588	13452	34830	36219	11193	104995	48064
95807	45576	114120	120059	43040	459501	199064

国有控股

State-controlled Enterprises

地区	Region	主营业务收入 Revenue from Principal Business	主营业务成本 Cost of Principal Business	主营业务税金及附加 Taxes and Other Charges on Principal Business	主营业务利润 Profits from Principal Business	其他业务利润 Profits from Other Business	销售费用 Selling Expenses	管理费用 Administrative Expenses
全　国	**National Total**	**187345991**	**166653600**	**670662**	**20021729**	**1663464**	**11506916**	**4504386**
北　京	Beijing	17881343	15689818	82636	2108889	309186	1302781	574618
天　津	Tianjin	4837669	4279739	15819	542111	35536	327292	185478
河　北	Hebei	5392934	4816806	22314	553814	44447	295657	159664
山　西	Shanxi	5006923	4627414	9880	369629	25697	302088	109580
内蒙古	Inner Mongolia	3893387	3604561	7514	281312	12966	228047	33430
辽　宁	Liaoning	4884902	4367948	18462	498492	30062	292400	157961
吉　林	Jilin	3003482	2736692	17601	249189	8215	143340	128093
黑龙江	Heilongjiang	1666241	1462666	8658	194917	6841	67242	66944
上　海	Shanghai	11052109	9680035	51956	1320118	178992	854045	590214
江　苏	Jiangsu	13959493	12768671	36387	1154435	85008	719490	197384
浙　江	Zhejiang	8389334	7533916	29267	826151	85837	505191	168348
安　徽	Anhui	6813691	6204092	18934	590665	38490	332494	146354
福　建	Fujian	4690464	4252466	12580	425418	26228	316265	76802
江　西	Jiangxi	1786792	1523092	7798	255902	9975	112329	82921
山　东	Shandong	9283850	8155041	33139	1095670	72029	510953	149319
河　南	Henan	4196770	3706789	19587	470394	17486	236932	104522
湖　北	Hubei	10258216	9050131	45688	1162397	195005	827059	265077
湖　南	Hunan	9117544	8399560	24258	693726	21318	402288	139421
广　东	Guangdong	19300278	16613205	59404	2627669	138545	1310123	358035
广　西	Guangxi	1577081	1363472	9362	204247	10804	99587	68304
海　南	Hainan	2372704	1944476	23771	404457	11295	163869	46921
重　庆	Chongqing	7669684	6717574	33006	919104	160522	598855	203466
四　川	Sichuan	9662803	8698895	13164	950744	45131	537012	166911
贵　州	Guizhou	4811576	4186837	12265	612474	42025	219241	55184
云　南	Yunnan	5402086	5007877	7843	386366	15553	237697	65496
西　藏	Tibet	818133	770683	6918	40532	902	28981	11859
陕　西	Shaanxi	4128311	3544798	27602	555911	20570	270403	123255
甘　肃	Gansu	2652048	2388846	7664	255538	3834	107250	25988
青　海	Qinghai	374404	335804	747	37853	305	15797	8210
宁　夏	Ningxia	60519	51360	357	8802	521	6043	4227
新　疆	Xinjiang	2401220	2170336	6081	224803	10139	136165	30400

3-4-5 Continued

单位：万元
Unit: 10000 yuan

财务费用 Financial Expenses	#利息支出 Interest Expenses	营业利润 Operating Profits	利润总额 Total Profits	应交所得税 Income Tax Payable	应付职工薪酬 Payables to Employees	应交增值税 VAT Payable
510765	**457294**	**6036804**	**6193598**	**1034606**	**6429463**	**3164170**
66338	128552	731248	759016	144161	863224	284764
17154	12722	65284	79639	27826	210090	92896
13471	12688	118482	116044	9550	180101	124009
12715	8743	-55320	-63679	12283	186124	25461
3975	2024	24765	30662	4254	119668	197021
2606	9862	181274	182370	25374	229109	29550
42585	37031	98074	96790	28327	83129	91972
8630	6709	69237	62269	13849	86191	14570
26483	35953	306245	336455	96041	496696	180036
33024	13643	323449	337497	38061	272241	308217
8484	13345	267675	272504	71575	304832	100833
10604	8415	141209	172418	13310	155944	52249
10056	8349	107327	114145	20807	185327	52958
-258	3130	73119	68670	4167	87994	31195
51832	32077	210153	208670	30401	263735	232660
16072	5800	125148	124673	16808	137631	82245
32934	36084	285720	317364	73227	455864	156882
24498	13841	184239	185439	20583	173600	101418
40467	23109	1297739	1315407	140055	706641	290219
5145	3721	51000	54794	8185	88317	21881
1746	456	206411	205858	53841	60770	20413
13298	10569	183723	208080	23362	177329	173040
6050	3384	332570	292598	30870	272515	89926
33285	3327	248115	255909	41585	82634	85768
6226	4796	110092	115301	21225	133724	50456
1553	139	-5691	-5173	400	22993	9683
10380	7863	186906	184418	41704	138975	58632
3000	2107	87288	83237	7508	145517	152345
113	455	14087	13412	2020	10965	7466
541	374	419	1863	258	7018	2353
7758	8026	66817	66948	12989	90565	43052

3-4-6 各地区限额以上零售业企业损益及分配(按登记注册类型分)

内资企业

Domestic Funded Enterprises

地　区	Region	主营业务收入 Revenue from Principal Business	主营业务成本 Cost of Principal Business	主营业务税金及附加 Taxes and Other Charges on Principal Business	主营业务利润 Profits from Principal Business	其他业务利润 Profits from Other Business	销售费用 Selling Expenses	管理费用 Administrative Expenses
全　国	**National Total**	**935911416**	**831317728**	**4285145**	**100308543**	**7655411**	**54422600**	**27293992**
北　京	Beijing	58415362	52706846	186682	5521834	1221967	4366677	1723332
天　津	Tianjin	16797093	15236113	42998	1517982	111091	1157205	540840
河　北	Hebei	25783171	23299754	91482	2391935	281005	1466528	835466
山　西	Shanxi	18906148	17335312	47948	1522888	117703	1001335	528350
内蒙古	Inner Mongolia	11835119	10726063	42850	1066206	75271	668179	308566
辽　宁	Liaoning	24379595	21979690	92155	2307750	166418	1333050	953236
吉　林	Jilin	14414420	12854288	63638	1496494	168028	654619	629854
黑龙江	Heilongjiang	13216638	11767363	70974	1378301	140647	576122	415330
上　海	Shanghai	39731045	34991019	131300	4608726	435068	3364312	1378072
江　苏	Jiangsu	83448592	74190466	344458	8913668	706925	4268602	2370180
浙　江	Zhejiang	60053675	53641563	177130	6234982	633887	4010302	1698917
安　徽	Anhui	33576988	30212215	123930	3240843	161274	1595993	880088
福　建	Fujian	42118174	37283286	197752	4637136	157179	2131085	1231141
江　西	Jiangxi	15288599	13490563	89032	1709004	100324	787801	468052
山　东	Shandong	75837748	67446358	418209	7973181	520505	3551280	1926807
河　南	Henan	42958558	37325562	327272	5305724	281184	2043218	1270131
湖　北	Hubei	45986948	40402639	293593	5290716	311041	2696548	1279547
湖　南	Hunan	43466654	38353310	302677	4810667	179859	2302259	1154221
广　东	Guangdong	88319474	76979331	331893	11008250	679855	6200982	2768306
广　西	Guangxi	15464963	13972900	52012	1440051	118903	813610	413459
海　南	Hainan	4697043	3996893	32242	667908	43216	322816	156176
重　庆	Chongqing	29156193	25403333	207810	3545050	288994	1780980	866103
四　川	Sichuan	44580934	39973671	154804	4452459	292994	2649648	1048123
贵　州	Guizhou	17580163	15738832	60717	1780614	85877	832577	350769
云　南	Yunnan	19528512	17630404	49291	1848817	89024	1036482	420420
西　藏	Tibet	1264731	1173108	8712	82911	1719	53426	31858
陕　西	Shaanxi	26870606	23506735	247601	3116270	148090	1412661	935913
甘　肃	Gansu	7963089	7084298	31294	847497	35112	425950	184518
青　海	Qinghai	2020404	1807634	6197	206573	20002	113481	66385
宁　夏	Ningxia	2764833	2413146	10443	341244	30310	214921	88223
新　疆	Xinjiang	9485944	8395033	48049	1042862	51939	589951	371609

Income and Distribution of Enterprises above Designated Size of Retail Trade by Region and Type of Registration

单位：万元
Unit: 10000 yuan

财务费用 Financial Expenses	#利息支出 Interest Expenses	营业利润 Operating Profits	利润总额 Total Profits	应交所得税 Income Tax Payable	应付职工薪酬 Payables to Employees	应交增值税 VAT Payable
6182222	**3256860**	**23122957**	**24681932**	**3870682**	**34559188**	**14491242**
348773	372553	676606	739639	231022	2386381	777969
108740	38729	-348707	-301886	-40305	553812	229392
228803	108107	277395	342410	73568	1358796	420169
155466	91354	-23282	-17142	35083	758569	248765
83764	30645	141568	186078	41952	514561	334161
256681	102342	256585	1363042	79220	894078	465168
160039	95458	330261	342483	61084	640301	209040
114284	63726	469282	456453	59284	367319	153820
129682	90231	684332	774116	203270	1436567	549139
547681	302898	2800091	2788098	459044	2220581	1605056
436541	329323	937026	1003742	285971	2759912	985445
187581	65621	780234	817653	83238	1056025	349687
212244	108109	1273856	1247040	125454	1246238	470369
106579	52709	441611	440032	36396	595294	199316
563714	248886	2296627	2306337	375080	2168922	1274574
391586	116138	1884217	1870113	232100	1430526	706215
321584	194809	1371214	1352070	233418	1597139	627747
288220	121249	1314953	1211901	117563	2948289	581198
428449	192820	2922252	3104041	496751	3215362	1555778
65051	39094	273228	271287	41938	518105	178384
26822	13962	231906	230844	66264	166319	59029
152255	79306	973878	995837	92816	867653	491848
244589	136675	963346	980796	141127	1836508	520884
106663	40736	512194	498219	80677	513015	309717
94903	68026	441351	441918	54604	673480	233241
1951	533	7360	12988	2340	40616	15055
150106	58353	891373	857736	117613	825275	372715
69850	31282	194703	199763	27348	347556	301859
77392	5508	32283	44372	8795	76610	32877
26393	13247	31207	32423	9951	101303	46004
95836	44431	84007	89528	38016	444076	186620

国有企业
State-owned Enterprises

地　区	Region	主营业务收入 Revenue from Principal Business	主营业务成本 Cost of Principal Business	主营业务税金及附加 Taxes and Other Charges on Principal Business	主营业务利润 Profits from Principal Business	其他业务利润 Profits from Other Business	销售费用 Selling Expenses	管理费用 Administrative Expenses
全　国	**National Total**	**9985357**	**8676325**	**63458**	**1245574**	**111162**	**594943**	**410489**
北　京	Beijing	985231	837469	3687	144075	46435	98630	72907
天　津	Tianjin	730308	641608	870	87830	4228	62191	23419
河　北	Hebei	73708	67970	1155	4583	1819	4308	4945
山　西	Shanxi	259780	240019	546	19215	3179	13507	9492
内蒙古	Inner Mongolia	35428	30581	76	4771	60	2610	2429
辽　宁	Liaoning	166193	141825	524	23844	4193	15270	13982
吉　林	Jilin	21304	19351	197	1756	181	798	1117
黑龙江	Heilongjiang	318852	285021	3021	30810	1272	7070	9810
上　海	Shanghai	273598	224372	1726	47500	12975	19895	25001
江　苏	Jiangsu	326251	289779	847	35625	2438	13130	14704
浙　江	Zhejiang	139871	118427	569	20875	3256	8087	8340
安　徽	Anhui	106002	98688	90	7224	2025	3920	3516
福　建	Fujian	105404	96281	247	8876	370	4814	3518
江　西	Jiangxi	72138	64702	96	7340	105	3731	2823
山　东	Shandong	653188	553294	2767	97127	565	33346	17741
河　南	Henan	579208	499863	7300	72045	756	22966	25836
湖　北	Hubei	706654	621045	5136	80473	963	40337	16354
湖　南	Hunan	840288	737451	7870	94967	9867	37716	24990
广　东	Guangdong	752721	599347	4654	148720	4343	43974	40927
广　西	Guangxi	134729	111761	1269	21699	2054	15017	4754
海　南	Hainan	9335	9918	51	-634		629	444
重　庆	Chongqing	392447	369846	401	22200	677	18510	2961
四　川	Sichuan	396408	357808	923	37677	1475	21130	9841
贵　州	Guizhou	86978	68087	389	18502	384	3230	4951
云　南	Yunnan	138974	123245	233	15496	515	10779	4553
西　藏	Tibet	194914	174792	6081	14041	42	5694	3943
陕　西	Shaanxi	1168005	1047904	11431	108670	5665	49348	37712
甘　肃	Gansu	75170	64806	895	9469	48	4105	3782
青　海	Qinghai							
宁　夏	Ningxia	15565	12238	36	3291	187	2025	1312
新　疆	Xinjiang	226705	168827	371	57507	1085	28175	14385

3-4-6 Continued 1

单位：万元
Unit: 10000 yuan

财务费用 Financial Expenses	#利息支出 Interest Expenses	营业利润 Operating Profits	利润总额 Total Profits	应交所得税 Income Tax Payable	应付职工薪酬 Payables to Employees	应交增值税 VAT Payable
29825	**15578**	**357315**	**386130**	**53429**	**475049**	**170071**
-1450	879	40371	47889	9926	96681	20148
-513	781	7019	15745	6143	42498	11637
-7	1	-2183	-1362	5	7669	1036
473	74	-3269	-1173	201	9053	678
-10	11	-100	1062	4	999	315
359	65	-2593	-219	547	11624	1002
61	-1	-39	43	1	716	194
1694	1663	13351	13266	526	8060	1706
-476	6	15892	16505	3873	22808	5450
1641	842	11843	15449	1548	12463	4130
79	459	8703	10500	1670	8982	2864
160	2	1773	1799	601	2838	753
122	39	918	1316	97	4040	807
323	311	811	2527	578	3094	638
4947	716	47396	50160	3759	20537	13761
3880	535	20910	19687	1918	28033	7941
2761	1103	22342	22812	1898	13446	3909
6108	304	30710	24317	2421	23143	9071
2613	1092	73897	75801	3418	40534	9708
469	779	4053	5665	1222	11112	3045
-5		-1644	-350		1100	69
582	603	780	1918	185	12144	42304
816	302	6679	-3078	1190	12558	2508
284	285	10461	11392	1998	3769	1344
861	640	793	4074	803	6452	605
12	14	5009	6022	88	5872	3008
4038	3921	25951	25965	3829	31100	18977
167	64	1839	1209	134	6726	608
	-1	294	1246	95	1776	455
-163	88	15348	15943	4751	25222	1400

集体企业
Collective-owned Enterprises

地 区	Region	主营业务收入 Revenue from Principal Business	主营业务成本 Cost of Principal Business	主营业务税金及附加 Taxes and Other Charges on Principal Business	主营业务利润 Profits from Principal Business	其他业务利润 Profits from Other Business	销售费用 Selling Expenses	管理费用 Administrative Expenses
全 国	**National Total**	**8096014**	**7103153**	**63361**	**929500**	**23089**	**292890**	**254123**
北 京	Beijing	228128	195890	806	31432	11093	27674	15965
天 津	Tianjin	110549	90040	384	20125		8392	1650
河 北	Hebei	354187	327918	1112	25157	200	10324	8078
山 西	Shanxi	275351	243240	1102	31009	1084	8843	11757
内蒙古	Inner Mongolia	121207	118308	63	2836	793	1008	684
辽 宁	Liaoning	76324	66726	203	9395	261	4380	2964
吉 林	Jilin	24664	19353	530	4781		696	3174
黑龙江	Heilongjiang	172899	153458	1845	17596		3853	2175
上 海	Shanghai	71706	55430	484	15792	2225	10224	6495
江 苏	Jiangsu	724808	626567	5901	92340	1212	20184	16159
浙 江	Zhejiang	142157	117356	797	24004	1051	9567	7690
安 徽	Anhui	42007	38484	156	3367	4	1233	1029
福 建	Fujian	297714	269735	1450	26529	223	10186	8212
江 西	Jiangxi	38644	33603	391	4650		634	735
山 东	Shandong	852470	703038	10621	138811	327	16174	22513
河 南	Henan	558157	500692	3978	53487	577	19677	11268
湖 北	Hubei	1452826	1294061	12818	145947	1770	35675	51093
湖 南	Hunan	360247	331899	4555	23793	770	9541	8367
广 东	Guangdong	813651	701208	4867	107576	443	37225	24147
广 西	Guangxi	276024	246834	1877	27313	19	8131	7171
海 南	Hainan	3027	2318	17	692		337	195
重 庆	Chongqing	41976	33782	440	7754	2	2709	2915
四 川	Sichuan	72527	62913	648	8966	2	2436	3737
贵 州	Guizhou	83599	73885	337	9377		1629	1579
云 南	Yunnan	370076	347553	928	21595	832	11572	6393
西 藏	Tibet							
陕 西	Shaanxi	473324	395848	6552	70924	20	28900	26353
甘 肃	Gansu	50877	47425	486	2966	181	1219	1183
青 海	Qinghai							
宁 夏	Ningxia	843	676	5	162		40	105
新 疆	Xinjiang	6045	4913	8	1124		427	337

3-4-6 Continued 2

单位：万元

Unit: 10000 yuan

财务费用 Financial Expenses	#利息支出 Interest Expenses	营业利润 Operating Profits	利润总额 Total Profits	应交所得税 Income Tax Payable	应付职工薪酬 Payables to Employees	应交增值税 VAT Payable
40909	**27711**	**377046**	**375130**	**52635**	**200325**	**99774**
570	701	-1343	-1297	1313	14137	3676
-19	2	10102	11644	2360	4506	3131
524	57	2705	5559	907	7117	3256
555	219	11040	11106	362	6440	3287
1		1144	1556	33	804	173
150	23	2138	2038	288	3840	1087
96	1	650	541	55	835	491
152	61	5506	1311	29	4119	280
-29		32059	32582	1297	9240	2016
8262	6056	47967	47278	7558	13206	11231
183	246	8131	9631	2838	6545	3038
196	156	937	941	93	1318	516
1172	636	6942	6897	201	6649	2837
126	100	968	941	1	1120	1465
4764	1878	95715	91976	12331	21086	11754
2315	137	23210	25809	1716	10601	1863
12723	13123	42847	42595	8546	30298	16238
1285	108	4736	4111	564	11213	2024
2494	619	41883	40798	8687	22407	15077
1869	863	9503	9621	372	4070	2244
3		157	157	36	255	100
100	59	2188	2699	596	2801	2330
102	37	3705	3259	326	2104	1330
571	657	5896	6022	1197	531	933
643	542	3762	3499	129	4608	880
1346	787	14212	13296	797	8197	8168
306	198	358	343	1	2011	260
1		17	17	2	48	9
448	445	-88	200		219	80

股份合作企业
Cooperative Enterprises

地 区	Region	主营业务收入 Revenue from Principal Business	主营业务成本 Cost of Principal Business	主营业务税金及附加 Taxes and Other Charges on Principal Business	主营业务利润 Profits from Principal Business	其他业务利润 Profits from Other Business	销售费用 Selling Expenses	管理费用 Administrative Expenses
全 国	**National Total**	**1558540**	**1344748**	**9520**	**204272**	**4400**	**58300**	**65853**
北 京	Beijing	282502	266457	187	15858	1231	6759	9249
天 津	Tianjin	18064	13796	118	4150		897	878
河 北	Hebei	115756	94273	901	20582	54	3576	7333
山 西	Shanxi	7418	6938	26	454			389
内蒙古	Inner Mongolia	2256	1901	2	353		114	81
辽 宁	Liaoning	16590	13246	66	3278	348	1715	896
吉 林	Jilin	62721	60076	372	2273		344	1354
黑龙江	Heilongjiang	44676	36359	583	7734	824	2953	2638
上 海	Shanghai	24401	20175	100	4126	254	1419	1489
江 苏	Jiangsu	28637	23568	110	4959		897	1167
浙 江	Zhejiang	143779	118373	638	24768	668	8219	5198
安 徽	Anhui	9425	8141	114	1170	98	437	637
福 建	Fujian	2253	2013	14	226		68	104
江 西	Jiangxi	17305	16026	85	1194	18	269	251
山 东	Shandong	118459	109615	1392	7452		5692	3383
河 南	Henan	6330	4971	59	1300		161	307
湖 北	Hubei	37464	33672	453	3339	614	809	1285
湖 南	Hunan	39713	12393	298	27022		587	1144
广 东	Guangdong	55496	44538	151	10807	68	2806	2022
广 西	Guangxi	1358	1006	6	346		100	115
海 南	Hainan							
重 庆	Chongqing	55089	47283	593	7213		1500	1207
四 川	Sichuan	39785	32788	626	6371	1	2175	1527
贵 州	Guizhou	17433	16257	45	1131	168	803	722
云 南	Yunnan	309995	296444	363	13188	54	8144	4100
西 藏	Tibet							
陕 西	Shaanxi	98710	62293	2209	34208		7320	17200
甘 肃	Gansu	2299	1599	7	693		473	214
青 海	Qinghai							
宁 夏	Ningxia							
新 疆	Xinjiang	626	547	2	77		63	963

单位：万元
Unit: 10000 yuan

财务费用 Financial Expenses	#利息支出 Interest Expenses	营业利润 Operating Profits	利润总额 Total Profits	应交所得税 Income Tax Payable	应付职工薪酬 Payables to Employees	应交增值税 VAT Payable
15315	**11179**	**50249**	**49344**	**8225**	**92132**	**29504**
502	243	741	930	351	4935	1675
12		2558	2473	143	1357	1011
9000	8816	802	1311	40	11895	436
3		62	63	16	210	209
		158	158	12	62	35
14	1	612	633	160	320	388
279	12	384	117	288	4734	99
269	247	1715	1736	19	21255	137
-252		2364	2283	642	1530	750
241	13	2652	2651	486	775	517
1023	616	10916	11031	2089	4963	3622
-10		105	163	30	435	133
1		52	52	2	141	46
50	3	548	528		350	350
1838	379	4645	4338	147	3854	941
132		992	991		319	16
278	4	1630	1697	359	1097	372
89	3	217	274		23393	53
106	30	1670	1703	356	2179	1037
		130	130	33	107	61
396	102	4726	3258	259	1713	1159
85	32	2420	2408	385	1286	901
-12	147	316	330	83	1191	463
544	518	871	1088	79	2686	291
719	13	8969	8969	2240	527	14732
2		22	22	6	452	70
6		-28	7		366	

联营企业
Joint Ownership Enterprises

地 区	Region	主营业务收入 Revenue from Principal Business	主营业务成本 Cost of Principal Business	主营业务税金及附加 Taxes and Other Charges on Principal Business	主营业务利润 Profits from Principal Business	其他业务利润 Profits from Other Business	销售费用 Selling Expenses	管理费用 Administrative Expenses
全 国	**National Total**	**844878**	**738660**	**4044**	**102174**	**231**	**30360**	**16392**
北 京	Beijing	10914	10082	19	813		283	10
天 津	Tianjin	15813	12180	85	3548		826	94
河 北	Hebei							
山 西	Shanxi							
内蒙古	Inner Mongolia							
辽 宁	Liaoning	12437	11115	16	1306	9	897	266
吉 林	Jilin							
黑龙江	Heilongjiang	62151	55183	159	6809		583	687
上 海	Shanghai	122212	108435	306	13471	115	4475	764
江 苏	Jiangsu	19690	17114	141	2435		632	145
浙 江	Zhejiang	65937	52329	294	13314	1	3132	368
安 徽	Anhui	8732	7484	26	1222		598	607
福 建	Fujian	1181	844	5	332	17	67	74
江 西	Jiangxi							
山 东	Shandong	144063	132413	1103	10547		6446	5352
河 南	Henan	7258	5522	43	1693	25	233	248
湖 北	Hubei	18461	18256	87	118		47	29
湖 南	Hunan	63314	52893	312	10109		3468	465
广 东	Guangdong	237219	208840	1228	27151	64	6287	4695
广 西	Guangxi							
海 南	Hainan							
重 庆	Chongqing	7165	6427	18	720		299	76
四 川	Sichuan	13701	11557	144	2000		410	339
贵 州	Guizhou	30292	24056	48	6188		1617	2062
云 南	Yunnan							
西 藏	Tibet							
陕 西	Shaanxi	1250	1154	2	94		10	8
甘 肃	Gansu	3088	2776	8	304		50	103
青 海	Qinghai							
宁 夏	Ningxia							
新 疆	Xinjiang							

3-4-6 Continued 4

单位：万元
Unit: 10000 yuan

财务费用 Financial Expenses	#利息支出 Interest Expenses	营业利润 Operating Profits	利润总额 Total Profits	应交所得税 Income Tax Payable	应付职工薪酬 Payables to Employees	应交增值税 VAT Payable
1454	**96**	**56657**	**57373**	**12206**	**29902**	**15355**
3		518	514	94	181	118
-67	-61	3284	3305	607	475	640
4		17	145	34	151	1343
358		4969	4971	14	500	80
-11	10	8358	8509	2020	2899	1992
43	1	1615	1615	192	737	259
-53	3	10368	10361	2466	1332	2237
9		21	14	8	342	223
-11		219	243	60	82	141
327	116	-341	116	1105	3599	1353
19	6	1192	1192	138	386	165
5	1	37	37		103	13
-83	-85	6673	6669	1268	1266	1669
421	22	15874	15850	3832	17005	4401
10	14	341	313	139	178	306
11	7	1244	1255	228	536	338
406		2103	2103	1	76	2
		76	76		18	6
63	62	89	85		36	69

有限责任公司

Limited Liability Corporations

地　区	Region	主营业务收入 Revenue from Principal Business	主营业务成本 Cost of Principal Business	主营业务税金及附加 Taxes and Other Charges on Principal Business	主营业务利润 Profits from Principal Business	其他业务利润 Profits from Other Business	销售费用 Selling Expenses	管理费用 Administr-ative Expenses
全　国	**National Total**	**436230529**	**388313910**	**1736913**	**46179706**	**3942442**	**27118323**	**12035446**
北　京	Beijing	38938771	35524358	117261	3297152	763299	2773153	952554
天　津	Tianjin	9516667	8541719	25477	949471	69893	775973	335789
河　北	Hebei	10521981	9554828	34413	932740	142181	587586	344917
山　西	Shanxi	4179253	3781348	11644	386261	29468	230554	136863
内蒙古	Inner Mongolia	5118066	4572430	21230	524406	39545	293501	148945
辽　宁	Liaoning	11218806	10049520	37646	1131640	79669	726870	420709
吉　林	Jilin	6630294	5861023	23057	746214	88606	338626	305131
黑龙江	Heilongjiang	6644391	5903769	32085	708537	76018	318936	203488
上　海	Shanghai	20582363	18182945	79280	2320138	247271	1724477	735466
江　苏	Jiangsu	31166155	27825833	108633	3231689	290085	1894396	805531
浙　江	Zhejiang	25872834	23034269	78689	2759876	363547	1836559	596578
安　徽	Anhui	14498167	13082771	56333	1359063	101017	792375	369159
福　建	Fujian	18426075	16248915	75843	2101317	73703	1073198	542754
江　西	Jiangxi	7799475	6904383	35290	859802	50319	398894	245847
山　东	Shandong	31193025	27934474	116581	3141970	216362	1664628	784187
河　南	Henan	24319562	21237854	161774	2919934	224274	1248294	747219
湖　北	Hubei	24113174	21353961	111624	2647589	89348	1399563	614961
湖　南	Hunan	11772075	10434686	59604	1277785	58898	672421	295489
广　东	Guangdong	47958306	41935222	160983	5862101	364081	3393051	1286769
广　西	Guangxi	7059408	6359126	22195	678087	75156	412594	150948
海　南	Hainan	3245451	2688483	30229	526739	36047	261335	129954
重　庆	Chongqing	10586122	9318319	53151	1214652	74287	588372	257672
四　川	Sichuan	21751780	19560361	63721	2127698	128869	1343193	475702
贵　州	Guizhou	7590445	6757082	24820	808543	35175	420659	169335
云　南	Yunnan	9689918	8807879	20762	861277	46310	491551	188014
西　藏	Tibet	628740	585165	1236	42339	876	23165	15423
陕　西	Shaanxi	15802015	13898547	130409	1773059	116877	875087	539119
甘　肃	Gansu	3427273	3042214	13398	371661	17227	192266	84834
青　海	Qinghai	1097875	962444	4437	130994	13534	75843	39730
宁　夏	Ningxia	1199832	1023036	5362	171434	14930	115995	42734
新　疆	Xinjiang	3682230	3346946	19746	315538	15570	175209	69625

3-4-6 Continued 5

单位：万元
Unit: 10000 yuan

财务费用 Financial Expenses	#利息支出 Interest Expenses	营业利润 Operating Profits	利润总额 Total Profits	应交所得税 Income Tax Payable	应付职工薪酬 Payables to Employees	应交增值税 VAT Payable
2688421	**1467527**	**9423542**	**9846273**	**1875280**	**15397854**	**6717386**
211542	218039	296932	354759	134470	1465946	484853
65820	18975	-371426	-346532	-61287	318261	123875
95757	43733	87412	133730	34520	697871	175177
34380	21341	29880	32190	15422	155305	86533
45438	14183	108728	122557	21515	220414	153483
122596	55304	36239	-24615	39538	322977	180746
63186	31631	122640	135365	20521	401295	48371
61726	35940	214118	218607	28683	159994	85190
72063	46949	275647	316991	102679	760289	255698
189236	96024	713442	723356	148632	842028	666778
131376	106980	604000	636342	144603	960431	363361
76513	25355	248869	299192	44902	483066	171871
80427	41813	534242	527253	61439	578828	217175
52094	29971	199841	208024	20322	292280	104484
235286	110848	765336	832361	157624	882569	608220
221895	69458	925420	931309	132708	853676	436400
157962	118659	608423	590019	126089	760193	327765
69442	35309	298940	283995	37285	336353	181850
226832	100185	1618712	1703541	303749	1617960	772616
22366	13704	153494	147853	25564	238447	88299
23923	12652	178357	177514	51333	141203	39594
57725	29944	314727	393402	31837	351217	140006
108311	61535	396785	384852	70749	1046849	236435
66842	23382	136372	135923	31953	244124	159351
38291	27517	237759	241345	36293	326067	149974
2178	311	4840	5371	518	20201	7467
84227	33951	477403	461697	71422	481569	209606
28091	16107	78209	82458	13122	205931	129578
10112	3448	21875	27423	7835	46997	17678
6569	4353	26804	28857	6090	38940	22357
26215	19926	79522	81134	15150	146573	72594

3-4-6 续表 6

股份有限公司

Share-holding Corporations Ltd.

地　区	Region	主营业务收入 Revenue from Principal Business	主营业务成本 Cost of Principal Business	主营业务税金及附加 Taxes and Other Charges on Principal Business	主营业务利润 Profits from Principal Business	其他业务利润 Profits from Other Business	销售费用 Selling Expenses	管理费用 Administrative Expenses
全　国	**National Total**	**121654787**	**108461044**	**501107**	**12692636**	**1402524**	**8044347**	**3165442**
北　京	Beijing	7413708	6622955	40170	750583	202160	587135	213406
天　津	Tianjin	1878350	1714685	5870	157795	3444	123028	60222
河　北	Hebei	3365893	3016145	14684	335064	39360	207299	96419
山　西	Shanxi	2802505	2656146	3729	142630	4802	157494	41162
内蒙古	Inner Mongolia	2601631	2430290	4468	166873	5181	155856	21423
辽　宁	Liaoning	4360651	3963131	21105	376415	39883	228722	146120
吉　林	Jilin	2730285	2447274	19130	263881	14159	163432	129590
黑龙江	Heilongjiang	2142306	1882568	9586	250152	50013	101430	90236
上　海	Shanghai	4876071	4325003	15259	535809	32356	402650	137310
江　苏	Jiangsu	11753103	10676431	48583	1028089	162692	545054	306130
浙　江	Zhejiang	4278229	3870010	11855	396364	59070	341046	110161
安　徽	Anhui	5047703	4609141	13938	424624	12084	218969	101791
福　建	Fujian	2332267	2121840	6789	203638	13523	149265	44114
江　西	Jiangxi	1219583	1024602	8610	186371	9635	106903	49262
山　东	Shandong	11237611	9889383	43061	1305167	136099	730375	255411
河　南	Henan	3887319	3427775	24962	434582	20632	257062	79014
湖　北	Hubei	6740100	5845548	30438	864114	186475	634969	218987
湖　南	Hunan	8803874	7868288	46244	889342	57020	673076	216512
广　东	Guangdong	9388847	8040575	34846	1313426	71714	681825	206352
广　西	Guangxi	1683578	1532894	7236	143448	16177	48568	56842
海　南	Hainan	1224394	1104070	1411	118913	4249	48375	17638
重　庆	Chongqing	4730880	4128525	28779	573576	134629	412582	141913
四　川	Sichuan	7614353	6824493	17691	772169	73819	510711	176513
贵　州	Guizhou	2725858	2402918	5095	317845	29265	124886	15298
云　南	Yunnan	1429365	1331603	2074	95688	1146	58918	14107
西　藏	Tibet	255413	256127	296	-1010	797	8688	4896
陕　西	Shaanxi	1215384	1091662	11747	111975	23	55236	37984
甘　肃	Gansu	1922935	1732049	4638	186248	5207	90698	18131
青　海	Qinghai	175974	162540	510	12924	1806	5103	7634
宁　夏	Ningxia	248967	195887	1752	51328	6150	39081	6482
新　疆	Xinjiang	1567649	1266486	16551	284612	8954	175911	144382

单位：万元
Unit: 10000 yuan

财务费用 Financial Expenses	#利息支出 Interest Expenses	营业利润 Operating Profits	利润总额 Total Profits	应交所得税 Income Tax Payable	应付职工薪酬 Payables to Employees	应交增值税 VAT Payable
474019	**416828**	**3567261**	**3542585**	**537461**	**5709158**	**2060780**
19768	51635	310977	294627	44573	340541	117705
11365	6725	-8024	-5066	2077	69140	28391
19645	15651	100723	99883	9810	111912	130947
2055	581	-80948	-87229	128	97540	11987
4687	2034	-5712	-2246	1804	87751	105142
10606	9490	180366	185409	21146	233137	38351
46069	40591	94833	89056	29857	95537	98857
13908	13060	118414	111534	21553	82754	23192
-3973	4427	248519	259851	40933	164008	101768
8448	83140	467456	446928	51648	245707	164551
44633	39715	17018	25578	28182	155903	58135
21546	8347	110213	109970	6417	103572	53238
10697	14954	34584	33975	5274	87255	21263
10277	1917	42962	42404	3159	62978	16368
58605	34166	164724	156473	28943	296430	187297
20150	6555	106504	103051	19915	110327	82495
18576	12522	208967	239366	53133	359414	116890
30447	17120	165432	164075	27483	1958031	100190
14576	8277	552750	560200	44405	343174	190903
4000	2116	49199	47677	2567	41233	19135
983	121	52802	51034	14174	15957	14499
7556	4231	145125	131549	19777	59866	84427
32317	24192	199484	201560	17971	279780	83153
2485	717	205012	204191	27169	36891	39312
2405	1253	14047	13939	1342	24888	10370
27	16	-13676	-13323	175	6215	2698
6854	3525	35196	29849	3945	48995	19089
17774	2869	63582	62730	2595	50175	112411
1128	508	1492	6217	415	5456	2339
2223	24	-13155	-17640	56	10073	1029
34182	6349	-1605	-3037	6835	124518	24648

私营企业
Private Enterprises

地　区	Region	主营业务收入 Revenue from Principal Business	主营业务成本 Cost of Principal Business	主营业务税金及附加 Taxes and Other Charges on Principal Business	主营业务利润 Profits from Principal Business	其他业务利润 Profits from Other Business	销售费用 Selling Expenses	管理费用 Administrative Expenses
全　国	**National Total**	**354840480**	**314492784**	**1879087**	**38468609**	**2169706**	**18168496**	**11248710**
北　京	Beijing	10554662	9248382	24553	1281727	197750	872924	459172
天　津	Tianjin	4526327	4221409	10193	294725	33526	185899	118640
河　北	Hebei	11338721	10226964	39101	1072656	97388	653120	373483
山　西	Shanxi	11369789	10396433	30893	942463	79169	590760	328431
内蒙古	Inner Mongolia	3939445	3557482	16887	365076	29546	213743	134293
辽　宁	Liaoning	8502209	7711335	32519	758355	41975	354367	366552
吉　林	Jilin	4881404	4392614	20098	468692	65081	150071	188478
黑龙江	Heilongjiang	3779562	3403559	22735	353268	12520	140901	106059
上　海	Shanghai	13774795	12069352	34140	1671303	139854	1200868	471097
江　苏	Jiangsu	38584305	34083738	173083	4327484	250287	1767178	1198669
浙　江	Zhejiang	29340835	26268049	84192	2988594	206295	1802023	968256
安　徽	Anhui	13799258	12314025	53184	1432049	46046	576102	400745
福　建	Fujian	20822815	18452244	111841	2258730	69343	871873	625613
江　西	Jiangxi	6122057	5432879	44429	644749	40057	276255	168459
山　东	Shandong	31360754	27892569	240526	3227659	167103	1082854	827451
河　南	Henan	13515748	11581308	128181	1806259	34920	491780	402918
湖　北	Hubei	12757985	11106029	128544	1523412	31735	578783	370919
湖　南	Hunan	21488507	18834103	182497	2471907	53283	901737	602751
广　东	Guangdong	28912472	25294422	121506	3496544	238733	2024458	1194241
广　西	Guangxi	6308219	5719679	19429	569111	25498	329199	193557
海　南	Hainan	214835	192104	534	22197	2920	12140	7947
重　庆	Chongqing	13241388	11408563	123129	1709696	78818	754357	456548
四　川	Sichuan	14507607	12965431	69503	1472673	88818	761413	373927
贵　州	Guizhou	7032244	6385129	29948	617167	20885	279294	156068
云　南	Yunnan	7485543	6633273	24656	827614	40168	452041	200473
西　藏	Tibet	184022	155726	1052	27244	4	15872	7586
陕　西	Shaanxi	7991834	6902946	84147	1004741	25505	392614	273224
甘　肃	Gansu	2464667	2179391	11721	273555	12443	135917	75552
青　海	Qinghai	744345	680545	1243	62557	4662	32518	19013
宁　夏	Ningxia	1299626	1181309	3289	115028	9044	57780	37590
新　疆	Xinjiang	3994500	3601792	11334	381374	26330	209655	140998

单位：万元
Unit: 10000 yuan

财务费用 Financial Expenses	#利息支出 Interest Expenses	营业利润 Operating Profits	利润总额 Total Profits	应交所得税 Income Tax Payable	应付职工薪酬 Payables to Employees	应交增值税 VAT Payable
2913374	**1313803**	**9033197**	**10184308**	**1318885**	**12508925**	**5362888**
117838	101057	28408	42215	40295	463863	149795
32142	12306	7589	16353	9652	117473	60707
103858	39806	87415	102962	28286	521950	109139
117925	69089	19713	27625	18955	489696	146052
33506	14414	37655	62971	18578	203765	74977
122726	37412	38971	1198965	17483	321312	242182
50238	23156	104658	110108	10355	135967	60910
36121	12747	108663	103807	8456	90183	42812
62362	38838	101286	137172	51773	475264	181415
333778	115677	1424048	1431900	244194	1051331	747811
258936	181133	274585	296826	104001	1618132	551949
88932	31720	411345	398593	31059	460841	122641
119388	50588	688309	668567	57206	555150	222899
43522	20373	193523	183043	12309	234471	75602
255927	100398	1198792	1150654	169736	927010	447004
142234	39310	796556	779284	75402	423011	176324
126651	48521	476372	446144	42982	425966	160496
179748	68437	802014	721977	47733	592635	285723
179333	82334	598068	687555	130848	1166104	558118
36347	21632	56832	60365	12176	222684	65601
1918	1188	2234	2489	721	7804	4767
85379	44339	502146	458576	39897	437763	219629
102582	50480	343362	381192	48848	489740	191924
36035	15512	151440	137748	18270	225911	108065
51458	37001	177014	170761	15910	306656	70788
-274	191	10913	14918	1559	8119	1879
52465	16133	325552	314272	35181	234224	102001
23406	11967	49980	52574	11487	80887	58811
66150	1553	8846	10662	546	24117	12859
17600	8871	17247	19944	3707	50464	22154
35142	17620	-10339	-5914	11280	146432	87854

其他企业

Other Enterprises

地　区	Region	主营业务收入 Revenue from Principal Business	主营业务成本 Cost of Principal Business	主营业务税金及附加 Taxes and Other Charges on Principal Business	主营业务利润 Profits from Principal Business	其他业务利润 Profits from Other Business	销售费用 Selling Expenses	管理费用 Administrative Expenses
全　国	**National Total**	**2700832**	**2187105**	**27657**	**486070**	**1862**	**114949**	**97541**
北　京	Beijing	1445	1252		193		120	70
天　津	Tianjin	1015	677		338			148
河　北	Hebei	12925	11655	115	1155	3	315	291
山　西	Shanxi	12052	11189	8	855		177	256
内蒙古	Inner Mongolia	17086	15070	125	1891	145	1347	713
辽　宁	Liaoning	26384	22790	76	3518	81	828	1748
吉　林	Jilin	63747	54596	255	8896		652	1009
黑龙江	Heilongjiang	51799	47447	959	3393		396	236
上　海	Shanghai	5900	5308	6	586	19	305	449
江　苏	Jiangsu	845643	647437	7160	191046	210	27132	27675
浙　江	Zhejiang	70034	62750	97	7187		1669	2326
安　徽	Anhui	65695	53480	89	12126		2359	2604
福　建	Fujian	130464	91414	1562	37488		21614	6752
江　西	Jiangxi	19398	14366	132	4900	191	1117	676
山　东	Shandong	278178	231572	2158	44448	50	11765	10769
河　南	Henan	84975	67577	976	16422		3045	3321
湖　北	Hubei	160283	130067	4492	25724	137	6366	5919
湖　南	Hunan	98635	81597	1297	15741	20	3713	4501
广　东	Guangdong	200764	155179	3657	41928	410	11355	9154
广　西	Guangxi	1646	1601		45			72
海　南	Hainan							
重　庆	Chongqing	101126	90588	1298	9240	580	2652	2811
四　川	Sichuan	184773	158321	1549	24903	9	8180	6537
贵　州	Guizhou	13315	11419	36	1860		461	755
云　南	Yunnan	104642	90408	275	13959		3476	2780
西　藏	Tibet	1643	1298	46	299		8	11
陕　西	Shaanxi	120085	106381	1104	12600		4146	4313
甘　肃	Gansu	16780	14039	141	2600	7	1222	719
青　海	Qinghai	2210	2105	7	98		18	7
宁　夏	Ningxia							
新　疆	Xinjiang	8190	5522	37	2631		511	919

单位：万元
Unit: 10000 yuan

财务费用 Financial Expenses	#利息支出 Interest Expenses	营业利润 Operating Profits	利润总额 Total Profits	应交所得税 Income Tax Payable	应付职工薪酬 Payables to Employees	应交增值税 VAT Payable
18898	**4138**	**257690**	**240789**	**12564**	**145845**	**35481**
		3	3		96	
		191	191		102	
27	42	522	326	1	382	177
75	49	241	276		325	18
141	3	-306	20	6	766	36
224	48	833	686	23	717	69
109	69	7135	7254	6	1217	118
54	7	2544	1221	4	454	423
-1		208	224	53	530	49
6033	1145	131068	118921	4788	54335	9780
364	171	3306	3474	121	3624	239
234	42	6972	6980	129	3614	313
448	79	8590	8737	1175	14094	5200
186	34	2959	2565	26	1001	409
2020	387	20360	20260	1437	13837	4243
959	137	9432	8790	303	4172	1011
2627	877	10596	9400	411	6621	2064
1182	53	6231	6483	810	2255	618
2075	260	19397	18592	1455	5999	3917
		17	-25	4	452	
509	14	3846	4121	126	1972	1687
366	91	9667	9348	1430	3656	4295
51	36	594	511	8	523	247
700	555	7106	7212	46	2124	332
7		273			208	4
457	22	4014	3611	197	20645	135
43	15	625	341	4	1339	52
2		70	70		40	1
6	3	1196	1196	1	745	44

港、澳、台商投资企业

Enterprises with Funds from Hong Kong,Macao and Taiwan

地　区	Region	主营业务收入 Revenue from Principal Business	主营业务成本 Cost of Principal Business	主营业务税金及附加 Taxes and Other Charges on Principal Business	主营业务利润 Profits from Principal Business	其他业务利润 Profits from Other Business	销售费用 Selling Expenses	管理费用 Administr-ative Expenses
全　国	**National Total**	**64504762**	**51658784**	**331865**	**12514113**	**1137802**	**8874330**	**3050902**
北　京	Beijing	3601042	2970345	19647	611050	83205	498336	181471
天　津	Tianjin	1790977	1507633	12400	270944	21094	247116	52786
河　北	Hebei	196100	161761	604	33735	1719	16086	3842
山　西	Shanxi	393738	332516	2046	59176	2170	33000	13543
内蒙古	Inner Mongolia	173721	145122	1201	27398	2858	14369	4754
辽　宁	Liaoning	1669292	1455408	8139	205745	15559	162837	70501
吉　林	Jilin	446041	378310	2067	65664	723	34522	21014
黑龙江	Heilongjiang	505618	434091	1989	69538	10863	53572	18298
上　海	Shanghai	12101125	8015471	88082	3997572	72789	2771169	966794
江　苏	Jiangsu	8692565	7437868	32179	1222518	135445	897039	318046
浙　江	Zhejiang	5199723	4326932	27433	845358	90096	556239	202214
安　徽	Anhui	1977878	1592644	6463	378771	10866	281831	64279
福　建	Fujian	2421814	1990303	9690	421821	14378	353689	116233
江　西	Jiangxi	565303	502228	1628	61447	22797	57410	14900
山　东	Shandong	2702290	2259042	11868	431380	33402	275969	57000
河　南	Henan	1854146	1565884	9564	278698	117552	110768	131535
湖　北	Hubei	1767647	1569758	4606	193283	167849	185135	69800
湖　南	Hunan	900425	734171	7894	158360	18563	103859	32240
广　东	Guangdong	9018766	7134498	37199	1847069	213440	1356070	398356
广　西	Guangxi	1177798	1006487	4130	167181	24009	110373	33969
海　南	Hainan	169218	143117	1315	24786	2297	16395	4062
重　庆	Chongqing	860819	698838	5659	156322	15776	107262	43684
四　川	Sichuan	1877586	1561058	11167	305361	24661	199879	85439
贵　州	Guizhou	433970	366267	2567	65136	17553	47712	9983
云　南	Yunnan	1019759	875516	4159	140084	9728	75411	32057
西　藏	Tibet	10264	9072	33	1159		142	200
陕　西	Shaanxi	2386194	1973226	14621	398347	67	269053	91675
甘　肃	Gansu	217866	184217	1662	31987	5536	19241	4906
青　海	Qinghai	62175	52786	325	9064	1068	5477	958
宁　夏	Ningxia	84319	74139	378	9802		6876	1377
新　疆	Xinjiang	226583	200076	1150	25357	1739	7493	4986

单位：万元
Unit: 10000 yuan

财务费用 Financial Expenses	#利息支出 Interest Expenses	营业利润 Operating Profits	利润总额 Total Profits	应交所得税 Income Tax Payable	应付职工薪酬 Payables to Employees	应交增值税 VAT Payable
223146	**199727**	**2657860**	**2792745**	**731366**	**3401307**	**1331523**
10047	9738	17858	4862	22204	217673	60848
13116	10369	30340	46609	22596	82720	56056
470	481	17205	9446	2677	6677	2266
2467	2052	15864	16486	5248	15639	5187
3014	136	12017	12136	-276	4203	2371
10846	2905	10389	19475	11186	68069	34585
15417	15101	14151	-35097	2577	12736	8694
3797	3757	8476	8540	3877	25610	21298
42466	9211	445026	487611	171920	912449	286913
44380	34115	167998	154733	73602	315854	120240
14174	17463	222368	240962	57749	236448	88054
1300	406	72391	66902	19338	57421	18563
-24197	1748	292859	301427	15828	159831	41615
2898	668	10453	14928	4140	18208	4778
8638	4868	141884	146370	43705	115270	67652
3998	1139	143771	149092	37833	50988	43140
-2554	1075	113946	119579	28269	68652	21498
7704	6619	87628	79811	10753	54788	24321
21902	42617	475992	473875	111636	632010	271108
2742	3406	48333	151014	11069	49997	24289
6921	6761	3332	3071	773	8036	3191
4084	3853	16815	21623	9525	39662	21075
9075	7454	54515	58062	15338	81132	28449
-1114	469	31651	31460	7410	21896	12715
3966	3501	50260	61385	12375	36298	21649
-34		850	849		365	-8
16547	9223	115860	111503	21092	89290	24478
155	55	13221	13432	4003	6308	5147
17		3680	3760	856	2966	1614
222	206	2897	3087	1063	3244	1897
682	331	15830	15752	3000	6866	7840

外商投资企业
Foreign Funded Enterprises

地 区	Region	主营业务收入 Revenue from Principal Business	主营业务成本 Cost of Principal Business	主营业务税金及附加 Taxes and Other Charges on Principal Business	主营业务利润 Profits from Principal Business	其他业务利润 Profits from Other Business	销售费用 Selling Expenses	管理费用 Administr-ative Expenses
全 国	**National Total**	**69742187**	**55942088**	**317417**	**13482682**	**1042439**	**9100047**	**2846368**
北 京	Beijing	9403654	7296368	52702	2054584	188659	1363005	368965
天 津	Tianjin	1436280	1160856	9636	265788	25811	164448	94414
河 北	Hebei	806380	729821	1852	74707	4214	54097	9741
山 西	Shanxi	73765	60828	288	12649	2133	12590	1617
内蒙古	Inner Mongolia	10006	8795	13	1198	924	3404	570
辽 宁	Liaoning	1159363	980759	7282	171322	19584	163670	49775
吉 林	Jilin	229809	197895	872	31042	1120	13179	11581
黑龙江	Heilongjiang	226344	181763	939	43642	9823	40171	13674
上 海	Shanghai	13385783	9225184	80391	4080208	160161	2477140	1162809
江 苏	Jiangsu	5817184	5127503	12880	676801	69899	641619	175592
浙 江	Zhejiang	3731382	3227074	17665	486643	106725	341254	159351
安 徽	Anhui	258398	226256	898	31244	11250	48310	9243
福 建	Fujian	2861940	2464711	7206	390023	28651	237545	31899
江 西	Jiangxi	456371	404353	1162	50856	3181	41448	12407
山 东	Shandong	1279575	1046628	8738	224209	37101	149247	92032
河 南	Henan	336407	311449	718	24240	4666	28890	4488
湖 北	Hubei	1015060	785182	5717	224161	21704	136186	52911
湖 南	Hunan	590885	493745	4024	93116	9485	57403	33547
广 东	Guangdong	17102133	13973157	62101	3066875	272594	2191553	327283
广 西	Guangxi	158706	131586	458	26662	138	20157	3423
海 南	Hainan	167011	138961	581	27469	5342	18580	3805
重 庆	Chongqing	1328643	1158642	4397	165604	17745	112499	36422
四 川	Sichuan	2684732	2185296	16355	483081	11060	316129	90666
贵 州	Guizhou	505706	415153	1957	88596	1567	49118	12977
云 南	Yunnan	844816	700008	2485	142323	20795	102512	18868
西 藏	Tibet	2735	2945		-210	34	347	24
陕 西	Shaanxi	3607700	3079998	15055	512647	2040	298997	59197
甘 肃	Gansu	9262	8142	9	1111	918	1835	584
青 海	Qinghai							
宁 夏	Ningxia	6327	4670	37	1620		680	241
新 疆	Xinjiang	245830	214360	999	30471	5115	14034	8262

单位：万元
Unit: 10000 yuan

财务费用 Financial Expenses	#利息支出 Interest Expenses	营业利润 Operating Profits	利润总额 Total Profits	应交所得税 Income Tax Payable	应付职工薪酬 Payables to Employees	应交增值税 VAT Payable
220687	**234997**	**2883722**	**3084183**	**707599**	**2858636**	**1428141**
55208	79277	522598	522979	126412	459039	144240
19956	17594	36358	46211	14634	63172	43989
3186	2921	-6895	-23459	425	22939	3601
776	612	196	233	44	5440	1101
344		-4076	-4995		1096	43
15717	8862	2444	-1996	9916	38430	18379
1623	834	9124	10003	2742	6287	9348
3380	1418	-5489	-3515	368	9203	1584
28350	21878	612263	671426	198926	647495	324193
12709	13494	201848	201229	37742	233188	74307
6675	35181	96215	100543	29890	142659	61577
4062	1668	-17769	-21765	358	19654	2344
9170	3282	88920	88262	21747	113875	42453
459	1148	946	-1373	784	18148	6659
4000	4105	23981	32832	7977	61502	22742
1702	1052	-2909	-3624	256	12305	2838
4884	7325	60604	62065	19689	63827	26191
13	475	16066	16581	2393	30534	10815
25901	18587	820925	968225	133051	602061	494227
-55	70	7056	6046	358	8852	1984
2496	4184	10129	10342	2187	9547	1711
4951	2456	33345	33374	8461	33360	25798
5608	2534	117023	117013	35499	108991	15971
3389	2524	25155	22756	5109	15642	10718
1811	1053	56100	54986	8604	47757	13790
12		-560	-560	40	183	-47
5134	1650	165469	165235	37784	74056	62848
-35		-355	-360		386	-29
-27		726	710	179	448	162
-712	813	14284	14779	2024	8560	4604

3-4-7 各地区限额以上零售业企业损益及分配(按国民经济行业分)

综合零售
Integrated Retail

地　区	Region	主营业务收入 Revenue from Principal Business	主营业务成本 Cost of Principal Business	主营业务税金及附加 Taxes and Other Charges on Principal Business	主营业务利润 Profits from Principal Business	其他业务利润 Profits from Other Business	销售费用 Selling Expenses	管理费用 Administrative Expenses
全　国	**National Total**	**202959353**	**171753504**	**1369588**	**29836261**	**5462749**	**21789475**	**9466073**
北　京	Beijing	12678185	10585562	71017	2021606	857769	1978987	644217
天　津	Tianjin	2073340	1842286	13590	217464	62631	273253	146898
河　北	Hebei	7059628	6044287	48313	967028	166576	692470	409874
山　西	Shanxi	3006640	2689953	13016	303671	50828	231746	119630
内蒙古	Inner Mongolia	1443424	1193516	11037	238871	27417	150469	74264
辽　宁	Liaoning	6133904	5282747	51255	799902	123445	587174	488901
吉　林	Jilin	3751528	3141444	32494	577590	58544	252403	316374
黑龙江	Heilongjiang	4028112	3413196	27729	587187	128998	270602	171867
上　海	Shanghai	13370630	10876253	77152	2417225	390670	1893711	857692
江　苏	Jiangsu	19630034	16923373	115113	2591548	489260	1922886	888544
浙　江	Zhejiang	10970284	9392814	62256	1515214	455306	1267895	478733
安　徽	Anhui	8418638	7311414	43033	1064191	85432	694221	331550
福　建	Fujian	6425981	5500873	36324	888784	75178	728525	245443
江　西	Jiangxi	2844454	2435688	24895	383871	74640	307994	99581
山　东	Shandong	17897414	15584497	122021	2190896	391300	1440787	699705
河　南	Henan	8465590	6966786	87743	1411061	276982	688756	477476
湖　北	Hubei	11706582	9820342	91700	1794540	400345	1155153	499203
湖　南	Hunan	9933902	8343693	96784	1493425	100625	939469	367490
广　东	Guangdong	16464814	13576304	71580	2816930	574690	2459892	547269
广　西	Guangxi	2995329	2521537	17115	456677	62846	349413	126920
海　南	Hainan	1452854	1069086	26842	356926	20751	178577	81161
重　庆	Chongqing	7285079	6156438	49231	1079410	205303	769530	294131
四　川	Sichuan	8083445	6824351	45214	1213880	132995	939324	268993
贵　州	Guizhou	2066366	1695880	14977	355509	44983	245580	72707
云　南	Yunnan	3249721	2809844	11589	428288	44434	259868	95716
西　藏	Tibet	76364	64904	777	10683	318	11170	9696
陕　西	Shaanxi	7133335	6075254	64796	993285	84207	654289	392055
甘　肃	Gansu	1372195	1164378	9947	197870	26284	129080	50230
青　海	Qinghai	424899	352246	3276	69377	12072	47139	17328
宁　夏	Ningxia	861780	698011	5228	158541	14043	124049	29607
新　疆	Xinjiang	1654902	1396547	23544	234811	23876	145063	162818

Income and Distribution of Enterprises above Designated Size of Retail Trade by Region and Sector

单位：万元

Unit: 10000 yuan

财务费用 Financial Expenses	#利息支出 Interest Expenses	营业利润 Operating Profits	利润总额 Total Profits	应交所得税 Income Tax Payable	应付职工薪酬 Payables to Employees	应交增值税 VAT Payable
1537583	**1039340**	**5949488**	**6027660**	**1394675**	**12104819**	**3223715**
136823	173941	326847	314860	102431	884451	211643
35768	28477	-83811	-59265	131	150994	25900
83985	36964	94713	119644	33640	458801	107377
46525	22434	-3120	1197	7058	146032	85208
25993	2702	52330	56706	11824	66078	17098
115709	31229	196320	122480	49204	353458	87864
88709	62692	167705	118188	33383	122637	48791
40614	34144	237399	229173	30939	150440	84006
38772	40525	365001	421596	129278	653657	172320
124100	98444	545925	527696	137636	878143	297696
73286	84821	271419	292532	94595	647440	132915
47927	11741	136581	148442	27619	334800	83192
-4468	18656	327654	330068	19018	362986	86183
22014	9465	39664	45531	8765	161696	36833
141646	76000	454121	458535	100088	769307	267434
72142	21916	428662	429887	81626	440853	169781
65054	46857	527739	543457	110223	699757	200792
73672	40524	309715	301928	41043	2080039	133804
64823	59505	579140	604636	159055	1074958	305861
16943	10873	53068	102129	10167	151755	46333
22746	17294	124741	125248	38164	80868	11642
29282	17998	199849	189636	35422	241704	146166
58079	40720	182909	193319	43025	390280	123950
13107	7989	85803	83743	17727	99458	47128
12889	9941	136555	132474	19546	151150	54535
43	-21	205	1289	641	7281	497
32788	22139	199906	200802	29795	327642	117423
8917	3136	50764	53378	11407	66485	77127
5972	1398	12017	14086	4122	21388	6537
5594	1526	-1933	-5765	2784	26692	9347
38128	5309	-68400	-69970	4319	103589	28332

食品、饮料及烟草制品专门零售
Special Retail of Food, Beverages and Tobaccos

地　区	Region	主营业务收入 Revenue from Principal Business	主营业务成本 Cost of Principal Business	主营业务税金及附加 Taxes and Other Charges on Principal Business	主营业务利润 Profits from Principal Business	其他业务利润 Profits from Other Business	销售费用 Selling Expenses	管理费用 Administr-ative Expenses
全　国	**National Total**	**38209825**	**30728721**	**295200**	**7185904**	**176178**	**3211251**	**1580110**
北　京	Beijing	1094624	743655	7398	343571	14802	194523	69991
天　津	Tianjin	359387	281173	1724	76490	1037	47626	24412
河　北	Hebei	200637	172948	695	26994	400	15557	7016
山　西	Shanxi	601659	538802	1786	61071	685	28130	20830
内蒙古	Inner Mongolia	311950	277457	753	33740	317	13807	16988
辽　宁	Liaoning	313350	263367	1599	48384	2196	19797	15289
吉　林	Jilin	366148	310570	1989	53589	2115	20664	22353
黑龙江	Heilongjiang	145164	124963	2609	17592	713	7659	4617
上　海	Shanghai	1121742	794392	4306	323044	7726	287511	69855
江　苏	Jiangsu	4142122	3373718	29261	739143	10910	215755	163112
浙　江	Zhejiang	981274	823686	3615	153973	11491	98447	52984
安　徽	Anhui	1729084	1508280	6443	214361	5087	84775	54093
福　建	Fujian	4188516	3427289	32648	728579	4536	281306	182281
江　西	Jiangxi	888376	709608	8396	170372	3171	51273	46759
山　东	Shandong	2832560	2405387	24115	403058	41497	117508	94706
河　南	Henan	1775959	1465037	18419	292503	11300	84722	56551
湖　北	Hubei	3111103	2473851	30394	606858	23758	243926	109312
湖　南	Hunan	1889282	1554080	19837	315365	9858	119266	83450
广　东	Guangdong	3997811	2457378	39184	1501249	7267	820621	196313
广　西	Guangxi	308954	265816	1232	41906	804	18060	20493
海　南	Hainan	28094	26212	56	1826		1145	1761
重　庆	Chongqing	1481063	1229922	9471	241670	5757	104681	50412
四　川	Sichuan	1542250	1312077	13311	216862	2130	117176	54692
贵　州	Guizhou	823477	697524	6741	119212	1138	29662	32312
云　南	Yunnan	2286628	2081266	8074	197288	6534	93954	47008
西　藏	Tibet	52010	39427	5853	6730	124	1533	3034
陕　西	Shaanxi	1305201	1093607	13812	197782	525	67427	63233
甘　肃	Gansu	218153	181503	1069	35581	38	14996	9864
青　海	Qinghai	22959	20075	62	2822	69	791	1433
宁　夏	Ningxia	42575	35179	180	7216	8	4871	1994
新　疆	Xinjiang	47713	40472	168	7073	185	4082	2962

3-4-7 Continued 1

单位：万元
Unit: 10000 yuan

财务费用 Financial Expenses	#利息支出 Interest Expenses	营业利润 Operating Profits	利润总额 Total Profits	应交所得税 Income Tax Payable	应付职工薪酬 Payables to Employees	应交增值税 VAT Payable
236523	**106955**	**2464654**	**2510170**	**308225**	**1816952**	**774946**
221	592	96892	98573	25044	135735	55924
823	55	5957	6780	4424	35697	12915
1429	887	4073	4247	345	13443	2305
4830	3569	8706	10156	1849	23454	6120
3130	1642	816	10155	1521	23331	3831
2451	1451	1375	3768	826	15576	5649
3758	2808	7872	10887	1313	15712	3544
812	587	5112	5102	460	6707	1709
3221	1642	14501	25947	8945	150306	30160
31840	13042	343567	335037	46698	182142	89305
6559	4405	14778	17180	3361	66470	23369
9676	3301	72999	72012	4533	70756	11581
19031	4740	257862	282937	16471	164369	50131
9063	3243	65135	61535	2831	56522	9055
20484	5499	192321	190298	21771	103168	56730
18333	3501	134107	132541	16051	62611	22043
22848	7371	248702	243141	35978	106783	71017
20107	5936	97172	84038	6038	78074	20479
-1359	5095	606569	622615	76734	186624	204403
2642	1842	1985	4895	962	18016	3247
337	335	-1407	-31	31	1808	783
10259	3378	78950	79595	6787	61267	16553
15915	13417	27189	35046	7854	79341	14479
4907	2478	57774	56610	9265	20175	11140
12796	10272	50207	53502	2690	54161	23912
3		2201	1089	74	2554	1828
8644	3733	60474	51928	4586	58991	17950
2080	1051	9067	8441	562	15183	3454
208	111	392	1022	1	1470	426
876	537	-499	694	26	2278	556
600	435	-195	430	194	4228	348

纺织、服装及日用品专门零售
Special Retail of Textiles, Garments and Daily Consumer Articles

地区	Region	主营业务收入 Revenue from Principal Business	主营业务成本 Cost of Principal Business	主营业务税金及附加 Taxes and Other Charges on Principal Business	主营业务利润 Profits from Principal Business	其他业务利润 Profits from Other Business	销售费用 Selling Expenses	管理费用 Administrative Expenses
全国	**National Total**	**50759752**	**35688134**	**363774**	**14707844**	**373088**	**9075587**	**3377958**
北京	Beijing	3159221	2096846	16681	1045694	48237	846312	192122
天津	Tianjin	1025795	796414	9980	219401	14441	178920	52675
河北	Hebei	521487	439175	4571	77741	8271	37947	36805
山西	Shanxi	872614	736578	3952	132084	8797	67086	62572
内蒙古	Inner Mongolia	320191	265917	2996	51278	10858	39795	11478
辽宁	Liaoning	829329	695330	4628	129371	8653	93278	56453
吉林	Jilin	362010	290262	4686	67062	5825	26750	38784
黑龙江	Heilongjiang	994160	834302	10749	149109	2289	60152	29595
上海	Shanghai	14082797	7810665	103488	6168644	95806	3930260	1467867
江苏	Jiangsu	3870189	3088344	25954	755891	16445	408218	149605
浙江	Zhejiang	3242182	2327539	16734	897909	22903	621052	192180
安徽	Anhui	844573	703986	4306	136281	2751	83137	28197
福建	Fujian	3746153	3082525	17477	646151	2356	285818	120551
江西	Jiangxi	507467	399316	5256	102895	8020	53043	25713
山东	Shandong	2495580	1982151	19976	493453	12151	195213	94994
河南	Henan	1169301	937278	14058	217965	4490	73062	45713
湖北	Hubei	1396125	1095600	12641	287884	13035	156681	62669
湖南	Hunan	1126095	920885	12316	192894	7165	97194	43594
广东	Guangdong	5455489	3484344	39505	1931640	41274	1229027	421958
广西	Guangxi	212696	167946	958	43792	775	28218	7629
海南	Hainan	31030	22784	120	8126	1545	6547	2892
重庆	Chongqing	1086730	821929	8670	256131	17652	131785	62547
四川	Sichuan	1091595	798911	6959	285725	7340	187651	63378
贵州	Guizhou	161052	125330	796	34926	1469	22466	7374
云南	Yunnan	344801	274554	1447	68800	1323	46817	20706
西藏	Tibet	25456	16017	245	9194	34	1782	85
陕西	Shaanxi	1223448	1012929	10780	199739	1669	108629	42381
甘肃	Gansu	116446	87201	933	28312	576	14211	4461
青海	Qinghai	61098	50224	276	10598	1827	8356	7943
宁夏	Ningxia	32910	26976	107	5827	1927	3782	2589
新疆	Xinjiang	351732	295876	2529	53327	3184	32398	22448

3-4-7 Continued 2

单位：万元
Unit: 10000 yuan

财务费用 Financial Expenses	#利息支出 Interest Expenses	营业利润 Operating Profits	利润总额 Total Profits	应交所得税 Income Tax Payable	应付职工薪酬 Payables to Employees	应交增值税 VAT Payable
318483	**165141**	**2499991**	**2516335**	**556301**	**3641023**	**1503642**
11655	11809	47231	54298	17656	290641	73821
18130	10304	-6341	-2280	6894	52759	36667
16074	10523	7911	688	508	26314	14679
16519	13903	1583	1927	3291	34098	12095
3515	1659	9330	9777	1836	14258	7302
11753	7389	-20560	-23596	3748	38179	15266
6202	5062	5110	9773	876	15370	6962
4841	4338	79064	77922	993	31540	15668
46336	15048	937664	973138	269859	1241377	554599
34299	5971	217733	213649	47034	183154	88862
16727	17483	109709	130888	29974	242386	108035
2756	567	24171	23774	4862	48826	15039
14543	3002	228686	195448	24016	146028	65508
7524	2401	12869	22031	3068	34203	12580
15957	9095	190223	192204	30126	132608	53351
10877	1967	90191	89434	9241	52175	20557
12203	6639	50950	51972	7326	79939	36406
7417	1227	52894	50421	4943	52997	18888
25514	15625	283136	272867	60698	586719	234775
3622	267	1049	4598	1237	9608	4888
314	281	-177	-1765	22	4548	936
9482	6281	56075	44510	6123	79447	27674
6348	3282	38066	36909	6771	86559	28560
1282	943	5840	5606	927	13483	3904
1715	1655	12511	12770	1721	63451	7644
-603		7964	10550	977	202	733
5224	1229	49467	45571	8033	46410	17933
1859	1909	7841	7711	1696	8195	10110
1050	974	-4738	770	23	4298	967
1321	1215	229	284	9	3576	379
4026	3093	4310	4486	1813	17675	8854

文化、体育用品及器材专门零售
Special Retail of Culture, Sports Appliances and Equipments

地 区	Region	主营业务收入 Revenue from Principal Business	主营业务成本 Cost of Principal Business	主营业务税金及附加 Taxes and Other Charges on Principal Business	主营业务利润 Profits from Principal Business	其他业务利润 Profits from Other Business	销售费用 Selling Expenses	管理费用 Administr-ative Expenses
全 国	**National Total**	**30563823**	**24647367**	**264592**	**5651864**	**293820**	**2628732**	**1744612**
北 京	Beijing	3849585	3270882	30656	548047	52524	328599	189906
天 津	Tianjin	564515	487373	5465	71677	22962	55092	49330
河 北	Hebei	472079	330803	3099	138177	5505	43863	44504
山 西	Shanxi	334880	274729	3054	57097	9411	38907	14687
内蒙古	Inner Mongolia	116472	90483	2303	23686	3252	10917	12280
辽 宁	Liaoning	677151	538381	5355	133415	3249	35047	87083
吉 林	Jilin	235778	195482	2062	38234	1703	12534	20268
黑龙江	Heilongjiang	368443	304229	2122	62092	4898	30085	17983
上 海	Shanghai	1977254	1299705	34782	642767	41192	475620	138978
江 苏	Jiangsu	3399776	2859083	20855	519838	26300	201967	128173
浙 江	Zhejiang	1239588	997760	12236	229592	11088	122135	83848
安 徽	Anhui	822772	691722	6780	124270	6012	46696	34859
福 建	Fujian	2474384	2130239	16237	327908	984	138265	103143
江 西	Jiangxi	967563	787673	4897	174993	7139	41156	69120
山 东	Shandong	1801857	1500232	23055	278570	9870	112492	63977
河 南	Henan	1541099	1178104	24696	338299	9330	104211	85556
湖 北	Hubei	762313	619394	7930	134989	9786	43603	47178
湖 南	Hunan	1092519	882569	10075	199875	3623	75231	68302
广 东	Guangdong	1712222	1299361	20092	392769	17429	199178	132343
广 西	Guangxi	374539	291864	2613	80062	4648	38606	25018
海 南	Hainan	31540	24317	502	6721	4496	4750	3653
重 庆	Chongqing	861579	624479	3904	233196	8006	55215	40466
四 川	Sichuan	1327434	987007	4428	335999	17765	142541	127755
贵 州	Guizhou	241780	199173	1284	41323	357	12142	14165
云 南	Yunnan	1529719	1391224	4502	133993	6899	62371	41942
西 藏	Tibet	5287	4469	5	813	416	465	683
陕 西	Shaanxi	1224450	943461	6534	274455	2954	150024	62517
甘 肃	Gansu	238538	198836	4181	35521	372	10202	15990
青 海	Qinghai	9713	7119	182	2412	83	1048	905
宁 夏	Ningxia	46819	37429	82	9308	310	5329	3936
新 疆	Xinjiang	262175	199785	624	61766	1257	30441	16063

单位：万元
Unit: 10000 yuan

财务费用 Financial Expenses	#利息支出 Interest Expenses	营业利润 Operating Profits	利润总额 Total Profits	应交所得税 Income Tax Payable	应付职工薪酬 Payables to Employees	应交增值税 VAT Payable
195388	**100148**	**1412872**	**1493771**	**168663**	**1806051**	**361261**
12062	13733	91786	109866	28909	221659	48779
6949	7089	52	10280	3574	37939	9407
1929	341	44863	42931	135	38964	2182
2388	133	12278	13163	2745	24298	3080
1096	457	3309	4580	101	10378	2861
4013	700	11831	17713	3819	24204	7770
1557	514	6694	6895	296	14794	1235
1726	232	15277	14720	2715	38942	3392
8583	5070	46602	53636	22557	141365	34665
20736	5460	220005	225907	21383	123495	47358
6011	9111	35514	38678	4985	100841	14354
3551	2303	49864	80790	2683	36975	8911
18353	11957	77413	73906	4980	85766	19718
-952	2359	68812	61835	960	57633	20751
20793	11679	91549	75689	11557	86390	27310
11259	2422	138880	140552	16642	87956	14978
7687	2675	44182	46194	5003	41004	11400
12127	4168	46497	45592	2188	61134	18572
7482	2293	99174	105854	16124	128667	26522
222	468	21520	22026	327	33662	3619
3118	3114	-10	406		3909	383
1133	-412	59205	74323	1968	39004	8474
5619	1239	104990	101173	1808	119032	7518
154	222	15374	15488	682	13111	1744
6350	5585	33214	34016	4713	57401	4443
-3		89	331	29	674	63
12725	899	54866	57528	2657	57160	4841
12966	929	7749	7268	247	80884	3820
27	26	469	591	22	6609	81
911	566	514	1004	43	5538	281
4816	4816	10310	10836	4810	26663	2749

医药及医疗器材专门零售
Special Retail of Medicines and Medical Appliances

地 区	Region	主营业务收入 Revenue from Principal Business	主营业务成本 Cost of Principal Business	主营业务税金及附加 Taxes and Other Charges on Principal Business	主营业务利润 Profits from Principal Business	其他业务利润 Profits from Other Business	销售费用 Selling Expenses	管理费用 Administrative Expenses
全 国	**National Total**	**49797856**	**42075798**	**221141**	**7500917**	**226835**	**4294122**	**1781188**
北 京	Beijing	2868225	2591520	6795	269910	23314	160975	82176
天 津	Tianjin	266211	222463	931	42817	1026	31343	13228
河 北	Hebei	923470	759437	3981	160052	3394	87258	51319
山 西	Shanxi	1884299	1622781	4625	256893	2858	190043	37398
内蒙古	Inner Mongolia	391745	311544	1924	78277	2190	45179	20588
辽 宁	Liaoning	1878705	1569076	6454	303175	5124	194953	66745
吉 林	Jilin	1090671	931962	3503	155206	7695	72982	41070
黑龙江	Heilongjiang	1513140	1322386	7036	183718	3579	65535	56712
上 海	Shanghai	2376723	2084892	6024	285807	18057	156009	70038
江 苏	Jiangsu	3287142	2751488	13922	521732	14662	282400	138234
浙 江	Zhejiang	2541185	2177601	7119	356465	16064	216621	110487
安 徽	Anhui	1689452	1466979	5943	216530	3403	107871	61459
福 建	Fujian	1412452	1248771	4730	158951	3617	77044	47003
江 西	Jiangxi	563721	456073	2889	104759	1024	62051	25807
山 东	Shandong	6229883	5387990	24896	816997	12827	422790	200485
河 南	Henan	1814873	1473821	15204	325848	4334	165785	69011
湖 北	Hubei	2220851	1899363	20269	301219	8273	162200	76351
湖 南	Hunan	2380106	1919386	17529	443191	13080	259162	85844
广 东	Guangdong	4179495	3248316	19359	911820	38418	560661	185450
广 西	Guangxi	2806041	2528602	7101	270338	3625	130890	63229
海 南	Hainan	52713	35123	367	17223	55	13084	3825
重 庆	Chongqing	1248134	1043074	5878	199182	8313	128808	47581
四 川	Sichuan	1334966	1103485	7101	224380	4862	143202	60549
贵 州	Guizhou	574108	440977	3360	129771	863	79120	26958
云 南	Yunnan	1128245	797816	6863	323566	13350	231182	42879
西 藏	Tibet	11446	8975	61	2410		1422	717
陕 西	Shaanxi	1128977	935913	9786	183278	7498	111254	37281
甘 肃	Gansu	518502	420381	2975	95146	393	60594	17387
青 海	Qinghai	63437	53563	162	9712		7498	3138
宁 夏	Ningxia	179184	153835	554	24795	707	14580	6974
新 疆	Xinjiang	1239755	1108205	3800	127750	4230	51626	31265

单位：万元
Unit: 10000 yuan

财务费用 Financial Expenses	#利息支出 Interest Expenses	营业利润 Operating Profits	利润总额 Total Profits	应交所得税 Income Tax Payable	应付职工薪酬 Payables to Employees	应交增值税 VAT Payable
349310	**280021**	**1583936**	**2901333**	**286181**	**2928766**	**1110382**
47415	83022	110619	111550	6763	120797	40508
932	117	-286	202	1320	19881	5930
4379	1017	21818	21834	4443	74289	38637
8249	6414	31927	32030	10263	122695	29207
1276	115	12980	12043	1846	27629	8578
11290	8460	42002	1226908	11393	89485	19453
11202	9963	38242	38459	8885	281179	18138
7015	4495	56758	58710	10207	59230	10038
3059	297	84644	88299	12897	108354	36164
22534	2276	107154	104660	22771	183031	76875
19963	18547	68774	71776	15704	160926	48833
14997	9349	38445	32025	5860	84032	37016
8534	6989	42875	44389	8368	72041	19386
5604	3061	12959	12571	1326	43333	9553
49960	32512	131714	158291	29448	213903	227592
16901	7158	80626	80330	11349	102643	37719
18649	22939	64849	67456	16185	97528	35054
22057	15547	152419	150999	16987	148649	68817
18347	8581	185889	204322	50556	327364	139365
8507	7483	77038	126731	6524	84024	37840
95	50	3358	3343	903	10112	2329
4909	2768	32619	33959	2837	75769	25605
7907	4588	22428	61257	4366	78577	21330
5538	3195	18175	18093	3348	44278	15932
8968	7325	50364	49344	7570	140367	20731
-2		387	620	84	650	503
6254	2623	38232	33050	2697	67569	17713
4782	3057	11611	11925	3176	32739	30104
820	12	-588	-525	283	5055	1301
1569	1192	2213	2647	614	12708	3238
7602	6868	43691	44035	7208	39929	26893

汽车、摩托车、燃料及零配件专门零售
Special Retail of Motor Vehicles, Motorcycles, Fuel and Parts

地区	Region	主营业务收入 Revenue from Principal Business	主营业务成本 Cost of Principal Business	主营业务税金及附加 Taxes and Other Charges on Principal Business	主营业务利润 Profits from Principal Business	其他业务利润 Profits from Other Business	销售费用 Selling Expenses	管理费用 Administr-ative Expenses
全国	**National Total**	**499417795**	**461655818**	**1397279**	**36364698**	**2467831**	**17069907**	**9190798**
北京	Beijing	24460648	22672745	77034	1710869	313458	911457	540512
天津	Tianjin	10621161	9832121	20525	768515	44629	438385	195786
河北	Hebei	15174545	14282373	26158	866014	87495	501863	224172
山西	Shanxi	10397112	9812919	16785	567408	43255	376817	210101
内蒙古	Inner Mongolia	8300474	7750892	20994	528588	29955	365178	119985
辽宁	Liaoning	13417843	12551488	27204	839151	37456	416644	257478
吉林	Jilin	7871696	7308708	16268	546720	86369	253281	163679
黑龙江	Heilongjiang	5292892	4946717	14844	331331	14925	155464	111746
上海	Shanghai	18589280	17280474	46646	1262160	63202	626890	409838
江苏	Jiangsu	45262351	41622909	116014	3523428	250863	1579412	844494
浙江	Zhejiang	38517591	35880658	92050	2544883	238640	1255417	754552
安徽	Anhui	16355821	15274530	32037	1049254	61620	489010	251728
福建	Fujian	16956950	15802873	46986	1107091	89002	565539	293175
江西	Jiangxi	7893322	7305150	27200	560972	26103	225551	151984
山东	Shandong	35089625	32082789	123135	2883701	87815	1093353	636334
河南	Henan	22700197	20820837	92480	1786880	78018	693717	409589
湖北	Hubei	19875616	18403546	83301	1388769	33117	633293	382727
湖南	Hunan	23001138	21236492	84993	1679653	63728	733038	395354
广东	Guangdong	58959895	53819661	157433	4982801	414652	2252118	1188715
广西	Guangxi	8146571	7606578	19903	520090	40696	257823	142578
海南	Hainan	3139483	2843303	5708	290472	21837	127071	58675
重庆	Chongqing	12226236	11252909	46368	926959	58560	401652	190649
四川	Sichuan	26494728	24488311	72943	1933474	147379	962980	418898
贵州	Guizhou	12842003	11823766	28862	989375	31323	418992	179599
云南	Yunnan	11289657	10516997	19871	752789	38320	420070	183326
西藏	Tibet	1044132	993376	1709	49047	860	32383	15724
陕西	Shaanxi	12290410	11228525	50272	1011613	27549	429050	239329
甘肃	Gansu	4966719	4568574	10713	387432	10204	163690	62562
青海	Qinghai	1294611	1204228	2154	88229	2515	42356	26476
宁夏	Ningxia	1437674	1325636	3610	108428	4336	42221	34152
新疆	Xinjiang	5507414	5115733	13078	378603	19950	205192	96881

3-4-7 Continued 5

单位：万元

Unit: 10000 yuan

财务费用 Financial Expenses	#利息支出 Interest Expenses	营业利润 Operating Profits	利润总额 Total Profits	应交所得税 Income Tax Payable	应付职工薪酬 Payables to Employees	应交增值税 VAT Payable
3132478	**1588056**	**9873501**	**10037665**	**1861688**	**12688915**	**7600792**
143641	110018	461383	469773	121364	671821	281977
49695	18514	152652	164083	44888	267825	177732
108642	57206	84632	112508	31124	337165	236264
67952	42030	-81100	-89139	9448	353770	103446
46091	21253	34224	65043	19906	325565	269218
116500	51619	31897	39226	26891	396928	336279
59250	27458	102197	109252	16609	167101	131296
57351	23660	39548	42989	14554	84908	43174
61178	32255	349948	382329	90462	378769	177282
326596	147841	1171732	1170651	211871	830750	929546
273181	199976	588800	600425	172155	1516558	621271
92240	34452	269514	272196	36353	340223	143445
91921	56159	276620	275669	52251	393775	163385
57281	29550	157318	159823	19429	183355	88261
261347	106158	737381	739905	130607	754676	521422
191000	69315	621741	618145	82005	472607	369979
146769	97314	305775	289514	70083	500066	196738
119160	53549	469670	416288	46963	480401	282310
290251	133635	1926124	2043379	286378	1424802	1099660
28922	16876	132897	128619	27334	209145	81501
7788	2847	124810	122648	29692	68183	42671
63491	39493	327996	360896	31843	292145	184787
139220	77637	627284	594658	111041	1071514	275948
52417	26505	236805	222901	27390	269448	225038
51898	34983	171419	187578	37354	237636	139211
2280	492	-2225	-1730	511	27238	11195
76092	29897	320286	292623	74235	276161	139826
31962	17403	109106	110583	12651	113185	174498
69381	2850	17459	21641	2892	34151	19842
15142	7875	26924	29841	6241	40813	25221
33840	19236	80684	85348	17163	168230	108369

家用电器及电子产品专门零售
Special Retail of Household Electric Appliances and Electronic Products

地区	Region	主营业务收入 Revenue from Principal Business	主营业务成本 Cost of Principal Business	主营业务税金及附加 Taxes and Other Charges on Principal Business	主营业务利润 Profits from Principal Business	其他业务利润 Profits from Other Business	销售费用 Selling Expenses	管理费用 Administrative Expenses
全国	**National Total**	**88181745**	**78493745**	**385802**	**9302198**	**438574**	**5334556**	**2466283**
北京	Beijing	18317018	16771827	35984	1509207	86181	1061719	268202
天津	Tianjin	1287177	1223762	1688	61727	2460	139876	87579
河北	Hebei	1542772	1375142	4477	163153	12458	97658	53057
山西	Shanxi	866147	784987	1801	79359	3874	51946	25923
内蒙古	Inner Mongolia	809419	708001	2220	99198	3647	47070	45962
辽宁	Liaoning	1759401	1567987	5074	186340	16930	105377	50484
吉林	Jilin	792892	706617	2489	83786	2998	43311	29619
黑龙江	Heilongjiang	1059844	952900	5437	101507	5815	46180	34448
上海	Shanghai	3765960	3319157	6604	440199	8640	320740	77141
江苏	Jiangsu	7531198	6674748	28353	828097	72986	507911	254114
浙江	Zhejiang	3690939	3316820	7058	367061	28289	239881	111425
安徽	Anhui	2493872	2230392	9015	254465	11010	141735	64468
福建	Fujian	2967953	2627908	10836	329209	7903	142069	74932
江西	Jiangxi	1389769	1264637	6706	118426	5248	65735	33815
山东	Shandong	7029756	6199600	34220	795936	20908	304133	153817
河南	Henan	4131782	3539179	39846	552757	16660	206540	134414
湖北	Hubei	3692949	3175017	27501	490431	2039	185718	128474
湖南	Hunan	2997597	2599161	30834	367602	5287	132176	82281
广东	Guangdong	7606381	6708076	24254	874051	41111	576694	380286
广西	Guangxi	1449154	1292233	5206	151715	25870	90472	44869
海南	Hainan	262340	229032	444	32864	1718	22604	9802
重庆	Chongqing	2893529	2574180	21736	297613	15805	147809	59852
四川	Sichuan	3401206	3026352	14316	360538	13850	238510	68646
贵州	Guizhou	838416	746346	3629	88441	747	47413	19573
云南	Yunnan	898905	788255	2365	108285	7530	75978	27522
西藏	Tibet	51232	47316	51	3865	1	4940	1860
陕西	Shaanxi	3479334	3017504	49977	411853	3468	189356	101087
甘肃	Gansu	362344	317939	1359	43046	736	29680	11354
青海	Qinghai	111186	95742	222	15222	4057	8077	6217
宁夏	Ningxia	242233	206087	1028	35118	7826	26088	8715
新疆	Xinjiang	459040	406841	1071	51128	2521	37160	16345

3-4-7 Continued 6

单位：万元
Unit: 10000 yuan

财务费用 Financial Expenses	#利息支出 Interest Expenses	营业利润 Operating Profits	利润总额 Total Profits	应交所得税 Income Tax Payable	应付职工薪酬 Payables to Employees	应交增值税 VAT Payable
362144	**217694**	**1720928**	**1679874**	**209398**	**2533258**	**1173475**
48174	56573	291856	308543	59634	371230	203242
19421	167	-426162	-425040	-85698	84232	8812
12099	3688	21322	22337	4497	55177	15942
4065	1019	853	2145	1139	27784	8825
3674	831	25904	27039	2186	41797	21642
11376	10017	20777	8278	1432	44506	15574
2594	733	12750	12203	1495	23090	6919
4520	739	28701	23035	3074	21110	11722
3674	1715	58217	67200	15245	104842	40539
6369	64803	211399	213582	30678	200686	137292
18629	11478	33031	38919	7755	126228	50677
10623	3711	50392	44837	4203	128906	28638
9724	3667	78980	78823	7327	83935	51557
3284	1792	18059	15529	1493	42044	15760
32197	9058	338543	321493	38873	131800	88086
29404	5054	195425	195269	20539	132736	59087
24698	11766	150820	143173	19676	97636	51237
23196	3029	137125	109505	3631	63256	41149
37116	10582	119077	132160	21114	284924	119554
5278	3511	18732	16838	2776	46807	17778
467	92	-5265	-4914	325	11362	4703
11607	4189	104715	102564	8445	67938	40873
16191	1778	63095	60856	6062	92258	29544
3587	2054	20751	18814	2583	66676	8135
4224	1523	10568	5401	1240	33576	14995
232	61	-1607	2	42	2189	190
10465	2811	131532	127402	26310	78743	59034
2969	556	1110	3403	686	13337	4022
242	36	1158	578	354	2770	668
1044	412	7147	7559	1424	11026	8643
1002	249	1922	2342	859	40656	8637

五金、家具及室内装饰材料专门零售

Special Retail of Hardware, Furniture and Interior Decoration Materials

地区	Region	主营业务收入 Revenue from Principal Business	主营业务成本 Cost of Principal Business	主营业务税金及附加 Taxes and Other Charges on Principal Business	主营业务利润 Profits from Principal Business	其他业务利润 Profits from Other Business	销售费用 Selling Expenses	管理费用 Administrative Expenses
全国	**National Total**	**29330258**	**24124884**	**381737**	**4823637**	**48751**	**1658150**	**1337542**
北京	Beijing	878674	574221	6241	298212	5431	190928	76967
天津	Tianjin	501886	389514	3367	109005	1053	35919	22311
河北	Hebei	239074	192554	1366	45154	36	15312	9206
山西	Shanxi	508854	450178	3837	54839	538	15664	16551
内蒙古	Inner Mongolia	142381	129190	789	12402	277	4500	4425
辽宁	Liaoning	253211	201602	2111	49498	109	20853	26425
吉林	Jilin	279330	247943	1870	29517	707	6804	16440
黑龙江	Heilongjiang	141660	116781	1667	23212	93	10469	13324
上海	Shanghai	720352	499760	6130	214462	2737	120786	112152
江苏	Jiangsu	3208146	2762097	21868	424181	897	128943	94998
浙江	Zhejiang	562440	450960	2862	108618	2389	65849	43225
安徽	Anhui	1012054	858523	15745	137786	1330	37791	41506
福建	Fujian	3059795	2690374	28105	341316	2657	95089	105473
江西	Jiangxi	449125	374349	5494	69282	41	16095	17162
山东	Shandong	2785259	2385383	49127	350749	3972	66840	67077
河南	Henan	1830360	1471808	28811	329741	916	82182	58945
湖北	Hubei	1275428	1016126	18303	240999	1818	85822	54993
湖南	Hunan	1147586	992763	13244	141579	2789	42906	36219
广东	Guangdong	2683429	2186691	23683	473055	10567	190596	140624
广西	Guangxi	257518	243124	1161	13233	264	4673	5136
海南	Hainan	13637	11548	39	2050	149	1640	1024
重庆	Chongqing	2931232	2387493	68441	475298	1420	147973	180462
四川	Sichuan	900156	755782	7583	136791	812	57772	39396
贵州	Guizhou	125859	103903	2611	19345	-2	3029	4022
云南	Yunnan	452059	393425	631	58003	288	9976	5710
西藏	Tibet							
陕西	Shaanxi	2473254	1944646	60645	467963	2995	86538	99379
甘肃	Gansu	92171	62694	1097	28380	513	12964	10807
青海	Qinghai	47127	44895	95	2137	1	1149	844
宁夏	Ningxia	7166	5064	31	2071	987	717	1055
新疆	Xinjiang	351034	181493	4782	164759	2967	98371	31684

单位：万元
Unit: 10000 yuan

财务费用 Financial Expenses	#利息支出 Interest Expenses	营业利润 Operating Profits	利润总额 Total Profits	应交所得税 Income Tax Payable	应付职工薪酬 Payables to Employees	应交增值税 VAT Payable
254727	**83463**	**1643576**	**1778906**	**205079**	**917151**	**527358**
4104	3647	30819	31145	11196	90205	34578
10041	1631	42012	52145	13514	12339	11481
1018	302	9973	3403	177	14124	2566
2834	1261	19732	23155	766	6487	3684
456	175	2233	1114	246	3511	1390
5492	2248	-1558	-1294	579	13585	5030
1633	826	3691	3068	311	9992	3485
3024	350	3295	3394	302	4326	1113
13676	3908	-15661	-14251	6259	48312	13111
26407	8437	173967	172968	26990	59133	50291
5974	5060	-1573	-1268	749	36469	14817
7813	1576	52536	50640	2591	24835	26777
19866	3909	123291	114393	5282	59490	35907
2516	1303	31429	29879	1167	17319	6116
23177	4768	193971	214660	37380	72523	51216
24995	2665	164467	158856	15618	67124	31579
19827	5902	80117	74285	11316	42718	16897
8575	1847	55311	53118	2737	26638	13313
10909	6583	139473	272099	17704	94876	48945
977	718	6130	5373	923	4459	1245
1024	830	-1486	-1506	52	1264	320
27111	9677	143561	142043	14478	53572	69811
7651	2706	30885	28690	4806	26001	13579
505	259	11581	11409	1262	3355	1626
606	340	42737	43404	162	10090	1654
17606	5503	266741	271884	22584	43791	52580
2195	2030	1499	1112	172	15679	590
	1	87	107		617	430
134	130	146	-182	2	625	136
4581	4871	34170	35063	5754	53692	13091

货摊、无店铺及其他零售
Stalls, Non-shop and Other Retails

地 区	Region	主营业务收入 Revenue from Principal Business	主营业务成本 Cost of Principal Business	主营业务税金及附加 Taxes and Other Charges on Principal Business	主营业务利润 Profits from Principal Business	其他业务利润 Profits from Other Business	销售费用 Selling Expenses	管理费用 Administr-ative Expenses
全 国	**National Total**	**80937962**	**69750642**	**255320**	**10932000**	**347835**	**7335197**	**2246696**
北 京	Beijing	4113878	3666301	7226	440351	92115	554517	209676
天 津	Tianjin	3324878	2829498	7764	487616	7756	368354	95822
河 北	Hebei	651959	594617	1278	56064	2802	44782	13095
山 西	Shanxi	901445	817730	1425	82290	1760	46587	35817
内蒙古	Inner Mongolia	182790	152980	1048	28762	1139	9038	7920
辽 宁	Liaoning	1945357	1745880	3896	195581	4399	186434	24652
吉 林	Jilin	340219	297506	1215	41498	3917	13591	13862
黑龙江	Heilongjiang	405186	367744	1710	35732	24	23719	7009
上 海	Shanghai	9213217	8266375	14640	932202	39988	801093	304114
江 苏	Jiangsu	7627381	6700078	18177	909126	29945	559768	202545
浙 江	Zhejiang	7239296	5827731	18297	1393268	44539	1020498	233049
安 徽	Anhui	2446998	1985290	7989	453719	6745	240898	85749
福 建	Fujian	6169743	5227448	21306	920989	13975	408664	207272
江 西	Jiangxi	806478	664650	6088	135740	917	63761	25419
山 东	Shandong	3657680	3224000	18270	415410	10668	223379	64742
河 南	Henan	1719950	1350046	16298	353606	1373	83902	68899
湖 北	Hubei	4728688	4254341	11877	462470	8422	351472	41352
湖 南	Hunan	1389739	1132196	28985	228558	1753	65081	57475
广 东	Guangdong	13380836	11306856	36103	2037877	20483	1459818	300989
广 西	Guangxi	250664	193275	1311	56078	3524	25984	14980
海 南	Hainan	21581	17565	58	3958	305	2375	1250
重 庆	Chongqing	1332073	1170390	4167	157516	1698	113288	20109
四 川	Sichuan	4967472	4423750	10471	533251	1582	376501	121920
贵 州	Guizhou	846778	687353	2979	156446	24120	71003	17019
云 南	Yunnan	213352	152547	595	60210	870	14188	6535
西 藏	Tibet	11804	10640	45	1119		221	282
陕 西	Shaanxi	2606092	2308120	10675	287297	19333	184144	49522
甘 肃	Gansu	305150	275152	691	29307	2450	11606	7354
青 海	Qinghai	47549	32326	94	15129	445	2544	3059
宁 夏	Ningxia	5137	3738	39	1360	166	842	818
新 疆	Xinjiang	84593	64519	603	19471	623	7144	4390

单位：万元

Unit: 10000 yuan

财务费用 Financial Expenses	#利息支出 Interest Expenses	营业利润 Operating Profits	利润总额 Total Profits	应交所得税 Income Tax Payable	应付职工薪酬 Payables to Employees	应交增值税 VAT Payable
239423	**110772**	**1515594**	**1613146**	**319445**	**2382198**	**975338**
9933	8232	-240371	-231128	6642	276553	32585
53	339	33917	44030	7878	38037	40593
2907	579	-1600	805	1800	370136	6083
5346	3255	1919	4943	3815	41030	3389
1892	1948	8383	6761	2211	7312	4654
4660	998	-12666	-12964	2429	24655	25246
2176	1337	9275	8663	3237	9449	6711
1557	355	7113	6432	287	4929	5882
21998	20860	-99296	-64741	18613	169528	101407
11889	4234	178456	179910	25328	129089	82379
37062	31086	135157	156118	44331	241702	120806
3363	696	140355	138072	14229	63748	15994
19713	4061	242254	241097	25315	151555	62661
3602	1348	46764	44852	2280	35545	11844
10791	3090	132668	134465	26913	81320	71828
22375	4331	170982	170567	17118	75115	26470
6180	1747	72631	74524	5586	64187	55895
9627	2517	97845	96403	6181	42425	19004
23168	12124	280586	288208	53075	340497	142029
624	532	16199	17139	3114	19478	8205
348	65	803	829	37	1848	166
4017	2243	21069	23309	2901	29829	18777
2342	1297	38036	43964	6231	83070	50395
27441	85	116895	119768	30014	20570	18505
1234	955	40138	39800	585	9703	1556
-20		636	1126	23	376	-8
1990	391	51199	53688	5592	32153	32741
2239	1267	8823	9015	754	8564	3251
-292	101	9708	9863	1956	3218	4239
-4		88	139	49	1739	261
1212	699	7628	7489	921	4838	1790

3-5-1 限额以上批发和零售业产业活动单位和个体经营户基本情况
Basic Conditions of Establishments and Getihus above Designated Size of Wholesale and Retail Trades

项　目	Item	单位数(个) Number of Units (unit)	年末从业人数(人) Engaged Persons the Year-end (person)
总　计	**Total**	**36567**	**614256**
一、批发业	**Wholesale Trade**	**4534**	**88334**
(一)按登记注册类型分	**by Type of Registration**		
1.内资企业	**Domestic Funded Enterprises**	**216**	**24855**
国有企业	State-owned Enterprises	71	6302
集体企业	Collective-owned Enterprises	4	289
股份合作企业	Cooperative Enterprises	NA	561
联营企业	Joint Ownership Enterprises		
国有联营企业	State Joint Ownership Enterprises		
集体联营企业	Collective Joint Ownership Enterprises		
国有与集体联营企业	Joint State-collective Enterprises		
其他联营企业	Other Joint Ownership Enterprises		
有限责任公司	Limited Liability Corporations	52	7533
国有独资公司	State Sole Funded Corporations	4	164
其他有限责任公司	Other Limited Liability Corporations	48	7369
股份有限公司	Share-holding Corporations Ltd.	38	6099
私营企业	Private Enterprises	41	2807
私营独资企业	Private-funded Enterprises	7	117
私营合伙企业	Private Partnership Enterprises	NA	55
私营有限责任公司	Private Limited Liability Corporations	31	2613
私营股份有限公司	Private Share-holding Corporations Ltd.	NA	22
其他内资企业	Other Domestic Funded Enterprises	7	1264
2.港、澳、台商投资企业	**Enterprises with Funds from Hongkong, Macao and Taiwan**	**44**	**6935**
合资经营企业	Joint-venture Enterprises	10	1091
合作经营企业	Cooperative Enterprises	NA	25
独资经营企业	Enterprises with Sole Investment	26	4617
投资股份有限公司	Share-holding Corporations Ltd. with Investment	6	808
其他港澳台商投资企业	Other Enterprises with Funds from Hongkong, Macao and Taiwan	NA	394
3.外商投资企业	**Foreign Funded Enterprises**	**69**	**12128**
中外合资经营企业	Joint-venture Enterprises	23	2537
中外合作经营企业	Cooperative Enterprises	NA	828
外资企业	Enterprises with Sole Foreign Investment	37	8063
外商投资股份有限公司	Share-holding Corporations Ltd. with Foreign Investment	5	598
其他外商投资企业	Other Foreign Funded Enterprises	NA	102
4.个体经营户	**Getihus**	**4205**	**44416**

项 目	Item	单位数 (个) Number of Units (unit)	年末从业人数 (人) Engaged Persons the Year-end (pcrson)
(二)按国民经济行业分	**by Sector**		
农、林、牧产品批发	Wholesale of Agricultural, Forestry and Livestock Products	390	5900
食品、饮料及烟草制品批发	Wholesale of Food, Beverages and Tobaccos	1635	33768
米、面制品及食用油批发	Wholesale of Rice, Flour and Edible Oil	113	1660
肉、禽、蛋、奶及水产品批发	Wholesale of Meal, Fowls, Eggs, Milk and Aquatic Products	419	7987
酒、饮料及茶叶批发	Wholesale of Wine, Beverages and Teas	248	7940
烟草制品批发	Wholesale of Tobaccos	9	832
纺织、服装及家庭用品批发	Wholesale of Textiles, Wearing Apparel and Household Articles	932	17033
服装批发	Wholesale of Garments	283	3510
鞋帽批发	Wholesale of Shoes and Hats	144	2021
家用电器批发	Wholesale of Household Electric Appliances	45	5599
文化、体育用品及器材批发	Wholesale of Culture, Sports Appliances and Equipments	171	2844
文具用品批发	Wholesale of Stationeries	16	202
体育用品及器材批发	Wholesale of Sports Appliances and Equipments	6	58
图书批发	Wholesale of Books		
医药及医疗器材批发	Wholesale of Medicines and Medical Appliances	66	4721
西药批发	Wholesale of Western Medicine	5	192
中药批发	Wholesale of Chinese Traditional Medicine	60	4523
矿产品、建材及化工产品批发	Wholesale of Mineral Products, Building Materials and Chemical Products	787	15013
煤炭及制品批发	Wholesale of Coal and Related Products	31	1756
石油及制品批发	Wholesale of Petroleum and Related Products	24	2854
金属及金属矿批发	Wholesale of Metal Materials	156	2383
建材批发	Wholesale of Building Materials	365	5084
化肥批发	Wholesale of Chemical Fertilizer	136	1934
农药批发	Wholesale of Pesticides	9	120
机械设备、五金产品及电子产品批发	Wholesale of Machinery, Hardware and Electronic Products	502	8267
计算机、软件及辅助设备批发	Wholesale of Computer, Software and Assistant Appliances	82	1726
通讯及广播电视设备批发	Wholesale of Communication, Radios and Televisions Equipments	50	495
贸易经纪与代理	Trade Broker and Agency	NA	14
其他批发业	Other Wholesale not Classified Elsewhere	49	774

项 目	Item	单位数 (个) Number of Units (unit)	年末从业人数 (人) Engaged Persons the Year-end (person)	零售业营业面积 (平方米) Business Area of Retail Trade at the Year-end (m^2)
二、零售业	**Retail Trade**	**32033**	**525922**	**24444368**
(一)按登记注册类型分	**by Type of Registration**			
1.内资企业	**Domestic Funded Enterprises**	**570**	**56508**	**3568160**
国有企业	State-owned Enterprises	103	11677	232226
集体企业	Collective-owned Enterprises	26	1555	54973
股份合作企业	Cooperative Enterprises	4	137	3653
联营企业	Joint Ownership Enterprises			
国有联营企业	State Joint Ownership Enterprises			
集体联营企业	Collective Joint Ownership Enterprises			
国有与集体联营企业	Joint State-collective Enterprises			
其他联营企业	Other Joint Ownership Enterprises			
有限责任公司	Limited Liability Corporations	188	23860	1304721
国有独资公司	State Sole Funded Corporations	5	1160	35802
其他有限责任公司	Other Limited Liability Corporations	183	22700	1268919
股份有限公司	Share-holding Corporations Ltd.	49	6780	679069
私营企业	Private Enterprises	177	10726	812608
私营独资企业	Private-funded Enterprises	21	987	43113
私营合伙企业	Private Partnership Enterprises	5	171	5150
私营有限责任公司	Private Limited Liability Corporations	140	8839	700779
私营股份有限公司	Private Share-holding Corporations Ltd.	11	729	63566
其他企业	Other Enterprises	23	1773	480910
2.港、澳、台商投资企业	**Enterprises with Funds from Hongkong, Macao and Taiwan**	**60**	**6410**	**278299**
合资经营企业	Joint-venture Enterprises	17	2486	139072
合作经营企业	Cooperative Enterprises			
独资经营企业	Enterprises with Sole Investment	38	3642	133432
投资股份有限公司	Share-holding Corporations Ltd. with Investment	5	282	5795
其他港澳台商投资企业	Other Enterprises with Funds from Hongkong, Macao and Taiwan			
3.外商投资企业	**Foreign Funded Enterprises**	**103**	**21191**	**760148**
中外合资经营企业	Joint-venture Enterprises	24	2953	172291
中外合作经营企业	Cooperative Enterprises	7	9499	73583
外资企业	Enterprises with Sole Foreign Investment	63	8074	283670
外商投资股份有限公司	Share-holding Corporations Ltd. with Foreign Investment	5	265	35224
其他外商投资企业	Other Foreign Funded Enterprises	4	400	195380
4.个体经营户	**Getihus**	**31300**	**441813**	**19837761**

项　　目	Item	单位数（个）Number of Units (unit)	年末从业人数（人）Engaged Persons the Year-end (person)	零售业营业面积（平方米）Business Area of Retail Trade at the Year-end (m²)
(二)按国民经济行业分	**by Sector**			
综合零售	Integrated Retail	8820	222703	11102530
百货零售	Retail of General Merchandise	3974	86317	5196940
超级市场零售	Retail of Supermarkets	3132	95498	4541527
食品、饮料及烟草制品专门零售	Special Retail of Food, Beverages and Tobaccos	3637	46343	1329697
粮油零售	Retail of Cereal and Oil	305	3786	151603
肉、禽、蛋、奶及水产品零售	Retail of Meat, Poultry, Eggs, Milk and Aquatic Products	552	6150	141474
酒、饮料及茶叶零售	Retail of Wine, Beverages and Teas	1250	13478	370187
烟草制品零售	Retail of Tobaccos	245	1741	43296
纺织、服装及日用品专门零售	Special Retail of Textiles, Garments and Daily Consumer Articles	4541	72972	2620130
服装零售	Retail of Garments	2394	43227	1774852
文化、体育用品及器材专门零售	Special Retail of Culture, Sports Appliances and Equipments	1713	26143	545872
体育用品及器材零售	Retail of Sports Appliances and Equipments	59	524	19168
图书、报刊零售	Retail of Books, Newspapers and Magazines	106	7773	90886
医药及医疗器材专门零售	Special Retail of Medicines and Medical Appliances	778	12760	310152
药品零售	Retail of Medicines	742	12419	296693
汽车、摩托车、燃料及零配件专门零售	Special Retail of Motor Vehicles, Motorcycles, Fuel and Parts	1747	19096	1267221
汽车零售	Retail of Motor Vehicles	277	3048	207249
机动车燃料零售	Retail of Automotive Fuels	755	10077	811942
家用电器及电子产品专门零售	Special Retail of Household Electric Appliances and Electronic Products	4030	50510	1663788
日用家电设备零售	Retail of Household Electric Appliances	2121	23005	1075566
计算机、软件及辅助设备零售	Retail of Computer, Software and Assistant Appliances	577	4893	84777
通信设备零售	Retail of Communication Equipments	497	14367	131311
五金、家具及室内装饰材料专门零售	Special Retail of Hardware, Furniture and Interior Decoration Materials	6254	67970	5250461
货摊、无店铺及其他零售业	Stalls, Non-shop and Other Retails	513	7425	354517
互联网零售	Retail on the Internet	30	248	13602
(三)按零售业态分	**by Mode of Business Operation**			
有店铺零售	Store-based Retailing	31962	514261	24405403
超市	Supermarket	6849	160420	6833597
大型超市	Hypermarket	160	18828	1613936
百货店	Department Store	2655	61471	3301160
专业店	Speciality Store	10609	131463	5516886
专卖店	Exclusive Shop	6515	75150	3176663
无店铺零售	Non-Store Selling	71	11661	38965

3-5-2 各地区限额以上批发和零售业产业活动单位和个体经营户基本情况

Basic Conditions of Establishments and Getihus above Designated Size of Wholesale and Retail Trades by Region

地 区	Region	批发业 Wholesale Trade		零售业 Retail Trade	
		单位数 (个) Number of Units (unit)	年末从业人数 (人) Engaged Persons at the Year-end (person)	单位数 (个) Number of Units (unit)	年末从业人数 (人) Engaged Persons at the Year-end (person)
全 国	**National Total**	**4534**	**88334**	**32033**	**525922**
北 京	Beijing	24	2097	28	9115
天 津	Tianjin	47	2495	339	2822
河 北	Hebei	39	2590	446	11318
山 西	Shanxi	33	637	696	17099
内蒙古	Inner Mongolia	26	635	401	10637
辽 宁	Liaoning	154	3207	712	13473
吉 林	Jilin	87	1630	1336	18542
黑龙江	Heilongjiang	88	1086	934	15332
上 海	Shanghai	7	3691	5	9936
江 苏	Jiangsu	731	8274	3991	45803
浙 江	Zhejiang	162	4018	657	13034
安 徽	Anhui	170	3514	1792	25287
福 建	Fujian	91	2021	920	16390
江 西	Jiangxi	88	3305	1080	22370
山 东	Shandong	537	7210	3859	48055
河 南	Henan	229	5878	3714	63537
湖 北	Hubei	30	2160	1850	39417
湖 南	Hunan	70	2194	1350	24687
广 东	Guangdong	1488	17961	2333	21950
广 西	Guangxi	79	2862	357	9115
海 南	Hainan	NA	5	15	711
重 庆	Chongqing	112	1627	1361	16029
四 川	Sichuan	103	3626	2122	34015
贵 州	Guizhou	15	1655	276	5499
云 南	Yunnan	22	319	378	9964
西 藏	Tibet			8	115
陕 西	Shaanxi	9	482	519	11128
甘 肃	Gansu	9	309	87	2572
青 海	Qinghai			8	247
宁 夏	Ningxia	NA	177	20	889
新 疆	Xinjiang	82	2669	439	6834

3-5-3 限额以上批发和零售业产业活动单位和个体经营户商品购、销、存情况

Total Purchases, Sales and Inventory of Establishments and Getihus above Designated Size of Wholesale and Retail Trades

单位：万元
Unit: 10000 yuan

项目	Item	商品购进额 Total Purchases Value	#进口 Imports	商品销售额 Total Sales Value	#出口 Exports	期末商品库存额 Inventory (year-end)
总计	**Total**	**138783051**	**1413540**	**156150900**	**1014292**	**7052995**
一、批发业	**Wholesale Trade**	**60187650**	**1350695**	**67890602**	**80195**	**2272596**
(一)按登记注册类型分	**by Type of Registration**					
1.内资企业	**Domestic Funded Enterprises**	**25165518**	**724388**	**26589562**	**62186**	**1003797**
国有企业	State-owned Enterprises	14760494	131748	15313842	58833	354873
集体企业	Collective-owned Enterprises	179419		198020		7072
股份合作企业	Cooperative Enterprises	46401		52134		742
联营企业	Joint Ownership Enterprises					
国有联营企业	State Joint Ownership Enterprises					
集体联营企业	Collective Joint Ownership Enterprises					
国有与集体联营企业	Joint State-collective Enterprises					
其他联营企业	Other Joint Ownership Enterprises					
有限责任公司	Limited Liability Corporations	4623921	592640	4815666		405647
国有独资公司	State Sole Funded Corporations	53392		56267		253
其他有限责任公司	Other Limited Liability Corporations	4570531	592640	4759398		405394
股份有限公司	Share-holding Corporations Ltd.	3264613		3549654	3353	169782
私营企业	Private Enterprises	2047619		2414884		54418
私营独资企业	Private-funded Enterprises	63363		64791		1381
私营合伙企业	Private Partnership Enterprises	201900		200958		980
私营有限责任公司	Private Limited Liability Corporations	1749357		2115667		52037
私营股份有限公司	Private Share-holding Corporations Ltd.	33000		33468		19
其他企业	Other Enterprises	243055		245369		11264
2.港、澳、台商投资企业	**Enterprises with Funds from Hongkong, Macao and Taiwan**	**3529264**	**620030**	**3702712**		**429446**
合资经营企业	Joint-venture Enterprises	394874		444532		10648
合作经营企业	Cooperative Enterprises	2018		3203		
独资经营企业	Enterprises with Sole Investment	2923511	620030	3041382		411200
投资股份有限公司	Share-holding Corporations Ltd. with Investment	175219		180508		225
其他港澳台商投资企业	Other Enterprises with Funds from Hongkong, Macao and Taiwan	33640		33088		7374
3.外商投资企业	**Foreign Funded Enterprises**	**2670416**	**1081**	**3891993**		**79146**
中外合资经营企业	Joint-venture Enterprises	354203	1081	933986		16693
中外合作经营企业	Cooperative Enterprises	60057		70244		3487
外资企业	Enterprises with Sole Foreign Investment	2134615		2748199		49452
外商投资股份有限公司	Share-holding Corporations Ltd. with Foreign Investment	103216		118257		7581
其他外商投资企业	Other Foreign Funded Enterprises	18324		21307		1930
4.个体经营户	**Getihus**	**28822454**	**5195**	**33706341**	**18009**	**760215**

单位：万元
Unit: 10000 yuan

项目	Item	商品购进额 Total Purchases Value	#进口 Imports	商品销售额 Total Sales Value	#出口 Exports	期末商品库存额 Inventory (year-end)
(二)按国民经济行业分	**by Sector**					
农、林、牧产品批发	Wholesale of Agricultural, Forestry and Livestock Products	2603019	4028	2906276		146186
食品、饮料及烟草制品批发	Wholesale of Food, Beverages and Tobaccos	14716985	98273	17500327		480622
米、面制品及食用油批发	Wholesale of Rice, Flour and Edible Oil	1351926		1427529		41577
肉、禽、蛋、奶及水产品批发	Wholesale of Meal, Fowls, Eggs, Milk and Aquatic Products	3616059	97306	4642103		99078
酒、饮料及茶叶批发	Wholesale of Wine, Beverages and Teas	2405412	10	2846281		149368
烟草制品批发	Wholesale of Tobaccos	368648		430249		22497
纺织、服装及家庭用品批发	Wholesale of Textiles, Wearing Apparel and Household Articles	7674206		9542260	98	258723
服装批发	Wholesale of Garments	1463024		2550060		96712
鞋帽批发	Wholesale of Shoes and Hats	1064760		1184953		21396
家用电器批发	Wholesale of Household Electrical Appliances	1469372		1766314	98	31379
文化、体育用品及器材批发	Wholesale of Culture, Sports Appliances and Equipments	3156370		3842739		314704
文具用品批发	Wholesale of Stationeries	55219		62132		2584
体育用品及器材批发	Wholesale of Sports Appliances and Equipments	25541		31021		1667
图书批发	Wholesale of Books					
医药及医疗器材批发	Wholesale of Medicines and Medical Appliances	1309213		1498847	3353	121360
西药批发	Wholesale of Western Medicine	34829		41166		3395
中药批发	Wholesale of Chinese Traditional Medicine	1272485		1455022	3353	117403
矿产品、建材及化工产品批发	Wholesale of Mineral Products, Building Materials and Chemical Products	22036771	131748	23271180	58833	508330
煤炭及制品批发	Wholesale of Coal and Related Products	3336343		3432631		42392
石油及制品批发	Wholesale of Petroleum and Related Products	9927865	131748	10283450	58833	71373
金属及金属矿批发	Wholesale of Metal Materials	3000318		3222021		263722
建材批发	Wholesale of Building Materials	2276020		2554636		62796
化肥批发	Wholesale of Chemical Fertilizer	1462608		1579408		46270
农药批发	Wholesale of Pesticides	36567		41110		2377
机械设备、五金产品及电子产品	Wholesale of Machinery, Hardware and Electronic Products	8261843	1116645	8875675	17911	423409
汽车批发	Wholesale of Motor Vehicles	28892		124763		3866
计算机、软件及辅助设备批发	Wholesale of Computer, Software and Assistant Appliances	4906989	1116645	5065814	7008	327403
通讯及广播电视设备批发	Wholesale of Communication, Radios and Televisions Equipments	362824		392123		10981
贸易经纪与代理	Trade Broker and Agency	19698		20602		58
其他批发业	Other Wholesale not Classified Elsewhere	409550		432698		19212

单位：万元
Unit: 10000 yuan

项 目	Item	商品购进额 Total Purchases Value	#进口 Imports	商品销售额 Total Sales Value	#出口 Exports	期末商品库存额 Inventory (year-end)
二、零售业	**Retail Trade**	**78595398**	**62845**	**88260294**	**934097**	**4780395**
(一)按登记注册类型分	**by Type of Registration**					
1.内资企业	**Domestic Funded Enterprises**	**15973201**	**16734**	**17168280**	**933428**	**601246**
国有企业	State-owned Enterprises	770803	15364	898054	1743	38378
集体企业	Collective-owned Enterprises	326190		373775		18979
股份合作企业	Cooperative Enterprises	54806		60596		664
联营企业	Joint Ownership Enterprises					
国有联营企业	State Joint Ownership Enterprises					
集体联营企业	Collective Joint Ownership Enterprises					
国有与集体联营企业	Joint State-collective Enterprises					
其他联营企业	Other Joint Ownership Enterprises					
有限责任公司	Limited Liability Corporations	12585492	1370	13219898	931609	423831
国有独资公司	State Sole Funded Corporations	41305		41408		732
其他有限责任公司	Other Limited Liability Corporations	12544186	1370	13178490	931609	423102
股份有限公司	Share-holding Corporations Ltd.	881831		977779		49620
私营企业	Private Enterprises	1245421		1452218	76	62545
私营独资企业	Private-funded Enterprises	207614		223994		15536
私营合伙企业	Private Partnership Enterprises	31586		33891		2000
私营有限责任公司	Private Limited Liability Corporations	929805		1110033	76	43489
私营股份有限公司	Private Share-holding Corporations Ltd.	76415		84304		1521
其他企业	Other Enterprises	108671		185966		7233
2.港、澳、台商投资企业	**Enterprises with Funds from Hongkong, Macao and Taiwan**	**519328**		**908193**		**62512**
合资经营企业	Joint-venture Enterprises	131634		404235		17298
合作经营企业	Cooperative Enterprises					
独资经营企业	Enterprises with Sole Investment	375412		480927		43670
投资股份有限公司	Share-holding Corporations Ltd. with Investment	12283		23031		1543
其他港澳台商投资企业	Other Enterprises with Funds from Hongkong, Macao and Taiwan					
3.外商投资企业	**Foreign Funded Enterprises**	**1992030**	**3828**	**2842204**		**260178**
中外合资经营企业	Joint-venture Enterprises	441111	3118	466509		86945
中外合作经营企业	Cooperative Enterprises	221427		291426		66568
外资企业	Enterprises with Sole Foreign Investment	1228236		1937546		105641
外商投资股份有限公司	Share-holding Corporations Ltd. with Foreign Investment	37650	710	59541		219
其他外商投资企业	Other Foreign Funded Enterprises	63607		87184		806
4.个体经营户	**Getihus**	**60110839**	**42283**	**67341617**	**669**	**3856459**

单位：万元
Unit: 10000 yuan

项 目	Item	商品购进额 Total Purchases Value	#进口 Imports	商品销售额 Total Sales Value	#出口 Exports	期末商品库存额 Inventory (year-end)
(二)按国民经济行业分	**by Sector**					
综合零售	Integrated Retail	18077148	25890	20615226	50	1312685
百货零售	Retail of General Merchandise	8100262	12733	9542939		489413
超级市场零售	Retail of Supermarkets	6842462	12416	7506317	50	605456
食品、饮料及烟草制品专门零售	Special Retail of Food, Beverages and Tobaccos	6920524	3047	8064437	76	901701
粮油零售	Retail of Cereal and Oil	677482		855850		35268
肉、禽、蛋、奶及水产品零售	Retail of Meat, Poultry, Eggs, Milk and Aquatic Products	1052529	645	1188062		531631
酒、饮料及茶叶零售	Retail of Wine, Beverages and Teas	2130377	1372	2368349		171270
烟草制品零售	Retail of Tobaccos	376507		411416		16865
纺织、服装及日用品专门零售	Special Retail of Textiles, Garments and Daily Consumer Articles	8696175	1831	10405318		520710
服装零售	Retail of Garments	4174609	1679	5036380		299455
文化、体育用品及器材专门零售	Special Retail of Culture, Sports Appliances and Equipments	4237414	2217	4729129	1743	265794
体育用品及器材零售	Retail of Sports Appliances and Equipments	102515		106742		6076
图书、报刊零售	Retail of Books, Newspapers and Magazines	297981	1580	337868	1743	14593
医药及医疗器材专门零售	Special Retail of Medicines and Medical Appliances	1481843		1685719		104237
药品零售	Retail of Medicines	1409855		1603090		98678
汽车、摩托车、燃料及零配件专门零售	Special Retail of Motor Vehicles, Motorcycles, Fuel and Parts	4853693	22209	5408827	619	225276
汽车零售	Retail of Motor Vehicles	772551	1220	887508		53395
机动车燃料零售	Retail of Fuel of Motor Vehicles	2609911	16902	2890888		105236
家用电器及电子产品专门零售	Special Retail of Household Electric and Electronic Products	19025994	688	20275604	931609	739562
日用家电设备零售	Retail of Household Electric Appliances	4047910	688	4524294		208901
计算机、软件及辅助设备零售	Retail of Computer, Software and Assistant Appliances	1098189		1271723		74732
通信设备零售	Retail of Communication Equipments	12169382		12561880	931609	364572
五金、家具及室内装饰材料专门零售	Special Retail of Hardware, Furniture and Interior Decoration Materials	14059464	6963	15651247		666674
货摊、无店铺及其他零售	Stalls, Non-shop and Other Retails	1243157		1424792		43761
互联网零售	Retail on the Internet	36048		39221		2607
(三)按零售业态分	**by Mode of Business Operation**					
有店铺零售	Store-based Retailing	67501871	62845	76560571	2488	4506523
超市	Supermarket	11785312	12595	13229544	50	837469
大型超市	Hypermarket	1671686	755	1745019		217139
百货店	Department Store	5883298	3099	7117581		340028
专业店	Speciality Store	25180440	7150	28005819	2362	1279341
专卖店	Exclusive Shop	12628165	24102	14518487	76	742695
无店铺零售	Non-Store Selling	11091395		11697364	931609	273203

3-5-4 各地区限额以上批发业产业活动单位和个体经营户商品购、销、存情况

Total Purchases, Sales and Inventory of Establishments and Getihus above Designated Size of Wholesale Trade by Region

单位：万元

Unit: 10000 yuan

地区	Region	商品购进额 Total Purchases Value	#进口 Imports	商品销售额 Total Sales Value	#出口 Exports	期末商品库存额 Inventory (year-end)
全国	**National Total**	**60187650**	**1350695**	**67890602**	**80195**	**2272596**
北京	Beijing	6458574	1212671	6580091		506790
天津	Tianjin	1211442	36605	1331824	18616	124091
河北	Hebei	783023		800197		11644
山西	Shanxi	315883		347768		7733
内蒙古	Inner Mongolia	1740285		1783361		7798
辽宁	Liaoning	836387		936540		42007
吉林	Jilin	304066		323145		22283
黑龙江	Heilongjiang	1353774		1617306		81349
上海	Shanghai	8722035		9104617		21903
江苏	Jiangsu	5631217	200	6722810		141991
浙江	Zhejiang	1881210	1081	2253404		65925
安徽	Anhui	952625		1062520		27024
福建	Fujian	810801		862520		21154
江西	Jiangxi	757809	945	860167		57689
山东	Shandong	3802524		4297240		112797
河南	Henan	3201012	4028	3429677		87977
湖北	Hubei	1193867		1439974		32561
湖南	Hunan	1271693		1433627		99043
广东	Guangdong	12794726		15430518	18009	547867
广西	Guangxi	965097		1221820		83283
海南	Hainan	690		650		51
重庆	Chongqing	1259581		1434240		12977
四川	Sichuan	1447922	95155	1996449	43570	52049
贵州	Guizhou	454246		467842		4058
云南	Yunnan	229269	10	255927		3477
西藏	Tibet					
陕西	Shaanxi	43390		58894		2279
甘肃	Gansu	26488		55482		1575
青海	Qinghai					
宁夏	Ningxia	50425		53309		950
新疆	Xinjiang	1687589		1728683		92271

3-5-5 各地区限额以上零售业产业活动单位和个体经营户商品购、销、存情况

Total Purchases, Sales and Inventory of Establishments and Getihus above Designated Size of Retail Trade by Region

单位：万元

Unit: 10000 yuan

地区	Region	商品购进额 Total Purchases Value	#进口 Imports	商品销售额 Total Sales Value	#出口 Exports	期末商品库存额 Inventory (year-end)
全国	**National Total**	**78595398**	**62845**	**88260294**	**934097**	**4780395**
北京	Beijing	10914144	1220	11416183	931609	283692
天津	Tianjin	668295		878828		148141
河北	Hebei	1194814	1140	1307845		74336
山西	Shanxi	1408609	6	1638012		92053
内蒙古	Inner Mongolia	652791		781644		46407
辽宁	Liaoning	1233394	1	1382746		230155
吉林	Jilin	1936871	502	2110688		122409
黑龙江	Heilongjiang	2622164		2942765		119614
上海	Shanghai	116118		418610		25051
江苏	Jiangsu	8762926	854	9857981	76	301269
浙江	Zhejiang	1426357	6437	1833152	2362	145944
安徽	Anhui	2340918	115	2621417		660649
福建	Fujian	1583356	14269	1813773		107175
江西	Jiangxi	1621646	521	1825923		125607
山东	Shandong	9300287		10321200		356394
河南	Henan	6496939	353	7347297	50	344060
湖北	Hubei	6649342	11008	7291841		383434
湖南	Hunan	3255241	231	3724643		153573
广东	Guangdong	5240918	1820	6127661		350320
广西	Guangxi	430702	8463	495762		61126
海南	Hainan	26127		31801		4273
重庆	Chongqing	2889678	352	3369987		94490
四川	Sichuan	3959409	5819	4423480		267242
贵州	Guizhou	375977		406218		45095
云南	Yunnan	858109	8	1052064		64226
西藏	Tibet	6523	77	7292		1405
陕西	Shaanxi	1460880	150	1580110		72242
甘肃	Gansu	134250		146906		18433
青海	Qinghai	43386		44458		1601
宁夏	Ningxia	76073		87622		17946
新疆	Xinjiang	909154	9499	972385		62033

3-6-1 按业态分连锁零售企业基本情况
Basic Conditions of Chain Retail Enterprises by Business Categories

业 态	Business Categories	门店总数（个）Number of Stores (unit)	从业人员（万人）Engaged Persons (10 000 persons)	营业面积（万平方米）Operating Area (10 000 sq.m)	商品销售额（亿元）Total Sales Value (100 million yuan)	#零售额 Retail Value
总 计	**Total**	**236103**	**234.9**	**17329.6**	**35629.1**	**27617.2**
便利店	Convenience Store	24060	9.0	190.8	482.9	434.3
折扣店	Discount Store	448	0.2	19.4	26.7	26.7
超市	Supermarket	29881	42.0	2112.9	3520.3	2985.2
大型超市	Hypermarket	6155	47.0	3539.8	4415.1	3984.4
仓储会员店	Warehouse Club	98	1.3	68.1	230.5	224.0
百货店	Department Store	6148	27.9	2842.9	3778.0	3235.0
专业店	Specialty Store	125362	84.8	7775.0	20392.8	14739.3
#加油站	Gas Station	33321	24.5	4841.9	12628.3	8848.4
专卖店	Franchised Store	31238	17.4	498.6	2152.7	1637.0
家居建材商店	Building Material Store	61	0.3	21.0	46.5	45.3
厂家直销中心	Factory Outlets Center	711	0.4	16.4	57.6	8.6
其他	Other Store	11941	4.7	244.7	526.1	297.5

3-6-2 按登记注册类型分连锁零售企业基本情况

Basic Conditions of Chain Retail Enterprises by Status of Registration

项 目	Item	门店总数（个）Number of Stores (unit)	从业人员（万人）Employed Person (10000 persons)	营业面积（万平方米）Operational Area (10000 sq.m)	商品销售额（亿元）Total Sales Value (100 million yuan)	#零售额 Retail Value
合 计	**Total**	**236103**	**234.9**	**17329.6**	**35629.1**	**27617.2**
内资企业	**Domestic Funded Enterprises**	**214398**	**185.2**	**13492.8**	**29323.8**	**22035.3**
国有企业	State-owned Enterprises	13348	11.0	1030.1	3835.9	2319.9
集体企业	Collective-owned Enterprises	739	0.9	51.1	85.1	55.2
股份合作企业	Cooperative Enterprises	389	0.4	47.7	123.5	93.9
联营企业	Joint Ownership Enterprises	238	0.1	3.1	10.5	10.1
国有联营企业	State Joint Ownership Enterprises	188	0.1	2.2	7.4	7.4
集体联营企业	Collective Joint Ownership Enterprises					
国有与集体联营企业	Joint State-collective Enterprises	5	0.0	0.1	0.1	0.1
其他联营企业	Other Joint Ownership Enterprises	45	0.0	0.8	3.0	2.6
有限责任公司	Limited Liability Corporations	82983	66.8	3874.0	8302.9	6168.2
国有独资公司	State Sole Funded Corporations	2205	1.9	243.8	749.1	346.4
其他有限责任公司	Other Limited Liability Corporations	80778	64.9	3630.2	7553.8	5821.8
股份有限公司	Share-holding Corporations Ltd.	50436	64.7	6794.1	13786.0	10632.4
私营企业	Private Enterprises	63696	39.6	1643.6	3122.6	2700.2
私营独资企业	Private-funded Enterprises	808	0.4	12.9	24.6	23.3
私营合伙企业	Private Partnership Enterprises	496	0.1	13.8	9.1	9.1
私营有限责任公司	Private Limited Liability Corporations	53261	33.3	1380.0	2655.8	2312.2
私营股份有限公司	Private Share-holding Corporations Ltd.	9131	5.8	237.0	433.0	355.5
其他企业	Other Enterprises	2569	1.6	49.1	57.3	55.5
港、澳、台商投资企业	**Enterprises with Funds from Hong Kong, Macao and Taiwan**	**11279**	**24.9**	**2251.8**	**2606.6**	**2347.5**
港、澳、台商合资经营企业	Joint-venture Enterprises	4257	3.7	223.8	357.8	328.3
港、澳、台商合作经营企业	Cooperative Enterprises	239	6.3	309.3	444.8	444.8
港、澳、台商独资经营企业	Enterprises with Sole Investment	5971	10.0	1037.2	1250.4	1020.8
港、澳、台商投资股份有限公	Share-holding Corporations Ltd. with Invest	278	0.2	11.8	19.0	19.0
其他港澳台商投资企业	Other Enterprises with Funds from Hongkon Macao and Taiwan	534	4.6	669.7	534.5	534.5
外商投资企业	**Foreign Funded Enterprises**	**10426**	**24.8**	**1585.0**	**3698.6**	**3234.3**
中外合资经营企业	Joint-venture Enterprises	4893	12.2	953.9	1879.7	1576.2
中外合作经营企业	Cooperative Enterprises	434	1.4	88.5	115.3	115.3
外资企业	Enterprises with Sole Foreign Investment	4908	10.9	497.9	1618.2	1464.2
外商投资股份有限公司	Share-holding Corporations Ltd. with Foreign Investment	187	0.4	44.3	75.7	74.8
其他外商投资企业	Other Foreign Funded Enterprises	4	0.0	0.4	9.7	3.8

3-6-3 按行业分连锁零售企业基本情况
Basic Conditions of Chain Retail Enterprises by Sector

项目	Item	门店总数（个）Number of Stores (unit)	从业人员（万人）Employed Person (10000 persons)	营业面积（万平方米）Operational Area (10000 sq.m)
总计	**Total**	**236103**	**234.9**	**17329.6**
一、批发业	**Wholesale Trade**	**38631**	**22.7**	**3040.0**
农、林、牧产品批发	Wholesale of Farm Produce and Livestock Products	4900	1.2	38.8
食品、饮料及烟草制品专门批发	Wholesale of Food, Beverages and Tobaccos	2403	2.4	38.1
纺织、服装及家庭用品批发	Wholesale of Textiles, Garments and Daily Consumer Articles	945	1.8	163.9
文化、体育用品及器材批发	Wholesale of Culture, Sports Appliances and Equipments	455	1.7	79.9
医药及医疗器材批发	Wholesale of Medicines and Medical Appliances	2485	0.9	22.0
矿产品、建材及化工产品批发	Wholesale of Mineral Products, Building Materials and	26459	13.8	2590.2
机械设备、五金产品及电子产品批发	Wholesale of Machinery, Hardware and Electronic Equipment	315	0.2	5.2
贸易经纪及代理	Trade Broker and Agency			
其他批发业	Other Wholesale not Classified Elsewhere	669	0.6	101.8
二、零售业	**Retail Trade**	**197472**	**212.3**	**14289.7**
综合零售	Integrated Retail	67642	130.2	8965.1
食品、饮料及烟草制品专门零售	Retail of Food, Beverages and Tobaccos	22393	8.4	126.3
纺织、服装及日用品专门零售	Special Retail of Textiles, Garments and Daily	18302	8.1	297.6
文化、体育用品及器材专门零售	Retail of Culture, Sports Appliances and Equipments	1811	3.5	128.6
医药及医疗器材专门零售	Retail of Medicines and Medical Appliances	63153	30.9	937.5
汽车、摩托车、燃料及零配件专门零售	Retail of Motor Vehicles, Motorcycles, Fuel	15442	13.3	2484.0
家用电器及电子产品专门零售	Special Retail of Household Electric Appliances and Electronic Products	7640	16.6	1291.2
五金、家具及室内装饰材料专门零售	Special Retail of Hardware, Furniture and Decoration Materials	383	0.8	47.0
货摊、无店铺及其他零售业	Non-shop and Other Retails	706	0.4	12.3

3-6-3 续表 Continued

项　目	Item	商品销售额（亿元）Total Sales (100 million yuan)	#零售额 Retail
总　计	**Total**	**35629.1**	**27617.2**
一、批发业	**Wholesale Trade**	**9410.3**	**5188.5**
农、林、牧产品批发	Wholesale of Farm Produce and Livestock Products	205.4	195.4
食品、饮料及烟草制品专门批发	Wholesale of Food, Beverages and Tobaccos	848.6	46.3
纺织、服装及家庭用品批发	Wholesale of Textiles, Garments and Daily Consumer Articles	289.8	135.1
文化、体育用品及器材批发	Wholesale of Culture, Sports Appliances and Equipments	366.8	130.2
医药及医疗器材批发	Wholesale of Medicines and Medical Appliances	78.0	24.2
矿产品、建材及化工产品批发	Wholesale of Mineral Products, Building Materials and	7296.5	4447.0
机械设备、五金产品及电子产品批发	Wholesale of Machinery, Hardware and Electronic Equipment	122.4	26.2
贸易经纪及代理	Trade Broker and Agency		
其他批发业	Other Wholesale not Classified Elsewhere	202.7	184.0
二、零售业	**Retail Trade**	**26218.8**	**22428.7**
综合零售	Integrated Retail	13070.4	11397.1
食品、饮料及烟草制品专门零售	Retail of Food, Beverages and Tobaccos	488.4	408.9
纺织、服装及日用品专门零售	Special Retail of Textiles, Garments and Daily	692.5	656.3
文化、体育用品及器材专门零售	Retail of Culture, Sports Appliances and Equipments	615.6	315.2
医药及医疗器材专门零售	Retail of Medicines and Medical Appliances	1588.6	1426.2
汽车、摩托车、燃料及零配件专门零售	Retail of Motor Vehicles, Motorcycles, Fuel	6095.5	4797.0
家用电器及电子产品专门零售	Special Retail of Household Electric Appliances and Electronic Products	3569.7	3332.7
五金、家具及室内装饰材料专门零售	Special Retail of Hardware, Furniture and Decoration Materials	85.7	84.5
货摊、无店铺及其他零售业	Non-shop and Other Retails	12.4	10.7

3-6-4 各地区连锁零售企业基本情况

Basic Conditions of Chain Retail Enterprises by Region

年份 Year	地区 Region	门店总数(个) Number of Stores (unit)	从业人数(万人) Employed Person (10 000 persons)	营业面积(万平方米) Selling Space (10 000 sq.m)	商品销售额(亿元) Total Revenue of Sales (100 million yuan)	#零售额 Retail Sales
	2004	77631	128.2	7202.6	8393.6	6163.1
	2005	105684	160.1	8687.5	12587.8	8569.5
	2006	128924	187.1	8979.0	14952.2	10764.8
	2007	145366	186.2	10044.0	17754.3	13066.8
	2008	168502	197.1	10197.8	20466.5	14369.7
	2009	175677	210.9	11809.2	22240.0	15860.3
	2010	176792	225.2	12756.8	27385.4	19009.5
	2011	195779	249.1	13670.7	34510.7	23812.5
	2012	192870	256.3	14765.9	35462.1	24605.3
	2013	204090	255.9	15640.3	38006.9	26340.8
	2014	206415	250.2	16221.3	37340.6	27356.5
	2015	209812	248.1	16862.4	35400.4	25749.3
	2016	232444	245.0	17960.1	35922.9	26856.2
	2017	236103	234.9	17329.6	35629.1	27617.2
北京	Beijing	8176	16.9	907.1	3165.8	2578.4
天津	Tianjin	2232	2.7	198.8	512.4	417.5
河北	Hebei	5879	5.5	648.6	1237.1	1035.8
山西	Shanxi	4167	3.8	312.3	460.4	367.6
内蒙古	Inner Mongolia	712	0.6	36.1	36.4	25.8
辽宁	Liaoning	6870	5.5	525.7	717.7	588.4
吉林	Jilin	2011	1.3	61.2	177.6	152.8
黑龙江	Heilongjiang	1845	1.9	61.3	244.5	167.2
上海	Shanghai	17706	22.5	1065.4	3198.4	2545.5
江苏	Jiangsu	21592	27.5	2317.2	4483.5	3164.8
浙江	Zhejiang	25291	14.1	1131.0	2116.2	1479.6
安徽	Anhui	9850	9.2	582.7	1674.7	1333.7
福建	Fujian	10492	11.4	1107.2	1513.8	1316.3
江西	Jiangxi	4840	5.2	344.3	1069.3	712.8
山东	Shandong	13948	17.9	1915.8	2070.9	1553.0
河南	Henan	6130	6.7	562.3	882.1	788.2
湖北	Hubei	9605	12.6	709.5	1961.0	1655.5
湖南	Hunan	9827	8.7	864.4	1210.4	1082.5
广东	Guangdong	27542	23.3	1454.4	3408.8	2903.5
广西	Guangxi	5904	4.3	460.8	847.3	496.3
海南	Hainan	835	0.5	39.5	191.2	116.1
重庆	Chongqing	12324	8.9	462.4	944.7	751.0
四川	Sichuan	11736	9.3	382.9	764.0	733.8
贵州	Guizhou	1409	1.1	46.1	66.8	65.1
云南	Yunnan	5705	3.5	205.8	462.7	382.4
西藏	Tibet	74	0.1	3.0	2.7	2.7
陕西	Shaanxi	3014	3.5	253.0	985.4	402.4
甘肃	Gansu	1156	0.9	76.3	173.8	149.8
青海	Qinghai	190	0.5	19.7	32.0	31.4
宁夏	Ningxia	1345	1.5	218.4	286.8	177.9
新疆	Xinjiang	3696	3.4	356.6	730.9	439.1

3-6-4 续表 Continued

年 份 Year	地 区 Region	商品购进总额（亿元）Total Purchases (100 million yuan)	统一配送商品购进额（亿元）Centralized Purchase and Delivery (100 million yuan)	自有配送中心配送商品购进额 Self Centralized Purchase and Delivery	非自有配送中心配送商品购进额 Non-self Centralized Purchase and Delivery
2004		7130.1	5545.6	4481.7	1063.9
2005		10734.6	8409.4	6696.1	1251.8
2006		13447.4	10565.7	7729.7	1384.0
2007		15917.0	12542.4	9057.0	1707.3
2008		17193.1	13782.1	8654.9	3118.8
2009		19343.7	14723.1	9616.9	2647.2
2010		24044.6	17412.5	10910.3	3373.4
2011		29653.0	22919.6	13458.8	3384.1
2012		30825.5	23975.8	13932.9	3522.8
2013		32258.7	25341.8	14598.7	4554.0
2014		31298.5	24582.4	14637.3	4265.7
2015		30556.8	23379.9	13656.3	3669.4
2016		31036.9	24173.7	13989.2	4342.3
2017		30520.8	23737.6	13994.0	3174.5
北 京	Beijing	2667.0	1934.0	1130.1	348.0
天 津	Tianjin	460.1	271.3	192.0	10.2
河 北	Hebei	1131.5	920.7	345.0	35.3
山 西	Shanxi	333.6	191.9	114.5	0.3
内蒙古	Inner Mongolia	33.4	21.7	10.8	0.2
辽 宁	Liaoning	716.3	502.3	75.7	142.2
吉 林	Jilin	144.6	137.8	118.2	1.0
黑龙江	Heilongjiang	241.3	220.8	53.2	14.9
上 海	Shanghai	2694.0	2246.1	944.0	240.2
江 苏	Jiangsu	4301.6	3773.2	3218.8	223.1
浙 江	Zhejiang	1928.9	1687.9	1486.5	131.3
安 徽	Anhui	1577.0	1124.0	481.3	48.6
福 建	Fujian	1204.2	779.7	267.7	330.9
江 西	Jiangxi	629.0	554.9	366.1	52.8
山 东	Shandong	1773.9	1252.8	738.4	135.6
河 南	Henan	796.9	439.7	240.0	26.0
湖 北	Hubei	1718.5	1119.6	860.8	92.7
湖 南	Hunan	866.3	741.8	453.2	106.0
广 东	Guangdong	2808.5	2246.9	1257.6	724.7
广 西	Guangxi	754.3	747.1	270.4	11.5
海 南	Hainan	174.2	170.5	0.6	
重 庆	Chongqing	679.0	470.3	315.5	107.0
四 川	Sichuan	694.8	468.8	231.4	40.4
贵 州	Guizhou	63.9	60.5	34.4	0.7
云 南	Yunnan	244.0	207.1	83.4	36.0
西 藏	Tibet	3.0	3.0		
陕 西	Shaanxi	761.5	588.3	297.7	76.5
甘 肃	Gansu	149.7	124.1	13.3	1.0
青 海	Qinghai	19.2	8.7	2.0	
宁 夏	Ningxia	323.7	173.3	80.4	1.4
新 疆	Xinjiang	627.2	548.6	311.2	236.1

住宿和餐饮业

HOTELS AND CATERING SERVICES

第4篇

4-1-1 限额以上住宿和餐饮业企业基本情况

Basic Conditions of Enterprises above Designated Size of Hotels and Catering Services

项 目	Item	法人单位数(个) Number of Corporation Enterprises (unit)	年末从业人数(人) Engaged Persons at the Year-end (person)	年末餐饮营业面积(平方米) Business Area of Catering Services at the Year-end (㎡)
总 计	**Total**	**45664**	**4053109**	**95904284**
一、住宿业	**Hotels**	**19780**	**1820851**	**42399355**
#国有控股	State-controlled Enterprises	2971	455089	7428220
(一)按登记注册类型分	**by Type of Registration**			
1.内资企业	**Domestic Funded Enterprises**	**18941**	**1637086**	**39864223**
国有企业	State-owned Enterprises	1487	191630	3424207
集体企业	Collective-owned Enterprises	250	19405	394973
股份合作企业	Cooperative Enterprises	51	4145	83860
联营企业	Joint Ownership Enterprises	16	1925	36886
国有联营企业	State Joint Ownership Enterprises	6	1361	14210
集体联营企业	Collective Joint Ownership Enterprises	6	301	13090
国有与集体联营企业	Joint State-collective Enterprises	NA	118	1906
其他联营企业	Other Joint Ownership Enterprises	NA	145	7680
有限责任公司	Limited Liability Corporations	6883	747253	16245944
国有独资公司	State Sole Funded Corporations	411	73871	1132619
其他有限责任公司	Other Limited Liability Corporations	6472	673382	15113325
股份有限公司	Share-holding Corporations Ltd.	495	56781	1203278
私营企业	Private Enterprises	9589	606523	18181788
私营独资企业	Private-funded Enterprises	968	38904	1371659
私营合伙企业	Private Partnership Enterprises	231	12604	409344
私营有限责任公司	Private Limited Liability Corporations	8013	528491	15647432
私营股份有限公司	Private Share-holding Corporations Ltd.	377	26524	753353
其他企业	Other Enterprises	170	9424	293287
2.港、澳、台商投资企业	**Enterprises with Funds from Hongkong, Macao and Taiwan**	**515**	**120574**	**1716140**
合资经营企业	Joint-venture Enterprises	211	53338	747247
合作经营企业	Cooperative Enterprises	42	10339	121206
独资经营企业	Enterprises with Sole Investment	231	51188	759337
投资股份有限公司	Share-holding Corporations Ltd. with Investment	23	4548	67928
其他港澳台商投资企业	Other Enterprises with Funds from Hongkong, Macao and Taiwan	8	1161	20422
3.外商投资企业	**Foreign Funded Enterprises**	**324**	**63191**	**818992**
中外合资经营企业	Joint-venture Enterprises	127	26091	367195
中外合作经营企业	Cooperative Enterprises	35	10495	87008
外资企业	Enterprises with Sole Foreign Investment	134	22997	304139
外商投资股份有限公司	Share-holding Corporations Ltd. with Foreign Investment	13	1019	20505
其他外商投资企业	Other Foreign Funded Enterprises	15	2589	40145
(二)按国民经济行业分	**by Sector**			
旅游饭店	Tourist Hotel	11663	1406118	30697286
一般旅馆	Fonda	7456	372781	10574827
其他住宿业	Others	661	41952	1127242

注：NA表示小于或等于3(下表同)。
Note: NA refers to less than or equal to three.The same applies to the tables following.

4-1-1 续表 Continued

项 目	Item	法人单位数(个) Number of Corporation Enterprises (unit)	年末从业人数(人) Engaged Persons at the Year-end (person)	年末餐饮营业面积(平方米) Business Area of Catering Services at the Year-end (㎡)
二、餐饮业	**Catering Services**	**25884**	**2232258**	**53504929**
#国有控股	State-controlled Enterprises	751	114416	2378533
(一)按登记注册类型分	**by Type of Registration**			
1.内资企业	**Domestic Funded Enterprises**	**24872**	**1655996**	**46823058**
国有企业	State-owned Enterprises	327	33651	818013
集体企业	Collective-owned Enterprises	151	7801	228564
股份合作企业	Cooperative Enterprises	76	5961	138082
联营企业	Joint Ownership Enterprises	8	335	9810
国有联营企业	State Joint Ownership Enterprises			
集体联营企业	Collective Joint Ownership Enterprises	6	235	7130
国有与集体联营企业	Joint State-collective Enterprises			
其他联营企业	Other Joint Ownership Enterprises	NA	100	2680
有限责任公司	Limited Liability Corporations	6459	550730	14379401
国有独资公司	State Sole Funded Corporations	108	18265	311805
其他有限责任公司	Other Limited Liability Corporations	6351	532465	14067596
股份有限公司	Share-holding Corporations Ltd.	377	63215	1319032
私营企业	Private Enterprises	17181	981971	29532010
私营独资企业	Private-funded Enterprises	2942	98002	3654593
私营合伙企业	Private Partnership Enterprises	328	14085	532928
私营有限责任公司	Private Limited Liability Corporations	13420	835611	24295525
私营股份有限公司	Private Share-holding Corporations Ltd.	491	34273	1048964
其他企业	Other Enterprises	293	12332	398146
2.港、澳、台商投资企业	**Enterprises with Funds from Hongkong, Macao and Taiwan**	**628**	**246662**	**2821395**
合资经营企业	Joint-venture Enterprises	118	52636	625337
合作经营企业	Cooperative Enterprises	19	6636	88032
独资经营企业	Enterprises with Sole Investment	475	186097	2084737
投资股份有限公司	Share-holding Corporations Ltd. with Investment	9	709	14001
其他港澳台商投资企业	Other Enterprises with Funds from Hongkong, Macao and Taiwan	7	584	9288
3.外商投资企业	**Foreign Funded Enterprises**	**384**	**329600**	**3860476**
中外合资经营企业	Joint-venture Enterprises	82	69163	778448
中外合作经营企业	Cooperative Enterprises	10	3591	26906
外资企业	Enterprises with Sole Foreign Investment	255	233058	2772946
外商投资股份有限公司	Share-holding Corporations Ltd. with Foreign Investment	16	11356	98261
其他外商投资企业	Other Foreign Funded Enterprises	21	12432	183915
(二)按国民经济行业分	**by Sector**			
正餐服务	Dinner	23977	1593776	46295288
快餐服务	Snack	950	475258	5373288
饮料及冷饮服务	Beverage and Cold Drink	226	64788	770925
其他餐饮业	Others	731	98436	1065428

4-1-2 各地区限额以上住宿业企业基本情况

Basic Conditions of Enterprises above Designated Size of Hotels by Region

地区	Region	住宿业 Hotels 法人单位数(个) Number of Corporation Enterprises (unit)	住宿业 Hotels 年末从业人数(人) Engaged Persons at the Year-end (person)	#国有控股 State-controlled Enterprises 法人单位数(个) Number of Corporation Enterprises (unit)	#国有控股 State-controlled Enterprises 年末从业人数(人) Engaged Persons at the Year-end (person)
全　国	**National Total**	**19780**	**1820851**	**2971**	**455089**
北　京	Beijing	959	119950	376	62747
天　津	Tianjin	229	19712	58	7831
河　北	Hebei	456	50017	122	15049
山　西	Shanxi	329	31472	72	11371
内蒙古	Inner Mongolia	294	25396	45	5606
辽　宁	Liaoning	451	38837	82	12271
吉　林	Jilin	201	17402	52	6107
黑龙江	Heilongjiang	209	17543	67	6882
上　海	Shanghai	721	73135	155	29515
江　苏	Jiangsu	1047	102728	197	31043
浙　江	Zhejiang	1320	130660	165	26506
安　徽	Anhui	548	42406	55	6948
福　建	Fujian	885	84864	102	18016
江　西	Jiangxi	524	41356	82	8429
山　东	Shandong	1119	102384	160	31565
河　南	Henan	1414	96593	120	16444
湖　北	Hubei	721	55531	59	7237
湖　南	Hunan	794	78188	78	12622
广　东	Guangdong	2259	245588	222	37026
广　西	Guangxi	560	46720	64	9097
海　南	Hainan	253	50264	34	6423
重　庆	Chongqing	457	38045	53	7540
四　川	Sichuan	1050	77966	91	13471
贵　州	Guizhou	635	39227	52	6726
云　南	Yunnan	611	55814	93	14876
西　藏	Tibet	68	5235	19	2347
陕　西	Shaanxi	868	69562	96	16540
甘　肃	Gansu	350	26817	66	8725
青　海	Qinghai	97	7543	22	2495
宁　夏	Ningxia	78	6922	12	1702
新　疆	Xinjiang	273	22974	100	11932

4-1-3 各地区限额以上住宿业企业基本情况(按登记注册类型分)
Basic Conditions of Enterprises above Designated Size of Hotels by Region and Type of Registration

地区	Region	内资企业 Domestic Funded Enterprises		国有企业 State-owned Enterprises	
		法人单位数(个) Number of Corporation Enterprises (unit)	年末从业人数(人) Engaged Persons at the Year-end (person)	法人单位数(个) Number of Corporation Enterprises (unit)	年末从业人数(人) Engaged Persons at the Year-end (person)
全　国	**National Total**	**18941**	**1637086**	**1487**	**191630**
北　京	Beijing	898	98429	184	26892
天　津	Tianjin	216	18077	27	2670
河　北	Hebei	450	48342	100	11419
山　西	Shanxi	329	31472	49	7860
内蒙古	Inner Mongolia	289	24429	26	2167
辽　宁	Liaoning	411	32799	53	7106
吉　林	Jilin	195	16248	40	4694
黑龙江	Heilongjiang	197	15548	42	4280
上　海	Shanghai	673	58611	40	5841
江　苏	Jiangsu	982	91571	70	8553
浙　江	Zhejiang	1259	117293	61	7589
安　徽	Anhui	536	39826	17	1476
福　建	Fujian	814	71050	43	5035
江　西	Jiangxi	509	39747	52	4576
山　东	Shandong	1091	97068	107	20215
河　南	Henan	1396	93748	77	10421
湖　北	Hubei	701	51650	30	3445
湖　南	Hunan	774	73568	45	5871
广　东	Guangdong	2047	201203	103	13920
广　西	Guangxi	542	42180	42	5024
海　南	Hainan	222	38623	8	995
重　庆	Chongqing	450	36196	14	2113
四　川	Sichuan	1034	74853	29	3632
贵　州	Guizhou	628	38373	20	1939
云　南	Yunnan	591	52789	40	4410
西　藏	Tibet	65	4778	11	1416
陕　西	Shaanxi	851	65423	52	5577
甘　肃	Gansu	348	26287	35	4405
青　海	Qinghai	95	7196	10	1299
宁　夏	Ningxia	77	6842	4	911
新　疆	Xinjiang	271	22867	56	5879

地区	Region	集体企业 Collective-owned Enterprises 法人单位数(个) Number of Corporation Enterprises (unit)	集体企业 Collective-owned Enterprises 年末从业人数(人) Engaged Persons at the Year-end (person)	股份合作企业 Cooperative Enterprises 法人单位数(个) Number of Corporation Enterprises (unit)	股份合作企业 Cooperative Enterprises 年末从业人数(人) Engaged Persons at the Year-end (person)
全国	**National Total**	**250**	**19405**	**51**	**4145**
北京	Beijing	33	3774	20	1357
天津	Tianjin	5	558	NA	570
河北	Hebei	9	666		
山西	Shanxi	7	624		
内蒙古	Inner Mongolia	NA	47	NA	80
辽宁	Liaoning	14	522	NA	35
吉林	Jilin	NA	99	NA	58
黑龙江	Heilongjiang	4	219	NA	374
上海	Shanghai	8	723		
江苏	Jiangsu	12	991		
浙江	Zhejiang	15	1161	4	199
安徽	Anhui	NA	141		
福建	Fujian	6	389	NA	187
江西	Jiangxi			NA	28
山东	Shandong	16	1190	NA	255
河南	Henan	29	2348	NA	161
湖北	Hubei	6	894	NA	26
湖南	Hunan	7	572	NA	145
广东	Guangdong	30	1622	5	227
广西	Guangxi	4	255	NA	28
海南	Hainan	NA	46	NA	113
重庆	Chongqing	6	485		
四川	Sichuan	4	433	NA	94
贵州	Guizhou	6	113		
云南	Yunnan	7	461	NA	33
西藏	Tibet	NA	46		
陕西	Shaanxi	7	447	NA	175
甘肃	Gansu	4	367		
青海	Qinghai	NA	50		
宁夏	Ningxia	NA	20		
新疆	Xinjiang	NA	142		

地 区	Region	联营企业 Joint Ownership Enterprises		有限责任公司 Limited Liability Corporations	
		法人单位数 (个) Number of Corporation Enterprises (unit)	年末从业人数 (人) Engaged Persons at the Year-end (person)	法人单位数 (个) Number of Corporation Enterprises (unit)	年末从业人数 (人) Engaged Persons at the Year-end (person)
全 国	**National Total**	**16**	**1925**	**6883**	**747253**
北 京	Beijing	NA	140	372	48737
天 津	Tianjin			79	8920
河 北	Hebei			101	13452
山 西	Shanxi			60	8443
内 蒙 古	Inner Mongolia	NA	57	116	12145
辽 宁	Liaoning	NA	50	145	13362
吉 林	Jilin			79	6965
黑 龙 江	Heilongjiang			78	5743
上 海	Shanghai	NA	49	211	28883
江 苏	Jiangsu	NA	128	316	40062
浙 江	Zhejiang	NA	75	374	50437
安 徽	Anhui			180	17580
福 建	Fujian	NA	498	304	34789
江 西	Jiangxi			205	19092
山 东	Shandong			345	37864
河 南	Henan	NA	48	633	44641
湖 北	Hubei			274	23955
湖 南	Hunan			226	28606
广 东	Guangdong	NA	150	830	101905
广 西	Guangxi			144	13886
海 南	Hainan			176	31707
重 庆	Chongqing			162	18301
四 川	Sichuan			385	32501
贵 州	Guizhou			174	16216
云 南	Yunnan	NA	164	209	25727
西 藏	Tibet			23	1800
陕 西	Shaanxi			376	35894
甘 肃	Gansu	NA	521	137	11236
青 海	Qinghai			34	2325
宁 夏	Ningxia			27	2449
新 疆	Xinjiang	NA	45	108	9630

4-1-3 续表 3 Continued 3

地 区	Region	股份有限公司 Share-holding Corporations Ltd. 法人单位数 (个) Number of Corporation Enterprises (unit)	股份有限公司 Share-holding Corporations Ltd. 年末从业人数 (人) Engaged Persons at the Year-end (person)	私营企业 Private Enterprises 法人单位数 (个) Number of Corporation Enterprises (unit)	私营企业 Private Enterprises 年末从业人数 (人) Engaged Persons at the Year-end (person)
全 国	**National Total**	**495**	**56781**	**9589**	**606523**
北 京	Beijing	8	1498	278	16004
天 津	Tianjin	4	440	97	4641
河 北	Hebei	9	942	231	21863
山 西	Shanxi	10	776	201	13593
内蒙古	Inner Mongolia	10	870	130	8808
辽 宁	Liaoning	13	917	179	10634
吉 林	Jilin	9	838	59	3472
黑龙江	Heilongjiang	6	1108	64	3769
上 海	Shanghai	17	2533	393	20310
江 苏	Jiangsu	40	6495	535	34533
浙 江	Zhejiang	18	3204	785	54478
安 徽	Anhui	8	908	325	19568
福 建	Fujian	12	1466	434	27900
江 西	Jiangxi	25	1604	216	13933
山 东	Shandong	46	4402	565	32581
河 南	Henan	48	3201	596	32660
湖 北	Hubei	19	2718	364	20466
湖 南	Hunan	19	2999	472	35105
广 东	Guangdong	47	6626	994	74782
广 西	Guangxi	21	2686	329	20204
海 南	Hainan	9	1262	26	4453
重 庆	Chongqing	11	1009	250	13968
四 川	Sichuan	31	3498	574	34274
贵 州	Guizhou	4	250	419	19669
云 南	Yunnan	13	1482	314	20318
西 藏	Tibet	4	185	23	1126
陕 西	Shaanxi	19	1350	388	21484
甘 肃	Gansu	7	502	161	9069
青 海	Qinghai	NA	411	46	3001
宁 夏	Ningxia			45	3462
新 疆	Xinjiang	6	601	96	6395

地 区	Region	港、澳、台商投资企业 Enterprises with Funds from Hongkong, Macao and Taiwan		外商投资企业 Foreign Funded Enterprises	
		法人单位数 (个) Number of Corporation Enterprises (unit)	年末从业人数 (人) Engaged Persons at the Year-end (person)	法人单位数 (个) Number of Corporation Enterprises (unit)	年末从业人数 (人) Engaged Persons at the Year-end (person)
全 国	**National Total**	**515**	**120574**	**324**	**63191**
北 京	Beijing	31	14289	30	7232
天 津	Tianjin	4	281	9	1354
河 北	Hebei	5	1131	NA	544
山 西	Shanxi				
内 蒙 古	Inner Mongolia	4	938	NA	29
辽 宁	Liaoning	16	4118	24	1920
吉 林	Jilin	NA	388	NA	766
黑 龙 江	Heilongjiang	9	1458	NA	537
上 海	Shanghai	29	7545	19	6979
江 苏	Jiangsu	37	6630	28	4527
浙 江	Zhejiang	36	10062	25	3305
安 徽	Anhui	9	2264	NA	316
福 建	Fujian	45	8544	26	5270
江 西	Jiangxi	10	1224	5	385
山 东	Shandong	17	3744	11	1572
河 南	Henan	14	2660	4	185
湖 北	Hubei	15	3357	5	524
湖 南	Hunan	16	3834	4	786
广 东	Guangdong	142	27915	70	16470
广 西	Guangxi	17	4473	NA	67
海 南	Hainan	21	8361	10	3280
重 庆	Chongqing	NA	612	4	1237
四 川	Sichuan	8	1596	8	1517
贵 州	Guizhou	4	393	NA	461
云 南	Yunnan	10	2123	10	902
西 藏	Tibet	NA	224	NA	233
陕 西	Shaanxi	7	2227	10	1912
甘 肃	Gansu	NA	183	NA	347
青 海	Qinghai			NA	347
宁 夏	Ningxia			NA	80
新 疆	Xinjiang			NA	107

4-1-4 各地区限额以上住宿业企业基本情况(按国民经济行业分)

Basic Conditions of Enterprises above Designated Size of Hotels by Region and Sector

地 区	Region	旅游饭店 Tourist Hotel		一般旅馆 Fonda		其他住宿业 Others	
		法人单位数(个) Number of Corporation Enterprises (unit)	年末从业人数(人) Engaged Persons at the Year-end (person)	法人单位数(个) Number of Corporation Enterprises (unit)	年末从业人数(人) Engaged Persons at the Year-end (person)	法人单位数(个) Number of Corporation Enterprises (unit)	年末从业人数(人) Engaged Persons at the Year-end (person)
全 国	**National Total**	**11663**	**1406118**	**7456**	**372781**	**661**	**41952**
北 京	Beijing	543	94144	389	22800	27	3006
天 津	Tianjin	100	12525	101	5190	28	1997
河 北	Hebei	276	33668	165	13381	15	2968
山 西	Shanxi	175	22007	143	8660	11	805
内蒙古	Inner Mongolia	188	18170	100	6772	6	454
辽 宁	Liaoning	288	31676	147	6111	16	1050
吉 林	Jilin	144	14164	47	2405	10	833
黑龙江	Heilongjiang	141	13786	56	3088	12	669
上 海	Shanghai	312	52424	380	19237	29	1474
江 苏	Jiangsu	607	85341	400	15192	40	2195
浙 江	Zhejiang	823	110170	471	19633	26	857
安 徽	Anhui	309	32422	220	9179	19	805
福 建	Fujian	557	68974	307	14709	21	1181
江 西	Jiangxi	318	30459	180	9903	26	994
山 东	Shandong	659	80706	430	20443	30	1235
河 南	Henan	702	61364	663	32627	49	2602
湖 北	Hubei	383	40286	319	14088	19	1157
湖 南	Hunan	480	60170	281	15615	33	2403
广 东	Guangdong	1346	196480	832	43306	81	5802
广 西	Guangxi	349	34516	196	11389	15	815
海 南	Hainan	238	48942	13	946	NA	376
重 庆	Chongqing	249	28334	188	8667	20	1044
四 川	Sichuan	569	55364	458	21503	23	1099
贵 州	Guizhou	399	30431	219	7884	17	912
云 南	Yunnan	388	42966	205	11480	18	1368
西 藏	Tibet	64	5042			4	193
陕 西	Shaanxi	491	50082	344	17266	33	2214
甘 肃	Gansu	232	21131	95	4712	23	974
青 海	Qinghai	72	6423	23	941	NA	179
宁 夏	Ningxia	61	6101	14	679	NA	142
新 疆	Xinjiang	200	17850	70	4975	NA	149

4-1-5 各地区限额以上餐饮业企业基本情况
Basic Conditions of Enterprises above Designated Size of Catering Services by Region

地区	Region	餐饮业 Catering Services		#国有控股 State-controlled Enterprises	
		法人单位数（个）Number of Corporation Enterprises (unit)	年末从业人数（人）Engaged Persons at the Year-end (person)	法人单位数（个）Number of Corporation Enterprises (unit)	年末从业人数（人）Engaged Persons at the Year-end (person)
全　国	**National Total**	**25884**	**2232258**	**751**	**114416**
北　京	Beijing	1299	253600	84	17444
天　津	Tianjin	351	39400	19	1627
河　北	Hebei	429	32554	28	2578
山　西	Shanxi	397	39508	30	3226
内蒙古	Inner Mongolia	326	26404	13	1650
辽　宁	Liaoning	343	29155	17	3777
吉　林	Jilin	223	12398	12	1551
黑龙江	Heilongjiang	101	5490	12	512
上　海	Shanghai	1655	237405	53	10380
江　苏	Jiangsu	1853	177071	85	10051
浙　江	Zhejiang	1579	139891	35	7501
安　徽	Anhui	1213	76554	19	5421
福　建	Fujian	1021	71862	13	2248
江　西	Jiangxi	447	24773	16	1526
山　东	Shandong	1767	121848	78	11162
河　南	Henan	1235	67165	14	1040
湖　北	Hubei	1363	94218	27	5304
湖　南	Hunan	930	60737	16	1332
广　东	Guangdong	3143	334200	42	9372
广　西	Guangxi	344	30917	13	992
海　南	Hainan	52	5363	NA	36
重　庆	Chongqing	1372	78943	12	1014
四　川	Sichuan	1474	96640	26	2400
贵　州	Guizhou	598	20419	9	1048
云　南	Yunnan	536	31165	15	2737
西　藏	Tibet	13	628		
陕　西	Shaanxi	1241	82975	29	5168
甘　肃	Gansu	362	22204	17	2145
青　海	Qinghai	53	3732	NA	209
宁　夏	Ningxia	67	5462	NA	219
新　疆	Xinjiang	97	9577	11	746

4-1-6 各地区限额以上餐饮业企业基本情况(按登记注册类型分)
Basic Conditions of Enterprises above Designated Size of Catering Services by Region and Type of Registration

地 区	Region	内资企业 Domestic Funded Enterprises			
				国有企业 State-owned Enterprises	
		法人单位数 (个) Number of Corporation Enterprises (unit)	年末从业人数 (人) Engaged Persons at the Year-end (person)	法人单位数 (个) Number of Corporation Enterprises (unit)	年末从业人数 (人) Engaged Persons at the Year-end (person)
全 国	**National Total**	**24872**	**1655996**	**327**	**33651**
北 京	Beijing	1194	140195	23	2348
天 津	Tianjin	326	22239	6	563
河 北	Hebei	426	32309	19	1507
山 西	Shanxi	395	35136	19	1437
内蒙古	Inner Mongolia	323	25440	10	1173
辽 宁	Liaoning	318	19449	9	3000
吉 林	Jilin	219	12316	7	1208
黑龙江	Heilongjiang	93	4690	10	402
上 海	Shanghai	1399	110174	14	1180
江 苏	Jiangsu	1787	125826	24	2195
浙 江	Zhejiang	1550	112881	7	503
安 徽	Anhui	1210	76318	5	390
福 建	Fujian	970	47540	5	658
江 西	Jiangxi	435	22351	9	724
山 东	Shandong	1736	113660	44	6109
河 南	Henan	1229	61951	7	317
湖 北	Hubei	1341	77691	12	691
湖 南	Hunan	924	55418	7	756
广 东	Guangdong	2860	223007	22	2907
广 西	Guangxi	336	25221	10	557
海 南	Hainan	45	4540	NA	36
重 庆	Chongqing	1364	69879	NA	69
四 川	Sichuan	1451	77162	10	830
贵 州	Guizhou	597	20411	NA	165
云 南	Yunnan	530	26267	7	454
西 藏	Tibet	13	628		
陕 西	Shaanxi	1226	74568	14	1007
甘 肃	Gansu	360	20681	13	1240
青 海	Qinghai	53	3732		
宁 夏	Ningxia	67	5462	NA	182
新 疆	Xinjiang	95	8854	8	1043

地　区	Region	集体企业 Collective-owned Enterprises		股份合作企业 Cooperative Enterprises	
		法人单位数（个） Number of Corporation Enterprises (unit)	年末从业人数（人） Engaged Persons at the Year-end (person)	法人单位数（个） Number of Corporation Enterprises (unit)	年末从业人数（人） Engaged Persons at the Year-end (person)
全　国	**National Total**	**151**	**7801**	**76**	**5961**
北　京	Beijing	15	815	21	1345
天　津	Tianjin	NA	85		
河　北	Hebei	NA	132	NA	264
山　西	Shanxi	NA	146	NA	45
内蒙古	Inner Mongolia	NA	70		
辽　宁	Liaoning	NA	69		
吉　林	Jilin	4	128		
黑龙江	Heilongjiang				
上　海	Shanghai	15	826	5	366
江　苏	Jiangsu	13	819	NA	84
浙　江	Zhejiang	NA	27	4	343
安　徽	Anhui	NA	176		
福　建	Fujian	NA	175		
江　西	Jiangxi			NA	98
山　东	Shandong	13	883	NA	90
河　南	Henan	10	310	NA	95
湖　北	Hubei	4	265	NA	105
湖　南	Hunan	NA	15	NA	132
广　东	Guangdong	27	1472	27	1234
广　西	Guangxi	4	226	NA	145
海　南	Hainan				
重　庆	Chongqing	20	762	NA	31
四　川	Sichuan	4	119	NA	1584
贵　州	Guizhou	NA	39		
云　南	Yunnan	NA	102		
西　藏	Tibet				
陕　西	Shaanxi	NA	140		
甘　肃	Gansu				
青　海	Qinghai				
宁　夏	Ningxia				
新　疆	Xinjiang				

地区	Region	联营企业 Joint Ownership Enterprises 法人单位数（个） Number of Corporation Enterprises (unit)	联营企业 年末从业人数（人） Engaged Persons at the Year-end (person)	有限责任公司 Limited Liability Corporations 法人单位数（个） Number of Corporation Enterprises (unit)	有限责任公司 年末从业人数（人） Engaged Persons at the Year-end (person)
全国	**National Total**	**8**	**335**	**6459**	**550730**
北京	Beijing			377	56684
天津	Tianjin			116	10469
河北	Hebei			81	7237
山西	Shanxi			62	7432
内蒙古	Inner Mongolia			134	10973
辽宁	Liaoning			85	5364
吉林	Jilin			82	5352
黑龙江	Heilongjiang			30	1326
上海	Shanghai	NA	29	175	22977
江苏	Jiangsu	NA	8	381	37811
浙江	Zhejiang	NA	58	231	28708
安徽	Anhui			322	25703
福建	Fujian			270	15380
江西	Jiangxi			153	10245
山东	Shandong	NA	31	492	36910
河南	Henan			479	25827
湖北	Hubei	NA	60	423	35652
湖南	Hunan			184	13065
广东	Guangdong	NA	92	725	79278
广西	Guangxi			81	9290
海南	Hainan			31	3498
重庆	Chongqing			295	17657
四川	Sichuan			390	26820
贵州	Guizhou			77	4476
云南	Yunnan			121	9085
西藏	Tibet			4	188
陕西	Shaanxi	NA	25	492	32164
甘肃	Gansu	NA	32	120	7448
青海	Qinghai			8	671
宁夏	Ningxia			15	1307
新疆	Xinjiang			23	1733

地区	Region	股份有限公司 Share-holding Corporations Ltd. 法人单位数(个) Number of Corporation Enterprises (unit)	股份有限公司 Share-holding Corporations Ltd. 年末从业人数(人) Engaged Persons at the Year-end (person)	私营企业 Private Enterprises 法人单位数(个) Number of Corporation Enterprises (unit)	私营企业 Private Enterprises 年末从业人数(人) Engaged Persons at the Year-end (person)
全国	**National Total**	**377**	**63215**	**17181**	**981971**
北京	Beijing	14	4138	744	74865
天津	Tianjin	5	967	197	10155
河北	Hebei	7	675	313	22494
山西	Shanxi	7	640	302	25249
内蒙古	Inner Mongolia	7	1940	167	11049
辽宁	Liaoning	5	379	211	10299
吉林	Jilin	10	559	113	4877
黑龙江	Heilongjiang	4	250	48	2682
上海	Shanghai	9	2131	1171	81648
江苏	Jiangsu	32	4082	1324	80449
浙江	Zhejiang	17	4737	1286	78357
安徽	Anhui	10	883	869	49156
福建	Fujian	7	516	667	30171
江西	Jiangxi	12	905	256	10189
山东	Shandong	33	11082	1135	57411
河南	Henan	36	2809	686	32201
湖北	Hubei	17	2354	845	37566
湖南	Hunan	9	798	716	40515
广东	Guangdong	31	4872	1955	129965
广西	Guangxi	8	625	231	14378
海南	Hainan	4	389	9	617
重庆	Chongqing	12	6403	1005	43974
四川	Sichuan	26	1666	1003	45695
贵州	Guizhou	4	283	506	15326
云南	Yunnan	8	1084	380	15245
西藏	Tibet			9	440
陕西	Shaanxi	25	6445	671	33773
甘肃	Gansu	10	609	213	11203
青海	Qinghai	5	527	40	2534
宁夏	Ningxia	NA	176	48	3737
新疆	Xinjiang	NA	291	61	5751

4-1-6 续表 4 Continued 4

地 区	Region	港、澳、台商投资企业 Enterprises with Funds from Hongkong, Macao and Taiwan 法人单位数(个) Number of Corporation Enterprises (unit)	港、澳、台商投资企业 年末从业人数(人) Engaged Persons at the Year-end (person)	外商投资企业 Foreign Funded Enterprises 法人单位数(个) Number of Corporation Enterprises (unit)	外商投资企业 年末从业人数(人) Engaged Persons at the Year-end (person)
全 国	**National Total**	**628**	**246662**	**384**	**329600**
北 京	Beijing	58	58975	47	54430
天 津	Tianjin	9	3001	16	14160
河 北	Hebei	NA	124	NA	121
山 西	Shanxi	NA	1283	NA	3089
内蒙古	Inner Mongolia	NA	180	NA	784
辽 宁	Liaoning	10	3771	15	5935
吉 林	Jilin	NA	20	NA	62
黑龙江	Heilongjiang	4	569	4	231
上 海	Shanghai	156	65988	100	61243
江 苏	Jiangsu	38	11374	28	39871
浙 江	Zhejiang	18	10795	11	16215
安 徽	Anhui	NA	86	NA	150
福 建	Fujian	33	7763	18	16559
江 西	Jiangxi	8	789	4	1633
山 东	Shandong	13	2752	18	5436
河 南	Henan	NA	160	4	5054
湖 北	Hubei	15	14734	7	1793
湖 南	Hunan	NA	150	NA	5169
广 东	Guangdong	214	52434	69	58759
广 西	Guangxi	6	514	NA	5182
海 南	Hainan	7	823		
重 庆	Chongqing	NA	143	6	8921
四 川	Sichuan	13	6199	10	13279
贵 州	Guizhou	NA	8		
云 南	Yunnan	NA	1025	NA	3873
西 藏	Tibet				
陕 西	Shaanxi	8	2933	7	5474
甘 肃	Gansu	NA	63	NA	1460
青 海	Qinghai				
宁 夏	Ningxia				
新 疆	Xinjiang	NA	6	NA	717

4-1-7 各地区限额以上餐饮业企业基本情况(按国民经济行业分)

Basic Conditions of Enterprises above Designated Size of Catering Services by Region and Sector

地 区	Region	正餐服务 Dinner		快餐服务 Snack	
		法人单位数 (个) Number of Corporation Enterprises (unit)	年末从业人数 (人) Engaged Persons at the Year-end (person)	法人单位数 (个) Number of Corporation Enterprises (unit)	年末从业人数 (人) Engaged Persons at the Year-end (person)
全 国	**National Total**	**23977**	**1593776**	**950**	**475258**
北 京	Beijing	1095	153237	101	76112
天 津	Tianjin	286	19051	24	17609
河 北	Hebei	419	29774	6	283
山 西	Shanxi	386	33886	9	5557
内 蒙 古	Inner Mongolia	319	25849	5	465
辽 宁	Liaoning	301	16081	27	11044
吉 林	Jilin	207	10242	7	1837
黑 龙 江	Heilongjiang	97	4523	NA	911
上 海	Shanghai	1400	129429	102	55383
江 苏	Jiangsu	1688	115121	90	50398
浙 江	Zhejiang	1450	100821	55	32897
安 徽	Anhui	1158	59041	36	16657
福 建	Fujian	935	46257	49	22431
江 西	Jiangxi	425	22487	16	2142
山 东	Shandong	1664	107002	70	10775
河 南	Henan	1154	56925	57	7958
湖 北	Hubei	1329	74463	18	13036
湖 南	Hunan	899	50944	16	9268
广 东	Guangdong	2812	212483	140	91572
广 西	Guangxi	321	20902	16	9682
海 南	Hainan	50	5165	NA	198
重 庆	Chongqing	1321	71967	20	4796
四 川	Sichuan	1419	74365	25	16214
贵 州	Guizhou	574	18832	7	207
云 南	Yunnan	518	24862	6	4613
西 藏	Tibet	9	424	NA	97
陕 西	Shaanxi	1187	73744	27	8361
甘 肃	Gansu	348	19707	6	2351
青 海	Qinghai	52	3702	NA	30
宁 夏	Ningxia	67	5462		
新 疆	Xinjiang	87	7028	8	2374

地区	Region	饮料及冷饮服务 Beverage and Cold Drink		其他餐饮业 Others	
		法人单位数 (个) Number of Corporation Enterprises (unit)	年末从业人数 (人) Engaged Persons at the Year-end (person)	法人单位数 (个) Number of Corporation Enterprises (unit)	年末从业人数 (人) Engaged Persons at the Year-end (person)
全国	**National Total**	**226**	**64788**	**731**	**98436**
北京	Beijing	25	7192	78	17059
天津	Tianjin	NA	61	40	2679
河北	Hebei			4	2497
山西	Shanxi			NA	65
内蒙古	Inner Mongolia			NA	90
辽宁	Liaoning	5	753	10	1277
吉林	Jilin	NA	20	8	299
黑龙江	Heilongjiang	NA	28	NA	28
上海	Shanghai	35	34495	118	18098
江苏	Jiangsu	15	1397	60	10155
浙江	Zhejiang	22	1065	52	5108
安徽	Anhui	8	210	11	646
福建	Fujian	10	435	27	2739
江西	Jiangxi	NA	34	4	110
山东	Shandong	NA	381	31	3690
河南	Henan	6	174	18	2108
湖北	Hubei	7	2298	9	4421
湖南	Hunan	7	168	8	357
广东	Guangdong	48	12719	143	17426
广西	Guangxi	6	253	NA	80
海南	Hainan				
重庆	Chongqing	NA	129	29	2051
四川	Sichuan	13	2640	17	3421
贵州	Guizhou	NA	46	14	1334
云南	Yunnan	NA	147	10	1543
西藏	Tibet	NA	27	NA	80
陕西	Shaanxi	NA	75	25	795
甘肃	Gansu	NA	41	6	105
青海	Qinghai				
宁夏	Ningxia				
新疆	Xinjiang			NA	175

4-2-1 限额以上住宿和餐饮业企业经营情况

项　目	Item	营业额 Business Revenue	客房收入 from Hotel Rooms
总　计	**Total**	**92767093**	**23661560**
一、住宿业	**Hotels**	**39639340**	**20512415**
#国有控股	State-controlled Enterprises	9941361	4552725
(一)按登记注册类型分	**by Type of Registration**		
1.内资企业	**Domestic Funded Enterprises**	**34162409**	**17782575**
国有企业	State-owned Enterprises	3598820	1589107
集体企业	Collective-owned Enterprises	397164	185862
股份合作企业	Cooperative Enterprises	85629	33971
联营企业	Joint Ownership Enterprises	37711	20632
国有联营企业	State Joint Ownership Enterprises	22113	12380
集体联营企业	Collective Joint Ownership Enterprises	4656	1870
国有与集体联营企业	Joint State-collective Enterprises	6645	3740
其他联营企业	Other Joint Ownership Enterprises	4298	2642
有限责任公司	Limited Liability Corporations	16076904	8114163
国有独资公司	State Sole Funded Corporations	1529998	704514
其他有限责任公司	Other Limited Liability Corporations	14546904	7409649
股份有限公司	Share-holding Corporations Ltd.	1219942	577065
私营企业	Private Enterprises	12585143	7173926
私营独资企业	Private-funded Enterprises	846375	479486
私营合伙企业	Private Partnership Enterprises	245347	107133
私营有限责任公司	Private Limited Liability Corporations	10939954	6300320
私营股份有限公司	Private Share-holding Corporations Ltd.	553466	286992
其他企业	Other Enterprises	161098	87853
2.港、澳、台商投资企业	**Enterprises with Funds from Hongkong, Macao and Taiwan**	**3571381**	**1738041**
合资经营企业	Joint-venture Enterprises	1468193	700008
合作经营企业	Cooperative Enterprises	386632	192582
独资经营企业	Enterprises with Sole Investment	1580900	774343
投资股份有限公司	Share-holding Corporations Ltd. with Investment	108001	57164
其他港澳台商投资企业	Other Enterprises with Funds from Hongkong, Macao and Taiwan	27651	13946
3.外商投资企业	**Foreign Funded Enterprises**	**1905553**	**991805**
中外合资经营企业	Joint-venture Enterprises	821630	415435
中外合作经营企业	Cooperative Enterprises	305565	153826
外资企业	Enterprises with Sole Foreign Investment	654658	358682
外商投资股份有限公司	Share-holding Corporations Ltd. with Foreign Investment	36686	22679
其他外商投资企业	Other Foreign Funded Enterprises	87017	41182
(二)按国民经济行业分	**by Sector**		
旅游饭店	Tourist Hotel	30594066	14623511
一般旅馆	Fonda	8132557	5374170
其他住宿业	Others	912719	514739

注：部分数据合计数由于单位取舍不同而产生的计算误差，未做机械调整(下表同)。
Note: Statistical discrepanies on totals figures due to rounding are not adjusted.The same applies to the tables following.

Business of Enterprises above Designated Size of Hotels and Catering Services

单位：万元

Unit: 10000 yuan

餐费收入 from Meals	商品销售额 from Commodities	其他收入 Others	客房数 (间) Hotel Rooms (unit)	床位数 (个) Hotel Beds (unit)	餐位数 (位) Seats for Meal (unit)
61354173	**2783989**	**4967368**	**4875495**	**7852993**	**72790627**
14033174	**1108657**	**3985099**	**3931662**	**6261588**	**8470925**
3559055	312572	1517015	674916	1135542	2099227
12244512	**905078**	**3230242**	**3694311**	**5905682**	**7961296**
1392185	80200	537335	217713	391863	1172675
139514	11074	60716	28061	52080	74450
31429	6222	14010	5899	11161	15792
14041	542	2499	2433	3952	6681
8071	473	1190	1455	2269	2753
2383	6	396	413	733	2080
1935	62	909	268	432	500
1652		4	297	518	1348
5751442	413895	1797400	1516130	2407525	3109548
564503	27271	233718	94222	157546	233518
5186945	386626	1563682	1421908	2249979	2876030
435982	66772	140128	169459	250385	294850
4421347	320549	669323	1738762	2761385	3238701
305527	32620	28749	124238	201745	298197
111538	12668	14011	26115	44034	67227
3784655	263014	591967	1510416	2389627	2702664
219627	12249	34601	77993	125979	170613
58584	5835	8838	15854	27331	48599
1202401	**139942**	**490998**	**142673**	**217375**	**346644**
512950	32164	223077	58162	87862	154937
121047	10712	62293	10784	16922	21426
516717	94134	195708	67216	102197	155265
40616	2835	7386	5126	8039	12075
11072	100	2533	1385	2355	2941
586264	**63636**	**263855**	**94678**	**138531**	**162985**
257652	5995	142549	36976	56134	73272
85569	41229	24942	9482	14546	27479
193904	15603	86472	42834	59728	52848
10942	267	2803	2530	3957	4440
38202	540	7094	2856	4166	4946
11669074	880986	3420493	2764111	4360743	6751369
2103309	184442	470646	1066199	1711841	1553286
260793	43227	93961	101352	189004	166270

项　目	Item	营业额 Business Revenue	客房收入 from Hotel Rooms
二、餐饮业	**Catering Services**	**53127754**	**3149148**
#国有控股	State-controlled Enterprises	2481108	274995
(一)按登记注册类型分	**by Type of Registration**		
1.内资企业	**Domestic Funded Enterprises**	**37501042**	**3056347**
国有企业	State-owned Enterprises	585950	131607
集体企业	Collective-owned Enterprises	239100	34357
股份合作企业	Cooperative Enterprises	138249	4420
联营企业	Joint Ownership Enterprises	10809	3341
国有联营企业	State Joint Ownership Enterprises		
集体联营企业	Collective Joint Ownership Enterprises	8250	2271
国有与集体联营企业	Joint State-collective Enterprises		
其他联营企业	Other Joint Ownership Enterprises	2559	1070
有限责任公司	Limited Liability Corporations	11870827	1134969
国有独资公司	State Sole Funded Corporations	407187	47295
其他有限责任公司	Other Limited Liability Corporations	11463639	1087675
股份有限公司	Share-holding Corporations Ltd.	1466291	92131
私营企业	Private Enterprises	22854323	1626556
私营独资企业	Private-funded Enterprises	2853319	152219
私营合伙企业	Private Partnership Enterprises	304512	19824
私营有限责任公司	Private Limited Liability Corporations	18891698	1389515
私营股份有限公司	Private Share-holding Corporations Ltd.	804794	65007
其他企业	Other Enterprises	335500	28971
2.港、澳、台商投资企业	**Enterprises with Funds from Hongkong, Macao and Taiwan**	**6650252**	**67302**
合资经营企业	Joint-venture Enterprises	1214595	14874
合作经营企业	Cooperative Enterprises	174286	6074
独资经营企业	Enterprises with Sole Investment	5227031	43383
投资股份有限公司	Share-holding Corporations Ltd. with Investment	15445	511
其他港澳台商投资企业	Other Enterprises with Funds from Hongkong, Macao and Taiwan	18896	2459
3.外商投资企业	**Foreign Funded Enterprises**	**8976463**	**25504**
中外合资经营企业	Joint-venture Enterprises	1872976	14000
中外合作经营企业	Cooperative Enterprises	74472	2280
外资企业	Enterprises with Sole Foreign Investment	6402112	5607
外商投资股份有限公司	Share-holding Corporations Ltd. with Foreign Investment	307708	3092
其他外商投资企业	Other Foreign Funded Enterprises	319195	525
(二)按国民经济行业分	**by Sector**		
正餐服务	Restaurant	36504012	3116384
快餐服务	Snack	12150511	10729
饮料及冷饮服务	Beverage and Cold Drink	2157981	1026
其他餐饮业	Others	2315249	21008

单位：万元
Unit: 10000 yuan

餐费收入 from Meals	商品销售额 from Commodities	其他收入 Others	客房数 (间) Hotel Rooms (unit)	床位数 (个) Hotel Beds (unit)	餐位数 (位) Seats for Meal (unit)
47320996	**1675332**	**982274**	**943833**	**1591405**	**64319702**
1765556	236356	204198	46323	80055	655366
32151735	**1468873**	**824085**	**929785**	**1568207**	**62028737**
403985	16650	33709	23997	42701	284919
179122	14031	11593	4507	8082	79669
119120	11405	3307	887	1552	40533
7419	51		799	1237	4045
5970	10		451	681	2045
1449	41		348	556	2000
9841441	489906	404513	251796	430780	47711472
234851	55892	69156	6629	11537	94683
9606596	434014	335356	245167	419243	47616789
1211365	129764	33039	17129	29765	306632
20102794	789772	335198	622358	1040078	13491222
2568492	112627	19983	67287	118305	1271753
274682	7183	2828	4724	7977	128072
16579629	619760	302799	512278	841250	11790731
679991	50206	9588	38069	72546	300666
286500	17307	2728	8312	14012	110245
6428191	**107084**	**47672**	**10207**	**16816**	**995483**
1173723	11312	14686	2887	4552	242873
163893	1955	2362	756	1307	17829
5062336	91541	29770	6101	10131	726570
14649	280	4	113	207	2807
13591	1996	851	350	619	5404
8741067	**99375**	**110519**	**3841**	**6382**	**1295482**
1842574	5918	10486	1562	2507	318534
51134	467	20591	165	248	6332
6277387	58673	60452	894	1576	911697
256462	33819	14335	1086	1897	31504
313514	500	4657	134	154	27415
31379746	1194394	813481	935504	1569583	18116718
11850214	185085	104487	4562	13988	44927402
2047596	100325	9036	295	464	257315
2043445	195531	55271	3472	7370	1018267

4-2-2 各地区限额以上住宿业企业经营情况

Business of Enterprises above Designated Size of Hotels by Region

单位：万元

Unit: 10000 yuan

地区	Region	营业额 Business Revenue	客房收入 from Hotel Rooms	餐费收入 from Meals	商品销售额 from Commodities	其他收入 Others
全国	**National Total**	**39639340**	**20512415**	**14033174**	**1108657**	**3985099**
北京	Beijing	3884934	2136278	928249	41847	778560
天津	Tianjin	433879	233207	123362	4598	72711
河北	Hebei	705204	304559	319574	11762	69308
山西	Shanxi	349609	166532	144237	4698	34141
内蒙古	Inner Mongolia	353589	174606	153988	1253	23742
辽宁	Liaoning	682763	339846	247004	12826	83086
吉林	Jilin	297094	155545	113594	5493	22462
黑龙江	Heilongjiang	312949	175919	99410	13767	23853
上海	Shanghai	2899291	1631149	713736	86902	467504
江苏	Jiangsu	2453657	1111697	1066180	88332	187448
浙江	Zhejiang	3250476	1684887	1281662	28028	255899
安徽	Anhui	715038	347359	304435	16314	46932
福建	Fujian	2030524	851073	889379	171345	118728
江西	Jiangxi	697811	359448	282735	16774	38853
山东	Shandong	2132053	1028601	917744	61606	124103
河南	Henan	1743492	915582	682250	58375	87285
湖北	Hubei	1178122	628681	436217	45544	67680
湖南	Hunan	1651051	811544	672738	71847	94922
广东	Guangdong	5614948	2859508	1805074	141051	809315
广西	Guangxi	782077	459720	244532	19595	58231
海南	Hainan	1121536	711833	328210	5285	76209
重庆	Chongqing	924958	468066	356940	31969	67983
四川	Sichuan	1509138	778093	568342	58353	104351
贵州	Guizhou	687036	427451	203891	20098	35597
云南	Yunnan	960156	555444	282544	30621	91547
西藏	Tibet	88122	56594	18895	557	12076
陕西	Shaanxi	1233725	594875	529640	46608	62603
甘肃	Gansu	420872	253783	140554	5234	21301
青海	Qinghai	85265	53618	24233	683	6731
宁夏	Ningxia	86329	42200	36426	1763	5941
新疆	Xinjiang	353642	194717	117399	5529	35997

4-2-2 续表 Continued

国有控股 单位：万元

State-controlled Enterprises Unit: 10000 yuan

地 区	Region	营业额 Business Revenue	客房收入 from Hotel Rooms	餐费收入 from Meals	商品销售额 from Commodities	其他收入 Others
全 国	**National Total**	**9941361**	**4552725**	**3559055**	**312572**	**1517015**
北 京	Beijing	1900556	926362	518292	22448	433453
天 津	Tianjin	149998	74447	48705	2168	24678
河 北	Hebei	217016	83976	101597	2725	28719
山 西	Shanxi	124802	54582	54852	1098	14271
内蒙古	Inner Mongolia	67359	24884	36274	358	5842
辽 宁	Liaoning	188675	74816	83683	1916	28260
吉 林	Jilin	83102	37051	35250	642	10159
黑龙江	Heilongjiang	113673	55589	37650	7943	12491
上 海	Shanghai	1143872	551451	303108	58651	230663
江 苏	Jiangsu	760333	288344	320837	49001	102152
浙 江	Zhejiang	638209	282165	262329	10478	83237
安 徽	Anhui	119499	50275	55113	3722	10389
福 建	Fujian	388353	171161	153404	39940	23849
江 西	Jiangxi	138311	66569	59399	4553	7791
山 东	Shandong	542260	225336	248839	9493	58592
河 南	Henan	250495	108295	106659	11564	23977
湖 北	Hubei	149872	69991	57830	3965	18086
湖 南	Hunan	276772	101049	128125	14826	32772
广 东	Guangdong	949754	477497	309235	8335	154687
广 西	Guangxi	135376	53829	50434	13745	17368
海 南	Hainan	133580	86251	37280	141	9909
重 庆	Chongqing	156775	65174	60102	2264	29236
四 川	Sichuan	200591	93077	70194	7433	29887
贵 州	Guizhou	126998	60461	50781	6678	9079
云 南	Yunnan	275703	126095	95717	14583	39308
西 藏	Tibet	36365	19654	7871	380	8460
陕 西	Shaanxi	266719	113870	120868	5819	26162
甘 肃	Gansu	158143	88243	55779	2111	12010
青 海	Qinghai	34083	19014	10537	576	3955
宁 夏	Ningxia	24584	12442	8860	658	2625
新 疆	Xinjiang	189533	90775	69451	4358	24948

4-2-3 各地区限额以上住宿业企业经营情况(按登记注册类型分)
Business of Enterprises above Designated Size of Hotels by Region and Type of Registration

内资企业
Domestic Funded Enterprises

单位：万元
Unit: 10000 yuan

地　区	Region	营业额 Business Revenue	客房收入 from Hotel Rooms	餐费收入 from Meals	商品销售额 from Commodities	其他收入 Others
全　国	**National Total**	**34162409**	**17782575**	**12244512**	**905078**	**3230242**
北　京	Beijing	2855751	1607614	708245	29237	510655
天　津	Tianjin	380747	202526	105324	4491	68406
河　北	Hebei	671548	290317	307492	8761	64978
山　西	Shanxi	349609	166532	144237	4698	34141
内蒙古	Inner Mongolia	327911	162851	142321	1253	21486
辽　宁	Liaoning	543604	269006	196485	7003	71110
吉　林	Jilin	269333	140666	101169	5298	22199
黑龙江	Heilongjiang	267188	151772	82935	12066	20415
上　海	Shanghai	2139380	1265972	518375	48888	306145
江　苏	Jiangsu	2183533	987728	936870	85850	173085
浙　江	Zhejiang	2896627	1532453	1117267	25685	221221
安　徽	Anhui	662928	323675	281609	15862	41781
福　建	Fujian	1653802	714253	752462	99464	87624
江　西	Jiangxi	671779	345041	273144	16121	37474
山　东	Shandong	1994908	964481	863526	57168	109732
河　南	Henan	1682079	889058	655749	56371	80901
湖　北	Hubei	1087456	577515	402793	45046	62102
湖　南	Hunan	1577154	774615	644359	70894	87287
广　东	Guangdong	4447782	2257084	1403939	99244	687515
广　西	Guangxi	683796	409099	202873	18645	53178
海　南	Hainan	807749	505128	237902	4343	60377
重　庆	Chongqing	876298	444094	343864	31090	57249
四　川	Sichuan	1427130	732153	544084	52417	98477
贵　州	Guizhou	676763	421924	199933	19777	35129
云　南	Yunnan	896646	517941	261989	29035	87681
西　藏	Tibet	72962	46944	14353	453	11212
陕　西	Shaanxi	1130612	547697	489969	42709	50236
甘　肃	Gansu	408605	247346	135587	5234	20438
青　海	Qinghai	80749	51166	22231	683	6669
宁　夏	Ningxia	85579	41874	36027	1763	5916
新　疆	Xinjiang	352401	194049	117399	5529	35423

4-2-3 续表 1 Continued 1

国有企业
State-owned Enterprises

单位：万元
Unit: 10000 yuan

地 区	Region	营业额 Business Revenue	客房收入 from Hotel Rooms	餐费收入 from Meals	商品销售额 from Commodities	其他收入 Others
全 国	**National Total**	**3598820**	**1589107**	**1392185**	**80200**	**537335**
北 京	Beijing	711508	353473	184293	8109	165634
天 津	Tianjin	42309	20868	11530	1722	8189
河 北	Hebei	145277	58027	72138	2023	13089
山 西	Shanxi	89556	38997	41560	873	8126
内蒙古	Inner Mongolia	22826	10167	10946	154	1559
辽 宁	Liaoning	103944	39309	46559	852	17225
吉 林	Jilin	67601	30432	30413	294	6462
黑龙江	Heilongjiang	68617	34147	24151	3187	7132
上 海	Shanghai	200461	79343	60253	3735	57131
江 苏	Jiangsu	165002	62900	81700	4763	15639
浙 江	Zhejiang	200385	91766	80910	1722	25987
安 徽	Anhui	23685	8456	12973	874	1382
福 建	Fujian	100282	48437	41583	355	9907
江 西	Jiangxi	70310	34966	31133	1717	2493
山 东	Shandong	346360	128126	178715	5194	34325
河 南	Henan	152814	63006	69780	7393	12635
湖 北	Hubei	53390	22583	25500	852	4455
湖 南	Hunan	127623	49413	64266	6310	7635
广 东	Guangdong	324784	150410	112310	3962	58103
广 西	Guangxi	73169	23536	26300	12126	11206
海 南	Hainan	11233	5955	3186	124	1968
重 庆	Chongqing	47198	17458	15502	536	13703
四 川	Sichuan	51971	23704	18017	2133	8118
贵 州	Guizhou	34487	17668	12733	780	3306
云 南	Yunnan	76749	33047	23690	5922	14089
西 藏	Tibet	20983	11704	3663	330	5287
陕 西	Shaanxi	85208	36268	42740	2189	4011
甘 肃	Gansu	71985	42098	26973	688	2227
青 海	Qinghai	12862	6452	4520	155	1736
宁 夏	Ningxia	12640	7064	3794	31	1751
新 疆	Xinjiang	83602	39327	30354	1096	12825

4-2-3 续表 2 Continued 2

集体企业 | 单位：万元
Collective-owned Enterprises | Unit: 10000 yuan

地　区	Region	营业额 Business Revenue	客房收入 from Hotel Rooms	餐费收入 from Meals	商品销售额 from Commodities	其他收入 Others
全　国	**National Total**	**397164**	**185862**	**139514**	**11074**	**60716**
北　京	Beijing	93791	48496	16013	178	29104
天　津	Tianjin	7643	2565	2152	2	2924
河　北	Hebei	12664	3687	8308	185	484
山　西	Shanxi	6143	3631	1968		543
内蒙古	Inner Mongolia	251	38	147	28	39
辽　宁	Liaoning	9919	3723	4258	72	1865
吉　林	Jilin	3771	1836	1935		
黑龙江	Heilongjiang	4198	2548	855	47	748
上　海	Shanghai	16394	5728	9785	10	871
江　苏	Jiangsu	25026	9197	13890	369	1571
浙　江	Zhejiang	23004	13754	5958	87	3205
安　徽	Anhui	1495	1057	428		9
福　建	Fujian	9424	3468	3812		2144
江　西	Jiangxi					
山　东	Shandong	32628	14307	15043	2033	1245
河　南	Henan	43051	19789	19195	941	3126
湖　北	Hubei	18198	8746	7668	640	1144
湖　南	Hunan	18370	7865	6005	3835	665
广　东	Guangdong	23482	9318	8846	437	4881
广　西	Guangxi	4729	2452	1115	278	884
海　南	Hainan	565	386			179
重　庆	Chongqing	9892	5739	3621	33	500
四　川	Sichuan	8483	4015	2350	107	2011
贵　州	Guizhou	5800	4270	1408	122	
云　南	Yunnan	5244	3472	1339		434
西　藏	Tibet	790	571			219
陕　西	Shaanxi	6793	2317	1866	1670	939
甘　肃	Gansu	3560	2159	894		508
青　海	Qinghai	199	121			78
宁　夏	Ningxia	232	232			
新　疆	Xinjiang	1425	374	655		396

股份合作企业
Cooperative Enterprises

单位：万元
Unit: 10000 yuan

地 区	Region	营业额 Business Revenue	客房收入 from Hotel Rooms	餐费收入 from Meals	商品销售额 from Commodities	其他收入 Others
全 国	**National Total**	**85629**	**33971**	**31429**	**6222**	**14010**
北 京	Beijing	30768	15970	4948	408	9441
天 津	Tianjin	9006	1505	3971	431	3099
河 北	Hebei					
山 西	Shanxi					
内蒙古	Inner Mongolia	422	231	130		61
辽 宁	Liaoning					
吉 林	Jilin	222	73	149		
黑龙江	Heilongjiang	10439	1848	3083	4605	903
上 海	Shanghai					
江 苏	Jiangsu					
浙 江	Zhejiang	2298	1619	660		19
安 徽	Anhui					
福 建	Fujian	1420	468	810	130	13
江 西	Jiangxi	4359	1870	2171	290	29
山 东	Shandong	5217	2015	3081	121	
河 南	Henan	1896	942	860	75	20
湖 北	Hubei	1094	648	439	6	2
湖 南	Hunan	3663	2550	940		173
广 东	Guangdong	1968	1189	746	32	1
广 西	Guangxi	231	200	1	2	28
海 南	Hainan	1156	581	420		154
重 庆	Chongqing					
四 川	Sichuan	1445	583	700	122	40
贵 州	Guizhou					
云 南	Yunnan	532	493	13		27
西 藏	Tibet					
陕 西	Shaanxi	9493	1186	8307		
甘 肃	Gansu					
青 海	Qinghai					
宁 夏	Ningxia					
新 疆	Xinjiang					

4-2-3 续表 4 Continued 4

联营企业
Joint Ownership Enterprises

单位：万元
Unit: 10000 yuan

地 区	Region	营业额 Business Revenue	客房收入 from Hotel Rooms	餐费收入 from Meals	商品销售额 from Commodities	其他收入 Others
全 国	**National Total**	**37711**	**20632**	**14041**	**542**	**2499**
北 京	Beijing	4264	2019	1612		633
天 津	Tianjin					
河 北	Hebei					
山 西	Shanxi					
内 蒙 古	Inner Mongolia	811	136	675		
辽 宁	Liaoning	766	357	409		
吉 林	Jilin					
黑 龙 江	Heilongjiang					
上 海	Shanghai	1206	429	502		275
江 苏	Jiangsu	4241	1746	2100	22	374
浙 江	Zhejiang	4938	2662	1935	62	280
安 徽	Anhui					
福 建	Fujian	10336	5937	3578	139	682
江 西	Jiangxi					
山 东	Shandong					
河 南	Henan	1741	1701	40		
湖 北	Hubei					
湖 南	Hunan					
广 东	Guangdong	2610	2031	150	313	116
广 西	Guangxi					
海 南	Hainan					
重 庆	Chongqing					
四 川	Sichuan					
贵 州	Guizhou					
云 南	Yunnan	2542	1545	859	6	133
西 藏	Tibet					
陕 西	Shaanxi					
甘 肃	Gansu	3776	1722	2054		
青 海	Qinghai					
宁 夏	Ningxia					
新 疆	Xinjiang	480	347	127		6

有限责任公司
Limited Liability Corporations

单位：万元
Unit: 10000 yuan

地 区	Region	营业额 Business Revenue	客房收入 from Hotel Rooms	餐费收入 from Meals	商品销售额 from Commodities	其他收入 Others
全 国	**National Total**	**16076904**	**8114163**	**5751442**	**413895**	**1797400**
北 京	Beijing	1497906	828013	398545	16469	254879
天 津	Tianjin	210684	103884	61758	1266	43776
河 北	Hebei	201427	86827	87925	1389	25286
山 西	Shanxi	92158	37249	41225	894	12790
内蒙古	Inner Mongolia	170582	77299	80564	512	12207
辽 宁	Liaoning	232679	115768	85846	3162	27902
吉 林	Jilin	119662	64416	42550	2967	9729
黑龙江	Heilongjiang	88340	54702	25898	1210	6531
上 海	Shanghai	1147146	607914	312285	25147	201800
江 苏	Jiangsu	919171	410181	411819	20029	77141
浙 江	Zhejiang	1178933	552158	496636	12725	117414
安 徽	Anhui	300252	146526	125210	6982	21533
福 建	Fujian	836798	354447	367022	66112	49217
江 西	Jiangxi	340513	170483	138160	6931	24938
山 东	Shandong	700828	335127	297147	20726	47828
河 南	Henan	783573	429802	288004	28119	37648
湖 北	Hubei	489539	270937	169433	9339	39829
湖 南	Hunan	581238	276679	239378	20726	44456
广 东	Guangdong	2451469	1154509	783139	67715	446106
广 西	Guangxi	239390	149362	65690	1969	22369
海 南	Hainan	663633	415667	198312	3548	46106
重 庆	Chongqing	404506	207006	152639	16795	28065
四 川	Sichuan	622836	317165	239458	19565	46648
贵 州	Guizhou	313872	172968	106065	11369	23470
云 南	Yunnan	481168	258645	151122	15600	55802
西 藏	Tibet	27278	16219	6948	63	4048
陕 西	Shaanxi	576340	277099	241089	24738	33414
甘 肃	Gansu	191254	107219	66587	3313	14135
青 海	Qinghai	27652	18935	5675	149	2892
宁 夏	Ningxia	35345	15361	16596	979	2410
新 疆	Xinjiang	150732	81596	48717	3389	17030

股份有限公司
Share-holding Corporations Ltd

单位：万元
Unit: 10000 yuan

地区	Region	营业额 Business Revenue	客房收入 from Hotel Rooms	餐费收入 from Meals	商品销售额 from Commodities	其他收入 Others
全国	**National Total**	**1219942**	**577065**	**435982**	**66772**	**140128**
北京	Beijing	44251	21018	11239	1062	10932
天津	Tianjin	5411	3389	1231		791
河北	Hebei	14945	6036	5727	247	2936
山西	Shanxi	9051	5358	2854	29	810
内蒙古	Inner Mongolia	9527	4956	4293	53	225
辽宁	Liaoning	17359	10307	5496	85	1472
吉林	Jilin	13475	7806	3168	104	2398
黑龙江	Heilongjiang	14117	10529	1435	171	1983
上海	Shanghai	74870	48214	20516	503	5637
江苏	Jiangsu	246236	83460	83636	35954	43185
浙江	Zhejiang	74403	33670	30035	3271	7428
安徽	Anhui	17647	8480	7723	148	1297
福建	Fujian	29536	15381	11646	180	2329
江西	Jiangxi	34415	16730	15744	1503	438
山东	Shandong	96437	45819	42569	4424	3624
河南	Henan	64538	32742	26146	3051	2598
湖北	Hubei	45229	21190	17780	2000	4259
湖南	Hunan	61949	27928	26905	1785	5331
广东	Guangdong	135767	66881	41901	1911	25073
广西	Guangxi	42521	20355	16768	1154	4244
海南	Hainan	23524	17842	4695	32	954
重庆	Chongqing	18777	11902	5979	98	799
四川	Sichuan	48644	18431	16886	6545	6783
贵州	Guizhou	5583	3559	1681	257	87
云南	Yunnan	27720	13856	10998	734	2132
西藏	Tibet	2857	2554	149	23	131
陕西	Shaanxi	21408	8422	10827	758	1402
甘肃	Gansu	4798	3278	1267	183	70
青海	Qinghai	7816	3760	3510	356	191
宁夏	Ningxia					
新疆	Xinjiang	7131	3212	3178	151	589

4-2-3 续表 7 Continued 7

私营企业
Private Enterprises

单位：万元
Unit: 10000 yuan

地 区	Region	营业额 Business Revenue	客房收入 from Hotel Rooms	餐费收入 from Meals	商品销售额 from Commodities	其他收入 Others
全 国	**National Total**	**12585143**	**7173926**	**4421347**	**320549**	**669323**
北 京	Beijing	472978	338384	91552	3011	40032
天 津	Tianjin	101483	67542	23829	1030	9082
河 北	Hebei	297235	135739	133394	4918	23183
山 西	Shanxi	151068	80147	56168	2882	11871
内蒙古	Inner Mongolia	121797	69210	44700	491	7395
辽 宁	Liaoning	176539	98326	53559	2301	22354
吉 林	Jilin	59338	34175	19636	1919	3608
黑龙江	Heilongjiang	80329	47156	27209	2846	3119
上 海	Shanghai	692459	519545	114224	19436	39254
江 苏	Jiangsu	808360	413351	337705	22933	34371
浙 江	Zhejiang	1411467	836367	500607	7604	66889
安 徽	Anhui	318349	157867	135081	7844	17558
福 建	Fujian	659309	282033	321529	32506	23241
江 西	Jiangxi	215908	117356	83532	5445	9575
山 东	Shandong	799814	431266	321814	24620	22115
河 南	Henan	626411	336416	249493	15638	24864
湖 北	Hubei	475109	249013	181701	32072	12322
湖 南	Hunan	780836	408841	304791	38203	29001
广 东	Guangdong	1473482	853615	445436	24657	149775
广 西	Guangxi	322994	212662	92769	3116	14447
海 南	Hainan	106996	64138	31288	640	10931
重 庆	Chongqing	390918	199196	163992	13548	14182
四 川	Sichuan	682456	363725	260616	23297	34818
贵 州	Guizhou	314106	220989	77748	7117	8252
云 南	Yunnan	299782	205829	72531	6684	14739
西 藏	Tibet	18322	14232	2624	38	1428
陕 西	Shaanxi	421526	218753	180372	13086	9314
甘 肃	Gansu	131022	89719	36795	1010	3498
青 海	Qinghai	30990	21082	8113	23	1772
宁 夏	Ningxia	37362	19216	15637	753	1755
新 疆	Xinjiang	106397	68036	32902	881	4578

4-2-3 续表 8 Continued 8

其他企业　　单位：万元

Other Enterprises　　Unit: 10000 yuan

地　区	Region	营业额 Business Revenue	客房收入 from Hotel Rooms	餐费收入 from Meals	商品销售额 from Commodities	其他收入 Others
全　国	**National Total**	**161098**	**87853**	**58584**	**5835**	**8838**
北　京	Beijing	285	242	43		
天　津	Tianjin	4210	2774	852	40	544
河　北	Hebei					
山　西	Shanxi	1633	1150	462	21	1
内蒙古	Inner Mongolia	1695	815	866	15	
辽　宁	Liaoning	2397	1217	359	530	293
吉　林	Jilin	5264	1928	3319	15	2
黑龙江	Heilongjiang	1146	843	304		
上　海	Shanghai	6844	4799	811	57	1177
江　苏	Jiangsu	15497	6892	6019	1782	804
浙　江	Zhejiang	1200	457	527	216	
安　徽	Anhui	1501	1290	195	15	2
福　建	Fujian	6697	4082	2483	42	91
江　西	Jiangxi	6275	3635	2404	235	1
山　东	Shandong	13625	7820	5157	51	597
河　南	Henan	8055	4660	2231	1154	10
湖　北	Hubei	4898	4399	273	137	90
湖　南	Hunan	3475	1339	2075	36	26
广　东	Guangdong	34221	19130	11413	217	3461
广　西	Guangxi	762	531	231		
海　南	Hainan	642	558			85
重　庆	Chongqing	5007	2794	2131	81	
四　川	Sichuan	11294	4530	6056	650	58
贵　州	Guizhou	2915	2471	299	132	14
云　南	Yunnan	2908	1055	1438	89	326
西　藏	Tibet	2733	1666	968		100
陕　西	Shaanxi	9844	3651	4768	269	1156
甘　肃	Gansu	2209	1152	1018	39	
青　海	Qinghai	1231	817	415		
宁　夏	Ningxia					
新　疆	Xinjiang	2635	1156	1467	12	

港、澳、台商投资企业
Enterprises with Funds from Hong Kong, Macao and Taiwan

单位：万元
Unit: 10000 yuan

地区	Region	营业额 Business Revenue	客房收入 from Hotel Rooms	餐费收入 from Meals	商品销售额 from Commodities	其他收入 Others
全国	**National Total**	**3571381**	**1738041**	**1202401**	**139942**	**490998**
北京	Beijing	675028	373425	142617	11782	147205
天津	Tianjin	7278	4785	2238	8	247
河北	Hebei	24648	10314	7756	3001	3578
山西	Shanxi					
内蒙古	Inner Mongolia	24744	10822	11667		2255
辽宁	Liaoning	96304	43690	39308	5518	7787
吉林	Jilin	6464	3122	3089	133	121
黑龙江	Heilongjiang	29434	15640	10576	860	2359
上海	Shanghai	476137	219375	130167	1328	125267
江苏	Jiangsu	157332	73028	76837	1248	6219
浙江	Zhejiang	277165	115159	130833	1784	29389
安徽	Anhui	46386	20736	20283	451	4917
福建	Fujian	258887	82101	87534	68625	20627
江西	Jiangxi	18112	9178	7500	260	1174
山东	Shandong	95562	41447	36502	4225	13388
河南	Henan	52596	21264	23018	1992	6321
湖北	Hubei	83004	46880	30665	390	5070
湖南	Hunan	58609	27978	23765	837	6029
广东	Guangdong	693853	329973	255732	33076	75072
广西	Guangxi	94908	47280	41658	949	5020
海南	Hainan	239030	160252	67028	452	11298
重庆	Chongqing	13449	9719	2405	11	1314
四川	Sichuan	31564	17761	10033	17	3753
贵州	Guizhou	6250	3448	2331	320	151
云南	Yunnan	46809	27808	16109	144	2748
西藏	Tibet	6639	4433	1962		244
陕西	Shaanxi	47062	16146	19104	2531	9280
甘肃	Gansu	4127	2277	1684		166
青海	Qinghai					
宁夏	Ningxia					
新疆	Xinjiang					

外商投资企业
Foreign Funded Enterprises

单位：万元
Unit: 10000 yuan

地区	Region	营业额 Business Revenue	客房收入 from Hotel Rooms	餐费收入 from Meals	商品销售额 from Commodities	其他收入 Others
全国	**National Total**	**1905553**	**991805**	**586264**	**63636**	**263855**
北京	Beijing	354154	155239	77387	828	120701
天津	Tianjin	45854	25896	15801	99	4058
河北	Hebei	9007	3929	4327		752
山西	Shanxi					
内蒙古	Inner Mongolia	934	934			
辽宁	Liaoning	42855	27150	11211	305	4189
吉林	Jilin	21297	11757	9336	63	142
黑龙江	Heilongjiang	16327	8507	5900	841	1079
上海	Shanghai	283774	145802	65194	36686	36092
江苏	Jiangsu	112793	50941	52474	1234	8143
浙江	Zhejiang	76684	37274	33562	559	5289
安徽	Anhui	5725	2948	2543	1	233
福建	Fujian	117835	54719	49382	3256	10478
江西	Jiangxi	7920	5230	2091	394	206
山东	Shandong	41584	22672	17716	213	983
河南	Henan	8818	5260	3483	12	62
湖北	Hubei	7661	4286	2759	108	508
湖南	Hunan	15288	8951	4615	116	1606
广东	Guangdong	473313	272451	145403	8732	46727
广西	Guangxi	3374	3341			33
海南	Hainan	74757	46454	23280	490	4533
重庆	Chongqing	35211	14253	10670	868	9420
四川	Sichuan	50444	28179	14225	5919	2122
贵州	Guizhou	4023	2079	1627		317
云南	Yunnan	16701	9696	4447	1441	1117
西藏	Tibet	8521	5217	2581	104	620
陕西	Shaanxi	56052	31032	20567	1367	3087
甘肃	Gansu	8140	4159	3283		698
青海	Qinghai	4515	2453	2001		61
宁夏	Ningxia	750	327	399		25
新疆	Xinjiang	1242	668			574

4-2-4 各地区限额以上住宿业企业经营情况(按国民经济行业分)
Business of Enterprises above Designated Size of Hotels by Region and Sector

旅游饭店 | 单位：万元
Tourist Hotel | Unit: 10000 yuan

地区	Region	营业额 Business Revenue	客房收入 from Hotel Rooms	餐费收入 from Meals	商品销售额 from Commodities	其他收入 Others
全国	**National Total**	**30594066**	**14623511**	**11669074**	**880986**	**3420493**
北京	Beijing	3050381	1503941	818314	35173	692954
天津	Tianjin	301770	151962	98255	1451	50103
河北	Hebei	491301	215775	218674	5935	50917
山西	Shanxi	249390	110524	110476	3474	24916
内蒙古	Inner Mongolia	254890	117561	115860	689	20780
辽宁	Liaoning	556702	259236	213620	10883	72963
吉林	Jilin	239779	122876	94717	3476	18709
黑龙江	Heilongjiang	236490	123972	79302	12445	20771
上海	Shanghai	2166883	1112747	609997	82984	361155
江苏	Jiangsu	2020103	822729	950733	76789	169852
浙江	Zhejiang	2581876	1155338	1175157	26030	225350
安徽	Anhui	533405	242671	238157	11239	41337
福建	Fujian	1655711	647686	751088	151973	104964
江西	Jiangxi	544846	258993	236270	13539	36044
山东	Shandong	1576786	684884	740924	45412	105566
河南	Henan	1047944	514110	439404	25218	69212
湖北	Hubei	793107	403786	314338	14930	60051
湖南	Hunan	1230999	569163	528002	56059	77774
广东	Guangdong	4603975	2164850	1600417	124969	713739
广西	Guangxi	572476	309600	199988	16900	45988
海南	Hainan	1100559	700213	321640	5274	73432
重庆	Chongqing	709308	325360	294966	27981	61001
四川	Sichuan	1058611	498584	432212	44109	83706
贵州	Guizhou	545474	324115	173270	16345	31745
云南	Yunnan	750043	417225	230032	23232	79553
西藏	Tibet	85090	54122	18375	549	12044
陕西	Shaanxi	874342	400201	386626	34094	53421
甘肃	Gansu	330997	184057	123580	3158	20203
青海	Qinghai	73987	45353	21444	672	6518
宁夏	Ningxia	78434	37426	34092	1616	5300
新疆	Xinjiang	278408	144451	99144	4387	30425

4-2-4 续表 1 Continued 1

一般旅馆 单位：万元
Fonda Unit: 10000 yuan

地 区	Region	营业额 Business Revenue	客房收入 from Hotel Rooms	餐费收入 from Meals	商品销售额 from Commodities	其他收入 Others
全 国	**National Total**	**8132557**	**5374170**	**2103309**	**184442**	**470646**
北 京	Beijing	718706	571982	82544	6227	57952
天 津	Tianjin	93546	58691	17332	2159	15365
河 北	Hebei	171992	72824	86007	2443	10719
山 西	Shanxi	92684	52854	30744	954	8133
内蒙古	Inner Mongolia	93648	54702	36539	312	2095
辽 宁	Liaoning	109751	71463	29652	1795	6841
吉 林	Jilin	44514	26342	13110	1723	3339
黑龙江	Heilongjiang	67178	46171	17759	1222	2025
上 海	Shanghai	673504	466999	99656	3890	102960
江 苏	Jiangsu	385649	263097	98320	10082	14150
浙 江	Zhejiang	651601	519079	101386	1987	29149
安 徽	Anhui	159851	94624	56107	4944	4176
福 建	Fujian	333049	184570	126598	10352	11529
江 西	Jiangxi	139713	91697	42181	3095	2740
山 东	Shandong	527756	325520	169243	15256	17738
河 南	Henan	643297	370615	223532	31581	17570
湖 北	Hubei	340715	208035	113446	13259	5975
湖 南	Hunan	364907	214500	123132	15274	12002
广 东	Guangdong	889940	615436	174982	13738	85784
广 西	Guangxi	192911	141245	42595	2679	6392
海 南	Hainan	15469	9857	4762	11	840
重 庆	Chongqing	191414	128855	52530	3520	6509
四 川	Sichuan	433878	270108	130846	13665	19259
贵 州	Guizhou	127497	93778	26904	3213	3603
云 南	Yunnan	194240	128602	47847	7070	10721
西 藏	Tibet					
陕 西	Shaanxi	312456	174366	120526	10936	6630
甘 肃	Gansu	73387	57350	13183	1767	1087
青 海	Qinghai	9969	7118	2628	11	213
宁 夏	Ningxia	6462	4179	1507	135	641
新 疆	Xinjiang	72872	49511	17711	1142	4509

其他住宿业
Others

单位：万元
Unit: 10000 yuan

地 区	Region	营业额 Business Revenue	客房收入 from Hotel Rooms	餐费收入 from Meals	商品销售额 from Commodities	其他收入 Others
全 国	**National Total**	**912719**	**514739**	**260793**	**43227**	**93961**
北 京	Beijing	115846	60354	27391	447	27654
天 津	Tianjin	38562	22554	7775	989	7244
河 北	Hebei	41911	15960	14894	3385	7672
山 西	Shanxi	7535	3155	3018	271	1092
内蒙古	Inner Mongolia	5051	2344	1589	252	866
辽 宁	Liaoning	16310	9148	3732	149	3282
吉 林	Jilin	12801	6327	5766	294	414
黑龙江	Heilongjiang	9282	5776	2349	100	1057
上 海	Shanghai	58903	51403	4084	28	3389
江 苏	Jiangsu	47905	25870	17127	1462	3446
浙 江	Zhejiang	16999	10470	5119	11	1400
安 徽	Anhui	21783	10063	10171	130	1419
福 建	Fujian	41765	18817	11693	9019	2236
江 西	Jiangxi	13251	8758	4284	140	70
山 东	Shandong	27511	18197	7577	937	799
河 南	Henan	52251	30858	19314	1575	503
湖 北	Hubei	44300	16860	8432	17354	1654
湖 南	Hunan	55146	27881	21605	514	5145
广 东	Guangdong	121033	79222	29675	2344	9792
广 西	Guangxi	16691	8875	1949	16	5851
海 南	Hainan	5509	1763	1808		1937
重 庆	Chongqing	24237	13852	9444	468	473
四 川	Sichuan	16649	9401	5283	579	1386
贵 州	Guizhou	14065	9559	3717	540	249
云 南	Yunnan	15873	9617	4665	318	1273
西 藏	Tibet	3032	2472	520	8	32
陕 西	Shaanxi	46926	20309	22488	1578	2552
甘 肃	Gansu	16488	12376	3792	308	12
青 海	Qinghai	1308	1147	162		
宁 夏	Ningxia	1434	596	827	11	
新 疆	Xinjiang	2362	755	544		1063

4-2-5 各地区限额以上餐饮业企业经营情况
Business of Enterprises above Designated Size of Catering Services by Region

单位：万元
Unit: 10000 yuan

地区	Region	营业额 Business Revenue	客房收入 from Hotel Rooms	餐费收入 from Meals	商品销售额 from Commodities	其他收入 Others
全国	**National Total**	**53127754**	**3149148**	**47320996**	**1675332**	**982274**
北京	Beijing	6516567	37540	6239501	93348	146178
天津	Tianjin	970088	43218	868822	15225	42824
河北	Hebei	422069	66405	331219	11224	13221
山西	Shanxi	502147	87163	389008	12514	13463
内蒙古	Inner Mongolia	488025	84366	389707	3604	10347
辽宁	Liaoning	1014836	43101	942749	12270	16716
吉林	Jilin	270593	41708	216005	4318	8561
黑龙江	Heilongjiang	117377	14228	95432	3949	3767
上海	Shanghai	7255530	62796	6987492	124395	80844
江苏	Jiangsu	4045205	376314	3438150	163044	67697
浙江	Zhejiang	3389099	299516	2939241	69781	80561
安徽	Anhui	1459187	166232	1183890	88815	20250
福建	Fujian	2108090	93986	1944229	51610	18264
江西	Jiangxi	444868	59870	362743	18866	3388
山东	Shandong	2814441	345348	2285081	122695	61317
河南	Henan	1459053	129782	1249616	50660	28996
湖北	Hubei	2531581	241496	2117424	118365	54295
湖南	Hunan	1386100	126898	1193609	48345	17248
广东	Guangdong	7610494	255032	6919056	287650	148757
广西	Guangxi	461054	31565	403902	19229	6357
海南	Hainan	93508	3551	83078	897	5983
重庆	Chongqing	2286065	123109	2024924	112108	25924
四川	Sichuan	2047917	140754	1779443	84402	43318
贵州	Guizhou	368425	26699	324362	10511	6853
云南	Yunnan	640699	23503	571477	28774	16946
西藏	Tibet	9695	1045	8559		92
陕西	Shaanxi	1796650	151666	1500228	111993	32763
甘肃	Gansu	333894	31935	294987	3717	3255
青海	Qinghai	45755	9843	35150	210	551
宁夏	Ningxia	71133	11297	57541	1442	853
新疆	Xinjiang	167609	19182	144371	1371	2685

国有控股
State-controlled Enterprises

单位：万元
Unit: 10000 yuan

地区	Region	营业额 Business Revenue	客房收入 from Hotel Rooms	餐费收入 from Meals	商品销售额 from Commodities	其他收入 Others
全国	**National Total**	**2481108**	**274995**	**1765556**	**236356**	**204198**
北京	Beijing	443302	4456	370520	13023	55302
天津	Tianjin	35241	3251	18137	1249	12603
河北	Hebei	34401	8422	24289	1329	362
山西	Shanxi	31492	11240	16766	242	3243
内蒙古	Inner Mongolia	16867	4471	9736	246	2414
辽宁	Liaoning	65918	2777	62362	530	248
吉林	Jilin	25485	11174	13152	1	1159
黑龙江	Heilongjiang	8426	3635	4217	55	519
上海	Shanghai	338461	11663	268654	44020	14120
江苏	Jiangsu	193961	45907	127988	6462	13604
浙江	Zhejiang	172652	14738	144563	1629	11721
安徽	Anhui	86149	4246	45122	32459	4323
福建	Fujian	38092	3913	30535	2761	884
江西	Jiangxi	23858	6771	16145	370	572
山东	Shandong	194120	49969	128694	5509	9948
河南	Henan	18520	1805	13686	2961	69
湖北	Hubei	101061	8005	20640	53132	19283
湖南	Hunan	22896	7393	15184	141	178
广东	Guangdong	266401	22047	188271	32131	23952
广西	Guangxi	19201	3216	7547	7386	1052
海南	Hainan	494		494		
重庆	Chongqing	63510	10099	49684	1980	1747
四川	Sichuan	43862	10028	26501	3392	3942
贵州	Guizhou	18148	602	16898	50	598
云南	Yunnan	63711	3744	39473	13956	6538
西藏	Tibet					
陕西	Shaanxi	112177	6819	81009	10815	13535
甘肃	Gansu	30989	10404	18327	493	1765
青海	Qinghai	1447	718	726	3	
宁夏	Ningxia	2656	516	2137		3
新疆	Xinjiang	7610	2966	4099	31	514

4-2-6 各地区限额以上餐饮业企业经营情况(按登记注册类型分)
Business of Enterprises above Designated Size of Catering Services by Region and Type of Registration

内资企业
Domestic Funded Enterprises

单位：万元
Unit: 10000 yuan

地　区	Region	营业额 Business Revenue	客房收入 from Hotel Rooms	餐费收入 from Meals	商品销售额 from Commodities	其他收入 Others
全　国	**National Total**	**37501042**	**3056347**	**32151735**	**1468873**	**824085**
北　京	Beijing	3558167	37540	3366935	51288	102405
天　津	Tianjin	512312	41730	418302	14913	37367
河　北	Hebei	419879	65905	329708	11224	13042
山　西	Shanxi	419445	87163	306306	12514	13463
内蒙古	Inner Mongolia	451647	84073	354130	3097	10347
辽　宁	Liaoning	400421	41898	333230	9411	15881
吉　林	Jilin	269726	41697	215150	4318	8561
黑龙江	Heilongjiang	99484	14228	78486	3002	3767
上　海	Shanghai	3295098	62328	3084143	96678	51946
江　苏	Jiangsu	2919049	365733	2358715	129173	65429
浙　江	Zhejiang	2650436	279147	2229456	69155	72678
安　徽	Anhui	1454456	164777	1181126	88775	19779
福　建	Fujian	1612830	73603	1479509	45441	14277
江　西	Jiangxi	363199	57251	284465	18094	3388
山　东	Shandong	2524783	336149	2013515	119766	55353
河　南	Henan	1378701	129782	1179615	50602	18702
湖　北	Hubei	1958444	237188	1554515	118142	48599
湖　南	Hunan	1228287	126417	1036547	48345	16978
广　东	Guangdong	4680356	238952	4108219	203069	130116
广　西	Guangxi	380120	31100	323565	19178	6277
海　南	Hainan	72465	3551	63480	822	4612
重　庆	Chongqing	2074734	123109	1815079	111520	25025
四　川	Sichuan	1649100	138249	1392989	82763	35099
贵　州	Guizhou	368031	26699	323968	10511	6853
云　南	Yunnan	553789	23503	490626	28629	11031
西　藏	Tibet	9695	1045	8559		92
陕　西	Shaanxi	1636783	151273	1348134	111703	25674
甘　肃	Gansu	302223	31935	263315	3717	3255
青　海	Qinghai	45755	9843	35150	210	551
宁　夏	Ningxia	71133	11297	57541	1442	853
新　疆	Xinjiang	140494	19182	117257	1371	2685

国有企业 单位：万元
State-controlled Enterprises Unit: 10000 yuan

地 区	Region	营业额 Business Revenue	客房收入 from Hotel Rooms	餐费收入 from Meals	商品销售额 from Commodities	其他收入 Others
全 国	**National Total**	**585950**	**131607**	**403985**	**16650**	**33709**
北 京	Beijing	50882	1785	43908	1278	3910
天 津	Tianjin	8288	1669	4551	1248	820
河 北	Hebei	20590	3785	15398	1156	250
山 西	Shanxi	11906	4245	7023	165	473
内蒙古	Inner Mongolia	9207	3672	4776	109	650
辽 宁	Liaoning	51033	2061	48704	21	247
吉 林	Jilin	21382	10112	10259	1	1010
黑龙江	Heilongjiang	6871	3011	3338	46	477
上 海	Shanghai	40098	3999	30366	1091	4642
江 苏	Jiangsu	54974	11185	35605	1400	6784
浙 江	Zhejiang	13392	967	11568	609	248
安 徽	Anhui	4544	1463	2762	176	143
福 建	Fujian	10183	1348	8789	27	20
江 西	Jiangxi	14262	3625	10548	88	1
山 东	Shandong	91463	33361	53267	2623	2213
河 南	Henan	5975	1068	4904		3
湖 北	Hubei	11898	3193	5898	633	2174
湖 南	Hunan	14602	5405	9069	25	103
广 东	Guangdong	57072	12528	39020	395	5129
广 西	Guangxi	5848	1781	3633	265	170
海 南	Hainan	494		494		
重 庆	Chongqing	3566	593	2973		
四 川	Sichuan	13669	3890	7672	1310	797
贵 州	Guizhou	895	58	630		207
云 南	Yunnan	13141	3603	8538	477	523
西 藏	Tibet					
陕 西	Shaanxi	24738	4184	16188	3133	1233
甘 肃	Gansu	16880	6385	9090	343	1061
青 海	Qinghai					
宁 夏	Ningxia	2483	466	2017		
新 疆	Xinjiang	5614	2165	2997	31	420

4-2-6 续表 2 Continued 2

集体企业
Collective-owned Enterprises

单位：万元
Unit: 10000 yuan

地 区	Region	营业额 Business Revenue	客房收入 from Hotel Rooms	餐费收入 from Meals	商品销售额 from Commodities	其他收入 Others
全 国	**National Total**	**239100**	**34357**	**179122**	**14031**	**11593**
北 京	Beijing	17273	1025	14103		2145
天 津	Tianjin	968		931	15	22
河 北	Hebei	1529	219	1245	65	
山 西	Shanxi	1834	1035	800		
内 蒙 古	Inner Mongolia	398	77	321		
辽 宁	Liaoning	958	37	906		15
吉 林	Jilin	1677	446	1186	30	16
黑 龙 江	Heilongjiang					
上 海	Shanghai	27448	676	25786		987
江 苏	Jiangsu	15759	3111	9763	749	2136
浙 江	Zhejiang	286		286		
安 徽	Anhui	2090		1861	219	9
福 建	Fujian	5795		2285	3510	
江 西	Jiangxi					
山 东	Shandong	26814	1697	22936	1687	494
河 南	Henan	11316	1590	9678	43	5
湖 北	Hubei	13413	118	13289	6	
湖 南	Hunan	1430	751	679		
广 东	Guangdong	53170	14036	31491	1893	5750
广 西	Guangxi	2610		2610		
海 南	Hainan					
重 庆	Chongqing	29975	389	24050	5527	9
四 川	Sichuan	1925	422	1243	260	
贵 州	Guizhou	306	71	235		
云 南	Yunnan	2500	785	1710		5
西 藏	Tibet					
陕 西	Shaanxi	19626	7872	11728	27	
甘 肃	Gansu					
青 海	Qinghai					
宁 夏	Ningxia					
新 疆	Xinjiang					

4-2-6 续表 3 Continued 3

股份合作企业
Cooperative Enterprises

单位：万元
Unit: 10000 yuan

地 区	Region	营业额 Business Revenue	客房收入 from Hotel Rooms	餐费收入 from Meals	商品销售额 from Commodities	其他收入 Others
全 国	**National Total**	**138249**	**4420**	**119120**	**11405**	**3307**
北 京	Beijing	31430	1079	30196	92	63
天 津	Tianjin					
河 北	Hebei	6669		6669		
山 西	Shanxi	413	182	216		15
内蒙古	Inner Mongolia					
辽 宁	Liaoning					
吉 林	Jilin					
黑龙江	Heilongjiang					
上 海	Shanghai	7095	75	6423	50	548
江 苏	Jiangsu	849	95	730	25	
浙 江	Zhejiang	8528	126	8402		
安 徽	Anhui					
福 建	Fujian					
江 西	Jiangxi	1112		890	223	
山 东	Shandong	1228	592	613	23	
河 南	Henan	1149		86	884	180
湖 北	Hubei	2260	430	1830		
湖 南	Hunan	2588		2588		
广 东	Guangdong	38459		38455	4	
广 西	Guangxi	1719	18	1619		81
海 南	Hainan					
重 庆	Chongqing	835		794	41	
四 川	Sichuan	33915	1823	19609	10063	2420
贵 州	Guizhou					
云 南	Yunnan					
西 藏	Tibet					
陕 西	Shaanxi					
甘 肃	Gansu					
青 海	Qinghai					
宁 夏	Ningxia					
新 疆	Xinjiang					

4-2-6 续表 4 Continued 4

联营企业
Joint Ownership Enterprises

单位：万元
Unit: 10000 yuan

地 区	Region	营业额 Business Revenue	客房收入 from Hotel Rooms	餐费收入 from Meals	商品销售额 from Commodities	其他收入 Others
全 国	**National Total**	**10809**	**3341**	**7419**	**51**	
北 京	Beijing					
天 津	Tianjin					
河 北	Hebei					
山 西	Shanxi					
内蒙古	Inner Mongolia					
辽 宁	Liaoning					
吉 林	Jilin					
黑龙江	Heilongjiang					
上 海	Shanghai	801	19	783		
江 苏	Jiangsu	305		305	1	
浙 江	Zhejiang	543	115	419	9	
安 徽	Anhui					
福 建	Fujian					
江 西	Jiangxi					
山 东	Shandong	70	30	39	1	
河 南	Henan					
湖 北	Hubei	4556	2107	2449		
湖 南	Hunan					
广 东	Guangdong	2254	1070	1144	40	
广 西	Guangxi					
海 南	Hainan					
重 庆	Chongqing					
四 川	Sichuan					
贵 州	Guizhou					
云 南	Yunnan					
西 藏	Tibet					
陕 西	Shaanxi	1785		1785		
甘 肃	Gansu	495		495		
青 海	Qinghai					
宁 夏	Ningxia					
新 疆	Xinjiang					

4-2-6 续表 5 Continued 5

有限责任公司
Limited Liability Corporations

单位：万元
Unit: 10000 yuan

地 区	Region	营业额 Business Revenue	客房收入 from Hotel Rooms	餐费收入 from Meals	商品销售额 from Commodities	其他收入 Others
全 国	**National Total**	**11870827**	**1134969**	**9841441**	**489906**	**404513**
北 京	Beijing	1472257	12211	1355167	34417	70462
天 津	Tianjin	234450	26299	189735	1739	16676
河 北	Hebei	97414	16729	73060	2185	5440
山 西	Shanxi	96629	18065	65617	5911	7038
内蒙古	Inner Mongolia	147462	42615	96875	1998	5974
辽 宁	Liaoning	110300	16442	85581	1324	6953
吉 林	Jilin	158533	17229	135524	1323	4456
黑龙江	Heilongjiang	27338	7230	18247	829	1033
上 海	Shanghai	639684	12297	600469	6431	20483
江 苏	Jiangsu	840945	156705	630297	26082	27861
浙 江	Zhejiang	667067	100394	485187	49224	32263
安 徽	Anhui	439522	53974	336096	40334	9119
福 建	Fujian	425900	39534	360931	15841	9594
江 西	Jiangxi	162327	28356	125891	5906	2175
山 东	Shandong	711483	128579	523590	29270	30045
河 南	Henan	482672	46682	405302	22413	8275
湖 北	Hubei	803121	94117	608305	69516	31183
湖 南	Hunan	253893	31296	211858	6357	4383
广 东	Guangdong	1713367	97004	1492703	71755	51904
广 西	Guangxi	145789	9343	118250	15543	2654
海 南	Hainan	56452	1584	51072	782	3013
重 庆	Chongqing	574637	25533	519585	17461	12058
四 川	Sichuan	553975	48380	470721	17436	17437
贵 州	Guizhou	95897	7164	81987	2375	4371
云 南	Yunnan	181761	2306	156176	19167	4113
西 藏	Tibet	4654		4654		
陕 西	Shaanxi	611119	69073	505853	22870	13323
甘 肃	Gansu	106958	14045	90921	788	1206
青 海	Qinghai	7590	2362	5224		4
宁 夏	Ningxia	18369	5665	12323	169	211
新 疆	Xinjiang	29262	3756	24240	460	806

4-2-6 续表 6 Continued 6

股份有限公司
Share-holding Corporations Ltd.

单位：万元
Unit: 10000 yuan

地　区	Region	营业额 Business Revenue	客房收入 from Hotel Rooms	餐费收入 from Meals	商品销售额 from Commodities	其他收入 Others
全　国	**National Total**	**1466291**	**92131**	**1211365**	**129764**	**33039**
北　京	Beijing	138337		132943	273	5121
天　津	Tianjin	39236	8157	16068	9281	5730
河　北	Hebei	5584	963	4560		61
山　西	Shanxi	3771	1448	2146	168	11
内蒙古	Inner Mongolia	104300	413	103842	13	32
辽　宁	Liaoning	7889	1770	5782	271	66
吉　林	Jilin	8113	1453	6213	119	328
黑龙江	Heilongjiang	2632		2400	232	
上　海	Shanghai	154369		115242	38594	533
江　苏	Jiangsu	89462	9264	72896	5089	2213
浙　江	Zhejiang	128775	9189	117063	914	1609
安　徽	Anhui	17177	3190	12418	1106	463
福　建	Fujian	7609	1023	5978	393	215
江　西	Jiangxi	13913	2459	10311	1057	87
山　东	Shandong	87634	14360	66960	4037	2278
河　南	Henan	54978	6873	42576	2905	2624
湖　北	Hubei	59765	2251	55614	1396	505
湖　南	Hunan	17664	279	16922		463
广　东	Guangdong	117968	1916	86694	27220	2138
广　西	Guangxi	7547	2503	4756	12	277
海　南	Hainan	4933	1148	3743	22	20
重　庆	Chongqing	80200	3543	71505	5066	86
四　川	Sichuan	32547	5501	24505	1984	558
贵　州	Guizhou	5740	2107	3550	73	10
云　南	Yunnan	15244	6	15146	65	27
西　藏	Tibet					
陕　西	Shaanxi	230617	9658	184628	29249	7083
甘　肃	Gansu	15875		15752	3	120
青　海	Qinghai	6491	1254	4962	185	90
宁　夏	Ningxia	1726	452	1258	14	2
新　疆	Xinjiang	6195	951	4932	23	289

4-2-6 续表 7 Continued 7

私营企业
Private Enterprises

单位：万元
Unit: 10000 yuan

地 区	Region	营业额 Business Revenue	客房收入 from Hotel Rooms	餐费收入 from Meals	商品销售额 from Commodities	其他收入 Others
全 国	**National Total**	**22854323**	**1626556**	**20102794**	**789772**	**335198**
北 京	Beijing	1847989	21439	1790618	15229	20703
天 津	Tianjin	228985	5605	206632	2630	14118
河 北	Hebei	288094	44209	228776	7819	7290
山 西	Shanxi	303964	61916	229851	6270	5927
内蒙古	Inner Mongolia	188729	36863	147212	977	3677
辽 宁	Liaoning	225285	21276	187613	7795	8600
吉 林	Jilin	72472	10299	58649	772	2751
黑龙江	Heilongjiang	62462	3988	54322	1895	2257
上 海	Shanghai	2407886	44471	2289962	49615	23837
江 苏	Jiangsu	1910179	184758	1603362	95638	26422
浙 江	Zhejiang	1830050	168162	1604964	18400	38524
安 徽	Anhui	991020	106102	827932	46940	10046
福 建	Fujian	1135454	31611	1073772	25623	4448
江 西	Jiangxi	169340	22279	135152	10785	1124
山 东	Shandong	1573661	150064	1321961	81407	20229
河 南	Henan	814445	72856	709621	24353	7615
湖 北	Hubei	1006116	131701	818367	41840	14209
湖 南	Hunan	931644	86288	791499	41836	12021
广 东	Guangdong	2642536	109873	2366805	101085	64772
广 西	Guangxi	216608	17456	192698	3359	3094
海 南	Hainan	10587	818	8171	18	1579
重 庆	Chongqing	1346443	91150	1161489	81154	12650
四 川	Sichuan	994842	76439	853630	51123	13649
贵 州	Guizhou	262586	17029	235240	8052	2264
云 南	Yunnan	334378	16048	303646	8389	6295
西 藏	Tibet	5042	1045	3906		92
陕 西	Shaanxi	715049	58160	600957	52054	3878
甘 肃	Gansu	159890	11427	145012	2584	868
青 海	Qinghai	31674	6227	24965	25	458
宁 夏	Ningxia	48044	4714	41441	1249	640
新 疆	Xinjiang	98869	12283	84569	856	1161

4-2-6 续表 8 Continued 8

其他企业
Other Enterprises

单位：万元
Unit: 10000 yuan

地 区	Region	营业额 Business Revenue	客房收入 from Hotel Rooms	餐费收入 from Meals	商品销售额 from Commodities	其他收入 Others
全 国	**National Total**	**335500**	**28971**	**286500**	**17307**	**2728**
北 京	Beijing					
天 津	Tianjin	385		385		
河 北	Hebei					
山 西	Shanxi	928	273	655		
内蒙古	Inner Mongolia	1552	432	1105		15
辽 宁	Liaoning	4956	311	4645		
吉 林	Jilin	7549	2158	3318	2074	
黑龙江	Heilongjiang	180		180		
上 海	Shanghai	17716	791	15113	897	916
江 苏	Jiangsu	6578	616	5758	190	13
浙 江	Zhejiang	1797	196	1568		34
安 徽	Anhui	104	48	56		
福 建	Fujian	27888	87	27755	47	
江 西	Jiangxi	2246	533	1674	36	2
山 东	Shandong	32430	7466	24151	720	94
河 南	Henan	8165	713	7447	5	
湖 北	Hubei	57314	3271	48763	4751	529
湖 南	Hunan	6465	2398	3932	128	7
广 东	Guangdong	55530	2525	51906	676	423
广 西	Guangxi					
海 南	Hainan					
重 庆	Chongqing	39077	1902	34683	2271	222
四 川	Sichuan	18228	1794	15609	588	238
贵 州	Guizhou	2607	270	2326	11	
云 南	Yunnan	6765	755	5410	532	69
西 藏	Tibet					
陕 西	Shaanxi	33850	2327	26996	4370	157
甘 肃	Gansu	2124	78	2046		
青 海	Qinghai					
宁 夏	Ningxia	512		501	11	
新 疆	Xinjiang	554	27	518		9

4-2-6 续表 9 Continued 9

港、澳、台商投资企业 单位：万元

Enterprises with Funds from Hongkong, Macao and Taiwan Unit: 10000 yuan

地区	Region	营业额 Business Revenue	客房收入 from Hotel Rooms	餐费收入 from Meals	商品销售额 from Commodities	其他收入 Others
全国	**National Total**	**6650252**	**67302**	**6428191**	**107084**	**47672**
北京	Beijing	1551747		1507597	34886	9263
天津	Tianjin	135554	1488	133976		90
河北	Hebei	1404	500	724		179
山西	Shanxi	18432		18432		
内蒙古	Inner Mongolia	3503		3503		
辽宁	Liaoning	151108		147826	2858	424
吉林	Jilin	182		182		
黑龙江	Heilongjiang	12844		12123	722	
上海	Shanghai	1744931		1738018	2390	4524
江苏	Jiangsu	277125	9042	264653	1711	1719
浙江	Zhejiang	206475	11358	190879	123	4115
安徽	Anhui	1543		1543		
福建	Fujian	267321	18097	239785	5494	3945
江西	Jiangxi	10642	2619	7344	679	
山东	Shandong	76080	7418	61132	1771	5759
河南	Henan	2783		2739	42	2
湖北	Hubei	541755	1327	538586	113	1729
湖南	Hunan	5257	481	4776		
广东	Guangdong	1333568	12209	1259834	54762	6763
广西	Guangxi	11795		11663	51	80
海南	Hainan	21043		19598	74	1370
重庆	Chongqing	33971		33877	1	93
四川	Sichuan	172224	2369	165012	1075	3767
贵州	Guizhou	394		394		
云南	Yunnan	27671		24497	145	3029
西藏	Tibet					
陕西	Shaanxi	40395	394	38993	187	821
甘肃	Gansu	502		502		
青海	Qinghai					
宁夏	Ningxia					
新疆	Xinjiang	3		3		

4-2-6 续表 10 Continued 10

外商投资企业
Foreign Funded Enterprises

单位：万元
Unit: 10000 yuan

地　区	Region	营业额 Business Revenue	客房收入 from Hotel Rooms	餐费收入 from Meals	商品销售额 from Commodities	其他收入 Others
全　国	**National Total**	**8976463**	**25504**	**8741067**	**99375**	**110519**
北　京	Beijing	1406653		1364969	7174	34510
天　津	Tianjin	322223		316543	312	5368
河　北	Hebei	786		786		
山　西	Shanxi	64270		64270		
内蒙古	Inner Mongolia	32875	294	32074	507	
辽　宁	Liaoning	463306	1203	461692		411
吉　林	Jilin	686	12	674		
黑龙江	Heilongjiang	5049		4824	226	
上　海	Shanghai	2215501	468	2165331	25327	24375
江　苏	Jiangsu	849031	1539	814782	32161	549
浙　江	Zhejiang	532187	9011	518905	503	3768
安　徽	Anhui	3187	1455	1221	40	471
福　建	Fujian	227939	2286	224935	675	43
江　西	Jiangxi	71027		70934	93	
山　东	Shandong	213579	1781	210435	1158	206
河　南	Henan	77570		67262	16	10292
湖　北	Hubei	31382	2982	24323	110	3968
湖　南	Hunan	152556		152286		270
广　东	Guangdong	1596570	3871	1551003	29819	11877
广　西	Guangxi	69139	466	68673		
海　南	Hainan					
重　庆	Chongqing	177360		175968	586	806
四　川	Sichuan	226593	136	221441	564	4452
贵　州	Guizhou					
云　南	Yunnan	59239		56353		2885
西　藏	Tibet					
陕　西	Shaanxi	119473		113101	104	6268
甘　肃	Gansu	31170		31170		
青　海	Qinghai					
宁　夏	Ningxia					
新　疆	Xinjiang	27112		27112		

4-2-7 各地区限额以上餐饮业企业经营情况(按国民经济行业分)

Business of Enterprises above Designated Size of Catering Services by Region and Sector

正餐服务 单位：万元

Dinner Unit: 10000 yuan

地 区	Region	营业额 Business Revenue	客房收入 from Hotel Rooms	餐费收入 from Meals	商品销售额 from Commodities	其他收入 Others
全 国	**National Total**	**36504012**	**3116384**	**31379746**	**1194394**	**813481**
北 京	Beijing	3943571	37376	3769556	40285	96354
天 津	Tianjin	411624	37041	329759	14672	30151
河 北	Hebei	403189	66405	313621	9942	13221
山 西	Shanxi	403657	86958	291491	11745	13463
内蒙古	Inner Mongolia	473812	82673	378311	2490	10339
辽 宁	Liaoning	318783	43058	250580	8845	16299
吉 林	Jilin	232071	41647	177545	4318	8561
黑龙江	Heilongjiang	96570	14228	74625	3949	3767
上 海	Shanghai	4073997	61745	3847303	104177	60769
江 苏	Jiangsu	2713435	370628	2165275	112834	64697
浙 江	Zhejiang	2405223	297445	2009461	24749	73568
安 徽	Anhui	1152457	165676	915020	56108	15653
福 建	Fujian	1472035	93660	1332467	31579	14329
江 西	Jiangxi	365268	59685	283443	18753	3386
山 东	Shandong	2359349	344973	1842391	113799	58186
河 南	Henan	1231561	127996	1042321	44244	16999
湖 北	Hubei	1880280	240856	1513686	71838	53900
湖 南	Hunan	1140155	126128	950213	46860	16955
广 东	Guangdong	4390567	250731	3905602	116227	118007
广 西	Guangxi	312383	31565	264014	12010	4793
海 南	Hainan	83647	3551	73217	897	5983
重 庆	Chongqing	2068750	121252	1818193	105549	23756
四 川	Sichuan	1589645	139940	1326993	82681	40031
贵 州	Guizhou	351449	26550	308263	9980	6656
云 南	Yunnan	523394	23503	460602	28258	11031
西 藏	Tibet	4478	1045	3342		92
陕 西	Shaanxi	1601117	151591	1311966	111235	26325
甘 肃	Gansu	288807	28822	253844	3693	2448
青 海	Qinghai	45131	9843	34527	210	551
宁 夏	Ningxia	71133	11297	57541	1442	853
新 疆	Xinjiang	96474	18516	74574	1025	2358

快餐服务
Snack

单位：万元
Unit: 10000 yuan

地区	Region	营业额 Business Revenue	客房收入 from Hotel Rooms	餐费收入 from Meals	商品销售额 from Commodities	其他收入 Others
全 国	**National Total**	**12150511**	**10729**	**11850214**	**185085**	**104487**
北 京	Beijing	1906660		1864939	15099	26622
天 津	Tianjin	476722		470704	538	5480
河 北	Hebei	3111		3060	52	
山 西	Shanxi	97063		96920	143	
内蒙古	Inner Mongolia	10702	1277	8318	1103	4
辽 宁	Liaoning	624844		624844		
吉 林	Jilin	31480		31480		
黑龙江	Heilongjiang	20148		20148		
上 海	Shanghai	1698159		1679192	3281	15687
江 苏	Jiangsu	1086785	683	1051386	33866	849
浙 江	Zhejiang	816599	1758	767616	42877	4348
安 徽	Anhui	290543	556	252689	32702	4597
福 建	Fujian	563017		547511	11642	3865
江 西	Jiangxi	78142		78028	112	2
山 东	Shandong	372990	155	365629	4090	3116
河 南	Henan	176621	1194	158904	6087	10436
湖 北	Hubei	435215	143	434740	190	142
湖 南	Hunan	234463	634	232570	970	288
广 东	Guangdong	2297343	21	2260689	22552	14082
广 西	Guangxi	145853		137613	7217	1023
海 南	Hainan	9861		9861		
重 庆	Chongqing	148732		147543	753	436
四 川	Sichuan	261258	529	257186	490	3053
贵 州	Guizhou	2908		2773	135	
云 南	Yunnan	85960		82693	381	2885
西 藏	Tibet	3898		3898		
陕 西	Shaanxi	166454		159558	459	6437
甘 肃	Gansu	42910	3113	38990		808
青 海	Qinghai	624		624		
宁 夏	Ningxia					
新 疆	Xinjiang	61446	666	60108	346	327

4-2-7 续表 2 Continued 2

饮料及冷饮服务

Beverage and Cold Drink

单位：万元

Unit: 10000 yuan

地 区	Region	营业额 Business Revenue	客房收入 from Hotel Rooms	餐费收入 from Meals	商品销售额 from Commodities	其他收入 Others
全 国	**National Total**	**2157981**	**1026**	**2047596**	**100325**	**9036**
北 京	Beijing	325973		290951	32092	2930
天 津	Tianjin	458		444	15	
河 北	Hebei					
山 西	Shanxi					
内蒙古	Inner Mongolia					
辽 宁	Liaoning	28822		25458	3364	
吉 林	Jilin	254		254		
黑龙江	Heilongjiang	239		239		
上 海	Shanghai	1053486		1050978	2090	418
江 苏	Jiangsu	25983		22215	2042	1726
浙 江	Zhejiang	23741	312	22810	602	17
安 徽	Anhui	2735		2735		
福 建	Fujian	14940		14382	534	24
江 西	Jiangxi	584	180	404		
山 东	Shandong	15883		14009	1874	
河 南	Henan	3624		3447	178	
湖 北	Hubei	98220		97910	310	
湖 南	Hunan	2235	50	2097	84	5
广 东	Guangdong	426674	200	369243	55198	2033
广 西	Guangxi	2314		1770	2	541
海 南	Hainan					
重 庆	Chongqing	5242		3189	1130	923
四 川	Sichuan	119757	284	118524	726	223
贵 州	Guizhou	1737		1457	84	196
云 南	Yunnan	3537		3537		
西 藏	Tibet	253		253		
陕 西	Shaanxi	745		745		
甘 肃	Gansu	545		545		
青 海	Qinghai					
宁 夏	Ningxia					
新 疆	Xinjiang					

4-2-7 续表 3 Continued 3

其他餐饮业
Others

单位：万元
Unit: 10000 yuan

地区	Region	营业额 Business Revenue	客房收入 from Hotel Rooms	餐费收入 from Meals	商品销售额 from Commodities	其他收入 Others
全国	**National Total**	**2315249**	**21008**	**2043445**	**195531**	**55271**
北京	Beijing	340363	164	314055	5872	20272
天津	Tianjin	81285	6177	67915		7193
河北	Hebei	15769		14538	1231	
山西	Shanxi	1428	205	598	626	
内蒙古	Inner Mongolia	3511	417	3078	11	5
辽宁	Liaoning	42387	43	41867	60	417
吉林	Jilin	6788	62	6726		
黑龙江	Heilongjiang	420		420		
上海	Shanghai	429888	1051	410020	14848	3970
江苏	Jiangsu	219003	5003	199275	14302	424
浙江	Zhejiang	143536		139354	1554	2629
安徽	Anhui	13451		13446	5	
福建	Fujian	58097	326	49868	7856	47
江西	Jiangxi	874	5	868	1	
山东	Shandong	66220	220	63053	2932	15
河南	Henan	47247	591	44944	151	1561
湖北	Hubei	117866	497	71088	46028	253
湖南	Hunan	9247	86	8730	431	
广东	Guangdong	495910	4080	383522	93673	14635
广西	Guangxi	504		504		
海南	Hainan					
重庆	Chongqing	63341	1857	55999	4676	810
四川	Sichuan	77256		76740	505	11
贵州	Guizhou	12330	149	11869	312	
云南	Yunnan	27808		24645	134	3029
西藏	Tibet	1066		1066		
陕西	Shaanxi	28334	75	27960	299	
甘肃	Gansu	1631		1608	24	
青海	Qinghai					
宁夏	Ningxia					
新疆	Xinjiang	9689		9689		

4-3-1 限额以上住宿和餐饮业企业年末资产负债
Assets and Liabilities of Enterprises above Designated Size of Hotels and Catering Services at the Year-end

单位：万元

Unit:10000 yuan

项 目	Item	流动资产合计 Total Working Capitals	#存货 Stock	固定资产原价 Original Value of Fixed Assets
总 计	**Total**	**71464804**	**4801069**	**102862964**
一、住宿业	**Hotels**	**48810357**	**2940827**	**79840824**
#国有控股	State-controlled Enterprises	10684927	605181	27690553
(一)按登记注册类型分	**by Type of Registration**			
1.内资企业	**Domestic Funded Enterprises**	**40749874**	**2197859**	**62879772**
国有企业	State-owned Enterprises	2986880	135627	9065530
集体企业	Collective-owned Enterprises	285380	11895	713451
股份合作企业	Cooperative Enterprises	78535	3032	114710
联营企业	Joint Ownership Enterprises	34413	963	60756
国有联营企业	State Joint Ownership Enterprises	23960	501	39625
集体联营企业	Collective Joint Ownership Enterprises	1351	361	12508
国有与集体联营企业	Joint State-collective Enterprises	8759	57	8290
其他联营企业	Other Joint Ownership Enterprises	344	42	332
有限责任公司	Limited Liability Corporations	22557925	1137931	35245728
国有独资公司	State Sole Funded Corporations	2054243	63696	4552612
其他有限责任公司	Other Limited Liability Corporations	20503681	1074241	30693121
股份有限公司	Share-holding Corporations Ltd.	1890029	214257	2515845
私营企业	Private Enterprises	12842310	688806	14943157
私营独资企业	Private-funded Enterprises	397961	28156	721313
私营合伙企业	Private Partnership Enterprises	101281	8364	188223
私营有限责任公司	Private Limited Liability Corporations	11855838	635143	13373000
私营股份有限公司	Private Share-holding Corporations Ltd.	487232	17148	660624
其他企业	Other Enterprises	74411	5356	220598
2.港、澳、台商投资企业	**Enterprises with Funds from Hongkong, Macao and Taiwan**	**5343408**	**660410**	**11300669**
合资经营企业	Joint-venture Enterprises	2225328	80087	4523776
合作经营企业	Cooperative Enterprises	444230	19027	1089012
独资经营企业	Enterprises with Sole Investment	2535388	556772	5297386
投资股份有限公司	Share-holding Corporations Ltd. with Investment	102409	2879	295897
其他港澳台商投资企业	Other Enterprises with Funds from Hongkong, Macao and Taiwan	36059	1654	94599
3.外商投资企业	**Foreign Funded Enterprises**	**2717071**	**82557**	**5660390**
中外合资经营企业	Joint-venture Enterprises	1083717	27983	2418002
中外合作经营企业	Cooperative Enterprises	439880	5091	937217
外资企业	Enterprises with Sole Foreign Investment	1138630	46490	2067341
外商投资股份有限公司	Share-holding Corporations Ltd. with Foreign Investment	23655	961	66651
其他外商投资企业	Other Foreign Funded Enterprises	31189	2033	171182
(二)按国民经济行业分	**by Sector**			
旅游饭店	Tourist Hotel	39893062	2620663	70359511
一般旅馆	Fonda	7280928	271992	8106014
其他住宿业	Others	1636369	48171	1375305

项　目	Item	累计折旧 Accumulated Depreciation	#本年折旧 Current Year Depreciation
总　计	**Total**	**41372356**	**4850480**
一、住宿业	**Hotels**	**33054801**	**3476218**
#国有控股	State-controlled Enterprises	11896541	1120015
(一)按登记注册类型分	**by Type of Registration**		
1.内资企业	**Domestic Funded Enterprises**	**25022959**	**2832250**
国有企业	State-owned Enterprises	4020156	312812
集体企业	Collective-owned Enterprises	376636	21656
股份合作企业	Cooperative Enterprises	61385	4214
联营企业	Joint Ownership Enterprises	37774	1830
国有联营企业	State Joint Ownership Enterprises	25030	1327
集体联营企业	Collective Joint Ownership Enterprises	5996	277
国有与集体联营企业	Joint State-collective Enterprises	6697	200
其他联营企业	Other Joint Ownership Enterprises	50	26
有限责任公司	Limited Liability Corporations	13668736	1650567
国有独资公司	State Sole Funded Corporations	1895266	208701
其他有限责任公司	Other Limited Liability Corporations	11773473	1441867
股份有限公司	Share-holding Corporations Ltd.	1123730	111948
私营企业	Private Enterprises	5636809	719558
私营独资企业	Private-funded Enterprises	249435	29931
私营合伙企业	Private Partnership Enterprises	76236	9963
私营有限责任公司	Private Limited Liability Corporations	5068661	642164
私营股份有限公司	Private Share-holding Corporations Ltd.	242479	37497
其他企业	Other Enterprises	97743	9672
2.港、澳、台商投资企业	**Enterprises with Funds from Hongkong, Macao and Taiwan**	**5336551**	**371500**
合资经营企业	Joint-venture Enterprises	2479654	129320
合作经营企业	Cooperative Enterprises	641118	39124
独资经营企业	Enterprises with Sole Investment	2075245	188799
投资股份有限公司	Share-holding Corporations Ltd. with Investment	108716	10244
其他港澳台商投资企业	Other Enterprises with Funds from Hongkong, Macao and Taiwan	31821	4012
3.外商投资企业	**Foreign Funded Enterprises**	**2695295**	**272472**
中外合资经营企业	Joint-venture Enterprises	1244735	112315
中外合作经营企业	Cooperative Enterprises	365172	36960
外资企业	Enterprises with Sole Foreign Investment	975034	112560
外商投资股份有限公司	Share-holding Corporations Ltd. with Foreign Investment	41670	3478
其他外商投资企业	Other Foreign Funded Enterprises	68687	7161
(二)按国民经济行业分	**by Sector**		
旅游饭店	Tourist Hotel	29785175	3027494
一般旅馆	Fonda	2725211	395468
其他住宿业	Others	544426	53260

注：限额以上住宿和餐饮业企业中，因包含了部分视同法人单位，财务指标数据存在资产≠负债+所有者权益的问题(下表同)。

Note: Of enterprises above designated size of Hotels and Catering Services, the financial data have the problem of total assets≠liabilies+total owners' equities, because some of them are regarded as legal entities. The same applies to the tables following.

单位：万元
Unit:10000 yuan

资产合计 Total Assets	负债合计 Total Liabilities	所有者权益合计 Total Owners' Equities	实收资本 Paicl-up Capitals	#国家资本 State-owned Capitals	#港澳台资本 Capitals from Hongkong, Macao and Taiwan	#外商资本 Foreign Capitals
176500497	**127908649**	**48600639**	**60920825**	**11891532**	**5753194**	**3009324**
126480581	**92791036**	**33689544**	**46172018**	**11042181**	**4735665**	**2123308**
35254305	20819947	14434358	14175635	10063072	115182	197524
103977016	**76963455**	**27013561**	**36599018**	**10396599**	**57339**	**131953**
10106755	5365003	4741758	4403185	3950848		
747334	522830	224505	162002	315		
180148	154155	25995	29633	4884		
75725	40683	35044	37018	30769		
53436	22471	30966	23766	22678		
11282	13144	-1862	3436			
10355	3842	6513	8091	8091		
653	1226	-573	1725			
58821936	44192533	14629402	18274740	5811964	42038	118450
6604170	3842447	2761727	2538640	1998553		
52217760	40350088	11867673	15736102	3813416	42038	118450
4720863	2828110	1892754	1706772	555103	10094	1425
29083111	23739894	5343217	11912089	25780	5206	12079
1062723	563254	499467	536041	2113		
262489	132381	130107	105837	7		
26569848	22186937	4382912	10909469	23656	5204	12078
1188053	857320	330734	360743	4	2	1
241150	120259	120894	73583	16939		
15138463	**10721685**	**4416775**	**6465018**	**322760**	**4595123**	**28495**
6034844	4936560	1098284	2024222	220102	1046039	21137
1063240	592785	470454	489440	88349	282950	64
7579524	4884901	2694619	3661057		3005024	7294
335737	223573	112168	232687	13840	213655	
125122	83869	41253	57617	469	47457	
7365102	**5105896**	**2259205**	**3107988**	**322823**	**83203**	**1962859**
3394970	2433119	961853	1077031	108249	32919	455825
1094068	979139	114929	559752	214573	19535	216576
2645834	1603247	1042587	1317197		30749	1151591
85500	55445	30055	27252			13334
144734	34945	109788	126754			125537
106289147	78684547	27604597	37442325	9029570	4496083	1857819
16998855	11669151	5329704	7469438	1765468	222146	261524
3192577	2437334	755244	1260254	247147	17436	3965

4-3-1 续表 2

项目	Item	流动资产合计 Working Assets	#存货 Stock	固定资产原价 Original Value of Fixed Assets
二、餐饮业	**Catering Services**	**22654447**	**1860244**	**23022143**
#国有控股	State-controlled Enterprises	1761082	206635	2266568
(一)按登记注册类型分	**by Type of Registration**			
1.内资企业	**Domestic Funded Enterprises**	**18866755**	**1601319**	**19410726**
国有企业	State-owned Enterprises	262223	23747	790407
集体企业	Collective-owned Enterprises	93355	4685	123307
股份合作企业	Cooperative Enterprises	88793	28092	57892
联营企业	Joint Ownership Enterprises	21906	245	2934
国有联营企业	State Joint Ownership Enterprises			
集体联营企业	Collective Joint Ownership Enterprises	17564	194	2794
国有与集体联营企业	Joint State-collective Enterprises			
其他联营企业	Other Joint Ownership Enterprises	4342	51	140
有限责任公司	Limited Liability Corporations	6959163	543026	7674321
国有独资公司	State Sole Funded Corporations	253095	17831	467548
其他有限责任公司	Other Limited Liability Corporations	6706068	525195	7206775
股份有限公司	Share-holding Corporations Ltd.	1127664	92288	809904
私营企业	Private Enterprises	10235557	901805	9841410
私营独资企业	Private-funded Enterprises	566372	71907	949872
私营合伙企业	Private Partnership Enterprises	74773	7459	92337
私营有限责任公司	Private Limited Liability Corporations	9225703	799002	8424379
私营股份有限公司	Private Share-holding Corporations Ltd.	368709	23440	374819
其他企业	Other Enterprises	78106	7436	110552
2.港、澳、台商投资企业	**Enterprises with Funds from Hongkong, Macao and Taiwan**	**2463878**	**130051**	**1960045**
合资经营企业	Joint-venture Enterprises	451180	20622	425968
合作经营企业	Cooperative Enterprises	55697	6943	49959
独资经营企业	Enterprises with Sole Investment	1895851	101936	1465051
投资股份有限公司	Share-holding Corporations Ltd. with Investment	56175	325	18244
其他港澳台商投资企业	Other Enterprises with Funds from Hongkong, Macao and Taiwan	4977	224	827
3.外商投资企业	**Foreign Funded Enterprises**	**1323812**	**128878**	**1651375**
中外合资经营企业	Joint-venture Enterprises	269850	22501	559465
中外合作经营企业	Cooperative Enterprises	28109	809	7721
外资企业	Enterprises with Sole Foreign Investment	887650	92053	1005512
外商投资股份有限公司	Share-holding Corporations Ltd. with Foreign Investment	67847	3197	25858
其他外商投资企业	Other Foreign Funded Enterprises	70356	10322	52822
(二)按国民经济行业分	**by Sector**			
正餐服务	Dinner	18856829	1581055	19976037
快餐服务	Snack	2180526	189772	2408923
饮料及冷饮服务	Beverage and Cold Drink	781463	38203	296255
其他餐饮业	Others	835632	51211	340930

4-3-1 Continued 2

单位：万元
Unit:10000 yuan

累计折旧 Accumulation Depreciation	#本年折旧 Current Year Depreciation	资产合计 Total Assets	负债合计 Total liabilities	所有者权益合计 Total Owners' Equities	实收资本 Paid-up Capitals	#国家资本 State-owned Capitals	#港澳台资本 Capitals from Hongkong, Macao and Taiwan	#外商资本 Foreign Capitals
8317551	**1374258**	**50019916**	**35117610**	**14911097**	**14748809**	**849348**	**1017526**	**886020**
847419	114122	4129586	2618861	1510730	1155423	674315	56	5620
6554394	**1069193**	**41474035**	**29827408**	**11655420**	**12200854**	**839634**	**7123**	**3951**
324879	42290	1022406	579527	442880	450814	377142		
57521	5981	192010	120713	71296	47484			
27721	3150	130782	96403	34376	14898	5000		
318	116	50674	31855	18820	15641			
310	115	40091	23280	16811	15347			
8	1	10583	8575	2009	294			
2532662	433498	15716997	12143088	3574175	4615660	342811	4715	1043
111784	22633	739847	492000	247849	137083	99000		
2420875	410865	14977154	11651093	3326329	4478577	243813	4715	1043
290368	32175	2439444	1399106	1040335	481727	95759	67	1917
3279863	545420	21739106	15375143	6372491	6512139	11357	2341	991
277153	44024	1507179	659798	847378	605006	103	3	3
28923	4017	173460	66230	107241	87655	5	168	
2850714	474894	19224610	14081682	5151490	5528624	9908	2129	988
123074	22485	833862	567440	266376	290852	1343	41	
41066	6564	182625	81577	101050	62499	7569		
924377	**183174**	**4986416**	**3129542**	**1856874**	**1451479**	**4071**	**991388**	**10502**
209972	24747	1090880	599353	491527	353791	2283	106072	5013
29892	19052	104481	138913	-34431	47122	1788	11611	
676840	138688	3708922	2349575	1359344	1018028		861089	5490
7219	606	76530	36742	39786	30543		12273	
454	84	5607	4960	648	1996		345	
838788	**121892**	**3559465**	**2160661**	**1398803**	**1096483**	**5644**	**19015**	**871566**
294598	47347	765477	443036	322440	225436	5644	14364	95379
5870	305	35605	21728	13876	17979		4547	9055
495705	66632	2438806	1489808	948998	758118		34	674010
14407	3275	156310	97903	58405	45184			44874
28205	4338	163269	108185	55084	49765		70	48250
6858310	1118702	42056232	30446286	11618741	12868603	753666	604305	459998
1187525	204819	5393940	3107112	2286829	1331555	63355	325713	318855
128260	26962	1339984	809465	530521	203721	3676	62822	80064
143462	23775	1229761	754756	475006	344935	28653	24687	27107

4-3-2 各地区限额以上住宿和餐饮业企业年末资产负债
Assets and Liabilities of Enterprises above Designated Size of Hotels and Catering Services by Region at the Year-end

单位：万元
Unit: 10000 yuan

地区	Region	资产总计 Total Assets	#流动资产合计 Total Working Capitals	#固定资产合计 Total Fixed Assets	负债合计 Total Liabilities	所有者权益合计 Total Owners' Equities
全国	**National Total**	**176500497**	**71464804**	**64868835**	**127908649**	**48600639**
北京	Beijing	18022373	7600464	5637813	13134599	4887774
天津	Tianjin	2710223	1310058	829496	2305708	404211
河北	Hebei	4053286	1742334	1582437	3440283	613002
山西	Shanxi	2382677	877823	1041954	2195937	186740
内蒙古	Inner Mongolia	2479261	792505	1142138	1814084	665177
辽宁	Liaoning	4359807	1631364	1779524	3702038	657769
吉林	Jilin	1474671	502259	782869	972372	502299
黑龙江	Heilongjiang	1234653	369063	643239	849057	385597
上海	Shanghai	13391105	6102593	3635664	8456250	4934807
江苏	Jiangsu	13054691	4345814	5512646	9563145	3493020
浙江	Zhejiang	13170737	4909996	5130767	10379079	2791658
安徽	Anhui	4876396	1810276	1740383	3556899	1319497
福建	Fujian	6376942	2456272	2460531	4108391	2268551
江西	Jiangxi	3199228	1179385	1217233	2146205	1053023
山东	Shandong	8677498	3182040	3798197	6209710	2467788
河南	Henan	5545691	2362120	2034233	3442968	2102723
湖北	Hubei	5617869	1934849	2284822	3730404	1887465
湖南	Hunan	5902604	2164027	2312251	3644778	2257826
广东	Guangdong	22721358	10608390	7084773	18361848	4367179
广西	Guangxi	2790624	1104287	1085724	2189821	600803
海南	Hainan	5190134	2484240	1630632	3582529	1607606
重庆	Chongqing	4156150	1869560	1433022	2917345	1238805
四川	Sichuan	7171135	2987618	2660898	5330319	1840816
贵州	Guizhou	2549893	1162990	870235	1647025	902868
云南	Yunnan	4892092	1926615	2030283	3297818	1594274
西藏	Tibet	439063	103301	280363	151981	287082
陕西	Shaanxi	5154978	1871909	2254141	3613015	1541963
甘肃	Gansu	2060567	970019	758022	1288779	771788
青海	Qinghai	606747	249571	266970	302970	303777
宁夏	Ningxia	591756	276920	245040	519530	72226
新疆	Xinjiang	1646288	576142	702535	1053762	592525

4-3-3 各地区限额以上住宿业企业年末资产负债
Assets and Liabilities of Enterprises above Designated Size of Hotels by Region at the Year-end

单位：万元
Unit: 10000 yuan

地区	Region	资产总计 Total Assets	#流动资产合计 Total Working Capitals	#固定资产合计 Total Fixed Assets	负债合计 Total Liabilities	所有者权益合计 Total Owners' Equities
全国	**National Total**	**126480581**	**48810357**	**49141133**	**92791036**	**33689544**
北京	Beijing	14125620	5137638	5191472	10266656	3858963
天津	Tianjin	1809516	836960	596428	1558356	251159
河北	Hebei	3256782	1381860	1315935	2784884	471898
山西	Shanxi	1274833	451331	605778	1161433	113399
内蒙古	Inner Mongolia	1282775	387672	683447	858496	424279
辽宁	Liaoning	3088404	1146533	1333521	2612533	475870
吉林	Jilin	1037786	337557	572872	786973	250813
黑龙江	Heilongjiang	1056499	285852	573168	733816	322683
上海	Shanghai	8907495	3356274	2916192	5000884	3906611
江苏	Jiangsu	8104873	2543905	3567343	5875489	2229384
浙江	Zhejiang	9328662	3292600	3811170	7366553	1962109
安徽	Anhui	2644835	922090	988402	2046856	597979
福建	Fujian	5167029	1879756	2132078	3368781	1798248
江西	Jiangxi	2507203	906673	991167	1705998	801205
山东	Shandong	4918704	1891087	2179114	3654614	1264090
河南	Henan	4208706	1795151	1566652	2792928	1415778
湖北	Hubei	3014848	950118	1277865	2011310	1003538
湖南	Hunan	4672642	1765606	1782669	2961774	1710869
广东	Guangdong	17235628	7648122	5817624	14584703	2650925
广西	Guangxi	2388156	914183	957750	1873996	514160
海南	Hainan	5085081	2426354	1603804	3469933	1615148
重庆	Chongqing	2805264	1291243	950538	2228552	576712
四川	Sichuan	4773934	1960737	1800230	3623968	1149967
贵州	Guizhou	2138826	951519	731481	1404347	734480
云南	Yunnan	4041363	1440132	1754574	2826189	1215174
西藏	Tibet	403061	92533	260058	132587	270474
陕西	Shaanxi	3499168	1162084	1666729	2606905	892263
甘肃	Gansu	1573682	782457	551343	1056287	517395
青海	Qinghai	471626	208642	209494	231051	240575
宁夏	Ningxia	440353	201379	200212	381281	59072
新疆	Xinjiang	1217227	462309	552023	822903	394324

4-3-3 续表 Continued

国有控股

State-controlled Enterprises

单位：万元

Unit: 10000 yuan

地区	Region	资产总计 Total Assets	#流动资产合计 Total Working Capitals	#固定资产合计 Total Fixed Assets	负债合计 Total Liabilities	所有者权益合计 Total Owners' Equities
全国	**National Total**	**35254305**	**10684927**	**16175531**	**20819947**	**14434358**
北京	Beijing	6100332	1722833	3074743	4010004	2090328
天津	Tianjin	754166	244100	352037	692652	61514
河北	Hebei	745575	193130	454836	415880	329695
山西	Shanxi	432360	134300	248646	347464	84895
内蒙古	Inner Mongolia	291412	64223	201134	126663	164749
辽宁	Liaoning	668846	171279	336844	357724	311122
吉林	Jilin	370847	64260	263331	245866	124981
黑龙江	Heilongjiang	345936	63456	229292	200815	145121
上海	Shanghai	4060130	1179653	1448456	1857330	2202800
江苏	Jiangsu	3329733	771167	1552371	1867794	1461939
浙江	Zhejiang	1991984	568765	855103	1034093	957892
安徽	Anhui	307979	89454	169653	204812	103166
福建	Fujian	973936	344382	403256	409380	564556
江西	Jiangxi	583666	143539	227363	287505	296162
山东	Shandong	1606801	662071	694052	1035826	570975
河南	Henan	690007	210832	337084	497316	192691
湖北	Hubei	665150	128912	240212	332301	332849
湖南	Hunan	1321131	678128	371215	832367	488764
广东	Guangdong	2862811	987000	1062918	1367929	1494882
广西	Guangxi	374722	96294	187221	273866	100856
海南	Hainan	634755	81086	424052	336131	298624
重庆	Chongqing	757444	374870	269927	573499	183945
四川	Sichuan	673379	213045	353256	349863	323516
贵州	Guizhou	338891	178273	103983	195284	143607
云南	Yunnan	1440335	521491	582104	1022109	418226
西藏	Tibet	188350	56382	112037	47539	140811
陕西	Shaanxi	1263847	164958	855122	993559	270288
甘肃	Gansu	578783	323276	202326	390243	188540
青海	Qinghai	171368	46579	118351	66212	105156
宁夏	Ningxia	141452	13308	122663	143973	-2521
新疆	Xinjiang	588177	193881	321943	303948	284229

4-3-4 各地区限额以上住宿业企业年末资产负债(按登记注册类型分)

Assets and Liabilities of Enterprises above Designated Size of Hotels by Region and Type of Registration at the Year-end

内资企业　　　　　　　　　　　　　　　　　　　　单位：万元

Domestic Funded Enterprises　　　　　　　　　　　Unit: 10000 yuan

地　区	Region	资产总计 Total Assets	#流动资产合计 Total Working Capitals	#固定资产合计 Total Fixed Assets	负债合计 Total Liabilities	所有者权益合计 Total Owners' Equities
全　国	**National Total**	**103977016**	**40749874**	**39966186**	**76963455**	**27013561**
北　京	Beijing	9864643	3902203	4017657	7777208	2087436
天　津	Tianjin	1713685	801604	540191	1458762	254923
河　北	Hebei	3071536	1350513	1178828	2605098	466438
山　西	Shanxi	1274833	451331	605778	1161433	113399
内蒙古	Inner Mongolia	1163850	378529	575979	791168	372682
辽　宁	Liaoning	2466273	970395	943205	2048767	417506
吉　林	Jilin	929697	292696	526746	705870	223827
黑龙江	Heilongjiang	790649	240190	387397	540988	249662
上　海	Shanghai	5617061	2054601	1621258	3262729	2354332
江　苏	Jiangsu	6867263	2201516	2915360	4716744	2150519
浙　江	Zhejiang	7880967	2798335	3013804	6345850	1535117
安　徽	Anhui	2225105	844059	822719	1679795	545309
福　建	Fujian	4051276	1575028	1627266	2578780	1472496
江　西	Jiangxi	2411033	891180	933437	1634375	776658
山　东	Shandong	4421938	1785249	1824472	3268493	1153444
河　南	Henan	3861745	1591213	1477569	2460011	1401735
湖　北	Hubei	2817444	880826	1184993	1862366	955078
湖　南	Hunan	4279063	1657290	1650367	2666747	1612316
广　东	Guangdong	12900248	5561265	4424839	11031154	1869094
广　西	Guangxi	1905647	762138	707837	1430503	475144
海　南	Hainan	3474552	1669610	999272	2494797	979755
重　庆	Chongqing	2592006	1203770	884375	2088604	503403
四　川	Sichuan	4487479	1892278	1609589	3414684	1072795
贵　州	Guizhou	2109672	947307	714488	1390770	718902
云　南	Yunnan	3733266	1355785	1576446	2684442	1048823
西　藏	Tibet	334495	84416	199890	125329	209165
陕　西	Shaanxi	3203570	1046125	1523068	2360136	843434
甘　肃	Gansu	1554726	777562	537283	1042924	511803
青　海	Qinghai	427670	197145	191855	223104	204566
宁　夏	Ningxia	391636	156260	198231	345205	46431
新　疆	Xinjiang	1153988	429455	551987	766619	387369

4-3-4 续表 1 Continued 1

国有企业 State-owned Enterprises

单位：万元 Unit: 10000 yuan

地区	Region	资产总计 Total Assets	#流动资产合计 Total Working Capitals	#固定资产合计 Total Fixed Assets	负债合计 Total Liabilities	所有者权益合计 Total Owners' Equities
全国	**National Total**	**10106755**	**2986880**	**5209389**	**5365003**	**4741758**
北京	Beijing	2116627	582077	1239951	1117802	998825
天津	Tianjin	108227	27382	57550	95356	12871
河北	Hebei	484208	105459	308768	333867	150342
山西	Shanxi	330478	111819	181221	265535	64943
内蒙古	Inner Mongolia	100457	20885	71749	40495	59962
辽宁	Liaoning	333785	84479	157481	140647	193138
吉林	Jilin	204447	43266	153995	106291	98156
黑龙江	Heilongjiang	212259	40227	157137	126554	85705
上海	Shanghai	775510	234656	185549	219608	555902
江苏	Jiangsu	570348	176554	297637	357245	213103
浙江	Zhejiang	463993	188126	198325	156282	307711
安徽	Anhui	23944	7172	14561	19545	4399
福建	Fujian	243823	68923	124469	133746	110077
江西	Jiangxi	203638	49420	108203	80353	123285
山东	Shandong	821073	251176	441842	364723	456351
河南	Henan	406832	111393	202249	268501	138331
湖北	Hubei	92046	31348	49409	55061	36986
湖南	Hunan	218503	76232	94318	120041	98463
广东	Guangdong	769578	279621	283429	407373	362205
广西	Guangxi	200145	47651	77223	129369	70776
海南	Hainan	19510	7998	9522	23556	-4045
重庆	Chongqing	162219	63246	90034	142222	19997
四川	Sichuan	153221	54157	58964	81742	71479
贵州	Guizhou	47603	18012	26724	28113	19490
云南	Yunnan	181206	82116	77468	98467	82739
西藏	Tibet	124098	24798	82250	28476	95622
陕西	Shaanxi	240012	41943	148269	119335	120678
甘肃	Gansu	126483	53387	60612	67476	59007
青海	Qinghai	47492	6059	40980	7056	40436
宁夏	Ningxia	89109	8059	79437	108811	-19702
新疆	Xinjiang	235881	89239	130063	121355	114526

4-3-4 续表 2 Continued 2

集体企业 单位：万元

Collective-owned Enterprises Unit: 10000 yuan

地区	Region	资产总计 Total Assets	#流动资产合计 Total Working Capitals	#固定资产合计 Total Fixed Assets	负债合计 Total Liabilities	所有者权益合计 Total Owners' Equities
全国	**National Total**	**747334**	**285380**	**361360**	**522830**	**224505**
北京	Beijing	215267	66976	129427	151876	63391
天津	Tianjin	41351	30134	10987	38895	2456
河北	Hebei	17979	5744	9632	8764	9215
山西	Shanxi	26908	6877	9509	25738	1170
内蒙古	Inner Mongolia	1421	773	648	131	1290
辽宁	Liaoning	16699	4274	6869	11576	5124
吉林	Jilin	1031	624	103	454	577
黑龙江	Heilongjiang	5985	3939	2000	7174	-1189
上海	Shanghai	30720	8367	18113	12359	18361
江苏	Jiangsu	62687	29703	18632	42672	20015
浙江	Zhejiang	42035	14505	21316	28503	13532
安徽	Anhui	3294	955	2018	261	3033
福建	Fujian	11441	5143	5413	6698	4743
江西	Jiangxi					
山东	Shandong	33433	10411	19249	15440	17992
河南	Henan	46771	18702	20220	33671	13101
湖北	Hubei	65560	22572	39725	27076	38484
湖南	Hunan	13746	9683	2771	3400	10346
广东	Guangdong	38682	13928	13785	49133	-10451
广西	Guangxi	6667	3223	2265	2586	4081
海南	Hainan	325	267	26	125	200
重庆	Chongqing	9451	3678	4940	9751	-300
四川	Sichuan	9907	5274	954	9193	714
贵州	Guizhou	12429	3119	9309	2450	9979
云南	Yunnan	7336	2743	3257	3833	3503
西藏	Tibet	2699	553	1506	1004	1695
陕西	Shaanxi	14341	9757	3198	21149	-6807
甘肃	Gansu	6729	2806	3728	7610	-881
青海	Qinghai	1068	244	824	895	173
宁夏	Ningxia	213	208	5	23	189
新疆	Xinjiang	1159	198	931	390	769

4-3-4 续表 3 Continued 3

股份合作企业

Cooperative Enterprises

单位：万元

Unit: 10000 yuan

地 区	Region	资产总计 Total Assets	#流动资产合计 Total Working Capitals	#固定资产合计 Total Fixed Assets	负债合计 Total Liabilities	所有者权益合计 Total Owners' Equities
全 国	**National Total**	**180148**	**78535**	**57053**	**154155**	**25995**
北 京	Beijing	102370	49434	26572	86417	15954
天 津	Tianjin	6482	4780	1272	1284	5198
河 北	Hebei					
山 西	Shanxi					
内蒙古	Inner Mongolia	431	257	174	269	162
辽 宁	Liaoning					
吉 林	Jilin	154	47		616	-462
黑龙江	Heilongjiang	22570	7260	8621	11077	11494
上 海	Shanghai					
江 苏	Jiangsu					
浙 江	Zhejiang	8081	2914	2575	5742	2338
安 徽	Anhui					
福 建	Fujian	663	462	183	135	528
江 西	Jiangxi	3140	490	2648	2959	181
山 东	Shandong	14357	8086	1266	12375	1982
河 南	Henan	4365	975	3180	1422	2943
湖 北	Hubei	7296	884	6412	8317	-1021
湖 南	Hunan	433	157		64	369
广 东	Guangdong	3701	645	1475	3974	-273
广 西	Guangxi	917	412	452	864	53
海 南	Hainan	760	246	499	15950	-15190
重 庆	Chongqing					
四 川	Sichuan	2462	792	1236	1343	1120
贵 州	Guizhou					
云 南	Yunnan	412	412		200	212
西 藏	Tibet					
陕 西	Shaanxi	1554	282	488	1147	407
甘 肃	Gansu					
青 海	Qinghai					
宁 夏	Ningxia					
新 疆	Xinjiang					

联营企业 单位：万元
Joint Ownership Enterprises Unit: 10000 yuan

地区	Region	资产总计 Total Assets	#流动资产合计 Total Working Capitals	#固定资产合计 Total Fixed Assets	负债合计 Total Liabilities	所有者权益合计 Total Owners' Equities
全国	**National Total**	**75725**	**34413**	**23572**	**40683**	**35044**
北京	Beijing	4305	3794	484	3960	345
天津	Tianjin					
河北	Hebei					
山西	Shanxi					
内蒙古	Inner Mongolia	947	228	379	2557	-1610
辽宁	Liaoning	830	192	639	130	700
吉林	Jilin					
黑龙江	Heilongjiang					
上海	Shanghai	6609	231	5035	9705	-3096
江苏	Jiangsu	1251	684	156	1291	-39
浙江	Zhejiang	6451	5258	1191	1059	5392
安徽	Anhui					
福建	Fujian	28277	12738	13466	10404	17874
江西	Jiangxi					
山东	Shandong					
河南	Henan	252	51	201	49	203
湖北	Hubei					
湖南	Hunan					
广东	Guangdong	10212	6505	808	1372	8840
广西	Guangxi					
海南	Hainan					
重庆	Chongqing					
四川	Sichuan					
贵州	Guizhou					
云南	Yunnan	2042	585	485	303	1739
西藏	Tibet					
陕西	Shaanxi					
甘肃	Gansu	13428	3754		8528	4901
青海	Qinghai					
宁夏	Ningxia					
新疆	Xinjiang	1121	393	728	1325	-205

有限责任公司
Limited Liability Corporations

单位：万元
Unit: 10000 yuan

地 区	Region	资产总计 Total Assets	#流动资产合计 Total Working Capitals	#固定资产合计 Total Fixed Assets	负债合计 Total Liabilities	所有者权益合计 Total Owners' Equities
全 国	**National Total**	**58821936**	**22557925**	**22676824**	**44192533**	**14629402**
北 京	Beijing	5830072	2172677	2384122	4757608	1072463
天 津	Tianjin	1280857	598976	397065	1056095	224762
河 北	Hebei	1222816	553454	473538	850752	372064
山 西	Shanxi	297204	105271	142431	309557	-12353
内 蒙 古	Inner Mongolia	581686	162759	292383	402324	179362
辽 宁	Liaoning	1213775	429808	562045	1020318	193457
吉 林	Jilin	428918	133771	230342	377546	51372
黑 龙 江	Heilongjiang	322195	123390	144428	242771	79424
上 海	Shanghai	3529588	1110431	1111422	2048355	1481233
江 苏	Jiangsu	3685488	984482	1644066	2318878	1366610
浙 江	Zhejiang	4093187	1291321	1742195	3197882	895305
安 徽	Anhui	1134086	443659	391225	944282	189804
福 建	Fujian	2353546	911899	902143	1522786	830760
江 西	Jiangxi	1386709	540192	433403	1010644	376064
山 东	Shandong	2096985	924355	830614	1775887	321098
河 南	Henan	2024890	858177	724929	1395536	629354
湖 北	Hubei	1540055	458560	594701	1009619	530436
湖 南	Hunan	1979223	642156	803817	1155166	824057
广 东	Guangdong	8312241	3551567	2989072	7360478	951763
广 西	Guangxi	746812	234572	344906	530392	216420
海 南	Hainan	3173472	1483922	925423	2139994	1033478
重 庆	Chongqing	1641001	817835	488807	1291842	349160
四 川	Sichuan	2356455	1035965	843306	1826946	529509
贵 州	Guizhou	1086173	529612	371548	764222	321952
云 南	Yunnan	2373949	869554	1041250	1798762	575187
西 藏	Tibet	129808	42567	79271	62084	67724
陕 西	Shaanxi	2162907	682803	1080410	1783849	379058
甘 肃	Gansu	935498	496124	301569	657409	278089
青 海	Qinghai	203458	80450	99083	137103	66354
宁 夏	Ningxia	133716	66882	52286	86923	46793
新 疆	Xinjiang	565166	220734	255024	356523	208643

股份有限公司
Share-holding Corporations Ltd.

单位：万元
Unit: 10000 yuan

地区	Region	资产总计 Total Assets	#流动资产合计 Total Working Capitals	#固定资产合计 Total Fixed Assets	负债合计 Total Liabilities	所有者权益合计 Total Owners' Equities
全国	**National Total**	**4720863**	**1890029**	**1469728**	**2828110**	**1892754**
北京	Beijing	145940	14065	43565	146010	-69
天津	Tianjin	42279	35546	3021	40258	2022
河北	Hebei	116941	68300	26718	92682	24259
山西	Shanxi	28838	6063	19349	16604	12233
内蒙古	Inner Mongolia	36413	12035	21361	15990	20423
辽宁	Liaoning	48467	9694	4352	55710	-7243
吉林	Jilin	41620	10384	20529	23206	18414
黑龙江	Heilongjiang	71091	7151	15729	47733	23358
上海	Shanghai	175025	45852	59254	77893	97131
江苏	Jiangsu	779746	263367	314479	530379	249367
浙江	Zhejiang	324946	151679	84588	183465	141482
安徽	Anhui	83968	34442	35869	70286	13682
福建	Fujian	59982	25613	21575	18562	41420
江西	Jiangxi	115574	31130	72178	83265	32309
山东	Shandong	231018	80797	128722	150748	80271
河南	Henan	145347	54809	70713	51255	94092
湖北	Hubei	249467	71261	81370	141320	108147
湖南	Hunan	740662	508239	48768	468307	272354
广东	Guangdong	665199	285735	100938	256318	408881
广西	Guangxi	122879	27569	55361	74105	48774
海南	Hainan	62321	26827	14277	24128	38193
重庆	Chongqing	54834	8326	40958	33654	21180
四川	Sichuan	199764	54636	108288	146157	53607
贵州	Guizhou	10708	7388	3319	7297	3411
云南	Yunnan	52511	20701	15242	30084	22427
西藏	Tibet	3675	554	1221	775	2900
陕西	Shaanxi	40332	5691	29198	18056	22276
甘肃	Gansu	12390	6589	5169	3727	8663
青海	Qinghai	20753	11921	5451	5969	14784
宁夏	Ningxia					
新疆	Xinjiang	38173	3665	18166	14167	24006

4-3-4 续表 7 Continued 7

私营企业
Private Enterprises

单位：万元
Unit: 10000 yuan

地 区	Region	资产总计 Total Assets	#流动资产合计 Total Working Capitals	#固定资产合计 Total Fixed Assets	负债合计 Total Liabilities	所有者权益合计 Total Owners' Equities
全 国	**National Total**	**29083111**	**12842310**	**10039910**	**23739894**	**5343217**
北 京	Beijing	1449183	1012617	193226	1512820	-63637
天 津	Tianjin	233184	103849	70007	224514	8670
河 北	Hebei	1229592	617557	360172	1319033	-89441
山 西	Shanxi	586908	220097	250296	541400	45508
内蒙古	Inner Mongolia	434797	179628	183581	324464	110332
辽 宁	Liaoning	851103	440939	211598	817704	33399
吉 林	Jilin	249287	103957	119689	196946	52341
黑龙江	Heilongjiang	156131	58090	59382	105445	50686
上 海	Shanghai	1091560	650287	239274	888128	203433
江 苏	Jiangsu	1723620	733878	609808	1454866	268755
浙 江	Zhejiang	2938934	1142989	961819	2772131	166803
安 徽	Anhui	979044	357548	378735	645170	333874
福 建	Fujian	1342297	542218	557655	876970	465327
江 西	Jiangxi	694194	268666	314215	452210	241984
山 东	Shandong	1211885	505373	395305	939810	272074
河 南	Henan	1229211	546035	453512	708692	520518
湖 北	Hubei	861254	295331	412659	620439	240815
湖 南	Hunan	1323321	419054	699544	917444	405877
广 东	Guangdong	3065869	1409878	1018248	2938669	127200
广 西	Guangxi	828027	448697	227629	693079	134947
海 南	Hainan	217111	150192	48668	289314	-72204
重 庆	Chongqing	715069	306744	254365	604996	110073
四 川	Sichuan	1739826	738181	586169	1343625	396201
贵 州	Guizhou	945710	388297	298531	585451	360260
云 南	Yunnan	1108149	378350	436004	747162	360987
西 藏	Tibet	69016	14558	33795	31653	37364
陕 西	Shaanxi	725696	302883	248968	402834	322862
甘 肃	Gansu	457563	214161	165300	297181	160382
青 海	Qinghai	151148	97437	43051	71118	80031
宁 夏	Ningxia	168598	81111	66503	149448	19151
新 疆	Xinjiang	305824	113708	142202	267178	38645

其他企业
Other Enterprises

单位：万元
Unit: 10000 yuan

地　区	Region	资产总计 Total Assets	#流动资产合计 Total Working Capitals	#固定资产合计 Total Fixed Assets	负债合计 Total Liabilities	所有者权益合计 Total Owners' Equities
全　国	**National Total**	**241150**	**74411**	**128360**	**120259**	**120894**
北　京	Beijing	879	564	310	715	164
天　津	Tianjin	1305	937	290	2361	-1055
河　北	Hebei					
山　西	Shanxi	4497	1205	2972	2599	1898
内蒙古	Inner Mongolia	7698	1965	5704	4937	2761
辽　宁	Liaoning	1614	1010	221	2682	-1068
吉　林	Jilin	4241	648	2088	812	3429
黑龙江	Heilongjiang	418	133	100	235	183
上　海	Shanghai	8050	4777	2611	6683	1368
江　苏	Jiangsu	44123	12847	30584	11414	32709
浙　江	Zhejiang	3340	1543	1797	786	2554
安　徽	Anhui	768	283	311	251	518
福　建	Fujian	11246	8033	2364	9480	1767
江　西	Jiangxi	7778	1282	2791	4944	2835
山　东	Shandong	13188	5050	7474	9511	3677
河　南	Henan	4078	1071	2565	885	3193
湖　北	Hubei	1767	870	717	535	1232
湖　南	Hunan	3176	1769	1149	2326	850
广　东	Guangdong	34767	13386	17085	13837	20930
广　西	Guangxi	201	14	1	108	93
海　南	Hainan	1053	159	858	1729	-676
重　庆	Chongqing	9432	3942	5271	6139	3292
四　川	Sichuan	25844	3272	10672	5678	20165
贵　州	Guizhou	7049	879	5056	3238	3811
云　南	Yunnan	7661	1324	2741	5631	2030
西　藏	Tibet	5199	1386	1847	1339	3860
陕　西	Shaanxi	18727	2766	12537	13766	4961
甘　肃	Gansu	2635	741	904	994	1641
青　海	Qinghai	3751	1035	2466	963	2788
宁　夏	Ningxia					
新　疆	Xinjiang	6665	1520	4874	5681	984

港、澳、台商投资企业 单位：万元
Enterprises with Funds from Hongkong, Macao and Taiwan Unit: 10000 yuan

地 区	Region	资产总计 Total Assets	#流动资产合计 Total Working Capitals	#固定资产合计 Total Fixed Assets	负债合计 Total Liabilities	所有者权益合计 Total Owners' Equities
全 国	**National Total**	**15138463**	**5343408**	**6183468**	**10721685**	**4416775**
北 京	Beijing	2384580	704420	739738	1465451	919128
天 津	Tianjin	56917	5728	50253	60659	-3742
河 北	Hebei	141738	21051	105742	118906	22832
山 西	Shanxi					
内 蒙 古	Inner Mongolia	118819	9059	107446	67307	51512
辽 宁	Liaoning	468563	101083	324746	284485	184078
吉 林	Jilin	35963	19957	1730	42447	-6484
黑 龙 江	Heilongjiang	216955	26116	162767	178488	38467
上 海	Shanghai	2282680	905066	737544	1185934	1096746
江 苏	Jiangsu	735084	237056	317783	779899	-44816
浙 江	Zhejiang	1109202	412949	594998	755337	353865
安 徽	Anhui	390015	75934	162699	341175	48839
福 建	Fujian	790045	230363	340728	561349	228696
江 西	Jiangxi	78867	9008	48170	53679	25188
山 东	Shandong	460395	94626	334986	352155	108239
河 南	Henan	332413	196723	84191	325869	6545
湖 北	Hubei	161433	52035	76561	118473	42960
湖 南	Hunan	299967	80599	70268	185812	114155
广 东	Guangdong	2561640	1129116	851290	2055324	506316
广 西	Guangxi	481546	151710	249778	442708	38838
海 南	Hainan	1498480	707617	547005	870040	628440
重 庆	Chongqing	53900	11858	37699	70883	-16982
四 川	Sichuan	64216	26417	22818	162102	-97886
贵 州	Guizhou	12208	2099	9948	8788	3420
云 南	Yunnan	222817	60137	127295	97388	125429
西 藏	Tibet	2136	2136		2743	-607
陕 西	Shaanxi	172589	67395	75141	133625	38963
甘 肃	Gansu	5295	3150	2144	659	4636
青 海	Qinghai					
宁 夏	Ningxia					
新 疆	Xinjiang					

外商投资企业

Foreign Funded Enterprises

单位：万元

Unit: 10000 yuan

地 区	Region	资产总计 Total Assets	#流动资产合计 Total Working Capitals	#固定资产合计 Total Fixed Assets	负债合计 Total Liabilities	所有者权益合计 Total Owners' Equities
全 国	**National Total**	**7365102**	**2717071**	**2991479**	**5105896**	**2259205**
北 京	Beijing	1876397	531015	434076	1023997	852399
天 津	Tianjin	38914	29629	5984	38935	-21
河 北	Hebei	43508	10296	31365	60880	-17372
山 西	Shanxi					
内蒙古	Inner Mongolia	107	83	23	21	86
辽 宁	Liaoning	153567	75054	65570	279281	-125714
吉 林	Jilin	72126	24904	44396	38656	33470
黑龙江	Heilongjiang	48895	19546	23004	14341	34554
上 海	Shanghai	1007754	396607	557389	552221	455533
江 苏	Jiangsu	502526	105333	334200	378846	123680
浙 江	Zhejiang	338493	81316	202367	265365	73128
安 徽	Anhui	29716	2097	2984	25886	3830
福 建	Fujian	325708	74365	164084	228652	97056
江 西	Jiangxi	17303	6485	9560	17944	-641
山 东	Shandong	36371	11211	19655	33965	2406
河 南	Henan	14548	7215	4891	7049	7499
湖 北	Hubei	35971	17257	16311	30471	5500
湖 南	Hunan	93612	27716	62034	109215	-15602
广 东	Guangdong	1773739	957741	541495	1498225	275515
广 西	Guangxi	962	334	135	785	177
海 南	Hainan	112049	49127	57527	105097	6952
重 庆	Chongqing	159357	75615	28464	69065	90292
四 川	Sichuan	222239	42042	167824	47181	175058
贵 州	Guizhou	16946	2113	7045	4789	12157
云 南	Yunnan	85281	24210	50833	44359	40921
西 藏	Tibet	66431	5981	60168	4515	61916
陕 西	Shaanxi	123009	48564	68521	113144	9865
甘 肃	Gansu	13661	1745	11916	12704	957
青 海	Qinghai	43956	11497	17640	7947	36008
宁 夏	Ningxia	48717	45119	1981	36076	12641
新 疆	Xinjiang	63239	32854	37	56284	6955

4-3-5 各地区限额以上住宿业企业年末资产负债(按国民经济行业分)

Assets and Liabilities of Enterprises above Designated Size of Hotels by Region and Sector at the Year-end

旅游饭店
Tourist Hotel

单位：万元
Unit: 10000 yuan

地　区	Region	资产总计 Total Assets	#流动资产合计 Total Working Capitals	#固定资产合计 Total Fixed Assets	负债合计 Total Liabilities	所有者权益合计 Total Owners' Equities
全　国	**National Total**	**106289147**	**39893062**	**42485188**	**78684547**	**27604597**
北　京	Beijing	11832076	4059866	4766973	8640953	3191122
天　津	Tianjin	1222950	434820	456410	956061	266889
河　北	Hebei	2404230	1016491	980177	2176623	227608
山　西	Shanxi	918003	318972	456278	883894	34109
内蒙古	Inner Mongolia	1014935	310499	560423	648493	366442
辽　宁	Liaoning	2644030	951595	1193757	2233782	410248
吉　林	Jilin	961511	318557	525439	730667	230844
黑龙江	Heilongjiang	918755	230566	509783	591416	327339
上　海	Shanghai	7668458	2655690	2624687	4124795	3543662
江　苏	Jiangsu	7400589	2270880	3273459	5316954	2083636
浙　江	Zhejiang	8345228	2965424	3399376	6595938	1749289
安　徽	Anhui	2227721	750478	836507	1774482	453239
福　建	Fujian	4565101	1621391	1954920	2992977	1572124
江　西	Jiangxi	2109371	737296	825697	1485652	623719
山　东	Shandong	4041433	1559645	1875301	2933784	1107649
河　南	Henan	2996986	1361702	1079037	2125925	871061
湖　北	Hubei	2373066	699346	1008107	1559801	813264
湖　南	Hunan	3072447	897525	1495198	2285725	786723
广　东	Guangdong	14777137	6412550	5116216	12716344	2060793
广　西	Guangxi	1847022	596918	829839	1425554	421468
海　南	Hainan	4931360	2409466	1468546	3382678	1548683
重　庆	Chongqing	2382221	1138961	780809	1915483	466738
四　川	Sichuan	3812824	1595226	1427516	2877388	935436
贵　州	Guizhou	1791346	805922	590179	1226190	565156
云　南	Yunnan	3541089	1261436	1513714	2521788	1019301
西　藏	Tibet	397048	91711	257672	130340	266707
陕　西	Shaanxi	2822177	948014	1363927	2222009	600168
甘　肃	Gansu	1374609	697712	457779	928613	445995
青　海	Qinghai	430003	194144	185808	212272	217731
宁　夏	Ningxia	419350	197947	192548	366603	52747
新　疆	Xinjiang	1046071	382312	479106	701363	344707

4-3-5 续表 1 Continued 1

一般旅馆 单位：万元
Fonda Unit: 10000 yuan

地区	Region	资产总计 Total Assets	#流动资产合计 Total Working Capitals	#固定资产合计 Total Fixed Assets	负债合计 Total Liabilities	所有者权益合计 Total Owners' Equities
全国	**National Total**	**16998855**	**7280928**	**5775709**	**11669151**	**5329704**
北京	Beijing	1750101	810698	326067	1106825	643276
天津	Tianjin	268738	188166	52051	242732	26006
河北	Hebei	720948	311984	280327	472088	248859
山西	Shanxi	325869	124453	129714	247706	78163
内蒙古	Inner Mongolia	259937	72881	119486	204911	55026
辽宁	Liaoning	325786	155505	104831	295458	30328
吉林	Jilin	69748	16139	44199	51919	17829
黑龙江	Heilongjiang	119300	50056	56931	81287	38013
上海	Shanghai	1142608	644028	271605	819410	323199
江苏	Jiangsu	646306	249596	267076	519457	126849
浙江	Zhejiang	968038	319527	407742	762940	205099
安徽	Anhui	354503	156491	115429	214762	139741
福建	Fujian	548335	234150	158663	331575	216760
江西	Jiangxi	351870	153929	148238	200713	151157
山东	Shandong	777910	273805	279307	631581	146329
河南	Henan	1145742	393021	471402	628387	517355
湖北	Hubei	554637	216134	239857	393069	161567
湖南	Hunan	878803	369712	245745	262724	616079
广东	Guangdong	2145059	1060063	601609	1647453	497606
广西	Guangxi	508180	307404	114134	427516	80664
海南	Hainan	62729	13489	47826	59100	3628
重庆	Chongqing	407342	145410	163069	289143	118198
四川	Sichuan	935005	359191	362659	735212	199793
贵州	Guizhou	324577	132437	134349	170420	154157
云南	Yunnan	448047	161486	215093	272263	175784
西藏	Tibet					
陕西	Shaanxi	569987	191838	248139	339788	230199
甘肃	Gansu	170441	74142	77087	110608	59833
青海	Qinghai	31225	14386	14226	17720	13506
宁夏	Ningxia	18447	2380	6340	13044	5404
新疆	Xinjiang	168637	78427	72508	119340	49297

其他住宿业
Others

单位：万元
Unit: 10000 yuan

地　区	Region	资产总计 Total Assets	#流动资产合计 Total Working Capitals	#固定资产合计 Total Fixed Assets	负债合计 Total Liabilities	所有者权益合计 Total Owners' Equities
全　国	**National Total**	**3192577**	**1636369**	**880240**	**2437334**	**755244**
北　京	Beijing	543443	267074	98432	518878	24565
天　津	Tianjin	317828	213975	87967	359564	-41736
河　北	Hebei	131604	53385	55431	136173	-4569
山　西	Shanxi	30961	7907	19786	29833	1128
内 蒙 古	Inner Mongolia	7903	4292	3538	5092	2810
辽　宁	Liaoning	118588	39433	34933	83293	35295
吉　林	Jilin	6527	2862	3235	4387	2140
黑 龙 江	Heilongjiang	18444	5230	6454	61113	-42669
上　海	Shanghai	96429	56557	19899	56680	39750
江　苏	Jiangsu	57977	23430	26808	39078	18899
浙　江	Zhejiang	15396	7649	4052	7675	7721
安　徽	Anhui	62610	15121	36467	57611	4999
福　建	Fujian	53593	24214	18496	44229	9364
江　西	Jiangxi	45962	15449	17232	19633	26329
山　东	Shandong	99360	57636	24506	89248	10112
河　南	Henan	65978	40428	16213	38616	27362
湖　北	Hubei	87146	34639	29900	58439	28707
湖　南	Hunan	721392	498368	41725	413325	308067
广　东	Guangdong	313431	175508	99799	220905	92526
广　西	Guangxi	32954	9861	13777	20925	12028
海　南	Hainan	90992	3400	87432	28155	62837
重　庆	Chongqing	15701	6871	6660	23925	-8224
四　川	Sichuan	26105	6320	10056	11367	14738
贵　州	Guizhou	22904	13160	6953	7737	15167
云　南	Yunnan	52227	17210	25767	32139	20089
西　藏	Tibet	6014	822	2386	2247	3767
陕　西	Shaanxi	107004	22232	54664	45108	61896
甘　肃	Gansu	28632	10602	16478	17065	11567
青　海	Qinghai	10397	112	9460	1060	9338
宁　夏	Ningxia	2556	1052	1324	1635	921
新　疆	Xinjiang	2519	1570	410	2199	320

4-3-6 各地区限额以上餐饮业企业年末资产负债

Assets and Liabilitiest of Enterprises above Designated Size of Catering Services by Region at the Year-end

单位：万元

Unit: 10000 yuan

地区	Region	资产总计 Total Assets	#流动资产合计 Total Working Capitals	#固定资产合计 Total Fixed Assets	负债合计 Total Liabilities	所有者权益合计 Total Owners' Equities
全国	**National Total**	**50019916**	**22654447**	**15727704**	**35117610**	**14911097**
北京	Beijing	3896754	2462826	446342	2867943	1028811
天津	Tianjin	900707	473098	233068	747352	153052
河北	Hebei	796504	360474	266502	655399	141105
山西	Shanxi	1107845	426491	436176	1034504	73341
内蒙古	Inner Mongolia	1196486	404834	458691	955588	240898
辽宁	Liaoning	1271404	484832	446003	1089505	181899
吉林	Jilin	436885	164702	209997	185399	251486
黑龙江	Heilongjiang	178154	83210	70070	115240	62913
上海	Shanghai	4483610	2746319	719473	3455365	1028197
江苏	Jiangsu	4949818	1801909	1945304	3687656	1263636
浙江	Zhejiang	3842075	1617395	1319598	3012526	829549
安徽	Anhui	2231561	888186	751980	1510043	721518
福建	Fujian	1209912	576516	328453	739609	470303
江西	Jiangxi	692024	272711	226066	440206	251818
山东	Shandong	3758794	1290954	1619083	2555097	1203698
河南	Henan	1336985	566969	467581	650040	686944
湖北	Hubei	2603021	984731	1006957	1719095	883927
湖南	Hunan	1229961	398421	529582	683004	546957
广东	Guangdong	5485730	2960268	1267149	3777145	1716254
广西	Guangxi	402468	190105	127975	315825	86643
海南	Hainan	105053	57886	26828	112595	-7542
重庆	Chongqing	1350887	578318	482484	688793	662093
四川	Sichuan	2397200	1026882	860668	1706351	690849
贵州	Guizhou	411066	211471	138754	242678	168388
云南	Yunnan	850729	486483	275709	471629	379100
西藏	Tibet	36002	10767	20305	19394	16608
陕西	Shaanxi	1655811	709825	587412	1006110	649701
甘肃	Gansu	486885	187562	206679	232492	254393
青海	Qinghai	135121	40929	57476	71918	63203
宁夏	Ningxia	151403	75540	44828	138249	13154
新疆	Xinjiang	429061	113833	150511	230860	198201

4-3-6 续表 Continued

国有控股
State-controlled Enterprises

单位：万元
Unit: 10000 yuan

地区	Region	资产总计 Total Assets	#流动资产合计 Total Working Capitals	#固定资产合计 Total Fixed Assets	负债合计 Total Liabilities	所有者权益合计 Total Owners' Equities
全国	**National Total**	**4129586**	**1761082**	**1485288**	**2618861**	**1510730**
北京	Beijing	558254	318673	92214	266350	291904
天津	Tianjin	51634	24638	18045	56031	-4397
河北	Hebei	61906	22693	27190	57444	4462
山西	Shanxi	184861	22193	102968	102918	81943
内蒙古	Inner Mongolia	114556	22801	32320	39239	75317
辽宁	Liaoning	62595	25475	25889	56680	5916
吉林	Jilin	77912	11505	54142	23018	54894
黑龙江	Heilongjiang	25680	1261	16802	26721	-1040
上海	Shanghai	468785	298353	69164	400238	68547
江苏	Jiangsu	368886	159703	166063	276455	92431
浙江	Zhejiang	278538	133076	88356	190416	88122
安徽	Anhui	82907	42142	21422	54660	28247
福建	Fujian	18431	13620	2837	9692	8740
江西	Jiangxi	69328	29119	23761	36882	32446
山东	Shandong	545297	112300	337072	319684	225613
河南	Henan	27497	13963	4257	12432	15066
湖北	Hubei	125596	86632	23759	77295	48301
湖南	Hunan	29945	7406	18653	15779	14165
广东	Guangdong	384721	189735	113098	241381	143340
广西	Guangxi	24580	10694	5535	27993	-3413
海南	Hainan	1424	293	1131	1774	-350
重庆	Chongqing	81989	39170	21860	43113	38876
四川	Sichuan	107244	43247	43672	81449	25796
贵州	Guizhou	12828	9417	2581	12173	655
云南	Yunnan	71319	35612	26190	30434	40886
西藏	Tibet					
陕西	Shaanxi	173966	68395	50342	90029	83937
甘肃	Gansu	66058	12396	51569	22352	43706
青海	Qinghai	7748	1281	6467	9214	-1466
宁夏	Ningxia	1936	750	1113	2922	-986
新疆	Xinjiang	43165	4539	36816	34093	9072

4-3-7 各地区限额以上餐饮业企业年末资产负债(按登记注册类型分)

Assets and Liabilities of Enterprises above Designated Size of Catering Services by Region and Type of Registration at the Year-end

内资企业　　　　单位：万元

Domestic Funded Enterprises　　　　Unit: 10000 yuan

地　区	Region	资产总计 Total Assets	#流动资产合计 Total Working Capitals	#固定资产合计 Total Fixed Assets	负债合计 Total Liabilities	所有者权益合计 Total Owners' Equities
全　国	**National Total**	**41474035**	**18866755**	**13771720**	**29827408**	**11655420**
北　京	Beijing	2454775	1660561	243938	2095049	359725
天　津	Tianjin	732313	434083	183690	642476	89534
河　北	Hebei	791508	359830	262666	651373	140134
山　西	Shanxi	1073208	420990	426611	1014376	58832
内蒙古	Inner Mongolia	1142760	368980	450712	927193	215567
辽　宁	Liaoning	1019812	406961	386879	900457	119354
吉　林	Jilin	435736	164019	209531	184491	251246
黑龙江	Heilongjiang	158598	71723	69126	110195	48403
上　海	Shanghai	2544784	1716577	388578	2063438	481299
江　苏	Jiangsu	4349744	1574050	1776093	3397716	953502
浙　江	Zhejiang	3325824	1468025	1075301	2597784	728040
安　徽	Anhui	2186973	885525	751520	1482174	704799
福　建	Fujian	860748	479655	215944	467420	393328
江　西	Jiangxi	607977	248205	188940	368978	238999
山　东	Shandong	3400472	1227023	1511784	2290758	1109713
河　南	Henan	1287301	555148	444714	604132	683169
湖　北	Hubei	2338504	907453	908390	1529232	809273
湖　南	Hunan	1172123	391398	500566	646651	525472
广　东	Guangdong	3715488	2072617	948658	2903837	819321
广　西	Guangxi	373257	180738	121177	303784	69473
海　南	Hainan	72188	44551	11710	77055	-4867
重　庆	Chongqing	1247720	522432	450107	654706	593014
四　川	Sichuan	2163570	929827	795681	1581508	582063
贵　州	Guizhou	410856	211447	138568	242511	168344
云　南	Yunnan	812055	463267	268777	453862	358193
西　藏	Tibet	36002	10767	20305	19394	16608
陕　西	Shaanxi	1576800	679212	566966	951375	625425
甘　肃	Gansu	475735	182723	205052	228437	247299
青　海	Qinghai	135121	40929	57476	71918	63203
宁　夏	Ningxia	151403	75540	44828	138249	13154
新　疆	Xinjiang	420680	112499	147432	226879	193801

4-3-7 续表 1 Continued 1

国有企业 State-owned Enterprises

单位：万元 Unit: 10000 yuan

地　区	Region	资产总计 Total Assets	#流动资产合计 Total Working Capitals	#固定资产合计 Total Fixed Assets	负债合计 Total Liabilities	所有者权益合计 Total Owners' Equities
全　国	**National Total**	**1022406**	**262223**	**500854**	**579527**	**442880**
北　京	Beijing	33204	21959	5985	25292	7911
天　津	Tianjin	15083	5132	6325	11029	4054
河　北	Hebei	42384	10501	24486	37674	4710
山　西	Shanxi	19510	4999	9689	14715	4795
内蒙古	Inner Mongolia	115270	18484	37642	37745	77525
辽　宁	Liaoning	36740	12000	23862	44510	-7769
吉　林	Jilin	69617	6547	53863	17428	52189
黑龙江	Heilongjiang	16031	-2216	16444	17883	-1853
上　海	Shanghai	20200	17079	1559	9923	10277
江　苏	Jiangsu	91923	29906	51128	81973	9950
浙　江	Zhejiang	16228	7102	3723	9777	6451
安　徽	Anhui	4646	2134	1397	3389	1257
福　建	Fujian	6371	4095	1660	2578	3793
江　西	Jiangxi	20533	4263	6422	10594	9939
山　东	Shandong	142926	45364	74604	106995	35930
河　南	Henan	5350	1705	2902	3215	2135
湖　北	Hubei	16961	6617	9173	6858	10103
湖　南	Hunan	11894	3460	6937	8679	3216
广　东	Guangdong	66163	24274	22660	36190	29973
广　西	Guangxi	7013	2278	4307	6290	723
海　南	Hainan	1424	293	1131	1774	-350
重　庆	Chongqing	1067	82	834	839	228
四　川	Sichuan	39680	11104	17662	34814	4866
贵　州	Guizhou	367	334	33	666	-299
云　南	Yunnan	6690	2377	3599	5176	1513
西　藏	Tibet					
陕　西	Shaanxi	19397	5612	11715	9083	10315
甘　肃	Gansu	53000	5659	46388	9602	43398
青　海	Qinghai					
宁　夏	Ningxia	1756	623	1096	763	994
新　疆	Xinjiang	140978	10456	53628	24073	116906

集体企业

Collective-owned Enterprises

单位：万元

Unit: 10000 yuan

地区	Region	资产总计 Total Assets	#流动资产合计 Total Working Capitals	#固定资产合计 Total Fixed Assets	负债合计 Total Liabilities	所有者权益合计 Total Owners' Equities
全国	**National Total**	**192010**	**93355**	**72062**	**120713**	**71296**
北京	Beijing	17979	5065	4376	13394	4586
天津	Tianjin	167	149	19	482	-315
河北	Hebei	2202	998	798	459	1744
山西	Shanxi	2924	1596	1164	1111	1813
内蒙古	Inner Mongolia	268	262	6	1006	-738
辽宁	Liaoning	334	207	127	634	-301
吉林	Jilin	1563	742	816	1344	218
黑龙江	Heilongjiang					
上海	Shanghai	26867	15579	8670	16691	10175
江苏	Jiangsu	27541	9288	15451	22453	5088
浙江	Zhejiang	53	53		177	-124
安徽	Anhui	478	423	55	6331	-5853
福建	Fujian	7622	6317	306	1214	6408
江西	Jiangxi					
山东	Shandong	20944	6565	12934	14004	6940
河南	Henan	7156	1617	5189	11616	-4459
湖北	Hubei	32742	18024	12268	7264	25478
湖南	Hunan	666	48	501	450	216
广东	Guangdong	29529	21858	2409	14641	14888
广西	Guangxi	688	484	139	428	260
海南	Hainan					
重庆	Chongqing	7543	2186	4680	2545	4998
四川	Sichuan	973	861	111	49	924
贵州	Guizhou	445	126	273	960	-515
云南	Yunnan	977	528	434	1335	-359
西藏	Tibet					
陕西	Shaanxi	2349	379	1336	2125	224
甘肃	Gansu					
青海	Qinghai					
宁夏	Ningxia					
新疆	Xinjiang					

4-3-7 续表 3 Continued 3

股份合作企业 单位：万元
Cooperative Enterprises Unit: 10000 yuan

地　区	Region	资产总计 Total Assets	#流动资产合计 Total Working Capitals	#固定资产合计 Total Fixed Assets	负债合计 Total Liabilities	所有者权益合计 Total Owners' Equities
全　国	**National Total**	**130782**	**88793**	**30354**	**96403**	**34376**
北　京	Beijing	23232	19510	1777	20673	2559
天　津	Tianjin					
河　北	Hebei	9752	1109	7415	8705	1047
山　西	Shanxi	148	74	74	19	128
内蒙古	Inner Mongolia					
辽　宁	Liaoning					
吉　林	Jilin					
黑龙江	Heilongjiang					
上　海	Shanghai	7369	5880	658	4713	2655
江　苏	Jiangsu	1145	523	591	695	450
浙　江	Zhejiang	3812	1955	867	6136	-2325
安　徽	Anhui					
福　建	Fujian					
江　西	Jiangxi	3599	3594	6	4503	-904
山　东	Shandong	1127	367	749	255	872
河　南	Henan	936	143	516	774	162
湖　北	Hubei	916	159	299	49	867
湖　南	Hunan	366	358		96	270
广　东	Guangdong	9462	6437	719	8125	1336
广　西	Guangxi	5127	4018	666	3181	1946
海　南	Hainan					
重　庆	Chongqing	192	132	46	26	166
四　川	Sichuan	63599	44534	15971	38453	25147
贵　州	Guizhou					
云　南	Yunnan					
西　藏	Tibet					
陕　西	Shaanxi					
甘　肃	Gansu					
青　海	Qinghai					
宁　夏	Ningxia					
新　疆	Xinjiang					

4-3-7 续表 4 Continued 4

联营企业
Joint Ownership Enterprises

单位：万元
Unit: 10000 yuan

地区	Region	资产总计 Total Assets	#流动资产合计 Total Working Capitals	#固定资产合计 Total Fixed Assets	负债合计 Total Liabilities	所有者权益合计 Total Owners' Equities
全国	**National Total**	**50674**	**21906**	**2635**	**31855**	**18820**
北京	Beijing					
天津	Tianjin					
河北	Hebei					
山西	Shanxi					
内蒙古	Inner Mongolia					
辽宁	Liaoning					
吉林	Jilin					
黑龙江	Heilongjiang					
上海	Shanghai	2211	175	2036	760	1451
江苏	Jiangsu	157	26	132	2	156
浙江	Zhejiang	246	144	102	46	200
安徽	Anhui					
福建	Fujian					
江西	Jiangxi					
山东	Shandong	954	803	141	241	713
河南	Henan					
湖北	Hubei	35647	15647		22174	13473
湖南	Hunan					
广东	Guangdong	10426	4316		8573	1853
广西	Guangxi					
海南	Hainan					
重庆	Chongqing					
四川	Sichuan					
贵州	Guizhou					
云南	Yunnan					
西藏	Tibet					
陕西	Shaanxi	63	35	14	12	51
甘肃	Gansu	970	760	210	47	923
青海	Qinghai					
宁夏	Ningxia					
新疆	Xinjiang					

有限责任公司
Limited Liability Corporations

单位：万元
Unit: 10000 yuan

地　区	Region	资产总计 Total Assets	#流动资产合计 Total Working Capitals	#固定资产合计 Total Fixed Assets	负债合计 Total Liabilities	所有者权益合计 Total Owners' Equities
全　国	**National Total**	**15716997**	**6959163**	**5530982**	**12143088**	**3574175**
北　京	Beijing	1023800	688084	116369	875020	148780
天　津	Tianjin	238246	161834	30923	254377	-16131
河　北	Hebei	207583	86576	76632	163105	44478
山　西	Shanxi	313881	83619	151565	284004	29877
内蒙古	Inner Mongolia	552428	174892	204789	559874	-7447
辽　宁	Liaoning	387521	171215	122590	325781	61740
吉　林	Jilin	155371	68113	62779	59194	96177
黑龙江	Heilongjiang	76493	47439	21865	62441	14052
上　海	Shanghai	618939	462872	80086	603037	15902
江　苏	Jiangsu	1805755	578068	848246	1495303	310452
浙　江	Zhejiang	869811	362835	356620	791790	78020
安　徽	Anhui	743693	312200	244147	519372	224321
福　建	Fujian	360914	197111	85057	223093	137821
江　西	Jiangxi	320176	138560	100440	189800	130375
山　东	Shandong	1633903	382172	909902	980678	653225
河　南	Henan	543057	258698	191109	298218	244838
湖　北	Hubei	1160753	484199	413141	936229	224524
湖　南	Hunan	228225	84172	86041	146389	81836
广　东	Guangdong	1814875	963830	527056	1497217	317927
广　西	Guangxi	146006	62804	47038	144787	1218
海　南	Hainan	37608	25350	4619	42933	-5324
重　庆	Chongqing	361077	169049	116330	187015	174062
四　川	Sichuan	775130	419526	218369	597935	177194
贵　州	Guizhou	83361	49428	23164	52563	30799
云　南	Yunnan	221501	92483	87095	117470	104031
西　藏	Tibet	3792	1379	716	1279	2513
陕　西	Shaanxi	742213	334823	291831	542167	200046
甘　肃	Gansu	152793	64323	57380	80784	72010
青　海	Qinghai	40133	4737	20840	16563	23570
宁　夏	Ningxia	29046	14383	5711	43729	-14683
新　疆	Xinjiang	68913	14389	28532	50941	17972

4-3-7 续表 6 Continued 6

股份有限公司

Share-holding Corporations Ltd.

单位：万元

Unit: 10000 yuan

地区	Region	资产总计 Total Assets	#流动资产合计 Total Working Capitals	#固定资产合计 Total Fixed Assets	负债合计 Total Liabilities	所有者权益合计 Total Owners' Equities
全国	**National Total**	**2439444**	**1127664**	**543500**	**1399106**	**1040335**
北京	Beijing	230481	123079	29592	58421	172060
天津	Tianjin	244576	114823	89782	190589	53986
河北	Hebei	13703	7961	5364	16637	-2934
山西	Shanxi	17708	12071	317	21127	-3419
内蒙古	Inner Mongolia	110152	48226	51940	46747	63405
辽宁	Liaoning	32130	3290	16590	39089	-6959
吉林	Jilin	22557	12831	7794	26439	-3882
黑龙江	Heilongjiang	3604	589	2154	2465	1139
上海	Shanghai	222119	124185	8523	127331	94787
江苏	Jiangsu	204115	132737	38974	168948	35168
浙江	Zhejiang	191237	64505	57324	108981	82256
安徽	Anhui	46041	14603	1646	37696	8345
福建	Fujian	7537	1297	4428	5011	2526
江西	Jiangxi	12816	6306	5578	6727	6089
山东	Shandong	142164	35837	38932	110555	31609
河南	Henan	128963	43034	19536	41187	87777
湖北	Hubei	59892	29273	10095	42169	17723
湖南	Hunan	16042	2298	10250	3259	12783
广东	Guangdong	200144	126387	12278	51308	148835
广西	Guangxi	14240	3400	10234	13539	701
海南	Hainan	13087	9850	1936	10843	2243
重庆	Chongqing	121323	22609	31265	67877	53446
四川	Sichuan	56643	19638	21890	45482	11161
贵州	Guizhou	9590	8987	255	8543	1047
云南	Yunnan	14953	12942	1677	11717	3236
西藏	Tibet					
陕西	Shaanxi	193046	92298	34204	70395	122650
甘肃	Gansu	19084	12047	5520	8354	10729
青海	Qinghai	18958	5824	10193	17958	1000
宁夏	Ningxia	15286	13298	1435	14560	726
新疆	Xinjiang	57253	23439	13794	25152	32102

私营企业　　单位：万元
Private Enterprises　　Unit: 10000 yuan

地　区	Region	资产总计 Total Assets	#流动资产合计 Total Working Capitals	#固定资产合计 Total Fixed Assets	负债合计 Total Liabilities	所有者权益合计 Total Owners' Equities
全　国	**National Total**	**21739106**	**10235557**	**7012347**	**15375143**	**6372491**
北　京	Beijing	1126079	802864	85840	1102249	23830
天　津	Tianjin	234191	152108	56642	185997	47891
河　北	Hebei	515883	252686	147971	424794	91090
山　西	Shanxi	716478	318048	262236	686873	29605
内蒙古	Inner Mongolia	358952	125307	153545	278687	80265
辽　宁	Liaoning	549663	214511	218758	478298	71365
吉　林	Jilin	171872	69857	75455	70229	101644
黑龙江	Heilongjiang	62242	25858	28487	27235	35007
上　海	Shanghai	1636969	1084813	284070	1291947	344975
江　苏	Jiangsu	2215673	821697	820128	1627431	589716
浙　江	Zhejiang	2239988	1029888	653820	1680509	559479
安　徽	Anhui	1392061	556132	504274	915361	476700
福　建	Fujian	470273	266636	121794	233010	237263
江　西	Jiangxi	247671	92691	76194	156941	90730
山　东	Shandong	1442576	744787	472659	1070675	371901
河　南	Henan	597110	248660	223359	248002	349109
湖　北	Hubei	1008669	348478	450725	509646	499023
湖　南	Hunan	911856	299841	395051	486907	424948
广　东	Guangdong	1563898	917668	372326	1281342	289956
广　西	Guangxi	200184	107755	58793	135559	64625
海　南	Hainan	20069	9058	4024	21504	-1435
重　庆	Chongqing	746893	326067	291560	393182	353712
四　川	Sichuan	1220055	430978	518612	862905	357150
贵　州	Guizhou	314762	151910	113771	178871	135892
云　南	Yunnan	564920	353721	174226	317031	247889
西　藏	Tibet	32210	9388	19589	18115	14094
陕　西	Shaanxi	598006	234159	219225	320801	277205
甘　肃	Gansu	245402	98333	94923	127814	117589
青　海	Qinghai	76031	30368	26443	37398	38633
宁　夏	Ningxia	105034	47152	36389	79124	25910
新　疆	Xinjiang	153436	64138	51458	126706	26730

4-3-7 续表 8 Continued 8

其他企业

Other Enterprises

单位：万元

Unit: 10000 yuan

地 区	Region	资产总计 Total Assets	#流动资产合计 Total Working Capitals	#固定资产合计 Total Fixed Assets	负债合计 Total Liabilities	所有者权益合计 Total Owners' Equities
全 国	**National Total**	**182625**	**78106**	**79000**	**81577**	**101050**
北 京	Beijing					
天 津	Tianjin	50	38		2	48
河 北	Hebei					
山 西	Shanxi	2560	584	1567	6527	-3967
内蒙古	Inner Mongolia	5691	1809	2790	3134	2557
辽 宁	Liaoning	13423	5739	4953	12145	1278
吉 林	Jilin	14756	5929	8826	9857	4900
黑龙江	Heilongjiang	229	53	176	171	57
上 海	Shanghai	10112	5994	2977	9035	1077
江 苏	Jiangsu	3435	1805	1445	912	2523
浙 江	Zhejiang	4450	1543	2847	367	4083
安 徽	Anhui	55	33		26	29
福 建	Fujian	8032	4200	2700	2514	5518
江 西	Jiangxi	3182	2792	300	413	2769
山 东	Shandong	15879	11128	1863	7355	8524
河 南	Henan	4729	1290	2103	1122	3607
湖 北	Hubei	22926	5056	12689	4844	18082
湖 南	Hunan	3073	1223	1786	871	2203
广 东	Guangdong	20992	7848	11210	6440	14552
广 西	Guangxi					
海 南	Hainan					
重 庆	Chongqing	9625	2308	5392	3222	6402
四 川	Sichuan	7490	3187	3067	1869	5621
贵 州	Guizhou	2330	662	1072	910	1421
云 南	Yunnan	3014	1216	1746	1132	1883
西 藏	Tibet					
陕 西	Shaanxi	21727	11905	8643	6793	14933
甘 肃	Gansu	4486	1602	630	1835	2651
青 海	Qinghai					
宁 夏	Ningxia	281	84	198	73	208
新 疆	Xinjiang	98	78	20	8	91

4-3-7 续表 9 Continued 9

港、澳、台商投资企业 单位：万元

Enterprises with Funds from Hongkong,Macao and Taiwan Unit: 10000 yuan

地　区	Region	资产总计 Total Assets	#流动资产合计 Total Working Capitals	#固定资产合计 Total Fixed Assets	负债合计 Total Liabilities	所有者权益合计 Total Owners' Equities
全　国	**National Total**	**4986416**	**2463878**	**1111892**	**3129542**	**1856874**
北　京	Beijing	1016731	611319	127971	476707	540024
天　津	Tianjin	69725	18119	23486	48519	21206
河　北	Hebei	4532	214	3831	3943	589
山　西	Shanxi	17450	1714	5635	13077	4373
内蒙古	Inner Mongolia	1681	1186	284	378	1303
辽　宁	Liaoning	85816	43802	21254	97957	-12140
吉　林	Jilin	388	314	74	78	310
黑龙江	Heilongjiang	16973	9354	839	4028	12945
上　海	Shanghai	1006759	564933	189817	698943	307816
江　苏	Jiangsu	269421	122670	96592	144558	124862
浙　江	Zhejiang	262944	63837	136022	234115	28829
安　徽	Anhui	367	182	185	148	218
福　建	Fujian	263837	80063	84229	219616	44221
江　西	Jiangxi	62196	23817	30153	60292	1904
山　东	Shandong	277632	41343	83845	216329	61303
河　南	Henan	7592	726	608	4657	2935
湖　北	Hubei	229553	64089	77897	161560	67994
湖　南	Hunan	1816	1198	359	738	1079
广　东	Guangdong	1168370	700885	175222	586900	581469
广　西	Guangxi	7623	6840	582	3529	4094
海　南	Hainan	32865	13335	15118	35541	-2675
重　庆	Chongqing	14106	9448	2627	8521	5584
四　川	Sichuan	124457	61738	22881	71158	53299
贵　州	Guizhou	210	24	186	167	44
云　南	Yunnan	16995	14723	2090	7119	9876
西　藏	Tibet					
陕　西	Shaanxi	24299	7672	8362	28901	-4603
甘　肃	Gansu	57	52	3	1	56
青　海	Qinghai					
宁　夏	Ningxia					
新　疆	Xinjiang	2021	281	1740	2062	-41

外商投资企业 单位：万元
Foreign Funded Enterprises Unit: 10000 yuan

地区	Region	资产总计 Total Assets	#流动资产合计 Total Working Capitals	#固定资产合计 Total Fixed Assets	负债合计 Total Liabilities	所有者权益合计 Total Owners' Equities
全国	**National Total**	**3559465**	**1323812**	**844096**	**2160661**	**1398803**
北京	Beijing	425248	190946	74433	296187	129061
天津	Tianjin	98669	20896	25892	56357	42313
河北	Hebei	464	429	5	83	382
山西	Shanxi	17186	3788	3930	7051	10136
内蒙古	Inner Mongolia	52044	34668	7695	28017	24028
辽宁	Liaoning	165776	34069	37870	91091	74685
吉林	Jilin	761	368	393	830	-70
黑龙江	Heilongjiang	2582	2133	106	1017	1565
上海	Shanghai	932066	464809	141078	692984	239082
江苏	Jiangsu	330653	105189	72619	145381	185272
浙江	Zhejiang	253308	85534	108274	180628	72680
安徽	Anhui	44222	2479	276	27720	16501
福建	Fujian	85327	16798	28280	52572	32755
江西	Jiangxi	21851	689	6973	10937	10914
山东	Shandong	80690	22588	23454	48009	32681
河南	Henan	42092	11095	22259	41251	841
湖北	Hubei	34964	13189	20671	28303	6660
湖南	Hunan	56022	5825	28656	35616	20406
广东	Guangdong	601872	186766	143270	286408	315464
广西	Guangxi	21589	2527	6216	8513	13076
海南	Hainan					
重庆	Chongqing	89061	46437	29750	25566	63494
四川	Sichuan	109174	35317	42106	53686	55488
贵州	Guizhou					
云南	Yunnan	21679	8493	4842	10648	11031
西藏	Tibet					
陕西	Shaanxi	54712	22941	12084	25833	28878
甘肃	Gansu	11093	4787	1624	4054	7039
青海	Qinghai					
宁夏	Ningxia					
新疆	Xinjiang	6360	1052	1340	1919	4441

4-3-8 各地区限额以上餐饮业企业年末资产负债(按国民经济行业)

Assets and Liabilities of Enterprises above Designated Size of Catering Services by Region and Sector at the Year-end

正餐服务 单位：万元

Dinner Unit: 10000 yuan

地区	Region	资产总计 Total Assets	#流动资产合计 Total Working Capitals	#固定资产合计 Total Fixed Assets	负债合计 Total Liabilities	所有者权益合计 Total Owners' Equities
全国	**National Total**	**42056232**	**18856829**	**14045459**	**30446286**	**11618741**
北京	Beijing	2647380	1703694	291555	2221051	426329
天津	Tianjin	649322	369686	170540	585671	63348
河北	Hebei	778184	351778	266048	642787	135397
山西	Shanxi	1052061	410485	420895	1004565	47496
内蒙古	Inner Mongolia	1144096	359386	452666	904856	239240
辽宁	Liaoning	969250	382425	361910	886669	82581
吉林	Jilin	412679	156955	199439	178180	234499
黑龙江	Heilongjiang	161989	78078	64710	103987	58002
上海	Shanghai	3073386	1998954	461010	2411492	661847
江苏	Jiangsu	4431491	1580589	1817696	3414934	1018030
浙江	Zhejiang	3377986	1448383	1208368	2666084	711902
安徽	Anhui	2028138	773071	700246	1382701	645437
福建	Fujian	961348	465375	274018	604006	357342
江西	Jiangxi	664557	269135	216952	427059	237498
山东	Shandong	3567824	1217377	1570643	2435765	1132059
河南	Henan	1216769	520046	417011	567200	649568
湖北	Hubei	2325089	873514	943633	1550005	775085
湖南	Hunan	1131623	377742	488116	625661	505962
广东	Guangdong	3788302	2138831	965582	2964430	831542
广西	Guangxi	335040	162855	110242	278861	56179
海南	Hainan	98451	51637	26544	109042	-10591
重庆	Chongqing	1206716	511198	435098	595334	611383
四川	Sichuan	2159967	921147	811293	1582084	577883
贵州	Guizhou	394771	200530	135042	234377	160394
云南	Yunnan	797301	459015	262512	447719	349582
西藏	Tibet	31887	9043	19590	17961	13927
陕西	Shaanxi	1555538	671673	555950	954007	601531
甘肃	Gansu	432357	177070	169420	222076	210281
青海	Qinghai	134621	40459	57446	71918	62703
宁夏	Ningxia	151403	75540	44828	138249	13154
新疆	Xinjiang	376706	101158	126456	217555	159151

快餐服务
Snack

单位：万元
Unit: 10000 yuan

地 区	Region	资产总计 Total Assets	#流动资产合计 Total Working Capitals	#固定资产合计 Total Fixed Assets	负债合计 Total Liabilities	所有者权益合计 Total Owners' Equities
全 国	**National Total**	**5393940**	**2180526**	**1304032**	**3107112**	**2286829**
北 京	Beijing	888750	486112	129091	447119	441631
天 津	Tianjin	176951	45491	52570	108217	68733
河 北	Hebei	1366	1060	137	403	964
山 西	Shanxi	50521	15480	10583	29356	21166
内蒙古	Inner Mongolia	47559	42843	3800	46373	1187
辽 宁	Liaoning	240498	67896	64425	186110	54388
吉 林	Jilin	19626	4863	8903	5516	14110
黑龙江	Heilongjiang	15469	4638	5159	10701	4768
上 海	Shanghai	679215	314509	159890	415564	263651
江 苏	Jiangsu	381007	140562	98902	210986	170021
浙 江	Zhejiang	380995	113388	95601	300855	80141
安 徽	Anhui	189511	108913	47067	123075	66436
福 建	Fujian	209452	84244	49502	124737	84715
江 西	Jiangxi	26376	3205	8395	12866	13510
山 东	Shandong	147123	46007	41001	97924	49199
河 南	Henan	82095	25790	34479	56738	25358
湖 北	Hubei	135505	20733	47506	93673	41831
湖 南	Hunan	93371	17724	40151	55128	38243
广 东	Guangdong	1157743	472433	248299	565211	592532
广 西	Guangxi	52189	16224	14231	26453	25736
海 南	Hainan	6602	6249	284	3554	3049
重 庆	Chongqing	71877	32975	18372	35933	35943
四 川	Sichuan	122597	45061	33433	69670	52927
贵 州	Guizhou	1902	1176	524	655	1247
云 南	Yunnan	31314	9719	9158	13926	17388
西 藏	Tibet	2850	1299	665	432	2418
陕 西	Shaanxi	80678	30098	24669	43261	37416
甘 肃	Gansu	51967	9544	36235	9561	42405
青 海	Qinghai	500	470	30		500
宁 夏	Ningxia					
新 疆	Xinjiang	48331	11820	20970	13115	35216

4-3-8 续表 2 Continued 2

饮料及冷饮服务

Beverage and Cold Drink

单位：万元

Unit: 10000 yuan

地　区	Region	资产总计 Total Assets	#流动资产合计 Total Working Capitals	#固定资产合计 Total Fixed Assets	负债合计 Total Liabilities	所有者权益合计 Total Owners' Equities
全　国	**National Total**	**1339984**	**781463**	**165803**	**809465**	**530521**
北　京	Beijing	226648	155512	17959	109719	116929
天　津	Tianjin	6041	5695	169	7749	-1708
河　北	Hebei					
山　西	Shanxi					
内蒙古	Inner Mongolia					
辽　宁	Liaoning	19002	12054	1600	4608	14395
吉　林	Jilin	621	510	111	101	520
黑龙江	Heilongjiang	363	162	201	279	84
上　海	Shanghai	556107	299440	78217	493032	63075
江　苏	Jiangsu	40488	19380	6563	20252	20236
浙　江	Zhejiang	17012	8705	1562	11960	5052
安　徽	Anhui	1543	683	421	1180	363
福　建	Fujian	8264	2888	2593	2872	5392
江　西	Jiangxi	174	42	132	91	83
山　东	Shandong	12297	7477	1031	3299	8999
河　南	Henan	2238	471	1768	236	2002
湖　北	Hubei	65575	33902	8435	23192	42383
湖　南	Hunan	1112	494	601	568	544
广　东	Guangdong	272125	169289	27417	86530	185595
广　西	Guangxi	15013	10884	3418	10485	4528
海　南	Hainan					
重　庆	Chongqing	1405	316	226	1649	-244
四　川	Sichuan	87171	49137	11592	28665	58506
贵　州	Guizhou	1547	1182	14	1257	290
云　南	Yunnan	2871	2321	517	868	2004
西　藏	Tibet	315	315		202	113
陕　西	Shaanxi	1163	241	905	50	1113
甘　肃	Gansu	889	363	351	621	267
青　海	Qinghai					
宁　夏	Ningxia					
新　疆	Xinjiang					

4-3-8 续表 3 Continued 3

其他餐饮业

Others

单位：万元

Unit: 10000 yuan

地 区	Region	资产总计 Total Assets	#流动资产合计 Total Working Capitals	#固定资产合计 Total Fixed Assets	负债合计 Total Liabilities	所有者权益合计 Total Owners' Equities
全 国	**National Total**	**1229761**	**835632**	**212417**	**754756**	**475006**
北 京	Beijing	133976	117508	7737	90054	43922
天 津	Tianjin	68393	52226	9790	45715	22678
河 北	Hebei	16954	7635	317	12209	4744
山 西	Shanxi	5262	526	4698	584	4679
内蒙古	Inner Mongolia	4831	2606	2225	4359	471
辽 宁	Liaoning	42654	22458	18068	12119	30535
吉 林	Jilin	3959	2374	1545	1602	2357
黑龙江	Heilongjiang	333	333		273	60
上 海	Shanghai	174902	133416	20356	135277	39624
江 苏	Jiangsu	96832	61378	22142	41484	55349
浙 江	Zhejiang	66081	46919	14066	33628	32454
安 徽	Anhui	12369	5518	4247	3087	9283
福 建	Fujian	30849	24010	2340	7995	22854
江 西	Jiangxi	917	330	588	191	726
山 东	Shandong	31550	20094	6409	18109	13441
河 南	Henan	35883	20662	14324	25866	10017
湖 北	Hubei	76852	56583	7383	52224	24627
湖 南	Hunan	3855	2462	714	1648	2208
广 东	Guangdong	267560	179715	25852	160974	106586
广 西	Guangxi	226	143	83	26	200
海 南	Hainan					
重 庆	Chongqing	70888	33829	28788	55877	15011
四 川	Sichuan	27465	11536	4350	25933	1532
贵 州	Guizhou	12846	8584	3175	6389	6457
云 南	Yunnan	19244	15427	3523	9117	10127
西 藏	Tibet	950	110	50	800	150
陕 西	Shaanxi	18433	7812	5888	8792	9640
甘 肃	Gansu	1673	584	673	234	1440
青 海	Qinghai					
宁 夏	Ningxia					
新 疆	Xinjiang	4024	854	3086	190	3834

4-4-1 限额以上住宿和餐饮业企业损益及分配

项 目	Item	主营业务收入 Revenue from Principal Business	主营业务成本 Cost of Principal Business
总 计	**Total**	**87355618**	**40889790**
一、住宿业	**Hotels**	**37315323**	**15015461**
#国有控股	State-controlled Enterprises	9392405	3477601
(一)按登记注册类型分	**by Type of Registration**		
1.内资企业	**Domestic Funded Enterprises**	**32089158**	**13250474**
国有企业	State-owned Enterprises	3370526	1215661
集体企业	Collective-owned Enterprises	376139	140075
股份合作企业	Cooperative Enterprises	73559	29264
联营企业	Joint Ownership Enterprises	35637	10723
国有联营企业	State Joint Ownership Enterprises	20813	6324
集体联营企业	Collective Joint Ownership Enterprises	4499	1802
国有与集体联营企业	Joint State-collective Enterprises	6193	1075
其他联营企业	Other Joint Ownership Enterprises	4133	1524
有限责任公司	Limited Liability Corporations	15197400	5938836
国有独资公司	State Sole Funded Corporations	1449262	573782
其他有限责任公司	Other Limited Liability Corporations	13748138	5365055
股份有限公司	Share-holding Corporations Ltd.	1152632	513242
私营企业	Private Enterprises	11732298	5318229
私营独资企业	Private-funded Enterprises	811046	498540
私营合伙企业	Private Partnership Enterprises	224789	131009
私营有限责任公司	Private Limited Liability Corporations	10168876	4417502
私营股份有限公司	Private Share-holding Corporations Ltd.	527589	271176
其他企业	Other Enterprises	150977	84447
2.港、澳、台商投资企业	**Enterprises with Funds from Hongkong, Macao and Taiwan**	**3397181**	**1153361**
合资经营企业	Joint-venture Enterprises	1401186	428493
合作经营企业	Cooperative Enterprises	371772	156708
独资经营企业	Enterprises with Sole Investment	1495941	519157
投资股份有限公司	Share-holding Corporations Ltd. with Investment	99114	37135
其他港澳台商投资企业	Other Enterprises with Funds from Hongkong, Macao and Taiwan	29178	11870
3.外商投资企业	**Foreign Funded Enterprises**	**1828982**	**611626**
中外合资经营企业	Joint-venture Enterprises	785413	191534
中外合作经营企业	Cooperative Enterprises	313484	156308
外资企业	Enterprises with Sole Foreign Investment	614074	216342
外商投资股份有限公司	Share-holding Corporations Ltd. with Foreign Investment	32092	8122
其他外商投资企业	Other Foreign Funded Enterprises	83923	39321
(二)按国民经济行业分	**by Sector**		
旅游饭店	Tourist Hotel	28936704	11127345
一般旅馆	Fonda	7519520	3492344
其他住宿业	Others	859102	395772

Income and Distribution of Enterprises above Designated Size of Hotels and Catering Services

单位：万元

Unit: 10000 yuan

主营业务税金及附加 Taxes and Other Charges on Principal Business	主营业务利润 Profits from Principal Business	其他业务利润 Profits from Other Business	销售费用 Selling Expenses	管理费用 Administrative Expenses
1172776	**45293052**	**1099768**	**25285759**	**16412952**
689399	**21610463**	**638161**	**10500711**	**10516976**
220922	5693882	157079	2918812	3084412
567883	**18270801**	**512544**	**9222024**	**8751621**
62977	2091888	52247	1138608	1126234
6132	229932	17486	123586	86378
1358	42937	2731	21442	17587
402	24512	121	16674	6230
292	14197		11068	2356
37	2660	29	1587	1066
49	5069	92	2558	2191
23	2586		1462	619
290250	8968314	243560	4412687	4527428
32653	842827	24347	405016	508464
257598	8125485	219216	4007668	4018965
25938	613452	35368	313807	309917
177945	6236124	158251	3167313	2647401
20380	292126	6483	100913	86755
5276	88504	2228	38032	30923
142334	5609040	143732	2922386	2427896
9960	246453	5813	105983	101833
2889	63641	2782	27914	30449
82393	**2161427**	**70347**	**815927**	**1166788**
38400	934293	35733	361969	469020
8135	206929	3260	69418	82337
32920	943864	26530	345821	581349
1670	60309	4577	33488	24644
1273	16035	245	5233	9439
39118	**1178238**	**55268**	**462762**	**598572**
22930	570949	37754	222161	283121
2593	154583	7215	73418	78226
12393	385339	8861	147576	203456
477	23493	131	7440	11221
726	43876	1308	12169	22549
554676	17254683	533348	8411209	8594831
117162	3910014	92431	1897179	1694258
17564	445766	12384	192324	227889

项　目	Item	财务费用 Financial Expenses	#利息支出 Interest Expenses
总　计	**Total**	**2314113**	**1427899**
一、住宿业	**Hotels**	**1708149**	**1147946**
#国有控股	State-controlled Enterprises	254127	219358
(一)按登记注册类型分	**by Type of Registration**		
1.内资企业	**Domestic Funded Enterprises**	**1446978**	**930995**
国有企业	State-owned Enterprises	26027	29105
集体企业	Collective-owned Enterprises	4329	2218
股份合作企业	Cooperative Enterprises	2909	1949
联营企业	Joint Ownership Enterprises	468	399
国有联营企业	State Joint Ownership Enterprises	515	397
集体联营企业	Collective Joint Ownership Enterprises	3	2
国有与集体联营企业	Joint State-collective Enterprises	-71	
其他联营企业	Other Joint Ownership Enterprises	22	
有限责任公司	Limited Liability Corporations	817994	564806
国有独资公司	State Sole Funded Corporations	47452	35975
其他有限责任公司	Other Limited Liability Corporations	770537	528832
股份有限公司	Share-holding Corporations Ltd.	50156	29183
私营企业	Private Enterprises	542904	301672
私营独资企业	Private-funded Enterprises	18921	8622
私营合伙企业	Private Partnership Enterprises	4388	2044
私营有限责任公司	Private Limited Liability Corporations	494219	275893
私营股份有限公司	Private Share-holding Corporations Ltd.	25384	15113
其他企业	Other Enterprises	2203	1666
2.港、澳、台商投资企业	**Enterprises with Funds from Hongkong, Macao and Taiwan**	**194741**	**164504**
合资经营企业	Joint-venture Enterprises	101415	76672
合作经营企业	Cooperative Enterprises	3776	4949
独资经营企业	Enterprises with Sole Investment	88231	80348
投资股份有限公司	Share-holding Corporations Ltd. with Investment	1112	1732
其他港澳台商投资企业	Other Enterprises with Funds from Hongkong, Macao and Taiwan	203	803
3.外商投资企业	**Foreign Funded Enterprises**	**66433**	**52452**
中外合资经营企业	Joint-venture Enterprises	32048	20321
中外合作经营企业	Cooperative Enterprises	16852	21081
外资企业	Enterprises with Sole Foreign Investment	15202	10493
外商投资股份有限公司	Share-holding Corporations Ltd. with Foreign Investment	398	363
其他外商投资企业	Other Foreign Funded Enterprises	1932	194
(二)按国民经济行业分	**by Sector**		
旅游饭店	Tourist Hotel	1456336	1010551
一般旅馆	Fonda	201426	104423
其他住宿业	Others	50391	32974

4-4-1 Continued 1

单位：万元
Unit: 10000 yuan

营业利润 Operating Profits	利润总额 Total Profits	应交所得税 Income Tax Payable	应付职工薪酬 Payables to Employees	应交增值税 VAT Payable
2400028	**2672531**	**1120108**	**20053572**	**1950216**
-301261	**-124478**	**439575**	**10000317**	**1005348**
-285875	-187405	124690	3062697	242008
-602428	**-433678**	**300981**	**8749970**	**859953**
-126541	-36841	35179	1170773	89383
20998	24284	5958	99260	10786
866	-1064	1031	23026	2454
1306	2147	581	12554	785
356	1154	194	8509	449
-20	5	55	1502	154
486	503	150	1833	90
485	485	182	710	92
-520214	-421911	144459	4190436	431826
-78401	-58746	16890	501154	40493
-441808	-363168	127571	3689284	391333
25700	-12748	13202	300794	24059
-8857	8499	99441	2913512	297753
85762	80027	11208	121050	14797
17799	17100	1762	38153	4482
-127689	-103083	81518	2653740	267666
15276	14450	4953	100569	10813
4314	3953	1130	39624	2911
96368	**102755**	**67714**	**805952**	**86906**
46576	51505	26158	363806	35902
55717	57301	17086	82994	7135
-10579	-11091	24015	326458	39362
2884	3247	353	26991	3324
1773	1796	100	5703	1184
204799	**206448**	**70882**	**444397**	**58490**
168532	168183	50928	205400	20447
-8819	-6533	3102	71381	5670
32587	34024	15790	136117	30839
4497	4217	1012	8714	573
8004	6553	49	22789	960
-536474	-353549	338826	8126771	769195
205744	218206	88918	1681760	214197
29470	10864	11832	191788	21954

项　目	Item	主营业务收入 Revenue from Principal Business	主营业务成本 Cost of Principal Business
二、餐饮业	**Catering Services**	**50040296**	**25874328**
#国有控股	State-controlled Enterprises	2271633	1181389
(一)按登记注册类型分	**by Type of Registration**		
1.内资企业	**Domestic Funded Enterprises**	**35365310**	**19835958**
国有企业	State-owned Enterprises	559016	316298
集体企业	Collective-owned Enterprises	229718	156420
股份合作企业	Cooperative Enterprises	120180	67274
联营企业	Joint Ownership Enterprises	10501	7282
国有联营企业	State Joint Ownership Enterprises		
集体联营企业	Collective Joint Ownership Enterprises	7942	5879
国有与集体联营企业	Joint State-collective Enterprises		
其他联营企业	Other Joint Ownership Enterprises	2559	1403
有限责任公司	Limited Liability Corporations	11151172	5793612
国有独资公司	State Sole Funded Corporations	365939	200116
其他有限责任公司	Other Limited Liability Corporations	10785233	5593498
股份有限公司	Share-holding Corporations Ltd.	1314300	709679
私营企业	Private Enterprises	21656585	12560931
私营独资企业	Private-funded Enterprises	2712117	1844123
私营合伙企业	Private Partnership Enterprises	295493	183595
私营有限责任公司	Private Limited Liability Corporations	17892333	10107202
私营股份有限公司	Private Share-holding Corporations Ltd.	756643	426016
其他企业	Other Enterprises	323847	224463
2.港、澳、台商投资企业	**Enterprises with Funds from Hongkong, Macao and Taiwan**	**6203992**	**2206492**
合资经营企业	Joint-venture Enterprises	1127472	468892
合作经营企业	Cooperative Enterprises	164593	72488
独资经营企业	Enterprises with Sole Investment	4879742	1652546
投资股份有限公司	Share-holding Corporations Ltd. with Investment	14511	6813
其他港澳台商投资企业	Other Enterprises with Funds from Hongkong, Macao and Taiwan	17670	5753
3.外商投资企业	**Foreign Funded Enterprises**	**8470999**	**3831883**
中外合资经营企业	Joint-venture Enterprises	1765263	766182
中外合作经营企业	Cooperative Enterprises	70703	54884
外资企业	Enterprises with Sole Foreign Investment	6042581	2756572
外商投资股份有限公司	Share-holding Corporations Ltd. with Foreign Investment	285932	126409
其他外商投资企业	Other Foreign Funded Enterprises	306520	127840
(二)按国民经济行业分	**by Sector**		
正餐服务	Dinner	34476939	18718389
快餐服务	Snack	11404614	5224585
饮料及冷饮服务	Beverage and Cold Drink	2017699	573451
其他餐饮业	Others	2141045	1357908

4-4-1 Continued 2

单位：万元
Unit: 10000 yuan

主营业务税金及附加 Taxes and Other Charges on Principal Business	主营业务利润 Profits from Principal Business	其他业务利润 Profits from Other Business	销售费用 Selling Expenses	管理费用 Administrative Expenses
483374	**23682594**	**461612**	**14785049**	**5895975**
25912	1064332	70415	681928	413464
450645	**15078707**	**354387**	**8849062**	**4482055**
9420	233298	14578	139137	124071
2469	70829	432	36563	22165
1026	51880	164	35924	16671
127	3092		890	1140
117	1946		436	762
10	1146		454	378
133348	5224212	151236	3277667	1576145
4038	161785	909	98046	76666
129310	5062425	150329	3179619	1499482
18435	586186	25712	350288	169847
277996	8817658	161295	4969625	2548630
56664	811330	7318	278366	207280
4553	107345	807	53976	28792
206507	7578624	144348	4458783	2224171
10273	320354	8823	178502	88389
7834	91550	973	38974	23387
12115	**3985385**	**47253**	**2942463**	**573616**
2385	656195	5171	467755	104623
1287	90818	15	66408	21213
8212	3218984	42065	2396759	443283
63	7635	3	4866	2202
170	11747		6677	2294
20623	**4618493**	**59969**	**2993526**	**840308**
1597	997484	8785	637665	167430
216	15603		5479	8644
17283	3268726	18345	2110272	606414
717	158806	1532	105678	31340
814	177866	31309	134435	26480
435892	15322658	355927	9135032	4507063
32542	6147487	94517	4184480	1047514
3856	1440392	5969	994601	124868
11092	772045	5198	470941	216535

项　目	Item	财务费用 Financial Expenses	#利息支出 Interest Expenses
二、餐饮业	**Catering Services**	**605964**	**279953**
#国有控股	State-controlled Enterprises	18033	6266
(一)按登记注册类型分	**by Type of Registration**		
1.内资企业	**Domestic Funded Enterprises**	**565160**	**258279**
国有企业	State-owned Enterprises	3342	994
集体企业	Collective-owned Enterprises	1623	391
股份合作企业	Cooperative Enterprises	959	414
联营企业	Joint Ownership Enterprises	36	2
国有联营企业	State Joint Ownership Enterprises		
集体联营企业	Collective Joint Ownership Enterprises	11	2
国有与集体联营企业	Joint State-collective Enterprises		
其他联营企业	Other Joint Ownership Enterprises	25	
有限责任公司	Limited Liability Corporations	181155	79009
国有独资公司	State Sole Funded Corporations	4829	398
其他有限责任公司	Other Limited Liability Corporations	176328	78614
股份有限公司	Share-holding Corporations Ltd.	40461	25509
私营企业	Private Enterprises	333039	149870
私营独资企业	Private-funded Enterprises	31553	9132
私营合伙企业	Private Partnership Enterprises	3147	502
私营有限责任公司	Private Limited Liability Corporations	279810	129076
私营股份有限公司	Private Share-holding Corporations Ltd.	18535	11161
其他企业	Other Enterprises	4546	2093
2.港、澳、台商投资企业	**Enterprises with Funds from Hongkong, Macao and Taiwan**	**37352**	**17082**
合资经营企业	Joint-venture Enterprises	8063	7891
合作经营企业	Cooperative Enterprises	998	162
独资经营企业	Enterprises with Sole Investment	28074	8882
投资股份有限公司	Share-holding Corporations Ltd. with Investment	195	144
其他港澳台商投资企业	Other Enterprises with Funds from Hongkong, Macao and Taiwan	23	3
3.外商投资企业	**Foreign Funded Enterprises**	**3455**	**4594**
中外合资经营企业	Joint-venture Enterprises	3713	2291
中外合作经营企业	Cooperative Enterprises	184	64
外资企业	Enterprises with Sole Foreign Investment	-1287	1546
外商投资股份有限公司	Share-holding Corporations Ltd. with Foreign Investment	624	2
其他外商投资企业	Other Foreign Funded Enterprises	221	691
(二)按国民经济行业分	**by Sector**		
正餐服务	Dinner	569288	267437
快餐服务	Snack	29488	7241
饮料及冷饮服务	Beverage and Cold Drink		2592
其他餐饮业	Others	7191	2685

单位：万元
Unit: 10000 yuan

营业利润 Operating Profits	利润总额 Total Profits	应交所得税 Income Tax Payablc	应付职工薪酬 Payables to Employccs	应交增值税 VAT Payable
2701292	**2797014**	**680532**	**10053254**	**944868**
51505	85415	28112	658570	55173
1450716	**1517887**	**340748**	**7174836**	**734950**
-28591	-6636	3608	143980	11693
11441	10195	2621	39413	4054
4219	4979	1408	22345	3988
1003	994	114	1056	14
739	730	54	718	13
264	264	60	338	1
278457	322317	118518	2807727	218853
-8324	-1537	2731	118503	10544
286779	323853	115786	2689227	208311
111068	110279	12237	434640	94545
1049931	1055097	200028	3684249	396203
296899	280157	32433	324690	48479
21671	20168	2789	48828	6456
693428	719240	156562	3173203	328613
37933	35535	8250	137537	12660
23189	20665	2215	41431	5609
491903	**490667**	**135939**	**1215462**	**19103**
78494	78329	24014	181985	-2071
-773	-889	2053	35428	5240
410964	409741	109817	990720	15150
378	683	15	3851	233
2840	2807	40	3475	552
758674	**788456**	**203850**	**1662960**	**190817**
193779	191863	51695	340767	3445
1242	1338	169	26316	4389
524554	554821	138493	1169414	179302
24745	29615	8290	58189	1655
14354	10820	5203	68274	2030
1354547	1440575	354996	7177196	739505
939561	942312	215380	1973419	31782
321929	331983	90214	491248	131284
85258	82141	19944	411392	42308

4-4-2 各地区限额以上住宿和餐饮业企业损益及分配

地区	Region	主营业务收入 Revenue from Principal Busines	主营业务成本 Cost of Principal Business	主营业务税金及附加 Taxes and Other Charges on Principal Business	主营业务利润 Profits from Principal Business	其他业务利润 Profits from Other Business	销售费用 Selling Expenses	管理费用 Administr-ative Expenses
全国	**National Total**	**87355618**	**40889790**	**1172776**	**45293052**	**1099768**	**25285759**	**16412952**
北京	Beijing	9792321	3533361	105194	6153766	103730	3670796	2025407
天津	Tianjin	1312543	581935	7287	723321	14671	458149	291460
河北	Hebei	1070909	471435	18231	581243	11122	378631	274361
山西	Shanxi	805345	361048	11255	433042	20853	299036	199397
内蒙古	Inner Mongolia	815843	389930	11260	414653	4839	241911	199403
辽宁	Liaoning	1645606	704765	25679	915162	26424	546075	385713
吉林	Jilin	538938	251117	10288	277533	42927	152401	134583
黑龙江	Heilongjiang	413518	180380	8348	224790	4740	126404	119316
上海	Shanghai	9453515	3743181	58308	5652026	218737	3463758	1654130
江苏	Jiangsu	6133185	2921332	73546	3138307	46461	1725368	1231637
浙江	Zhejiang	6029258	2558716	51337	3419205	97292	1914950	1332467
安徽	Anhui	2083202	1107530	33923	941749	18501	504384	352742
福建	Fujian	3912266	2150349	57870	1704047	57395	880146	627571
江西	Jiangxi	1114179	553688	22530	537961	17907	256929	216072
山东	Shandong	4700200	2533708	67420	2099072	71144	1086845	790310
河南	Henan	3005523	1674460	70765	1260298	28904	515224	441726
湖北	Hubei	3448911	1817467	58269	1573175	25839	856079	466730
湖南	Hunan	2883633	1556277	72064	1255292	25237	563176	502023
广东	Guangdong	12556094	5710843	125014	6720237	81417	3956052	2163226
广西	Guangxi	1163659	489501	19364	654794	18151	375666	258952
海南	Hainan	1178239	340157	24330	813752	23628	371546	449875
重庆	Chongqing	2977310	1768545	52612	1156153	16021	488119	371105
四川	Sichuan	3357891	1722155	55213	1580523	46872	844440	555836
贵州	Guizhou	998653	538532	17306	442815	7461	179706	207577
云南	Yunnan	1493295	795513	34837	662945	20277	314048	346441
西藏	Tibet	90467	31422	880	58165	371	36219	37478
陕西	Shaanxi	2888056	1652243	53177	1182636	22313	648790	444870
甘肃	Gansu	719848	382457	15281	322110	10270	180187	135188
青海	Qinghai	126280	60684	1795	63801	6297	41013	33046
宁夏	Ningxia	150780	71290	2277	77213	3195	52972	38977
新疆	Xinjiang	496151	235769	7116	253266	6772	156739	125333

Income and Distribution of Enterprises above Designated Size of Hotels and Catering Services by Region

单位：万元

Unit: 10000 yuan

财务费用 Financial Expenses	#利息支出 Interest Expenses	营业利润 Operating Profits	利润总额 Total Profits	应交所得税 Income Tax Payable	应付职工薪酬 Payables to Employees	应交增值税 VAT Payable
2314113	**1427899**	**2400028**	**2672531**	**1120108**	**20053572**	**1950216**
189019	189620	522518	575700	208429	2651228	138124
35055	16046	-25671	-16020	13511	334302	20587
62699	21289	-129294	-115341	4315	323694	23725
30349	19964	-101777	-97335	4045	387889	14469
19448	13518	-46715	-68198	2678	202287	58861
62654	29053	-93606	-66435	17871	245850	24354
18940	9704	-24486	-16062	2045	504150	8036
11640	6485	-26525	-22067	3820	79416	9353
109793	65208	617935	687517	191231	1855433	296119
159173	61349	65906	93323	72043	1220472	113854
231702	165930	59195	106732	65865	1648145	115677
75266	38649	27263	47566	29254	445853	35183
94734	49151	139955	131594	45815	703246	55409
46415	22156	28323	29578	5745	451852	93948
126881	64623	117697	144869	57032	942311	97476
86569	28835	232180	254788	43422	544643	64177
81318	37220	193042	183359	37783	630490	66424
94805	54312	152603	98243	22003	547052	49756
299376	207751	396624	463491	156447	2898874	280032
43204	33700	-10266	-7864	9193	264268	29959
46656	34510	-10810	-36588	10253	322984	38889
69139	46201	258213	232612	30541	447679	69401
117187	69495	107757	106130	33797	625941	67646
52465	34211	8212	12931	8592	208242	51674
55817	52666	-33708	-43190	11709	370481	35814
1375	851	-10441	-9069	374	31937	2539
46192	19499	56614	54905	22506	687808	52086
21785	16900	-5354	-3989	5173	179055	16998
5662	3790	-13140	-11222	294	63705	3484
6703	4617	-20202	-19616	516	73813	2892
12092	10596	-32014	-17811	3806	160472	13270

4-4-3 各地区限额以上住宿业企业损益及分配

地区	Region	主营业务收入 Revenue from Principal Business	主营业务成本 Cost of Principal Business	主营业务税金及附加 Taxes and Other Charges on Principal Business	主营业务利润 Profits from Principal Business	其他业务利润 Profits from Other Business	销售费用 Selling Expenses	管理费用 Administr-ative Expenses
全国	**National Total**	**37315323**	**15015461**	**689399**	**21610463**	**638161**	**10500711**	**10516976**
北京	Beijing	3675242	1014153	91565	2569524	53066	1128717	1313725
天津	Tianjin	393455	147650	3979	241826	4468	123982	174592
河北	Hebei	674022	270244	12587	391191	6219	253750	209692
山西	Shanxi	328373	122960	5903	199510	11583	131176	109838
内蒙古	Inner Mongolia	349449	135216	5927	208306	-1448	121245	103715
辽宁	Liaoning	661448	221770	12419	427259	19271	237750	255040
吉林	Jilin	279554	120942	5362	153250	10295	83798	86973
黑龙江	Heilongjiang	297713	116536	6091	175086	4295	94517	105282
上海	Shanghai	2752448	859037	44234	1849177	140600	750953	874092
江苏	Jiangsu	2303130	905631	36812	1360687	24694	700200	703694
浙江	Zhejiang	2873990	940778	32652	1900560	70102	980608	891555
安徽	Anhui	682055	323259	13606	345190	11927	166445	184564
福建	Fujian	1900492	885391	35790	979311	16678	479299	434513
江西	Jiangxi	681365	307057	15712	358596	10808	163542	167277
山东	Shandong	2033414	951042	31218	1051154	49981	549016	455740
河南	Henan	1639323	843595	37356	758372	16406	316704	319352
湖北	Hubei	1114243	521896	22090	570257	12267	285899	241494
湖南	Hunan	1565155	791147	42613	731395	16514	301928	368062
广东	Guangdong	5324586	2154919	74826	3094841	44959	1514817	1352622
广西	Guangxi	728950	260957	14359	453634	13823	246462	207144
海南	Hainan	1088353	301916	23186	763251	17076	336843	434450
重庆	Chongqing	872221	420462	16629	435130	7127	200528	181214
四川	Sichuan	1411919	628984	26789	756146	28930	387774	347464
贵州	Guizhou	645963	314888	12731	318344	3756	135422	161570
云南	Yunnan	887744	410638	24046	453060	15789	213604	284699
西藏	Tibet	80837	26895	765	53177	295	34109	35191
陕西	Shaanxi	1171395	579435	21777	570183	14292	302236	276853
甘肃	Gansu	398462	201956	9445	187061	5656	100423	91488
青海	Qinghai	82172	37024	1313	43835	4518	27470	26084
宁夏	Ningxia	82660	36693	1642	44325	644	31725	23412
新疆	Xinjiang	335190	162390	5975	166825	3570	99769	95585

Income and Distribution of Enterprises above Designated Size of Hotels by Region

单位：万元
Unit: 10000 yuan

财务费用 Financial Expenses	#利息支出 Interest Expenses	营业利润 Operating Profits	利润总额 Total Profits	应交所得税 Income Tax Payable	应付职工薪酬 Payables to Employees	应交增值税 VAT Payable
1708149	**1147946**	**-301261**	**-124478**	**439575**	**10000317**	**1005348**
165876	173065	156379	176863	101829	1143785	93221
21212	6538	-56350	-48354	1493	131667	9616
49735	17084	-119014	-107066	2365	226866	16033
18219	12114	-56387	-52006	762	277129	7656
6695	6667	-23411	-44657	1173	102597	8655
46587	24425	-121794	-93678	2068	135983	16667
14459	7497	-28112	-18664	689	63233	4871
8201	4633	-27542	-22560	2991	62121	7838
79090	58892	266824	296049	74038	601039	120137
106411	45010	-106065	-87570	16922	551547	53898
172302	135042	-81075	-49687	24429	1032375	67222
40704	24069	-37427	-32471	14959	165671	13331
78846	43283	19182	25683	21562	424697	33030
39149	18885	-3832	-703	1963	250287	15076
69242	37287	-6185	14926	20895	451064	41992
62074	22622	74558	98944	23230	338490	36414
43685	23010	16463	12795	6698	233187	28783
70660	44771	48618	9484	11633	312970	27163
253704	189105	47216	78472	57421	1347750	151882
35813	29705	-26253	-23852	3160	176553	22914
45692	33766	-10273	-36117	9479	294670	36907
47970	34940	12405	2607	8271	172381	33079
77761	48049	-31179	-26397	9476	320609	35162
46429	30039	-20466	-16368	5525	146647	45660
46251	39032	-75865	-83498	5469	262773	24161
1156	831	-10814	-9523	272	29057	2429
27108	11042	-27573	-25967	6200	422373	25503
16784	13408	-20359	-19065	2160	98958	12064
4154	2740	-10992	-9419	244	50115	2075
4305	3402	-13989	-13990	248	55752	1616
7875	6993	-27949	-18689	1951	117971	10293

4-4-3 续表

国有控股

State-controlled Enterprises

地　区	Region	主营业务收入 Revenue from Principal Business	主营业务成本 Cost of Principal Business	主营业务税金及附加 Taxes and Other Charges on Principal Business	主营业务利润 Profits from Principal Business	其他业务利润 Profits from Other Business	销售费用 Selling Expenses	管理费用 Administrative Expenses
全　国	**National Total**	**9392405**	**3477601**	**220922**	**5693882**	**157079**	**2918812**	**3084412**
北　京	Beijing	1804332	461725	57223	1285384	12172	558819	701460
天　津	Tianjin	141653	63592	1586	76475	1626	38766	61565
河　北	Hebei	202035	89678	4510	107847	2365	82331	59558
山　西	Shanxi	118806	39371	3471	75964	9175	50438	46763
内蒙古	Inner Mongolia	68156	31270	1577	35309	-10125	22909	20669
辽　宁	Liaoning	177201	66132	3253	107816	12461	59452	73513
吉　林	Jilin	78787	31633	1877	45277	3205	30372	30662
黑龙江	Heilongjiang	108300	50985	2106	55209	2716	31341	36102
上　海	Shanghai	1098468	356617	20642	721209	54186	314531	347891
江　苏	Jiangsu	712898	283616	17972	411310	10708	227139	249875
浙　江	Zhejiang	597387	186304	10046	401037	7156	211168	190178
安　徽	Anhui	111855	48291	2159	61405	520	36672	34352
福　建	Fujian	359046	147303	5289	206454	5860	119660	94158
江　西	Jiangxi	132867	57115	3093	72659	1142	42836	39659
山　东	Shandong	510494	199828	8171	302495	9838	189571	139275
河　南	Henan	236055	96354	5777	133924	4257	70835	68401
湖　北	Hubei	143191	64052	3648	75491	1972	36572	35988
湖　南	Hunan	255842	119496	8268	128078	3732	52006	89951
广　东	Guangdong	895211	318998	17301	558912	5417	267015	256814
广　西	Guangxi	122941	51586	3057	68298	2417	45193	36309
海　南	Hainan	135661	43445	4747	87469	-164	27040	59909
重　庆	Chongqing	149991	72500	2977	74514	385	44613	42412
四　川	Sichuan	190122	71310	3246	115566	3219	71664	58379
贵　州	Guizhou	118217	65129	2360	50728	1395	26760	29505
云　南	Yunnan	254761	121470	10591	122700	4956	65084	91741
西　藏	Tibet	31571	9357	264	21950	29	17157	12639
陕　西	Shaanxi	252214	123927	7159	121128	660	71123	78576
甘　肃	Gansu	150669	77300	4028	69341	765	40334	35826
青　海	Qinghai	32797	16802	563	15432	4066	12109	9957
宁　夏	Ningxia	23218	13883	499	8836		9484	5718
新　疆	Xinjiang	177659	98532	3462	75665	968	45818	46607

4-4-3 Continued

单位：万元
Unit: 10000 yuan

财务费用 Financial Expenses	#利息支出 Interest Expenses	营业利润 Operating Profits	利润总额 Total Profits	应交所得税 Income Tax Payable	应付职工薪酬 Payables to Employees	应交增值税 VAT Payable
254127	**219358**	**-285875**	**-187405**	**124690**	**3062697**	**242008**
60770	70687	-13421	-2909	32192	642610	46200
9952	5611	-32574	-25768	616	62962	3159
2898	1260	-33059	-27058	623	72605	5082
2347	1758	-23035	-20053	108	52311	3309
1005	619	-8622	-16524	256	33768	1822
3376	3326	-23981	-22256	241	44344	5738
1524	-16	-15814	-9994	233	23129	2132
892	533	-8997	-5842	1014	27333	3271
14282	16467	94125	118405	29899	308372	26941
22062	8799	-63712	-43345	5134	202610	15835
27004	19485	-12350	-13655	8829	186913	16165
5612	1351	-13283	-11964	291	35754	2319
4039	2066	3202	4959	5308	115434	5574
1153	509	-8499	-1945	805	35716	2597
7014	12965	-28167	-10982	2844	161320	12453
6145	1987	-7073	-2548	1273	70728	5585
7691	7216	-2843	-2531	587	38332	3720
8732	6916	24302	-7247	3907	67884	4773
16232	15188	55437	65988	18950	299952	25846
3634	3125	-12172	-11950	577	49034	5142
815	661	978	463	4396	42617	4036
9941	5667	-20941	-20507	278	46237	4457
6062	4532	-17939	-15537	1556	72830	5742
6977	6712	-10705	-9766	1027	38787	3477
14390	14995	-41661	-39465	972	76239	7824
4	13	-2378	-1449	225	13336	1145
4726	2483	-28794	-28392	224	78772	5959
4434	4195	-11776	-10410	836	36490	4844
114	7	-4585	-4289	52	15443	1074
36	15	-6136	-6271	20	40063	538
264	226	-11402	-4563	1417	70772	5249

4-4-4 各地区限额以上住宿业企业损益及分配(按登记注册类型分)

内资企业

Domestic Funded Enterprises

地　区	Region	主营业务收入 Revenue from Principal Business	主营业务成本 Cost of Principal Business	主营业务税金及附加 Taxes and Other Charges on Principal Business	主营业务利润 Profits from Principal Business	其他业务利润 Profits from Other Business	销售费用 Selling Expenses	管理费用 Administrative Expense
全　国	**National Total**	**32089158**	**13250474**	**567883**	**18270801**	**512544**	**9222024**	**8751621**
北　京	Beijing	2701399	754644	52353	1894402	42750	904189	994624
天　津	Tianjin	343433	131810	3833	207790	4459	114300	154764
河　北	Hebei	642127	259259	11284	371584	6128	249366	190168
山　西	Shanxi	328373	122960	5903	199510	11583	131176	109838
内蒙古	Inner Mongolia	323995	120681	5833	197481	-4599	116830	95180
辽　宁	Liaoning	524309	187874	8762	327673	6482	188055	194143
吉　林	Jilin	253486	111694	4794	136998	10282	74352	78954
黑龙江	Heilongjiang	256247	107616	4656	143975	4173	81296	77297
上　海	Shanghai	2005425	559922	27399	1418104	105938	652811	638304
江　苏	Jiangsu	2049451	822820	32326	1194305	14799	616583	606246
浙　江	Zhejiang	2530302	847489	28700	1654113	61952	870676	775827
安　徽	Anhui	632003	309239	13169	309595	5310	155051	149442
福　建	Fujian	1547195	742093	31434	773668	14965	393055	331561
江　西	Jiangxi	657100	297495	15465	344140	7547	155425	160403
山　东	Shandong	1911150	923330	28993	958827	43946	516502	396314
河　南	Henan	1584789	824036	36111	724642	13532	298706	293466
湖　北	Hubei	1029427	493184	20518	515725	12191	258990	213482
湖　南	Hunan	1493589	764753	40542	688294	16496	278183	349509
广　东	Guangdong	4213139	1709748	58080	2445311	34011	1226683	1056987
广　西	Guangxi	638683	242222	10300	386161	12132	218057	163146
海　南	Hainan	768456	210808	12812	544836	11540	265264	312379
重　庆	Chongqing	827033	404223	15095	407715	5901	191345	168399
四　川	Sichuan	1341354	601723	25964	713667	22749	373634	320010
贵　州	Guizhou	636140	310156	12304	313680	3756	133990	157976
云　南	Yunnan	828497	394378	22782	411337	15708	195987	256797
西　藏	Tibet	65914	22787	722	42405	295	31566	23697
陕　西	Shaanxi	1075468	540381	19939	515148	14168	277987	252662
甘　肃	Gansu	386851	198329	9092	179430	5656	96363	87139
青　海	Qinghai	77790	36343	1155	40292	4518	24628	24751
宁　夏	Ningxia	81976	36293	1635	44048	644	31549	23206
新　疆	Xinjiang	334057	162184	5928	165945	3532	99425	94950

Income and Distribution of Enterprises above Designated Size of Hotels by Region and Type of Registration

单位：万元

Unit: 10000 yuan

财务费用 Financial Expense	#利息支出 Interest Expenses	营业利润 Operating Profit	利润总额 Total Profit	应交所得税 Income Tax Payable	应付职工薪酬 Payables to Employees	应交增值税 VAT Payable
1446978	**930995**	**-602428**	**-433678**	**300981**	**8749970**	**859953**
106952	110788	-74297	-55517	34080	860942	70413
21380	6458	-61493	-53228	1049	116766	8622
47837	16583	-113034	-101091	2332	216027	15186
18219	12114	-56387	-52006	762	277129	7656
10385	6611	-23872	-30652	1173	97085	8205
42247	20133	-105964	-81177	1408	111012	13709
12800	7471	-25649	-16146	616	58588	4580
6378	2269	-15830	-10717	1857	54645	7243
37653	20474	158755	185005	47722	470874	99959
84695	42206	-72727	-52254	16053	483789	48317
142928	109559	-84318	-57256	18983	947070	58035
38943	19874	-21802	-24142	14959	152973	12402
53374	33078	25204	31381	16983	345488	27048
38337	18579	-3422	306	1924	244445	14985
55364	32007	-1816	20831	18936	422110	38031
57752	20728	87066	102297	23102	323858	35486
42261	21118	14567	12061	7656	209764	27023
64293	38987	54248	14999	11560	296371	25789
235359	166694	-8823	17574	38614	1087029	118113
31797	23385	-18126	-16080	3055	157621	19730
24944	14127	-16638	-40859	5521	220107	27917
45471	34749	4504	-1019	5552	161693	19711
77105	47652	-38400	-33310	7550	303064	32873
45877	29521	-19553	-15453	5444	144107	45417
44772	38375	-71859	-79387	5251	244563	22996
1157	831	-7549	-6257	272	24326	2219
25877	10091	-33752	-32032	3970	399526	22570
16761	13398	-19559	-18514	2156	95990	11893
3885	2740	-10132	-8525	244	50047	1996
4303	3402	-13883	-13884	248	55546	1616
7872	6993	-27887	-18626	1949	117415	10213

4-4-4 续表 1

国有企业

State-owned Enterprises

地 区	Region	主营业务收入 Revenue from Principal Business	主营业务成本 Cost of Principal Business	主营业务税金及附加 Taxes and Other Charges on Principal Business	主营业务利润 Profits from Principal Business	其他业务利润 Profits from Other Business	销售费用 Selling Expenses	管理费用 Administrative Expenses
全 国	**National Total**	**3370526**	**1215661**	**62977**	**2091888**	**52247**	**1138608**	**1126234**
北 京	Beijing	675642	164901	15559	495182	5337	215353	275603
天 津	Tianjin	39182	19082	417	19683	1	12810	11809
河 北	Hebei	135918	60374	2845	72699	2286	60861	41328
山 西	Shanxi	85692	26278	2657	56757	7948	36328	32026
内蒙古	Inner Mongolia	22952	11685	651	10616	-10751	8233	6295
辽 宁	Liaoning	95920	35957	1166	58797	692	32011	40642
吉 林	Jilin	64269	27257	906	36106	3233	22462	21349
黑龙江	Heilongjiang	66157	28343	1392	36422	1988	21747	23133
上 海	Shanghai	183223	34814	2082	146327	3806	59783	79686
江 苏	Jiangsu	153642	65091	1916	86635	1611	55063	60544
浙 江	Zhejiang	186847	52824	2843	131180	4924	68589	58362
安 徽	Anhui	23077	12175	175	10727	139	7127	5452
福 建	Fujian	94043	32504	1096	60443	1761	33521	28295
江 西	Jiangxi	68840	36524	1938	30378	891	18904	15790
山 东	Shandong	316632	134639	3943	178050	9309	105906	90502
河 南	Henan	143545	60624	3869	79052	4191	44572	38210
湖 北	Hubei	50545	21144	982	28419	1972	17780	11592
湖 南	Hunan	120049	62084	2561	55404	482	26581	29223
广 东	Guangdong	300689	96528	4912	199249	4560	101203	97461
广 西	Guangxi	66012	23656	1655	40701	2083	28002	19099
海 南	Hainan	10420	2545	108	7767		4696	4237
重 庆	Chongqing	50145	21611	791	27743	85	15428	15218
四 川	Sichuan	49450	18641	995	29814	802	20693	14229
贵 州	Guizhou	31705	17223	828	13654	651	5851	7214
云 南	Yunnan	67759	28498	1941	37320	2436	21266	22672
西 藏	Tibet	17739	5055	222	12462		10693	5901
陕 西	Shaanxi	79307	34764	1544	42999	481	23328	21306
甘 肃	Gansu	68419	30482	1633	36304	15	19466	18725
青 海	Qinghai	12579	7622	132	4825	1206	5954	4422
宁 夏	Ningxia	12065	3705	41	8319		9120	3514
新 疆	Xinjiang	78062	39031	1177	37854	108	25277	22395

单位：万元
Unit: 10000 yuan

财务费用 Financial Expenses	#利息支出 Interest Expenses	营业利润 Operating Profits	利润总额 Total Profits	应交所得税 Income Tax Payable	应付职工薪酬 Payables to Employees	应交增值税 VAT Payable
26027	**29105**	**-126541**	**-36841**	**35179**	**1170773**	**89383**
2282	5403	9415	17886	8322	259482	18302
457	6	-4353	-4158	364	28771	1392
1791	885	-27719	-21299	511	49433	3496
2010	1386	-14084	-11075	50	33108	2180
103	5	-3364	-13192	174	7911	725
441	276	-11273	-9606	95	29193	1549
543	-12	-7125	-3334	232	18661	2024
534	478	-7334	-3892	387	16012	1784
-5852	31	22173	37600	9026	58370	5803
1840	1241	-28133	-12467	622	44082	4559
1107	2060	7582	7447	3215	60761	3325
13	1	-1488	-1227	8	5337	264
88	307	983	2090	1355	30453	1821
479	71	-4186	-2601	114	16958	1068
140	849	-15021	-560	2167	104116	6289
3690	1041	-5204	-2805	604	41766	3221
388	147	-1040	-419	295	16012	1235
1701	1011	-2579	-982	1070	27528	2084
4804	5362	10054	22427	4198	113786	9302
2363	2214	-5205	-4678	189	26058	3904
135	6	-852	-450	77	4690	527
3123	3002	-5160	-5316	55	13125	2230
401	779	-4429	-4068	139	16624	1564
334	233	908	1036	365	9263	800
538	695	-6303	-5759	327	14169	1793
-28	3	-861	-571	156	7901	753
2084	1209	-3101	-3416	172	22482	1722
447	381	-2992	-2876	448	17303	2686
13		-4099	-3754		7404	246
32	15	-4340	-4497	2	35603	121
26	20	-7411	-2325	440	34411	2614

集体企业

Collective-owned Enterprises

地　区	Region	主营业务收入 Revenue from Principal Business	主营业务成本 Cost of Principal Business	主营业务税金及附加 Taxes and Other Charges on Principal Business	主营业务利润 Profits from Principal Business	其他业务利润 Profits from Other Business	销售费用 Selling Expenses	管理费用 Administrative Expenses
全　国	**National Total**	**376139**	**140075**	**6132**	**229932**	**17486**	**123586**	**86378**
北　京	Beijing	88122	11363	619	76140	12832	43330	24625
天　津	Tianjin	8359	4948	73	3338	14	1227	2632
河　北	Hebei	12028	5019	213	6796	973	4152	2222
山　西	Shanxi	4755	1896	108	2751		1723	2394
内蒙古	Inner Mongolia	251	103	1	147		141	112
辽　宁	Liaoning	9524	5040	114	4370		2794	2233
吉　林	Jilin	3640	2050	19	1571		828	700
黑龙江	Heilongjiang	4160	954	107	3099	3	1103	1415
上　海	Shanghai	15366	6605	266	8495	5	4694	4035
江　苏	Jiangsu	24153	8735	212	15206	478	10747	3170
浙　江	Zhejiang	22868	6449	244	16175	1551	9447	7019
安　徽	Anhui	1445	685	7	753		340	300
福　建	Fujian	7274	4743	104	2427	51	1333	481
江　西	Jiangxi							
山　东	Shandong	31291	17258	710	13323	575	5429	4547
河　南	Henan	41351	25027	680	15644		6817	4772
湖　北	Hubei	17061	5584	769	10708	427	4194	5092
湖　南	Hunan	17625	5797	167	11661	1	4754	4905
广　东	Guangdong	21384	9502	311	11571	479	7458	5795
广　西	Guangxi	4363	1677	113	2573		1742	815
海　南	Hainan	564	367	5	192			98
重　庆	Chongqing	9159	3926	180	5053		3456	1332
四　川	Sichuan	8404	2477	91	5836	97	3353	2090
贵　州	Guizhou	5800	2363	501	2936		346	527
云　南	Yunnan	4981	1455	36	3490		1792	1848
西　藏	Tibet	790	538	4	248			238
陕　西	Shaanxi	6452	3619	302	2531		868	1319
甘　肃	Gansu	3392	1380	147	1865		688	1232
青　海	Qinghai	199	102	9	88		29	107
宁　夏	Ningxia	232		1	231		83	105
新　疆	Xinjiang	1146	413	19	714		718	218

单位：万元

Unit: 10000 yuan

财务费用 Financial Expenses	#利息支出 Interest Expenses	营业利润 Operating Profits	利润总额 Total Profits	应交所得税 Income Tax Payable	应付职工薪酬 Payables to Employees	应交增值税 VAT Payable
4329	**2218**	**20998**	**24284**	**5958**	**99260**	**10786**
-85	34	9684	9834	2811	34104	3212
33		-537	-344	10	2773	194
138		285	288	1	3142	304
26		-1287	-977		1753	67
		-106	-106		146	8
11	1	-549	-467	30	2131	122
1		42	42	20	362	86
-11	1	612	596	90	554	142
27		-9	-4	86	3558	379
403	25	1597	1515	264	5165	586
3	1	-60	58	137	6223	753
34		85	58	43	482	52
47	56	603	614	39	1546	142
473	24	2879	3021	733	3711	804
1052	657	3204	3954	507	8377	959
587	512	1240	1361	234	5353	342
178	2	1931	1604	311	2118	239
586	481	-1273	190	130	6926	938
-4	1	80	84	142	939	218
1		93	93	12	238	51
79	22	681	719	132	2082	271
91	74	305	473	42	2446	292
162		1901	1901	137	389	
32	26	-168	-109	14	1539	331
42		-32	7	6	282	29
420	300	-147	-87		1299	149
1	1	-62	-52	13	810	76
1		-49	-40		139	
		44	44	11	71	7
1		11	14	3	602	33

股份合作企业

Cooperative Enterprises

地 区	Region	主营业务收入 Revenue from Principal Business	主营业务成本 Cost of Principal Business	主营业务税金及附加 Taxes and Other Charges on Principal Business	主营业务利润 Profits from Principal Business	其他业务利润 Profits from Other Business	销售费用 Selling Expenses	管理费用 Administr-ative Expenses
全 国	**National Total**	**73559**	**29264**	**1358**	**42937**	**2731**	**21442**	**17587**
北 京	Beijing	28748	8498	532	19718	361	10761	8327
天 津	Tianjin	315	138		177		39	114
河 北	Hebei							
山 西	Shanxi							
内 蒙 古	Inner Mongolia	422	210	3	209		56	149
辽 宁	Liaoning							
吉 林	Jilin	215	88	9	118		29	100
黑 龙 江	Heilongjiang	9848	3028	112	6708		3095	3334
上 海	Shanghai							
江 苏	Jiangsu							
浙 江	Zhejiang	2205	695	18	1492	18	937	534
安 徽	Anhui							
福 建	Fujian	1410	722	51	637		379	241
江 西	Jiangxi	4359	1554	72	2733		1185	740
山 东	Shandong	4923	2161	19	2743	2352	1385	1127
河 南	Henan	1875	833	46	996		635	392
湖 北	Hubei	1032	867		165		2	708
湖 南	Hunan	3663	2516	293	854		155	124
广 东	Guangdong	1876	421	22	1433		983	913
广 西	Guangxi	208	4	11	193		116	150
海 南	Hainan	1083	248	4	831		1064	226
重 庆	Chongqing							
四 川	Sichuan	1378	793	62	523		418	272
贵 州	Guizhou							
云 南	Yunnan	506	297	49	160			52
西 藏	Tibet							
陕 西	Shaanxi	9493	6191	55	3247		203	84
甘 肃	Gansu							
青 海	Qinghai							
宁 夏	Ningxia							
新 疆	Xinjiang							

4-4-4 Continued 3

单位：万元
Unit: 10000 yuan

财务费用 Financial Expenses	#利息支出 Interest Expense	营业利润 Operating Profits	利润总额 Total Profits	应交所得税 Income Tax Payable	应付职工薪酬 Payables to Employees	应交增值税 VAT Payable
2909	**1949**	**866**	**-1064**	**1031**	**23026**	**2454**
335	632	1014	1132	388	10321	1207
-4	-4	28	32		3159	
		4	4		161	11
		-11	-11		75	6
7	7	850	889	609	3240	888
426	421	-355	-359	7	729	70
7		-3	19	4	567	10
45		762			87	
195		36	41		1082	22
27	12	137	133	13	532	59
755		-1300	-1306		175	34
97		479			577	
7	5	-471	-475	10	763	19
1		-50	-50		78	
848	848	-1306	-1303		497	65
29	28	-162	89		220	32
1		108	101		143	30
133		1106			620	1

联营企业
Joint Ownership Enterprises

地 区	Region	主营业务收入 Revenue from Principal Business	主营业务成本 Cost of Principal Business	主营业务税金及附加 Taxes and Other Charges on Principal Business	主营业务利润 Profits from Principal Business	其他业务利润 Profits from Other Business	销售费用 Selling Expenses	管理费用 Administr-ative Expenses
全 国	**National Total**	**35637**	**10723**	**402**	**24512**	**121**	**16674**	**6230**
北 京	Beijing	3929	591	15	3323	92	2051	1266
天 津	Tianjin							
河 北	Hebei							
山 西	Shanxi							
内蒙古	Inner Mongolia	766	386	1	379		294	110
辽 宁	Liaoning	766	481		285		125	134
吉 林	Jilin							
黑龙江	Heilongjiang							
上 海	Shanghai	1139	388	26	725		441	471
江 苏	Jiangsu	3999	964	4	3031	29	2260	273
浙 江	Zhejiang	4676	1068	40	3568		1958	1528
安 徽	Anhui							
福 建	Fujian	9736	1794	263	7679		5720	1148
江 西	Jiangxi							
山 东	Shandong							
河 南	Henan	1721	939	17	765		11	16
湖 北	Hubei							
湖 南	Hunan							
广 东	Guangdong	2297	139	22	2136		1866	75
广 西	Guangxi							
海 南	Hainan							
重 庆	Chongqing							
四 川	Sichuan							
贵 州	Guizhou							
云 南	Yunnan	2403	600	12	1791		832	810
西 藏	Tibet							
陕 西	Shaanxi							
甘 肃	Gansu	3725	3268		457		966	179
青 海	Qinghai							
宁 夏	Ningxia							
新 疆	Xinjiang	480	105	2	373		150	220

单位：万元
Unit: 10000 yuan

财务费用 Financial Expenses	#利息支出 Interest Expenses	营业利润 Operating Profits	利润总额 Total Profits	应交 所得税 Income Tax Payable	应付职工 薪酬 Payables to Employees	应交 增值税 VAT Payable
468	**399**	**1306**	**2147**	**581**	**12554**	**785**
8		91	100	110	1080	120
		-25	-25		194	13
1		-1	-1		157	7
2		-189	-185		343	25
10	2	488	509	126	1403	94
-69		153	161	40	1252	28
446	397	365	394	4	4005	136
12		727	727	182	211	34
10		185	228	59	774	196
4		242	238	60	1061	81
43		-732			1921	51
1		2	1		153	

有限责任公司
Limited Liability Corporations

地 区	Region	主营业务收入 Revenue from Principal Business	主营业务成本 Cost of Principal Business	主营业务税金及附加 Taxes and Other Charges on Principal Business	主营业务利润 Profits from Principal Business	其他业务利润 Profits from Other Business	销售费用 Selling Expenses	管理费用 Administr-ative Expenses
全 国	**National Total**	**15197400**	**5938836**	**290250**	**8968314**	**243560**	**4412687**	**4527428**
北 京	Beijing	1419087	415605	32414	971068	17092	453897	522482
天 津	Tianjin	189345	71789	2770	114786	1920	59978	105170
河 北	Hebei	194089	70052	4402	119635	1562	74586	60235
山 西	Shanxi	85968	33269	1490	51209	1278	34933	28830
内 蒙 古	Inner Mongolia	170738	64891	3181	102666	4137	61552	52379
辽 宁	Liaoning	226035	75635	4553	145847	4138	83405	94588
吉 林	Jilin	113332	45917	2461	64954	4572	35942	37740
黑 龙 江	Heilongjiang	84011	34444	1568	47999	895	29172	27729
上 海	Shanghai	1074375	306940	20564	746871	75152	328698	335695
江 苏	Jiangsu	867915	290520	15844	561551	2922	283018	303962
浙 江	Zhejiang	1108558	363329	13798	731431	20279	368748	362153
安 徽	Anhui	281419	126941	6613	147865	3303	81012	79428
福 建	Fujian	780019	358881	17589	403549	10714	211014	179410
江 西	Jiangxi	335081	135462	6618	193001	3310	92109	92846
山 东	Shandong	676482	281227	10801	384454	11338	213555	157078
河 南	Henan	742331	361280	14991	366060	6377	155240	169905
湖 北	Hubei	460365	193837	8370	258158	2063	125968	114967
湖 南	Hunan	551250	250043	17141	284066	5073	109916	170051
广 东	Guangdong	2328246	975189	32533	1320524	12057	631629	573274
广 西	Guangxi	224404	81433	3754	139217	4989	71950	62396
海 南	Hainan	631979	173683	11876	446420	10455	190766	270744
重 庆	Chongqing	377115	170195	6571	200349	1609	97015	89521
四 川	Sichuan	582119	243539	11670	326910	9227	179018	153677
贵 州	Guizhou	289212	137863	5719	145630	2236	65429	73924
云 南	Yunnan	444886	202362	13558	228966	10287	105547	152486
西 藏	Tibet	25204	9903	148	15153	66	10652	10226
陕 西	Shaanxi	548823	259214	10042	279567	8642	161127	150923
甘 肃	Gansu	181132	96206	4444	80482	2168	46529	39401
青 海	Qinghai	25880	14041	595	11244	3251	5971	8529
宁 夏	Ningxia	33955	17746	664	15545	444	9707	8609
新 疆	Xinjiang	144045	77400	3508	63137	2004	34604	39070

单位：万元

Unit: 10000 yuan

财务费用 Financial Expenses	#利息支出 Interest Expenses	营业利润 Operating Profits	利润总额 Total Profits	应交所得税 Income Tax Payable	应付职工薪酬 Payables to Employees	应交增值税 VAT Payable
817994	**564806**	**-520214**	**-421911**	**144459**	**4190436**	**431826**
80284	84797	-67575	-53452	19755	429827	33542
17519	5671	-49173	-44133	454	54619	5157
15931	6708	-28614	-26209	648	59199	4780
6860	3728	-18112	-17265	138	34410	2098
5602	4152	-16734	-14554	748	55594	4457
16166	7089	-63463	-47108	504	42396	8861
8099	4746	-14858	-10279	170	26083	1393
2895	792	-9744	-9548	323	19240	1853
26639	10110	102124	116215	27756	268838	75511
33988	20705	-42539	-38435	6840	228783	19880
74351	57762	-45430	-41908	9760	293116	28741
20246	10195	-28214	-27449	899	78905	5642
31607	22046	3388	11230	10089	185305	14895
23783	12900	-12775	-7675	1253	173085	9318
28115	22632	-12518	-4065	4194	176006	14469
27419	11771	18012	30157	10622	162959	19618
21110	12523	2728	209	3191	103492	11828
30935	21513	-17037	-13562	4113	125308	10748
165122	120296	-31725	-24659	20012	582614	63734
13877	10404	-5059	-5827	1843	54345	6141
16583	7611	7895	-16606	5343	183996	18964
26115	19765	-11966	-13031	2233	88461	8262
36340	20996	-32082	-24226	3599	153113	15451
30443	21216	-22065	-18594	2684	70211	7152
30649	27876	-52475	-55434	3641	122824	15854
733	663	-4199	-3534	76	9240	659
13063	4282	-38098	-36281	1483	296672	11932
8288	7318	-13277	-14188	915	40747	5195
2440	2008	-4880	-4097	53	10555	1008
176	29	-2090	-2062	66	9483	773
2616	2502	-9659	-5541	1054	51010	3910

股份有限公司
Share-holding Corporations Ltd.

地　区	Region	主营业务收入 Revenue from Principal Business	主营业务成本 Cost of Principal Business	主营业务税金及附加 Taxes and Other Charges on Principal Business	主营业务利润 Profits from Principal Business	其他业务利润 Profits from Other Business	销售费用 Selling Expenses	管理费用 Administr-ative Expenses
全　国	**National Total**	**1152632**	**513242**	**25938**	**613452**	**35368**	**313807**	**309917**
北　京	Beijing	38814	21361	675	16778	2491	4866	29727
天　津	Tianjin	5303	1069	125	4109		2733	2026
河　北	Hebei	14225	4753	312	9160		4461	5932
山　西	Shanxi	8696	3993	115	4588		2657	2672
内蒙古	Inner Mongolia	9307	3643	66	5598	17	3963	3133
辽　宁	Liaoning	16748	4399	133	12216	1	8114	4081
吉　林	Jilin	12778	3394	450	8934	1945	5056	3771
黑龙江	Heilongjiang	14142	2609	387	11146	1	5347	7035
上　海	Shanghai	68905	25813	1348	41744	19216	23109	19294
江　苏	Jiangsu	228995	120072	6231	102692	583	52827	53041
浙　江	Zhejiang	69042	21217	1412	46413	768	24331	22666
安　徽	Anhui	16556	9751	483	6322		1104	4318
福　建	Fujian	28120	10205	404	17511	54	9374	7410
江　西	Jiangxi	34134	17454	1135	15545	1163	3957	9035
山　东	Shandong	93296	44464	1199	47633	1645	26095	18262
河　南	Henan	61887	29201	1691	30995	670	13312	9876
湖　北	Hubei	41778	16229	1080	24469	455	14686	10337
湖　南	Hunan	60327	31464	1919	26944	2903	11885	15945
广　东	Guangdong	129754	46524	2419	80811	82	38865	35410
广　西	Guangxi	38921	15865	420	22636	152	11285	11111
海　南	Hainan	23096	13518	385	9193	2	6311	3226
重　庆	Chongqing	18702	8905	365	9432	2283	3848	4665
四　川	Sichuan	45195	20878	963	23354	796	14227	12159
贵　州	Guizhou	5487	3070	397	2020		418	942
云　南	Yunnan	25586	12063	625	12898		7693	6656
西　藏	Tibet	2518	1036	86	1396	141	575	589
陕　西	Shaanxi	21088	12872	623	7593		4165	1882
甘　肃	Gansu	4944	1766	335	2843		2318	948
青　海	Qinghai	7320	1550	-2	5772		3785	2383
宁　夏	Ningxia							
新　疆	Xinjiang	6968	4104	157	2707		2440	1385

单位：万元
Unit: 10000 yuan

财务费用 Financial Expenses	#利息支出 Interest Expenses	营业利润 Operating Profits	利润总额 Total Profits	应交所得税 Income Tax Payable	应付职工薪酬 Payables to Employees	应交增值税 VAT Payable
50156	**29183**	**25700**	**-12748**	**13202**	**300794**	**24059**
1045	934	-16284	-21247	111	30004	1354
14		-668	-690	1	2005	86
105		-1014	-873	111	4574	546
33	19	-683	-62	2	2735	303
80	3	-1593	-1498	11	2241	248
27	2	488	517		4740	463
350	294	-132	13	9	2990	242
638	389	-1874	-1858	40	3083	1303
1539	1723	-1109	-663	843	22564	1375
16876	4837	-11435	-9649	2188	45465	3508
4250	3981	-2831	-2715	440	21638	1127
1789	1778	-832	751	333	3530	607
19	50	1022	1099	272	8344	344
1905	394	1092	494	50	5473	509
2210	900	1914	2307	641	15837	2160
2112	1779	6445	5934	1828	11789	919
2872	2133	-2535	-2141	295	11786	1329
3260	1990	40989	4046	2807	14661	722
3941	3298	22696	22278	2536	36988	2574
2154	2083	-373	-812	2	10885	1142
50	1	-311	-209	50	6490	304
584	145	543	379	29	3335	477
3090	2206	-6013	-6388	256	10913	1000
31	2	629	726	93	660	15
402	10	-1813	-1998	142	6683	603
20		184	420	14	612	68
269	4	1258	1113	71	4092	374
187		-611	-602	2	1258	42
9		-19	96	22	2952	119
295	228	-1430	-1516	3	2467	196

4-4-4 续表 7

私营企业
Private Enterprises

地　区	Region	主营业务收入 Revenue from Principal Business	主营业务成本 Cost of Principal Business	主营业务税金及附加 Taxes and Other Charges on Principal Business	主营业务利润 Profits from Principal Business	其他业务利润 Profits from Other Business	销售费用 Selling Expenses	管理费用 Administr-ative Expenses
全　国	**National Total**	**11732298**	**5318229**	**177945**	**6236124**	**158251**	**3167313**	**2647401**
北　京	Beijing	446781	132162	2539	312080	4546	173759	132363
天　津	Tianjin	97317	32590	430	64297	2523	37198	31791
河　北	Hebei	285867	119062	3512	163293	1307	105306	80452
山　西	Shanxi	141598	57114	1502	82982	2356	54566	43471
内蒙古	Inner Mongolia	117979	39056	1871	77052	1852	42022	32732
辽　宁	Liaoning	172975	64960	2764	105251	1615	61296	51896
吉　林	Jilin	55729	30068	863	24798	401	9858	15071
黑龙江	Heilongjiang	76823	37824	1045	37954	1286	20562	14407
上　海	Shanghai	655745	183094	2961	469690	7758	235554	195943
江　苏	Jiangsu	756237	334200	8048	413989	9175	206870	178658
浙　江	Zhejiang	1134966	401054	10339	723573	34412	396645	323552
安　徽	Anhui	308039	159133	5850	143056	1868	65220	59393
福　建	Fujian	620085	329172	11767	279146	2385	130426	114074
江　西	Jiangxi	208500	102675	5504	100321	2183	38279	41477
山　东	Shandong	775728	435155	12025	328548	17836	162815	123556
河　南	Henan	585214	340653	14565	229996	2294	77915	69859
湖　北	Hubei	454036	252401	9205	192430	7273	96184	70301
湖　南	Hunan	737255	410701	18395	308159	7959	124411	127908
广　东	Guangdong	1396076	561929	17287	816860	16989	439721	338541
广　西	Guangxi	304013	119380	4341	180292	4908	104524	69499
海　南	Hainan	100712	20448	433	79831	1084	62182	33421
重　庆	Chongqing	366995	196816	7013	163166	1814	71351	57309
四　川	Sichuan	644523	308461	12030	324032	11070	154216	136651
贵　州	Guizhou	301203	148535	4837	147831	869	60873	74753
云　南	Yunnan	279125	146772	6506	125847	2985	58460	71905
西　藏	Tibet	17717	6020	211	11486	11	7610	5806
陕　西	Shaanxi	400764	218072	7245	175447	4337	86751	74316
甘　肃	Gansu	123145	64070	2482	56593	3473	25915	26416
青　海	Qinghai	30582	12140	383	18059	61	8888	9281
宁　夏	Ningxia	35724	14842	930	19952	201	12640	10977
新　疆	Xinjiang	100845	39670	1062	60113	1420	35296	31622

4-4-4 Continued 7

单位：万元

Unit: 10000 yuan

财务费用 Financial Expenses	#利息支出 Interest Expenses	营业利润 Operating Profits	利润总额 Total Profits	应交所得税 Income Tax Payable	应付职工薪酬 Payables to Employees	应交增值税 VAT Payable
542904	**301672**	**-8857**	**8499**	**99441**	**2913512**	**297753**
23082	18986	-10348	-9478	2583	95942	12667
3347	785	-6684	-3830	213	23607	1786
29874	8991	-55972	-52998	1061	99678	6060
9289	6981	-22029	-22436	572	204323	2974
4594	2451	-2167	-1394	240	30140	2733
25576	12751	-31201	-24533	778	31293	2668
3796	2442	-3671	-2632	160	10043	819
2298	602	1540	2978	408	12366	1230
15347	8609	35163	31380	9847	114444	16713
31535	15397	8440	7350	5984	153205	19405
62862	45334	-43638	-20203	5383	563016	23984
16857	7901	8580	3657	13659	64144	5831
20944	10023	18508	15888	5192	113358	9520
12050	5189	11054	9503	503	44588	4058
24027	7485	19579	18989	10922	119141	14051
23320	5223	63369	63823	9343	97517	10627
16515	5804	14809	13688	3554	72578	12242
28120	14470	30970	24280	3240	125150	11886
60695	37236	-10406	-4874	11523	339048	40791
13403	8680	-7572	-4852	863	65019	8326
7325	5661	-22082	-22309	39	23990	7966
15020	11312	19606	15475	3103	53492	8378
37105	23568	3385	509	3461	118285	14310
14758	7982	-691	-287	2165	63095	37368
13105	9741	-11632	-16616	1043	97487	4177
386	158	-1736	-1790	20	5016	546
9436	3882	6334	7758	2072	72970	8160
7787	5694	-2045	-850	779	33765	3749
1423	733	-1361	-1006	122	28428	588
4096	3357	-7497	-7368	169	10389	715
4932	4244	-9462	-9323	440	27995	3425

其他企业
Other Enterprises

地区	Region	主营业务收入 Revenue from Principal Business	主营业务成本 Cost of Principal Business	主营业务税金及附加 Taxes and Other Charges on Principal Business	主营业务利润 Profits from Principal Business	其他业务利润 Profits from Other Business	销售费用 Selling Expenses	管理费用 Administr-ative Expenses
全国	**National Total**	**150977**	**84447**	**2889**	**63641**	**2782**	**27914**	**30449**
北京	Beijing	277	163	1	113		172	232
天津	Tianjin	3612	2193	17	1402		315	1221
河北	Hebei							
山西	Shanxi	1665	410	31	1224		969	445
内蒙古	Inner Mongolia	1581	707	60	814	146	570	270
辽宁	Liaoning	2341	1402	32	907	37	310	569
吉林	Jilin	3522	2920	86	516	132	177	223
黑龙江	Heilongjiang	1106	414	46	646		269	245
上海	Shanghai	6672	2267	153	4252		533	3181
江苏	Jiangsu	14510	3238	71	11201		5799	6598
浙江	Zhejiang	1140	855	7	278		21	14
安徽	Anhui	1467	555	43	869		248	551
福建	Fujian	6508	4073	159	2276		1290	502
江西	Jiangxi	6187	3826	198	2163		991	515
山东	Shandong	12798	8425	296	4077	892	1318	1241
河南	Henan	6867	5478	252	1137		205	436
湖北	Hubei	4609	3122	112	1375		176	485
湖南	Hunan	3421	2149	65	1207	79	480	1352
广东	Guangdong	32818	19515	575	12728	-156	4958	5518
广西	Guangxi	762	206	5	551		439	76
海南	Hainan	602		2	600		245	428
重庆	Chongqing	4917	2771	175	1971	110	247	354
四川	Sichuan	10285	6935	153	3197	756	1710	931
贵州	Guizhou	2735	1102	21	1612		1074	617
云南	Yunnan	3251	2330	56	865		397	368
西藏	Tibet	1947	235	51	1661	78	2036	938
陕西	Shaanxi	9541	5650	128	3763	708	1544	2832
甘肃	Gansu	2095	1156	52	887		480	238
青海	Qinghai	1231	889	38	304			29
宁夏	Ningxia							
新疆	Xinjiang	2510	1461	4	1045		941	40

4-4-4 Continued 8

单位：万元

Unit: 10000 yuan

财务费用 Financial Expenses	#利息支出 Interest Expenses	营业利润 Operating Profits	利润总额 Total Profits	应交所得税 Income Tax Payable	应付职工薪酬 Payables to Employees	应交增值税 VAT Payable
2203	**1666**	**4314**	**3953**	**1130**	**39624**	**2911**
1	1	-293	-292		183	9
13		-106	-104	7	1833	7
1		-191	-191		801	34
6		114	112		697	12
25	15	34	21	1	1102	38
10		105	55	25	373	9
17		119	119		151	44
-49		600	662	163	2758	152
42		-1144	-1077	29	5687	285
		263	263		335	7
4		67	68	18	576	7
217	199	339	46	28	1910	180
75	26	631	585	4	4255	32
205	117	1315	1097	279	2218	235
121	246	375	375	3	707	47
36		665	668	87	368	15
2	1	-504	-387	18	1029	110
194	16	2117	2458	145	6129	560
3	3	53	54	16	296	
2		-75	-75		208	40
551	504	800	754	1	1197	94
49	1	596	302	52	1463	224
149	88	-236	-236		491	81
42	26	182	190	25	659	126
4	6	-905	-790		1274	165
473	413	-1105	-1119	174	1391	233
8	4	160	54		186	94
		276	276	46	570	36
2		62	65	9	777	35

港、澳、台商投资企业

Enterprises with Funds from Hongkong, Macao and Taiwan

地　区	Region	主营业务收入 Revenue from Principal Business	主营业务成本 Cost of Principal Business	主营业务税金及附加 Taxes and Other Charges on Principal Business	主营业务利润 Profits from Principal Business	其他业务利润 Profits from Other Business	销售费用 Selling Expenses	管理费用 Administr-ative Expenses
全　国	**National Total**	**3397181**	**1153361**	**82393**	**2161427**	**70347**	**815927**	**1166788**
北　京	Beijing	639027	184636	22119	432272	10316	153489	207111
天　津	Tianjin	6840	3493	41	3306	-3	295	2911
河　北	Hebei	23254	9177	937	13140	90	4225	12249
山　西	Shanxi							
内蒙古	Inner Mongolia	24520	14517	93	9910	3151	3834	8254
辽　宁	Liaoning	95824	23303	2844	69677	12451	35237	40081
吉　林	Jilin	5839	1494	18	4327	13	1913	2398
黑龙江	Heilongjiang	25259	6639	1000	17620	27	8850	21494
上　海	Shanghai	451219	182878	15286	253055	3461	42236	126643
江　苏	Jiangsu	148664	47222	1603	99839	8338	48028	64559
浙　江	Zhejiang	271657	66877	3304	201476	6275	89338	88800
安　徽	Anhui	44467	10668	240	33559	6590	10429	34127
福　建	Fujian	241071	110555	2418	128098	568	50303	66565
江　西	Jiangxi	16748	6951	157	9640	1057	5321	4930
山　东	Shandong	84022	15907	1883	66232	5231	19307	49925
河　南	Henan	48611	15439	1183	31989	2874	17134	25720
湖　北	Hubei	78025	25817	1500	50708	76	24997	25332
湖　南	Hunan	57174	20248	1473	35453	18	20776	12771
广　东	Guangdong	658579	269712	9972	378895	3589	159628	179103
广　西	Guangxi	87393	18271	3896	65226	1570	26984	43558
海　南	Hainan	241544	67418	9203	164923	816	52802	99516
重　庆	Chongqing	12802	2731	207	9864		4476	6915
四　川	Sichuan	30195	12551	575	17069	3839	9150	6640
贵　州	Guizhou	6022	3227	303	2492		690	1291
云　南	Yunnan	43487	11140	842	31505		13019	19885
西　藏	Tibet	6639	715	21	5903		2023	3094
陕　西	Shaanxi	44406	19788	1156	23462		10450	11910
甘　肃	Gansu	3893	1987	119	1787		993	1006
青　海	Qinghai							
宁　夏	Ningxia							
新　疆	Xinjiang							

单位：万元
Unit: 10000 yuan

财务费用 Financial Expenses	#利息支出 Interest Expenses	营业利润 Operating Profits	利润总额 Total Profits	应交所得税 Income Tax Payable	应付职工薪酬 Payables to Employees	应交增值税 VAT Payable
194741	**164504**	**96368**	**102755**	**67714**	**805952**	**86906**
38972	40843	59161	58734	20820	180961	13789
-695	5	21	26	114	2003	123
1931	563	-5174	-5166	33	7823	601
-3689	56	408	-14057		5382	450
2888	3300	-9212	-5612	470	17052	1860
929		-904	-903		912	256
2373	2353	-14990	-15148	64	6971	206
29880	27939	100828	102481	21792	84643	12067
12561	-778	-23151	-25852	416	37758	2794
22784	21465	12002	15936	4600	67028	8367
1649	4195	-15586	-8280		11455	841
20077	7424	-6912	-7792	2858	47086	3952
544	289	-232	-851	39	4465	73
13284	5281	-8595	-9370	1760	20198	3286
4270	1875	-13166	-4011	124	13816	842
1400	1892	2643	1484	-961	21777	1608
3812	3230	-1835	-1630	69	12198	1098
11870	16650	34947	40308	10798	155528	20726
3996	6320	-8493	-8134	57	18333	2990
20073	19636	-5115	-5413	3958	52955	6589
3124	138	-807	-4650		3402	392
347	208	951	787	194	6285	1249
542	518	-28	-27	79	1396	143
340	401	-641	-666	200	12799	714
		786	786		1587	20
1469	691	-317	-253	226	11337	1859
10	10	-221	28	4	802	11

外商投资企业
Foreign Funded Enterprises

地区	Region	主营业务收入 Revenue from Principal Business	主营业务成本 Cost of Principal Business	主营业务税金及附加 Taxes and Other Charges on Principal Business	主营业务利润 Profits from Principal Business	其他业务利润 Profits from Other Business	销售费用 Selling Expenses	管理费用 Administr-ative Expenses
全国	**National Total**	**1828982**	**611626**	**39118**	**1178238**	**55268**	**462762**	**598572**
北京	Beijing	334815	74873	17093	242849		71040	111990
天津	Tianjin	43182	12346	104	30732	12	9387	16918
河北	Hebei	8641	1807	367	6467		159	7275
山西	Shanxi							
内蒙古	Inner Mongolia	934	18	1	915		581	281
辽宁	Liaoning	41315	10593	812	29910	338	14458	20816
吉林	Jilin	20228	7754	551	11923		7533	5621
黑龙江	Heilongjiang	16208	2281	434	13493	96	4371	6491
上海	Shanghai	295804	116237	1548	178019	31202	55906	109145
江苏	Jiangsu	105014	35589	2882	66543	1557	35589	32889
浙江	Zhejiang	72031	26413	648	44970	1875	20594	26928
安徽	Anhui	5584	3352	196	2036	26	966	996
福建	Fujian	112225	32743	1937	77545	1145	35941	36387
江西	Jiangxi	7517	2610	90	4817	2204	2795	1944
山东	Shandong	38242	11806	342	26094	803	13208	9501
河南	Henan	5923	4121	62	1740		864	166
湖北	Hubei	6790	2896	72	3822		1912	2680
湖南	Hunan	14392	6146	598	7648		2969	5783
广东	Guangdong	452867	175459	6774	270634	7359	128506	116532
广西	Guangxi	2874	464	163	2247	121	1421	440
海南	Hainan	78353	23690	1171	53492	4720	18777	22555
重庆	Chongqing	32387	13507	1326	17554	1226	4707	5900
四川	Sichuan	40370	14710	251	25409	2341	4990	20814
贵州	Guizhou	3801	1505	124	2172		742	2304
云南	Yunnan	15760	5120	421	10219	81	4597	8017
西藏	Tibet	8285	3394	23	4868		520	8400
陕西	Shaanxi	51521	19266	683	31572	124	13799	12281
甘肃	Gansu	7719	1640	234	5845		3068	3344
青海	Qinghai	4382	680	158	3544		2842	1333
宁夏	Ningxia	684	400	7	277		176	206
新疆	Xinjiang	1134	206	46	882	38	344	635

4-4-4 Continued 10

单位：万元

Unit: 10000 yuan

财务费用 Financial Expenses	#利息支出 Interest Expenses	营业利润 Operating Profits	利润总额 Total Profits	应　交 所得税 Income Tax Payable	应付职工 薪　酬 Payables to Employees	应　交 增值税 VAT Payable
66433	**52452**	**204799**	**206448**	**70882**	**444397**	**58490**
19953	21434	171515	173646	46929	101882	9019
527	76	5122	4849	331	12897	872
-33	-62	-807	-808		3017	246
		53	53		130	
1452	992	-6618	-6889	191	7918	1097
730	27	-1560	-1616	72	3733	35
-550	12	3277	3305	1069	505	389
11557	10480	7241	8563	4525	45522	8111
9154	3582	-10187	-9464	453	30000	2786
6589	4017	-8759	-8367	847	18277	820
113		-38	-49		1243	88
5395	2781	890	2094	1721	32122	2031
268	16	-179	-158		1377	18
594		4227	3464	198	8757	675
52	19	658	658	4	816	86
24		-747	-749	4	1646	152
2556	2555	-3795	-3884	4	4401	276
6475	5761	21092	20590	8008	105194	13044
20		366	362	48	600	194
676	4	11480	10155		21608	2401
-625	52	8708	8276	2719	7287	12975
309	190	6271	6126	1732	11260	1040
10		-884	-888	3	1144	100
1139	255	-3365	-3446	18	5411	452
-2		-4051	-4052		3145	190
-237	261	6496	6319	2004	11509	1074
13		-579	-579		2166	160
269		-860	-894		68	79
2		-106	-107		206	
3		-62	-62	2	556	80

4-4-5 各地区限额以上住宿业企业损益及分配(按国民经济行业分)

旅游饭店

Tourist Hotel

地 区	Region	主营业务收入 Revenue from Principal Business	主营业务成本 Cost of Principal Business	主营业务税金及附加 Taxes and Other Charges on Principal Business	主营业务利润 Profits from Principal Business	其他业务利润 Profits from Other Business	销售费用 Selling Expenses	管理费用 Administr-ative Expenses
全 国	**National Total**	**28936704**	**11127345**	**554676**	**17254683**	**533348**	**8411209**	**8594831**
北 京	Beijing	2879117	772346	82216	2024555	36490	869007	1070779
天 津	Tianjin	272779	98696	2413	171670	4267	84082	131273
河 北	Hebei	469395	177152	9396	282847	4122	186483	156926
山 西	Shanxi	233577	87706	4608	141263	9020	99266	76365
内蒙古	Inner Mongolia	253364	97934	4156	151274	-2368	86335	79269
辽 宁	Liaoning	539496	177851	10775	350870	17234	193037	213965
吉 林	Jilin	224642	96201	4147	124294	9286	69670	70973
黑龙江	Heilongjiang	224040	83050	4887	136103	4263	75641	83548
上 海	Shanghai	2059135	654968	39442	1364725	131558	543382	646166
江 苏	Jiangsu	1900651	714780	32917	1152954	23547	591953	613409
浙 江	Zhejiang	2436300	784168	27757	1624375	61776	831285	761391
安 徽	Anhui	505118	225313	9762	270043	10841	133229	154628
福 建	Fujian	1546982	700400	30262	816320	14230	403206	370495
江 西	Jiangxi	532782	230685	11496	290601	9472	132963	141350
山 东	Shandong	1504977	657628	21722	825627	41249	441468	384764
河 南	Henan	987262	467966	21879	497417	12302	233527	224184
湖 北	Hubei	751482	316972	14800	419710	10681	217213	185641
湖 南	Hunan	1169340	558755	30563	580022	10377	244659	299025
广 东	Guangdong	4368932	1704030	63591	2601311	34008	1258960	1124330
广 西	Guangxi	530964	187308	11623	332033	8627	178486	164084
海 南	Hainan	1068369	297566	22205	748598	17503	328283	422623
重 庆	Chongqing	659508	314115	12639	332754	4106	159951	137944
四 川	Sichuan	985406	415373	19047	550986	21953	281953	259903
贵 州	Guizhou	511148	238235	10098	262815	3261	111321	134877
云 南	Yunnan	692096	304293	19908	367895	14207	176514	241559
西 藏	Tibet	77945	25896	641	51408	266	32378	34789
陕 西	Shaanxi	829859	394846	15727	419286	9578	227702	211006
甘 肃	Gansu	313586	159394	8320	145872	4185	78503	75688
青 海	Qinghai	70938	28466	1226	41246	4469	25864	23653
宁 夏	Ningxia	74599	33585	1456	39558	601	28406	21638
新 疆	Xinjiang	262915	121667	4997	136251	2237	86482	78586

Income and Distribution of Enterprises above Designated Size of Hotels by Region and Sector

单位：万元

Unit: 10000 yuan

财务费用 Financial Expenses	#利息支出 Interest Expenses	营业利润 Operating Profits	利润总额 Total Profits	应交所得税 Income Tax Payable	应付职工薪酬 Payables to Employees	应交增值税 VAT Payable
1456336	**1010551**	**-536474**	**-353549**	**338826**	**8126771**	**769195**
128627	134136	136507	144910	86317	953370	73021
13177	6433	-37735	-32428	605	94129	6346
41182	14357	-95042	-88050	1751	143895	11669
13360	8616	-44735	-41332	270	251720	5546
3095	4678	-18089	-40700	827	80372	6399
41081	21874	-106783	-83044	1663	113245	14839
13166	7282	-26486	-17213	549	53099	3975
6106	3587	-24425	-20660	2562	50691	5586
67375	52151	190441	225629	54371	478149	97107
97925	43560	-107189	-81816	12863	470811	43207
151936	126512	-65449	-31662	21190	933019	57397
35684	21822	-44800	-39212	13634	135130	9786
72921	39904	-189	5378	17229	354742	26842
36198	16997	-12749	-7491	1659	112843	11739
58645	34822	-41880	-27949	11342	356579	29127
43730	17160	6743	29773	10432	227918	22647
33781	19048	-3110	-2918	3378	178873	21673
61780	40797	-15248	-13801	7318	248722	20339
227305	172684	61111	77394	48347	1117936	122977
28202	26302	-30713	-30754	1922	133660	17169
45641	33756	-4521	-30652	9471	288155	36310
42470	32171	-9038	-17397	6715	133465	28098
60366	37574	-27796	-25672	7991	235801	25640
41543	27502	-21356	-16775	4016	117210	11348
38980	34029	-77529	-82293	4406	218980	18993
1015	830	-10849	-9568	254	28134	2316
22636	9056	-33196	-31129	4445	360966	18183
14656	11851	-22567	-21965	1402	81166	9786
3612	2598	-9280	-7739	204	27603	1782
4235	3346	-13908	-13883	206	54094	1503
5906	514	5116	-347	2001	92294	7845

一般旅馆
Fonda

地　区	Region	主营业务收入 Revenue from Principal Business	主营业务成本 Cost of Principal Business	主营业务税金及附加 Taxes and Other Charges on Principal Business	主营业务利润 Profits from Principal Business	其他业务利润 Profits from Other Business	销售费用 Selling Expenses	管理费用 Administr-ative Expenses
全　国	**National Total**	**7519520**	**3492344**	**117162**	**3910014**	**92431**	**1897179**	**1694258**
北　京	Beijing	683013	214349	5988	462676	15911	230281	206096
天　津	Tianjin	90221	38296	902	51023	59	30529	25662
河　北	Hebei	166617	79610	2484	84523	810	58909	37801
山　西	Shanxi	88379	32093	1182	55104	2009	29337	32328
内蒙古	Inner Mongolia	91324	35022	1727	54575	927	33146	23608
辽　宁	Liaoning	104781	37593	1302	65886	1661	37584	34687
吉　林	Jilin	42850	20055	1088	21707	877	10583	12017
黑龙江	Heilongjiang	64673	29896	936	33841	33	14939	18200
上　海	Shanghai	639049	182604	4560	451885	6683	198036	210884
江　苏	Jiangsu	357640	168411	3486	185743	979	96868	81302
浙　江	Zhejiang	422315	150701	4815	266799	8256	143725	127194
安　徽	Anhui	155271	85581	2843	66847	1085	30359	26661
福　建	Fujian	314078	156233	5075	152770	2065	71146	59746
江　西	Jiangxi	135543	69511	3990	62042	1213	28745	22290
山　东	Shandong	503203	276044	8914	218245	8731	103934	66709
河　南	Henan	602715	349959	13801	238955	3659	75635	88073
湖　北	Hubei	320014	172639	6642	140733	-70	65558	51747
湖　南	Hunan	343460	201174	10338	131948	6137	51246	53704
广　东	Guangdong	839159	405271	9533	424355	9052	221774	196101
广　西	Guangxi	182550	71083	2517	108950	5196	63811	39890
海　南	Hainan	14789	3341	345	11103	-426	6809	6413
重　庆	Chongqing	190001	92376	3578	94047	2607	38295	40093
四　川	Sichuan	411108	206743	7563	196802	6102	100031	84533
贵　州	Guizhou	121513	68310	2407	50796	495	22335	23716
云　南	Yunnan	182060	98907	3961	79192	1564	34673	39304
西　藏	Tibet							
陕　西	Shaanxi	297750	165595	5130	127025	4714	62886	51980
甘　肃	Gansu	68779	33292	890	34597	1471	17954	13773
青　海	Qinghai	9958	5445	86	4427	49	1606	2426
宁　夏	Ningxia	6681	2253	117	4311	44	3193	1512
新　疆	Xinjiang	70026	39957	962	29107	538	13252	15808

单位：万元
Unit: 10000 yuan

财务费用 Financial Expenses	#利息支出 Interest Expenses	营业利润 Operating Profits	利润总额 Total Profits	应交所得税 Income Tax Payable	应付职工薪酬 Payables to Employees	应交增值税 VAT Payable
201426	**104423**	**205744**	**218206**	**88918**	**1681760**	**214197**
13442	15698	28238	32724	14409	162446	17279
606	108	-4281	-5000	455	26017	2438
5665	2226	-23392	-19157	387	71296	3465
4826	3495	-11660	-10704	477	23667	1990
3558	1961	-5189	-3489	346	20804	2170
4108	1382	-10596	-9427	364	17711	1824
1193	134	-1853	-1569	29	6831	532
2067	1024	-826	511	382	10030	2097
11125	6316	69586	63640	17557	114184	21375
8175	1320	-254	-7159	3538	71223	9001
20232	8495	-16364	-18849	3073	95885	9473
4133	1357	5616	4746	814	27461	2595
5474	3336	18335	18740	3747	64034	5704
2559	1557	8702	7335	295	134319	2893
8700	2429	38152	43979	9070	89508	12097
17233	4954	61384	62879	11906	101568	13151
8996	3559	17885	14054	3210	50137	5986
7668	2959	21631	17340	1738	52332	5963
21875	13205	-12877	110	8167	199399	25198
7325	3138	-1026	1326	932	40218	5005
40	11	-2125	-1844	1	4692	455
5414	2763	18556	17909	1186	33625	4269
17245	10422	-3545	-836	1452	80575	9181
4804	2532	1090	601	1481	27340	33970
6763	4835	2223	-894	983	39624	4807
3874	1772	7667	6401	1698	54771	6549
1768	1381	2041	2974	674	14614	1983
542	142	129	161	40	20960	259
49	35	-127	-100	43	1447	111
1967	1877	-1376	1804	464	25042	2377

其他住宿业
Others

地 区	Region	主营业务收入 Revenue from Principal Business	主营业务成本 Cost of Principal Business	主营业务税金及附加 Taxes and Other Charges on Principal Business	主营业务利润 Profits from Principal Business	其他业务利润 Profits from Other Business	销售费用 Selling Expenses	管理费用 Administr-ative Expenses
全 国	**National Total**	**859102**	**395772**	**17564**	**445766**	**12384**	**192324**	**227889**
北 京	Beijing	113111	27458	3361	82292	665	29430	36850
天 津	Tianjin	30455	10658	664	19133	142	9371	17657
河 北	Hebei	38011	13482	708	23821	1287	8358	14965
山 西	Shanxi	6418	3162	113	3143	554	2573	1145
内 蒙 古	Inner Mongolia	4760	2261	44	2455	-7	1764	837
辽 宁	Liaoning	17171	6326	342	10503	376	7129	6388
吉 林	Jilin	12062	4686	128	7248	132	3545	3983
黑 龙 江	Heilongjiang	9001	3590	267	5144		3938	3534
上 海	Shanghai	54264	21465	232	32567	2359	9535	17042
江 苏	Jiangsu	44839	22440	409	21990	169	11379	8983
浙 江	Zhejiang	15375	5909	79	9387	69	5597	2970
安 徽	Anhui	21666	12364	1001	8301		2858	3275
福 建	Fujian	39432	28758	453	10221	383	4947	4273
江 西	Jiangxi	13041	6860	227	5954	123	1834	3636
山 东	Shandong	25234	17370	583	7281	1	3614	4268
河 南	Henan	49346	25671	1676	21999	444	7542	7096
湖 北	Hubei	42747	32286	648	9813	1656	3127	4106
湖 南	Hunan	52356	31217	1712	19427		6022	15333
广 东	Guangdong	116494	45617	1702	69175	1900	34082	32191
广 西	Guangxi	15436	2566	219	12651		4165	3171
海 南	Hainan	5195	1009	636	3550		1752	5414
重 庆	Chongqing	22711	13970	411	8330	414	2282	3177
四 川	Sichuan	15405	6868	180	8357	875	5790	3028
贵 州	Guizhou	13302	8343	226	4733		1766	2977
云 南	Yunnan	13587	7438	176	5973	18	2417	3836
西 藏	Tibet	2892	999	124	1769	29	1731	402
陕 西	Shaanxi	43786	18995	921	23870		11648	13868
甘 肃	Gansu	16098	9270	235	6593		3966	2027
青 海	Qinghai	1277	3113	1	-1837			4
宁 夏	Ningxia	1381	855	70	456		127	262
新 疆	Xinjiang	2249	766	16	1467	795	35	1191

4-4-5 Continued 2

单位：万元

Unit: 10000 yuan

财务费用 Financial Expenses	#利息支出 Interest Expenses	营业利润 Operating Profits	利润总额 Total Profits	应交所得税 Income Tax Payable	应付职工薪酬 Payables to Employees	应交增值税 VAT Payable
50391	**32974**	**29470**	**10864**	**11832**	**191788**	**21954**
23808	23231	-8367	-772	1104	27969	2921
7430	-4	-14334	-10927	433	11521	832
2888	501	-580	142	227	11676	898
32	4	8	30	16	1743	120
42	28	-134	-468		1421	86
1399	1170	-4414	-1207	40	5027	3
101	82	227	118	111	3303	365
27	22	-2292	-2411	47	1400	155
590	424	6797	6780	2110	8707	1655
310	130	1378	1405	520	9512	1690
134	35	738	823	166	3472	352
887	891	1758	1995	511	3079	950
452	42	1037	1565	585	5920	484
393	331	215	-547	10	3125	443
1897	37	-2457	-1104	483	4977	767
1111	508	6431	6292	892	9004	616
909	403	1687	1658	110	4177	1125
1212	1016	42235	5946	2577	11915	861
4524	3216	-1018	968	906	30415	3707
287	265	5486	5576	306	2675	740
11		-3626	-3620	7	1823	143
85	6	2887	2095	370	5292	712
150	53	162	111	33	4233	341
82	4	-200	-194	28	2097	342
508	167	-559	-311	81	4169	360
141		35	44	18	923	113
598	214	-2044	-1239	56	6636	772
359	176	168	-74	85	3178	295
		-1841	-1841		1552	33
21	21	46	-7		211	2
3	1	41	38		636	71

4-4-6 各地区限额以上餐饮业企业损益及分配

地　区	Region	主营业务收入 Revenue from Principal Business	主营业务成本 Cost of Principal Business	主营业务税金及附加 Taxes and Other Charges on Principal Business	主营业务利润 Profits from Principal Business	其他业务利润 Profits from Other Business	销售费用 Selling Expenses	管理费用 Administrative Expenses
全　国	**National Total**	**50040296**	**25874328**	**483374**	**23682594**	**461612**	**14785049**	**5895975**
北　京	Beijing	6117080	2519208	13629	3584243	50664	2542078	711682
天　津	Tianjin	919088	434285	3308	481495	10203	334167	116868
河　北	Hebei	396886	201190	5643	190053	4903	124881	64669
山　西	Shanxi	476972	238088	5351	233533	9271	167860	89559
内蒙古	Inner Mongolia	466394	254714	5332	206348	6288	120665	95688
辽　宁	Liaoning	984159	482996	13260	487903	7153	308325	130673
吉　林	Jilin	259384	130175	4926	124283	32632	68603	47610
黑龙江	Heilongjiang	115804	63844	2258	49702	444	31886	14035
上　海	Shanghai	6701067	2884144	14074	3802849	78137	2712806	780037
江　苏	Jiangsu	3830056	2015701	36735	1777620	21767	1025168	527943
浙　江	Zhejiang	3155267	1617938	18686	1518643	27190	934342	440912
安　徽	Anhui	1401147	784272	20317	596558	6575	337939	168178
福　建	Fujian	2011774	1264957	22081	724736	40717	400847	193058
江　西	Jiangxi	432813	246631	6818	179364	7099	93388	48796
山　东	Shandong	2666787	1582666	36202	1047919	21164	537829	334570
河　南	Henan	1366200	830864	33409	501927	12499	198519	122373
湖　北	Hubei	2334668	1295570	36179	1002919	13572	570180	225236
湖　南	Hunan	1318479	765129	29451	523899	8723	261249	133960
广　东	Guangdong	7231508	3555925	50187	3625396	36458	2441235	810604
广　西	Guangxi	434709	228544	5005	201160	4328	129205	51809
海　南	Hainan	89886	38241	1144	50501	6552	34703	15424
重　庆	Chongqing	2105089	1348083	35983	721023	8894	287591	189891
四　川	Sichuan	1945972	1093171	28423	824378	17942	456666	208372
贵　州	Guizhou	352690	223644	4575	124471	3705	44284	46006
云　南	Yunnan	605551	384875	10791	209885	4488	100445	61742
西　藏	Tibet	9630	4527	114	4989	76	2110	2287
陕　西	Shaanxi	1716661	1072807	31399	612455	8022	346554	168017
甘　肃	Gansu	321386	180502	5836	135048	4613	79764	43700
青　海	Qinghai	44108	23660	482	19966	1779	13543	6963
宁　夏	Ningxia	68120	34598	635	32887	2551	21247	15565
新　疆	Xinjiang	160961	73379	1141	86441	3203	56970	29748

Income and Distribution of Enterprises above Designated Size of Catering Services by Region

单位：万元
Unit: 10000 yuan

财务费用 Financial Expenses	#利息支出 Interest Expenses	营业利润 Operating Profits	利润总额 Total Profits	应交所得税 Income Tax Payable	应付职工薪酬 Payables to Employees	应交增值税 VAT Payable
605964	**279953**	**2701292**	**2797014**	**680532**	**10053254**	**944868**
23143	16555	366139	398837	106599	1507443	44903
13843	9508	30679	32334	12018	202636	10971
12964	4205	-10280	-8275	1950	96828	7692
12130	7850	-45390	-45329	3283	110759	6812
12753	6851	-23304	-23541	1505	99690	50206
16067	4628	28188	27244	15803	109867	7688
4481	2206	3626	2602	1357	440917	3165
3439	1852	1017	493	829	17296	1515
30703	6316	351111	391468	117193	1254393	175982
52762	16339	171971	180893	55122	668925	59956
59401	30889	140269	156419	41436	615770	48455
34562	14580	64690	80037	14295	280183	21852
15888	5868	120773	105911	24253	278550	22379
7266	3272	32156	30280	3782	201566	78872
57639	27336	123882	129943	36137	491246	55484
24495	6213	157623	155844	20192	206153	27764
37632	14209	176579	170565	31084	397303	37640
24144	9541	103985	88759	10370	234082	22593
45672	18646	349408	385019	99026	1551124	128150
7391	3995	15987	15989	6033	87715	7045
964	744	-537	-471	774	28314	1982
21169	11262	245809	230005	22270	275297	36322
39426	21445	138936	132527	24321	305332	32484
6036	4172	28678	29299	3067	61595	6014
9566	13634	42157	40309	6240	107707	11653
219	20	373	454	102	2879	110
19084	8457	84187	80871	16306	265436	26583
5002	3492	15005	15077	3012	80097	4934
1508	1050	-2148	-1802	50	13589	1409
2398	1215	-6213	-5625	268	18061	1276
4217	221	3603	-2	2389	42501	2977

国有控股

State-controlled Enterprises

地　区	Region	主营业务收入 Revenue from Principal Business	主营业务成本 Cost of Principal Business	主营业务税金及附加 Taxes and Other Charges on Principal Business	主营业务利润 Profits from Principal Business	其他业务利润 Profits from Other Business	销售费用 Selling Expenses	管理费用 Administrative Expenses
全　国	**National Total**	**2271633**	**1181389**	**25912**	**1064332**	**70415**	**681928**	**413464**
北　京	Beijing	438483	174764	3748	259971	13451	167818	73416
天　津	Tianjin	33279	19663	244	13372	5	8291	7514
河　北	Hebei	31479	17897	487	13095	117	8927	7793
山　西	Shanxi	29792	17629	886	11277	1053	10760	10829
内蒙古	Inner Mongolia	16166	10762	286	5118		4260	7769
辽　宁	Liaoning	64293	52018	784	11491	347	2839	8220
吉　林	Jilin	24521	8625	501	15395		4955	13605
黑龙江	Heilongjiang	7215	4134	241	2840		1305	1825
上　海	Shanghai	248671	118715	1308	128648	40719	83637	50339
江　苏	Jiangsu	182340	75934	1776	104630	285	64232	51479
浙　江	Zhejiang	161011	78731	478	81802	815	55724	22657
安　徽	Anhui	78777	43251	575	34951	19	33125	7338
福　建	Fujian	35414	19637	133	15644	150	11484	4001
江　西	Jiangxi	23619	10830	222	12567	1302	7806	4014
山　东	Shandong	183849	107128	3475	73246	6527	51220	44827
河　南	Henan	17431	10958	279	6194	1	3941	1717
湖　北	Hubei	96948	50301	1286	45361	89	34904	7945
湖　南	Hunan	22148	12358	829	8961	5	4558	5537
广　东	Guangdong	247848	150354	2525	94969	2528	52187	32105
广　西	Guangxi	17021	8210	108	8703		4159	6193
海　南	Hainan	480	325	13	142		164	82
重　庆	Chongqing	46373	26420	919	19034	174	8046	7952
四　川	Sichuan	43042	20647	828	21567		11294	10706
贵　州	Guizhou	15678	12127	162	3389	201	1019	1594
云　南	Yunnan	58139	43168	737	14234	825	3115	7076
西　藏	Tibet							
陕　西	Shaanxi	106295	64635	2233	39427	256	27949	9123
甘　肃	Gansu	29403	13603	657	15143	1384	11172	5034
青　海	Qinghai	1880	1763	64	53	124	29	594
宁　夏	Ningxia	2642	1539	11	1092		1202	272
新　疆	Xinjiang	7396	5263	117	2016	38	1806	1908

4-4-6 Continued

单位：万元
Unit: 10000 yuan

财务费用 Financial Expenses	#利息支出 Interest Expenses	营业利润 Operating Profits	利润总额 Total Profits	应交所得税 Income Tax Payable	应付职工薪酬 Payables to Employees	应交增值税 VAT Payable
18033	**6266**	**51505**	**85415**	**28112**	**658570**	**55173**
282	1250	45086	50496	10969	164894	11315
136	34	-2685	-1633	153	8566	732
470	52	-3956	-3695	21	9918	367
333	4	-21472	-20027	142	10500	508
44	26	-6922	-6089	28	5632	447
1042	77	-646	-46	372	5389	652
-22	5	-3009	-2811	12	6675	212
141		-335	-241	162	1794	101
5051	4	4876	8764	4869	64245	5126
1784	1305	-11097	-8501	1321	53268	5108
493	356	32121	33966	1299	54197	3169
17	73	1378	1297	494	27324	3243
11	5	621	832	163	12752	349
-5	50	805	1089	1	5476	479
3320	547	-23308	-13831	880	50561	2772
144	53	734	746	61	3289	276
72	65	2743	2859	622	15331	3553
496	20	-1576	-497	110	5441	381
1962	359	31718	34863	3336	76003	7027
668	182	-1948	-1941		3674	382
-1		-103	-102		147	2
120	65	3305	5319	552	6871	1629
906	340	-43	-20	93	11812	1163
-28	-3	1200	1210	438	5357	192
185	276	5614	6424	913	13750	3246
227	1054	2123	-196	925	23406	1762
164	64	-901	-783	173	6914	488
4	2	-594	-462		615	77
3		-501	-320	1	892	138
14	1	-1723	-1255	2	3877	277

4-4-7 各地区限额以上餐饮业企业损益及分配(按登记注册类型分)

内资企业
Domestic Funded Enterprises

地 区	Region	主营业务收入 Revenue from Principal Business	主营业务成本 Cost of Principal Business	主营业务税金及附加 Taxes and Other Charges on Principal Business	主营业务利润 Profits from Principal Business	其他业务利润 Profits from Other Business	销售费用 Selling Expenses	管理费用 Administrative Expenses
全 国	**National Total**	**35365310**	**19835958**	**450645**	**15078707**	**354387**	**8849062**	**4482055**
北 京	Beijing	3359284	1477185	11529	1870570	35415	1330422	452969
天 津	Tianjin	484497	242519	2923	239055	6682	168575	72727
河 北	Hebei	395007	200182	5637	189188	4903	123743	64466
山 西	Shanxi	398952	203407	5319	190226	9271	139290	83854
内蒙古	Inner Mongolia	430377	234505	5093	190779	6288	115036	88423
辽 宁	Liaoning	400906	227288	12928	160690	6488	93611	74872
吉 林	Jilin	258533	129848	4907	123778	32632	68445	47433
黑龙江	Heilongjiang	99259	57873	2129	39257	82	24954	11603
上 海	Shanghai	3020482	1504858	9873	1505751	71274	1031598	408190
江 苏	Jiangsu	2728512	1504557	30146	1193809	13383	663905	419442
浙 江	Zhejiang	2463763	1320102	17950	1125711	19647	697332	364110
安 徽	Anhui	1396583	781392	19966	595225	6575	337234	166660
福 建	Fujian	1551878	1058655	20482	472741	4946	226206	142148
江 西	Jiangxi	352804	207888	6711	138205	7099	68474	41105
山 东	Shandong	2380416	1451706	35799	892911	21007	441890	300051
河 南	Henan	1292603	793688	33326	465589	12499	173103	110601
湖 北	Hubei	1800134	1069348	35413	695373	13530	361989	177037
湖 南	Hunan	1165366	691488	28965	444913	8723	217428	119340
广 东	Guangdong	4468670	2446854	39145	1982671	23915	1262370	589020
广 西	Guangxi	358597	194324	4881	159392	4308	107036	44613
海 南	Hainan	69424	32640	515	36269	1529	25824	8654
重 庆	Chongqing	1930001	1216379	35357	678265	4955	270398	174997
四 川	Sichuan	1563119	927275	27408	608436	13127	322819	176122
贵 州	Guizhou	352317	223334	4575	124408	3705	44262	45995
云 南	Yunnan	524272	341695	10559	172018	4145	80678	53732
西 藏	Tibet	9630	4527	114	4989	76	2110	2287
陕 西	Shaanxi	1570817	1005198	30935	534684	6037	293606	150604
甘 肃	Gansu	291498	167453	5827	118218	4613	71714	41268
青 海	Qinghai	44108	23660	482	19966	1779	13543	6963
宁 夏	Ningxia	68120	34598	635	32887	2551	21247	15565
新 疆	Xinjiang	135381	61532	1116	72733	3203	50220	27204

Income and Distribution of Enterprises above Designated Size of Catering Services by Region and Type of Registration

单位：万元
Unit: 10000 yuan

财务费用 Financial Expenses	#利息支出 Interest Expenses	营业利润 Operating Profits	利润总额 Total Profits	应交所得税 Income Tax Payable	应付职工薪酬 Payables to Employees	应交增值税 VAT Payable
565160	**258279**	**1450716**	**1517887**	**340748**	**7174836**	**734950**
19485	9657	118706	130342	37707	806394	49306
12970	9768	-3118	-146	4760	112257	10552
12963	4205	-9981	-7981	1945	96181	7627
11671	7850	-53385	-53164	1417	98844	6769
12774	6851	-24071	-16966	1473	94967	7349
13346	4586	-20936	-20805	2359	57884	6617
4460	2186	3476	2645	1353	440671	3152
3352	1850	24	-460	527	16420	1209
23326	2355	91357	120042	35329	544578	46874
48618	15681	58078	66328	26239	526441	55696
53361	28169	55358	67992	19982	482434	45371
34554	14580	65586	80961	14287	279004	21515
10779	3618	92977	84014	15062	189537	18157
7141	3214	24010	21808	1480	185429	78671
52858	23375	105174	110618	29482	452549	54802
24043	6210	159056	153120	19553	193684	27194
34467	14021	131410	125896	19558	279716	36048
23922	9431	84273	68950	10352	210395	20869
44466	18120	124788	158425	40659	970730	109975
7408	3991	2815	2526	2719	76337	6977
999	744	837	878	491	24372	1870
21197	10994	230944	216125	19404	240909	35571
39160	21436	86971	78120	11250	253854	31757
6036	4172	28649	29270	3067	61578	6014
9724	13632	31784	29902	3897	92393	9540
219	20	373	454	102	2879	110
18608	8203	73871	71196	13843	238388	25345
5127	3492	8532	8713	1410	76164	4916
1508	1050	-2148	-1802	50	13589	1409
2398	1215	-6213	-5625	268	18061	1276
4220	3603	-8481	-3489	723	38197	2412

国有企业

State-owned Enterprises

地区	Region	主营业务收入 Revenue from Principal Business	主营业务成本 Cost of Principal Business	主营业务税金及附加 Taxes and Other Charges on Principal Business	主营业务利润 Profits from Principal Business	其他业务利润 Profits from Other Business	销售费用 Selling Expenses	管理费用 Administrative Expenses
全国	**National Total**	**559016**	**316298**	**9420**	**233298**	**14578**	**139137**	**124071**
北京	Beijing	47141	25601	357	21183	861	13822	8273
天津	Tianjin	7753	2487	144	5122	4	3395	2190
河北	Hebei	18328	10710	420	7198	88	5675	3354
山西	Shanxi	11120	5525	163	5432	1053	3067	5147
内蒙古	Inner Mongolia	8993	4636	93	4264		4242	7281
辽宁	Liaoning	50653	43999	672	5982		1318	5820
吉林	Jilin	20575	6520	210	13845		4133	11869
黑龙江	Heilongjiang	5726	3620	235	1871		482	1571
上海	Shanghai	36826	23465	88	13273	4100	7541	5294
江苏	Jiangsu	51334	23974	944	26416	97	16170	11651
浙江	Zhejiang	12472	5671	26	6775		2204	4239
安徽	Anhui	4533	2271	29	2233		1653	873
福建	Fujian	9835	5921	50	3864	56	2976	954
江西	Jiangxi	14319	7237	129	6953	495	4952	1915
山东	Shandong	88075	44083	1901	42091	5732	30833	20696
河南	Henan	5496	4135	149	1212	2	472	128
湖北	Hubei	11802	6449	545	4808	89	2415	2355
湖南	Hunan	14219	8542	575	5102	5	2322	3079
广东	Guangdong	54724	31035	1062	22627	379	11572	10841
广西	Guangxi	5645	2683	74	2888		1844	1372
海南	Hainan	480	325	13	142		164	82
重庆	Chongqing	3452	2423	14	1015		36	311
四川	Sichuan	14216	6763	123	7330		3156	5084
贵州	Guizhou	601	512	13	76	197	249	423
云南	Yunnan	10875	7597	158	3120	36	1396	1781
西藏	Tibet							
陕西	Shaanxi	23800	15552	524	7724	20	3264	1706
甘肃	Gansu	16367	8770	591	7006	1384	5433	2257
青海	Qinghai							
宁夏	Ningxia	2469	1472	10	987		1056	210
新疆	Xinjiang	7187	4320	108	2759	-20	3295	3315

4-4-7 Continued 1

单位：万元
Unit: 10000 yuan

财务费用 Financial Expenses	#利息支出 Interest Expenses	营业利润 Operating Profits	利润总额 Total Profits	应交所得税 Income Tax Payable	应付职工薪酬 Payables to Employees	应交增值税 VAT Payable
3342	**994**	**-28591**	**-6636**	**3608**	**143980**	**11693**
19	21	-466	1439	338	15924	1767
97	5	-609	228	17	2775	211
437	10	-2167	-1957	19	4730	177
59	2	-2834	-1482	1	3970	267
12		-7210	-6369		5081	214
1079	74	-2225	-1647	-215	3258	35
1	5	-2187	-2000	2	5338	99
31		-72	22	84	1464	51
-54	4	1931	2017	368	8394	717
220	205	-1120	-206	372	11958	1902
-89		641	665	273	3598	146
-29	6	-432	-418		1435	115
	1	-156	-41		3553	52
42	34	34	110		2084	270
386	71	-9186	-2675	652	25534	1111
103	1	521	521	7	632	78
33	27	285	312	25	2628	100
296	14	-594	20	86	2957	241
163	216	-1038	1666	795	17031	1861
38	29	-361	-361		1704	159
-1		-103	-102		147	2
20		658	658	66	219	104
163	65	-809	-810	19	3192	373
		-383	-378		276	23
109	104	788	1673		1389	264
73	35	2686	2695	691	2766	744
116	64	-821	-821	6	4347	274
3		-397	-158	1	755	129
15	1	-2965	763	1	6841	207

集体企业

Collective-owned Enterprises

地 区	Region	主营业务收入 Revenue from Principal Business	主营业务成本 Cost of Principal Business	主营业务税金及附加 Taxes and Other Charges on Principal Business	主营业务利润 Profits from Principal Business	其他业务利润 Profits from Other Business	销售费用 Selling Expenses	管理费用 Administrative Expenses
全 国	**National Total**	**229718**	**156420**	**2469**	**70829**	**432**	**36563**	**22165**
北 京	Beijing	16434	8569	85	7780	12	4500	2087
天 津	Tianjin	940	495	2	443		60	438
河 北	Hebei	1528	1165	15	348		139	61
山 西	Shanxi	1592	546	12	1034	2	518	364
内蒙古	Inner Mongolia	398	196	2	200		147	70
辽 宁	Liaoning	917	545	11	361	15	214	417
吉 林	Jilin	1605	1001	31	573		331	77
黑龙江	Heilongjiang							
上 海	Shanghai	25003	11770	82	13151		8240	3322
江 苏	Jiangsu	14943	6659	203	8081		4928	3313
浙 江	Zhejiang	278	162	1	115		115	62
安 徽	Anhui	2078	1168	19	891	28	1028	352
福 建	Fujian	5135	1970	53	3112		1441	1004
江 西	Jiangxi							
山 东	Shandong	25478	17519	552	7407	2	3071	3118
河 南	Henan	10572	7249	359	2964	345	978	581
湖 北	Hubei	13452	11676	2	1774		84	1822
湖 南	Hunan	1388	1174	11	203		30	19
广 东	Guangdong	51605	35107	581	15917	23	8501	2958
广 西	Guangxi	2558	1293	49	1216		753	248
海 南	Hainan							
重 庆	Chongqing	29745	25915	218	3612	5	496	1164
四 川	Sichuan	1852	1015	85	752		343	328
贵 州	Guizhou	297	114	1	182			198
云 南	Yunnan	2355	1956	17	382		500	72
西 藏	Tibet							
陕 西	Shaanxi	19565	19156	78	331		146	90
甘 肃	Gansu							
青 海	Qinghai							
宁 夏	Ningxia							
新 疆	Xinjiang							

单位：万元
Unit: 10000 yuan

财务费用 Financial Expenses	#利息支出 Interest Expenses	营业利润 Operating Profits	利润总额 Total Profits	应交所得税 Income Tax Payable	应付职工薪酬 Payables to Employees	应交增值税 VAT Payable
1623	**391**	**11441**	**10195**	**2621**	**39413**	**4054**
31	2	1175	1315	63	4111	382
3		-57	-57		324	13
4		145	26	2	397	10
3		174	175		359	46
		-16	-10		157	25
		-80	-256	7	128	25
12	12	93	57		341	11
-24	2	2303	2334	684	7122	320
10	10	-170	-94	71	3532	300
4	4	-47	-1	3	91	8
6		-495	-415	40	616	21
11		656	656	164	1658	407
155	144	1085	771	312	4577	767
1213	152	240	239	39	995	62
43	13	-275	-1081	5	1079	7
19	9	135	135	34	82	20
46	27	4461	4483	1069	7284	1318
4	2	239	156	21	601	65
78	10	1875	1669	106	4820	163
		116	117		335	39
		-15	-15		105	9
1		-191	-99	1	148	11
4	4	90	90		551	25

4-4-7 续表 3

股份合作企业
Cooperative Enterprises

地区	Region	主营业务收入 Revenue from Principal Business	主营业务成本 Cost of Principal Business	主营业务税金及附加 Taxes and Other Charges on Principal Business	主营业务利润 Profits from Principal Business	其他业务利润 Profits from Other Business	销售费用 Selling Expenses	管理费用 Administrative Expenses
全国	**National Total**	**120180**	**67274**	**1026**	**51880**	**164**	**35924**	**16671**
北京	Beijing	30022	16100	101	13821		8597	4541
天津	Tianjin							
河北	Hebei	6307	3376	48	2883		1772	662
山西	Shanxi	386	203	2	181		148	40
内蒙古	Inner Mongolia							
辽宁	Liaoning							
吉林	Jilin							
黑龙江	Heilongjiang							
上海	Shanghai	6200	2854	44	3302		2324	1915
江苏	Jiangsu	810	534	4	272		142	117
浙江	Zhejiang	8148	5208	139	2801		1970	1135
安徽	Anhui							
福建	Fujian							
江西	Jiangxi	1065	469	5	591		617	
山东	Shandong	1157	399	4	754		342	396
河南	Henan	1137	676	1	460	3	125	201
湖北	Hubei	2075	998	303	774			221
湖南	Hunan	932	439	59	434		330	41
广东	Guangdong	36773	21898	201	14674		9818	3371
广西	Guangxi	1697	1382	5	310	161	89	200
海南	Hainan							
重庆	Chongqing	829	557	3	269		90	112
四川	Sichuan	22642	12181	107	10354		9560	3719
贵州	Guizhou							
云南	Yunnan							
西藏	Tibet							
陕西	Shaanxi							
甘肃	Gansu							
青海	Qinghai							
宁夏	Ningxia							
新疆	Xinjiang							

单位：万元

Unit: 10000 yuan

财务费用 Financial Expenses	#利息支出 Interest Expenses	营业利润 Operating Profits	利润总额 Total Profits	应交所得税 Income Tax Payable	应付职工薪酬 Payables to Employees	应交增值税 VAT Payable
959	**414**	**4219**	**4979**	**1408**	**22345**	**3988**
-85	15	767	740	190	6352	740
396		53	52	10	812	190
1		7	7		108	12
11		-331	75	24	1871	213
1		14	14	1	231	26
153	143	-457	-299	2	1345	197
4		-30	-32	1	372	
-1		17	20		367	30
79		54	54	1	253	8
7	7	547	547	137	308	112
		63	62		573	
273	6	1212	1142	413	5795	1243
4	4	-2	-6	6	500	101
		67	67		138	7
116	239	2238	2536	623	3320	1109

联营企业

Joint Ownership Enterprises

地 区	Region	主营业务收入 Revenue from Principal Business	主营业务成本 Cost of Principal Business	主营业务税金及附加 Taxes and Other Charges on Principal Business	主营业务利润 Profits from Principal Business	其他业务利润 Profits from Other Business	销售费用 Selling Expenses	管理费用 Administr-ative Expenses
全 国	**National Total**	**10501**	**7282**	**127**	**3092**		**890**	**1140**
北 京	Beijing							
天 津	Tianjin							
河 北	Hebei							
山 西	Shanxi							
内 蒙 古	Inner Mongolia							
辽 宁	Liaoning							
吉 林	Jilin							
黑 龙 江	Heilongjiang							
上 海	Shanghai	793	403	1	389		216	154
江 苏	Jiangsu	305	273	1	31			6
浙 江	Zhejiang	527	414	14	99			83
安 徽	Anhui							
福 建	Fujian							
江 西	Jiangxi							
山 东	Shandong	70	15	2	53		17	21
河 南	Henan							
湖 北	Hubei	4298	3467	73	758		3	450
湖 南	Hunan							
广 东	Guangdong	2254	1130	9	1115		454	372
广 西	Guangxi							
海 南	Hainan							
重 庆	Chongqing							
四 川	Sichuan							
贵 州	Guizhou							
云 南	Yunnan							
西 藏	Tibet							
陕 西	Shaanxi	1774	1370	7	397		2	14
甘 肃	Gansu	480	210	20	250		198	40
青 海	Qinghai							
宁 夏	Ningxia							
新 疆	Xinjiang							

单位：万元
Unit: 10000 yuan

财务费用 Financial Expenses	#利息支出 Interest Expenses	营业利润 Operating Profits	利润总额 Total Profits	应交所得税 Income Tax Payable	应付职工薪酬 Payables to Employees	应交增值税 VAT Payable
36	**2**	**1003**	**994**	**114**	**1056**	**14**
1		18	25	2	101	1
1		25	25		39	1
		16	16		170	1
		16			57	
2	2	304	304	52	242	7
24		239	239	60	299	
8		374	374		80	4
		11	11		68	

有限责任公司

Limited Liability Corporations

地 区	Region	主营业务收入 Revenue from Principal Business	主营业务成本 Cost of Principal Business	主营业务税金及附加 Taxes and Other Charges on Principal Business	主营业务利润 Profits from Principal Business	其他业务利润 Profits from Other Business	销售费用 Selling Expenses	管理费用 Administrative Expenses
全 国	**National Total**	**11151172**	**5793612**	**133348**	**5224212**	**151236**	**3277667**	**1576145**
北 京	Beijing	1399827	578055	5340	816432	19700	560574	206187
天 津	Tianjin	217927	97004	608	120315	971	86861	33937
河 北	Hebei	93375	44871	941	47563	1234	30449	19933
山 西	Shanxi	91001	50006	1522	39473	2015	29944	18979
内 蒙 古	Inner Mongolia	141968	66775	2702	72491	3290	45727	44186
辽 宁	Liaoning	106673	52264	8296	46113	590	33126	22370
吉 林	Jilin	152310	76990	2759	72561	32009	45408	22303
黑 龙 江	Heilongjiang	29436	16766	513	12157		5842	5013
上 海	Shanghai	584454	260310	909	323235	24053	232347	102845
江 苏	Jiangsu	790897	361881	9160	419856	7759	246608	165573
浙 江	Zhejiang	623476	318467	3286	301723	8319	199289	89017
安 徽	Anhui	416641	220221	4992	191428	1821	127077	50144
福 建	Fujian	405691	242167	5068	158456	3224	80579	42944
江 西	Jiangxi	156937	89108	2811	65018	1360	36337	18894
山 东	Shandong	665880	360166	9710	296004	9383	167923	119720
河 南	Henan	455210	265814	9698	179698	3541	85267	48986
湖 北	Hubei	701006	378802	10144	312060	9659	198225	81469
湖 南	Hunan	241851	144218	5463	92170	315	47776	27949
广 东	Guangdong	1631902	879880	10262	741760	4484	487864	203504
广 西	Guangxi	134070	64099	1088	68883	1804	49795	15598
海 南	Hainan	53975	25705	348	27922	222	21322	5741
重 庆	Chongqing	530901	313081	9420	208400	1601	112927	41192
四 川	Sichuan	520908	288950	9790	222168	4920	129213	58587
贵 州	Guizhou	90471	54536	960	34975	15	12408	14098
云 南	Yunnan	171944	105896	3228	62820	2553	35604	16861
西 藏	Tibet	4593	2270	23	2300		280	961
陕 西	Shaanxi	584081	350548	11757	221776	2634	128963	69685
甘 肃	Gansu	101524	59930	2109	39485	563	23151	13588
青 海	Qinghai	7326	4132	35	3159	128	2130	1905
宁 夏	Ningxia	17592	8510	58	9024		4676	7556
新 疆	Xinjiang	27325	12190	348	14787	3069	9975	6420

单位：万元
Unit: 10000 yuan

财务费用 Financial Expenses	#利息支出 Interest Expenses	营业利润 Operating Profits	利润总额 Total Profits	应交所得税 Income Tax Payable	应付职工薪酬 Payables to Employees	应交增值税 VAT Payable
181155	**79009**	**278457**	**322317**	**118518**	**2807727**	**218853**
4547	3260	70132	75660	21414	335521	20732
2111	1391	2063	3158	3747	58462	6041
2176	1155	-4034	-2809	461	26544	1488
1561	875	-21702	-23638	473	21123	1418
6923	5597	-24005	-20108	946	42594	3912
3138	1111	-10913	-10153	1120	17824	2427
1175	724	4104	3633	912	418870	1671
2183	1700	-532	-1286	318	7410	520
3950	408	13152	22530	11885	139911	8245
17000	6769	-17616	-14101	8136	177038	16495
18396	7425	-51	1085	3674	122744	10589
8413	2059	13486	14256	4597	115806	7813
5357	858	28404	26509	5066	65317	5746
2433	1438	7937	7772	905	30240	2059
18798	5460	-4939	-2553	5480	150477	15110
7183	2952	40368	40060	7052	81963	11702
13746	7078	24217	25179	7452	133567	14901
3692	1224	13007	10218	2104	65293	4481
22760	9966	35376	60879	14423	386192	40839
3258	913	1013	920	1799	29235	2110
286	115	573	587	441	20936	1430
4458	2180	53133	52803	5615	65419	9764
12552	6893	29350	26830	3600	97150	12169
953	768	7631	7075	922	17551	1470
1910	1219	10594	9874	2071	30509	3654
42	16	1018	1030	102	849	33
9034	3554	13082	11936	3162	102685	8541
1524	1033	1384	1491	458	31070	1919
164		-1037	-915		2597	737
1061	691	-4237	-4209	2	4637	239
371	177	-2501	-1396	181	8193	598

股份有限公司

Share-holding Corporations Ltd.

地 区	Region	主营业务收入 Revenue from Principal Business	主营业务成本 Cost of Principal Business	主营业务税金及附加 Taxes and Other Charges on Principal Business	主营业务利润 Profits from Principal Business	其他业务利润 Profits from Other Business	销售费用 Selling Expenses	管理费用 Administr-ative Expenses
全 国	**National Total**	**1314300**	**709679**	**18435**	**586186**	**25712**	**350288**	**169847**
北 京	Beijing	129994	37458	916	91620	404	63423	20753
天 津	Tianjin	36291	21422	849	14020	2611	7095	4585
河 北	Hebei	5204	2328	46	2830	1	2033	513
山 西	Shanxi	3526	1802	87	1637		1374	839
内 蒙 古	Inner Mongolia	99689	74281	423	24985	343	13891	3938
辽 宁	Liaoning	7520	3149	182	4189	333	5091	1385
吉 林	Jilin	7779	4059	146	3574		1854	1991
黑 龙 江	Heilongjiang	2300	1351	95	854	82	446	377
上 海	Shanghai	80057	40274	1002	38781	15780	22553	12681
江 苏	Jiangsu	80686	38069	872	41745	542	23104	14590
浙 江	Zhejiang	118860	52728	544	65588	162	42592	19142
安 徽	Anhui	16443	10538	455	5450	289	2002	1347
福 建	Fujian	6985	4000	143	2842		663	1606
江 西	Jiangxi	13695	8867	446	4382	331	1436	1265
山 东	Shandong	83263	41111	1247	40905	2039	21664	14134
河 南	Henan	50748	26614	725	23409	500	11555	4958
湖 北	Hubei	55628	25617	521	29490	45	21728	4555
湖 南	Hunan	18186	10819	602	6765		3069	1685
广 东	Guangdong	105511	52952	892	51667	2260	32913	12567
广 西	Guangxi	7873	4574	190	3109		2055	1190
海 南	Hainan	4701	1894	49	2758		1366	941
重 庆	Chongqing	75760	40253	468	35039		14954	12125
四 川	Sichuan	30197	17016	638	12543	-15	8236	3992
贵 州	Guizhou	5584	2147	277	3160	5	790	683
云 南	Yunnan	14700	7969	474	6257		2873	2223
西 藏	Tibet							
陕 西	Shaanxi	223850	162526	5757	55567		34164	11635
甘 肃	Gansu	15495	8597	277	6621		3864	11339
青 海	Qinghai	6725	4203	106	2416		2602	753
宁 夏	Ningxia	1596	711	3	882		688	185
新 疆	Xinjiang	5454	2350	3	3101		210	1870

单位：万元

Unit: 10000 yuan

财务费用 Financial Expenses	#利息支出 Interest Expenses	营业利润 Operating Profits	利润总额 Total Profits	应交所得税 Income Tax Payable	应付职工薪酬 Payables to Employees	应交增值税 VAT Payable
40461	**25509**	**111068**	**110279**	**12237**	**434640**	**94545**
475	383	17365	17458	2615	51896	2570
9889	8291	-1879	-1866	15	6336	689
742	730	-1111	-1108	38	1793	77
555	520	-1131	-961		1504	77
3126		4994	6369	100	7049	55
58		-2307	-1867	4	1169	123
582		-773	-712	4	1650	122
2		30	29	2	415	7
2712		11861	11837	593	14724	1982
4216	-83	730	1106	689	16605	1243
2120	1833	25316	26934	888	36022	1885
117	73	1084	1153	84	4226	437
12	4	561	-20	6	1580	183
68	32	1605	736	60	121836	72190
6939	6658	-1760	-3584	538	55561	1442
2722	1236	4350	2101	581	10017	906
1457	57	2718	2731	188	10048	1591
368	28	1797	1395	218	1559	683
-793	25	30926	30454	2295	26580	2846
168	139	-280	-265	7	1490	198
67		475	501	37	1095	142
2422	2814	5538	5917	557	17957	2618
203	145	-300	371	149	6678	652
409	397	1324	1207	266	653	21
624	504	580	192	5	2961	411
696	1233	9855	10339	2063	28920	1145
4	11	373	400	44	1913	153
234	234	-1192	-972		749	49
215	215	-206	-172		508	39
52	30	525	576	191	1146	9

私营企业
Private Enterprises

地 区	Region	主营业务收入 Revenue from Principal Business	主营业务成本 Cost of Principal Business	主营业务税金及附加 Taxes and Other Charges on Principal Business	主营业务利润 Profits from Principal Business	其他业务利润 Profits from Other Business	销售费用 Selling Expenses	管理费用 Administrative Expenses
全 国	**National Total**	**21656585**	**12560931**	**277996**	**8817658**	**161295**	**4969625**	**2548630**
北 京	Beijing	1735866	811402	4730	919734	14438	679506	211128
天 津	Tianjin	221215	120910	1296	99009	3096	71131	31513
河 北	Hebei	270265	137730	4166	128369	3580	83676	39943
山 西	Shanxi	290410	144659	3498	142253	5985	103716	58043
内蒙古	Inner Mongolia	177783	87629	1840	88314	2655	50729	32834
辽 宁	Liaoning	230420	124817	3682	101921	5540	52342	44516
吉 林	Jilin	69123	38266	1647	29210	623	14102	10726
黑龙江	Heilongjiang	61627	36042	1278	24307		18133	4633
上 海	Shanghai	2270262	1155686	7703	1106873	27285	752527	280889
江 苏	Jiangsu	1783350	1069322	18868	695160	4985	372207	222833
浙 江	Zhejiang	1698299	936261	13851	748187	11167	450832	250350
安 徽	Anhui	956784	547095	14472	395217	4437	205472	113940
福 建	Fujian	1097329	783067	14610	299652	1664	139642	94655
江 西	Jiangxi	164543	101219	3283	60041	4912	24471	18776
山 东	Shandong	1485281	965550	22019	497712	3853	215791	139209
河 南	Henan	761447	483195	22181	256071	7891	74404	55082
湖 北	Hubei	956540	599059	21732	335749	3738	137727	84453
湖 南	Hunan	882481	523283	22056	337142	8404	162247	85382
广 东	Guangdong	2531970	1391810	24439	1115721	16390	701308	349893
广 西	Guangxi	206755	120294	3475	82986	2343	52499	26005
海 南	Hainan	10269	4715	105	5449	1307	2973	1891
重 庆	Chongqing	1251936	807336	24439	420161	3347	139080	118657
四 川	Sichuan	955804	589399	16187	350218	8221	170705	103198
贵 州	Guizhou	252776	164231	3284	85261	3488	30685	30408
云 南	Yunnan	317640	213468	6577	97595	1556	39778	32184
西 藏	Tibet	5038	2257	91	2690	76	1830	1327
陕 西	Shaanxi	684427	432028	12151	240248	3383	123373	64824
甘 肃	Gansu	156049	88927	2793	64329	2575	38713	13872
青 海	Qinghai	30058	15326	342	14390	1651	8811	4305
宁 夏	Ningxia	45951	23549	547	21855	2551	14755	7562
新 疆	Xinjiang	94887	42399	654	51834	154	36460	15599

单位：万元

Unit: 10000 yuan

财务费用 Financial Expenses	#利息支出 Interest Expenses	营业利润 Operating Profits	利润总额 Total Profits	应交所得税 Income Tax Payable	应付职工薪酬 Payables to Employees	应交增值税 VAT Payable
333039	**149870**	**1049931**	**1055097**	**200028**	**3684249**	**396203**
14498	5976	29734	33731	13087	392590	23114
840	80	-2656	-1628	981	44361	3597
9208	2309	-2867	-2186	1415	61906	5686
9492	6452	-27150	-27262	942	71381	4921
2707	1254	2061	3047	423	39615	3129
8799	3344	-5356	-7180	1443	34543	3995
2111	873	1889	1319	409	14016	1112
1136	150	591	767	122	7040	624
16644	1882	62642	81303	21733	367028	34943
27121	8758	76114	79479	16958	315392	35666
32777	18764	29925	39618	15142	317464	32425
26047	12442	51942	66384	9567	156900	13129
5367	2751	60722	56088	9798	115152	11647
4575	1710	14176	12933	509	30281	3917
26192	11038	117328	116037	21854	211998	35853
12623	1864	113061	109696	11833	98851	14403
18661	6770	97760	92208	11379	128796	18852
19479	8156	69674	57003	7911	139570	15311
21240	7335	50847	56659	21254	516674	60217
3936	2905	2206	2081	887	42807	4345
646	629	-107	-108	12	2194	296
13926	5911	165178	151857	12853	148996	22411
26009	14090	54293	47081	6534	141786	17146
4636	3008	19690	21038	1820	42663	4437
7023	11787	19525	17767	1798	56598	5127
178	4	-645	-575		2030	77
7693	2738	46565	44567	7812	101005	14255
3466	2370	7602	7779	894	38455	2498
1111	816	82	85	50	10243	623
1119	309	-1386	-1088	265	12043	869
3779	3395	-3509	-3403	343	21871	1578

其他企业
Other Enterprises

地 区	Region	主营业务收入 Revenue from Principal Business	主营业务成本 Cost of Principal Business	主营业务税金及附加 Taxes and Other Charges on Principal Business	主营业务利润 Profits from Principal Business	其他业务利润 Profits from Other Business	销售费用 Selling Expenses	管理费用 Administr-ative Expenses
全 国	**National Total**	**323847**	**224463**	**7834**	**91550**	**973**	**38974**	**23387**
北 京	Beijing							
天 津	Tianjin	371	200	25	146		34	64
河 北	Hebei							
山 西	Shanxi	917	667	35	215	215	523	442
内蒙古	Inner Mongolia	1547	988	33	526		300	115
辽 宁	Liaoning	4723	2514	86	2123	9	1520	363
吉 林	Jilin	7142	3012	113	4017		2618	468
黑龙江	Heilongjiang	169	94	8	67		51	8
上 海	Shanghai	16888	10096	45	6747	57	5849	1091
江 苏	Jiangsu	6187	3845	94	2248		746	1359
浙 江	Zhejiang	1703	1192	90	421		330	81
安 徽	Anhui	104	98	1	5		3	3
福 建	Fujian	26903	21530	559	4814	3	905	984
江 西	Jiangxi	2246	987	36	1223		660	255
山 东	Shandong	31211	22862	365	7984		2249	2758
河 南	Henan	7994	6005	214	1775	217	302	664
湖 北	Hubei	55335	43282	2094	9959		1808	1713
湖 南	Hunan	6308	3012	198	3098		1655	1185
广 东	Guangdong	53931	33043	1699	19189	378	9939	5515
广 西	Guangxi							
海 南	Hainan							
重 庆	Chongqing	37378	26814	795	9769	3	2816	1436
四 川	Sichuan	17500	11952	480	5068		1607	1214
贵 州	Guizhou	2589	1794	40	755		130	184
云 南	Yunnan	6759	4809	105	1845		527	612
西 藏	Tibet							
陕 西	Shaanxi	33320	24018	661	8641		3695	2649
甘 肃	Gansu	1582	1019	38	525	91	354	172
青 海	Qinghai							
宁 夏	Ningxia	512	356	18	138		73	52
新 疆	Xinjiang	528	274	2	252		280	

4-4-7 Continued 8

单位：万元
Unit: 10000 yuan

财务费用 Financial Expenses	#利息支出 Interest Expenses	营业利润 Operating Profits	利润总额 Total Profits	应交所得税 Income Tax Payable	应付职工薪酬 Payables to Employees	应交增值税 VAT Payable
4546	**2093**	**23189**	**20665**	**2215**	**41431**	**5609**
30		20	20			1
1		-750	-3		399	28
5		105	105	4	470	14
272	58	-55	298		962	13
578	573	349	349	27	455	138
1		8	8		91	7
85	59	-219	-79	40	5426	454
50	22	100	105	11	1646	63
		15	-27		1001	121
					21	
33	5	2789	821	29	2277	122
19		288	289	5	617	235
387	3	2614	2603	646	3979	491
121	4	462	448	41	973	36
518	67	5854	5696	321	3049	478
68		190	118		362	134
753	546	2766	2903	350	10875	1651
294	78	4496	3154	207	3360	504
116	5	2082	1995	324	1392	269
38		402	343	60	330	54
58	18	489	495	22	787	73
1100	640	1219	1197	114	2382	631
16	15	-17	-146	8	311	72
		13	2		119	
3		-31	-29	6	147	20

港、澳、台商投资企业
Enterprises with Funds from Hongkong, Macao and Taiwan

地 区	Region	主营业务收入 Revenue from Principal Business	主营业务成本 Cost of Principal Business	主营业务税金及附加 Taxes and Other Charges on Principal Business	主营业务利润 Profits from Principal Business	其他业务利润 Profits from Other Business	销售费用 Selling Expenses	管理费用 Administrative Expenses
全 国	**National Total**	**6203992**	**2206492**	**12115**	**3985385**	**47253**	**2942463**	**573616**
北 京	Beijing	1453202	455515	1384	996303	4725	730177	113651
天 津	Tianjin	130080	41942	123	88015	36	70922	7144
河 北	Hebei	1155	557	3	595		956	140
山 西	Shanxi	17388	5431	26	11931		10256	576
内 蒙 古	Inner Mongolia	3503	1277		2226		1866	240
辽 宁	Liaoning	145760	49060	102	96598		75167	10175
吉 林	Jilin	176	82	7	87		62	12
黑 龙 江	Heilongjiang	12252	4340	68	7844	362	6295	1409
上 海	Shanghai	1606338	596004	2141	1008193	5504	767514	180536
江 苏	Jiangsu	264952	102017	909	162026	7808	123308	26880
浙 江	Zhejiang	191370	62632	245	128493	1547	99489	17981
安 徽	Anhui	1456	790		666		488	144
福 建	Fujian	250009	99531	1203	149275	4855	108240	28456
江 西	Jiangxi	9074	4221	69	4784		3951	1516
山 东	Shandong	72679	24905	140	47634	156	36511	9984
河 南	Henan	2639	1037	3	1599		1729	429
湖 北	Hubei	511132	213088	359	297685	34	199862	45995
湖 南	Hunan	5076	3999	150	927		293	364
广 东	Guangdong	1255060	449928	3737	801395	9664	581743	100631
广 西	Guangxi	11137	4349	55	6733	10	5315	1259
海 南	Hainan	20462	5601	630	14231	5023	8879	6770
重 庆	Chongqing	5237	1865	6	3366	3940	3173	3490
四 川	Sichuan	168395	43026	450	124919	1604	84268	10993
贵 州	Guizhou	373	310		63		22	12
云 南	Yunnan	25635	17426	195	8014		3151	2116
西 藏	Tibet							
陕 西	Shaanxi	38966	17381	103	21482	1985	18608	2443
甘 肃	Gansu	483	176	2	305		168	171
青 海	Qinghai							
宁 夏	Ningxia							
新 疆	Xinjiang	3	2	5	-4		50	99

单位：万元
Unit: 10000 yuan

财务费用 Financial Expenses	#利息支出 Interest Expenses	营业利润 Operating Profits	利润总额 Total Profits	应交所得税 Income Tax Payable	应付职工薪酬 Payables to Employees	应交增值税 VAT Payable
37352	**17082**	**491903**	**490667**	**135939**	**1215462**	**19103**
2460	4738	151957	150105	41074	369780	-2910
1168	6	8781	7321	268	24903	172
1		-322	-318		470	48
453		647	400		2756	
-9		130	129	32	532	
2712	4	7369	6541	2635	26949	337
1		14	14	3	21	4
77		63	22	7	310	200
6023	2504	81291	85534	25905	254707	-2876
3253	706	13406	13427	3587	47439	2891
6222	2165	10393	10399	1801	37429	1116
2		32	32	8	245	
4585	1567	16589	14571	5231	43466	1306
89	58	-777	-746	4	2277	201
4943	3729	-3637	-3304	960	14810	385
3		-562	-573		1114	20
3216	184	45743	45444	11338	112291	1047
75	2	196	196	1	275	165
1054	1568	127221	129223	34873	246499	13480
22	4	630	834	164	2626	70
-35		-1374	-1349	283	3943	112
-158	-164	891	705	191	1073	195
780		30491	29544	7086	8017	504
		29	29		18	
-28	2	2930	2940	488	6460	1822
442	9	-41	-266		6856	796
1		-35	-35		180	18
		-152	-152		16	

外商投资企业

Foreign Funded Enterprises

地区	Region	主营业务收入 Revenue from Principal Business	主营业务成本 Cost of Principal Business	主营业务税金及附加 Taxes and Other Charges on Principal Business	主营业务利润 Profits from Principal Business	其他业务利润 Profits from Other Business	销售费用 Selling Expenses	管理费用 Administr-ative Expenses
全国	**National Total**	**8470999**	**3831883**	**20623**	**4618493**	**59969**	**2993526**	**840308**
北京	Beijing	1304594	586508	716	717370	10524	481480	145062
天津	Tianjin	304511	149824	262	154425	3484	94670	36997
河北	Hebei	724	452	4	268		182	63
山西	Shanxi	60632	29250	6	31376		18314	5128
内蒙古	Inner Mongolia	32514	18932	240	13342		3763	7026
辽宁	Liaoning	437493	206648	231	230614	665	139548	45626
吉林	Jilin	675	245	13	417		95	165
黑龙江	Heilongjiang	4294	1632	61	2601		637	1023
上海	Shanghai	2074248	783282	2060	1288906	1358	913694	191312
江苏	Jiangsu	836592	409126	5680	421786	575	237955	81622
浙江	Zhejiang	500135	235203	491	264441	5996	137522	58822
安徽	Anhui	3109	2091	350	668		217	1374
福建	Fujian	209887	106772	395	102720	30916	66401	22454
江西	Jiangxi	70935	34523	39	36373		20963	6174
山东	Shandong	213692	106054	264	107374		59428	24535
河南	Henan	70958	36139	81	34738		23687	11344
湖北	Hubei	23402	13134	407	9861	8	8329	2204
湖南	Hunan	148037	69643	337	78057		43528	14256
广东	Guangdong	1507779	659143	7305	841331	2879	597122	120953
广西	Guangxi	64975	29872	69	35034	10	16854	5936
海南	Hainan							
重庆	Chongqing	169850	129839	620	39391		14019	11404
四川	Sichuan	214458	122870	565	91023	3211	49579	21257
贵州	Guizhou							
云南	Yunnan	55645	25754	37	29854	343	16616	5894
西藏	Tibet							
陕西	Shaanxi	106878	50228	362	56288		34340	14971
甘肃	Gansu	29405	12873	7	16525		7883	2261
青海	Qinghai							
宁夏	Ningxia							
新疆	Xinjiang	25577	11846	21	13710		6700	2445

4-4-7 Continued 10

单位：万元
Unit: 10000 yuan

财务费用 Financial Expenses	#利息支出 Interest Expenses	营业利润 Operating Profits	利润总额 Total Profits	应交所得税 Income Tax Payable	应付职工薪酬 Payables to Employees	应交增值税 VAT Payable
3455	**4594**	**758674**	**788456**	**203850**	**1662960**	**190817**
1198	2161	95476	118390	27819	331268	-1493
-295	-265	25017	25159	6990	65476	247
		23	23	5	177	17
6		7348	7435	1866	9160	44
-11		638	-6704		4191	42857
8	38	41755	41508	10809	25035	734
21	20	136	-57	1	226	9
11	2	931	931	296	566	107
1354	1457	178463	185891	55959	455109	131983
891	-48	100487	101139	25296	95045	1370
-183	555	74518	78027	19653	95907	1968
6		-928	-956		933	337
525	683	11207	7327	3960	45547	2916
36		8923	9218	2299	13860	
-162	232	22345	22629	5695	23887	296
450	3	-872	3297	639	11355	550
-50	4	-574	-775	188	5295	545
147	107	19516	19613	17	23411	1559
152	-1042	97399	97371	23493	333895	4695
-39		12542	12628	3151	8752	-2
130	432	13974	13175	2675	33316	556
-514	10	21474	24863	5986	43462	223
-130		7443	7466	1855	8855	291
33	245	10357	9941	2463	20192	442
-126		6508	6398	1603	3752	
-3		4568	4519	1132	4288	566

4-4-8 各地区限额以上餐饮业企业损益及分配(按国民经济行业分)

正餐服务

Dinner

地　区	Region	主营业务收入 Revenue from Principal Business	主营业务成本 Cost of Principal Business	主营业务税金及附加 Taxes and Other Charges on Principal Business	主营业务利润 Profits from Principal Business	其他业务利润 Profits from Other Business	销售费用 Selling Expenses	管理费用 Administrative Expenses
全　国	**National Total**	**34476939**	**18718389**	**435892**	**15322658**	**355927**	**9135032**	**4507063**
北　京	Beijing	3725729	1560573	11086	2154070	30160	1513835	496976
天　津	Tianjin	385758	185785	2386	197587	5976	144059	59622
河　北	Hebei	379387	193555	5551	180281	4848	117633	62635
山　西	Shanxi	384035	195431	5244	183360	9271	136435	82883
内蒙古	Inner Mongolia	452669	246553	5172	200944	6107	117675	93184
辽　宁	Liaoning	317444	162964	12265	142215	7123	89749	64528
吉　林	Jilin	222374	108893	4698	108783	29038	57742	45083
黑龙江	Heilongjiang	95029	56934	2229	35866	444	19613	12984
上　海	Shanghai	3762852	1631962	11286	2119604	70223	1540401	511893
江　苏	Jiangsu	2543588	1378357	28593	1136638	19162	634360	404569
浙　江	Zhejiang	2235492	1157327	16963	1061202	23111	645961	357495
安　徽	Anhui	1116765	653391	19163	444211	6284	213325	151088
福　建	Fujian	1424660	928017	20440	476203	4769	232536	143140
江　西	Jiangxi	353366	206985	6626	139755	6784	70386	42126
山　东	Shandong	2225943	1350614	34486	840843	20617	413249	295815
河　南	Henan	1158381	712413	30409	415559	12269	148395	100270
湖　北	Hubei	1757692	1050698	34929	672065	13503	337406	178915
湖　南	Hunan	1080658	655187	25554	399917	8723	182631	115243
广　东	Guangdong	4193424	2150257	38249	2004918	23158	1321714	558382
广　西	Guangxi	295850	165348	4644	125858	2581	81369	40999
海　南	Hainan	80175	35414	1142	43619	6552	32254	11634
重　庆	Chongqing	1922939	1256022	34821	632096	4955	231528	171830
四　川	Sichuan	1505465	888354	27346	589765	12961	307730	176570
贵　州	Guizhou	336682	211312	4440	120930	3691	43558	44496
云　南	Yunnan	495975	331717	10386	153872	4488	69424	49694
西　藏	Tibet	4473	2068	81	2324	76	1711	1308
陕　西	Shaanxi	1535945	976370	30106	529469	7064	297450	148021
甘　肃	Gansu	278667	162750	5501	110416	4456	64731	40067
青　海	Qinghai	43508	23310	456	19742	1779	13483	6863
宁　夏	Ningxia	68120	34598	635	32887	2551	21247	15565
新　疆	Xinjiang	93894	45230	1005	47659	3203	33442	23185

Income and Distribution of Enterprises above Designated Size of Catering Services by Region and Sector

单位：万元

Unit: 10000 yuan

财务费用 Financial Expenses	#利息支出 Interest Expenses	营业利润 Operating Profits	利润总额 Total Profits	应交所得税 Income Tax Payable	应付职工薪酬 Payables to Employees	应交增值税 VAT Payable
569288	**267437**	**1354547**	**1440575**	**354996**	**7177196**	**739505**
23549	14148	159982	181025	51996	931076	38916
12692	9761	-6752	-3481	4134	95225	8559
12915	4204	-10724	-8758	1898	89836	7414
11621	7850	-56390	-53807	1202	96075	6748
12619	6652	-23118	-23371	1341	97863	50002
13156	4432	-26085	-26016	1855	53939	6270
4191	2195	1961	925	1167	434014	2990
2746	1852	1199	665	829	14876	1410
25735	3954	84516	118366	47632	703453	47318
48879	15980	44174	53001	24657	497109	52695
54736	30005	56253	71701	19932	447842	42799
33919	14491	45823	57713	11633	225431	18803
14021	4680	85600	75837	14647	186943	17904
7195	3251	22565	20376	1440	185632	78782
55522	26868	82901	89918	26941	424686	52564
22155	5801	146003	141446	18426	178308	23880
35233	14166	130491	124461	19737	275523	34529
22162	8003	79909	64258	9757	194107	20271
42665	17898	115135	152024	42584	941056	102123
6455	3447	-2016	-1846	1385	63236	6450
937	744	-1152	-1095	574	27358	1972
20359	10557	228411	214926	19045	250977	33742
38885	21299	83435	74756	10278	242368	31686
5899	4150	27496	28154	3013	58074	5870
9738	13612	28878	27305	3282	87562	9511
182		-877	-795		1828	68
18248	8188	67853	67769	13482	237284	26432
4955	3492	9145	9199	1387	72896	4788
1438	1050	-2142	-1796	50	13459	1409
2398	1215	-6213	-5625	268	18061	1276
4083	3492	-11714	-6660	424	31099	2324

快餐服务

Snack

地区	Region	主营业务收入 Revenue from Principal Business	主营业务成本 Cost of Principal Business	主营业务税金及附加 Taxes and Other Charges on Principal Business	主营业务利润 Profits from Principal Business	其他业务利润 Profits from Other Business	销售费用 Selling Expenses	管理费用 Administrative Expenses
全国	**National Total**	**11404614**	**5224585**	**32542**	**6147487**	**94517**	**4184480**	**1047514**
北京	Beijing	1767828	683517	1274	1083037	19852	790379	159569
天津	Tianjin	453150	202821	382	249947	4227	171816	45035
河北	Hebei	2967	1281	57	1629		1153	161
山西	Shanxi	91599	41612	57	49930		31382	6635
内蒙古	Inner Mongolia	10451	5369	144	4938	181	2747	2078
辽宁	Liaoning	599222	288138	781	310303		203900	54602
吉林	Jilin	30673	16122	195	14356	3594	10422	2088
黑龙江	Heilongjiang	20136	6599	21	13516		12058	797
上海	Shanghai	1566579	723149	1020	842410	1374	569152	167757
江苏	Jiangsu	1052977	501293	6475	545209	1773	327243	107827
浙江	Zhejiang	764818	362636	853	401329	3099	256506	64927
安徽	Anhui	268809	119363	956	148490	290	122830	16017
福建	Fujian	518237	299204	1089	217944	35855	149319	44961
江西	Jiangxi	78024	38710	173	39141	106	22812	6556
山东	Shandong	364824	183063	1037	180724	532	113424	30965
河南	Henan	162263	86290	2445	73528	4	46209	16071
湖北	Hubei	410522	193909	290	216323	42	148044	39631
湖南	Hunan	226028	103218	3715	119095		75992	17523
广东	Guangdong	2166204	961257	8924	1196023	12922	856820	180515
广西	Guangxi	136009	61617	280	74112	941	46691	10474
海南	Hainan	9711	2827	2	6882		2449	3790
重庆	Chongqing	117146	51313	577	65256	3940	44536	10182
四川	Sichuan	248522	136588	368	111566	4813	67632	24161
贵州	Guizhou	2852	1639	37	1176	14	422	494
云南	Yunnan	80558	34572	48	45938		29056	6650
西藏	Tibet	3898	1931	21	1946		375	229
陕西	Shaanxi	152035	76089	889	75057	958	47395	18028
甘肃	Gansu	40570	16604	301	23665		14371	3361
青海	Qinghai	600	350	26	224		60	100
宁夏	Ningxia							
新疆	Xinjiang	57402	23504	105	33793		19285	6330

单位：万元

Unit: 10000 yuan

财务费用 Financial Expenses	#利息支出 Interest Expenses	营业利润 Operating Profits	利润总额 Total Profits	应交所得税 Income Tax Payable	应付职工薪酬 Payables to Employees	应交增值税 VAT Payable
29488	**7241**	**939561**	**942312**	**215380**	**1973419**	**31782**
562	2200	151675	153004	39196	372778	-3766
825	-258	34363	32954	7019	93163	333
5		315	289	6	706	39
506		10829	8607	2081	14593	61
-65	1	181	197	164	1579	188
2790	4	45307	44474	11663	39426	550
254	7	1435	1450	182	5690	104
693		-32	-26		2253	98
2531	532	127770	130443	26088	216988	-120
2908	-42	111116	111175	27241	138093	3604
4148	674	78482	78714	19640	138671	1826
563	89	17926	21297	2565	52194	2853
1729	1185	28130	23069	7731	80896	3619
64	21	9427	9765	2329	15380	81
1516	441	34467	33671	7638	52914	1730
1827	140	9218	13397	1428	18365	1248
2212		23194	23399	5569	99511	137
1888	1490	23142	23563	552	37726	2188
3139	420	141292	140259	32797	449578	12566
465	82	17593	17705	4648	23356	458
28		615	624	200	956	10
-148	-124	14302	13911	2513	14010	1263
348	-14	21535	23882	5889	48028	92
22	19	251	263	3	417	-36
-125	8	10367	10081	2538	12180	292
21	4	1321	1321	102	555	14
549	251	12311	11838	2584	25918	1587
40		5887	5851	1609	6767	110
70		-6	-6		130	
123	111	7148	7141	1405	10598	653

饮料及冷饮服务
Beverage and Cold Drink

地 区	Region	主营业务收入 Revenue from Principal Business	主营业务成本 Cost of Principal Business	主营业务税金及附加 Taxes and Other Charges on Principal Business	主营业务利润 Profits from Principal Business	其他业务利润 Profits from Other Business	销售费用 Selling Expenses	管理费用 Administr-ative Expenses
全 国	**National Total**	**2017699**	**573451**	**3856**	**1440392**	**5969**	**994601**	**124868**
北 京	Beijing	304851	75244	393	229214	701	157939	24280
天 津	Tianjin	447	143	5	299		578	17
河 北	Hebei							
山 西	Shanxi							
内 蒙 古	Inner Mongolia							
辽 宁	Liaoning	27465	6473	42	20950		13575	1574
吉 林	Jilin	247	148	9	90		72	7
黑 龙 江	Heilongjiang	232	65	1	166		216	85
上 海	Shanghai	969216	267602	1059	700555	3097	513551	49857
江 苏	Jiangsu	24218	10963	255	13000	788	9740	3204
浙 江	Zhejiang	22643	9925	227	12491		5315	6497
安 徽	Anhui	2631	1714	52	865		500	216
福 建	Fujian	14528	8545	148	5835	29	3780	2386
江 西	Jiangxi	524	267	9	248	209	153	15
山 东	Shandong	14846	3555	6	11285		7461	416
河 南	Henan	3427	2241	37	1149		255	263
湖 北	Hubei	93333	22737	147	70449		44924	3598
湖 南	Hunan	2074	1179	72	823		289	348
广 东	Guangdong	404220	126586	657	276977	61	176710	25570
广 西	Guangxi	2345	1071	81	1193	806	1145	336
海 南	Hainan							
重 庆	Chongqing	5072	2193	58	2821		1257	16
四 川	Sichuan	119386	28865	451	90070	121	55624	5479
贵 州	Guizhou	1645	1435	6	204		48	124
云 南	Yunnan	2847	1647	102	1098		780	386
西 藏	Tibet	253	182	8	63		25	31
陕 西	Shaanxi	709	423	8	278		308	116
甘 肃	Gansu	540	248	23	269	157	356	47
青 海	Qinghai							
宁 夏	Ningxia							
新 疆	Xinjiang							

单位：万元
Unit: 10000 yuan

财务费用 Financial Expenses	#利息支出 Interest Expenses	营业利润 Operating Profits	利润总额 Total Profits	应交所得税 Income Tax Payable	应付职工薪酬 Payables to Employees	应交增值税 VAT Payable
	2592	**321929**	**331983**	**90214**	**491248**	**131284**
-1270	21	47229	57380	13658	127252	2745
2		-297	-401		262	
-2		5805	5823	1525	11106	219
1		9	9	2	25	6
		-135	-133		102	7
1699	1738	136541	138911	41582	244611	123934
295	265	288	972	237	3937	267
37		658	681	282	4553	491
40		131	94	17	738	56
20	2	-335	-311	76	1615	114
		80	80	11	76	8
-20		3429	3296	847	1734	35
40	2	575	574	98	556	69
86		21822	21450	5312	12028	544
20	6	179	144	13	627	17
-1362	70	75284	74970	19452	78175	2444
471	467	415	135		882	137
7		1517	-367		405	
-60	16	29038	28844	7100	1731	140
1		31	15		227	42
-10	5	-58	-58		133	
		8	8		146	8
		-146	6		277	
5		-139	-139	2	50	1

其他餐饮业

Others

地　区	Region	主营业务收入 Revenue from Principal Business	主营业务成本 Cost of Principal Business	主营业务税金及附加 Taxes and Other Charges on Principal Business	主营业务利润 Profits from Principal Business	其他业务利润 Profits from Other Business	销售费用 Selling Expenses	管理费用 Administr-ative Expenses
全　国	**National Total**	**2141045**	**1357908**	**11092**	**772045**	**5198**	**470941**	**216535**
北　京	Beijing	318672	199874	876	117922	-50	79926	30857
天　津	Tianjin	79732	45536	536	33660		17714	12194
河　北	Hebei	14532	6354	35	8143	56	6095	1872
山　西	Shanxi	1339	1045	51	243		43	41
内蒙古	Inner Mongolia	3275	2792	16	467		243	427
辽　宁	Liaoning	40028	25421	172	14435	30	1102	9970
吉　林	Jilin	6091	5011	25	1055		366	432
黑龙江	Heilongjiang	408	246	8	154			168
上　海	Shanghai	402420	261431	709	140280	3443	89701	50531
江　苏	Jiangsu	209273	125089	1412	82772	43	53825	12343
浙　江	Zhejiang	132314	88049	642	43623	980	26561	11993
安　徽	Anhui	12943	9805	146	2992		1284	857
福　建	Fujian	54350	29192	404	24754	65	15211	2571
江　西	Jiangxi	899	670	11	218		37	99
山　东	Shandong	61173	45434	673	15066	14	3696	7375
河　南	Henan	42128	29919	518	11691	226	3660	5770
湖　北	Hubei	73122	28226	813	44083	27	39807	3093
湖　南	Hunan	9719	5546	110	4063		2338	846
广　东	Guangdong	467660	317825	2357	147478	316	85992	46137
广　西	Guangxi	504	509		-5			
海　南	Hainan							
重　庆	Chongqing	59932	38555	527	20850		10269	7863
四　川	Sichuan	72599	39364	259	32976	48	25681	2162
贵　州	Guizhou	11511	9258	92	2161		255	892
云　南	Yunnan	26171	16940	256	8975		1185	5011
西　藏	Tibet	1006	346	4	656			720
陕　西	Shaanxi	27971	19926	397	7648		1401	1853
甘　肃	Gansu	1608	900	11	697		306	224
青　海	Qinghai							
宁　夏	Ningxia							
新　疆	Xinjiang	9665	4645	32	4988		4243	234

单位：万元

Unit: 10000 yuan

财务费用 Financial Expenses	#利息支出 Interest Expenses	营业利润 Operating Profits	利润总额 Total Profits	应交所得税 Income Tax Payable	应付职工薪酬 Payables to Employees	应交增值税 VAT Payable
7191	**2685**	**85258**	**82141**	**19944**	**411392**	**42308**
303	187	7253	7428	1749	76337	7009
324	4	3366	3262	865	13986	2079
45		129	194	46	6287	239
4		170	-129		91	4
199	198	-367	-367		247	17
122	192	3162	2963	760	5397	650
35	4	221	218	6	1188	66
		-14	-14		65	
738	92	2284	3747	1891	89341	4850
681	136	16393	15744	2987	29787	3390
479	209	4876	5323	1581	24704	3340
40		811	933	81	1820	141
118	1	7378	7317	1799	9096	742
7		84	59	2	478	1
620	27	3086	3058	710	11912	1155
474	271	1826	427	241	8924	2566
101	43	1072	1255	467	10241	2431
75	42	755	794	49	1622	118
1229	258	17697	17765	4193	82315	11018
		-5	-5		241	
951	829	1579	1536	713	9905	1317
253	144	4928	5045	1054	13205	566
114	4	900	867	51	2876	139
-37	9	2971	2980	420	7832	1850
16	16	-80	-80		350	20
286	18	4170	1258	240	1957	-1436
2	1	112	166	14	384	36
12		501	397	25	804	

4-5-1 限额以上住宿和餐饮业产业活动单位和个体经营户基本情况

Basic Conditions of Establishments and Getihus above Designated Size of Hotels and Catering Services

项 目	Item	单位数（个）Number of Units (unit)	年末从业人数（人）Engaged Persons at the Year-end (person)
总 计	**Total**	**38044**	**1105178**
一、住宿业	**Hotels**	**5461**	**300269**
（一）按登记注册类型分	**by Type of Registration**		
1.内资企业	**Domestic Funded Enterprises**	**1091**	**178031**
国有企业	State-owned Enterprises	224	28124
集体企业	Collective-owned Enterprises	16	1075
股份合作企业	Cooperative Enterprises	7	3274
联营企业	Joint Ownership Enterprises	6	638
国有联营企业	State Joint Ownership Enterprises	NA	33
集体联营企业	Collective Joint Ownership Enterprises	NA	149
国有与集体联营企业	Joint State-collective Enterprises		
其他联营企业	Other Joint Ownership Enterprises	4	456
有限责任公司	Limited Liability Corporations	438	79108
国有独资公司	State Sole Funded Corporations	22	3333
其他有限责任公司	Other Limited Liability Corporations	416	75775
股份有限公司	Share-holding Corporations Ltd.	73	14071
私营企业	Private Enterprises	282	45103
私营独资企业	Private-funded Enterprises	24	2775
私营合伙企业	Private Partnership Enterprises	5	190
私营有限责任公司	Private Limited Liability Corporations	239	40365
私营股份有限公司	Private Share-holding Corporations Ltd.	14	1773
其他内资企业	Other Domestic Funded Enterprises	45	6638
2.港、澳、台商投资企业	**Enterprises with Funds from Hongkong, Macao and Taiwan**	**54**	**16400**
合资经营企业	Joint-venture Enterprises	21	6798
合作经营企业	Cooperative Enterprises	NA	938
独资经营企业	Enterprises with Sole Investment	25	7102
投资股份有限公司	Share-holding Corporations Ltd. with Investment	4	1137
其他港澳台商投资企业	Other Enterprises with Funds from Hongkong, Macao and Taiwan	NA	425
3.外商投资企业	**Foreign Funded Enterprises**	**53**	**15012**
中外合资经营企业	Joint-venture Enterprises	23	6862
中外合作经营企业	Cooperative Enterprises	NA	1395
外资企业	Enterprises with Sole Foreign Investment	19	4292
外商投资股份有限公司	Share-holding Corporations Ltd. With Foreign Investment	NA	746
其他外商投资企业	Other Foreign Funded Enterprises	5	1717
4.个体经营户	**Getihus**	**4263**	**90826**
（二）按国民经济行业分	**by Sector**		
旅游饭店	Tourist Hotel	1926	211283
一般旅馆	Fonda	3274	79876
其他住宿业	Others	261	9110

项　目	Item	单位数(个) Number of Units (unit)	年末从业人数(人) Engaged Persons at the Year-end (person)	年末餐饮营业面积(平方米) Business Area of Catering Services at the Year-end (㎡)
二、餐饮业	**Catering Services**	**32583**	**804909**	**26353338**
(一)按登记注册类型分	**by Type of Registration**			
1.内资企业	**Domestic Funded Enterprises**	**566**	**62004**	**2005791**
国有企业	State-owned Enterprises	97	10936	336397
集体企业	Collective-owned Enterprises	22	1303	54788
股份合作企业	Cooperative Enterprises	NA	47	510
联营企业	Joint Ownership Enterprises	NA	211	22580
国有联营企业	State Joint Ownership Enterprises	NA	176	21280
集体联营企业	Collective Joint Ownership Enterprises			
国有与集体联营企业	Joint State-collective Enterprises			
其他联营企业	Other Joint Ownership Enterprises	NA	35	1300
有限责任公司	Limited Liability Corporations	173	21434	621991
国有独资公司	State Sole Funded Corporations	7	594	56100
其他有限责任公司	Other Limited Liability Corporations	166	20840	565891
股份有限公司	Share-holding Corporations Ltd.	31	5194	196236
私营企业	Private Enterprises	184	17617	519689
私营独资企业	Private-funded Enterprises	40	2772	123870
私营合伙企业	Private Partnership Enterprises	9	398	8934
私营有限责任公司	Private Limited Liability Corporations	128	13537	379395
私营股份有限公司	Private Share-holding Corporations Ltd.	7	910	7490
其他企业	Other Enterprises	54	5262	253600

项 目	Item	单位数(个) Number of Units (unit)	年末从业人数(人) Engaged Persons at the Year-end (person)	年末餐饮营业面积(平方米) Business Area of Catering Services at the Year-end (㎡)
2.港、澳、台商投资企业	**Enterprises with Funds from Hongkong, Macao and Taiwan**	**19**	**3775**	**53994**
合资经营企业	Joint-venture Enterprises	4	766	23000
合作经营企业	Cooperative Enterprises			
独资经营企业	Enterprises with Sole Investment	12	2534	27153
投资股份有限公司	Share-holding Corporations Ltd. with Investment			
其他港澳台商投资企业	Other Enterprises with Funds from Hongkong, Macao and Taiwan	NA	475	3841
3.外商投资企业	**Foreign Funded Enterprises**	**37**	**15428**	**116110**
中外合资经营企业	Joint-venture Enterprises	NA	180	16114
中外合作经营企业	Cooperative Enterprises	NA	9127	4088
外资企业	Enterprises with Sole Foreign Investment	27	5577	74056
外商投资股份有限公司	Share-holding Corporations Ltd. With Foreign Investment	4	498	12457
其他外商投资企业	Other Foreign Funded Enterprises	NA	46	9395
4.个体经营户	**Getihus**	**31961**	**723702**	**24177443**
(二)按国民经济行业分	**by Sector**			
正餐服务	Dinner	30762	753902	25160591
快餐服务	Snack	1021	30980	612792
饮料及冷饮服务	Beverage and Cold Drink	251	9232	183261
其他餐饮业	Others	541	10532	388043

4-5-2 各地区限额以上住宿和餐饮业产业活动单位和个体经营户基本情况

Basic Conditions of Establishments and Getihus above Designated Size of Hotels and Catering Services by Region

地区	Region	住宿业 Hotels		餐饮业 Catering Services	
		单位数（个） Number of Units (unit)	年末从业人数（人） Engaged Persons at the Year-end (person)	单位数（个） Number of Units (unit)	年末从业人数（人） Engaged Persons at the Year-end (person)
全国	**National Total**	**5461**	**300269**	**32583**	**804909**
北京	Beijing	118	22897	53	2806
天津	Tianjin	19	2626	200	4766
河北	Hebei	75	8162	421	14394
山西	Shanxi	55	5677	371	13258
内蒙古	Inner Mongolia	130	4467	533	18109
辽宁	Liaoning	145	14368	1207	28229
吉林	Jilin	177	6130	1038	19629
黑龙江	Heilongjiang	204	4719	924	17888
上海	Shanghai	46	13684	5	9244
江苏	Jiangsu	369	23841	3783	81098
浙江	Zhejiang	246	20757	1412	39119
安徽	Anhui	225	13302	1718	38383
福建	Fujian	93	8053	1026	20071
江西	Jiangxi	187	9206	904	25427
山东	Shandong	402	11185	3540	65372
河南	Henan	645	16151	3462	82663
湖北	Hubei	221	7263	1549	35601
湖南	Hunan	250	10743	1029	31288
广东	Guangdong	400	19260	2538	70325
广西	Guangxi	213	8063	776	24215
海南	Hainan	42	1738	131	5201
重庆	Chongqing	152	8028	1736	34479
四川	Sichuan	315	18319	2040	58986
贵州	Guizhou	137	6631	351	10037
云南	Yunnan	218	11931	572	15102
西藏	Tibet	6	370	13	313
陕西	Shaanxi	101	8046	386	12614
甘肃	Gansu	33	1307	154	5641
青海	Qinghai	12	1391	6	355
宁夏	Ningxia	17	2395	52	1521
新疆	Xinjiang	208	9559	653	18775

4-5-3 限额以上住宿和餐饮业产业活动单位和个体经营户经营情况

项目	Item	营业额 Business Revenue	客房收入 from Hotel Rooms
总计	**Total**	**35545330**	**6058882**
一、住宿业	**Hotels**	**8577582**	**5031997**
(一)按登记注册类型分	**by Type of Registration**		
1.内资企业	**Domestic Funded Enterprises**	**4371796**	**2313447**
国有企业	State-owned Enterprises	617720	310642
集体企业	Collective-owned Enterprises	26806	11389
股份合作企业	Cooperative Enterprises	54703	26373
联营企业	Joint Ownership Enterprises	13434	5629
国有联营企业	State Joint Ownership Enterprises	1127	635
集体联营企业	Collective Joint Ownership Enterprises	775	461
国有与集体联营企业	Joint State-collective Enterprises		
其他联营企业	Other Joint Ownership Enterprises	11532	4533
有限责任公司	Limited Liability Corporations	1994322	1061788
国有独资公司	State Sole Funded Corporations	94202	53929
其他有限责任公司	Other Limited Liability Corporations	1900123	1007861
股份有限公司	Share-holding Corporations Ltd.	370695	213040
私营企业	Private Enterprises	1124592	591917
私营独资企业	Private-funded Enterprises	78997	31969
私营合伙企业	Private Partnership Enterprises	3627	3007
私营有限责任公司	Private Limited Liability Corporations	1001918	534785
私营股份有限公司	Private Share-holding Corporations Ltd.	40050	22158
其他企业	Other Enterprises	169533	92676
2.港、澳、台商投资企业	**Enterprises with Funds from Hongkong, Macao and Taiwan**	**580460**	**299453**
合资经营企业	Joint-venture Enterprises	209569	99987
合作经营企业	Cooperative Enterprises	45442	29358
独资经营企业	Enterprises with Sole Investment	282219	144995
投资股份有限公司	Share-holding Corporations Ltd. with Investment	28351	14681
其他港澳台商投资企业	Other Enterprises with Funds from Hongkong, Macao and Taiwan	14881	10431
3.外商投资企业	**Foreign Funded Enterprises**	**574660**	**296619**
中外合资经营企业	Joint-venture Enterprises	259212	131027
中外合作经营企业	Cooperative Enterprises	72417	36373
外资企业	Enterprises with Sole Foreign Investment	143379	79091
外商投资股份有限公司	Share-holding Corporations Ltd. With Foreign Investment	22567	12994
其他外商投资企业	Other Foreign Funded Enterprises	77085	37135
4.个体经营户	**Getihus**	**3050666**	**2122478**
(二)按国民经济行业分	**by Sector**		
旅游饭店	Tourist Hotel	5722763	3057477
一般旅馆	Fonda	2576665	1816543
其他住宿业	Others	278154	157977

Business of Establishments and Getihus above Designated Size of Hotels and Catering Services

单位：万元

Unit: 10000 yuan

餐费收入 from Meals	商品销售额 from Commodities	其他收入 Others	客房数 (间) Hotel Rooms (unit)	床位数 (个) Hotel Beds (unit)	餐位数 (位) Seats for Meal (unit)
27441634	**1520736**	**524078**	**723972**	**1182584**	**9278617**
2963045	**204548**	**377993**	**589893**	**944066**	**1174621**
1711129	**68279**	**278940**	**322599**	**470176**	**690512**
233667	19077	54336	34862	58674	97932
12426	272	2719	1107	1988	3773
24019	88	4223	3828	5350	6370
5300	178	2326	924	1451	2158
491			150	270	800
274	38	2	115	196	450
4535	140	2324	659	985	908
765415	18603	148514	109882	177187	266402
30622	325	9328	3939	6011	6887
734793	18279	139185	105943	171176	259515
123175	11325	23155	17935	32399	40721
477808	15346	39528	144946	178208	241268
37369	4684	4976	3365	5778	9243
589	17	16	499	738	908
423571	10270	33293	138517	167529	226675
16279	377	1240	2565	4163	4442
69323	3392	4142	9115	14919	31888
249465	**6790**	**24757**	**16611**	**23128**	**39410**
94559	4543	10483	6477	8732	14217
14398		1687	1308	1677	1226
125831	1504	9893	7328	10254	19376
10662	691	2316	1039	1703	3634
4018	53	379	459	762	957
244745	**7605**	**25694**	**15788**	**22350**	**32898**
109167	6931	12090	7138	10377	13852
33530		2515	1253	1603	1658
56658	380	7253	4868	6709	11142
8631	196	747	1038	1447	1838
36762	99	3092	1491	2214	4408
757706	**121874**	**48603**	**234895**	**428412**	**411801**
2237454	122762	305072	378431	567284	820086
632992	72772	54359	193795	344362	314408
92599	9014	18562	17667	32420	40127

项 目	Item	营业额 Business Revenue	客房收入 from Hotel Rooms
二、餐饮业	**Catering Services**	**26967750**	**1026884**
(一)按登记注册类型分	**by Type of Registration**		
1.内资企业	**Domestic Funded Enterprises**	**1403494**	**336303**
国有企业	State-owned Enterprises	229757	39397
集体企业	Collective-owned Enterprises	32472	6557
股份合作企业	Cooperative Enterprises	3206	621
联营企业	Joint Ownership Enterprises	7689	921
国有联营企业	State Joint Ownership Enterprises	6051	921
集体联营企业	Collective Joint Ownership Enterprises		
国有与集体联营企业	Joint State-collective Enterprises		
其他联营企业	Other Joint Ownership Enterprises	1638	
有限责任公司	Limited Liability Corporations	447699	151651
国有独资公司	State Sole Funded Corporations	7775	2639
其他有限责任公司	Other Limited Liability Corporations	439924	149011
股份有限公司	Share-holding Corporations Ltd.	135110	27238
私营企业	Private Enterprises	389952	83398
私营独资企业	Private-funded Enterprises	74801	10279
私营合伙企业	Private Partnership Enterprises	14016	349
私营有限责任公司	Private Limited Liability Corporations	279298	68101
私营股份有限公司	Private Share-holding Corporations Ltd.	21841	4671
其他内资企业	Other Domestic Funded Enterprises	157612	26526
2.港、澳、台商投资企业	**Enterprises with Funds from Hongkong, Macao and Taiwan**	**111172**	**20365**
合资经营企业	Joint-venture Enterprises	37245	8517
合作经营企业	Cooperative Enterprises		
独资经营企业	Enterprises with Sole Investment	64779	8024
投资股份有限公司	Share-holding Corporations Ltd. with Investment		
其他港澳台商投资企业	Other Enterprises with Funds from Hongkong, Macao and Taiwan	9149	3824
3.外商投资企业	**Foreign Funded Enterprises**	**290502**	**14950**
中外合资经营企业	Joint-venture Enterprises	1897	765
中外合作经营企业	Cooperative Enterprises	87586	
外资企业	Enterprises with Sole Foreign Investment	189343	11563
外商投资股份有限公司	Share-holding Corporations Ltd. With Foreign Investment	11054	2282
其他外商投资企业	Other Foreign Funded Enterprises	624	340
4.个体经营户	**Getihus**	**25162582**	**655264**
(二)按国民经济行业分	**by Sector**		
正餐服务	Restaurant	25299188	1002077
快餐服务	Snack Counter	897472	12810
饮料及冷饮服务	Beverage and Cold Drink	377410	970
其他餐饮业	Others	393680	11027

4-5-3 Continued

单位：万元
Unit: 10000 yuan

餐费收入 from Meals	商品销售额 from Commodities	其他收入 Others	客房数 (间) Hotel Rooms (unit)	床位数 (个) Hotel Beds (unit)	餐位数 (位) Seats for Meal (unit)
24478586	**1316195**	**146085**	**134079**	**238518**	**8103996**
975050	**47051**	**45088**	**44558**	**74803**	**469046**
166986	10445	12933	5382	9037	118320
23817	1933	167	1285	2370	19056
2549	37		50	110	452
6702	66		770	3560	4160
5064	66		770	3560	3900
1638					260
269746	11696	14608	18910	29753	101715
4178	672	285	710	1167	2005
265568	11024	14323	18200	28586	99710
102186	944	4744	2513	4056	39860
288706	11069	6782	12632	20666	112371
56760	7023	740	1724	2890	24941
12887	755	26	102	204	3879
203080	2895	5222	9969	16139	80189
15982	394	794	837	1433	3362
114361	10870	5856	3016	5251	73112
78665	**10728**	**1415**	**2168**	**3450**	**13346**
21366	6642	721	481	771	3000
52178	4059	519	1041	1593	8980
5123	27	175	646	1086	1366
253448	**20696**	**1408**	**1527**	**2283**	**43741**
1116		17	172	327	1100
87586					6050
156120	20639	1020	1021	1476	34985
8379	57	336	284	406	1506
248		35	50	74	100
23171426	**1237719**	**98175**	**85826**	**157982**	**7577863**
22925247	1231565	140296	132259	235329	7699224
852603	28494	3565	815	1498	219561
335877	39344	1221	165	288	61170
364859	16729	1003	840	1403	124041

4-5-4 各地区限额以上住宿业产业活动单位和个体经营户经营情况
Business of Establishments and Getihus above Designated Size of Hotels by Region

单位：万元
Unit: 10000 yuan

地区	Region	营业额 Business Revenue	客房收入 from Hotel Rooms	餐费收入 from Meals	商品销售额 from Commodities	其他收入 Others
全国	**National Total**	**8577582**	**5031997**	**2963045**	**204548**	**377993**
北京	Beijing	924486	529439	304870	3435	86741
天津	Tianjin	73475	38269	26913	419	7874
河北	Hebei	116194	53184	51687	4057	7267
山西	Shanxi	68564	30117	31053	1940	5455
内蒙古	Inner Mongolia	110300	66181	41102	1167	1850
辽宁	Liaoning	308582	150224	132528	8962	16867
吉林	Jilin	189603	111254	65581	5224	7545
黑龙江	Heilongjiang	235306	183050	30804	10931	10521
上海	Shanghai	623870	357566	226531	6430	33343
江苏	Jiangsu	740543	435536	267444	16892	20671
浙江	Zhejiang	604674	308825	255691	4941	35217
安徽	Anhui	271231	157652	92913	7997	12668
福建	Fujian	219446	109693	97445	4698	7610
江西	Jiangxi	274059	146997	102172	17332	7557
山东	Shandong	412411	252947	141935	11544	5986
河南	Henan	548102	377926	146052	15168	8956
湖北	Hubei	272179	166991	85227	12189	7773
湖南	Hunan	316816	184882	112102	11450	8382
广东	Guangdong	561214	366148	167938	10102	17027
广西	Guangxi	121770	83486	33575	1336	3372
海南	Hainan	29907	17083	11814	480	530
重庆	Chongqing	290499	169317	104031	7223	9928
四川	Sichuan	476165	275160	163549	20895	16561
贵州	Guizhou	126151	83742	35923	2733	3753
云南	Yunnan	222325	147564	60651	4604	9506
西藏	Tibet	3786	2394	1015	55	322
陕西	Shaanxi	151441	70069	66397	9333	5642
甘肃	Gansu	23023	14544	8033	383	63
青海	Qinghai	32978	17829	12498	21	2630
宁夏	Ningxia	43106	20823	19375	279	2629
新疆	Xinjiang	185376	103105	66196	2328	13747

4-5-5 各地区限额以上餐饮业产业活动单位和个体经营户经营情况

Business of Establishments and Getihus above Designated Size of Catering Services by Region

单位：万元
Unit: 10000 yuan

地区	Region	营业额 Business Revenue	客房收入 from Hotel Rooms	餐费收入 from Meals	商品销售额 from Commodities	其他收入 Others
全国	**National Total**	**26967750**	**1026884**	**24478586**	**1316195**	**146085**
北京	Beijing	62371	843	61120	242	166
天津	Tianjin	132796	350	126086	4156	2203
河北	Hebei	289808	22260	254762	10631	2156
山西	Shanxi	200648	23826	167900	5911	3012
内蒙古	Inner Mongolia	388207	37676	340576	8504	1451
辽宁	Liaoning	617134	17791	577222	16039	6081
吉林	Jilin	838498	19864	782583	34350	1701
黑龙江	Heilongjiang	682839	10439	585326	67130	19944
上海	Shanghai	94137	3998	89822		316
江苏	Jiangsu	3876537	147380	3439256	272137	17764
浙江	Zhejiang	1069204	75229	956397	30066	7511
安徽	Anhui	1000526	34134	932759	30462	3171
福建	Fujian	846190	12387	817563	15524	716
江西	Jiangxi	612008	17300	540036	53559	1113
山东	Shandong	3368982	61827	3026189	264167	16798
河南	Henan	2564965	75396	2361092	119790	8687
湖北	Hubei	1819822	85288	1634293	91730	8512
湖南	Hunan	1222472	79888	1106317	29872	6396
广东	Guangdong	1626327	27437	1571428	17633	9829
广西	Guangxi	355795	7581	342256	4727	1231
海南	Hainan	110548	1466	103472	4819	791
重庆	Chongqing	1870626	31130	1762747	72486	4263
四川	Sichuan	1929254	156817	1641091	116840	14506
贵州	Guizhou	195689	1197	190575	3622	295
云南	Yunnan	328014	5203	311971	9230	1611
西藏	Tibet	5747	514	5233		
陕西	Shaanxi	325410	30961	271239	20289	2922
甘肃	Gansu	78874	3362	74747	636	130
青海	Qinghai	3005		3005		
宁夏	Ningxia	33443	462	32312	365	303
新疆	Xinjiang	417874	34878	369211	11278	2506

4-6-1 按登记注册类型分连锁餐饮企业基本情况

Basic Conditions of Chain Catering Enterprises by Status of Registration

项　目	Item	门店总数（个）Number of Stores (unit)	从业人员（万人）Employed Person (10000 persons)	营业面积（万平方米）Operational Area (10000 sq.m)
合　计	**Total**	**27478**	**78.0**	**1075.4**
内资企业	**Domestic Funded Enterprises**	**8637**	**27.2**	**456.6**
国有企业	State-owned Enterprises	127	0.3	3.4
集体企业	Collective-owned Enterprises	3	0.1	1.2
股份合作企业	Cooperative Enterprises	9	0.0	0.8
联营企业	Joint Ownership Enterprises			
国有联营企业	State Joint Ownership Enterprises			
集体联营企业	Collective Joint Ownership Enterprises			
国有与集体联营企业	Joint State-collective Enterprises			
其他联营企业	Other Joint Ownership Enterprises			
有限责任公司	Limited Liability Corporations	3728	8.7	165.3
国有独资公司	State Sole Funded Corporations	33	0.1	1.5
其他有限责任公司	Other Limited Liability Corporations	3695	8.6	163.8
股份有限公司	Share-holding Corporations Ltd.	1121	5.6	102.5
私营企业	Private Enterprises	3640	12.4	183.2
私营独资企业	Private-funded Enterprises	141	0.4	6.4
私营合伙企业	Private Partnership Enterprises			
私营有限责任公司	Private Limited Liability Corporations	3470	11.9	174.4
私营股份有限公司	Private Share-holding Corporations Ltd.	29	0.1	2.4
其他企业	Other Enterprises	9	0.0	0.3
港、澳、台商投资企业	**Enterprises with Funds from Hong Kong, Macao and Taiwan**	**6565**	**18.4**	**183.6**
港、澳、台商合资经营企业	Joint-venture Enterprises	1030	4.0	35.7
港、澳、台商合作经营企业	Cooperative Enterprises	4	0.1	1.7
港、澳、台商独资经营企业	Enterprises with Sole Investment	5507	14.3	145.3
港、澳、台商投资股份有限公司	Share-holding Corporations Ltd. with Investment	24	0.1	0.9
其他港澳台商投资企业	Other Enterprises with Funds from Hongkong, Macao and Taiwan			
外商投资企业	**Foreign Funded Enterprises**	**12276**	**32.5**	**435.2**
中外合资经营企业	Joint-venture Enterprises	2119	6.2	71.4
中外合作经营企业	Cooperative Enterprises			
外资企业	Enterprises with Sole Foreign Investment	9682	24.3	326.0
外商投资股份有限公司	Share-holding Corporations Ltd. With Foreign Investment	79	1.0	8.4
其他外商投资企业	Other Foreign Funded Enterprises	396	1.0	29.4

4-6-1 续表 Continued

项 目	Item	餐位数(万个) Number of Dining-seats (10000 units)	营业额(亿元) Business Revenue (100 million yuan)	#餐费及商品销售收入 From Meals and Commodities
合 计	**Total**	**337.9**	**1735.5**	**1722.8**
内资企业	**Domestic Funded Enterprises**	**144.3**	**502.1**	**491.2**
国有企业	State-owned Enterprises	1.1	7.2	7.1
集体企业	Collective-owned Enterprises	0.3	1.2	1.1
股份合作企业	Cooperative Enterprises	0.3	0.8	0.8
联营企业	Joint Ownership Enterprises			
国有联营企业	State Joint Ownership Enterprises			
集体联营企业	Collective Joint Ownership Enterprises			
国有与集体联营企业	Joint State-collective Enterprises			
其他联营企业	Other Joint Ownership Enterprises			
有限责任公司	Limited Liability Corporations	51.3	169.4	166.9
国有独资公司	State Sole Funded Corporations	0.4	1.9	1.9
其他有限责任公司	Other Limited Liability Corporations	50.8	167.5	165.0
股份有限公司	Share-holding Corporations Ltd.	23.9	133.3	127.4
私营企业	Private Enterprises	67.5	190.2	187.9
私营独资企业	Private-funded Enterprises	2.0	8.9	8.8
私营合伙企业	Private Partnership Enterprises			
私营有限责任公司	Private Limited Liability Corporations	65.0	180.4	178.1
私营股份有限公司	Private Share-holding Corporations Ltd.	0.5	1.0	1.0
其他企业	Other Enterprises	0.1	0.0	0.0
港、澳、台商投资企业	**Enterprises with Funds from Hong Kong, Macao and Taiwan**	**57.9**	**422.5**	**421.6**
港、澳、台商合资经营企业	Joint-venture Enterprises	9.7	89.5	89.2
港、澳、台商合作经营企业	Cooperative Enterprises	0.2	2.5	2.5
港、澳、台商独资经营企业	Enterprises with Sole Investment	47.7	329.4	328.8
港、澳、台商投资股份有限公司	Share-holding Corporations Ltd. with Investment	0.3	1.1	1.1
其他港、澳、台商投资企业	Other Enterprises with Funds from Hongkong, Macao and Taiwan			
外商投资企业	**Foreign Funded Enterprises**	**135.7**	**810.9**	**810.0**
中外合资经营企业	Joint-venture Enterprises	23.1	172.9	172.9
中外合作经营企业	Cooperative Enterprises			
外资企业	Enterprises with Sole Foreign Investment	98.1	593.3	592.6
外商投资股份有限公司	Share-holding Corporations Ltd. with Foreign Investment	2.6	24.3	24.1
其他外商投资企业	Other Foreign Funded Enterprises	11.9	20.4	20.4

4-6-2 按行业分连锁餐饮企业基本情况
Basic Conditions of Chain Catering Enterprises by Sector

行　业	Sector	门店总数（个）Number of Stores (unit)	从业人数（万人）Engaged Persons (10000 persons)	营业面积（万平方米）Operating Area (10000 sq.m)
总　计	**Total**	**27478**	**78.0**	**1075.4**
正餐服务	Restaurant	6826	27.7	499.1
快餐服务	Snack Counter	16139	45.1	510.5
饮料及冷饮服务	Beverages and Cold Drinks	3926	4.6	60.4
其他餐饮业	Others	587	0.6	5.4

4-6-2 续表 Continued

行　业	sector	餐位数（万个）Number of Dining-seats (10000 units)	营业额（亿元）Business Revenue (100 million yuan)	#餐费及商品销售收入 From Meals and Commodities
总　计	**Total**	**337.9**	**1735.5**	**1722.8**
正餐服务	Restaurant	151.6	540.2	530.2
快餐服务	Snack Counter	162.0	1008.7	1006.3
饮料及冷饮服务	Beverages and Cold Drinks	21.6	166.7	166.4
其他餐饮业	Others	2.8	19.9	19.9

4-6-3 各地区连锁餐饮企业基本情况
Basic Conditions of Chain Catering Enterprises by Region

年份 Year	地区 Region	门店总数（个）Number of Stores (unit)	从业人数（万人）Employed Person (10000 persons)	营业面积（万平方米）Operational Area (10000 sq.m)	餐位数（万个）Number of dining-seat (10000 units)	营业额（亿元）Business Revenue (100 million yuan)
	2004	7578	37.9	352.6	180.1	348.2
	2005	9748	50.1	478.1	245.8	454.4
	2006	11360	55.7	588.2	274.8	563.8
	2007	12743	62.6	629.2	280.0	640.0
	2008	12561	66.1	651.9	253.1	806.9
	2009	13739	65.2	691.6	248.9	879.3
	2010	15333	70.6	742.6	263.8	955.4
	2011	16285	83.3	821.4	277.1	1120.4
	2012	18153	80.6	869.2	286.5	1283.3
	2013	20554	80.3	937.1	319.5	1319.6
	2014	22494	78.0	1020.0	338.6	1391.0
	2015	23721	71.4	970.9	333.6	1526.6
	2016	25634	75.6	1036.9	341.1	1635.1
	2017	27478	78.0	1075.4	337.9	1735.5
北 京	Beijing	5133	14.4	204.4	57.1	380.2
天 津	Tianjin	573	1.6	21.1	6.4	42.6
河 北	Hebei	18	0.1	3.7	0.6	1.6
山 西	Shanxi	109	0.6	6.5	2.0	7.5
内蒙古	Inner Mongolia	120	0.3	7.3	2.3	13.7
辽 宁	Liaoning	730	1.0	27.6	8.6	57.7
吉 林	Jilin	19	0.0	0.9	0.2	0.6
黑龙江	Heilongjiang	65	0.2	2.8	0.8	3.6
上 海	Shanghai	3888	7.7	126.5	36.9	245.5
江 苏	Jiangsu	1598	4.8	50.3	16.3	101.6
浙 江	Zhejiang	1940	4.6	69.0	22.0	107.6
安 徽	Anhui	747	1.4	35.9	6.5	21.1
福 建	Fujian	703	2.2	20.7	5.4	34.8
江 西	Jiangxi	151	0.7	6.2	0.7	9.3
山 东	Shandong	646	2.0	38.1	9.0	53.7
河 南	Henan	217	0.7	6.6	3.0	11.0
湖 北	Hubei	1089	5.0	56.9	15.0	69.7
湖 南	Hunan	1133	4.7	64.7	26.2	61.4
广 东	Guangdong	4158	10.9	134.6	39.1	267.6
广 西	Guangxi	247	0.9	5.9	2.3	12.5
海 南	Hainan	7	0.0	0.3	0.1	0.9
重 庆	Chongqing	2460	9.2	130.1	52.6	131.2
四 川	Sichuan	973	2.6	28.8	11.4	57.0
贵 州	Guizhou	18	0.1	1.9	0.4	0.7
云 南	Yunnan	249	0.8	6.6	3.8	15.1
西 藏	Tibet	3	0.0	0.0	0.0	0.1
陕 西	Shaanxi	282	1.2	12.6	7.5	17.8
甘 肃	Gansu	37	0.2	1.4	0.4	3.3
青 海	Qinghai					
宁 夏	Ningxia					
新 疆	Xinjiang	165	0.3	4.1	1.2	6.0

年份 Year	地区 Region	#餐费收入及商品销售额 From Meals and Commodities	商品购进总额（亿元） Total Purchases Value (100 million yuan)	统一配送商品购进额（亿元） Centralized Purchase and Delivery (100 million yuan)	#自有配送中心配送商品购进额 Self Centralized Purchase and Delivery	#非自有配送中心配送商品购进额 Non-self Centralized Purchase and Delivery
	2004	345.3	124.6	89.3	64.7	24.6
	2005	447.2	171.5	109.1	77.9	31.0
	2006	563.2	201.2	127.5	93.6	33.7
	2007	639.3	274.9	168.8	110.0	30.9
	2008	796.2	271.6	192.5	118.7	35.3
	2009	878.5	362.0	239.8	138.0	50.7
	2010	952.9	455.8	298.8	159.5	51.4
	2011	1098.7	518.9	343.1	190.0	65.1
	2012	1280.3	561.4	388.5	202.3	86.0
	2013	1316.0	571.2	400.7	183.0	80.8
	2014	1387.0	583.4	413.9	193.4	68.8
	2015	1505.2	577.0	462.5	212.1	68.2
	2016	1625.1	612.4	494.1	202.6	78.8
	2017	1722.8	613.3	489.5	206.0	76.2
北京	Beijing	376.9	118.5	100.5	53.5	21.7
天津	Tianjin	42.6	17.8	4.3	0.3	
河北	Hebei	1.5	0.8	0.0		
山西	Shanxi	7.5	3.6	2.9	2.9	
内蒙古	Inner Mongolia	13.7	10.1	0.3	0.1	0.0
辽宁	Liaoning	57.7	49.7	45.1	2.0	
吉林	Jilin	0.6	0.2	0.1		0.0
黑龙江	Heilongjiang	3.6	0.9	0.8	0.1	0.7
上海	Shanghai	245.5	78.8	60.8	6.4	4.5
江苏	Jiangsu	101.4	33.0	30.3	16.6	11.8
浙江	Zhejiang	107.5	39.4	37.0	26.3	8.6
安徽	Anhui	20.9	7.0	6.9	3.1	0.5
福建	Fujian	34.8	13.8	11.7	4.1	0.9
江西	Jiangxi	9.3	4.4	4.2	0.2	
山东	Shandong	48.2	16.8	14.3	11.2	1.1
河南	Henan	11.0	5.5	5.0		0.2
湖北	Hubei	68.0	20.5	17.9	11.2	5.3
湖南	Hunan	60.2	20.6	13.8	10.2	3.0
广东	Guangdong	267.4	77.1	70.1	28.4	3.2
广西	Guangxi	12.5	5.3	5.3	2.0	2.3
海南	Hainan	0.9	0.3	0.3		0.3
重庆	Chongqing	130.9	58.9	29.9	17.4	8.2
四川	Sichuan	57.0	15.2	15.0	2.1	0.7
贵州	Guizhou	0.7	0.3	0.3		
云南	Yunnan	15.1	4.1	2.5		1.7
西藏	Tibet	0.1	0.0			
陕西	Shaanxi	17.8	7.2	6.9	5.4	0.7
甘肃	Gansu	3.3	1.4	1.3	1.3	
青海	Qinghai					
宁夏	Ningxia					
新疆	Xinjiang	6.0	2.3	2.0	1.2	0.8

国际收支

BALANCE OF PAYMENTS

第5篇

5-1 国际收支概况
Brief Table of BOP of China

单位：亿美元

Unit: USD 100 million

年 份 Year	经常项目差额 Current Account Balance	资本和金融项目差额 Capital and Financial Account Balance	净误差与遗漏 Net Errors and Omissions
1982	56.74	-59.53	2.79
1983	42.40	-40.67	-1.73
1984	20.30	-32.21	11.91
1985	-114.17	139.07	-24.90
1986	-70.35	82.67	-12.32
1987	3.00	10.71	-13.71
1988	-38.03	48.14	-10.11
1989	-43.18	42.26	0.92
1990	119.97	-88.63	-31.34
1991	132.71	-65.10	-67.61
1992	64.01	18.51	-82.52
1993	-119.04	217.07	-98.03
1994	76.58	21.17	-97.75
1995	16.18	162.12	-178.30
1996	72.42	83.05	-155.47
1997	369.63	-146.67	-222.96
1998	314.71	-127.35	-187.36
1999	211.14	-33.26	-177.88
2000	204.32	-86.26	-118.05
2001	174.05	-125.50	-48.56
2002	354.22	-432.16	77.94
2003	430.52	-512.75	82.24
2004	689.41	-819.08	129.67
2005	1323.78	-1553.00	229.21
2006	2318.43	-2354.71	36.28
2007	3531.83	-3664.73	132.90
2008	4205.69	-4394.13	188.44
2009	2432.57	-2018.74	-413.83
2010	2378.10	-1848.74	-529.36
2011	1360.97	-1223.31	-137.66
2012	2153.92	-1283.17	-870.74
2013	1482.04	-852.79	-629.25
2014	2360.47	-1691.74	-668.73
2015	3041.64	-912.07	-2129.58
2016	2022.03	272.50	-2294.53
2017	1648.87	570.03	-2218.89

注：根据《国际收支和国际投资头寸手册》(第六版)编制，资本和金融账户中包含储备资产。

Note：The table is compiled according to BPM6. Reserve asstes are included in capital and financial account.

5-2 国际收支平衡表
Balance of Payments

单位：万美元
Unit: USD 10000

项 目	Item	2016	2017
1. 经常账户	**Current account**	**20220342**	**16488665**
贷方	Credit	245464052	270886516
借方	Debit	-225243710	-254397851
1.A货物和服务	Goods and services	25573709	21072844
贷方	Credit	219792247	242291100
借方	Debit	-194218538	-221218256
1.A.a 货物	Goods	48888300	47614571
贷方	Credit	198951864	221645786
借方	Debit	-150063564	-174031216
1.A.b 服务	Services	-23314591	-26541727
贷方	Credit	20840383	20645314
借方	Debit	-44154974	-47187041
1.A.b.1 加工服务	Manufacturing services on physical inputs owned by others	1838178	1793079
贷方	Credit	1853990	1810669
借方	Debit	-15812	-17590
1.A.b.2 维护和维修服务	Maintenance and repair services n.i.e	323969	367478
贷方	Credit	520219	595021
借方	Debit	-196250	-227543
1.A.b.3 运输	Transport	-4675309	-5605983
贷方	Credit	3382713	3724262
借方	Debit	-8058022	-9330246
1.A.b.4 旅行	Travel	-20568036	-22511548
贷方	Credit	4443158	3261734
借方	Debit	-25011195	-25773282
1.A.b.5 建设	Construction	415672	361783
贷方	Credit	1266061	1221051
借方	Debit	-850389	-859269
1.A.b.6 保险和养老金服务	Insurance and pension services	-884890	-740239
贷方	Credit	406379	407061
借方	Debit	-1291269	-1147300
1.A.b.7 金融服务	Financial services	114070	180160
贷方	Credit	317418	340071
借方	Debit	-203349	-159911
1.A.b.8 知识产权使用费	Charges for the use of intellectual property	-2281838	-2388189
贷方	Credit	116120	477873

注：1.根据《国际收支和国际投资头寸手册》(第六版)编制。
2."贷方"按正值列示，"借方"按负值列示，差额等于"贷方"加上"借方"，本表除标注"贷方"和"借方"的项目外，其他项目均指差额。

Note: 1. The table is compiled according to BPM6.
2. "Credit" is presented as positive value while "debit" as negative value; the difference is the sum of the "Credit" and the "Debit"; all items here in refer to difference, unless marked with "Credit" or "Debit".

5-2 续表 1 continued 1

单位：万美元
Unit: USD 10000

项　目	Item	2016	2017
借方	Debit	-2397958	-2866062
1.A.b.9 电信、计算机和信息服务	Telecommunications, computer, and information services	1269488	768096
贷方	Credit	2543249	2697677
借方	Debit	-1273761	-1929581
1.A.b.10 其他商业服务	Other business services	1471254	1607560
贷方	Credit	5795671	5863835
借方	Debit	-4324417	-4256274
1.A.b.11 个人、文化和娱乐服务	Personal, cultural, and recreational services	-139821	-198473
贷方	Credit	74233	75942
借方	Debit	-214054	-274415
1.A.b.12 别处未提及的政府服务	Government goods and services n.i.e	-197328	-175450
贷方	Credit	121171	170118
借方	Debit	-318499	-345568
1.B 初次收入	Primary income	-4401340	-3444429
贷方	Credit	22581796	25733553
借方	Debit	-26983137	-29177982
1.B.1 雇员报酬	Compensation of employees	2067239	1499271
贷方	Credit	2688328	2168258
借方	Debit	-621089	-668987
1.B.2 投资收益	Investment income	-6503135	-4991346
贷方	Credit	19837423	23491996
借方	Debit	-26340559	-28483343
1.B.3 其他初次收入	Other primary income	34556	47647
贷方	Credit	56045	73300
借方	Debit	-21489	-25653
1.C 二次收入	Secondary income	-952026	-1139750
贷方	Credit	3090009	2861862
借方	Debit	-4042035	-4001613
2. 资本和金融账户	**Capital and financial account**	**2724993**	**5700259**
2.1 资本账户	Capital account	-34441	-9361
贷方	Credit	31794	23069
借方	Debit	-66235	-32431
2.2 金融账户	Financial account	2759434	5709620
资产	Assets	-23198495	-37824697
负债	Liabilities	25957929	43534317
2.2.1 非储备性质的金融账户	Financial account excluding reserve assets	-41607025	14861194
资产	Financial assets excluding reserve assets	-67564954	-28673122
负债	Liabilities	25957929	43534317
2.2.1.1 直接投资	Direct investment	-4167488	6630948
2.2.1.1.1 资产	Assets	-21642446	-10191410

5-2 续表 2 continued 2

单位：万美元
Unit: USD 10000

项　目	Item	2016	2017
2.2.1.1.1.1 股权	Equity and investment fund shares	-14700100	-9970025
2.2.1.1.1.2 关联企业债务	Debt instruments	-6942347	-221385
2.2.1.1.2负债	Liabilities	17474958	16822358
2.2.1.1.2.1 股权	Equity and investment fund shares	16492970	14218156
2.2.1.1.2.2 关联企业债务	Debt instruments	981989	2604202
2.2.1.2 证券投资	Portfolio investment	-5227062	743131
2.2.1.2.1 资产	Assets	-10276958	-10938663
2.2.1.2.1.1 股权	Equity and investment fund shares	-3823823	-3769690
2.2.1.2.1.2 债券	Debt securities	-6453135	-7168973
2.2.1.2.2 负债	Liabilities	5049896	11681794
2.2.1.2.2.1 股权	Equity and investment fund shares	2341607	3395413
2.2.1.2.2.2 债券	Debt securities	2708289	8286381
2.2.1.3 金融衍生工具	Financial derivatives (other than reserves) and employee stock options	-538403	47117
2.2.1.3.1 资产	Assets	-654966	147373
2.2.1.3.2 负债	Liabilities	116563	-100256
2.2.1.4 其他投资	Other investment	-31674073	7439998
2.2.1.4.1 资产	Assets	-34990584	-7690422
2.2.1.4.1.1 其他股权	Other equity	-163	4044
2.2.1.4.1.2 货币和存款	Currency and deposits	-6427961	-3703339
2.2.1.4.1.3 贷款	Loans	-11026662	-3973194
2.2.1.4.1.4 保险和养老金	Insurance, pension, and standardized guarantee schemes	-26614	-1087
2.2.1.4.1.5 贸易信贷	Trade credit and advances	-10080000	-1940000
2.2.1.4.1.6 其他	Other accounts receivable	-7429183	1923154
2.2.1.4.2 负债	Liabilities	3316511	15130420
2.2.1.4.2.1 其他股权	Other equity		
2.2.1.4.2.2 货币和存款	Currency and deposits	906226	10545454
2.2.1.4.2.3 贷款	Loans	-1736136	4957067
2.2.1.4.2.4 保险和养老金	Insurance, pension, and standardized guarantee schemes	-66755	66553
2.2.1.4.2.5 贸易信贷	Trade credit and advances	1620000	-120000
2.2.1.4.2.6 其他	Other accounts payable	2593175	-318655
2.2.1.4.2.7 特别提款权	Special drawing rights	0	
2.2.2 储备资产	Reserve assets	44366460	-9151574
2.2.2.1 货币黄金	Monetary gold		
2.2.2.2 特别提款权	Special drawing rights	32624	-73936
2.2.2.3 在国际货币基金组织的储备头寸	Reserve position in the IMF	-534220	219040
2.2.2.4 外汇储备	Foreign exchange reserves	44868055	-9296678
2.2.2.5 其他储备资产	Other reserve assets		
3.净误差与遗漏	**Net errors and omissions**	**-22945336**	**-22188923**

5-3 外债概况
Notes of China's External Debt at the Year-end

单位：亿美元

Unit: USD 100 million

年 份 Year	合 计 Outstanding Debt	中长期外债 Long-term Debt	短期外债 Short-term Debt
1985	158.3	94.1	64.2
1986	214.8	167.1	47.7
1987	302.0	244.8	57.2
1988	400.0	326.9	73.1
1989	413.0	370.3	42.7
1990	525.5	457.8	67.7
1991	605.6	502.6	103.0
1992	693.2	584.7	108.5
1993	835.7	700.2	135.5
1994	928.1	823.9	104.2
1995	1065.9	946.8	119.1
1996	1162.8	1021.7	141.1
1997	1309.6	1128.2	181.4
1998	1460.4	1287.0	173.4
1999	1518.3	1366.5	151.8
2000	1457.3	1326.5	130.8
2001	2033.0	1195.3	837.7
2002	2026.3	1155.5	870.8
2003	2193.6	1165.9	1027.7
2004	2629.9	1242.9	1387.1
2005	2965.4	1249.0	1716.4
2006	3385.9	1393.6	1992.3
2007	3892.2	1535.3	2356.8
2008	3901.6	1638.8	2262.8
2009	4286.5	1693.9	2592.6
2010	5489.4	1732.4	3757.0
2011	6950.0	1941.0	5009.0
2012	7369.9	1960.6	5409.3
2013	8631.7	1865.4	6766.3
2014	17799.0	4817.0	12982.0
2015	13829.8	4955.7	8874.1
2016	14158.0	5497.6	8660.4
2017	17106.2	6115.8	10990.4
构成 Proportion (%)			
1985	100.0	59.4	40.6
1986	100.0	77.8	22.2
1987	100.0	81.1	18.9
1988	100.0	81.7	18.3
1989	100.0	89.7	10.3
1990	100.0	87.1	12.9
1991	100.0	83.0	17.0
1992	100.0	84.3	15.7
1993	100.0	83.8	16.2
1994	100.0	88.8	11.2
1995	100.0	88.8	11.2
1996	100.0	87.9	12.1
1997	100.0	86.1	13.9
1998	100.0	88.1	11.9
1999	100.0	90.0	10.0
2000	100.0	91.0	9.0
2001	100.0	58.8	41.2
2002	100.0	57.0	43.0
2003	100.0	53.2	46.8
2004	100.0	47.3	52.7
2005	100.0	42.1	57.9
2006	100.0	41.2	58.8
2007	100.0	39.4	60.6
2008	100.0	42.0	58.0
2009	100.0	39.5	60.5
2010	100.0	31.6	68.4
2011	100.0	27.9	72.1
2012	100.0	26.6	73.4
2013	100.0	21.6	78.4
2014	100.0	27.1	72.9
2015	100.0	35.8	64.2
2016	100.0	38.8	61.2
2017	100.0	35.8	64.2

注：2015年，中国按照国际货币基金组织的数据公布特殊标准(SDDS)调整了外债统计口径并对外公布全口径外债统计口径并对外公布全口径外债数据，将人民币外债纳入统计，并按签约期限划分中长期和短期外债。为保证数据的可比性，将2014年末外债数据相应调整为全口径外债数据(下同)。

Note: In accordance with the Special Data Dissemination Standard(SDDS) of the IMF, China adjusted the statistical coverage of external debt and disseminatied the full-scale data on China's external debt in 2015,including RMB-denominated external debt, which wa classified into medium-and long-term external debt and short-term external debt by contract term. To ensure data comparability, the external debt data at the end of 2014 have been adjusted to the full-scale data.

5-4 外债风险指标
Risk Indicators on Foreign Debts

单位：%
Unit: %

年 份 Year	偿债率 Debt Servicing Ratio	负债率 External Debt/GDP Ratio	债务率 External Debt/Foreign Exchange Income Ratio
1985	2.7	5.1	56.0
1986	15.4	7.2	72.1
1987	9.0	9.3	77.1
1988	6.5	9.9	87.1
1989	8.3	9.1	86.4
1990	8.7	13.4	91.6
1991	8.5	14.7	91.9
1992	7.1	14.1	87.9
1993	10.2	13.6	96.5
1994	9.1	16.5	78.0
1995	7.6	14.6	72.4
1996	6.0	13.5	67.7
1997	7.3	13.7	63.2
1998	10.9	14.2	70.4
1999	11.2	13.9	68.7
2000	9.2	12.1	52.1
2001	7.5	15.3	67.9
2002	7.9	13.9	55.5
2003	6.9	13.3	45.2
2004	3.2	13.5	40.2
2005	3.1	13.1	35.4
2006	2.1	12.4	31.9
2007	2.0	11.0	29.0
2008	1.8	8.6	24.7
2009	2.9	8.5	32.2
2010	1.6	9.1	29.2
2011	1.7	9.3	33.3
2012	1.6	8.7	32.8
2013	1.6	9.1	35.6
2014	2.6	17.2	69.9
2015	5.0	12.5	58.6
2016	6.1	12.6	64.4
2017	6.9	14.0	70.6

注：1.偿债率指当年外债还本付息额与当年国际收支口径的货物与服务贸易出口收入的比率。
2.负债率指年末外债余额与当年国内生产总值的比率。
3.债务率指年末外债余额与当年国际收支口径的货物与服务贸易出口收入的比率。

Note: a) Debt Servicing Ratio refers to the ratio of the repayment amount of the external debt principal and interest to the export revenue from trade in goods and services for the year in the balance of payments.
b) External Debt/GDP Ratio refers to the ratio of outstanding external debt as of the end of the year to the GDP for the year.
c) External Debt/Foreign Exchange Income Ratio refers to the ratio of outstanding external debt as of the end of the year to the export revenue from trade in goods and services for the year in the balance of payments.

5-5 人民币市场汇率(年平均汇价)

Reference Exchange Rate of Renminbi(Period Average)

单位：人民币元

Unit: RMB yuan

年 份 Year	美 元 US Dollar (100)	欧 元 EURO (100)	日 元 Japanese Yen (100)	港 币 Hong Kong Dollar (100)	英 镑 Pound (100)
1981	170.50		0.77	30.41	
1982	189.25		0.76	31.15	
1983	197.57		0.83	27.36	
1984	232.70		0.98	29.71	
1985	293.66		1.25	37.57	
1986	345.28		2.07	44.22	
1987	372.21		2.58	47.74	
1988	372.21		2.91	47.70	
1989	376.51		2.74	48.28	
1990	478.32		3.32	61.39	
1991	532.33		3.96	68.45	
1992	551.46		4.36	71.24	
1993	576.20		5.20	74.41	
1994	861.87		8.44	111.53	
1995	835.10		8.92	107.96	
1996	831.42		7.64	107.51	
1997	828.98		6.86	107.09	
1998	827.91		6.35	106.88	
1999	827.83		7.29	106.66	
2000	827.84		7.69	106.18	
2001	827.70		6.81	106.08	
2002	827.70	800.58	6.62	106.07	
2003	827.70	936.13	7.15	106.24	
2004	827.68	1029.00	7.66	106.23	
2005	819.17	1019.53	7.45	105.30	
2006	797.18	1001.90	6.86	102.62	
2007	760.40	1041.75	6.46	97.46	1522.13
2008	694.51	1022.27	6.74	89.19	1286.64
2009	683.10	952.70	7.30	88.12	1071.97
2010	676.95	897.25	7.73	87.13	1045.72
2011	645.88	900.11	8.11	82.97	1036.39
2012	631.25	810.67	7.90	81.38	1000.12
2013	619.32	822.19	6.33	79.85	967.93
2014	614.28	816.51	5.82	79.22	1012.91
2015	622.84	691.41	5.15	80.34	953.44
2016	664.23	734.26	6.12	85.58	898.55
2017	675.18	763.03	6.02	86.64	869.88

5-6 人民币市场汇率(年末价)

Reference Exchange Rate of Renminbi(End of Period)

单位：人民币元

Unit: RMB yuan

年 份 Year	美 元 US Dollar (100)	欧 元 EURO (100)	日 元 Japanese Yen (100)	港 币 Hong Kong Dollar (100)	英镑 Pound (100)
1981	174.55		0.79	30.80	
1982	192.27		0.82	29.80	
1983	198.09		0.85	25.30	
1984	257.55		1.13	35.90	
1985	320.15		1.59	40.79	
1986	372.21		2.33	47.68	
1987	372.21		3.01	47.90	
1988	372.21		2.98	47.61	
1989	472.21		3.29	60.48	
1990	522.21		3.87	67.00	
1991	543.42		4.32	69.42	
1992	575.18		4.61	74.31	
1993	580.00		5.21	75.09	
1994	844.62		8.48	109.14	
1995	831.74		8.05	107.96	
1996	829.84		7.20	107.24	
1997	827.96		6.35	106.99	
1998	827.87		7.17	106.78	
1999	827.93		8.09	106.51	
2000	827.81		7.24	106.06	
2001	827.66		6.30	106.06	
2002	827.73	863.60	6.90	106.11	
2003	827.67	1033.83	7.73	106.57	
2004	827.65	1126.27	7.97	106.37	
2005	807.02	957.97	6.87	104.03	
2006	780.87	1026.65	6.56	100.47	
2007	730.46	1066.69	6.11	93.64	1458.07
2008	683.46	965.90	7.57	88.19	987.98
2009	682.82	979.71	7.38	88.05	1097.80
2010	662.27	880.65	8.13	85.09	1021.82
2011	630.09	816.25	8.11	81.07	971.16
2012	628.55	831.76	7.30	81.09	1016.11
2013	609.69	841.89	5.78	78.62	1005.56
2014	611.90	745.56	5.14	78.89	954.37
2015	649.36	709.52	5.39	83.78	961.59
2016	693.70	730.68	5.96	89.45	850.94
2017	653.42	780.23	5.79	83.59	877.92

5-7 国家外汇储备和外债余额

Foreign Exchange Reserves and Outstanding External Debt

年 份 Year	黄金储备 (万盎司) Gold Reserves (10000 Ounces)	外汇储备 (亿美元) Foreign Exchange Reserves (USD 100 million)	外债余额 (亿美元) Outstanding External Debt (USD 100 million)
1979	1280	8.4	
1980	1280	-13.0	
1981	1267	27.1	
1982	1267	69.9	
1983	1267	89.0	
1984	1267	82.2	
1985	1267	26.4	158.3
1986	1267	20.7	214.8
1987	1267	29.2	302.0
1988	1267	33.7	400.0
1989	1267	55.5	413.0
1990	1267	110.9	525.5
1991	1267	217.1	605.6
1992	1267	194.4	693.2
1993	1267	212.0	835.7
1994	1267	516.2	928.1
1995	1267	736.0	1065.9
1996	1267	1050.3	1162.8
1997	1267	1398.9	1309.6
1998	1267	1449.6	1460.4
1999	1267	1546.8	1518.3
2000	1267	1655.7	1457.3
2001	1608	2121.7	2033.0
2002	1929	2864.1	2026.3
2003	1929	4032.5	2193.6
2004	1929	6099.3	2629.9
2005	1929	8188.7	2965.4
2006	1929	10663.4	3385.9
2007	1929	15282.5	3892.2
2008	1929	19460.3	3901.6
2009	3389	23991.5	4286.5
2010	3389	28473.4	5489.4
2011	3389	31811.5	6950.0
2012	3389	33115.9	7369.9
2013	3389	38213.2	8631.7
2014	3389	38430.2	17799.0
2015	5666	33303.6	13829.8
2016	5924	30105.2	14158.0
2017	5924	31399.5	17106.2

对外贸易

FOREIGN TRADE

第6篇

6-1 进出口额(按人民币计算)
Total Value of Imports and Exports by RMB

单位：亿元人民币

Unit: RMB 100 million

年 份 Year	进出口总额 Total	出口额 Exports	进口额 Imports	差额(+顺差,-逆差) Balance
1950	41.3	20.0	21.3	-1.3
1955	109.8	48.7	61.1	-12.4
1960	128.4	63.3	65.1	-1.8
1961	90.7	47.7	43.0	4.7
1962	80.9	47.1	33.8	13.3
1963	85.7	50.0	35.7	14.3
1964	97.5	55.4	42.1	13.3
1965	118.4	63.1	55.3	7.8
1966	127.1	66.0	61.1	4.9
1967	112.2	58.8	53.4	5.4
1968	108.5	57.6	50.9	6.7
1969	107.0	59.8	47.2	12.6
1970	112.9	56.8	56.1	0.7
1971	120.9	68.5	52.4	16.1
1972	146.9	82.9	64.0	18.9
1973	220.5	116.9	103.6	13.3
1974	292.2	139.4	152.8	-13.4
1975	290.4	143.0	147.4	-4.4
1976	264.1	134.8	129.3	5.5
1977	272.5	139.7	132.8	6.9
1978	355.0	167.6	187.4	-19.8
1979	454.6	211.7	242.9	-31.2
1980	570.0	271.2	298.8	-27.6
1981	735.3	367.6	367.7	-0.1
1982	771.4	413.8	357.5	56.3
1983	860.2	438.3	421.8	16.5
1984	1201.0	580.6	620.5	-39.9
1985	2066.7	808.9	1257.9	-449.0
1986	2580.4	1082.1	1498.3	-416.2
1987	3084.2	1470.0	1614.2	-144.3
1988	3821.8	1766.7	2055.1	-288.4
1989	4155.9	1956.1	2199.9	-243.8
1990	5560.1	2985.8	2574.3	411.6
1991	7225.8	3827.1	3398.7	428.5
1992	9119.6	4676.3	4443.3	233.0
1993	11271.0	5284.8	5986.2	-701.4
1994	20381.9	10421.8	9960.1	461.8
1995	23499.9	12451.8	11048.1	1403.7
1996	24133.9	12576.4	11557.4	1019.0
1997	26967.2	15160.7	11806.6	3354.1
1998	26849.7	15223.5	11626.1	3597.4
1999	29896.2	16159.8	13736.5	2423.3
2000	39273.3	20634.4	18638.8	1995.6
2001	42183.6	22024.4	20159.2	1865.3
2002	51378.2	26947.9	24430.3	2517.6
2003	70483.5	36287.9	34195.6	2092.3
2004	95539.1	49103.3	46435.8	2667.6
2005	116921.8	62648.1	54273.7	8374.4
2006	140974.7	77597.9	63376.9	14221.0
2007	166924.1	93627.1	73296.9	20330.2
2008	179921.5	100394.9	79526.5	20868.4
2009	150648.1	82029.7	68618.4	13411.3
2010	201722.3	107022.8	94699.5	12323.3
2011	236402.0	123240.6	113161.4	10079.2
2012	244160.2	129359.3	114801.0	14558.3
2013	258168.9	137131.4	121037.5	16094.0
2014	264241.8	143883.8	120358.0	23525.7
2015	245502.9	141166.8	104336.1	36830.7
2016	243386.5	138419.3	104967.2	33452.1
2017	278101.0	153311.2	124789.8	28521.4

注：1.本表1979年以前为外贸业务统计数，1980年以后为海关进出口统计数。以下诸表同。

2.进出口差额负数为入超。

Note: a) Figures before 1980 are recorded by the Ministry of Foreign Trade and figures since 1980 are recorded by General Administration of Customs. The same to the following tables.

b) Negative figures in balance refer to unfavourable positions.

6-2 进出口额(按美元计算)

Total Value of Imports and Exports By USD

单位：亿美元
Unit: USD 100 million

年 份 Year	进出口总额 Total	出口额 Exports	进口额 Imports	差额(+顺差,-逆差) Balance
1950	11.3	5.5	5.8	-0.3
1955	31.4	14.1	17.3	-3.2
1960	38.1	18.6	19.5	-0.9
1961	29.4	14.9	14.5	0.4
1962	26.6	14.9	11.7	3.2
1963	29.2	16.5	12.7	3.8
1964	34.7	19.2	15.5	3.7
1965	42.5	22.3	20.2	2.1
1966	46.2	23.7	22.5	1.2
1967	41.6	21.4	20.2	1.2
1968	40.5	21.0	19.5	1.5
1969	40.3	22.0	18.3	3.7
1970	45.9	22.6	23.3	-0.7
1971	48.4	26.4	22.0	4.4
1972	63.0	34.4	28.6	5.8
1973	109.8	58.2	51.6	6.6
1974	145.7	69.5	76.2	-6.7
1975	147.5	72.6	74.9	-2.3
1976	134.3	68.5	65.8	2.7
1977	148.0	75.9	72.1	3.8
1978	206.4	97.5	108.9	-11.4
1979	293.3	136.6	156.7	-20.1
1980	381.4	181.2	200.2	-19.0
1981	440.2	220.1	220.2	-0.1
1982	416.1	223.2	192.9	30.4
1983	436.2	222.3	213.9	8.4
1984	535.5	261.4	274.1	-12.7
1985	696.0	273.5	422.5	-149.0
1986	738.5	309.4	429.0	-119.6
1987	826.5	394.4	432.2	-37.8
1988	1027.8	475.2	552.7	-77.5
1989	1116.8	525.4	591.4	-66.0
1990	1154.4	620.9	533.5	87.5
1991	1356.3	718.4	637.9	80.5
1992	1655.3	849.4	805.9	43.6
1993	1957.0	917.4	1039.6	-122.2
1994	2366.2	1210.1	1156.2	53.9
1995	2808.6	1487.8	1320.8	167.0
1996	2898.8	1510.5	1388.3	122.2
1997	3251.6	1827.9	1423.7	404.2
1998	3239.5	1837.1	1402.4	434.8
1999	3606.3	1949.3	1657.0	292.3
2000	4743.0	2492.0	2250.9	241.1
2001	5096.5	2661.0	2435.5	225.5
2002	6207.7	3256.0	2951.7	304.3
2003	8509.9	4382.3	4127.6	254.7
2004	11545.5	5933.3	5612.3	321.0
2005	14219.1	7619.5	6599.5	1020.0
2006	17604.4	9689.8	7914.6	1775.2
2007	21761.8	12200.6	9561.2	2639.4
2008	25632.6	14306.9	11325.6	2981.3
2009	22075.4	12016.1	10059.2	1956.9
2010	29740.0	15777.5	13962.5	1815.1
2011	36418.6	18983.8	17434.8	1549.0
2012	38671.2	20487.1	18184.1	2303.1
2013	41589.9	22090.0	19499.9	2590.2
2014	43015.3	23422.9	19592.4	3830.6
2015	39530.3	22734.7	16795.6	5939.0
2016	36855.6	20976.3	15879.3	5097.1
2017	41071.6	22633.7	18437.9	4195.8

6-3 进出口额指数(按美元计算)
Indices of Total Value of Imports and Exports by USD

(1980年=100) (Year of 1980 =100)

年 份 Year	进出口总额 Total	出口额 Exports	进口额 Imports
1980	100.00	100.00	100.00
1981	115.42	121.47	109.99
1982	109.10	123.18	96.35
1983	114.37	122.68	106.84
1984	140.40	144.26	136.91
1985	182.49	150.94	211.04
1986	193.63	170.75	214.29
1987	216.70	217.66	215.88
1988	269.48	262.25	276.07
1989	292.82	289.96	295.40
1990	302.66	342.67	266.46
1991	355.62	396.48	318.64
1992	433.99	468.76	402.52
1993	513.12	506.31	519.28
1994	620.40	667.80	577.50
1995	736.40	821.08	659.76
1996	760.04	833.60	693.47
1997	852.55	1008.79	711.14
1998	849.37	1013.86	700.48
1999	945.54	1075.78	827.67
2000	1243.57	1375.29	1124.35
2001	1336.26	1468.53	1216.55
2002	1627.60	1796.89	1474.38
2003	2231.22	2418.48	2061.74
2004	3027.15	3274.43	2803.34
2005	3728.12	4205.04	3296.47
2006	4615.73	5347.56	3953.35
2007	5705.76	6733.22	4775.80
2008	6720.65	7895.66	5657.15
2009	5787.98	6631.41	5024.59
2010	7797.59	8707.25	6974.26
2011	9548.67	10476.72	8708.71
2012	10139.27	11306.37	9082.94
2013	10904.54	12190.97	9740.20
2014	11278.26	12926.56	9786.39
2015	10364.53	12546.73	8389.43
2016	9663.23	11576.33	7931.70
2017	10768.65	12491.01	9209.75

6-4 进出口额增长速度(按美元计算)

Growth Rates of Import and Export Value by USD

(上年=100) (Percentage change over previous year)

年 份 Year	进出口总额 Total (%)	出口额 Exports (%)	进口额 Imports (%)
1980	30.0	32.7	27.8
1981	15.4	21.5	10.0
1982	-5.5	1.4	-12.4
1983	4.8	-0.4	10.9
1984	22.8	17.6	28.1
1985	30.0	4.6	54.1
1986	6.1	13.1	1.5
1987	11.9	27.5	0.7
1988	24.4	20.5	27.9
1989	8.7	10.6	7.0
1990	3.4	18.2	-9.8
1991	17.5	15.7	19.6
1992	22.0	18.2	26.3
1993	18.2	8.0	29.0
1994	20.9	31.9	11.2
1995	18.7	23.0	14.2
1996	3.2	1.5	5.1
1997	12.2	21.0	2.5
1998	-0.4	0.5	-1.5
1999	11.3	6.1	18.2
2000	31.5	27.8	35.8
2001	7.5	6.8	8.2
2002	21.8	22.4	21.2
2003	37.1	34.6	39.8
2004	35.7	35.4	36.0
2005	23.2	28.4	17.6
2006	23.8	27.2	19.9
2007	23.6	25.9	20.8
2008	17.8	17.3	18.5
2009	-13.9	-16.0	-11.2
2010	34.7	31.3	38.8
2011	22.5	20.3	24.9
2012	6.2	7.9	4.3
2013	7.5	7.8	7.2
2014	3.4	6.0	0.5
2015	-8.1	-2.9	-14.3
2016	-6.8	-7.7	-5.5
2017	11.4	7.9	16.1

6-5 中国出口额占国内生产总值的比重
China's Export Proportion in GDP

单位：亿元人民币
Unit: RMB 100 million

年 份 Year	国内生产总值 GDP	出 口 额 Exports	出口占国内生产总值的比重(%) Exports Proportion(%)
1980	4587.6	271.2	5.9
1981	4935.8	367.6	7.4
1982	5373.4	413.8	7.7
1983	6020.9	438.3	7.3
1984	7278.5	580.6	8.0
1985	9098.9	808.9	8.9
1986	10376.2	1082.1	10.4
1987	12174.6	1470.0	12.1
1988	15180.4	1766.7	11.6
1989	17179.7	1956.1	11.4
1990	18872.9	2985.8	15.8
1991	22005.6	3827.1	17.4
1992	27194.5	4676.3	17.2
1993	35673.2	5284.8	14.8
1994	48637.5	10421.8	21.4
1995	61339.9	12451.8	20.3
1996	71813.6	12576.4	17.5
1997	79715.0	15160.7	19.0
1998	85195.5	15223.5	17.9
1999	90564.4	16159.8	17.8
2000	100280.1	20634.4	20.6
2001	110863.1	22024.4	19.9
2002	121717.4	26947.9	22.1
2003	137422.0	36287.9	26.4
2004	161840.2	49103.3	30.3
2005	187318.9	62648.1	33.4
2006	219438.5	77597.9	35.4
2007	270232.3	93627.1	34.6
2008	319515.5	100394.9	31.4
2009	349081.4	82029.7	23.5
2010	413030.3	107022.8	25.9
2011	489300.6	123240.6	25.2
2012	540367.4	129359.3	23.9
2013	595244.4	137131.4	23.0
2014	643974.0	143883.8	22.3
2015	689052.1	141166.8	20.5
2016	743585.5	138419.3	18.6
2017	827121.7	153311.2	18.5

6–6 中国出口额占世界出口总额的比重和位次
China's Export Share and Ranking in the World

单位：亿美元
Unit: USD 100 million

年 份 Year	世界出口总额 World Exports	中国出口额 China Exports	中国出口额占世界出口总额的比重(%) China's Share (%)	位 次 Ranking
1980	20361	181	0.9	26
1981	20144	220	1.1	19
1982	18858	223	1.2	17
1983	18460	222	1.2	17
1984	19557	261	1.3	18
1985	19529	274	1.4	17
1986	21385	309	1.4	16
1987	25155	394	1.6	16
1988	28689	475	1.7	16
1989	30989	525	1.7	14
1990	34897	621	1.8	15
1991	35114	718	2.0	13
1992	37792	849	2.2	11
1993	37947	917	2.4	11
1994	43283	1210	2.8	11
1995	51676	1488	2.9	11
1996	54061	1510	2.8	11
1997	55923	1828	3.3	10
1998	55031	1837	3.3	9
1999	57194	1949	3.4	9
2000	64562	2492	3.9	7
2001	61933	2661	4.3	6
2002	64979	3256	5.0	5
2003	75878	4382	5.8	4
2004	92244	5933	6.4	3
2005	105101	7620	7.2	3
2006	121312	9690	8.0	3
2007	140263	12201	8.7	2
2008	161653	14307	8.9	2
2009	125606	12016	9.6	1
2010	153111	15778	10.3	1
2011	183380	18984	10.4	1
2012	184960	20487	11.1	1
2013	189565	22090	11.7	1
2014	189703	23423	12.3	1
2015	165247	22735	13.8	1
2016	160323	20976	13.1	1
2017	177067	22634	12.8	1

注：根据WTO网站公布的数据对历年“世界出口总额”进行了调整。
Note: "World Exports" from 1980 to 2017 is adjusted according to the statistics from WTO website.

6-7 分贸易方式进出口总额
Imports and Exports by Customs Regime

单位：万美元

Unit: USD 10000

贸易方式	Customs Regime	2016		2017	
		出口 Exports	进口 Imports	出口 Exports	进口 Imports
合　计	**Total**	**209763119**	**158792622**	**226337133**	**184379294**
一般贸易	Ordinary Trade	113136852	90064043	123002023	108536506
国家间、国际组织无偿援助和赠送的物资	Aid or Donation between Governments or by International Organizations	47223	1937	53821	258
其他捐赠物资	Other Donation	616	838	221	533
来料加工装配贸易	Processing and Assembling with Materials Provided Abroad	7590496	8518544	7989943	8469668
进料加工贸易	Processing with Imported Materials	63942613	31125291	67886853	34658080
寄售代销贸易	Goods on Consignment	24			166
边境小额贸易	Border Trade	2641057	703681	3023696	889442
加工贸易进口设备	Equipment Imported for Processing and Assembling		46383		74956
对外承包工程出口货物	Contracting Projects	1330286		1539426	
租赁贸易	Goods on Lease	19196	286041	15487	197009
外商投资企业作为投资进口的设备、物品	Equipment or Materials Invested by Foreign-invested Enterprises		408592		445940
出料加工贸易	Outward Processing	22088	26490	20633	32659
易货贸易	Barter Trade	179	793	1515	9697
免税外汇商品	Duty-free Commodities		2250		2128
保税监管场所进出境货物	Customs Trade through Bonded Supervision Areas	3836556	9632714	4109823	11544799
海关特殊监管区域物流货物	Logistics Goods By Customs Special Control Area	9397020	15761390	9972192	17142594
海关特殊监管区域进口设备	Equipment Imported Into Customs Special Control Area		489338		643828
其他	Others	7798913	1724298	8721502	1731033

6-8 一般贸易与加工贸易进出口额

Imports and Exports by Conventional Trade and Processing Trade

单位：亿美元

Unit: USD 100 million

年份 Year	一般贸易 Conventional Trade		加工贸易 Processing Trade		其他贸易 Other Trading Forms	
	出口 Exports	进口 Imports	出口 Exports	进口 Imports	出口 Exports	进口 Imports
1981	208.00	203.66	11.31	15.04	0.79	1.50
1982	206.69	170.17	15.77	21.28	0.74	1.45
1983	201.60	187.68	20.01	24.01	0.69	2.21
1984	231.62	238.49	29.29	31.47	0.49	4.14
1985	237.30	372.72	33.16	42.74	3.04	7.04
1986	250.95	352.07	51.41	63.90	7.04	13.13
1987	296.43	287.72	81.38	95.02	16.59	49.36
1988	325.96	352.08	128.33	137.46	20.91	63.16
1989	315.52	356.14	188.04	156.78	21.84	78.48
1990	354.60	262.00	254.20	187.60	12.10	83.90
1991	381.20	295.40	324.30	250.30	13.60	92.20
1992	436.80	336.20	396.07	315.14	16.53	154.56
1993	432.00	380.45	442.36	363.60	43.04	295.55
1994	615.60	355.20	569.80	475.70	24.70	325.20
1995	713.61	433.81	737.18	583.59	37.01	303.40
1996	628.24	393.63	843.27	622.75	38.99	371.92
1997	779.74	390.30	996.02	702.06	52.14	331.34
1998	742.35	436.80	1044.54	685.99	50.22	279.58
1999	791.35	670.40	1108.82	735.78	49.14	250.81
2000	1051.81	1000.79	1376.52	925.58	63.70	324.57
2001	1118.81	1134.56	1474.34	939.74	67.83	361.23
2002	1361.87	1291.11	1799.27	1222.00	94.82	438.59
2003	1820.34	1877.00	2418.49	1629.35	143.45	621.22
2004	2436.06	2481.45	3279.70	2216.95	217.50	913.89
2005	3150.63	2796.33	4164.67	2740.12	304.23	1063.08
2006	4162.33	3330.74	5103.55	3214.72	423.81	1369.15
2007	5393.55	4286.64	6175.60	3684.74	623.20	1590.20
2008	6628.62	5720.93	6751.14	3783.77	927.17	1820.92
2009	5298.12	5344.70	5868.62	3222.91	849.37	1491.62
2010	7206.12	7692.76	7402.79	4174.82	1168.63	2094.86
2011	9170.34	10076.21	8352.84	4697.56	1460.64	2661.07
2012	9878.99	10223.86	8626.77	4812.75	1981.38	3147.43
2013	10873.26	11098.59	8600.40	4966.62	2616.38	3434.68
2014	12033.91	11089.40	8842.18	5240.85	2546.84	3262.09
2015	12147.92	9224.02	7975.30	4466.10	2611.47	3105.53
2016	11313.69	9006.40	7153.31	3964.38	2509.32	2908.47
2017	12300.20	10853.65	7587.68	4312.77	2745.83	3271.50

6-9 一般贸易与加工贸易进出口增长速度
Growth Rates of Imports and Exports by Conventional Trade and Processing Trade

(上年=100) (Percentage change over previous year)

年 份 Year	一般贸易 Conventional Trade		加工贸易 Processing Trade		其他贸易 Other Trading Forms	
	出 口(%) Exports	进 口(%) Imports	出 口(%) Exports	进 口(%) Imports	出 口(%) Exports	进 口(%) Imports
1982	-0.6	-16.4	39.4	41.5	-6.3	-3.3
1983	-2.5	10.3	26.9	12.8	-6.8	52.4
1984	14.9	27.1	46.4	31.1	-29.0	87.3
1985	2.5	56.3	13.2	35.8	520.4	70.0
1986	5.8	-5.5	55.0	49.5	131.6	86.5
1987	18.1	-18.3	58.3	48.7	135.7	275.9
1988	10.0	22.4	57.7	44.7	26.0	28.0
1989	-3.2	1.2	46.5	14.1	4.4	24.3
1990	12.4	-26.4	35.2	19.7	-44.6	6.9
1991	7.5	12.7	27.6	33.4	12.4	9.9
1992	14.6	13.8	22.1	25.9	21.5	67.6
1993	-1.1	13.2	11.7	15.4	160.4	91.2
1994	42.5	-6.6	28.8	30.8	-42.6	10.0
1995	15.9	22.1	29.4	22.7	49.8	-6.7
1996	-12.0	-9.3	14.4	6.7	5.3	22.6
1997	24.1	-0.8	18.1	12.7	33.7	-10.9
1998	-4.8	11.9	4.9	-2.3	-3.7	-15.6
1999	6.6	53.5	6.2	7.3	-2.2	-10.3
2000	32.9	49.3	24.1	25.8	29.6	29.4
2001	6.4	13.4	7.1	1.5	6.5	11.3
2002	21.7	13.8	22.0	30.0	39.8	21.4
2003	33.7	45.4	34.4	33.3	51.3	41.6
2004	33.8	32.2	35.6	36.1	51.6	47.1
2005	29.3	12.7	27.0	23.6	39.9	16.3
2006	32.1	19.1	22.5	17.3	39.3	28.8
2007	29.6	28.7	21.0	14.6	47.0	16.1
2008	22.9	33.5	9.3	2.7	48.8	14.6
2009	-20.1	-6.6	-13.1	-14.8	-8.4	-18.1
2010	36.0	43.9	26.1	29.5	37.6	40.4
2011	27.3	31.0	12.8	12.5	25.0	27.0
2012	7.7	1.5	3.3	2.5	35.7	18.3
2013	10.1	8.6	-0.3	3.2	32.0	9.1
2014	10.7	-0.1	2.8	5.5	-2.7	-5.0
2015	0.9	-16.8	-9.8	-14.8	2.5	-4.8
2016	-6.9	-2.4	-10.3	-11.2	-3.9	-6.3
2017	8.7	20.5	6.1	8.8	9.4	12.5

6-10 按国际贸易标准分类的进出口简表
Brief Table of Imports and Exports by SITC

单位：亿美元
Unit: USD 100 million

年 份 Year	初级产品 Primary Goods		工业制成品 Manufactured Goods	
	出 口 Exports	进 口 Imports	出 口 Exports	进 口 Imports
1980	91.14	69.59	90.05	130.58
1981	102.48	80.44	117.59	139.71
1982	100.50	76.34	122.71	116.51
1983	96.20	58.08	126.06	155.82
1984	119.34	52.08	142.05	222.02
1985	138.28	52.89	135.22	369.63
1986	112.72	56.49	196.70	372.55
1987	132.31	69.15	262.06	363.01
1988	144.06	100.68	331.10	452.07
1989	150.78	117.54	374.60	473.86
1990	158.86	98.53	462.05	434.92
1991	161.45	108.34	556.98	529.57
1992	170.04	132.55	679.36	673.30
1993	166.66	142.10	750.78	897.49
1994	197.08	164.86	1012.98	991.28
1995	214.85	244.17	1272.95	1076.67
1996	219.25	254.41	1291.23	1133.92
1997	239.53	286.20	1588.39	1137.50
1998	204.89	229.49	1632.20	1172.88
1999	199.41	268.46	1749.90	1388.53
2000	254.60	467.39	2237.43	1783.55
2001	263.38	457.43	2397.60	1978.10
2002	285.40	492.71	2970.56	2458.99
2003	348.12	727.63	4034.16	3399.96
2004	405.49	1172.67	5527.77	4439.62
2005	490.37	1477.14	7129.16	5122.39
2006	529.19	1871.29	9160.17	6043.32
2007	615.09	2430.85	11562.67	7128.65
2008	779.57	3623.95	13527.36	7701.67
2009	631.12	2898.04	11384.83	7161.19
2010	816.86	4338.50	14960.69	9623.94
2011	1005.45	6042.69	17978.36	11392.15
2012	1005.58	6349.34	19481.56	11834.71
2013	1072.68	6580.81	21017.36	12919.09
2014	1126.92	6469.40	22296.01	13122.95
2015	1039.27	4720.57	21695.41	12075.07
2016	1051.87	4410.55	19924.44	11468.71
2017	1177.33	5796.38	21456.38	12641.55

6-11 按国际贸易标准分类的进出口增长速度
Growth Rates of Imports and Exports by SITC

(上年=100) (Percentage change over previous year)

年 份 Year	初级产品 Primary Goods		工业制成品 Manufactured Goods	
	出 口 Exports (%)	进 口 Imports (%)	出 口 Exports (%)	进 口 Imports (%)
1981	12.4	15.6	30.6	7.0
1982	-1.9	-5.1	4.4	-16.6
1983	-4.3	-23.9	2.7	33.7
1984	24.1	-10.3	12.7	42.5
1985	15.9	1.6	-4.8	66.5
1986	-18.5	6.8	45.5	0.8
1987	17.4	22.4	33.2	-2.6
1988	8.9	45.6	26.3	24.5
1989	4.7	16.7	13.1	4.8
1990	5.4	-16.2	23.3	-8.2
1991	1.6	10.0	20.5	21.8
1992	5.3	22.3	22.0	27.1
1993	-2.0	7.2	10.5	33.3
1994	18.3	16.0	34.9	10.5
1995	9.0	48.1	25.7	8.6
1996	2.0	4.2	1.4	5.3
1997	9.2	12.5	23.0	0.3
1998	-14.5	-19.8	2.8	3.1
1999	-2.7	17.0	7.2	18.4
2000	27.7	74.1	27.9	28.4
2001	3.4	-2.1	7.2	10.9
2002	8.4	7.7	23.9	24.3
2003	22.0	47.7	35.8	38.3
2004	16.5	61.2	37.0	30.6
2005	20.9	26.0	29.0	15.4
2006	7.9	26.7	28.5	18.0
2007	16.2	29.9	26.2	18.0
2008	26.7	49.1	17.0	8.0
2009	-19.0	-20.0	-15.8	-7.0
2010	29.4	49.7	31.4	34.4
2011	23.1	39.3	20.2	18.4
2012	0.0	5.1	8.4	3.9
2013	6.7	3.6	7.9	9.2
2014	5.1	-1.7	6.1	1.6
2015	-7.8	-27.0	-2.7	-8.0
2016	1.2	-6.6	-8.2	-5.0
2017	11.9	31.4	7.7	10.2

6–12 按国际贸易标准分类的出口商品金额
Value of Exports by SITC

单位：亿美元
Unit: USD 100 million

商品分类	Category	2015	2016	2017
总 额	**Total**	**22734.68**	**20976.31**	**22633.71**
一、初级产品	**Primary Goods**	**1039.27**	**1051.87**	**1177.33**
食品及活动物	Food and Live Animals	581.54	610.98	626.26
饮料及烟类	Beverages and Tobacco	33.09	35.39	34.68
非食用原料(燃料除外)	Crude Materials,Inedible,Except Fuels	139.17	131.02	154.40
矿物燃料、润滑油及有关原料	Mineral Fuels，Lubricants and Related Materials	279.02	268.73	353.89
动植物油、脂及蜡	Animal and Vegetable Oils，Fats and Waxes	6.45	5.75	8.10
二、工业制成品	**Manufactured Goods**	**21695.41**	**19924.44**	**21456.38**
化学成品及有关产品	Chemicals and Related Products	1295.80	1219.29	1412.93
按原料分类的制成品	Manufactured Goods Classified Chiefly by Material	3910.18	3512.45	3685.64
机械及运输设备	Machinery and Transport Equipment	10591.18	9842.12	10823.29
杂项制品	Miscellaneous Manufactured Articles	5874.45	5294.88	5476.92
未分类的商品	Products Not Classified	23.81	55.70	57.60

6–13 按国际贸易标准分类的进口商品金额
Value of Imports by SITC

单位：亿美元
Unit: USD 100 million

商品分类	Category	2015	2016	2017
总 额	**Total**	**16795.64**	**15879.26**	**18437.93**
一、初级产品	**Primary Goods**	**4720.57**	**4410.55**	**5796.38**
食品及活动物	Food and Live Animals	505.01	491.56	543.14
饮料及烟类	Beverages and Tobacco	57.74	60.96	70.28
非食用原料(燃料除外)	Crude Materials,Inedible,Except Fuels	2097.10	2025.45	2610.00
矿物燃料、润滑油及有关原料	Mineral Fuels，Lubricants and Related Materials	1985.89	1765.26	2496.17
动植物油、脂及蜡	Animal and Vegetable Oils，Fats and Waxes	74.83	67.32	76.78
二、工业制成品	**Manufactured Goods**	**12075.07**	**11468.71**	**12641.55**
化学成品及有关产品	Chemicals and Related Products	1712.66	1641.17	1937.31
按原料分类的制成品	Manufactured Goods Classified Chiefly by Material	1330.11	1219.20	1351.47
机械及运输设备	Machinery and Transport Equipment	6824.18	6578.25	7348.65
杂项制品	Miscellaneous Manufactured Articles	1346.92	1261.41	1343.32
未分类的商品	Products Not Classified	861.20	768.68	660.79

6-14 按国际贸易标准分类的出口商品构成
Composition of Exports by SITC

单位：%
Unit: %

商品分类	Category	2015	2016	2017
总　额	**Total**	**100.00**	**100.00**	**100.00**
一、初级产品	**Primary Goods**	**4.57**	**5.01**	**5.20**
食品及活动物	Food and Live Animals	2.56	2.91	2.77
饮料及烟类	Beverages and Tobacco	0.15	0.17	0.15
非食用原料(燃料除外)	Crude Materials,Inedible,Except Fuels	0.61	0.62	0.68
矿物燃料、润滑油及有关原料	Mineral Fuels，Lubricants and Related Materials	1.23	1.28	1.56
动植物油、脂及蜡	Animal and Vegetable Oils，Fats and Waxes	0.03	0.03	0.04
二、工业制成品	**Manufactured Goods**	**95.43**	**94.99**	**94.80**
化学成品及有关产品	Chemicals and Related Products	5.70	5.81	6.24
按原料分类的制成品	Manufactured Goods Classified Chiefly by Material	17.20	16.74	16.28
机械及运输设备	Machinery and Transport Equipment	46.59	46.92	47.82
杂项制品	Miscellaneous Manufactured Articles	25.84	25.24	24.20
未分类的商品	Products Not Classified	0.10	0.27	0.25

6-15 按国际贸易标准分类的进口商品构成
Composition of Imports by SITC

单位：%
Unit: %

商品分类	Category	2015	2016	2017
总　额	**Total**	**100.00**	**100.00**	**100.00**
一、初级产品	**Primary Goods**	**28.11**	**27.78**	**31.44**
食品及活动物	Food and Live Animals	3.01	3.10	2.95
饮料及烟类	Beverages and Tobacco	0.34	0.38	0.38
非食用原料(燃料除外)	Crude Materials,Inedible,Except Fuels	12.49	12.76	14.16
矿物燃料、润滑油及有关原料	Mineral Fuels，Lubricants and Related Materials	11.82	11.12	13.54
动植物油、脂及蜡	Animal and Vegetable Oils，Fats and Waxes	0.45	0.42	0.42
二、工业制成品	**Manufactured Goods**	**71.89**	**72.22**	**68.56**
化学成品及有关产品	Chemicals and Related Products	10.20	10.34	10.51
按原料分类的制成品	Manufactured Goods Classified Chiefly by Material	7.92	7.68	7.33
机械及运输设备	Machinery and Transport Equipment	40.63	41.43	39.86
杂项制品	Miscellaneous Manufactured Articles	8.02	7.94	7.29
未分类的商品	Products Not Classified	5.13	4.84	3.58

6-16 按商品类章分出口商品金额

Value of Exports of Goods by HS Section and Division

商品分类	HS Section and Division	2016 亿元人民币 RMB 100 million	2016 亿美元 USD 100 million	2017 亿元人民币 RMB 100 million	2017 亿美元 USD 100 million
总　　额	**Total**	**138419.29**	**20976.31**	**153311.19**	**22633.71**
第一类　活动物；动物产品	**LIVE ANIMALS；ANIMAL PRODUCTS**	**1162.51**	**176.18**	**1194.06**	**176.28**
01章　活动物	Live animals	42.67	6.47	38.06	5.62
02章　肉及食用杂碎	Meat and edible meat offal	59.57	9.02	62.10	9.16
03章　鱼、甲壳动物、软体动物及其他水生无脊椎动物	Fish and crustaceans molluscs and other aquatic invertebrates	904.48	137.06	897.71	132.53
04章　乳品；蛋品；天然蜂蜜；其他食用动物产品	Dairy produce；birds' eggs；natural honey；edible products of animal origin，not elsewhere specified or included	38.87	5.90	39.85	5.88
05章　其他动物产品	Products of animal origin，not elsewhere specified or included	116.92	17.72	156.34	23.09
第二类　植物产品	**VEGETABLE PRODUCTS**	**1612.90**	**244.05**	**1701.14**	**251.39**
06章　活树及其他活植物；鳞茎、根及类似品；插花及装饰用簇叶	Live tree and other plants；bulbs，roots and the like; cut flowers and ornamental foliage	21.81	3.30	22.91	3.38
07章　食用蔬菜、根及块茎	Edible vegetables and certain roots and tubers	696.69	105.47	756.45	111.64
08章　食用水果及坚果；甜瓜或柑桔属水果的果皮	Edible fruit and nuts；peel of citrus fruit or melons	364.70	54.99	359.66	53.37
09章　咖啡、茶、马黛茶及调味香料	Coffee，tea，mate and spices	196.74	29.82	198.65	29.31
10章　谷物	Cereals	28.34	4.29	45.34	6.70
11章　制粉工业产品；麦芽；淀粉；菊粉；面筋	Products of the milling industry；malt；starches；inulin；wheat gluten	37.29	5.65	38.87	5.75
12章　含油子仁及果实；杂项子仁及果实；工业用或药用植物；稻草、秸秆及饲料	Oil seeds and oleaginous fruits；miscellaneous grains，seeds and fruit；industrial or medicinal plants；straw and fodder	176.54	26.74	179.04	26.46
13章　虫胶；树胶、树脂及其他植物液、汁	Lac；gums，resins and other vegetable saps and extracts	82.85	12.58	91.35	13.48
14章　编结用植物材料；其他植物产品	Vegetable plaiting materials；vegetable products not elsewhere specified or included	7.95	1.21	8.88	1.31
第三类　动、植物油、脂及其分解产品；精制的食用油脂；动、植物蜡	**ANIMAL OR VEGETABLE FATS AND OILS AND THEIR CLEAVAGE PRODUCTS；PREPARED EDIBLE FATS；ANIMAL OR VEGETABLE WAXES**	**39.59**	**6.00**	**56.79**	**8.39**
15章　动、植物油、脂及其分解产品；精制的食用油脂；动、植物蜡	Animal or vegetable fats and oils and their cleavage products；prepared edible fats；animal or vegetable waxes	39.59	6.00	56.79	8.39
第四类　食品；饮料、酒及醋；烟草、烟草及烟草代用品的制品	**PREPARED FOODSTUFFS；BEVERAGES, SPIRITS AND VINEGAR；TOBACCO AND MANUFACTURED TOBACCO SUBSTITUTES**	**1882.89**	**285.47**	**2030.08**	**299.76**
16章　肉、鱼、甲壳动物、软体动物及其他水生无脊椎动物的制品	Preparations of meat，of fish or of crustaceans，molluscs or other aquatic invertebrates	524.00	79.42	610.87	90.24
17章　糖及糖食	Sugars and sugar confectionery	112.62	17.07	119.19	17.59
18章　可可及可可制品	Cocoa and cocoa preparations	28.18	4.26	25.39	3.76
19章　谷物、粮食粉、淀粉或乳的制品；糕饼点心	Preparations of cereals，flour，starch or milk；pastry-cooks' products	104.23	15.79	111.75	16.50

6-16 续表 1 Continued 1

商品分类	HS Section and Division	2016 亿 元 人民币 RMB 100 million	2016 亿美元 USD 100 million	2017 亿 元 人民币 RMB 100 million	2017 亿美元 USD 100 million
20章 蔬菜、水果、坚果或植物其他部分的制品	Preparations of vegetables, fruit, nuts or other parts of plants	483.81	73.38	521.12	76.94
21章 杂项食品	Miscellaneous edible preparations	211.53	32.07	220.88	32.60
22章 饮料、酒及醋	Beverages, spirits and vinegar	145.20	22.03	150.86	22.27
23章 食品工业的残渣及废料；配制的动物饲料	Residues and waste from the food industries; prepared animal fodder	182.21	27.68	180.25	26.59
24章 烟草及烟草代用品的制品	Tobacco and manufactured tobacco substitutes	91.12	13.77	89.78	13.27
第五类 矿产品	**MINERAL PRODUCTS**	**1983.69**	**301.33**	**2666.53**	**393.26**
25章 盐；硫磺；泥土及石料；石膏料、石灰及水泥	Salt; sulphur; earths and stone; plastering materials, lime and cement	196.48	29.87	218.02	32.18
26章 矿砂、矿渣及矿灰	Ores, slag and ash	17.79	2.70	48.50	7.17
27章 矿物燃料、矿物油及其蒸馏产品；沥青物质；矿物蜡	Mineral fuels, mineral oils and products of their distillation; bituminous substances; mineral waxes	1769.42	268.76	2400.01	353.91
第六类 化学工业及其相关工业的产品	**PRODUCTS OF THE CHEMICAL OR INDUSTRIES ALLIED**	**6545.36**	**993.18**	**7755.52**	**1144.52**
28章 无机化学品；贵金属、稀土金属、放射性元素及其同位素的有机及无机化合物	Inorganic chemicals; organic or inorganic compounds of precious metals, of rare- earth metals, of radioactive elements or of isotopes	799.88	121.37	1016.37	150.04
29章 有机化学品	Organic chemicals	2779.20	421.65	3370.52	497.36
30章 药品	Pharmaceutical products	463.15	70.12	498.76	73.64
31章 肥料	Fertilizers	429.60	65.57	410.29	60.43
32章 鞣料浸膏及染料浸膏；鞣酸及其衍生物；染料、颜料及其他着色料；油漆及清漆；油灰及其他类似胶粘剂；墨水、油墨	Tanning or dyeing extracts; tannins and their derivatives; dyes, pigments and other colouring matter; paints and varnishes; putty and other mastics; inks	401.51	60.90	473.89	69.91
33章 精油及香膏；芳香料制品及化妆盥洗品	Essential oils and retinoid; perfumery, cosmetic or toilet preparations	283.12	42.89	327.26	48.32
34章 肥皂、有机表面活性剂、洗涤剂、润滑剂、人造蜡、调制蜡、光洁剂、蜡烛及类似品、塑型用膏、"牙科用蜡"及牙科用熟石膏制剂	Soap, organic surface-active agents, washing preparations, lubricating preparations, artificial waxes, prepared waxes, polishing or scouring preparations, candles and similar articles, modelling pastes, "dental waxes" and dental preparations with a basis of plast	213.35	32.34	239.74	35.38
35章 蛋白类物质；改性淀粉；胶；酶	Albuminoidal substances; modified starches; glues; enzymes	164.55	24.94	192.57	28.41
36章 炸药；烟火制品；火柴；引火合金；易燃材料制品	Explosives; pyrotechnic products; matches; pyrophoric alloys; certain combustible preparations	54.10	8.22	55.96	8.25
37章 照相及电影用品	Photographic or cinematographic goods	70.58	10.71	73.35	10.83
38章 杂项化学产品	Miscellaneous chemical products	886.34	134.47	1096.79	161.94
第七类 塑料及其制品，橡胶及其制品	**PLASTICS AND ARTICLES THEREOF RUBBER AND ARTICLES THEREOF**	**5349.13**	**811.07**	**6143.81**	**906.55**
39章 塑料及其制品	Plastics and articles thereof	4114.04	623.74	4744.22	700.00
40章 橡胶及其制品	Rubber and articles thereof	1235.09	187.33	1399.59	206.54
第八类 生皮、皮革、毛皮及其制品；鞍具及挽具；旅行用品、手提包及类似品；动物肠线(蚕胶丝除外)制品	**RAW HIDES AND SKINS, LEATHER, FUR SKINS AND ARTICLES THEREOF; SADDLERY AND HARNESS; TRAVEL GOODS, HANDBAGS AND SIMILAR CONTAINERS; ARTICLES OF ANIMAL GUT(OTHER THAN SILK-WORM GUT)**	**2072.44**	**313.98**	**2246.50**	**331.39**
41章 生皮(毛皮除外)及皮革	Raw hides and skins(other than fur skins) and leather	41.31	6.27	41.73	6.15

商品分类		HS Section and Division	2016		2017	
			亿 元 人民币 RMB 100 million	亿美元 USD 100 million	亿 元 人民币 RMB 100 million	亿美元 USD 100 million
42章	皮革制品；鞍具及挽具；旅行用品、手提包及类似容器；动物肠线(蚕胶丝除外)制品	Articles of leather；saddlery and harness；travel goods，hand bags and similar containers；articles of animal gut (other than silk-worm gut)	1805.72	273.69	1958.27	288.72
43章	毛皮、人造毛皮及其制品	Fur skins and artificial fur；manufactures thereof	225.41	34.02	246.50	36.52
第九类	**木及木制品；木炭；软木及软木制品；稻草，秸秆、针茅或其他编结材料制品；篮筐及柳条编结品**	**WOOD AND ARTICLES OF WOOD；WOOD CHAR-COAL；CORK AND ARTICLES OF CORK；MANUFACTURES OF STRAW，OF ESPARTO OR OF OTHER PLAITING MATERIALS；BASKET WARE AND WICKERWORK**	**992.34**	**150.50**	**1027.73**	**151.57**
44章	木及木制品；木炭	Wood and articles of wood；wood charcoal	893.29	135.47	924.79	136.40
45章	软木及软木制品	Cork and articles of cork	1.40	0.21	1.43	0.21
46章	稻草、秸秆、针茅或其他编结材料制品；篮筐及柳条编结品	Manufactures of straw，of esparto or of other plaiting Materials；basket ware and wickerwork	97.65	14.82	101.51	14.96
第十类	**木浆及其他纤维状纤维素浆；纸及纸板的废碎品；纸、纸板及其制品**	**PULP OF WOOD OR OF OTHER FIBROUS CELLULOSIC MATERIAL；WASTE AND SCRAP OF PAPER OR PAPERBOARD；PAPER AND PAPERBOARD AND ARTICLES THEREOF**	**1408.77**	**213.40**	**1474.43**	**217.52**
47章	木浆及其他纤维状纤维素浆；纸及纸板的废碎品	Pulp of wood or of other fibrous cellulosic material；waste and scrap of paper or paperboard	7.22	1.10	9.15	1.35
48章	纸及纸板；纸浆、纸或纸板制品	Paper and paperboard；articles of paper pulp，of paper or paperboard	1163.02	176.17	1219.51	179.89
49章	书籍、报纸、印刷图画及其他印制品；手稿、打字稿及设计图纸	Printed books，newspapers，pictures and other products of the printing industry；manuscripts，typescripts and plans	238.52	36.13	245.77	36.29
第十一类	**纺织原料及纺织制品**	**TEXTILES AND TEXTILE ARTICLES**	**16703.95**	**2532.63**	**17444.89**	**2573.21**
50章	蚕丝	Silk	76.28	11.58	75.38	11.12
51章	羊毛、动物细毛或粗毛；马毛纱线及其机织物	Wool，fine or coarse animal hair；horsehair yarn and woven fabric	140.79	21.41	135.60	19.99
52章	棉花	Cotton	986.22	149.67	1025.24	151.27
53章	其他植物纺织纤维；纸纱线及其机织物	Other vegetable textile fibres；paper yarn and woven fabrics of paper yarn	69.65	10.55	71.33	10.55
54章	化学纤维长丝	Man-made filaments	1092.41	165.69	1217.50	179.54
55章	化学纤维短纤	Man-made short fibres	798.50	121.16	818.13	120.61
56章	絮胎、毡呢及无纺织物；特种纱线；线、绳、索、缆及其制品	Wadding，felt and nonwoven；special yarns；twine，cordage，ropes and cables and articles thereof	323.60	49.11	344.63	50.84
57章	地毯及纺织材料的其他铺地制品	Carpets and other textile floor coverings	166.44	25.23	183.13	27.02
58章	特种机织物；簇绒织物；花边；装饰毯；装饰带；刺绣品	Special woven fabrics；tufted textile fabrics；lace；tapestries；trimmings；embroidery	295.72	44.86	321.30	47.40
59章	浸渍、涂布、包覆或层压的纺织物；工业用纺织制品	Impregnated，coated，covered or laminated textile fabrics；textile articles of a kind suitable for industrial use	454.85	69.01	501.01	73.90
60章	针织物及钩编织物	Knitted or crocheted fabrics	951.02	144.21	1118.93	165.06
61章	针织或钩编的服装及衣着附件	Articles of apparel and clothing accessories，knitted or crocheted	4909.68	744.22	4865.76	718.24
62章	非针织或非钩编的服装及衣着附件	Articles of apparel and clothing accessories，not knitted or crocheted	4755.56	720.69	4980.24	734.09

商品分类	HS Section and Division	2016 亿元人民币 RMB 100 million	2016 亿美元 USD 100 million	2017 亿元人民币 RMB 100 million	2017 亿美元 USD 100 million
63章 其他纺织制成品；成套物品；旧衣着及旧纺织品；碎织物	Other made up textile articles；sets；worn clothing and worn textile articles；rags articles；rags	1683.22	255.24	1786.70	263.58
第十二类 鞋、帽、伞、杖、鞭及其零件；已加工的羽毛及其制品；人造花；人发制品	**FOOTWEAR，HEADGEAR，UMBRELLAS，SUN UMBRELLAS，WALKING-STICKS，SEAT-STICKS，WHIPS，RIDING-CROPS AND PARTS THEREOF；PREPARED FEATHERS AND ARTICLES MADE THEREWITH；ARTIFICIAL FLOWERS；ARTICLES OF HUMAN HAIR**	**3921.37**	**594.43**	**4147.04**	**611.06**
64章 鞋靴、护腿和类似品及其零件	Footwear，gaiters and the like；parts of such articles	3114.04	472.08	3270.84	481.86
65章 帽类及其零件	Headgear and parts thereof	290.50	44.05	297.82	43.90
66章 雨伞、阳伞、手杖、鞭子、马鞭及其零件	Umbrellas，sun umbrellas，walking-sticks，seat-sticks，whips，riding-crops and parts thereof	178.97	27.18	178.09	26.21
67章 已加工羽毛、羽绒及其制品；人造花；人发制品	Prepared feathers and down and articles made of feathers or of down；artificial flowers；articles of human hair	337.86	51.12	400.28	59.08
第十三类 石料、石膏、水泥、石棉、云母及类似材料的制品；陶瓷产品；玻璃及其制品	**ARTICLES OF STONE，PLASTER，CEMENT，ASBESTOS，MICA OR SIMILAR MATERIALS；CERAMIC PRODUCTS；GLASS AND GLASSWARE**	**2921.08**	**442.72**	**3110.30**	**459.03**
68章 石料、石膏、水泥、石棉、云母及类似材料的制品	Articles of stone，plaster，cement，asbestos，mica or similar materials；ceramic products；glass and glassware	708.28	107.38	736.64	108.71
69章 陶瓷产品	Ceramic products	1205.93	182.68	1308.09	193.14
70章 玻璃及其制品	Glass and glassware	1006.87	152.66	1065.58	157.18
第十四类 天然或养殖珍珠、宝石或半宝石、贵金属、包贵金属及其制品；仿首饰；硬币	**NATURAL OR CULTURED PEARLS，PRECIOUS OR SEMI-PRECIOUS STONES，PRECIOUS METALS，METALS CLAD WITH PRECIOUS METAL AND STONES，PRECIOUS METALS，METALS CLAD WITH PRECIOUS METAL AND ARTICLES THEREOF；IMITATION JEWELLERY；COIN**	**1441.52**	**217.31**	**1216.54**	**179.81**
71章 天然或养殖珍珠、宝石或半宝石、贵金属、包贵金属及其制品；仿首饰；硬币	Natural or cultured pearls，precious or semi-precious stones，precious metals，metals clad with precious metal and articles thereof；imitation jewellery；coin	1441.52	217.31	1216.54	179.81
第十五类 贱金属及其制品	**BASE METALS AND ARTICLES OF BASE METAL**	**10179.35**	**1544.12**	**11194.45**	**1650.97**
72章 钢铁	Iron and steel	2848.41	432.57	2918.42	429.84
73章 钢铁制品	Articles of iron or steel	3422.02	519.01	3844.56	567.28
74章 铜及其制品	Copper and articles thereof	381.90	57.95	437.46	64.57
75章 镍及其制品	Nickel and articles thereof	21.51	3.25	28.33	4.18
76章 铝及其制品	Aluminium and articles thereof	1398.39	212.10	1530.96	225.85
78章 铅及其制品	Lead and articles thereof	4.78	0.73	5.73	0.85
79章 锌及其制品	Zinc and articles thereof	17.96	2.72	16.51	2.43
80章 锡及其制品	Tin and articles thereof	4.40	0.66	4.04	0.60
81章 其他贱金属、金属陶瓷及其制品	Other base metals；cermets；articles thereof	165.01	25.00	218.86	32.29
82章 贱金属工具、器具、利口器、餐匙、餐叉及其零件	Tools，implements，cutlery，spoons and forks，of base metal；parts thereof of base metal	880.22	133.42	1017.27	150.13
83章 贱金属杂项制品	Miscellaneous articles of base metal	1034.75	156.69	1172.30	172.95

6-16 续表 4 Continued 4

商品分类	HS Section and Division	2016 亿元人民币 RMB 100 million	2016 亿美元 USD 100 million	2017 亿元人民币 RMB 100 million	2017 亿美元 USD 100 million
第十六类 机器、机械器具、电气设备及其零件；录音机及放声机、电视图像、声音的录制和重放设备及其零件、附件	**MACHINERY AND MECHANICAL APPLIANCES；ELECTRICAL EQUIPMENT；PARTS THEREOF；SOUND RECORDERS AND REPRODUCERS，TELEVISION IMAGE AND SOUND RECORDERS AND REPRODUCERS；AND PARTS AND ACCESSORIES OF RECORDERS AND REPRODUCERS；AND PARTS AND ACCESSORIES OF SUCH ARTICLES**	**59207.50**	**8969.75**	**66431.72**	**9815.69**
84章 核反应堆、锅炉、机器、机械器具及其零件	Nuclear reactors，boilers，machinery and mechanical appliances；parts thereof	22678.25	3437.90	25958.67	3832.44
85章 电机、电气设备及其零件；录音机及放声机、电视图像、声音的录制和重放设备及其零件、附件	Electrical machinery and equipment and parts thereof；sound recorders and reproducers，television image and sound recorders and reproducers，and parts and accessories of such articles	36529.25	5531.85	40473.06	5983.25
第十七类 车辆、航空器、船舶及有关运输设备	**VEHICLES，AIRCRAFT，VESSELS AND ASSOCIATED TRANSPORT EQUIPMENT**	**6122.58**	**928.87**	**7108.05**	**1048.09**
86章 铁道及电车道机车、车辆及其零件；铁道及电车轨道固定装置及其零件、附件；各种机械(包括电动机械)交通信号设备	Railway or tramway locomotives，rolling-stock and parts thereof；railway or tramway track fixtures and fittings and parts thereof；mechanical(including electro-mechanical) traffic signalling equipment of all kinds	452.36	68.59	740.92	109.46
87章 车辆及其零件、附件，但铁道及电车道车辆除外	Vehicles other than railway or tramway rolling-stock，and parts and accessories thereof	3967.22	601.49	4557.15	672.63
88章 航空器、航天器及其零件	Aircraft，spacecraft，and parts thereof	221.29	33.65	249.09	36.67
89章 船舶及浮动结构体	Ships，boats and floating structures	1481.71	225.15	1560.89	229.33
第十八类 光学、照相、电影、计量、检验、医疗或外科用仪器及设备、精密仪器及设备；钟表；乐器；上述物品的零件、附件	**OPTICAL，PHOTOGRAPHIC，CINEMATOGRAPHIC，MEASURING，CHECKING，PRECISION，MEDICAL OR SURGICAL INSTRUMENTS AND APPARATUS；CLOCKS AND WATCHES；MUSICAL INSTRUMENTS；PARTS AND ACCESSORIES THEREOF**	**4909.09**	**743.90**	**5204.33**	**768.20**
90章 光学、照相、电影、计量、检验、医疗或外科用仪器及设备、精密仪器及设备；上述物品的零件、附件	Optical，photographic，cinematographic，measuring，checking，precision medical or surgical instruments and apparatus；parts and accessories thereof	4453.84	674.88	4784.01	706.16
91章 钟表及其零件	Clocks and watches and parts thereof	351.62	53.31	315.51	46.55
92章 乐器及其零件、附件	Musical instruments；parts and accessories of such articles	103.63	15.70	104.82	15.48
第十九类 武器、弹药及其零件、附件	**ARMS AND AMMUNITION；PARTS AND ACCESSORIES THEREOF**	**9.18**	**1.39**	**8.99**	**1.33**
93章 武器、弹药及其零件、附件	Arms and ammunition；parts and accessories thereof	9.18	1.39	8.99	1.33
第二十类 杂项制品	**MISCELLANEOUS MANUFACTURED ARTICLES**	**9642.83**	**1460.61**	**10782.00**	**1591.58**
94章 家具；寝具、褥垫、弹簧床垫、软坐垫及类似的填充制品；未列名灯具及照明装置；发光标志、发光名牌及类似品；活动房屋	Furniture；bedding，mattresses，mattress supports，cushions and similar stuffed furnishings；lamps and lighting fittings，not elsewhere specified or included；illuminated signs，illuminated	5774.91	875.14	6031.97	889.73
95章 玩具、游戏品、运动用品及其零件、附件	Toys，games and sports requisites；parts and accessories thereof	2889.05	437.07	3692.86	545.93
96章 杂项制品	Miscellaneous manufactured articles	978.88	148.40	1057.17	155.92
第二十一类 艺术品、收藏品及古物	**WORKS OF ART，COLLECTORS' PIECES AND ANTIQUES**	**14.21**	**2.15**	**8.68**	**1.28**
97章 艺术品、收藏品及古物	Works of art，collectors' pieces and antiques	14.21	2.15	8.68	1.28
第二十二类 特殊交易品及未分类商品	**COMMODITIES AND TRANSACTIONS NOT CLASSIFIED ACCORDING TO KIND**	**297.03**	**43.27**	**357.62**	**52.85**
98章 特殊交易品及未分类商品	Commodities and transactions not classified according to kind	297.03	43.27	357.62	52.85

6-17 按商品类章分进口商品金额
Value of Imports of Goods by HS Section and Division

商品分类	HS Section and Division	2016 亿元人民币 RMB 100 million	2016 亿美元 USD 100 million	2017 亿元人民币 RMB 100 million	2017 亿美元 USD 100 million
总　　额	**Total**	**104967.17**	**15879.26**	**124789.81**	**18437.93**
第一类　活动物；动物产品	**LIVE ANIMALS；ANIMAL PRODUCTS**	**1426.94**	**216.14**	**1598.33**	**236.05**
01章　活动物	Live animals	26.21	3.94	24.56	3.64
02章　肉及食用杂碎	Meat and edible meat offal	677.24	102.63	642.64	94.87
03章　鱼、甲壳动物、软体动物及其他水生无脊椎动物	Fish and crustaceans molluscs and other aquatic invertebrates	457.26	69.18	545.89	80.71
04章　乳品；蛋品；天然蜂蜜；其他食用动物产品	Dairy produce；birds' eggs；natural honey；edible products of animal origin，not elsewhere specified or included	231.76	35.17	343.73	50.70
05章　其他动物产品	Products of animal origin，not elsewhere specified or included	34.47	5.22	41.51	6.14
第二类　植物产品	**VEGETABLE PRODUCTS**	**3557.91**	**538.90**	**4169.25**	**614.81**
06章　活树及其他活植物；鳞茎、根及类似品；插花及装饰用簇叶	Live tree and other plants；bulbs、roots and the like；cut flowers and ornamental foliage	14.96	2.26	18.91	2.81
07章　食用蔬菜、根及块茎	Edible vegetables and certain roots and tubers	122.76	18.64	136.46	20.16
08章　食用水果及坚果；甜瓜或柑桔属水果的果皮	Edible fruit and nuts；peel of citrus fruit or melons	386.36	58.65	434.02	63.95
09章　咖啡、茶、马黛茶及调味香料	Coffee，tea，mate and spices	44.25	6.67	32.01	4.72
10章　谷物	Cereals	372.30	56.61	434.28	64.01
11章　制粉工业产品；麦芽；淀粉；菊粉；面筋	Products of the milling industry；malt；starches；inulin；wheat gluten	58.91	8.92	65.72	9.70
12章　含油子仁及果实；杂项子仁及果实；工业用或药用植物；稻草、秸秆及饲料	Oil seeds and oleaginous fruits；miscellaneous grains，seeds and fruit；industrial or medicinal plants；straw and fodder	2530.77	382.95	3018.64	445.14
13章　虫胶；树胶、树脂及其他植物液、汁	Lac；gums，resins and other vegetable saps and extracts	14.13	2.14	17.31	2.56
14章　编结用植物材料；其他植物产品	Vegetable plaiting materials；vegetable products not elsewhere specified or included	13.47	2.04	11.90	1.75
第三类　动、植物油、脂及其分解产品；精制的食用油脂；动、植物蜡	**ANIMAL OR VEGETABLE FATS AND OILS AND THEIR CLEAVAGE PRODUCTS；PREPARED EDIBLE FATS；ANIMAL OR VEGETABLE WAXES**	**465.99**	**70.41**	**560.71**	**82.85**
15章　动、植物油、脂及其分解产品；精制的食用油脂；动、植物蜡	Animal or vegetable fats and oils and their cleavage products；prepared edible fats；animal or vegetable waxes	465.99	70.41	560.71	82.85
第四类　食品；饮料、酒及醋；烟草、烟草及烟草代用品的制品	**PREPARED FOODSTUFFS；BEVERAGES, SPIRITS AND VINEGAR；TOBACCO AND MANUFACTURED TOBACCO SUBSTITUTES**	**1296.11**	**196.09**	**1482.72**	**219.22**
16章　肉、鱼、甲壳动物、软体动物及其他水生无脊椎动物的制品	Preparations of meat，of fish or of crustaceans，molluscs or other aquatic invertebrates	12.12	1.83	16.19	2.39
17章　糖及糖食	Sugars and sugar confectionery	96.45	14.60	95.70	14.08
18章　可可及可可制品	Cocoa and cocoa preparations	45.40	6.86	44.45	6.60
19章　谷物、粮食粉、淀粉或乳的制品；糕饼点心	Preparations of cereals，flour，starch or milk；pastry-cooks' products	302.08	45.59	383.57	56.86

6-17 续表 1 Continued 1

商品分类	HS Section and Division	2016 亿元人民币 RMB 100 million	2016 亿美元 USD 100 million	2017 亿元人民币 RMB 100 million	2017 亿美元 USD 100 million
20章 蔬菜、水果、坚果或植物其他部分的制品	Preparations of vegetables, fruit, nuts or other parts of plants	64.89	9.82	73.84	10.93
21章 杂项食品	Miscellaneous edible preparations	143.29	21.64	161.25	23.88
22章 饮料、酒及醋	Beverages, spirits and vinegar	316.23	47.87	356.83	52.88
23章 食品工业的残渣及废料；配制的动物饲料	Residues and waste from the food industries; prepared animal fodder	201.88	30.62	230.58	33.98
24章 烟草及烟草代用品的制品	Tobacco and manufactured tobacco substitutes	113.77	17.28	120.28	17.63
第五类 矿产品	**MINERAL PRODUCTS**	**18220.59**	**2756.90**	**25917.15**	**3824.70**
25章 盐；硫磺；泥土及石料；石膏料、石灰及水泥	Salt; sulphur; earths and stone; plastering materials, lime and cement	308.53	46.74	430.61	63.67
26章 矿砂、矿渣及矿灰	Ores, slag and ash	6244.34	944.79	8573.22	1264.78
27章 矿物燃料、矿物油及其蒸馏产品；沥青物质；矿物蜡	Mineral fuels, mineral oils and products of their distillation; bituminous substances; mineral waxes	11667.73	1765.36	16913.32	2496.25
第六类 化学工业及其相关工业的产品	**PRODUCTS OF THE CHEMICAL OR INDUSTRIES ALLIED**	**7256.27**	**1097.91**	**8973.18**	**1325.51**
28章 无机化学品；贵金属、稀土金属、放射性元素及其同位素的有机及无机化合物	Inorganic chemicals; organic or inorganic compounds of precious metals, of rare- earth metals, of radioactive elements or of isotopes	596.25	90.25	705.53	104.34
29章 有机化学品	Organic chemicals	2900.79	439.06	3782.29	558.38
30章 药品	Pharmaceutical products	1374.77	207.71	1717.97	253.65
31章 肥料	Fertilizers	158.74	24.08	156.85	23.14
32章 鞣料浸膏及染料浸膏；鞣酸及其衍生物；染料、颜料及其他着色料；油漆及清漆；油灰及其他类似胶粘剂；墨水、油墨	Tanning or dyeing extracts; tannins and their derivatives; dyes, pigments and other colouring matter; paints and varnishes; putty and other mastics; inks	279.91	42.36	314.77	46.52
33章 精油及香膏；芳香料制品及化妆盥洗品	Essential oils and retinoid; perfumery, cosmetic or toilet preparations	364.33	55.07	516.78	76.58
34章 肥皂、有机表面活性剂、洗涤剂、润滑剂、人造蜡、调制蜡、光洁剂、蜡烛及类似品、塑型用膏、"牙科用蜡"及牙科用熟石膏制剂	Soap, organic surface-active agents, washing preparations, lubricating preparations, artificial waxes, prepared waxes, polishing or scouring preparations, candles and similar articles, modelling pastes, "dental waxes" and dental preparations with a basis of plast	260.24	39.39	301.65	44.61
35章 蛋白类物质；改性淀粉；胶；酶	Albuminoidal substances; modified starches; glues; enzymes	204.20	30.88	226.87	33.55
36章 炸药；烟火制品；火柴；引火合金；易燃材料制品	Explosives; pyrotechnic products; matches; pyrophoric alloys; certain combustible preparations	11.76	1.78	11.13	1.64
37章 照相及电影用品	Photographic or cinematographic goods	147.15	22.28	160.64	23.73
38章 杂项化学产品	Miscellaneous chemical products	958.12	145.06	1078.71	159.38
第七类 塑料及其制品，橡胶及其制品	**PLASTICS AND ARTICLES THEREOF RUBBER AND ARTICLES THEREOF**	**4941.72**	**747.62**	**5937.43**	**876.83**
39章 塑料及其制品	Plastics and articles thereof	4034.31	610.49	4667.10	689.29
40章 橡胶及其制品	Rubber and articles thereof	907.41	137.14	1270.33	187.54
第八类 生皮、皮革、毛皮及其制品；鞍具及挽具；旅行用品、手提包及类似品；动物肠线(蚕胶丝除外)制品	**RAW HIDES AND SKINS, LEATHER, FUR SKINS AND ARTICLES THEREOF; SADDLERY AND HARNESS; TRAVEL GOODS, HANDBAGS AND SIMILAR CONTAINERS; ARTICLES OF ANIMAL GUT(OTHER THAN SILK-WORM GUT)**	**606.47**	**91.89**	**645.09**	**95.21**
41章 生皮(毛皮除外)及皮革	Raw hides and skins(other than fur skins) and leather	380.01	57.59	383.07	56.49

6–17 续表 2 Continued 2

商品分类	HS Section and Division	2016 亿元人民币 RMB 100 million	2016 亿美元 USD 100 million	2017 亿元人民币 RMB 100 million	2017 亿美元 USD 100 million
42章 皮革制品；鞍具及挽具；旅行用品、手提包及类似容器；动物肠线(蚕胶丝除外)制品	Articles of leather；saddlery and harness；travel goods，hand bags and similar containers；articles of animal gut (other than silk-worm gut)	145.82	22.02	178.02	26.31
43章 毛皮、人造毛皮及其制品	Fur skins and artificial fur；manufactures thereof	80.65	12.27	84.00	12.42
第九类 木及木制品；木炭；软木及软木制品；稻草，秸秆、针茅或其他编结材料制品；篮筐及柳条编结品	**WOOD AND ARTICLES OF WOOD；WOOD CHAR-COAL；CORK AND ARTICLES OF CORK；MANUFACTURES OF STRAW，OF ESPARTO OR OF OTHER PLAITING MATERIALS；BASKET WARE AND WICKERWORK**	**1299.70**	**196.81**	**1589.68**	**234.84**
44章 木及木制品；木炭	Wood and articles of wood；wood charcoal	1296.13	196.27	1585.49	234.22
45章 软木及软木制品	Cork and articles of cork	2.74	0.41	3.21	0.48
46章 稻草、秸秆、针茅或其他编结材料制品；篮筐及柳条编结品	Manufactures of straw，of esparto or of other plaiting Materials；basket ware and wickerwork	0.83	0.13	0.98	0.15
第十类 木浆及其他纤维状纤维素浆；纸及纸板的废碎品；纸、纸板及其制品	**PULP OF WOOD OR OF OTHER FIBROUS CELLULOSIC MATERIAL；WASTE AND SCRAP OF PAPER OR PAPERBOARD；PAPER AND PAPERBOARD AND ARTICLES THEREOF**	**1507.21**	**228.19**	**1890.25**	**279.10**
47章 木浆及其他纤维状纤维素浆；纸及纸板的废碎品	Pulp of wood or of other fibrous cellulosic material；waste and scrap of paper or paperboard	1137.78	172.30	1437.88	212.14
48章 纸及纸板；纸浆、纸或纸板制品	Paper and paperboard；articles of paper pulp，of paper or paperboard	260.82	39.47	336.64	49.82
49章 书籍、报纸、印刷图画及其他印制品；手稿、打字稿及设计图纸	Printed books，newspapers，pictures and other products of the printing industry；manuscripts，typescripts and plans	108.61	16.42	115.73	17.14
第十一类 纺织原料及纺织制品	**TEXTILES AND TEXTILE ARTICLES**	**1875.98**	**283.96**	**2105.55**	**310.99**
50章 蚕丝	Silk	3.77	0.57	3.42	0.51
51章 羊毛、动物细毛或粗毛；马毛纱线及其机织物	Wool，fine or coarse animal hair；horsehair yarn and woven fabric	207.45	31.46	246.05	36.32
52章 棉花	Cotton	511.74	77.44	583.68	86.15
53章 其他植物纺织纤维；纸纱线及其机织物	Other vegetable textile fibres；paper yarn and woven fabrics of paper yarn	52.45	7.95	54.62	8.06
54章 化学纤维长丝	Man-made filaments	192.41	29.13	203.65	30.09
55章 化学纤维短纤	Man-made short fibres	134.71	20.40	160.87	23.76
56章 絮胎、毡呢及无纺织物；特种纱线；线、绳、索、缆及其制品	Wadding，felt and nonwoven；special yarns；twine，cordage，ropes and cables and articles thereof	77.37	11.71	87.85	12.99
57章 地毯及纺织材料的其他铺地制品	Carpets and other textile floor coverings	9.04	1.37	8.99	1.33
58章 特种机织物；簇绒织物；花边；装饰毯；装饰带；刺绣品	Special woven fabrics；tufted textile fabrics；lace；tapestries；trimmings；embroidery	35.85	5.43	35.29	5.21
59章 浸渍、涂布、包覆或层压的纺织物；工业用纺织制品	Impregnated，coated，covered or laminated textile fabrics；textile articles of a kind suitable for industrial use	113.63	17.21	120.92	17.87
60章 针织物及钩编织物	Knitted or crocheted fabrics	112.54	17.04	114.53	16.91
61章 针织或钩编的服装及衣着附件	Articles of apparel and clothing accessories，knitted or crocheted	157.97	23.89	189.28	27.99
62章 非针织或非钩编的服装及衣着附件	Articles of apparel and clothing accessories，not knitted or crocheted	237.39	35.88	262.12	38.75

商品分类		HS Section and Division	2016		2017	
			亿元人民币 RMB 100 million	亿美元 USD 100 million	亿元人民币 RMB 100 million	亿美元 USD 100 million
63章	其他纺织制成品；成套物品；旧衣着及旧纺织品；碎织物	Other made up textile articles; sets; worn clothing and worn textile articles; rags articles; rags	29.68	4.49	34.27	5.06
第十二类	**鞋、帽、伞、杖、鞭及其零件；已加工的羽毛及其制品；人造花；人发制品**	**FOOTWEAR, HEADGEAR, UMBRELLAS, SUN UMBRELLAS, WALKING-STICKS, SEAT-STICKS, WHIPS, RIDING-CROPS AND PARTS THEREOF; PREPARED FEATHERS AND ARTICLES MADE THEREWITH; ARTIFICIAL FLOWERS; ARTICLES OF HUMAN HAIR**	**221.97**	**33.56**	**268.08**	**39.61**
64章	鞋靴、护腿和类似品及其零件	Footwear, gaiters and the like; parts of such articles	202.64	30.63	247.08	36.51
65章	帽类及其零件	Headgear and parts thereof	4.17	0.63	5.38	0.80
66章	雨伞、阳伞、手杖、鞭子、马鞭及其零件	Umbrellas, sun umbrellas, walking-sticks, seat-sticks, whips, riding-crops and parts thereof	0.82	0.12	0.81	0.12
67章	已加工羽毛、羽绒及其制品；人造花；人发制品	Prepared feathers and down and articles made of feathers or of down; artificial flowers; articles of human hair	14.35	2.17	14.81	2.19
第十三类	**石料、石膏、水泥、石棉、云母及类似材料的制品；陶瓷产品；玻璃及其制品**	**ARTICLES OF STONE, PLASTER, CEMENT, ASBESTOS, MICA OR SIMILAR MATERIALS; CERAMIC PRODUCTS; GLASS AND GLASSWARE**	**606.64**	**91.84**	**670.36**	**99.12**
68章	石料、石膏、水泥、石棉、云母及类似材料的制品	Articles of stone, plaster, cement, asbestos, mica or similar materials; ceramic products; glass and glassware	103.54	15.66	112.90	16.70
69章	陶瓷产品	Ceramic products	52.20	7.90	69.07	10.23
70章	玻璃及其制品	Glass and glassware	450.90	68.29	488.39	72.19
第十四类	**天然或养殖珍珠、宝石或半宝石、贵金属、包贵金属及其制品；仿首饰；硬币**	**NATURAL OR CULTURED PEARLS, PRECIOUS OR SEMI-PRECIOUS STONES, PRECIOUS METALS, METALS CLAD WITH PRECIOUS METAL AND STONES, PRECIOUS METALS, METALS CLAD WITH PRECIOUS METAL AND ARTICLES THEREOF; IMITATION JEWELLERY; COIN**	**5255.64**	**793.27**	**4425.68**	**652.88**
71章	天然或养殖珍珠、宝石或半宝石、贵金属、包贵金属及其制品；仿首饰；硬币	Natural or cultured pearls, precious or semi-precious stones, precious metals, metals clad with precious metal and articles thereof; imitation jewellery; coin	5255.64	793.27	4425.68	652.88
第十五类	**贱金属及其制品**	**BASE METALS AND ARTICLES OF BASE METAL**	**5215.57**	**789.58**	**6463.60**	**955.64**
72章	钢铁	Iron and steel	1118.38	169.18	1454.18	214.76
73章	钢铁制品	Articles of iron or steel	632.58	95.76	677.23	100.20
74章	铜及其制品	Copper and articles thereof	2196.22	332.59	2793.09	412.85
75章	镍及其制品	Nickel and articles thereof	326.64	49.57	313.49	46.43
76章	铝及其制品	Aluminium and articles thereof	393.31	59.46	447.76	66.18
78章	铅及其制品	Lead and articles thereof	3.50	0.53	17.98	2.65
79章	锌及其制品	Zinc and articles thereof	77.19	11.71	167.86	24.97
80章	锡及其制品	Tin and articles thereof	20.34	3.07	14.17	2.09
81章	其他贱金属、金属陶瓷及其制品	Other base metals; cermets; articles thereof	119.17	18.04	209.42	30.98
82章	贱金属工具、器具、利口器、餐匙、餐叉及其零件	Tools, implements, cutlery, spoons and forks, of base metal; parts thereof of base metal	212.26	32.11	246.13	36.43
83章	贱金属杂项制品	Miscellaneous articles of base metal	115.98	17.55	122.28	18.10

商品分类	HS Section and Division	2016 亿元人民币 RMB 100 million	2016 亿美元 USD 100 million	2017 亿元人民币 RMB 100 million	2017 亿美元 USD 100 million
第十六类 机器、机械器具、电气设备及其零件；录音机及放声机、电视图像、声音的录制和重放设备及其零件、附件	**MACHINERY AND MECHANICAL APPLIANCES；ELECTRICAL EQUIPMENT；PARTS THEREOF；SOUND RECORDERS AND REPRODUCERS，TELEVISION IMAGE AND SOUND RECORDERS AND REPRODUCERS；AND PARTS AND ACCESSORIES OF RECORDERS AND REPRODUCERS；AND PARTS AND ACCESSORIES OF SUCH ARTICLES**	**37046.85**	**5605.45**	**42425.45**	**6274.55**
84章 核反应堆、锅炉、机器、机械器具及其零件	Nuclear reactors，boilers，machinery and mechanical appliances；parts thereof	9755.37	1476.60	11461.33	1695.32
85章 电机、电气设备及其零件；录音机及放声机、电视图像、声音的录制和重放设备及其零件、附件	Electrical machinery and equipment and parts thereof；sound recorders and reproducers，television image and sound recorders and reproducers，and parts and accessories of such articles	27291.47	4128.85	30964.12	4579.22
第十七类 车辆、航空器、船舶及有关运输设备	**VEHICLES，AIRCRAFT，VESSELS AND ASSOCIATED TRANSPORT EQUIPMENT**	**6435.30**	**973.34**	**7255.34**	**1072.68**
86章 铁道及电车道机车、车辆及其零件；铁道及电车轨道固定装置及其零件、附件；各种机械(包括电动机械)交通信号设备	Railway or tramway locomotives，rolling-stock and parts thereof；railway or tramway track fixtures and fittings and parts thereof；mechanical(including electro-mechanical) traffic signalling equipment of all kinds	70.01	10.63	51.41	7.63
87章 车辆及其零件、附件，但铁道及电车道车辆除外	Vehicles other than railway or tramway rolling-stock，and parts and accessories thereof	4728.20	715.06	5362.19	792.46
88章 航空器、航天器及其零件	Aircraft，spacecraft，and parts thereof	1510.51	228.40	1722.48	254.93
89章 船舶及浮动结构体	Ships，boats and floating structures	126.58	19.24	119.26	17.66
第十八类 光学、照相、电影、计量、检验、医疗或外科用仪器及设备、精密仪器及设备；钟表；乐器；上述物品的零件、附件	**OPTICAL，PHOTOGRAPHIC，CINEMATOGRAPHIC，MEASURING，CHECKING，PRECISION，MEDICAL OR SURGICAL INSTRUMENTS AND APPARATUS；CLOCKS AND WATCHES；MUSICAL INSTRUMENTS；PARTS AND ACCESSORIES THEREOF**	**6358.26**	**961.93**	**6848.49**	**1011.99**
90章 光学、照相、电影、计量、检验、医疗或外科用仪器及设备、精密仪器及设备；上述物品的零件、附件	Optical，photographic，cinematographic，measuring，checking，precision medical or surgical instruments and apparatus；parts and accessories thereof	6126.30	926.89	6596.06	974.69
91章 钟表及其零件	Clocks and watches and parts thereof	207.10	31.28	225.18	33.27
92章 乐器及其零件、附件	Musical instruments；parts and accessories of such articles	24.86	3.76	27.25	4.03
第十九类 武器、弹药及其零件、附件	**ARMS AND AMMUNITION；PARTS AND ACCESSORIES THEREOF**	**0.90**	**0.13**	**0.48**	**0.07**
93章 武器、弹药及其零件、附件	Arms and ammunition；parts and accessories thereof	0.90	0.13	0.48	0.07
第二十类 杂项制品	**MISCELLANEOUS MANUFACTURED ARTICLES**	**497.34**	**75.18**	**565.20**	**83.65**
94章 家具；寝具、褥垫、弹簧床垫、软坐垫及类似的填充制品；未列名灯具及照明装置；发光标志、发光名牌及类似品；活动房屋	Furniture；bedding，mattresses，mattress supports，cushions and similar stuffed furnishings；lamps and lighting fittings，not elsewhere specified or included；illuminated signs，illuminated	212.94	32.19	249.78	37.01
95章 玩具、游戏品、运动用品及其零件、附件	Toys，games and sports requisites；parts and accessories thereof	126.57	19.10	137.31	20.30
96章 杂项制品	Miscellaneous manufactured articles	157.83	23.89	178.10	26.34
第二十一类 艺术品、收藏品及古物	**WORKS OF ART，COLLECTORS' PIECES AND ANTIQUES**	**9.06**	**1.37**	**5.16**	**0.77**
97章 艺术品、收藏品及古物	Works of art，collectors' pieces and antiques	9.06	1.37	5.16	0.77
第二十二类 特殊交易品及未分类商品	**COMMODITIES AND TRANSACTIONS NOT CLASSIFIED ACCORDING TO KIND**	**864.75**	**128.81**	**992.65**	**146.85**
98章 特殊交易品及未分类商品	Commodities and transactions not classified according to kind	864.75	128.81	992.65	146.85

6-18 一般贸易进出口商品分类金额(2017年)
Value of Imports and Exports in Ordinary by HS(2017)

商品分类	HS Section and Division	出口 Exports 亿元人民币 RMB 100 million	出口 Exports 亿美元 USD 100 million	进口 Imports 亿元人民币 RMB 100 million	进口 Imports 亿美元 USD 100 million
总　额	**Total**	**83320.58**	**12300.20**	**73472.73**	**10853.65**
第一类　活动物；动物产品	**LIVE ANIMALS；ANIMAL PRODUCTS**	**860.36**	**127.00**	**1154.75**	**170.56**
01章　活动物	Live animals	37.61	5.55	24.34	3.61
02章　肉及食用杂碎	Meat and edible meat offal	60.99	9.00	561.34	82.91
03章　鱼、甲壳动物、软体动物及其他水生无脊椎动物	Fish and crustaceans molluscs and other aquatic invertebrates	596.66	88.08	241.78	35.76
04章　乳品；蛋品；天然蜂蜜；其他食用动物产品	Dairy produce；birds' eggs；natural honey；edible products of animal origin，not elsewhere specified or included	39.00	5.76	308.15	45.46
05章　其他动物产品	Products of animal origin，not elsewhere specified or included	126.11	18.62	19.14	2.83
第二类　植物产品	**VEGETABLE PRODUCTS**	**1477.17**	**218.26**	**3871.67**	**570.86**
06章　活树及其他活植物；鳞茎、根及类似品；插花及装饰用簇叶	Live tree and other plants；bulbs，roots and the like; cut flowers and ornamental foliage	22.47	3.32	18.19	2.70
07章　食用蔬菜、根及块茎	Edible vegetables and certain roots and tubers	674.86	99.58	129.14	19.08
08章　食用水果及坚果；甜瓜或柑桔属水果的果皮	Edible fruit and nuts；peel of citrus fruit or melons	278.33	41.32	352.87	51.93
09章　咖啡、茶、马黛茶及调味香料	Coffee，tea，mate and spices	187.31	27.63	18.26	2.70
10章　谷物	Cereals	34.82	5.14	409.56	60.37
11章　制粉工业产品；麦芽；淀粉；菊粉；面筋	Products of the milling industry；malt；starches；inulin；wheat gluten	30.97	4.58	57.00	8.41
12章　含油子仁及果实；杂项子仁及果实；工业用或药用植物；稻草、秸秆及饲料	Oil seeds and oleaginous fruits；miscellaneous grains，seeds and fruit；industrial or medicinal plants；straw and fodder	165.20	24.41	2860.80	421.85
13章　虫胶；树胶、树脂及其他植物液、汁	Lac；gums，resins and other vegetable saps and extracts	74.83	11.04	14.65	2.17
14章　编结用植物材料；其他植物产品	Vegetable plaiting materials；vegetable products not elsewhere specified or included	8.37	1.23	11.20	1.65
第三类　动、植物油、脂及其分解产品；精制的食用油脂；动、植物蜡	**ANIMAL OR VEGETABLE FATS AND OILS AND THEIR CLEAVAGE PRODUCTS；PREPARED EDIBLE FATS；ANIMAL OR VEGETABLE WAXES**	**45.39**	**6.71**	**484.86**	**71.64**
15章　动、植物油、脂及其分解产品；精制的食用油脂；动、植物蜡	Animal or vegetable fats and oils and their cleavage products；prepared edible fats；animal or vegetable waxes	45.39	6.71	484.86	71.64
第四类　食品；饮料、酒及醋；烟草、烟草及烟草代用品的制品	**PREPARED FOODSTUFFS；BEVERAGES, SPIRITS AND VINEGAR; TOBACCO AND MANUFACTURED TOBACCO SUBSTITUTES**	**1722.78**	**254.38**	**1080.65**	**159.71**
16章　肉、鱼、甲壳动物、软体动物及其他水生无脊椎动物的制品	Preparations of meat，of fish or of crustaceans，molluscs or other aquatic invertebrates	525.85	77.68	9.06	1.34
17章　糖及糖食	Sugars and sugar confectionery	100.57	14.84	57.84	8.52
18章　可可及可可制品	Cocoa and cocoa preparations	13.19	1.95	28.20	4.18
19章　谷物、粮食粉、淀粉或乳的制品；糕饼点心	Preparations of cereals，flour，starch or milk；pastry-cooks' products	85.31	12.59	309.53	45.88

商品分类	HS Section and Division	出口 Exports 亿元人民币 RMB 100 million	出口 Exports 亿美元 USD 100 million	进口 Imports 亿元人民币 RMB 100 million	进口 Imports 亿美元 USD 100 million
20章 蔬菜、水果、坚果或植物其他部分的制品	Preparations of vegetables, fruit, nuts or other parts of plants	459.50	67.84	65.29	9.67
21章 杂项食品	Miscellaneous edible preparations	183.38	27.07	124.97	18.51
22章 饮料、酒及醋	Beverages, spirits and vinegar	109.81	16.21	170.37	25.26
23章 食品工业的残渣及废料；配制的动物饲料	Residues and waste from the food industries; prepared animal fodder	160.88	23.74	225.62	33.24
24章 烟草及烟草代用品的制品	Tobacco and manufactured tobacco substitutes	84.29	12.46	89.76	13.12
第五类 矿产品	**MINERAL PRODUCTS**	**1074.60**	**159.21**	**20312.82**	**2998.71**
25章 盐；硫磺；泥土及石料；石膏料、石灰及水泥	Salt; sulphur; earths and stone; plastering materials, lime and cement	212.56	31.37	405.39	59.95
26章 矿砂、矿渣及矿灰	Ores, slag and ash	14.03	2.07	7208.07	1062.95
27章 矿物燃料、矿物油及其蒸馏产品；沥青物质；矿物蜡	Mineral fuels, mineral oils and products of their distillation; bituminous substances; mineral waxes	848.01	125.77	12699.36	1875.82
第六类 化学工业及其相关工业的产品	**PRODUCTS OF THE CHEMICAL OR INDUSTRIES ALLIED**	**6592.11**	**972.84**	**6075.78**	**897.72**
28章 无机化学品；贵金属、稀土金属、放射性元素及其同位素的有机及无机化合物	Inorganic chemicals; organic or inorganic compounds of precious metals, of rare- earth metals, of radioactive elements or of isotopes	903.86	133.39	548.18	81.05
29章 有机化学品	Organic chemicals	2957.05	436.42	2831.99	418.18
30章 药品	Pharmaceutical products	294.92	43.56	764.65	112.97
31章 肥料	Fertilizers	392.96	57.87	135.39	20.00
32章 鞣料浸膏及染料浸膏；鞣酸及其衍生物；染料、颜料及其他着色料；油漆及清漆；油灰及其他类似胶粘剂；墨水、油墨	Tanning or dyeing extracts; tannins and their derivatives; dyes, pigments and other colouring matter; paints and varnishes; putty and other mastics; inks	447.66	66.04	229.62	33.96
33章 精油及香膏；芳香料制品及化妆盥洗品	Essential oils and retinoid; perfumery, cosmetic or toilet preparations	209.01	30.86	291.95	43.29
34章 肥皂、有机表面活性剂、洗涤剂、润滑剂、人造蜡、调制蜡、光洁剂、蜡烛及类似品、塑型用膏、"牙科用蜡"及牙科用熟石膏制剂	Soap, organic surface-active agents, washing preparations, lubricating preparations, artificial waxes, prepared waxes, polishing or scouring preparations, candles and similar articles, modelling pastes, "dental waxes" and dental preparations with a basis of plast	185.59	27.39	257.34	38.06
35章 蛋白类物质；改性淀粉；胶；酶	Albuminoidal substances; modified starches; glues; enzymes	146.82	21.66	145.02	21.45
36章 炸药；烟火制品；火柴；引火合金；易燃材料制品	Explosives; pyrotechnic products; matches; pyrophoric alloys; certain combustible preparations	54.99	8.10	8.62	1.27
37章 照相及电影用品	Photographic or cinematographic goods	48.64	7.18	95.92	14.17
38章 杂项化学产品	Miscellaneous chemical products	950.61	140.37	767.10	113.32
第七类 塑料及其制品，橡胶及其制品	**PLASTICS AND ARTICLES THEREOF RUBBER AND ARTICLES THEREOF**	**3260.48**	**481.39**	**3778.67**	**558.28**
39章 塑料及其制品	Plastics and articles thereof	2818.46	416.11	2975.49	439.58
40章 橡胶及其制品	Rubber and articles thereof	442.02	65.29	803.18	118.70
第八类 生皮、皮革、毛皮及其制品；鞍具及挽具；旅行用品、手提包及类似品；动物肠线(蚕胶丝除外)制品	**RAW HIDES AND SKINS, LEATHER, FUR SKINS AND ARTICLES THEREOF; SADDLERY AND HARNESS; TRAVEL GOODS, HANDBAGS AND SIMILAR CONTAINERS; ARTICLES OF ANIMAL GUT(OTHER THAN SILK-WORM GUT)**	**1559.22**	**230.23**	**402.20**	**59.39**
41章 生皮(毛皮除外)及皮革	Raw hides and skins(other than fur skins) and leather	8.02	1.18	198.29	29.26

商品分类	HS Section and Division	出口 Exports 亿元人民币 RMB 100 million	出口 Exports 亿美元 USD 100 million	进口 Imports 亿元人民币 RMB 100 million	进口 Imports 亿美元 USD 100 million
42章 皮革制品；鞍具及挽具；旅行用品、手提包及类似容器；动物肠线(蚕胶丝除外)制品	Articles of leather；saddlery and harness；travel goods，hand bags and similar containers；articles of animal gut (other than silk-worm gut)	1320.17	194.81	131.50	19.43
43章 毛皮、人造毛皮及其制品	Fur skins and artificial fur；manufactures thereof	231.03	34.24	72.42	10.70
第九类 木及木制品；木炭；软木及软木制品；稻草，秸秆、针茅或其他编结材料制品；篮筐及柳条编结品	**WOOD AND ARTICLES OF WOOD；WOOD CHAR-COAL；CORK AND ARTICLES OF CORK；MANUFACTURES OF STRAW，OF ESPARTO OR OF OTHER PLAITING MATERIALS；BASKET WARE AND WICKERWORK**	**897.34**	**132.33**	**1297.21**	**191.72**
44章 木及木制品；木炭	Wood and articles of wood；wood charcoal	799.52	117.91	1293.81	191.22
45章 软木及软木制品	Cork and articles of cork	1.34	0.20	3.04	0.45
46章 稻草、秸秆、针茅或其他编结材料制品；篮筐及柳条编结品	Manufactures of straw，of esparto or of other plaiting Materials；basket ware and wickerwork	96.48	14.22	0.37	0.05
第十类 木浆及其他纤维状纤维素浆；纸及纸板的废碎品；纸、纸板及其制品	**PULP OF WOOD OR OF OTHER FIBROUS CELLULOSIC MATERIAL；WASTE AND SCRAP OF PAPER OR PAPERBOARD；PAPER AND PAPERBOARD AND ARTICLES THEREOF**	**786.86**	**116.21**	**1422.41**	**210.00**
47章 木浆及其他纤维状纤维素浆；纸及纸板的废碎品	Pulp of wood or of other fibrous cellulosic material；waste and scrap of paper or paperboard	8.11	1.20	1092.58	161.16
48章 纸及纸板；纸浆、纸或纸板制品	Paper and paperboard；articles of paper pulp，of paper or paperboard	640.10	94.54	241.89	35.82
49章 书籍、报纸、印刷图画及其他印制品；手稿、打字稿及设计图纸	Printed books，newspapers，pictures and other products of the printing industry；manuscripts，typescripts and plans	138.65	20.48	87.95	13.03
第十一类 纺织原料及纺织制品	**TEXTILES AND TEXTILE ARTICLES**	**13319.44**	**1964.90**	**1234.20**	**182.41**
50章 蚕丝	Silk	73.59	10.85	1.26	0.19
51章 羊毛、动物细毛或粗毛；马毛纱线及其机织物	Wool，fine or coarse animal hair；horsehair yarn and woven fabric	92.11	13.56	164.87	24.35
52章 棉花	Cotton	822.09	121.34	345.60	51.05
53章 其他植物纺织纤维；纸纱线及其机织物	Other vegetable textile fibres；paper yarn and woven fabrics of paper yarn	66.29	9.81	44.20	6.53
54章 化学纤维长丝	Man-made filaments	1032.74	152.33	91.42	13.51
55章 化学纤维短纤	Man-made short fibres	630.02	92.86	97.44	14.40
56章 絮胎、毡呢及无纺织物；特种纱线；线、绳、索、缆及其制品	Wadding，felt and nonwoven；special yarns；twine，cordage，ropes and cables and articles thereof	280.86	41.44	53.79	7.96
57章 地毯及纺织材料的其他铺地制品	Carpets and other textile floor coverings	157.74	23.28	4.37	0.65
58章 特种机织物；簇绒织物；花边；装饰毯；装饰带；刺绣品	Special woven fabrics；tufted textile fabrics；lace；tapestries；trimmings；embroidery	265.74	39.21	8.68	1.29
59章 浸渍、涂布、包覆或层压的纺织物；工业用纺织制品	Impregnated，coated，covered or laminated textile fabrics；textile articles of a kind suitable for industrial use	441.07	65.07	57.61	8.52
60章 针织物及钩编织物	Knitted or crocheted fabrics	851.18	125.52	23.05	3.41
61章 针织或钩编的服装及衣着附件	Articles of apparel and clothing accessories，Knitted or crocheted	3838.92	566.68	142.95	21.14
62章 非针织或非钩编的服装及衣着附件	Articles of apparel and clothing accessories，not knitted or crocheted	3280.60	483.70	181.05	26.78

商品分类	HS Section and Division	出口 Exports 亿元人民币 RMB 100 million	出口 Exports 亿美元 USD 100 million	进口 Imports 亿元人民币 RMB 100 million	进口 Imports 亿美元 USD 100 million
63章 其他纺织制成品；成套物品；旧衣着及旧纺织品；碎织物	Other made up textile articles；sets；worn clothing and worn textile articles；rags articles；rags	1486.50	219.28	17.91	2.64
第十二类 鞋、帽、伞、杖、鞭及其零件；已加工的羽毛及其制品；人造花；人发制品	**FOOTWEAR，HEADGEAR，UMBRELLAS，SUN UMBRELLAS，WALKING-STICKS，SEAT-STICKS，WHIPS，RIDING-CROPS AND PARTS THEREOF；PREPARED FEATHERS AND ARTICLES MADE THEREWITH；ARTIFICIAL FLOWERS；ARTICLES OF HUMAN HAIR**	**2635.19**	**388.55**	**215.15**	**31.79**
64章 鞋靴、护腿和类似品及其零件	Footwear，gaiters and the like；parts of such articles	1985.43	292.67	210.24	31.06
65章 帽类及其零件	Headgear and parts thereof	211.55	31.20	3.75	0.56
66章 雨伞、阳伞、手杖、鞭子、马鞭及其零件	Umbrellas，sun umbrellas，walking-sticks，seat-sticks，whips，riding-crops and parts thereof	141.31	20.80	0.56	0.08
67章 已加工羽毛、羽绒及其制品；人造花；人发制品	Prepared feathers and down and articles made of feathers or of down；artificial flowers；articles of human hair	296.90	43.88	0.61	0.09
第十三类 石料、石膏、水泥、石棉、云母及类似材料的制品；陶瓷产品；玻璃及其制品	**ARTICLES OF STONE，PLASTER，CEMENT，ASBESTOS，MICA OR SIMILAR MATERIALS；CERAMIC PRODUCTS；GLASS AND GLASSWARE**	**2435.38**	**359.65**	**348.35**	**51.56**
68章 石料、石膏、水泥、石棉、云母及类似材料的制品	Articles of stone，plaster，cement，asbestos，mica or similar materials；ceramic products；glass and glassware	632.47	93.38	74.27	10.99
69章 陶瓷产品	Ceramic products	1025.38	151.54	47.64	7.06
70章 玻璃及其制品	Glass and glassware	777.53	114.73	226.43	33.50
第十四类 天然或养殖珍珠、宝石或半宝石、贵金属、包贵金属及其制品；仿首饰；硬币	**NATURAL OR CULTURED PEARLS，PRECIOUS OR SEMI-PRECIOUS STONES，PRECIOUS METALS，METALS CLAD WITH PRECIOUS METAL AND STONES，PRECIOUS METALS，METALS CLAD WITH PRECIOUS METAL AND ARTICLES THEREOF；IMITATION JEWELLERY；COIN**	**119.94**	**17.70**	**2454.44**	**361.62**
71章 天然或养殖珍珠、宝石或半宝石、贵金属、包贵金属及其制品；仿首饰；硬币	Natural or cultured pearls，precious or semi-precious stones，precious metals，metals clad with precious metal and articles thereof；imitation jewellery；coin	119.94	17.70	2454.44	361.62
第十五类 贱金属及其制品	**BASE METALS AND ARTICLES OF BASE METAL**	**8822.03**	**1301.34**	**4421.85**	**653.83**
72章 钢铁	Iron and steel	2658.69	391.52	1108.93	163.78
73章 钢铁制品	Articles of iron or steel	3019.90	445.78	459.99	68.10
74章 铜及其制品	Copper and articles thereof	124.68	18.39	1941.95	287.00
75章 镍及其制品	Nickel and articles thereof	9.09	1.34	206.24	30.57
76章 铝及其制品	Aluminium and articles thereof	1308.83	193.12	252.77	37.39
78章 铅及其制品	Lead and articles thereof	2.51	0.37	3.19	0.48
79章 锌及其制品	Zinc and articles thereof	10.57	1.56	75.80	11.27
80章 锡及其制品	Tin and articles thereof	1.96	0.29	3.62	0.53
81章 其他贱金属、金属陶瓷及其制品	Other base metals；cermets；articles thereof	198.03	29.20	112.18	16.63
82章 贱金属工具、器具、利口器、餐匙、餐叉及其零件	Tools，implements，cutlery，spoons and forks，of base metal；parts thereof of base metal	720.99	106.46	170.43	25.23
83章 贱金属杂项制品	Miscellaneous articles of base metal	766.78	113.31	86.74	12.85

商品分类	HS Section and Division	出口 Exports 亿元人民币 RMB 100 million	亿美元 USD 100 million	进口 Imports 亿元人民币 RMB 100 million	亿美元 USD 100 million
第十六类 机器、机械器具、电气设备及其零件；录音机及放声机、电视图像、声音的录制和重放设备及其零件、附件	**MACHINERY AND MECHANICAL APPLIANCES; ELECTRICAL EQUIPMENT; PARTS THEREOF; SOUND RECORDERS AND REPRODUCERS, TELEVISION IMAGE AND SOUND RECORDERS AND REPRODUCERS; AND PARTS AND ACCESSORIES OF RECORDERS AND REPRODUCERS; AND PARTS AND ACCESSORIES OF SUCH ARTICLES**	**24720.83**	**3651.56**	**16169.35**	**2390.95**
84章 核反应堆、锅炉、机器、机械器具及其零件	Nuclear reactors, boilers, machinery and mechanical appliances; parts thereof	9699.39	1431.75	6984.96	1033.79
85章 电机、电气设备及其零件；录音机及放声机、电视图像、声音的录制和重放设备及其零件、附件	Electrical machinery and equipment and parts thereof; sound recorders and reproducers, television image and sound recorders and reproducers, and parts and accessories of such articles	15021.44	2219.80	9184.39	1357.16
第十七类 车辆、航空器、船舶及有关运输设备	**VEHICLES, AIRCRAFT, VESSELS AND ASSOCIATED TRANSPORT EQUIPMENT**	**3952.07**	**583.41**	**5158.95**	**762.43**
86章 铁道及电车道机车、车辆及其零件；铁道及电车轨道固定装置及其零件、附件；各种机械(包括电动机械)交通信号设备	Railway or tramway locomotives, rolling-stock and parts thereof; railway or tramway track fixtures and fittings and parts thereof; mechanical(including electro-mechanical) traffic signalling equipment of all kinds	355.70	52.59	45.71	6.78
87章 车辆及其零件、附件，但铁道及电车道车辆除外	Vehicles other than railway or tramway rolling-stock, and parts and accessories thereof	3466.51	511.73	4784.80	706.97
88章 航空器、航天器及其零件	Aircraft, spacecraft, and parts thereof	89.91	13.21	260.45	38.59
89章 船舶及浮动结构体	Ships, boats and floating structures	39.95	5.89	67.99	10.08
第十八类 光学、照相、电影、计量、检验、医疗或外科用仪器及设备、精密仪器及设备；钟表；乐器；上述物品的零件、附件	**OPTICAL, PHOTOGRAPHIC, CINEMATOGRAPHIC, MEASURING, CHECKING, PRECISION, MEDICAL OR SURGICAL INSTRUMENTS AND APPARATUS; CLOCKS AND WATCHES; MUSICAL INSTRUMENTS; PARTS AND ACCESSORIES THEREOF**	**1859.70**	**274.68**	**3053.39**	**451.52**
90章 光学、照相、电影、计量、检验、医疗或外科用仪器及设备、精密仪器及设备；上述物品的零件、附件	Optical, photographic, cinematographic, measuring, checking, precision medical or surgical instruments and apparatus; parts and accessories thereof	1706.75	252.08	2952.25	436.56
91章 钟表及其零件	Clocks and watches and parts thereof	94.24	13.92	80.25	11.87
92章 乐器及其零件、附件	Musical instruments; parts and accessories of such articles	58.71	8.68	20.89	3.09
第十九类 武器、弹药及其零件、附件	**ARMS AND AMMUNITION; PARTS AND ACCESSORIES THEREOF**	**8.89**	**1.31**	**0.47**	**0.07**
93章 武器、弹药及其零件、附件	Arms and ammunition; parts and accessories thereof	8.89	1.31	0.47	0.07
第二十类 杂项制品	**MISCELLANEOUS MANUFACTURED ARTICLES**	**7130.36**	**1052.54**	**388.76**	**57.57**
94章 家具；寝具、褥垫、弹簧床垫、软坐垫及类似的填充制品；未列名灯具及照明装置；发光标志、发光名牌及类似品；活动房屋	Furniture; bedding, mattresses, mattress supports, cushions and similar stuffed furnishings; lamps and lighting fittings, not elsewhere specified or included; illuminated signs, illuminated	4683.01	691.15	176.85	26.22
95章 玩具、游戏品、运动用品及其零件、附件	Toys, games and sports requisites; parts and accessories thereof	1721.84	254.35	73.01	10.80
96章 杂项制品	Miscellaneous manufactured articles	725.51	107.04	138.90	20.55
第二十一类 艺术品、收藏品及古物	**WORKS OF ART, COLLECTORS' PIECES AND ANTIQUES**	**6.65**	**0.98**	**3.39**	**0.50**
97章 艺术品、收藏品及古物	Works of art, collectors' pieces and antiques	6.65	0.98	3.39	0.50
第二十二类 特殊交易品及未分类商品	**COMMODITIES AND TRANSACTIONS NOT CLASSIFIED ACCORDING TO KIND**	**33.70**	**5.02**	**143.41**	**20.83**
98章 特殊交易品及未分类商品	Commodities and transactions not classified according to kind	33.70	5.02	143.41	20.83

6-19 加工贸易进出口商品分类金额(2017年)
Value of Imports and Exports in Processing Trade by HS(2017)

商品分类	HS Section and Division	出口 Exports 亿元人民币 RMB 100 million	出口 Exports 亿美元 USD 100 million	进口 Imports 亿元人民币 RMB 100 million	进口 Imports 亿美元 USD 100 million
总　额	**Total**	**51376.40**	**7587.68**	**29183.31**	**4312.77**
第一类　活动物；动物产品	**LIVE ANIMALS；ANIMAL PRODUCTS**	**316.48**	**46.74**	**172.44**	**25.50**
01章　活动物	Live animals				
02章　肉及食用杂碎	Meat and edible meat offal	0.33	0.05	2.91	0.43
03章　鱼、甲壳动物、软体动物及其他水生无脊椎动物	Fish and crustaceans molluscs and other aquatic invertebrates	286.57	42.31	151.05	22.34
04章　乳品；蛋品；天然蜂蜜；其他食用动物产品	Dairy produce；birds' eggs；natural honey；edible products of animal origin，not elsewhere specified or included	0.05	0.01	0.53	0.08
05章　其他动物产品	Products of animal origin，not elsewhere specified or included	29.54	4.37	17.95	2.66
第二类　植物产品	**VEGETABLE PRODUCTS**	**50.57**	**7.46**	**102.55**	**15.14**
06章　活树及其他活植物；鳞茎、根及类似品；插花及装饰用簇叶	Live tree and other plants；bulbs，roots and the like；cut flowers and ornamental foliage	0.36	0.05	0.00	0.00
07章　食用蔬菜、根及块茎	Edible vegetables and certain roots and tubers	2.54	0.37	1.52	0.22
08章　食用水果及坚果；甜瓜或柑桔属水果的果皮	Edible fruit and nuts；peel of citrus fruit or melons	20.37	3.01	34.14	5.07
09章　咖啡、茶、马黛茶及调味香料	Coffee，tea，mate and spices	4.29	0.63	2.52	0.37
10章　谷物	Cereals			14.74	2.16
11章　制粉工业产品；麦芽；淀粉；菊粉；面筋	Products of the milling industry；malt；starches；inulin；wheat gluten	5.27	0.77	5.20	0.76
12章　含油子仁及果实；杂项子仁及果实；工业用或药用植物；稻草、秸秆及饲料	Oil seeds and oleaginous fruits；miscellaneous grains，seeds and fruit；industrial or medicinal plants；straw and fodder	2.47	0.36	43.46	6.40
13章　虫胶；树胶、树脂及其他植物液、汁	Lac；gums，resins and other vegetable saps and extracts	15.21	2.25	0.75	0.11
14章　编结用植物材料；其他植物产品	Vegetable plaiting materials；vegetable products not elsewhere specified or included	0.07	0.01	0.23	0.03
第三类　动、植物油、脂及其分解产品；精制的食用油脂；动、植物蜡	**ANIMAL OR VEGETABLE FATS AND OILS AND THEIR CLEAVAGE PRODUCTS；PREPARED EDIBLE FATS；ANIMAL OR VEGETABLE WAXES**	**8.26**	**1.22**	**18.48**	**2.73**
15章　动、植物油、脂及其分解产品；精制的食用油脂；动、植物蜡	Animal or vegetable fats and oils and their cleavage products；prepared edible fats；animal or vegetable waxes	8.26	1.22	18.48	2.73
第四类　食品；饮料、酒及醋；烟草、烟草及烟草代用品的制品	**PREPARED FOODSTUFFS；BEVERAGES, SPIRITS AND VINEGAR；TOBACCO AND MANUFACTURED TOBACCO SUBSTITUTES**	**219.65**	**32.43**	**19.81**	**2.93**
16章　肉、鱼、甲壳动物、软体动物及其他水生无脊椎动物的制品	Preparations of meat，of fish or of crustaceans，molluscs or other aquatic invertebrates	83.14	12.28	3.93	0.58
17章　糖及糖食	Sugars and sugar confectionery	12.14	1.79	6.68	0.99
18章　可可及可可制品	Cocoa and cocoa preparations	10.99	1.63	3.71	0.55
19章　谷物、粮食粉、淀粉或乳的制品；糕饼点心	Preparations of cereals，flour，starch or milk；pastry-cooks' products	16.72	2.47	0.24	0.04

商品分类	HS Section and Division	出口 Exports 亿元人民币 RMB 100 million	出口 Exports 亿美元 USD 100 million	进口 Imports 亿元人民币 RMB 100 million	进口 Imports 亿美元 USD 100 million
20章 蔬菜、水果、坚果或植物其他部分的制品	Preparations of vegetables, fruit, nuts or other parts of plants	57.08	8.42	1.80	0.27
21章 杂项食品	Miscellaneous edible preparations	19.99	2.95	1.77	0.26
22章 饮料、酒及醋	Beverages, spirits and vinegar	1.73	0.26	0.59	0.09
23章 食品工业的残渣及废料；配制的动物饲料	Residues and waste from the food industries; prepared animal fodder	17.80	2.62	1.08	0.16
24章 烟草及烟草代用品的制品	Tobacco and manufactured tobacco substitutes	0.07	0.01		
第五类 矿产品	**MINERAL PRODUCTS**	**732.93**	**107.30**	**2169.98**	**319.47**
25章 盐；硫磺；泥土及石料；石膏料、石灰及水泥	Salt; sulphur; earths and stone; plastering materials, lime and cement	0.00	0.00	6.07	0.90
26章 矿砂、矿渣及矿灰	Ores, slag and ash			599.32	88.73
27章 矿物燃料、矿物油及其蒸馏产品；沥青物质；矿物蜡	Mineral fuels, mineral oils and products of their distillation; bituminous substances; mineral waxes	732.93	107.30	1564.60	229.84
第六类 化学工业及其相关工业的产品	**PRODUCTS OF THE CHEMICAL OR INDUSTRIES ALLIED**	**901.52**	**133.04**	**1144.73**	**169.02**
28章 无机化学品；贵金属、稀土金属、放射性元素及其同位素的有机及无机化合物	Inorganic chemicals; organic or inorganic compounds of precious metals, of rare- earth metals, of radioactive elements or of isotopes	93.05	13.77	87.07	12.89
29章 有机化学品	Organic chemicals	357.64	52.72	589.51	86.97
30章 药品	Pharmaceutical products	178.98	26.43	58.27	8.61
31章 肥料	Fertilizers			0.00	0.00
32章 鞣料浸膏及染料浸膏；鞣酸及其衍生物；染料、颜料及其他着色料；油漆及清漆；油灰及其他类似胶粘剂；墨水、油墨	Tanning or dyeing extracts; tannins and their derivatives; dyes, pigments and other colouring matter; paints and varnishes; putty and other mastics; inks	3.43	0.51	60.40	8.91
33章 精油及香膏；芳香料制品及化妆盥洗品	Essential oils and retinoid; perfumery, cosmetic or toilet preparations	77.76	11.48	14.16	2.09
34章 肥皂、有机表面活性剂、洗涤剂、润滑剂、人造蜡、调制蜡、光洁剂、蜡烛及类似品、塑型用膏、"牙科用蜡"及牙科用熟石膏制剂	Soap, organic surface-active agents, washing preparations, lubricating preparations, artificial waxes, prepared waxes, polishing or scouring preparations, candles and similar articles, modelling pastes, "dental waxes" and dental preparations with a basis of plast	29.98	4.42	18.92	2.79
35章 蛋白类物质；改性淀粉；胶；酶	Albuminoidal substances; modified starches; glues; enzymes	28.20	4.16	58.61	8.66
36章 炸药；烟火制品；火柴；引火合金；易燃材料制品	Explosives; pyrotechnic products; matches; pyrophoric alloys; certain combustible preparations	0.81	0.12	2.45	0.36
37章 照相及电影用品	Photographic or cinematographic goods	18.01	2.66	58.37	8.62
38章 杂项化学产品	Miscellaneous chemical products	113.65	16.77	196.96	29.11
第七类 塑料及其制品, 橡胶及其制品	**PLASTICS AND ARTICLES THEREOF RUBBER AND ARTICLES THEREOF**	**2114.77**	**312.02**	**1495.21**	**220.64**
39章 塑料及其制品	Plastics and articles thereof	1246.10	183.87	1244.47	183.70
40章 橡胶及其制品	Rubber and articles thereof	868.68	128.16	250.74	36.94
第八类 生皮、皮革、毛皮及其制品；鞍具及挽具；旅行用品、手提包及类似品；动物肠线(蚕胶丝除外)制品	**RAW HIDES AND SKINS, LEATHER, FUR SKINS AND ARTICLES THEREOF; SADDLERY AND HARNESS; TRAVEL GOODS, HANDBAGS AND SIMILAR CONTAINERS; ARTICLES OF ANIMAL GUT(OTHER THAN SILK-WORM GUT)**	**258.60**	**38.13**	**187.23**	**27.60**
41章 生皮(毛皮除外)及皮革	Raw hides and skins(other than fur skins) and leather	31.43	4.63	175.28	25.83

6-19 续表 2 Continued 2

商品分类		HS Section and Division	出口 Exports 亿元 人民币 RMB 100 million	出口 Exports 亿美元 USD 100 million	进口 Imports 亿元 人民币 RMB 100 million	进口 Imports 亿美元 USD 100 million
42章	皮革制品；鞍具及挽具；旅行用品、手提包及类似容器；动物肠线(蚕胶丝除外)制品	Articles of leather；saddlery and harness；travel goods, hand bags and similar containers；articles of animal gut (other than silk-worm gut)	212.74	31.38	7.48	1.10
43章	毛皮、人造毛皮及其制品	Fur skins and artificial fur；manufactures thereof	14.43	2.13	4.47	0.66
第九类	**木及木制品；木炭；软木及软木制品；稻草，秸秆、针茅或其他编结材料制品；篮筐及柳条编结品**	**WOOD AND ARTICLES OF WOOD；WOOD CHAR-COAL；CORK AND ARTICLES OF CORK；MANUFACTURES OF STRAW, OF ESPARTO OR OF OTHER PLAITING MATERIALS ；BASKET WARE AND WICKERWORK**	**90.72**	**13.39**	**45.10**	**6.66**
44章	木及木制品；木炭	Wood and articles of wood；wood charcoal	88.98	13.13	44.87	6.62
45章	软木及软木制品	Cork and articles of cork	0.00	0.00	0.06	0.01
46章	稻草、秸秆、针茅或其他编结材料制品；篮筐及柳条编结品	Manufactures of straw, of esparto or of other plaiting Materials；basket ware and wickerwork	1.74	0.26	0.18	0.03
第十类	**木浆及其他纤维状纤维素浆；纸及纸板的废碎品；纸、纸板及其制品**	**PULP OF WOOD OR OF OTHER FIBROUS CELLULOSIC MATERIAL；WASTE AND SCRAP OF PAPER OR PAPERBOARD；PAPER AND PAPERBOARD AND ARTICLES THEREOF**	**499.12**	**73.62**	**290.06**	**42.86**
47章	木浆及其他纤维状纤维素浆；纸及纸板的废碎品	Pulp of wood or of other fibrous cellulosic material；waste and scrap of paper or paperboard			201.88	29.84
48章	纸及纸板；纸浆、纸或纸板制品	Paper and paperboard；articles of paper pulp, of paper or paperboard	415.37	61.25	77.68	11.48
49章	书籍、报纸、印刷图画及其他印制品；手稿、打字稿及设计图纸	Printed books, newspapers, pictures and other products of the printing industry；manuscripts, typescripts and plans	83.75	12.36	10.49	1.55
第十一类	**纺织原料及纺织制品**	**TEXTILES AND TEXTILE ARTICLES**	**1767.46**	**260.68**	**622.09**	**91.79**
50章	蚕丝	Silk	0.11	0.02	2.07	0.31
51章	羊毛、动物细毛或粗毛；马毛纱线及其机织物	Wool, fine or coarse animal hair；horsehair yarn and woven fabric	39.78	5.88	59.88	8.84
52章	棉花	Cotton	133.12	19.62	168.72	24.87
53章	其他植物纺织纤维；纸纱线及其机织物	Other vegetable textile fibres；paper yarn and woven fabrics of paper yarn	4.53	0.67	6.43	0.95
54章	化学纤维长丝	Man-made filaments	109.86	16.19	100.95	14.91
55章	化学纤维短纤	Man-made short fibres	84.29	12.41	56.16	8.29
56章	絮胎、毡呢及无纺织物；特种纱线；线、绳、索、缆及其制品	Wadding, felt and nonwoven；special yarns；twine, cordage, ropes and cables and articles thereof	36.88	5.44	28.51	4.21
57章	地毯及纺织材料的其他铺地制品	Carpets and other textile floor coverings	8.39	1.24	1.17	0.17
58章	特种机织物；簇绒织物；花边；装饰毯；装饰带；刺绣品	Special woven fabrics；tufted textile fabrics；lace；tapestries；trimmings；embroidery	20.30	3.00	25.07	3.70
59章	浸渍、涂布、包覆或层压的纺织物；工业用纺织制品	Impregnated, coated, covered or laminated textile fabrics；textile articles of a kind suitable for industrial use	38.97	5.74	57.66	8.51
60章	针织物及钩编织物	Knitted or crocheted fabrics	156.18	23.04	89.74	13.25
61章	针织或钩编的服装及衣着附件	Articles of apparel and clothing accessories, Knitted or crocheted	380.44	56.13	3.53	0.52
62章	非针织或非钩编的服装及衣着附件	Articles of apparel and clothing accessories, not knitted or crocheted	617.32	91.07	16.46	2.42

6–19 续表 3 Continued 3

商品分类	HS Section and Division	出口 Exports 亿元人民币 RMB 100 million	出口 Exports 亿美元 USD 100 million	进口 Imports 亿元人民币 RMB 100 million	进口 Imports 亿美元 USD 100 million
63章 其他纺织制成品；成套物品；旧衣着及旧纺织品；碎织物	Other made up textile articles；sets；worn clothing and worn textile articles；rags articles；rags	137.28	20.24	5.76	0.85
第十二类 鞋、帽、伞、杖、鞭及其零件；已加工的羽毛及其制品；人造花；人发制品	**FOOTWEAR，HEADGEAR，UMBRELLAS，SUN UMBRELLAS，WALKING-STICKS，SEAT-STICKS，WHIPS，RIDING-CROPS AND PARTS THEREOF；PREPARED FEATHERS AND ARTICLES MADE THEREWITH；ARTIFICIAL FLOWERS；ARTICLES OF HUMAN HAIR**	**656.21**	**96.71**	**39.03**	**5.77**
64章 鞋靴、护腿和类似品及其零件	Footwear，gaiters and the like；parts of such articles	559.78	82.50	24.67	3.65
65章 帽类及其零件	Headgear and parts thereof	36.07	5.32	0.61	0.09
66章 雨伞、阳伞、手杖、鞭子、马鞭及其零件	Umbrellas，sun umbrellas，walking-sticks，seat-sticks，whips，riding-crops and parts thereof	11.51	1.69	0.03	0.00
67章 已加工羽毛、羽绒及其制品；人造花；人发制品	Prepared feathers and down and articles made of feathers or of down；artificial flowers；articles of human hair	48.84	7.21	13.71	2.02
第十三类 石料、石膏、水泥、石棉、云母及类似材料的制品；陶瓷产品；玻璃及其制品	**ARTICLES OF STONE，PLASTER，CEMENT，ASBESTOS，MICA OR SIMILAR MATERIALS；CERAMIC PRODUCTS；GLASS AND GLASSWARE**	**132.45**	**19.53**	**218.55**	**32.27**
68章 石料、石膏、水泥、石棉、云母及类似材料的制品	Articles of stone，plaster，cement，asbestos，mica or similar materials；ceramic products；glass and glassware	32.23	4.74	24.50	3.62
69章 陶瓷产品	Ceramic products	11.46	1.69	11.44	1.69
70章 玻璃及其制品	Glass and glassware	88.77	13.09	182.61	26.96
第十四类 天然或养殖珍珠、宝石或半宝石、贵金属、包贵金属及其制品；仿首饰；硬币	**NATURAL OR CULTURED PEARLS，PRECIOUS OR SEMI-PRECIOUS STONES，PRECIOUS METALS，METALS CLAD WITH PRECIOUS METAL AND STONES，PRECIOUS METALS，METALS CLAD WITH PRECIOUS METAL AND ARTICLES THEREOF；IMITATION JEWELLERY；COIN**	**993.25**	**146.86**	**926.44**	**137.01**
71章 天然或养殖珍珠、宝石或半宝石、贵金属、包贵金属及其制品；仿首饰；硬币	Natural or cultured pearls，precious or semi-precious stones，precious metals，metals clad with precious metal and articles thereof；imitation jewellery；coin	993.25	146.86	926.44	137.01
第十五类 贱金属及其制品	**BASE METALS AND ARTICLES OF BASE METAL**	**1044.31**	**154.07**	**1275.23**	**188.42**
72章 钢铁	Iron and steel	171.88	25.35	283.83	41.93
73章 钢铁制品	Articles of iron or steel	250.05	36.86	148.87	21.99
74章 铜及其制品	Copper and articles thereof	278.29	41.09	479.34	70.84
75章 镍及其制品	Nickel and articles thereof	13.90	2.05	49.45	7.30
76章 铝及其制品	Aluminium and articles thereof	130.26	19.21	173.70	25.65
78章 铅及其制品	Lead and articles thereof	2.46	0.36	1.75	0.26
79章 锌及其制品	Zinc and articles thereof	1.47	0.22	17.44	2.57
80章 锡及其制品	Tin and articles thereof	0.17	0.02	7.36	1.09
81章 其他贱金属、金属陶瓷及其制品	Other base metals；cermets；articles thereof	12.12	1.79	66.48	9.84
82章 贱金属工具、器具、利口器、餐匙、餐叉及其零件	Tools，implements，cutlery，spoons and forks，of base metal；parts thereof of base metal	84.41	12.46	22.15	3.27
83章 贱金属杂项制品	Miscellaneous articles of base metal	99.30	14.65	24.86	3.67

商品分类	HS Section and Division	出口 Exports		进口 Imports	
		亿元人民币 RMB 100 million	亿美元 USD 100 million	亿元人民币 RMB 100 million	亿美元 USD 100 million
第十六类 机器、机械器具、电气设备及其零件；录音机及放声机、电视图像、声音的录制和重放设备及其零件、附件	**MACHINERY AND MECHANICAL APPLIANCES；ELECTRICAL EQUIPMENT；PARTS THEREOF；SOUND RECORDERS AND REPRODUCERS，TELEVISION IMAGE AND SOUND RECORDERS AND REPRODUCERS；AND PARTS AND ACCESSORIES OF RECORDERS AND REPRODUCERS；AND PARTS AND ACCESSORIES OF SUCH ARTICLES**	**34023.06**	**5028.23**	**17660.39**	**2612.15**
84章 核反应堆、锅炉、机器、机械器具及其零件	Nuclear reactors，boilers，machinery and mechanical appliances；parts thereof	12506.91	1845.80	1858.81	274.67
85章 电机、电气设备及其零件；录音机及放声机、电视图像、声音的录制和重放设备及其零件、附件	Electrical machinery and equipment and parts thereof；sound recorders and reproducers，television image and sound recorders and reproducers，and parts and accessories of such articles	21516.14	3182.43	15801.58	2337.47
第十七类 车辆、航空器、船舶及有关运输设备	**VEHICLES，AIRCRAFT，VESSELS AND ASSOCIATED TRANSPORT EQUIPMENT**	**2625.02**	**386.34**	**254.33**	**37.70**
86章 铁道及电车道机车、车辆及其零件；铁道及电车轨道固定装置及其零件、附件；各种机械(包括电动机械)交通信号设备	Railway or tramway locomotives，rolling-stock and parts thereof；railway or tramway track fixtures and fittings and parts thereof；mechanical(including electro-mechanical) traffic signalling equipment of all kinds	340.06	50.24	4.19	0.62
87章 车辆及其零件、附件，但铁道及电车道车辆除外	Vehicles other than railway or tramway rolling-stock，and parts and accessories thereof	774.56	114.32	115.77	17.14
88章 航空器、航天器及其零件	Aircraft，spacecraft，and parts thereof	103.43	15.29	110.09	16.34
89章 船舶及浮动结构体	Ships，boats and floating structures	1406.97	206.48	24.27	3.59
第十八类 光学、照相、电影、计量、检验、医疗或外科用仪器及设备、精密仪器及设备；钟表；乐器；上述物品的零件、附件	**OPTICAL，PHOTOGRAPHIC，CINEMATOGRAPHIC，MEASURING，CHECKING，PRECISION，MEDICAL OR SURGICAL INSTRUMENTS AND APPARATUS；CLOCKS AND WATCHES；MUSICAL INSTRUMENTS；PARTS AND ACCESSORIES THEREOF**	**2744.08**	**404.88**	**2449.24**	**361.48**
90章 光学、照相、电影、计量、检验、医疗或外科用仪器及设备、精密仪器及设备；上述物品的零件、附件	Optical，photographic，cinematographic，measuring，checking，precision medical or surgical instruments and apparatus；parts and accessories thereof	2565.04	378.46	2388.05	352.47
91章 钟表及其零件	Clocks and watches and parts thereof	148.25	21.87	57.88	8.53
92章 乐器及其零件、附件	Musical instruments；parts and accessories of such articles	30.78	4.55	3.31	0.49
第十九类 武器、弹药及其零件、附件	**ARMS AND AMMUNITION；PARTS AND ACCESSORIES THEREOF**	**0.01**	**0.00**		
93章 武器、弹药及其零件、附件	Arms and ammunition；parts and accessories thereof	0.01	0.00		
第二十类 杂项制品	**MISCELLANEOUS MANUFACTURED ARTICLES**	**2197.93**	**325.03**	**92.42**	**13.65**
94章 家具；寝具、褥垫、弹簧床垫、软坐垫及类似的填充制品；未列名灯具及照明装置；发光标志、发光名牌及类似品；活动房屋	Furniture；bedding，mattresses，mattress supports，cushions and similar stuffed furnishings；lamps and lighting fittings，not elsewhere specified or included；illuminated signs，illuminated	603.81	89.05	20.72	3.06
95章 玩具、游戏品、运动用品及其零件、附件	Toys，games and sports requisites；parts and accessories thereof	1464.38	216.84	47.65	7.04
96章 杂项制品	Miscellaneous manufactured articles	129.75	19.13	24.05	3.55
第二十一类 艺术品、收藏品及古物	**WORKS OF ART，COLLECTORS' PIECES AND ANTIQUES**	**0.00**	**0.00**		
97章 艺术品、收藏品及古物	Works of art，collectors' pieces and antiques	0.00	0.00		
第二十二类 特殊交易品及未分类商品	**COMMODITIES AND TRANSACTIONS NOT CLASSIFIED ACCORDING TO KIND**				
98章 特殊交易品及未分类商品	Commodities and transactions not classified according to kind				

6-20 对香港地区进出口商品分类金额
Value of Exports and Imports from Hongkong by HS

单位：亿美元

Unit: USD 100 million

商品分类	HS Section and Division	2016		2017	
		出 口 Exports	进 口 Imports	出 口 Exports	进 口 Imports
总　额	**Total**	**2872.53**	**167.01**	**2792.11**	**73.17**
第一类 活动物；动物产品	**LIVE ANIMALS；ANIMAL PRODUCTS**	**28.32**	**0.07**	**26.58**	**0.03**
01章 活动物	Live animals	5.37	0.00	4.74	0.00
02章 肉及食用杂碎	Meat and edible meat offal	6.80		6.99	
03章 鱼、甲壳动物、软体动物及其他水生无脊椎动物	Fish and crustaceans molluscs and other aquatic invertebrates	13.69	0.07	12.14	0.02
04章 乳品；蛋品；天然蜂蜜；其他食用动物产品	Dairy produce；birds' eggs；natural honey；edible products of animal origin，not elsewhere specified or included	1.77	0.00	1.67	0.00
05章 其他动物产品	Products of animal origin，not elsewhere specified or included	0.69	0.00	1.04	0.00
第二类 植物产品	**VEGETABLE PRODUCTS**	**28.49**	**0.02**	**30.96**	**0.01**
06章 活树及其他活植物；鳞茎、根及类似品；插花及装饰用簇叶	Live tree and other plants；bulbs，roots and the like；cut flowers and ornamental foliage	0.13		0.11	
07章 食用蔬菜、根及块茎	Edible vegetables and certain roots and tubers	14.21		20.00	
08章 食用水果及坚果；甜瓜或柑桔属水果的果皮	Edible fruit and nuts；peel of citrus fruit or melons	4.80	0.00	3.62	0.00
09章 咖啡、茶、马黛茶及调味香料	Coffee，tea，mate and spices	4.28	0.01	3.00	0.01
10章 谷物	Cereals	0.15		0.11	
11章 制粉工业产品；麦芽；淀粉；菊粉；面筋	Products of the milling industry；malt；starches；inulin；wheat gluten	0.61	0.00	0.54	
12章 含油子仁及果实；杂项子仁及果实；工业用或药用植物；稻草、秸秆及饲料	Oil seeds and oleaginous fruits；miscellaneous grains，seeds and fruit；industrial or medicinal plants；straw and fodder	3.55	0.00	2.66	0.00
13章 虫胶；树胶、树脂及其他植物液、汁	Lac；gums，resins and other vegetable saps and extracts	0.63	0.00	0.79	0.00
14章 编结用植物材料；其他植物产品	Vegetable plaiting materials；vegetable products not elsewhere specified or included	0.15		0.14	
第三类 动、植物油、脂及其分解产品；精制的食用油脂；动、植物蜡	**ANIMAL OR VEGETABLE FATS AND OILS AND THEIR CLEAVAGE PRODUCTS；PREPARED EDIBLE FATS；ANIMAL OR VEGETABLE WAXES**	**0.65**	**0.04**	**0.95**	**0.03**
15章 动、植物油、脂及其分解产品；精制的食用油脂；动、植物蜡	Animal or vegetable fats and oils and their cleavage products；prepared edible fats；animal or vegetable waxes	0.65	0.04	0.95	0.03
第四类 食品；饮料、酒及醋；烟草、烟草及烟草代用品的制品	**PREPARED FOODSTUFFS；BEVERAGES, SPIRITS AND VINEGAR；TOBACCO AND MANUFACTURED TOBACCO SUBSTITUTES**	**41.41**	**2.79**	**39.26**	**3.17**
16章 肉、鱼、甲壳动物、软体动物及其他水生无脊椎动物的制品	Preparations of meat，of fish or of crustaceans，molluscs or other aquatic invertebrates	10.02	0.00	10.85	0.00
17章 糖及糖食	Sugars and sugar confectionery	0.50	0.08	0.48	0.07
18章 可可及可可制品	Cocoa and cocoa preparations	0.98	0.01	0.67	0.01
19章 谷物、粮食粉、淀粉或乳的制品；糕饼点心	Preparations of cereals，flour，starch or milk；pastry-cooks' products	3.75	1.23	3.91	1.60

6-20 续表 1 Continued 1

单位：亿美元
Unit: USD 100 million

商品分类	HS Section and Division	2016 出口 Exports	2016 进口 Imports	2017 出口 Exports	2017 进口 Imports
20章 蔬菜、水果、坚果或植物其他部分的制品	Preparations of vegetables, fruit，nuts or other parts of plants	2.09	0.06	2.57	0.05
21章 杂项食品	Miscellaneous edible preparations	6.14	0.38	4.20	0.47
22章 饮料、酒及醋	Beverages，spirits and vinegar	14.98	0.24	14.13	0.34
23章 食品工业的残渣及废料；配制的动物饲料	Residues and waste from the food industries；prepared animal fodder	0.09	0.00	0.08	0.00
24章 烟草及烟草代用品的制品	Tobacco and manufactured tobacco substitutes	2.87	0.79	2.38	0.63
第五类 矿产品	**MINERAL PRODUCTS**	**56.69**	**1.94**	**70.15**	**1.97**
25章 盐；硫磺；泥土及石料；石膏料、石灰及水泥	Salt；sulphur；earths and stone；plastering materials, lime and cement	1.83	0.02	2.98	0.00
26章 矿砂、矿渣及矿灰	Ores，slag and ash	0.08		0.08	
27章 矿物燃料、矿物油及其蒸馏产品；沥青物质；矿物蜡	Mineral fuels，mineral oils and products of their distillation; bituminous substances; mineral waxes	54.79	1.91	67.08	1.96
第六类 化学工业及其相关工业的产品	**PRODUCTS OF THE CHEMICAL OR INDUSTRIES ALLIED**	**21.63**	**5.70**	**23.51**	**6.30**
28章 无机化学品；贵金属、稀土金属、放射性元素及其同位素的有机及无机化合物	Inorganic chemicals；organic or inorganic compounds of precious metals，of rare- earth metals, of radioactive elements or of isotopes	1.92	0.57	2.26	0.88
29章 有机化学品	Organic chemicals	2.26	0.01	2.46	0.03
30章 药品	Pharmaceutical products	3.28	3.42	4.20	3.76
31章 肥料	Fertilizers	0.02		0.04	
32章 鞣料浸膏及染料浸膏；鞣酸及其衍生物；染料、颜料及其他着色料；油漆及清漆；油灰及其他类似胶粘剂；墨水、油墨	Tanning or dyeing extracts；tannins and their derivatives；dyes，pigments and other colouring matter；paints and varnishes；putty and other mastics；inks	1.90	0.09	1.71	0.08
33章 精油及香膏；芳香料制品及化妆盥洗品	Essential oils and retinoid；perfumery，cosmetic or toilet preparations	3.45	0.77	4.21	0.72
34章 肥皂、有机表面活性剂、洗涤剂、润滑剂、人造蜡、调制蜡、光洁剂、蜡烛及类似品、塑型用膏、“牙科用蜡”及牙科用熟石膏制剂	Soap，organic surface-active agents，washing preparations，lubricating preparations，artificial waxes，prepared waxes，polishing or scouring preparations，candles and similar articles，modelling pastes，“dental waxes” and dental preparations with a basis of plast	2.02	0.27	1.67	0.28
35章 蛋白类物质；改性淀粉；胶；酶	Albuminoidal substances；modified starches；glues；enzymes	1.96	0.03	2.19	0.03
36章 炸药；烟火制品；火柴；引火合金；易燃材料制品	Explosives；pyrotechnic products；matches；pyrophoric alloys；certain combustible preparations	0.03	0.00	0.03	0.00
37章 照相及电影用品	Photographic or cinematographic goods	1.00	0.03	0.83	0.04
38章 杂项化学产品	Miscellaneous chemical products	3.81	0.52	3.90	0.49
第七类 塑料及其制品，橡胶及其制品	**PLASTICS AND ARTICLES THEREOF RUBBER AND ARTICLES THEREOF**	**47.14**	**12.40**	**46.59**	**9.13**
39章 塑料及其制品	Plastics and articles thereof	44.25	12.28	43.99	8.99
40章 橡胶及其制品	Rubber and articles thereof	2.89	0.13	2.61	0.15
第八类 生皮、皮革、毛皮及其制品；鞍具及挽具；旅行用品、手提包及类似品；动物肠线(蚕胶丝除外)制品	**RAW HIDES AND SKINS，LEATHER，FUR SKINS AND ARTICLES THEREOF；SADDLERY AND HARNESS；TRAVEL GOODS，HANDBAGS AND SIMILAR CONTAINERS；ARTICLES OF ANIMAL GUT(OTHER THAN SILK-WORM GUT)**	**24.08**	**0.45**	**22.08**	**0.24**
41章 生皮(毛皮除外)及皮革	Raw hides and skins(other than fur skins) and leather	2.37	0.28	2.11	0.13

单位：亿美元

Unit: USD 100 million

商品分类		HS Section and Division	2016		2017	
			出 口 Exports	进 口 Imports	出 口 Exports	进 口 Imports
42章	皮革制品；鞍具及挽具；旅行用品、手提包及类似容器；动物肠线(蚕胶丝除外)制品	Articles of leather；saddlery and harness；travel goods, hand bags and similar containers；articles of animal gut (other than silk-worm gut)	20.43	0.09	18.65	0.02
43章	毛皮、人造毛皮及其制品	Fur skins and artificial fur；manufactures thereof	1.28	0.08	1.32	0.09
第九类	**木及木制品；木炭；软木及软木制品；稻草，秸秆、针茅或其他编结材料制品；篮筐及柳条编结品**	**WOOD AND ARTICLES OF WOOD；WOOD CHAR-COAL；CORK AND ARTICLES OF CORK；MANUFACTURES OF STRAW，OF ESPARTO OR OF OTHER PLAITING MATERIALS；BASKET WARE AND WICKERWORK**	**2.90**	**0.00**	**3.52**	**0.00**
44章	木及木制品；木炭	Wood and articles of wood；wood charcoal	2.79	0.00	3.39	0.00
45章	软木及软木制品	Cork and articles of cork	0.00	0.00	0.00	
46章	稻草、秸秆、针茅或其他编结材料制品；篮筐及柳条编结品	Manufactures of straw，of esparto or of other plaiting Materials；basket ware and wickerwork	0.11	0.00	0.13	0.00
第十类	**木浆及其他纤维状纤维素浆；纸及纸板的废碎品；纸、纸板及其制品**	**PULP OF WOOD OR OF OTHER FIBROUS CELLULOSIC MATERIAL；WASTE AND SCRAP OF PAPER OR PAPERBOARD；PAPER AND PAPERBOARD AND ARTICLES THEREOF**	**20.86**	**3.00**	**20.51**	**3.32**
47章	木浆及其他纤维状纤维素浆；纸及纸板的废碎品	Pulp of wood or of other fibrous cellulosic material；waste and scrap of paper or paperboard	0.01	1.49	0.00	1.80
48章	纸及纸板；纸浆、纸或纸板制品	Paper and paperboard；articles of paper pulp，of paper or paperboard	13.17	0.34	13.61	0.30
49章	书籍、报纸、印刷图画及其他印制品；手稿、打字稿及设计图纸	Printed books，newspapers，pictures and other products of the printing industry；manuscripts，typescripts and plans	7.68	1.17	6.90	1.23
第十一类	**纺织原料及纺织制品**	**TEXTILES AND TEXTILE ARTICLES**	**142.66**	**1.50**	**125.98**	**1.14**
50章	蚕丝	Silk	0.66	0.02	0.59	0.01
51章	羊毛、动物细毛或粗毛；马毛纱线及其机织物	Wool，fine or coarse animal hair；horsehair yarn and woven fabric	3.42	0.01	2.94	0.01
52章	棉花	Cotton	15.53	0.22	11.15	0.17
53章	其他植物纺织纤维；纸纱线及其机织物	Other vegetable textile fibres；paper yarn and woven fabrics of paper yarn	1.35	0.00	0.70	0.00
54章	化学纤维长丝	Man-made filaments	3.46	0.09	3.04	0.08
55章	化学纤维短纤	Man-made short fibres	3.43	0.06	2.73	0.03
56章	絮胎、毡呢及无纺织物；特种纱线；线、绳、索、缆及其制品	Wadding，felt and nonwoven；special yarns；twine，cordage，ropes and cables and articles thereof	1.47	0.08	1.53	0.09
57章	地毯及纺织材料的其他铺地制品	Carpets and other textile floor coverings	0.55	0.00	0.41	0.00
58章	特种机织物；簇绒织物；花边；装饰毯；装饰带；刺绣品	Special woven fabrics；tufted textile fabrics；lace；tapestries；trimmings；embroidery	5.93	0.21	6.15	0.19
59章	浸渍、涂布、包覆或层压的纺织物；工业用纺织制品	Impregnated，coated，covered or laminated textile fabrics；textile articles of a kind suitable for industrial use	3.38	0.11	2.97	0.09
60章	针织物及钩编织物	Knitted or crocheted fabrics	16.00	0.29	17.67	0.28
61章	针织或钩编的服装及衣着附件	Articles of apparel and clothing accessories，knitted or crocheted	41.26	0.18	40.10	0.09
62章	非针织或非钩编的服装及衣着附件	Articles of apparel and clothing accessories，not knitted or crocheted	41.14	0.21	32.49	0.06

单位：亿美元
Unit: USD 100 million

商品分类	HS Section and Division	2016 出口 Exports	2016 进口 Imports	2017 出口 Exports	2017 进口 Imports
63章 其他纺织制成品；成套物品；旧衣着及旧纺织品；碎织物	Other made up textile articles；sets；worn clothing and worn textile articles；rags articles；rags	5.08	0.01	3.51	0.02
第十二类 鞋、帽、伞、杖、鞭及其零件；已加工的羽毛及其制品；人造花；人发制品	**FOOTWEAR，HEADGEAR，UMBRELLAS，SUN UMBRELLAS，WALKING-STICKS，SEAT-STICKS，WHIPS，RIDING-CROPS AND PARTS THEREOF；PREPARED FEATHERS AND ARTICLES MADE THEREWITH；ARTIFICIAL FLOWERS；ARTICLES OF HUMAN HAIR**	**18.80**	**0.16**	**17.51**	**0.10**
64章 鞋靴、护腿和类似品及其零件	Footwear，gaiters and the like；parts of such articles	15.41	0.15	14.44	0.09
65章 帽类及其零件	Headgear and parts thereof	1.59	0.00	1.35	0.00
66章 雨伞、阳伞、手杖、鞭子、马鞭及其零件	Umbrellas，sun umbrellas，walking-sticks，seat-sticks，whips，riding-crops and parts thereof	0.74	0.00	0.56	0.00
67章 已加工羽毛、羽绒及其制品；人造花；人发制品	Prepared feathers and down and articles made of feathers or of down；artificial flowers；articles of human hair	1.05	0.00	1.15	0.01
第十三类 石料、石膏、水泥、石棉、云母及类似材料的制品；陶瓷产品；玻璃及其制品	**ARTICLES OF STONE，PLASTER，CEMENT，ASBESTOS，MICA OR SIMILAR MATERIALS；CERAMIC PRODUCTS；GLASS AND GLASSWARE**	**22.40**	**0.21**	**22.82**	**0.36**
68章 石料、石膏、水泥、石棉、云母及类似材料的制品	Articles of stone，plaster，cement，asbestos，mica or similar materials；ceramic products；glass and glassware	5.30	0.00	5.82	0.00
69章 陶瓷产品	Ceramic products	2.87	0.01	3.55	0.00
70章 玻璃及其制品	Glass and glassware	14.23	0.20	13.46	0.36
第十四类 天然或养殖珍珠、宝石或半宝石、贵金属、包贵金属及其制品；仿首饰；硬币	**NATURAL OR CULTURED PEARLS，PRECIOUS OR SEMI-PRECIOUS STONES，PRECIOUS METALS，METALS CLAD WITH PRECIOUS METAL AND STONES，PRECIOUS METALS，METALS CLAD WITH PRECIOUS METAL AND ARTICLES THEREOF；IMITATION JEWELLERY；COIN**	**147.27**	**105.41**	**116.03**	**9.10**
71章 天然或养殖珍珠、宝石或半宝石、贵金属、包贵金属及其制品；仿首饰；硬币	Natural or cultured pearls，precious or semi-precious stones，precious metals，metals clad with precious metal and articles thereof；imitation jewellery；coin	147.27	105.41	116.03	9.10
第十五类 贱金属及其制品	**BASE METALS AND ARTICLES OF BASE METAL**	**47.00**	**15.09**	**47.67**	**20.19**
72章 钢铁	Iron and steel	8.39	0.09	7.67	0.19
73章 钢铁制品	Articles of iron or steel	14.93	0.09	17.32	0.10
74章 铜及其制品	Copper and articles thereof	3.63	10.55	3.69	14.73
75章 镍及其制品	Nickel and articles thereof	0.41	0.00	0.15	0.00
76章 铝及其制品	Aluminium and articles thereof	7.98	4.14	8.59	4.90
78章 铅及其制品	Lead and articles thereof	0.03	0.00	0.05	0.00
79章 锌及其制品	Zinc and articles thereof	0.33	0.02	0.26	0.05
80章 锡及其制品	Tin and articles thereof	0.07	0.03	0.17	0.02
81章 其他贱金属、金属陶瓷及其制品	Other base metals；cermets；articles thereof	0.58	0.08	0.38	0.13
82章 贱金属工具、器具、利口器、餐匙、餐叉及其零件	Tools，implements，cutlery，spoons and forks，of base metal；parts thereof of base metal	3.52	0.02	3.66	0.01
83章 贱金属杂项制品	Miscellaneous articles of base metal	7.14	0.06	5.74	0.05

单位：亿美元
Unit: USD 100 million

商品分类	HS Section and Division	2016 出口 Exports	2016 进口 Imports	2017 出口 Exports	2017 进口 Imports
第十六类 机器、机械器具、电气设备及其零件；录音机及放声机、电视图像、声音的录制和重放设备及其零件、附件	**MACHINERY AND MECHANICAL APPLIANCES; ELECTRICAL EQUIPMENT; PARTS THEREOF; SOUND RECORDERS AND REPRODUCERS, TELEVISION IMAGE AND SOUND RECORDERS AND REPRODUCERS; AND PARTS AND ACCESSORIES OF RECORDERS AND REPRODUCERS; AND PARTS AND ACCESSORIES OF SUCH ARTICLES**	**1908.92**	**12.46**	**1851.34**	**10.76**
84章 核反应堆、锅炉、机器、机械器具及其零件	Nuclear reactors, boilers, machinery and mechanical appliances; parts thereof	426.71	4.74	438.87	1.62
85章 电机、电气设备及其零件；录音机及放声机、电视图像、声音的录制和重放设备及其零件、附件	Electrical machinery and equipment and parts thereof; sound recorders and reproducers, television image and sound recorders and reproducers, and parts and accessories of such articles	1482.21	7.71	1412.47	9.13
第十七类 车辆、航空器、船舶及有关运输设备	**VEHICLES, AIRCRAFT, VESSELS AND ASSOCIATED TRANSPORT EQUIPMENT**	**69.23**	**0.13**	**100.03**	**0.11**
86章 铁道及电车道机车、车辆及其零件；铁道及电车轨道固定装置及其零件、附件；各种机械(包括电动机械)交通信号设备	Railway or tramway locomotives, rolling-stock and parts thereof; railway or tramway track fixtures and fittings and parts thereof; mechanical(including electro-mechanical) traffic signalling equipment of all kinds	10.15	0.05	23.19	0.00
87章 车辆及其零件、附件，但铁道及电车道车辆除外	Vehicles other than railway or tramway rolling-stock, and parts and accessories thereof	8.39	0.03	7.07	0.06
88章 航空器、航天器及其零件	Aircraft, spacecraft, and parts thereof	4.48	0.02	6.83	0.03
89章 船舶及浮动结构体	Ships, boats and floating structures	46.23	0.03	62.93	0.02
第十八类 光学、照相、电影、计量、检验、医疗或外科用仪器及设备、精密仪器及设备；钟表；乐器；上述物品的零件、附件	**OPTICAL, PHOTOGRAPHIC, CINEMATOGRAPHIC, MEASURING, CHECKING, PRECISION, MEDICAL OR SURGICAL INSTRUMENTS AND APPARATUS; CLOCKS AND WATCHES; MUSICAL INSTRUMENTS; PARTS AND ACCESSORIES THEREOF**	**174.12**	**3.24**	**165.77**	**2.97**
90章 光学、照相、电影、计量、检验、医疗或外科用仪器及设备、精密仪器及设备；上述物品的零件、附件	Optical, photographic, cinematographic, measuring, checking, precision medical or surgical instruments and apparatus; parts and accessories thereof	148.41	1.51	143.73	2.04
91章 钟表及其零件	Clocks and watches and parts thereof	25.17	1.72	21.55	0.92
92章 乐器及其零件、附件	Musical instruments; parts and accessories of such articles	0.53	0.00	0.49	0.00
第十九类 武器、弹药及其零件、附件	**ARMS AND AMMUNITION; PARTS AND ACCESSORIES THEREOF**	**0.10**		**0.10**	**0.00**
93章 武器、弹药及其零件、附件	Arms and ammunition; parts and accessories thereof	0.10		0.10	0.00
第二十类 杂项制品	**MISCELLANEOUS MANUFACTURED ARTICLES**	**67.84**	**0.38**	**59.16**	**0.35**
94章 家具；寝具、褥垫、弹簧床垫、软坐垫及类似的填充制品；未列名灯具及照明装置；发光标志、发光名牌及类似品；活动房屋	Furniture; bedding, mattresses, mattress supports, cushions and similar stuffed furnishings; lamps and lighting fittings, not elsewhere specified or included; illuminated signs, illuminated	36.76	0.07	27.20	0.03
95章 玩具、游戏品、运动用品及其零件、附件	Toys, games and sports requisites; parts and accessories thereof	24.14	0.02	24.26	0.03
96章 杂项制品	Miscellaneous manufactured articles	6.94	0.29	7.70	0.28
第二十一类 艺术品、收藏品及古物	**WORKS OF ART, COLLECTORS' PIECES AND ANTIQUES**	**0.41**	**0.04**	**0.15**	**0.04**
97章 艺术品、收藏品及古物	Works of art, collectors' pieces and antiques	0.41	0.04	0.15	0.04
第二十二类 特殊交易品及未分类商品	**COMMODITIES AND TRANSACTIONS NOT CLASSIFIED ACCORDING TO KIND**	**1.61**	**1.97**	**1.45**	**3.86**
98章 特殊交易品及未分类商品	Commodities and transactions not classified according to kind	1.61	1.97	1.45	3.86

6-21 对台湾地区进出口商品分类金额

Value of Exports and Imports from Taiwan Province by HS

单位：亿美元

Unit: USD 100 million

商品分类	HS Section and Division	2016		2017	
		出口 Exports	进口 Imports	出口 Exports	进口 Imports
总　额	**Total**	**402.41**	**1388.47**	**439.79**	**1559.61**
第一类　活动物；动物产品	**LIVE ANIMALS；ANIMAL PRODUCTS**	**10.61**	**1.52**	**8.82**	**1.90**
01章　活动物	Live animals	0.00	0.01	0.00	0.01
02章　肉及食用杂碎	Meat and edible meat offal				
03章　鱼、甲壳动物、软体动物及其他水生无脊椎动物	Fish and crustaceans molluscs and other aquatic invertebrates	10.01	1.18	8.07	1.37
04章　乳品；蛋品；天然蜂蜜；其他食用动物产品	Dairy produce；birds' eggs；natural honey；edible products of animal origin，not elsewhere specified or included	0.01	0.08	0.00	0.05
05章　其他动物产品	Products of animal origin，not elsewhere specified or included	0.60	0.25	0.74	0.47
第二类　植物产品	**VEGETABLE PRODUCTS**	**3.20**	**1.48**	**3.14**	**1.50**
06章　活树及其他活植物；鳞茎、根及类似品；插花及装饰用簇叶	Live tree and other plants；bulbs，roots and the like；cut flowers and ornamental foliage	0.01	0.02	0.02	0.04
07章　食用蔬菜、根及块茎	Edible vegetables and certain roots and tubers	0.65	0.02	0.54	0.02
08章　食用水果及坚果；甜瓜或柑桔属水果的果皮	Edible fruit and nuts；peel of citrus fruit or melons	0.33	1.05	0.26	0.93
09章　咖啡、茶、马黛茶及调味香料	Coffee，tea，mate and spices	0.36	0.29	0.38	0.44
10章　谷物	Cereals	0.12	0.01	0.18	0.00
11章　制粉工业产品；麦芽；淀粉；菊粉；面筋	Products of the milling industry；malt；starches；inulin；wheat gluten	0.15	0.01	0.18	0.01
12章　含油子仁及果实；杂项子仁及果实；工业用或药用植物；稻草、秸秆及饲料	Oil seeds and oleaginous fruits；miscellaneous grains，seeds and fruit；industrial or medicinal plants；straw and fodder	1.33	0.04	1.33	0.03
13章　虫胶；树胶、树脂及其他植物液、汁	Lac；gums，resins and other vegetable saps and extracts	0.18	0.03	0.20	0.03
14章　编结用植物材料；其他植物产品	Vegetable plaiting materials；vegetable products not elsewhere specified or included	0.07	0.01	0.05	0.01
第三类　动、植物油、脂及其分解产品；精制的食用油脂；动、植物蜡	**ANIMAL OR VEGETABLE FATS AND OILS AND THEIR CLEAVAGE PRODUCTS；PREPARED EDIBLE FATS；ANIMAL OR VEGETABLE WAXES**	**0.05**	**0.06**	**0.05**	**0.07**
15章　动、植物油、脂及其分解产品；精制的食用油脂；动、植物蜡	Animal or vegetable fats and oils and their cleavage products；prepared edible fats；animal or vegetable waxes	0.05	0.06	0.05	0.07
第四类　食品；饮料、酒及醋；烟草、烟草及烟草代用品的制品	**PREPARED FOODSTUFFS；BEVERAGES, SPIRITS AND VINEGAR；TOBACCO AND MANUFACTURED TOBACCO SUBSTITUTES**	**8.80**	**4.36**	**12.40**	**4.30**
16章　肉、鱼、甲壳动物、软体动物及其他水生无脊椎动物的制品	Preparations of meat，of fish or of crustaceans，molluscs or other aquatic invertebrates	5.75	0.09	9.19	0.09
17章　糖及糖食	Sugars and sugar confectionery	0.13	0.22	0.16	0.20
18章　可可及可可制品	Cocoa and cocoa preparations	0.06	0.03	0.07	0.01
19章　谷物、粮食粉、淀粉或乳的制品；糕饼点心	Preparations of cereals，flour，starch or milk；pastry-cooks' products	0.10	1.19	0.11	1.16

6-21 续表 1 Continued 1

单位：亿美元
Unit: USD 100 million

商品分类		HS Section and Division	2016		2017	
			出 口 Exports	进 口 Imports	出 口 Exports	进 口 Imports
20章	蔬菜、水果、坚果或植物其他部分的制品	Preparations of vegetables, fruit，nuts or other parts of plants	1.70	0.15	1.59	0.20
21章	杂项食品	Miscellaneous edible preparations	0.31	1.31	0.42	1.48
22章	饮料、酒及醋	Beverages，spirits and vinegar	0.36	1.03	0.44	0.95
23章	食品工业的残渣及废料；配制的动物饲料	Residues and waste from the food industries；prepared animal fodder	0.25	0.10	0.28	0.09
24章	烟草及烟草代用品的制品	Tobacco and manufactured tobacco substitutes	0.13	0.24	0.14	0.12
第五类	**矿产品**	**MINERAL PRODUCTS**	**4.01**	**6.72**	**4.96**	**8.06**
25章	盐；硫磺；泥土及石料；石膏料、石灰及水泥	Salt；sulphur；earths and stone；plastering materials，lime and cement	1.66	0.22	1.81	0.37
26章	矿砂、矿渣及矿灰	Ores，slag and ash	0.22	1.37	0.08	1.72
27章	矿物燃料、矿物油及其蒸馏产品；沥青物质；矿物蜡	Mineral fuels，mineral oils and products of their distillation; bituminous substances; mineral waxes	2.14	5.13	3.07	5.97
第六类	**化学工业及其相关工业的产品**	**PRODUCTS OF THE CHEMICAL OR INDUSTRIES ALLIED**	**40.64**	**77.86**	**41.69**	**89.00**
28章	无机化学品；贵金属、稀土金属、放射性元素及其同位素的有机及无机化合物	Inorganic chemicals；organic or inorganic compounds of precious metals，of rare- earth metals, of radioactive elements or of isotopes	5.63	5.30	5.85	5.75
29章	有机化学品	Organic chemicals	11.31	47.49	13.51	56.86
30章	药品	Pharmaceutical products	0.32	1.32	0.44	2.09
31章	肥料	Fertilizers	0.68	0.01	0.48	0.01
32章	鞣料浸膏及染料浸膏；鞣酸及其衍生物；染料、颜料及其他着色料；油漆及清漆；油灰及其他类似胶粘剂；墨水、油墨	Tanning or dyeing extracts；tannins and their derivatives；dyes，pigments and other colouring matter；paints and varnishes；putty and other mastics；inks	2.59	3.85	2.77	4.25
33章	精油及香膏；芳香料制品及化妆盥洗品	Essential oils and retinoid；perfumery，cosmetic or toilet preparations	1.22	1.26	1.19	1.47
34章	肥皂、有机表面活性剂、洗涤剂、润滑剂、人造蜡、调制蜡、光洁剂、蜡烛及类似品、塑型用膏、“牙科用蜡”及牙科用熟石膏制剂	Soap，organic surface-active agents，washing preparations，lubricating preparations，artificial waxes，prepared waxes，polishing or scouring preparations，candles and similar articles，modelling pastes，“dental waxes” and dental preparations with a basis of plast	1.11	1.80	1.25	1.70
35章	蛋白类物质；改性淀粉；胶；酶	Albuminoidal substances；modified starches；glues；enzymes	1.18	2.01	1.32	2.21
36章	炸药；烟火制品；火柴；引火合金；易燃材料制品	Explosives；pyrotechnic products；matches；pyrophoric alloys；certain combustible preparations	0.14	0.00	0.19	
37章	照相及电影用品	Photographic or cinematographic goods	0.77	1.78	0.89	2.11
38章	杂项化学产品	Miscellaneous chemical products	15.68	13.05	13.82	12.55
第七类	**塑料及其制品，橡胶及其制品**	**PLASTICS AND ARTICLES THEREOF RUBBER AND ARTICLES THEREOF**	**12.61**	**78.33**	**14.17**	**92.88**
39章	塑料及其制品	Plastics and articles thereof	10.75	74.97	11.98	89.19
40章	橡胶及其制品	Rubber and articles thereof	1.86	3.37	2.19	3.68
第八类	**生皮、皮革、毛皮及其制品；鞍具及挽具；旅行用品、手提包及类似品；动物肠线（蚕胶丝除外）制品**	**RAW HIDES AND SKINS，LEATHER，FUR SKINS AND ARTICLES THEREOF；SADDLERY AND HARNESS；TRAVEL GOODS，HANDBAGS AND SIMILAR CONTAINERS；ARTICLES OF ANIMAL GUT(OTHER THAN SILK-WORM GUT)**	**2.77**	**1.78**	**2.42**	**1.48**
41章	生皮(毛皮除外)及皮革	Raw hides and skins(other than fur skins) and leather	0.09	1.68	0.07	1.37

6-21 续表 2 Continued 2

单位：亿美元
Unit: USD 100 million

商品分类	HS Section and Division	2016 出口 Exports	2016 进口 Imports	2017 出口 Exports	2017 进口 Imports
42章 皮革制品；鞍具及挽具；旅行用品、手提包及类似容器；动物肠线(蚕胶丝除外)制品	Articles of leather；saddlery and harness；travel goods，hand bags and similar containers；articles of animal gut (other than silk-worm gut)	2.67	0.10	2.34	0.11
43章 毛皮、人造毛皮及其制品	Fur skins and artificial fur；manufactures thereof	0.01	0.00	0.01	0.00
第九类 木及木制品；木炭；软木及软木制品；稻草，秸秆、针茅或其他编结材料制品；篮筐及柳条编结品	**WOOD AND ARTICLES OF WOOD；WOOD CHAR-COAL；CORK AND ARTICLES OF CORK；MANUFACTURES OF STRAW，OF ESPARTO OR OF OTHER PLAITING MATERIALS；BASKET WARE AND WICKERWORK**	**2.46**	**0.31**	**2.53**	**0.46**
44章 木及木制品；木炭	Wood and articles of wood；wood charcoal	2.27	0.29	2.35	0.45
45章 软木及软木制品	Cork and articles of cork	0.00	0.00	0.01	0.00
46章 稻草、秸秆、针茅或其他编结材料制品；篮筐及柳条编结品	Manufactures of straw，of esparto or of other plaiting Materials；basket ware and wickerwork	0.19	0.02	0.17	0.01
第十类 木浆及其他纤维状纤维素浆；纸及纸板的废碎品；纸、纸板及其制品	**PULP OF WOOD OR OF OTHER FIBROUS CELLULOSIC MATERIAL；WASTE AND SCRAP OF PAPER OR PAPERBOARD；PAPER AND PAPERBOARD AND ARTICLES THEREOF**	**4.22**	**3.77**	**4.79**	**4.88**
47章 木浆及其他纤维状纤维素浆；纸及纸板的废碎品	Pulp of wood or of other fibrous cellulosic material；waste and scrap of paper or paperboard	0.00	0.27	0.00	0.31
48章 纸及纸板；纸浆、纸或纸板制品	Paper and paperboard；articles of paper pulp，of paper or paperboard	3.99	2.61	4.57	3.70
49章 书籍、报纸、印刷图画及其他印制品；手稿、打字稿及设计图纸	Printed books，newspapers，pictures and other products of the printing industry；manuscripts，typescripts and plans	0.23	0.89	0.22	0.87
第十一类 纺织原料及纺织制品	**TEXTILES AND TEXTILE ARTICLES**	**14.58**	**24.27**	**16.15**	**24.42**
50章 蚕丝	Silk	0.02	0.00	0.01	0.00
51章 羊毛、动物细毛或粗毛；马毛纱线及其机织物	Wool，fine or coarse animal hair；horsehair yarn and woven fabric	0.14	0.05	0.13	0.03
52章 棉花	Cotton	0.28	3.07	0.26	3.03
53章 其他植物纺织纤维；纸纱线及其机织物	Other vegetable textile fibres；paper yarn and woven fabrics of paper yarn	0.01	0.01	0.01	0.00
54章 化学纤维长丝	Man-made filaments	0.96	8.05	1.17	8.22
55章 化学纤维短纤	Man-made short fibres	0.52	2.11	0.84	2.15
56章 絮胎、毡呢及无纺织物；特种纱线；线、绳、索、缆及其制品	Wadding，felt and nonwoven；special yarns；twine，cordage，ropes and cables and articles thereof	0.71	1.33	0.77	1.39
57章 地毯及纺织材料的其他铺地制品	Carpets and other textile floor coverings	0.28	0.02	0.26	0.02
58章 特种机织物；簇绒织物；花边；装饰毯；装饰带；刺绣品	Special woven fabrics；tufted textile fabrics；lace；tapestries；trimmings；embroidery	0.19	0.81	0.17	0.79
59章 浸渍、涂布、包覆或层压的纺织物；工业用纺织制品	Impregnated，coated，covered or laminated textile fabrics；textile articles of a kind suitable for industrial use	0.62	3.33	0.73	3.48
60章 针织物及钩编织物	Knitted or crocheted fabrics	0.08	4.87	0.09	4.65
61章 针织或钩编的服装及衣着附件	Articles of apparel and clothing accessories，knitted or crocheted	4.71	0.13	5.04	0.15
62章 非针织或非钩编的服装及衣着附件	Articles of apparel and clothing accessories，not knitted or crocheted	4.36	0.23	4.96	0.24

6-21 续表 3 Continued 3

单位：亿美元

Unit: USD 100 million

商品分类	HS Section and Division	2016		2017	
		出口 Exports	进口 Imports	出口 Exports	进口 Imports
63章 其他纺织制成品；成套物品；旧衣着及旧纺织品；碎织物	Other made up textile articles；sets；worn clothing and worn textile articles；rags articles；rags	1.70	0.28	1.70	0.27
第十二类 鞋、帽、伞、杖、鞭及其零件；已加工的羽毛及其制品；人造花；人发制品	**FOOTWEAR，HEADGEAR，UMBRELLAS，SUN UMBRELLAS，WALKING-STICKS，SEAT-STICKS，WHIPS，RIDING-CROPS AND PARTS THEREOF；PREPARED FEATHERS AND ARTICLES MADE THEREWITH；ARTIFICIAL FLOWERS；ARTICLES OF HUMAN HAIR**	**3.11**	**0.35**	**2.91**	**0.33**
64章 鞋靴、护腿和类似品及其零件	Footwear，gaiters and the like；parts of such articles	2.33	0.27	2.27	0.25
65章 帽类及其零件	Headgear and parts thereof	0.20	0.04	0.16	0.04
66章 雨伞、阳伞、手杖、鞭子、马鞭及其零件	Umbrellas，sun umbrellas，walking-sticks，seat-sticks，whips，riding-crops and parts thereof	0.51	0.03	0.39	0.03
67章 已加工羽毛、羽绒及其制品；人造花；人发制品	Prepared feathers and down and articles made of feathers or of down；artificial flowers；articles of human hair	0.07	0.00	0.09	0.00
第十三类 石料、石膏、水泥、石棉、云母及类似材料的制品；陶瓷产品；玻璃及其制品	**ARTICLES OF STONE，PLASTER，CEMENT，ASBESTOS，MICA OR SIMILAR MATERIALS；CERAMIC PRODUCTS；GLASS AND GLASSWARE**	**7.50**	**14.04**	**6.49**	**15.42**
68章 石料、石膏、水泥、石棉、云母及类似材料的制品	Articles of stone，plaster，cement，asbestos，mica or similar materials；ceramic products；glass and glassware	2.40	1.02	1.68	1.05
69章 陶瓷产品	Ceramic products	1.87	0.37	2.10	0.40
70章 玻璃及其制品	Glass and glassware	3.23	12.65	2.71	13.97
第十四类 天然或养殖珍珠、宝石或半宝石、贵金属、包贵金属及其制品；仿首饰；硬币	**NATURAL OR CULTURED PEARLS，PRECIOUS OR SEMI-PRECIOUS STONES，PRECIOUS METALS，METALS CLAD WITH PRECIOUS METAL AND STONES，PRECIOUS METALS，METALS CLAD WITH PRECIOUS METAL AND ARTICLES THEREOF；IMITATION JEWELLERY；COIN**	**0.65**	**3.57**	**0.48**	**1.41**
71章 天然或养殖珍珠、宝石或半宝石、贵金属、包贵金属及其制品；仿首饰；硬币	Natural or cultured pearls，precious or semi-precious stones，precious metals，metals clad with precious metal and articles thereof；imitation jewellery；coin	0.65	3.57	0.48	1.41
第十五类 贱金属及其制品	**BASE METALS AND ARTICLES OF BASE METAL**	**37.31**	**46.99**	**42.62**	**54.92**
72章 钢铁	Iron and steel	18.86	12.25	18.45	14.68
73章 钢铁制品	Articles of iron or steel	4.90	5.42	5.59	6.46
74章 铜及其制品	Copper and articles thereof	6.29	19.63	9.90	24.71
75章 镍及其制品	Nickel and articles thereof	0.55	0.52	1.26	0.21
76章 铝及其制品	Aluminium and articles thereof	2.15	3.76	2.39	3.45
78章 铅及其制品	Lead and articles thereof	0.13	0.02	0.23	0.03
79章 锌及其制品	Zinc and articles thereof	0.12	0.12	0.12	0.15
80章 锡及其制品	Tin and articles thereof	0.04	0.25	0.00	0.24
81章 其他贱金属、金属陶瓷及其制品	Other base metals；cermets；articles thereof	0.94	0.32	1.19	0.35
82章 贱金属工具、器具、利口器、餐匙、餐叉及其零件	Tools，implements，cutlery，spoons and forks，of base metal；parts thereof of base metal	1.73	3.23	1.89	3.35
83章 贱金属杂项制品	Miscellaneous articles of base metal	1.60	1.48	1.59	1.28

6-21 续表 4 Continued 4

单位：亿美元
Unit: USD 100 million

商品分类	HS Section and Division	2016 出口 Exports	2016 进口 Imports	2017 出口 Exports	2017 进口 Imports
第十六类 机器、机械器具、电气设备及其零件；录音机及放声机、电视图像、声音的录制和重放设备及其零件、附件	**MACHINERY AND MECHANICAL APPLIANCES；ELECTRICAL EQUIPMENT；PARTS THEREOF；SOUND RECORDERS AND REPRODUCERS，TELEVISION IMAGE AND SOUND RECORDERS AND REPRODUCERS；AND PARTS AND ACCESSORIES OF RECORDERS AND REPRODUCERS；AND PARTS AND ACCESSORIES OF SUCH ARTICLES**	**207.10**	**974.85**	**229.17**	**1094.13**
84章 核反应堆、锅炉、机器、机械器具及其零件	Nuclear reactors，boilers，machinery and mechanical appliances；parts thereof	54.34	85.37	64.64	119.02
85章 电机、电气设备及其零件；录音机及放声机、电视图像、声音的录制和重放设备及其零件、附件	Electrical machinery and equipment and parts thereof；sound recorders and reproducers，television image and sound recorders and reproducers，and parts and accessories of such articles	152.76	889.49	164.53	975.11
第十七类 车辆、航空器、船舶及有关运输设备	**VEHICLES，AIRCRAFT，VESSELS AND ASSOCIATED TRANSPORT EQUIPMENT**	**8.99**	**5.08**	**10.30**	**5.50**
86章 铁道及电车道机车、车辆及其零件；铁道及电车轨道固定装置及其零件、附件；各种机械(包括电动机械)交通信号设备	Railway or tramway locomotives，rolling-stock and parts thereof；railway or tramway track fixtures and fittings and parts thereof；mechanical(including electro-mechanical) traffic signalling equipment of all kinds	0.48	0.02	1.57	0.02
87章 车辆及其零件、附件，但铁道及电车道车辆除外	Vehicles other than railway or tramway rolling-stock，and parts and accessories thereof	8.32	4.99	8.48	5.37
88章 航空器、航天器及其零件	Aircraft，spacecraft，and parts thereof	0.04	0.05	0.03	0.02
89章 船舶及浮动结构体	Ships，boats and floating structures	0.15	0.02	0.23	0.09
第十八类 光学、照相、电影、计量、检验、医疗或外科用仪器及设备、精密仪器及设备；钟表；乐器；上述物品的零件、附件	**OPTICAL，PHOTOGRAPHIC，CINEMATOGRAPHIC，MEASURING，CHECKING，PRECISION，MEDICAL OR SURGICAL INSTRUMENTS AND APPARATUS；CLOCKS AND WATCHES；MUSICAL INSTRUMENTS；PARTS AND ACCESSORIES THEREOF**	**18.16**	**136.26**	**19.48**	**151.37**
90章 光学、照相、电影、计量、检验、医疗或外科用仪器及设备、精密仪器及设备；上述物品的零件、附件	Optical，photographic，cinematographic，measuring，checking，precision medical or surgical instruments and apparatus；parts and accessories thereof	17.86	136.02	19.19	151.13
91章 钟表及其零件	Clocks and watches and parts thereof	0.15	0.07	0.16	0.07
92章 乐器及其零件、附件	Musical instruments；parts and accessories of such articles	0.15	0.16	0.14	0.17
第十九类 武器、弹药及其零件、附件	**ARMS AND AMMUNITION；PARTS AND ACCESSORIES THEREOF**	**0.00**	**0.00**	**0.00**	**0.00**
93章 武器、弹药及其零件、附件	Arms and ammunition；parts and accessories thereof	0.00	0.00	0.00	0.00
第二十类 杂项制品	**MISCELLANEOUS MANUFACTURED ARTICLES**	**13.02**	**4.92**	**13.01**	**5.93**
94章 家具；寝具、褥垫、弹簧床垫、软坐垫及类似的填充制品；未列名灯具及照明装置；发光标志、发光名牌及类似品；活动房屋	Furniture；bedding，mattresses，mattress supports，cushions and similar stuffed furnishings；lamps and lighting fittings，not elsewhere specified or included；illuminated signs，illuminated	8.88	1.37	8.16	1.66
95章 玩具、游戏品、运动用品及其零件、附件	Toys，games and sports requisites；parts and accessories thereof	2.36	2.58	3.16	3.24
96章 杂项制品	Miscellaneous manufactured articles	1.78	0.98	1.70	1.03
第二十一类 艺术品、收藏品及古物	**WORKS OF ART，COLLECTORS' PIECES AND ANTIQUES**	**0.05**	**0.01**	**0.01**	**0.01**
97章 艺术品、收藏品及古物	Works of art，collectors' pieces and antiques	0.05	0.01	0.01	0.01
第二十二类 特殊交易品及未分类商品	**COMMODITIES AND TRANSACTIONS NOT CLASSIFIED ACCORDING TO KIND**	**0.56**	**0.74**	**4.20**	**1.64**
98章 特殊交易品及未分类商品	Commodities and transactions not classified according to kind	0.56	0.74	4.20	1.64

6-22 对日本进出口商品分类金额

Value of Exports and Imports from Japan by HS

单位：亿美元

Unit: USD 100 million

商品分类	HS Section and Division	2016		2017	
		出口 Exports	进口 Imports	出口 Exports	进口 Imports
总　额	**Total**	**1294.10**	**1456.71**	**1372.59**	**1657.94**
第一类　活动物；动物产品	**LIVE ANIMALS；ANIMAL PRODUCTS**	**22.80**	**2.89**	**23.88**	**2.88**
01章　活动物	Live animals	0.05	0.03	0.05	0.10
02章　肉及食用杂碎	Meat and edible meat offal	0.00		0.00	
03章　鱼、甲壳动物、软体动物及其他水生无脊椎动物	Fish and crustaceans molluscs and other aquatic invertebrates	20.08	2.78	21.12	2.70
04章　乳品；蛋品；天然蜂蜜；其他食用动物产品	Dairy produce；birds' eggs；natural honey；edible products of animal origin，not elsewhere specified or included	1.22	0.01	1.02	0.00
05章　其他动物产品	Products of animal origin，not elsewhere specified or included	1.45	0.08	1.69	0.08
第二类　植物产品	**VEGETABLE PRODUCTS**	**23.12**	**1.23**	**23.35**	**1.44**
06章　活树及其他活植物；鳞茎、根及类似品；插花及装饰用簇叶	Live tree and other plants；bulbs，roots and the like; cut flowers and ornamental foliage	0.98	0.42	0.99	0.52
07章　食用蔬菜、根及块茎	Edible vegetables and certain roots and tubers	12.92	0.00	13.15	0.00
08章　食用水果及坚果；甜瓜或柑桔属水果的果皮	Edible fruit and nuts；peel of citrus fruit or melons	1.49	0.08	1.52	0.06
09章　咖啡、茶、马黛茶及调味香料	Coffee，tea，mate and spices	1.50	0.05	1.56	0.06
10章　谷物	Cereals	0.45	0.02	0.33	0.01
11章　制粉工业产品；麦芽；淀粉；菊粉；面筋	Products of the milling industry；malt；starches；inulin；wheat gluten	0.32	0.02	0.32	0.04
12章　含油子仁及果实；杂项子仁及果实；工业用或药用植物；稻草、秸秆及饲料	Oil seeds and oleaginous fruits；miscellaneous grains，seeds and fruit；industrial or medicinal plants；straw and fodder	3.53	0.60	3.35	0.71
13章　虫胶；树胶、树脂及其他植物液、汁	Lac；gums，resins and other vegetable saps and extracts	1.72	0.04	1.90	0.03
14章　编结用植物材料；其他植物产品	Vegetable plaiting materials；vegetable products not elsewhere specified or included	0.21	0.00	0.23	0.00
第三类　动、植物油、脂及其分解产品；精制的食用油脂；动、植物蜡	**ANIMAL OR VEGETABLE FATS AND OILS AND THEIR CLEAVAGE PRODUCTS；PREPARED EDIBLE FATS；ANIMAL OR VEGETABLE WAXES**	**0.29**	**0.07**	**0.26**	**0.06**
15章　动、植物油、脂及其分解产品；精制的食用油脂；动、植物蜡	Animal or vegetable fats and oils and their cleavage products；prepared edible fats；animal or vegetable waxes	0.29	0.07	0.26	0.06
第四类　食品；饮料、酒及醋；烟草、烟草及烟草代用品的制品	**PREPARED FOODSTUFFS；BEVERAGES, SPIRITS AND VINEGAR；TOBACCO AND MANUFACTURED TOBACCO SUBSTITUTES**	**52.96**	**3.01**	**53.45**	**3.35**
16章　肉、鱼、甲壳动物、软体动物及其他水生无脊椎动物的制品	Preparations of meat，of fish or of crustaceans，molluscs or other aquatic invertebrates	24.87	0.23	26.83	0.15
17章　糖及糖食	Sugars and sugar confectionery	0.13	0.12	0.13	0.17
18章　可可及可可制品	Cocoa and cocoa preparations	0.24	0.08	0.25	0.07
19章　谷物、粮食粉、淀粉或乳的制品；糕饼点心	Preparations of cereals，flour，starch or milk；pastry-cooks' products	2.18	0.55	2.30	0.65

6-22 续表 1 Continued 1

单位：亿美元
Unit: USD 100 million

商品分类	HS Section and Division	2016		2017	
		出口 Exports	进口 Imports	出口 Exports	进口 Imports
20章 蔬菜、水果、坚果或植物其他部分的制品	Preparations of vegetables, fruit, nuts or other parts of plants	16.12	0.04	16.63	0.04
21章 杂项食品	Miscellaneous edible preparations	2.16	0.96	2.06	1.04
22章 饮料、酒及醋	Beverages, spirits and vinegar	0.34	0.48	0.35	0.67
23章 食品工业的残渣及废料；配制的动物饲料	Residues and waste from the food industries; prepared animal fodder	6.62	0.10	4.80	0.06
24章 烟草及烟草代用品的制品	Tobacco and manufactured tobacco substitutes	0.31	0.46	0.09	0.50
第五类 矿产品	**MINERAL PRODUCTS**	**16.12**	**14.69**	**27.43**	**15.03**
25章 盐；硫磺；泥土及石料；石膏料、石灰及水泥	Salt; sulphur; earths and stone; plastering materials, lime and cement	4.29	1.93	5.08	2.08
26章 矿砂、矿渣及矿灰	Ores, slag and ash	0.54	0.05	3.91	0.03
27章 矿物燃料、矿物油及其蒸馏产品；沥青物质；矿物蜡	Mineral fuels, mineral oils and products of their distillation; bituminous substances; mineral waxes	11.29	12.72	18.44	12.92
第六类 化学工业及其相关工业的产品	**PRODUCTS OF THE CHEMICAL OR INDUSTRIES ALLIED**	**65.76**	**144.34**	**74.19**	**173.83**
28章 无机化学品；贵金属、稀土金属、放射性元素及其同位素的有机及无机化合物	Inorganic chemicals; organic or inorganic compounds of precious metals, of rare- earth metals, of radioactive elements or of isotopes	15.98	5.78	20.54	7.15
29章 有机化学品	Organic chemicals	27.94	58.32	30.82	69.60
30章 药品	Pharmaceutical products	2.46	7.31	2.39	9.21
31章 肥料	Fertilizers	2.12	0.07	2.13	0.07
32章 鞣料浸膏及染料浸膏；鞣酸及其衍生物；染料、颜料及其他着色料；油漆及清漆；油灰及其他类似胶粘剂；墨水、油墨	Tanning or dyeing extracts; tannins and their derivatives; dyes, pigments and other colouring matter; paints and varnishes; putty and other mastics; inks	2.43	8.73	2.39	10.27
33章 精油及香膏；芳香料制品及化妆盥洗品	Essential oils and retinoid; perfumery, cosmetic or toilet preparations	3.13	8.82	3.10	15.12
34章 肥皂、有机表面活性剂、洗涤剂、润滑剂、人造蜡、调制蜡、光洁剂、蜡烛及类似品、塑型用膏、"牙科用蜡"及牙科用熟石膏制剂	Soap, organic surface-active agents, washing preparations, lubricating preparations, artificial waxes, prepared waxes, polishing or scouring preparations, candles and similar articles, modelling pastes, "dental waxes" and dental preparations with a basis of plast	2.41	9.04	2.51	10.27
35章 蛋白类物质；改性淀粉；胶；酶	Albuminoidal substances; modified starches; glues; enzymes	1.43	8.15	1.57	9.02
36章 炸药；烟火制品；火柴；引火合金；易燃材料制品	Explosives; pyrotechnic products; matches; pyrophoric alloys; certain combustible preparations	0.26	0.11	0.31	0.13
37章 照相及电影用品	Photographic or cinematographic goods	0.58	9.61	0.60	10.44
38章 杂项化学产品	Miscellaneous chemical products	7.02	28.39	7.83	32.55
第七类 塑料及其制品，橡胶及其制品	**PLASTICS AND ARTICLES THEREOF RUBBER AND ARTICLES THEREOF**	**46.43**	**102.15**	**49.68**	**112.64**
39章 塑料及其制品	Plastics and articles thereof	40.23	87.40	42.98	97.03
40章 橡胶及其制品	Rubber and articles thereof	6.20	14.75	6.70	15.60
第八类 生皮、皮革、毛皮及其制品；鞍具及挽具；旅行用品、手提包及类似品；动物肠线(蚕胶丝除外)制品	**RAW HIDES AND SKINS, LEATHER, FUR SKINS AND ARTICLES THEREOF; SADDLERY AND HARNESS; TRAVEL GOODS, HANDBAGS AND SIMILAR CONTAINERS; ARTICLES OF ANIMAL GUT(OTHER THAN SILK-WORM GUT)**	**19.31**	**0.55**	**19.35**	**0.47**
41章 生皮(毛皮除外)及皮革	Raw hides and skins(other than fur skins) and leather	0.15	0.38	0.12	0.34

6-22 续表 2 Continued 2

单位：亿美元
Unit: USD 100 million

商品分类	HS Section and Division	2016		2017	
		出 口 Exports	进 口 Imports	出 口 Exports	进 口 Imports
42章 皮革制品；鞍具及挽具；旅行用品、手提包及类似容器；动物肠线(蚕胶丝除外)制品	Articles of leather；saddlery and harness；travel goods，hand bags and similar containers；articles of animal gut (other than silk-worm gut)	18.81	0.17	18.85	0.13
43章 毛皮、人造毛皮及其制品	Fur skins and artificial fur；manufactures thereof	0.35	0.01	0.37	0.00
第九类 木及木制品；木炭；软木及软木制品；稻草，秸秆、针茅或其他编结材料制品；篮筐及柳条编结品	**WOOD AND ARTICLES OF WOOD；WOOD CHAR-COAL；CORK AND ARTICLES OF CORK；MANUFACTURES OF STRAW，OF ESPARTO OR OF OTHER PLAITING MATERIALS；BASKET WARE AND WICKERWORK**	**14.63**	**0.96**	**14.50**	**1.41**
44章 木及木制品；木炭	Wood and articles of wood；wood charcoal	12.36	0.95	12.37	1.40
45章 软木及软木制品	Cork and articles of cork	0.02	0.01	0.02	0.01
46章 稻草、秸秆、针茅或其他编结材料制品；篮筐及柳条编结品	Manufactures of straw，of esparto or of other plaiting Materials；basket ware and wickerwork	2.25	0.00	2.11	0.00
第十类 木浆及其他纤维状纤维素浆；纸及纸板的废碎品；纸、纸板及其制品	**PULP OF WOOD OR OF OTHER FIBROUS CELLULOSIC MATERIAL；WASTE AND SCRAP OF PAPER OR PAPERBOARD；PAPER AND PAPERBOARD AND ARTICLES THEREOF**	**12.95**	**13.56**	**12.90**	**15.15**
47章 木浆及其他纤维状纤维素浆；纸及纸板的废碎品	Pulp of wood or of other fibrous cellulosic material；waste and scrap of paper or paperboard	0.10	7.16	0.15	7.99
48章 纸及纸板；纸浆、纸或纸板制品	Paper and paperboard；articles of paper pulp，of paper or paperboard	11.51	5.22	11.71	6.09
49章 书籍、报纸、印刷图画及其他印制品；手稿、打字稿及设计图纸	Printed books，newspapers，pictures and other products of the printing industry；manuscripts，typescripts and plans	1.35	1.17	1.05	1.08
第十一类 纺织原料及纺织制品	**TEXTILES AND TEXTILE ARTICLES**	**196.53**	**25.77**	**196.99**	**26.54**
50章 蚕丝	Silk	0.79	0.06	0.92	0.04
51章 羊毛、动物细毛或粗毛；马毛纱线及其机织物	Wool，fine or coarse animal hair；horsehair yarn and woven fabric	2.41	1.42	2.14	1.33
52章 棉花	Cotton	1.23	1.88	1.13	1.68
53章 其他植物纺织纤维；纸纱线及其机织物	Other vegetable textile fibres；paper yarn and woven fabrics of paper yarn	0.39	0.11	0.40	0.09
54章 化学纤维长丝	Man-made filaments	1.90	6.63	2.03	6.79
55章 化学纤维短纤	Man-made short fibres	1.26	4.38	1.22	4.94
56章 絮胎、毡呢及无纺织物；特种纱线；线、绳、索、缆及其制品	Wadding，felt and nonwoven；special yarns；twine，cordage，ropes and cables and articles thereof	4.49	3.23	5.23	3.61
57章 地毯及纺织材料的其他铺地制品	Carpets and other textile floor coverings	3.26	0.07	3.40	0.09
58章 特种机织物；簇绒织物；花边；装饰毯；装饰带；刺绣品	Special woven fabrics；tufted textile fabrics；lace；tapestries；trimmings；embroidery	0.65	1.10	0.62	1.11
59章 浸渍、涂布、包覆或层压的纺织物；工业用纺织制品	Impregnated，coated，covered or laminated textile fabrics；textile articles of a kind suitable for industrial use	1.88	2.79	1.96	3.04
60章 针织物及钩编织物	Knitted or crocheted fabrics	0.40	2.78	0.44	2.55
61章 针织或钩编的服装及衣着附件	Articles of apparel and clothing accessories，Knitted or crocheted	81.50	0.42	79.85	0.42
62章 非针织或非钩编的服装及衣着附件	Articles of apparel and clothing accessories，not knitted or crocheted	72.14	0.57	72.85	0.47

单位：亿美元
Unit: USD 100 million

商品分类	HS Section and Division	2016 出口 Exports	2016 进口 Imports	2017 出口 Exports	2017 进口 Imports
63章 其他纺织制成品；成套物品；旧衣着及旧纺织品；碎织物	Other made up textile articles；sets；worn clothing and worn textile articles；rags articles；rags	24.23	0.33	24.80	0.37
第十二类 鞋、帽、伞、杖、鞭及其零件；已加工的羽毛及其制品；人造花；人发制品	**FOOTWEAR，HEADGEAR，UMBRELLAS，SUN UMBRELLAS，WALKING-STICKS，SEAT-STICKS，WHIPS，RIDING-CROPS AND PARTS THEREOF；PREPARED FEATHERS AND ARTICLES MADE THEREWITH；ARTIFICIAL FLOWERS；ARTICLES OF HUMAN HAIR**	**29.36**	**0.48**	**28.42**	**0.56**
64章 鞋靴、护腿和类似品及其零件	Footwear，gaiters and the like；parts of such articles	23.01	0.13	22.50	0.15
65章 帽类及其零件	Headgear and parts thereof	2.75	0.04	2.61	0.05
66章 雨伞、阳伞、手杖、鞭子、马鞭及其零件	Umbrellas，sun umbrellas，walking-sticks，seat-sticks，whips，riding-crops and parts thereof	2.51	0.01	2.24	0.00
67章 已加工羽毛、羽绒及其制品；人造花；人发制品	Prepared feathers and down and articles made of feathers or of down；artificial flowers；articles of human hair	1.08	0.30	1.07	0.36
第十三类 石料、石膏、水泥、石棉、云母及类似材料的制品；陶瓷产品；玻璃及其制品	**ARTICLES OF STONE，PLASTER，CEMENT，ASBESTOS，MICA OR SIMILAR MATERIALS；CERAMIC PRODUCTS；GLASS AND GLASSWARE**	**17.63**	**21.40**	**17.80**	**21.50**
68章 石料、石膏、水泥、石棉、云母及类似材料的制品	Articles of stone，plaster，cement，asbestos，mica or similar materials；ceramic products；glass and glassware	6.78	5.09	6.46	5.14
69章 陶瓷产品	Ceramic products	5.17	1.99	5.53	2.29
70章 玻璃及其制品	Glass and glassware	5.68	14.33	5.81	14.07
第十四类 天然或养殖珍珠、宝石或半宝石、贵金属、包贵金属及其制品；仿首饰；硬币	**NATURAL OR CULTURED PEARLS，PRECIOUS OR SEMI-PRECIOUS STONES，PRECIOUS METALS，METALS CLAD WITH PRECIOUS METAL AND STONES，PRECIOUS METALS，METALS CLAD WITH PRECIOUS METAL AND ARTICLES THEREOF；IMITATION JEWELLERY；COIN**	**1.67**	**8.27**	**1.60**	**14.72**
71章 天然或养殖珍珠、宝石或半宝石、贵金属、包贵金属及其制品；仿首饰；硬币	Natural or cultured pearls，precious or semi-precious stones，precious metals，metals clad with precious metal and articles thereof；imitation jewellery；coin	1.67	8.27	1.60	14.72
第十五类 贱金属及其制品	**BASE METALS AND ARTICLES OF BASE METAL**	**69.88**	**126.95**	**77.26**	**141.78**
72章 钢铁	Iron and steel	7.89	51.39	9.83	59.79
73章 钢铁制品	Articles of iron or steel	29.94	21.43	31.19	24.07
74章 铜及其制品	Copper and articles thereof	2.47	29.39	2.83	30.50
75章 镍及其制品	Nickel and articles thereof	0.19	1.91	0.20	1.72
76章 铝及其制品	Aluminium and articles thereof	15.33	8.72	18.16	9.89
78章 铅及其制品	Lead and articles thereof	0.05	0.05	0.02	0.04
79章 锌及其制品	Zinc and articles thereof	0.12	0.61	0.16	0.83
80章 锡及其制品	Tin and articles thereof	0.01	0.40	0.04	0.41
81章 其他贱金属、金属陶瓷及其制品	Other base metals；cermets；articles thereof	2.98	1.75	3.69	1.88
82章 贱金属工具、器具、利口器、餐匙、餐叉及其零件	Tools，implements，cutlery，spoons and forks，of base metal；parts thereof of base metal	4.94	9.32	5.31	10.50
83章 贱金属杂项制品	Miscellaneous articles of base metal	5.96	1.99	5.83	2.14

6-22 续表 4 Continued 4

单位：亿美元
Unit: USD 100 million

商品分类	HS Section and Division	2016		2017	
		出 口 Exports	进 口 Imports	出 口 Exports	进 口 Imports
第十六类 机器、机械器具、电气设备及其零件；录音机及放声机、电视图像、声音的录制和重放设备及其零件、附件	**MACHINERY AND MECHANICAL APPLIANCES；ELECTRICAL EQUIPMENT；PARTS THEREOF；SOUND RECORDERS AND REPRODUCERS，TELEVISION IMAGE AND SOUND RECORDERS AND REPRODUCERS；AND PARTS AND ACCESSORIES OF RECORDERS AND REPRODUCERS；AND PARTS AND ACCESSORIES OF SUCH ARTICLES**	**532.40**	**676.58**	**563.70**	**767.51**
84章 核反应堆、锅炉、机器、机械器具及其零件	Nuclear reactors，boilers，machinery and mechanical appliances；parts thereof	205.68	272.05	222.98	345.49
85章 电机、电气设备及其零件；录音机及放声机、电视图像、声音的录制和重放设备及其零件、附件	Electrical machinery and equipment and parts thereof；sound recorders and reproducers，television image and sound recorders and reproducers，and parts and accessories of such articles	326.71	404.53	340.71	422.02
第十七类 车辆、航空器、船舶及有关运输设备	**VEHICLES，AIRCRAFT，VESSELS AND ASSOCIATED TRANSPORT EQUIPMENT**	**43.07**	**142.77**	**45.82**	**169.94**
86章 铁道及电车道机车、车辆及其零件；铁道及电车轨道固定装置及其零件、附件；各种机械(包括电动机械)交通信号设备	Railway or tramway locomotives，rolling-stock and parts thereof；railway or tramway track fixtures and fittings and parts thereof；mechanical(including electro-mechanical) traffic signalling equipment of all kinds	2.28	2.34	1.70	1.04
87章 车辆及其零件、附件，但铁道及电车道车辆除外	Vehicles other than railway or tramway rolling-stock，and parts and accessories thereof	38.84	138.46	41.85	164.95
88章 航空器、航天器及其零件	Aircraft，spacecraft，and parts thereof	0.70	0.09	0.82	0.08
89章 船舶及浮动结构体	Ships，boats and floating structures	1.25	1.87	1.46	3.87
第十八类 光学、照相、电影、计量、检验、医疗或外科用仪器及设备、精密仪器及设备；钟表；乐器；上述物品的零件、附件	**OPTICAL，PHOTOGRAPHIC，CINEMATOGRAPHIC，MEASURING，CHECKING，PRECISION，MEDICAL OR SURGICAL INSTRUMENTS AND APPARATUS；CLOCKS AND WATCHES；MUSICAL INSTRUMENTS；PARTS AND ACCESSORIES THEREOF**	**47.12**	**148.40**	**49.40**	**165.11**
90章 光学、照相、电影、计量、检验、医疗或外科用仪器及设备、精密仪器及设备；上述物品的零件、附件	Optical，photographic，cinematographic，measuring，checking，precision medical or surgical instruments and apparatus；parts and accessories thereof	43.20	142.87	45.43	159.22
91章 钟表及其零件	Clocks and watches and parts thereof	2.93	4.39	3.07	4.60
92章 乐器及其零件、附件	Musical instruments；parts and accessories of such articles	0.99	1.14	0.90	1.29
第十九类 武器、弹药及其零件、附件	**ARMS AND AMMUNITION；PARTS AND ACCESSORIES THEREOF**	**0.01**	**0.00**	**0.02**	**0.00**
93章 武器、弹药及其零件、附件	Arms and ammunition；parts and accessories thereof	0.01	0.00	0.02	0.00
第二十类 杂项制品	**MISCELLANEOUS MANUFACTURED ARTICLES**	**78.62**	**17.91**	**88.22**	**20.71**
94章 家具；寝具、褥垫、弹簧床垫、软坐垫及类似的填充制品；未列名灯具及照明装置；发光标志、发光名牌及类似品；活动房屋	Furniture；bedding，mattresses，mattress supports，cushions and similar stuffed furnishings；lamps and lighting fittings，not elsewhere specified or included；illuminated signs，illuminated	47.31	2.43	46.88	2.45
95章 玩具、游戏品、运动用品及其零件、附件	Toys，games and sports requisites；parts and accessories thereof	24.05	1.60	33.77	2.18
96章 杂项制品	Miscellaneous manufactured articles	7.26	13.88	7.57	16.09
第二十一类 艺术品、收藏品及古物	**WORKS OF ART，COLLECTORS' PIECES AND ANTIQUES**	**0.01**	**0.02**	**0.03**	**0.03**
97章 艺术品、收藏品及古物	Works of art，collectors' pieces and antiques	0.01	0.02	0.03	0.03
第二十二类 特殊交易品及未分类商品	**COMMODITIES AND TRANSACTIONS NOT CLASSIFIED ACCORDING TO KIND**	**1.14**	**3.89**	**4.33**	**3.29**
98章 特殊交易品及未分类商品	Commodities and transactions not classified according to kind	1.14	3.89	4.33	3.29

6–23 对欧洲联盟进出口商品分类金额
Value of Exports to and Imports from EU by HS

单位：亿美元
Unit: USD 100 million

商品分类	HS Section and Division	2016 出口 Exports	2016 进口 Imports	2017 出口 Exports	2017 进口 Imports
总　额	**Total**	**3392.56**	**2081.36**	**3720.31**	**2449.70**
第一类　活动物；动物产品	**LIVE ANIMALS；ANIMAL PRODUCTS**	**27.18**	**49.45**	**29.56**	**43.26**
01章　活动物	Live animals	0.01	0.57	0.02	0.45
02章　肉及食用杂碎	Meat and edible meat offal	0.17	36.10	0.22	25.35
03章　鱼、甲壳动物、软体动物及其他水生无脊椎动物	Fish and crustaceans molluscs and other aquatic invertebrates	19.40	2.13	19.79	2.96
04章　乳品；蛋品；天然蜂蜜；其他食用动物产品	Dairy produce；birds' eggs；natural honey；edible products of animal origin，not elsewhere specified or included	1.51	8.93	1.69	12.30
05章　其他动物产品	Products of animal origin，not elsewhere specified or included	6.09	1.73	7.85	2.20
第二类　植物产品	**VEGETABLE PRODUCTS**	**23.56**	**6.88**	**23.20**	**6.70**
06章　活树及其他活植物；鳞茎、根及类似品；插花及装饰用簇叶	Live tree and other plants；bulbs，roots and the like；cut flowers and ornamental foliage	0.45	1.17	0.52	1.38
07章　食用蔬菜、根及块茎	Edible vegetables and certain roots and tubers	6.52	0.13	6.13	0.06
08章　食用水果及坚果；甜瓜或柑桔属水果的果皮	Edible fruit and nuts；peel of citrus fruit or melons	3.60	1.11	3.68	1.24
09章　咖啡、茶、马黛茶及调味香料	Coffee，tea，mate and spices	4.82	0.37	4.97	0.47
10章　谷物	Cereals	0.05	1.52	0.06	0.55
11章　制粉工业产品；麦芽；淀粉；菊粉；面筋	Products of the milling industry；malt；starches；inulin；wheat gluten	0.50	0.63	0.48	0.72
12章　含油子仁及果实；杂项子仁及果实；工业用或药用植物；稻草、秸秆及饲料	Oil seeds and oleaginous fruits；miscellaneous grains，seeds and fruit；industrial or medicinal plants；straw and fodder	4.76	1.18	4.25	1.47
13章　虫胶；树胶、树脂及其他植物液、汁	Lac；gums，resins and other vegetable saps and extracts	2.39	0.77	2.62	0.80
14章　编结用植物材料；其他植物产品	Vegetable plaiting materials；vegetable products not elsewhere specified or included	0.45	0.01	0.50	0.01
第三类　动、植物油、脂及其分解产品；精制的食用油脂；动、植物蜡	**ANIMAL OR VEGETABLE FATS AND OILS AND THEIR CLEAVAGE PRODUCTS；PREPARED EDIBLE FATS；ANIMAL OR VEGETABLE WAXES**	**1.19**	**3.03**	**2.88**	**3.10**
15章　动、植物油、脂及其分解产品；精制的食用油脂；动、植物蜡	Animal or vegetable fats and oils and their cleavage products；prepared edible fats；animal or vegetable waxes	1.19	3.03	2.88	3.10
第四类　食品；饮料、酒及醋；烟草、烟草及烟草代用品的制品	**PREPARED FOODSTUFFS；BEVERAGES, SPIRITS AND VINEGAR；TOBACCO AND MANUFACTURED TOBACCO SUBSTITUTES**	**26.89**	**63.17**	**28.17**	**77.14**
16章　肉、鱼、甲壳动物、软体动物及其他水生无脊椎动物的制品	Preparations of meat，of fish or of crustaceans，molluscs or other aquatic invertebrates	4.13	0.08	4.28	0.09
17章　糖及糖食	Sugars and sugar confectionery	0.78	0.67	0.85	0.77
18章　可可及可可制品	Cocoa and cocoa preparations	0.58	2.34	0.26	2.30
19章　谷物、粮食粉、淀粉或乳的制品；糕饼点心	Preparations of cereals，flour，starch or milk；pastry-cooks' products	1.59	25.88	1.53	32.82

6-23 续表 1 Continued 1

单位：亿美元
Unit: USD 100 million

商品分类	HS Section and Division	2016 出口 Exports	2016 进口 Imports	2017 出口 Exports	2017 进口 Imports
20章 蔬菜、水果、坚果或植物其他部分的制品	Preparations of vegetables, fruit, nuts or other parts of plants	8.61	1.18	8.85	1.51
21章 杂项食品	Miscellaneous edible preparations	2.66	3.50	2.89	5.16
22章 饮料、酒及醋	Beverages, spirits and vinegar	1.05	27.65	1.09	32.26
23章 食品工业的残渣及废料；配制的动物饲料	Residues and waste from the food industries；prepared animal fodder	5.34	1.39	6.32	1.79
24章 烟草及烟草代用品的制品	Tobacco and manufactured tobacco substitutes	2.14	0.46	2.11	0.45
第五类 矿产品	**MINERAL PRODUCTS**	**15.15**	**61.35**	**20.28**	**92.06**
25章 盐；硫磺；泥土及石料；石膏料、石灰及水泥	Salt；sulphur；earths and stone；plastering materials, lime and cement	3.22	5.03	3.91	6.69
26章 矿砂、矿渣及矿灰	Ores, slag and ash	0.20	10.61	0.21	15.26
27章 矿物燃料、矿物油及其蒸馏产品；沥青物质；矿物蜡	Mineral fuels, mineral oils and products of their distillation; bituminous substances; mineral waxes	11.73	45.71	16.17	70.11
第六类 化学工业及其相关工业的产品	**PRODUCTS OF THE CHEMICAL OR INDUSTRIES ALLIED**	**156.98**	**279.27**	**184.23**	**338.78**
28章 无机化学品；贵金属、稀土金属、放射性元素及其同位素的有机及无机化合物	Inorganic chemicals；organic or inorganic compounds of precious metals, of rare- earth metals, of radioactive elements or of isotopes	13.02	11.35	16.00	14.51
29章 有机化学品	Organic chemicals	92.25	46.65	106.07	54.93
30章 药品	Pharmaceutical products	13.62	138.64	17.25	172.52
31章 肥料	Fertilizers	0.45	2.95	0.50	2.69
32章 鞣料浸膏及染料浸膏；鞣酸及其衍生物；染料、颜料及其他着色料；油漆及清漆；油灰及其他类似胶粘剂；墨水、油墨	Tanning or dyeing extracts；tannins and their derivatives；dyes, pigments and other colouring matter；paints and varnishes； putty and other mastics；inks	8.78	11.42	11.39	12.34
33章 精油及香膏； 芳香料制品及化妆盥洗品	Essential oils and retinoid；perfumery, cosmetic or toilet preparations	8.35	19.87	8.99	27.37
34章 肥皂、有机表面活性剂、洗涤剂、润滑剂、人造蜡、调制蜡、光洁剂、蜡烛及类似品、塑型用膏、“牙科用蜡”及牙科用熟石膏制剂	Soap, organic surface-active agents, washing preparations, lubricating preparations, artificial waxes, prepared waxes, polishing or scouring preparations, candles and similar articles, modelling pastes, “dental waxes” and dental preparations with a basis of plast	4.16	11.84	4.78	13.77
35章 蛋白类物质；改性淀粉；胶；酶	Albuminoidal substances；modified starches；glues；enzymes	2.49	7.06	3.00	7.64
36章 炸药；烟火制品；火柴；引火合金；易燃材料制品	Explosives；pyrotechnic products；matches；pyrophoric alloys；certain combustible preparations	2.54	0.38	2.63	0.42
37章 照相及电影用品	Photographic or cinematographic goods	0.96	1.56	0.98	1.23
38章 杂项化学产品	Miscellaneous chemical products	10.35	27.56	12.63	31.38
第七类 塑料及其制品，橡胶及其制品	**PLASTICS AND ARTICLES THEREOF RUBBER AND ARTICLES THEREOF**	**121.30**	**94.99**	**136.96**	**104.70**
39章 塑料及其制品	Plastics and articles thereof	87.28	73.71	97.69	80.64
40章 橡胶及其制品	Rubber and articles thereof	34.02	21.28	39.27	24.06
第八类 生皮、皮革、毛皮及其制品；鞍具及挽具；旅行用品、手提包及类似品；动物肠线（蚕胶丝除外）制品	**RAW HIDES AND SKINS, LEATHER, FUR SKINS AND ARTICLES THEREOF；SADDLERY AND HARNESS；TRAVEL GOODS, HANDBAGS AND SIMILAR CONTAINERS；ARTICLES OF ANIMAL GUT(OTHER THAN SILK-WORM GUT)**	**66.76**	**29.83**	**70.19**	**33.30**
41章 生皮(毛皮除外)及皮革	Raw hides and skins(other than fur skins) and leather	0.27	10.34	0.39	10.49

6-23 续表 2 Continued 2

单位：亿美元
Unit: USD 100 million

商品分类	HS Section and Division	2016		2017	
		出口 Exports	进口 Imports	出口 Exports	进口 Imports
42章 皮革制品；鞍具及挽具；旅行用品、手提包及类似容器；动物肠线(蚕胶丝除外)制品	Articles of leather；saddlery and harness；travel goods, hand bags and similar containers；articles of animal gut (other than silk-worm gut)	64.87	12.81	68.12	16.59
43章 毛皮、人造毛皮及其制品	Fur skins and artificial fur；manufactures thereof	1.62	6.68	1.68	6.22
第九类 木及木制品；木炭；软木及软木制品；稻草，秸秆、针茅或其他编结材料制品；篮筐及柳条编结品	**WOOD AND ARTICLES OF WOOD；WOOD CHAR-COAL；CORK AND ARTICLES OF CORK；MANUFACTURES OF STRAW，OF ESPARTO OR OF OTHER PLAITING MATERIALS ；BASKET WARE AND WICKERWORK**	**29.26**	**13.36**	**29.39**	**19.29**
44章 木及木制品；木炭	Wood and articles of wood；wood charcoal	23.59	12.96	23.66	18.84
45章 软木及软木制品	Cork and articles of cork	0.06	0.39	0.06	0.43
46章 稻草、秸秆、针茅或其他编结材料制品；篮筐及柳条编结品	Manufactures of straw，of esparto or of other plaiting Materials；basket ware and wickerwork	5.61	0.01	5.67	0.01
第十类 木浆及其他纤维状纤维素浆；纸及纸板的废碎品；纸、纸板及其制品	**PULP OF WOOD OR OF OTHER FIBROUS CELLULOSIC MATERIAL；WASTE AND SCRAP OF PAPER OR PAPERBOARD；PAPER AND PAPERBOARD AND ARTICLES THEREOF**	**27.97**	**43.62**	**29.38**	**51.39**
47章 木浆及其他纤维状纤维素浆；纸及纸板的废碎品	Pulp of wood or of other fibrous cellulosic material；waste and scrap of paper or paperboard	0.38	27.94	0.48	33.60
48章 纸及纸板；纸浆、纸或纸板制品	Paper and paperboard；articles of paper pulp，of paper or paperboard	20.41	11.78	21.67	13.30
49章 书籍、报纸、印刷图画及其他印制品；手稿、打字稿及设计图纸	Printed books，newspapers，pictures and other products of the printing industry；manuscripts，typescripts and plans	7.18	3.90	7.23	4.50
第十一类 纺织原料及纺织制品	**TEXTILES AND TEXTILE ARTICLES**	**473.84**	**38.82**	**472.63**	**42.73**
50章 蚕丝	Silk	2.90	0.09	2.78	0.13
51章 羊毛、动物细毛或粗毛；马毛纱线及其机织物	Wool，fine or coarse animal hair；horsehair yarn and woven fabric	4.91	3.95	5.23	3.89
52章 棉花	Cotton	5.54	1.03	6.41	1.11
53章 其他植物纺织纤维；纸纱线及其机织物	Other vegetable textile fibres；paper yarn and woven fabrics of paper yarn	1.62	4.12	1.79	3.91
54章 化学纤维长丝	Man-made filaments	19.66	2.62	21.11	2.99
55章 化学纤维短纤	Man-made short fibres	8.50	4.39	9.00	5.06
56章 絮胎、毡呢及无纺织物；特种纱线；线、绳、索、缆及其制品	Wadding，felt and nonwoven；special yarns；twine，cordage，ropes and cables and articles thereof	6.54	2.35	7.03	2.54
57章 地毯及纺织材料的其他铺地制品	Carpets and other textile floor coverings	4.21	0.24	4.47	0.27
58章 特种机织物；簇绒织物；花边；装饰毯；装饰带；刺绣品	Special woven fabrics；tufted textile fabrics；lace；tapestries；trimmings；embroidery	4.98	0.43	5.17	0.53
59章 浸渍、涂布、包覆或层压的纺织物；工业用纺织制品	Impregnated，coated，covered or laminated textile fabrics；textile articles of a kind suitable for industrial use	7.35	4.17	7.56	4.32
60章 针织物及钩编织物	Knitted or crocheted fabrics	8.60	0.84	8.91	0.97
61章 针织或钩编的服装及衣着附件	Articles of apparel and clothing accessories，Knitted or crocheted	167.82	4.63	162.54	5.65
62章 非针织或非钩编的服装及衣着附件	Articles of apparel and clothing accessories，not knitted or crocheted	181.59	9.38	179.47	10.60

单位：亿美元
Unit: USD 100 million

商品分类	HS Section and Division	2016 出口 Exports	2016 进口 Imports	2017 出口 Exports	2017 进口 Imports
63章 其他纺织制成品；成套物品；旧衣着及旧纺织品；碎织物	Other made up textile articles；sets；worn clothing and worn textile articles；rags articles；rags	49.62	0.57	51.16	0.75
第十二类 鞋、帽、伞、杖、鞭及其零件；已加工的羽毛及其制品；人造花；人发制品	**FOOTWEAR，HEADGEAR，UMBRELLAS，SUN UMBRELLAS，WALKING-STICKS，SEAT-STICKS，WHIPS，RIDING-CROPS AND PARTS THEREOF；PREPARED FEATHERS AND ARTICLES MADE THEREWITH；ARTIFICIAL FLOWERS；ARTICLES OF HUMAN HAIR**	**127.56**	**7.17**	**131.63**	**7.73**
64章 鞋靴、护腿和类似品及其零件	Footwear，gaiters and the like；parts of such articles	102.20	6.93	103.65	7.49
65章 帽类及其零件	Headgear and parts thereof	11.24	0.18	11.43	0.20
66章 雨伞、阳伞、手杖、鞭子、马鞭及其零件	Umbrellas，sun umbrellas，walking-sticks，seat-sticks，whips，riding-crops and parts thereof	5.97	0.02	5.98	0.02
67章 已加工羽毛、羽绒及其制品；人造花；人发制品	Prepared feathers and down and articles made of feathers or of down；artificial flowers；articles of human hair	8.15	0.04	10.57	0.03
第十三类 石料、石膏、水泥、石棉、云母及类似材料的制品；陶瓷产品；玻璃及其制品	**ARTICLES OF STONE，PLASTER，CEMENT，ASBESTOS，MICA OR SIMILAR MATERIALS；CERAMIC PRODUCTS；GLASS AND GLASSWARE**	**57.77**	**15.80**	**63.23**	**17.96**
68章 石料、石膏、水泥、石棉、云母及类似材料的制品	Articles of stone，plaster，cement，asbestos，mica or similar materials；ceramic products；glass and glassware	14.38	3.97	14.60	4.00
69章 陶瓷产品	Ceramic products	22.87	2.37	27.33	3.26
70章 玻璃及其制品	Glass and glassware	20.53	9.46	21.29	10.70
第十四类 天然或养殖珍珠、宝石或半宝石、贵金属、包贵金属及其制品；仿首饰；硬币	**NATURAL OR CULTURED PEARLS，PRECIOUS OR SEMI-PRECIOUS STONES，PRECIOUS METALS，METALS CLAD WITH PRECIOUS METAL AND STONES，PRECIOUS METALS，METALS CLAD WITH PRECIOUS METAL AND ARTICLES THEREOF；IMITATION JEWELLERY；COIN**	**10.89**	**18.60**	**8.76**	**17.33**
71章 天然或养殖珍珠、宝石或半宝石、贵金属、包贵金属及其制品；仿首饰；硬币	Natural or cultured pearls，precious or semi-precious stones，precious metals，metals clad with precious metal and articles thereof；imitation jewellery；coin	10.89	18.60	8.76	17.33
第十五类 贱金属及其制品	**BASE METALS AND ARTICLES OF BASE METAL**	**211.17**	**117.44**	**231.92**	**152.18**
72章 钢铁	Iron and steel	33.65	19.78	30.10	24.40
73章 钢铁制品	Articles of iron or steel	72.78	33.00	82.01	34.40
74章 铜及其制品	Copper and articles thereof	5.54	33.15	6.57	49.84
75章 镍及其制品	Nickel and articles thereof	0.67	3.69	0.78	5.80
76章 铝及其制品	Aluminium and articles thereof	29.63	8.88	33.71	10.12
78章 铅及其制品	Lead and articles thereof	0.00	0.10	0.00	0.26
79章 锌及其制品	Zinc and articles thereof	0.30	0.55	0.35	5.78
80章 锡及其制品	Tin and articles thereof	0.15	0.05	0.02	0.05
81章 其他贱金属、金属陶瓷及其制品	Other base metals；cermets；articles thereof	8.28	1.61	10.51	2.03
82章 贱金属工具、器具、利口器、餐匙、餐叉及其零件	Tools，implements，cutlery，spoons and forks，of base metal；parts thereof of base metal	31.23	9.76	35.66	11.39
83章 贱金属杂项制品	Miscellaneous articles of base metal	28.94	6.86	32.21	8.13

6-23 续表 4 Continued 4

单位：亿美元

Unit: USD 100 million

商品分类	HS Section and Division	2016 出口 Exports	2016 进口 Imports	2017 出口 Exports	2017 进口 Imports
第十六类 机器、机械器具、电气设备及其零件；录音机及放声机、电视图像、声音的录制和重放设备及其零件、附件	**MACHINERY AND MECHANICAL APPLIANCES；ELECTRICAL EQUIPMENT；PARTS THEREOF；SOUND RECORDERS AND REPRODUCERS，TELEVISION IMAGE AND SOUND RECORDERS AND REPRODUCERS；AND PARTS AND CCESSORIES OF RECORDERS AND EPRODUCERS；AND PARTS AND ACCESSORIES OF SUCH ARTICLES**	**1417.59**	**609.93**	**1585.58**	**716.60**
84章 核反应堆、锅炉、机器、机械器具及其零件	Nuclear reactors，boilers，machinery and mechanical appliances；parts thereof	646.87	369.55	749.72	428.08
85章 电机、电气设备及其零件；录音机及放声机、电视图像、声音的录制和重放设备及其零件、附件	Electrical machinery and equipment and parts thereof；sound recorders and reproducers，television image and sound recorders and reproducers，and parts and accessories of such articles	770.72	240.39	835.87	288.52
第十七类 车辆、航空器、船舶及有关运输设备	**VEHICLES，AIRCRAFT，VESSELS AND ASSOCIATED TRANSPORT EQUIPMENT**	**136.83**	**445.66**	**172.31**	**514.18**
86章 铁道及电车道机车、车辆及其零件；铁道及电车轨道固定装置及其零件、附件；各种机械(包括电动机械)交通信号设备	Railway or tramway locomotives，rolling-stock and parts thereof；railway or tramway track fixtures and fittings and parts thereof；mechanical(including electro- mechanical) traffic signalling equipment of all kinds	11.38	7.03	22.04	5.75
87章 车辆及其零件、附件，但铁道及电车道车辆除外	Vehicles other than railway or tramway rolling-stock，and parts and accessories thereof	81.98	351.30	98.85	403.63
88章 航空器、航天器及其零件	Aircraft，spacecraft，and parts thereof	8.20	84.10	8.12	103.06
89章 船舶及浮动结构体	Ships，boats and floating structures	35.26	3.24	43.31	1.74
第十八类 光学、照相、电影、计量、检验、医疗或外科用仪器及设备、精密仪器及设备；钟表；乐器；上述物品的零件、附件	**OPTICAL，PHOTOGRAPHIC，CINEMATOGRAPHIC，MEASURING，CHECKING，PRECISION，MEDICAL OR SURGICAL INSTRUMENTS AND APPARATUS；CLOCKS AND WATCHES；MUSICAL INSTRUMENTS；PARTS AND ACCESSORIES THEREOF**	**133.41**	**160.48**	**139.31**	**177.87**
90章 光学、照相、电影、计量、检验、医疗或外科用仪器及设备、精密仪器及设备；上述物品的零件、附件	Optical，photographic，cinematographic，measuring，checking，precision medical or surgical instruments and apparatus；parts and accessories thereof	123.50	159.30	130.48	176.67
91章 钟表及其零件	Clocks and watches and parts thereof	6.14	0.50	5.16	0.51
92章 乐器及其零件、附件	Musical instruments；parts and accessories of such articles	3.78	0.68	3.68	0.69
第十九类 武器、弹药及其零件、附件	**ARMS AND AMMUNITION；PARTS AND ACCESSORIES THEREOF**	**0.22**	**0.11**	**0.20**	**0.05**
93章 武器、弹药及其零件、附件	Arms and ammunition；parts and accessories thereof	0.22	0.11	0.20	0.05
第二十类 杂项制品	**MISCELLANEOUS MANUFACTURED ARTICLES**	**321.08**	**20.52**	**352.76**	**26.04**
94章 家具；寝具、褥垫、弹簧床垫、软坐垫及类似的填充制品；未列名灯具及照明装置；发光标志、发光名牌及类似品；活动房屋	Furniture；bedding，mattresses，mattress supports，cushions and similar stuffed furnishings；lamps and lighting fittings，not elsewhere specified or included；illuminated signs，illuminated	189.02	15.65	191.28	19.98
95章 玩具、游戏品、运动用品及其零件、附件	Toys，games and sports requisites；parts and accessories thereof	108.10	2.90	135.91	3.47
96章 杂项制品	Miscellaneous manufactured articles	23.96	1.97	25.58	2.58
第二十一类 艺术品、收藏品及古物	**WORKS OF ART，COLLECTORS' PIECES AND ANTIQUES**	**0.49**	**0.60**	**0.30**	**0.28**
97章 艺术品、收藏品及古物	Works of art，collectors' pieces and antiques	0.49	0.60	0.30	0.28
第二十二类 特殊交易品及未分类商品	**COMMODITIES AND TRANSACTIONS NOT CLASSIFIED ACCORDING TO KIND**	**2.26**	**0.41**	**7.43**	**7.04**
98章 特殊交易品及未分类商品	Commodities and transactions not classified according to kind	2.26	0.41	7.43	7.04

6-24 对美国进出口商品分类金额
Value of Exports and Imports from United States by HS

单位：亿美元

Unit: USD 100 million

商品分类	HS Section and Division	2016		2017	
		出口 Exports	进口 Imports	出口 Exports	进口 Imports
总　额	**Total**	**3852.71**	**1344.45**	**4297.30**	**1539.46**
第一类　活动物；动物产品	**LIVE ANIMALS；ANIMAL PRODUCTS**	**20.06**	**27.82**	**20.06**	**30.57**
01章　活动物	Live animals	0.36	0.05	0.27	0.16
02章　肉及食用杂碎	Meat and edible meat offal	0.02	13.53	0.04	11.87
03章　鱼、甲壳动物、软体动物及其他水生无脊椎动物	Fish and crustaceans molluscs and other aquatic invertebrates	17.25	10.28	16.96	13.15
04章　乳品；蛋品；天然蜂蜜；其他食用动物产品	Dairy produce；birds' eggs；natural honey；edible products of animal origin，not elsewhere specified or included	0.15	2.69	0.15	4.28
05章　其他动物产品	Products of animal origin，not elsewhere specified or included	2.28	1.28	2.65	1.12
第二类　植物产品	**VEGETABLE PRODUCTS**	**15.78**	**166.48**	**15.94**	**169.57**
06章　活树及其他活植物；鳞茎、根及类似品；插花及装饰用簇叶	Live tree and other plants；bulbs，roots and the like; cut flowers and ornamental foliage	0.35	0.05	0.43	0.04
07章　食用蔬菜、根及块茎	Edible vegetables and certain roots and tubers	7.22	0.45	7.69	0.45
08章　食用水果及坚果；甜瓜或柑桔属水果的果皮	Edible fruit and nuts；peel of citrus fruit or melons	1.63	5.76	1.42	7.66
09章　咖啡、茶、马黛茶及调味香料	Coffee，tea，mate and spices	2.19	0.14	2.27	0.18
10章　谷物	Cereals	0.02	15.26	0.02	15.10
11章　制粉工业产品；麦芽；淀粉；菊粉；面筋	Products of the milling industry；malt；starches；inulin；wheat gluten	0.08	0.23	0.10	0.24
12章　含油子仁及果实；杂项子仁及果实；工业用或药用植物；稻草、秸秆及饲料	Oil seeds and oleaginous fruits；miscellaneous grains，seeds and fruit；industrial or medicinal plants；straw and fodder	1.64	144.30	1.47	145.60
13章　虫胶；树胶、树脂及其他植物液、汁	Lac；gums，resins and other vegetable saps and extracts	2.56	0.23	2.43	0.21
14章　编结用植物材料；其他植物产品	Vegetable plaiting materials；vegetable products not elsewhere specified or included	0.10	0.05	0.11	0.09
第三类　动、植物油、脂及其分解产品；精制的食用油脂；动、植物蜡	**ANIMAL OR VEGETABLE FATS AND OILS AND THEIR CLEAVAGE PRODUCTS；PREPARED EDIBLE FATS；ANIMAL OR VEGETABLE WAXES**	**0.76**	**1.49**	**0.84**	**1.39**
15章　动、植物油、脂及其分解产品；精制的食用油脂；动、植物蜡	Animal or vegetable fats and oils and their cleavage products；prepared edible fats；animal or vegetable waxes	0.76	1.49	0.84	1.39
第四类　食品；饮料、酒及醋；烟草、烟草及烟草代用品的制品	**PREPARED FOODSTUFFS；BEVERAGES, SPIRITS AND VINEGAR；TOBACCO AND MANUFACTURED TOBACCO SUBSTITUTES**	**35.71**	**26.24**	**38.28**	**17.68**
16章　肉、鱼、甲壳动物、软体动物及其他水生无脊椎动物的制品	Preparations of meat，of fish or of crustaceans，molluscs or other aquatic invertebrates	12.34	0.06	14.03	0.05
17章　糖及糖食	Sugars and sugar confectionery	1.77	0.60	1.81	0.79
18章　可可及可可制品	Cocoa and cocoa preparations	0.27	0.35	0.34	0.29
19章　谷物、粮食粉、淀粉或乳的制品；糕饼点心	Preparations of cereals，flour，starch or milk；pastry-cooks' products	1.85	1.20	1.84	1.20

单位：亿美元
Unit: USD 100 million

商品分类	HS Section and Division	2016		2017	
		出口 Exports	进口 Imports	出口 Exports	进口 Imports
20章 蔬菜、水果、坚果或植物其他部分的制品	Preparations of vegetables, fruit，nuts or other parts of plants	10.66	2.67	10.89	2.72
21章 杂项食品	Miscellaneous edible preparations	3.85	3.73	4.27	4.36
22章 饮料、酒及醋	Beverages，spirits and vinegar	0.62	4.99	0.63	1.34
23章 食品工业的残渣及废料；配制的动物饲料	Residues and waste from the food industries；prepared animal fodder	4.21	10.83	4.34	5.22
24章 烟草及烟草代用品的制品	Tobacco and manufactured tobacco substitutes	0.13	1.82	0.13	1.70
第五类 矿产品	**MINERAL PRODUCTS**	**15.88**	**38.56**	**16.22**	**91.13**
25章 盐；硫磺；泥土及石料；石膏料、石灰及水泥	Salt；sulphur；earths and stone；plastering materials, lime and cement	3.14	2.27	3.47	3.21
26章 矿砂、矿渣及矿灰	Ores，slag and ash	0.06	12.29	0.16	15.13
27章 矿物燃料、矿物油及其蒸馏产品；沥青物质；矿物蜡	Mineral fuels，mineral oils and products of their distillation; bituminous substances; mineral waxes	12.67	24.01	12.59	72.79
第六类 化学工业及其相关工业的产品	**PRODUCTS OF THE CHEMICAL OR INDUSTRIES ALLIED**	**118.32**	**125.35**	**139.46**	**145.82**
28章 无机化学品；贵金属、稀土金属、放射性元素及其同位素的有机及无机化合物	Inorganic chemicals；organic or inorganic compounds of precious metals，of rare- earth metals, of radioactive elements or of isotopes	10.35	11.06	12.38	9.00
29章 有机化学品	Organic chemicals	57.92	30.19	74.48	36.71
30章 药品	Pharmaceutical products	13.03	25.80	12.57	33.76
31章 肥料	Fertilizers	2.59	0.36	1.06	0.56
32章 鞣料浸膏及染料浸膏；鞣酸及其衍生物；染料、颜料及其他着色料；油漆及清漆；油灰及其他类似胶粘剂；墨水、油墨	Tanning or dyeing extracts；tannins and their derivatives；dyes，pigments and other colouring matter；paints and varnishes；putty and other mastics；inks	5.22	4.84	5.45	4.99
33章 精油及香膏；芳香料制品及化妆盥洗品	Essential oils and retinoid；perfumery，cosmetic or toilet preparations	10.69	6.68	12.78	8.96
34章 肥皂、有机表面活性剂、洗涤剂、润滑剂、人造蜡、调制蜡、光洁剂、蜡烛及类似品、塑型用膏、“牙科用蜡”及牙科用熟石膏制剂	Soap，organic surface-active agents，washing preparations，lubricating preparations，artificial waxes，prepared waxes，polishing or scouring preparations，candles and similar articles，modelling pastes，“dental waxes” and dental preparations with a basis of plast	3.14	8.35	3.47	8.78
35章 蛋白类物质；改性淀粉；胶；酶	Albuminoidal substances；modified starches；glues；enzymes	2.35	4.23	2.92	4.88
36章 炸药；烟火制品；火柴；引火合金；易燃材料制品	Explosives；pyrotechnic products；matches；pyrophoric alloys；certain combustible preparations	2.94	0.88	2.81	0.58
37章 照相及电影用品	Photographic or cinematographic goods	0.35	5.04	0.31	5.11
38章 杂项化学产品	Miscellaneous chemical products	9.74	27.91	11.22	32.49
第七类 塑料及其制品，橡胶及其制品	**PLASTICS AND ARTICLES THEREOF RUBBER AND ARTICLES THEREOF**	**163.13**	**71.56**	**185.32**	**81.47**
39章 塑料及其制品	Plastics and articles thereof	131.04	60.84	153.15	69.73
40章 橡胶及其制品	Rubber and articles thereof	32.08	10.72	32.17	11.74
第八类 生皮、皮革、毛皮及其制品；鞍具及挽具；旅行用品、手提包及类似品；动物肠线(蚕胶丝除外)制品	**RAW HIDES AND SKINS，LEATHER，FUR SKINS AND ARTICLES THEREOF；SADDLERY AND HARNESS；TRAVEL GOODS，HANDBAGS AND SIMILAR CONTAINERS；ARTICLES OF ANIMAL GUT(OTHER THAN SILK-WORM GUT)**	**64.92**	**12.85**	**68.24**	**12.58**
41章 生皮(毛皮除外)及皮革	Raw hides and skins(other than fur skins) and leather	0.23	11.78	0.25	11.99

6-24 续表 2 Continued 2

单位：亿美元
Unit: USD 100 million

商品分类	HS Section and Division	2016 出口 Exports	2016 进口 Imports	2017 出口 Exports	2017 进口 Imports
42章 皮革制品；鞍具及挽具；旅行用品、手提包及类似容器；动物肠线(蚕胶丝除外)制品	Articles of leather；saddlery and harness；travel goods，hand bags and similar containers；articles of animal gut (other than silk-worm gut)	64.09	0.47	67.50	0.18
43章 毛皮、人造毛皮及其制品	Fur skins and artificial fur；manufactures thereof	0.59	0.60	0.48	0.41
第九类 木及木制品；木炭；软木及软木制品；稻草，秸秆、针茅或其他编结材料制品；篮筐及柳条编结品	**WOOD AND ARTICLES OF WOOD；WOOD CHAR-COAL；CORK AND ARTICLES OF CORK；MANUFACTURES OF STRAW，OF ESPARTO OR OF OTHER PLAITING MATERIALS；BASKET WARE AND WICKERWORK**	**41.16**	**25.16**	**39.88**	**30.70**
44章 木及木制品；木炭	Wood and articles of wood；wood charcoal	37.77	25.16	36.50	30.69
45章 软木及软木制品	Cork and articles of cork	0.07	0.00	0.06	0.00
46章 稻草、秸秆、针茅或其他编结材料制品；篮筐及柳条编结品	Manufactures of straw，of esparto or of other plaiting Materials；basket ware and wickerwork	3.32	0.00	3.31	0.00
第十类 木浆及其他纤维状纤维素浆；纸及纸板的废碎品；纸、纸板及其制品	**PULP OF WOOD OR OF OTHER FIBROUS CELLULOSIC MATERIAL；WASTE AND SCRAP OF PAPER OR PAPERBOARD；PAPER AND PAPERBOARD AND ARTICLES THEREOF**	**37.20**	**50.64**	**41.38**	**57.43**
47章 木浆及其他纤维状纤维素浆；纸及纸板的废碎品	Pulp of wood or of other fibrous cellulosic material；waste and scrap of paper or paperboard	0.02	37.95	0.07	43.73
48章 纸及纸板；纸浆、纸或纸板制品	Paper and paperboard；articles of paper pulp，of paper or paperboard	25.65	7.98	28.73	8.68
49章 书籍、报纸、印刷图画及其他印制品；手稿、打字稿及设计图纸	Printed books，newspapers，pictures and other products of the printing industry；manuscripts，typescripts and plans	11.53	4.71	12.59	5.02
第十一类 纺织原料及纺织制品	**TEXTILES AND TEXTILE ARTICLES**	**421.22**	**12.78**	**424.43**	**18.41**
50章 蚕丝	Silk	0.29	0.00	0.27	0.00
51章 羊毛、动物细毛或粗毛；马毛纱线及其机织物	Wool，fine or coarse animal hair；horsehair yarn and woven fabric	0.31	0.09	0.41	0.17
52章 棉花	Cotton	2.62	6.23	2.77	10.73
53章 其他植物纺织纤维；纸纱线及其机织物	Other vegetable textile fibres；paper yarn and woven fabrics of paper yarn	0.35	0.01	0.29	0.00
54章 化学纤维长丝	Man-made filaments	5.57	1.21	6.59	1.32
55章 化学纤维短纤	Man-made short fibres	4.84	1.14	4.58	2.04
56章 絮胎、毡呢及无纺织物；特种纱线；线、绳、索、缆及其制品	Wadding，felt and nonwoven；special yarns；twine，cordage，ropes and cables and articles thereof	6.19	1.69	6.77	1.81
57章 地毯及纺织材料的其他铺地制品	Carpets and other textile floor coverings	5.28	0.20	5.91	0.21
58章 特种机织物；簇绒织物；花边；装饰毯；装饰带；刺绣品	Special woven fabrics；tufted textile fabrics；lace；tapestries；trimmings；embroidery	3.70	0.21	3.68	0.21
59章 浸渍、涂布、包覆或层压的纺织物；工业用纺织制品	Impregnated，coated，covered or laminated textile fabrics；textile articles of a kind suitable for industrial use	5.70	0.98	6.31	1.19
60章 针织物及钩编织物	Knitted or crocheted fabrics	7.19	0.13	6.36	0.13
61章 针织或钩编的服装及衣着附件	Articles of apparel and clothing accessories，Knitted or crocheted	160.88	0.21	160.00	0.09
62章 非针织或非钩编的服装及衣着附件	Articles of apparel and clothing accessories，not knitted or crocheted	143.04	0.34	140.56	0.18

单位：亿美元
Unit: USD 100 million

商品分类	HS Section and Division	2016		2017	
		出口 Exports	进口 Imports	出口 Exports	进口 Imports
63章 其他纺织制成品；成套物品；旧衣着及旧纺织品；碎织物	Other made up textile articles；sets；worn clothing and worn textile articles；rags articles；rags	75.26	0.35	79.92	0.34
第十二类 鞋、帽、伞、杖、鞭及其零件；已加工的羽毛及其制品；人造花；人发制品	**FOOTWEAR，HEADGEAR，UMBRELLAS，SUN UMBRELLAS，WALKING-STICKS，SEAT-STICKS，WHIPS，RIDING-CROPS AND PARTS THEREOF；PREPARED FEATHERS AND ARTICLES MADE THEREWITH；ARTIFICIAL FLOWERS；ARTICLES OF HUMAN HAIR**	**158.18**	**1.26**	**159.63**	**1.16**
64章 鞋靴、护腿和类似品及其零件	Footwear，gaiters and the like；parts of such articles	121.38	1.12	119.79	1.02
65章 帽类及其零件	Headgear and parts thereof	12.03	0.03	12.07	0.05
66章 雨伞、阳伞、手杖、鞭子、马鞭及其零件	Umbrellas，sun umbrellas，walking-sticks，seat-sticks，whips，riding-crops and parts thereof	4.63	0.01	4.98	0.00
67章 已加工羽毛、羽绒及其制品；人造花；人发制品	Prepared feathers and down and articles made of feathers or of down；artificial flowers；articles of human hair	20.14	0.09	22.79	0.10
第十三类 石料、石膏、水泥、石棉、云母及类似材料的制品；陶瓷产品；玻璃及其制品	**ARTICLES OF STONE，PLASTER，CEMENT，ASBESTOS，MICA OR SIMILAR MATERIALS；CERAMIC PRODUCTS；GLASS AND GLASSWARE**	**63.61**	**12.90**	**73.38**	**12.53**
68章 石料、石膏、水泥、石棉、云母及类似材料的制品	Articles of stone，plaster，cement，asbestos，mica or similar materials；ceramic products；glass and glassware	14.64	2.21	18.58	2.55
69章 陶瓷产品	Ceramic products	23.85	1.02	27.76	1.25
70章 玻璃及其制品	Glass and glassware	25.11	9.67	27.03	8.72
第十四类 天然或养殖珍珠、宝石或半宝石、贵金属、包贵金属及其制品；仿首饰；硬币	**NATURAL OR CULTURED PEARLS，PRECIOUS OR SEMI-PRECIOUS STONES，PRECIOUS METALS，METALS CLAD WITH PRECIOUS METAL AND STONES，PRECIOUS METALS，METALS CLAD WITH PRECIOUS METAL AND ARTICLES THEREOF；IMITATION JEWELLERY；COIN**	**37.23**	**26.94**	**35.88**	**52.90**
71章 天然或养殖珍珠、宝石或半宝石、贵金属、包贵金属及其制品；仿首饰；硬币	Natural or cultured pearls，precious or semi-precious stones，precious metals，metals clad with precious metal and articles thereof；imitation jewellery；coin	37.23	26.94	35.88	52.90
第十五类 贱金属及其制品	**BASE METALS AND ARTICLES OF BASE METAL**	**196.95**	**45.95**	**225.10**	**54.67**
72章 钢铁	Iron and steel	5.36	2.25	5.98	3.69
73章 钢铁制品	Articles of iron or steel	89.60	10.40	102.03	11.73
74章 铜及其制品	Copper and articles thereof	3.83	12.86	4.41	16.56
75章 镍及其制品	Nickel and articles thereof	0.29	2.53	0.26	3.07
76章 铝及其制品	Aluminium and articles thereof	30.89	10.70	37.42	12.00
78章 铅及其制品	Lead and articles thereof	0.02	0.03	0.01	0.03
79章 锌及其制品	Zinc and articles thereof	0.34	0.26	0.37	0.23
80章 锡及其制品	Tin and articles thereof	0.03	0.03	0.01	0.03
81章 其他贱金属、金属陶瓷及其制品	Other base metals；cermets；articles thereof	3.03	2.87	4.10	2.91
82章 贱金属工具、器具、利口器、餐匙、餐叉及其零件	Tools，implements，cutlery，spoons and forks，of base metal；parts thereof of base metal	31.63	2.40	35.51	2.72
83章 贱金属杂项制品	Miscellaneous articles of base metal	31.94	1.62	35.01	1.70

6–24 续表 4 Continued 4

单位：亿美元
Unit: USD 100 million

商品分类	HS Section and Division	2016 出口 Exports	2016 进口 Imports	2017 出口 Exports	2017 进口 Imports
第十六类 机器、机械器具、电气设备及其零件；录音机及放声机、电视图像、声音的录制和重放设备及其零件、附件	**MACHINERY AND MECHANICAL APPLIANCES；ELECTRICAL EQUIPMENT；PARTS THEREOF；SOUND RECORDERS AND REPRODUCERS, TELEVISION IMAGE AND SOUND RECORDERS AND REPRODUCERS；AND PARTS AND CCESSORIES OF RECORDERS AND EPRODUCERS；AND PARTS AND ACCESSORIES OF SUCH ARTICLES**	**1724.46**	**303.29**	**1985.28**	**338.59**
84章 核反应堆、锅炉、机器、机械器具及其零件	Nuclear reactors，boilers，machinery and mechanical appliances；parts thereof	793.74	145.02	916.38	164.72
85章 电机、电气设备及其零件；录音机及放声机、电视图像、声音的录制和重放设备及其零件、附件	Electrical machinery and equipment and parts thereof；sound recorders and reproducers，television image and sound recorders and reproducers，and parts and accessories of such articles	930.72	158.27	1068.90	173.87
第十七类 车辆、航空器、船舶及有关运输设备	**VEHICLES，AIRCRAFT，VESSELS AND ASSOCIATED TRANSPORT EQUIPMENT**	**168.04**	**273.49**	**196.81**	**292.31**
86章 铁道及电车道机车、车辆及其零件；铁道及电车轨道固定装置及其零件、附件；各种机械(包括电动机械)交通信号设备	Railway or tramway locomotives，rolling-stock and parts thereof；railway or tramway track fixtures and fittings and parts thereof；mechanical(including electro-mechanical) traffic signalling equipment of all kinds	14.78	0.49	31.85	0.38
87章 车辆及其零件、附件，但铁道及电车道车辆除外	Vehicles other than railway or tramway rolling-stock，and parts and accessories thereof	138.95	139.84	151.17	150.94
88章 航空器、航天器及其零件	Aircraft，spacecraft，and parts thereof	11.12	132.85	12.58	140.63
89章 船舶及浮动结构体	Ships，boats and floating structures	3.18	0.31	1.20	0.36
第十八类 光学、照相、电影、计量、检验、医疗或外科用仪器及设备、精密仪器及设备；钟表；乐器；上述物品的零件、附件	**OPTICAL，PHOTOGRAPHIC，CINEMATOGRAPHIC，MEASURING，CHECKING，PRECISION，MEDICAL OR SURGICAL INSTRUMENTS AND APPARATUS；CLOCKS AND WATCHES；MUSICAL INSTRUMENTS；PARTS AND ACCESSORIES THEREOF**	**108.80**	**112.15**	**106.39**	**117.60**
90章 光学、照相、电影、计量、检验、医疗或外科用仪器及设备、精密仪器及设备；上述物品的零件、附件	Optical，photographic，cinematographic，measuring，checking，precision medical or surgical instruments and apparatus；parts and accessories thereof	98.37	111.86	96.72	117.34
91章 钟表及其零件	Clocks and watches and parts thereof	5.57	0.12	4.88	0.03
92章 乐器及其零件、附件	Musical instruments；parts and accessories of such articles	4.86	0.17	4.78	0.24
第十九类 武器、弹药及其零件、附件	**ARMS AND AMMUNITION；PARTS AND ACCESSORIES THEREOF**	**0.88**	**0.01**	**0.82**	**0.01**
93章 武器、弹药及其零件、附件	Arms and ammunition；parts and accessories thereof	0.88	0.01	0.82	0.01
第二十类 杂项制品	**MISCELLANEOUS MANUFACTURED ARTICLES**	**453.60**	**5.65**	**510.32**	**5.37**
94章 家具；寝具、褥垫、弹簧床垫、软坐垫及类似的填充制品；未列名灯具及照明装置；发光标志、发光名牌及类似品；活动房屋	Furniture；bedding，mattresses，mattress supports，cushions and similar stuffed furnishings；lamps and lighting fittings，not elsewhere specified or included；illuminated signs，illuminated	273.26	2.99	291.89	2.72
95章 玩具、游戏品、运动用品及其零件、附件	Toys，games and sports requisites；parts and accessories thereof	147.59	1.54	186.08	1.70
96章 杂项制品	Miscellaneous manufactured articles	32.75	1.11	32.34	0.95
第二十一类 艺术品、收藏品及古物	**WORKS OF ART，COLLECTORS' PIECES AND ANTIQUES**	**0.55**	**0.20**	**0.40**	**0.11**
97章 艺术品、收藏品及古物	Works of art，collectors' pieces and antiques	0.55	0.20	0.40	0.11
第二十二类 特殊交易品及未分类商品	**COMMODITIES AND TRANSACTIONS NOT CLASSIFIED ACCORDING TO KIND**	**2.56**	**2.35**	**13.24**	**7.45**
98章 特殊交易品及未分类商品	Commodities and transactions not classified according to kind	2.56	2.35	13.24	7.45

6-25 我国同各国(地区)海关进出口总额

China's Foreign Trade with Related Countries and Territories

单位：万美元

Unit: USD 10000

国别（地区）	Region	2016		2017	
		出口总额 Exports	进口总额 Imports	出口总额 Exports	进口总额 Imports
总　计	**Total**	**209763119**	**158792622**	**226337133**	**184379294**
亚洲	**Asia**	**104111685**	**90579344**	**109634007**	**103018441**
阿富汗	Afghanistan	43129	453	54121	343
巴林	Bahrain	79080	6372	90252	12395
孟加拉国	Bangladesh	1430223	86940	1516902	87515
不丹	Bhutan	485	13	624	18
文莱	Brunei	51103	22155	63759	35181
缅甸	Myanmar	818868	409771	894846	452635
柬埔寨	Cambodia	393016	83051	478320	100758
塞浦路斯	Cyprus	46236	4779	52431	5334
朝鲜	Korea DPR	308054	257246	324510	173099
中国香港	Hong Kong, China	28725302	1670067	27921137	731718
印度	India	5841534	1176413	6804225	1634537
印度尼西亚	Indonesia	3212613	2141404	3475739	2857431
伊朗	Iran	1641866	1482719	1858482	1855369
伊拉克	Iraq	754818	1066327	833042	1381411
以色列	Israel	818106	317290	891847	420624
日本	Japan	12941000	14567069	13725893	16579401
约旦	Jordan	295483	21116	280361	27919
科威特	Kuwait	300179	637028	311277	893495
老挝	Laos	98710	135961	141935	160500
黎巴嫩	Lebanon	210071	1767	201061	2304
中国澳门	Macao, China	314118	14034	316895	10400
马来西亚	Malaysia	3767178	4926964	4171228	5442614
马尔代夫	Maldives	32094	24	29563	62
蒙古	Mongolia	98864	362260	123561	516731
尼泊尔	Nepal	86627	2241	96696	1785
阿曼	Oman	214809	1204102	231645	1338328
巴基斯坦	Pakistan	1723446	191259	1825079	183322
巴勒斯坦	Palestine	5931	31	6906	12
菲律宾	Philippines	2984267	1739589	3206593	1923918
卡塔尔	Qatar	151637	401237	168233	640027
沙特阿拉伯	Saudi Arabia	1865528	2362602	1837501	3176187
新加坡	Singapore	4451167	2601425	4501930	3424962
韩国	Korea Rep.	9372895	15897453	10270378	17755315
斯里兰卡	Sri Lanka	428833	27344	408800	31003
叙利亚	Syria	91535	326	110281	133
泰国	Thailand	3719508	3853234	3854173	4159608
土耳其	Turkey	1668951	278542	1812151	378343
阿联酋	United Arab Emirates	3007253	999436	2872397	1231116
也门共和国	Republic of Yemen	169241	16603	164304	65996
越南	Vietnam	6110413	3717160	7161725	5037462
中华人民共和国	P. R. China		12802993		13236937
中国台湾	Taiwan, China	4024120	13884723	4397853	15596059
东帝汶	Timor Leste	16432	29	13260	157
哈萨克斯坦	Kazakhstan	829259	480508	1156444	637869
吉尔吉斯斯坦	Kirghizia	560546	7124	533681	8706

6-25 续表 1 Continued 1

单位：万美元
Unit: USD 10000

国 别（地 区）	Region	2016 出口总额 Exports	2016 进口总额 Imports	2017 出口总额 Exports	2017 进口总额 Imports
塔吉克斯坦	Tadzhikistan	172510	3125	130138	4674
土库曼斯坦	Turkmenistan	33848	556330	36812	657513
乌兹别克斯坦	Uzbekistan	200755	160706	274942	147145
亚洲其他国家(地区)	Other Countries (Regions) in Asia	51	0.2	79	71
非洲	**Africa**	**9227200**	**5668990**	**9471762**	**7592715**
阿尔及利亚	Algeria	764811	33189	678475	44832
安哥拉	Angola	168065	1396612	225745	2069871
贝宁	Benin	203950	5539	192651	9159
博茨瓦那	Botswana	20973	6214	23270	3355
布隆迪	Burundi	4506	274	4525	693
喀麦隆	Cameroon	155725	40223	138861	50850
加那利群岛	Canary Is.	402	1	334	27
佛得角	Cape Verde	4870	8	6924	1
中非	Central Africa	1547	3157	1296	2811
塞卜泰(休达)	Ceuta	99		30	0
乍得	Chad	9359	11491	11536	27991
科摩罗	Comoros	4840	1	6776	4
刚果(布)	Congo	74068	233300	49784	396207
吉布提	Djibouti	214844	13	217541	2
埃及	Egypt	1043728	55321	948564	134193
赤道几内亚	Eq. Guinea	14829	63185	16622	148384
埃塞俄比亚	Ethiopia	321469	41942	266456	35758
加蓬	Gabon	37724	143908	44619	229361
冈比亚	Gambia	31511	9010	39865	9905
加纳	Ghana	466703	130965	482480	185294
几内亚	Guinea	114450	63006	123996	146675
几内亚比绍	Guinea-Bissau	2125	16	3372	40
科特迪瓦共和国	Cote d'lvoire	158469	10138	169255	15791
肯尼亚	Kenya	558800	9714	503465	16682
利比里亚	Liberia	159269	4817	210367	2886
利比亚	Libya	118476	34562	102797	136266
马达加斯加	Madagascar	94314	16079	100749	22709
马拉维	Malawi	22828	2612	26194	2733
马里	Mali	36673	9870	33725	6788
毛里塔尼亚	Mauritania	86974	74756	85915	78651
毛里求斯	Mauritius	75877	1971	76215	2244
摩洛哥	Morocco	307918	55346	317623	65060
莫桑比克	Mozambique	130871	47936	130675	52872
纳米比亚	Namibia	26869	16579	27214	29754
尼日尔	Niger	10080	12424	9788	9908
尼日利亚	Nigeria	971533	90701	1215316	162405
留尼汪	Reunion	17302	1	15352	3
卢旺达	Rwanda	10860	3314	12867	2888
圣多美和普林西比	Sao Tome & Principe	641	2	690	0.1
塞内加尔	Senegal	219450	16159	204071	14970
塞舌尔	Seychelles	5573	8	4882	147
塞拉利昂	Sierra Leone	24220	23956	24243	33802
索马里	Somalia	39196	1096	47350	1180
南非	South Africa	1285352	2222889	1480877	2438860
西撒哈拉	Western Sahara	19	0	179	0

6-25 续表 2 Continued 2

单位：万美元
Unit: USD 10000

国 别（地 区）	Region	2016		2017	
		出口总额 Exports	进口总额 Imports	出口总额 Exports	进口总额 Imports
苏丹	Sudan	212984	50471	222176	59080
坦桑尼亚	Tanzania	356712	31583	311955	33586
多哥	Togo	191930	10533	188635	7319
突尼斯	Tunisia	129613	13885	132799	19816
乌干达	Uganda	82390	3762	77737	3341
布基纳法索	Burkina Faso	14109	1400	18305	2044
刚果(金)	Congo DR	99258	208496	96998	328999
赞比亚	Zambia	49022	218350	70947	312275
津巴布韦	Zimbabwe	38772	72688	44382	87203
莱索托	Lesotho	5472	1964	6130	2485
梅利利亚	Melilla	1052		1032	0.1
斯威士兰	Swaziland	4246	33	3423	434
厄立特里亚	Eritrea	6933	17548	4295	17069
马约特岛	Mayotte	3826		4151	1
南苏丹共和国	Republic of South Sudan	4627	145975	5194	127005
非洲其他国家(地区)	Other Countries (Regions) in Africa	4094	2	75	48
欧洲	**Europe**	**38991655**	**28784681**	**42897540**	**32713136**
比利时	Belgium	1473612	687406	1573812	754990
丹麦	Denmark	541321	423815	651102	421178
英国	United Kingdom	5572079	1868145	5671352	2232896
德国	Germany	6525905	8610903	7113440	9694011
法国	France	2468616	2250332	2766510	2679734
爱尔兰	Ireland	278037	529698	291263	811793
意大利	Italy	2638835	1671319	2919996	2049794
卢森堡	Luxembourg	125566	30557	70094	30804
荷兰	Netherlands	5745937	980980	6713167	1127204
希腊	Greece	420269	28311	475138	43004
葡萄牙	Portugal	400428	158282	344522	213918
西班牙	Spain	2132043	613575	2291494	802777
阿尔巴尼亚	Albania	50672	12860	45403	19622
安道尔	Andorra	131	11	127	10
奥地利	Austria	224287	502654	252713	586591
保加利亚	Bulgaria	105654	59011	116905	96918
芬兰	Finland	287858	345505	284570	425933
直布罗陀	Gibraltar	723	0.2	397	4
匈牙利	Hungary	542517	346423	604935	407722
冰岛	Iceland	13473	9439	11183	11009
列支敦士登	Liechtenstein	3725	11177	4623	12659
马耳他	Malta	156602	40013	209594	41091
摩纳哥	Monaco	1326	760	1326	754
挪威	Norway	260562	323067	248899	312926
波兰	Poland	1510002	253772	1787305	335351
罗马尼亚	Romania	344872	145522	377796	182432
圣马力诺	San Marino	479	665	555	314
瑞典	Sweden	631928	615769	702573	788382
瑞士	Switzerland	316930	3983367	316050	3289242
爱沙尼亚	Estonia	96417	21179	100635	26034
拉脱维亚	Latvia	106272	13221	114824	17724
立陶宛	Lithuania	129167	16401	160027	25515
格鲁吉亚	Georgia	74544	5356	91262	6759

6–25 续表 3 Continued 3

单位：万美元
Unit: USD 10000

国别（地区）	Region	2016 出口总额 Exports	2016 进口总额 Imports	2017 出口总额 Exports	2017 进口总额 Imports
亚美尼亚	Armenia	11119	28062	14385	30268
阿塞拜疆	Azerbaijan	34600	41208	38697	57745
白俄罗斯	Byelorussia	109017	43519	93336	51538
摩尔多瓦	Moldavia	7681	2437	9792	3396
俄罗斯	Russia	3735577	3226015	4283060	4139029
乌克兰	Ukraine	422023	249080	504065	233964
斯洛文尼亚	Slovenia	227026	43686	288693	49535
克罗地亚	Croatia	101724	16144	115964	18308
捷克	Czech	806175	295154	879297	369571
斯洛伐克	Slovak	286234	241017	272948	258496
马其顿	Macedonia	9014	4671	7804	8669
波黑	Bosnia & Herzegovina	6413	4355	7882	5725
梵蒂冈城国	Vatican City State	29	3	8	
法罗群岛	Faroe Islands	174	10311	207	9980
塞尔维亚	Serbia	43224	16270	54564	21159
黑山	Montenegro	10835	3258	13246	6640
欧洲其他国家(地区)	Other Countries (Regions) in Europe	1	0.1	1	17
拉丁美洲	**Latin America**	**11393614**	**10307123**	**13081617**	**12777394**
安提瓜和巴布达	Antigua and Barbuda	13345	4	4487	1
阿根廷	Argentina	720370	511810	906721	475423
阿鲁巴岛	Aruba	2529	38	2430	1
巴哈马	Bahamas	35956	5160	27849	2101
巴巴多斯	Barbados	7243	1864	10780	2477
伯利兹	Belize	8999	94	8725	41
玻利维亚	Bolivia	61055	32609	72917	35458
博内尔	Bonaire	67	0	112	0.1
巴西	Brazil	2197927	4585505	2895054	5885716
开曼群岛	Cayman Is.	16911	2	25697	1
智利	Chile	1280674	1860496	1440985	2117553
哥伦比亚	Colombia	675612	254463	743975	388544
多米尼克	Dominica	3377	99	4913	71
哥斯达黎加	Costa Rica	149530	69741	149508	79162
古巴	Cuba	178311	27375	135704	39799
库腊索岛	Curacao	2315	0.3	2969	1
多米尼加共和国	Dominica Rep.	156721	13026	170295	16759
厄瓜多尔	Ecuador	225803	93992	296321	112774
法属圭亚那	French Guyana	1314	5	1581	21
格林纳达	Granada	734	1	1070	1
瓜德罗普岛	Guadeloupe	3358	1	3760	1
危地马拉	Guatemala	185561	10007	195940	10684
圭亚那	Guyana	17836	2826	18864	3839
海地	Haiti	45403	639	53257	761
洪都拉斯	Honduras	72067	2785	84482	2394
牙买加	Jamaica	50614	1573	51657	4809
马提尼克岛	Martinique	2364	2	2716	6
墨西哥	Mexico	3236742	1032474	3590539	1180324
蒙特塞拉特	Montserrat	34	1	22	5
尼加拉瓜	Nicaragua	62421	1789	62414	2840
巴拿马	Panama	634409	3765	662697	6203
巴拉圭	Paraguay	116971	2238	156056	3302
秘鲁	Peru	599156	949081	695887	1336737
波多黎各	Puerto Rico	59616	67499	59777	49634
萨巴	Saba	6		1	0

6-25 续表 4 Continued 4

单位：万美元
Unit: USD 10000

国别（地区）	Region	2016 出口总额 Exports	2016 进口总额 Imports	2017 出口总额 Exports	2017 进口总额 Imports
圣卢西亚	Saint Lucia	1695	4	1592	6
圣马丁岛	Saint Martin Is.	682	0	955	0
圣文森特和格林纳丁斯	Saint Vincent & Grenadines	1748	6	4209	44
萨尔瓦多	El Salvador	77233	4583	77255	11637
苏里南	Surinam	13673	2929	17755	2624
特立尼达和多巴哥	Trinidad and Tobago	34636	17494	42989	18233
特克斯和凯科斯群岛	Turks & Caicos Is.	91		272	0.3
乌拉圭	Uruguay	177325	194810	215152	265022
委内瑞拉	Venezuela	251954	556282	174641	721992
英属维尔京群岛	Virgin Is. (E)	3713	1	1184	11
圣其茨–尼维斯	St. Kitts-Nevis	420	44	869	70
圣皮埃尔和密克隆	St. Pierre and Miquelon	1		4	3
荷属安地列斯群岛	Andreas Is. (N)	4937	10	4433	5
拉美其他国家(地区)	Other Countries (Regions) in Latin America	156		147	307
北美洲	**North America**	**41284094**	**15288329**	**46124082**	**17450192**
加拿大	Canada	2733885	1833683	3137546	2042301
美国	United States	38527101	13444514	42973038	15394552
格陵兰	Greenland	57	10120	249	13338
百慕大群岛	Bermuda	23025	7	13202	1
北美洲其他国家(地区)	Other Countries (Regions) in North America	26	4	47	
大洋洲及太平洋群岛	**Oceanic and Pacific Islands**	**4754871**	**8061357**	**5126407**	**10789470**
澳大利亚	Australia	3732740	7089501	4143823	9500912
库克群岛	Cook Islands	322	120	742	577
斐济	Fiji	38405	1718	36550	1752
盖比群岛	Gambier Is.	0.4		3	0
瑙鲁	Nauru	141	2	42	28
新喀里多尼亚	New Caledonia (Fr)	8566	50353	8533	79467
瓦努阿图	Vanuatu	6374	501	6559	1424
新西兰	New Zealand	476828	714063	510010	939110
诺福克岛	Norfolk Islands	261	0.3	223	0.1
巴布亚新几内亚	Papua New Guinea	64805	163069	77499	207033
社会群岛	Society Is.	281		305	
所罗门群岛	Solomon Is.	8656	37627	9258	55482
汤加	Tonga	3033	2	2794	58
土阿莫土群岛	Tuamotu Archipelago		0.1		
萨摩亚	Samoa	6959	80	6388	53
基里巴斯	Kiribati	2487	949	1540	41
图瓦卢	Tuvalu	563	3	1835	1
密克罗尼西亚联邦	Micronesia Commonwealth	1418	689	2629	1166
马绍尔群岛共和国	Marshall. Is.	395078	2008	309641	1827
帕劳共和国	Republic of Palau	1918	4	1683	0.1
法属波利尼西亚	Polynesia (F)	5175	665	5932	541
瓦利斯和浮图纳	Wallis and Futuna	77	0	30	0
大洋洲其他国家(地区)	Other Countries (Regions) in Oceania	785	0	388	
国别（地区)不详	**Others**	**1**	**102800**	**1717**	**37946**
东南亚国家联盟	**ASEAN**	**25606841**	**19630714**	**27950248**	**23595068**
欧洲联盟	**EU**	**33925619**	**20813570**	**37203099**	**24497040**
亚太经济合作组织	**APEC**	**133747074**	**108137132**	**143602794**	**123638158**

6–26 主要出口商品数量和金额
Major Export Commodities in Quantity and Value

单位：万美元

Unit: USD 10000

商　品	Commodities	单　位	Unit	数量 Quantity		金额 Value	
				2016	2017	2016	2017
活猪(种猪除外)	Live Hogs	万头	10000 heads	155	157	51303	45015
活家禽	Live Poultry	万只	10000 heads	440	230	1532	223
牛肉	Beef	吨	tn	4143	922	4026	790
猪肉	Pork	万吨	10000 tn	5	5	25357	25857
冻鸡	Frozen Chicken	万吨	10000 tn	12	13	23134	24135
水海产品	Aquatic Products	万吨	10000 tn	409	421	1999627	2040740
鲜蛋	Fresh Eggs	百万个	million pc.	1303	1369	11878	11384
谷物及谷物粉	Cereals and Cereals Flour	万吨	10000 tn	67	156	48921	75656
#稻谷和大米	Rice	万吨	10000 tn	48	120	37893	59685
玉米	Maize	吨	tn	4071	85921	288	2224
蔬菜	Vegetables	万吨	10000 tn	827	925	1229467	1315237
#鲜或冷藏蔬菜	Fresh Vegetables	万吨	10000 tn	538	621	540698	530850
橘、橙	Mandarins and Oranges	吨	tn	723683	561681	103679	83597
苹果	Apples	吨	tn	1339079	1334636	146586	145637
松子仁	Pine nut Kernels	吨	tn	13771	16153	27216	24325
大豆	Soybean	万吨	10000 tn	13	11	10843	9116
花生及花生仁	Peanuts	万吨	10000 tn	12	15	19118	22479
食用植物油(含棕榈油)	Edible Vegetable Oil	吨	tn	126048	200055	16822	22970
食糖	Sugar	吨	tn	149052	157933	8318	9059
天然蜂蜜	Natural Honey	吨	tn	128330	129274	27656	27071
茶叶	Tea	吨	tn	328699	355258	148502	160996
辣椒干	Dried Chillies	吨	tn	80202	61716	15810	12148
猪肉罐头	Canned Pork	吨	tn	38963	43095	12168	13210
蘑菇罐头	Canned Mushroom	吨	tn	236456	226418	40119	38471
啤酒	Beer	万升	10000 liters	29158	36095	19273	22760
肠衣	Casings	吨	tn	96537	105955	107292	134741
填充用羽毛及羽绒	Feathers and Dawn for Stuffing	吨	tn	43678	53376	43152	63085
中药材及中式成药	Medical Materials and Medicaments of Chinese Type	吨	tn	151930	155553	123801	121802
烤烟	Flue-cured Tobacco	吨	tn	119950	146865	47177	51415

6-26 续表 1 Continued 1

单位：万美元
Unit: USD 10000

商 品	Commodities	单 位	Unit	数量 Quantity 2016	2017	金额 Value 2016	2017
纸烟	Cigarette	万条	10000 items	13976	12468	63475	57578
锯材	Wood Sawn	万立方米	10000 cu.m	26	28	19323	20208
生丝	Raw Silk	吨	tn	6927	5936	31568	32809
山羊绒	Cashmere	吨	tn	2995	3072	19700	18891
棉花	Cotton	吨	tn	7757	17083	1525	3358
天然石墨	Natural Graphite	万吨	10000 tn	24	34	22848	26570
天然碳酸镁及氧化镁	Magnesian Ores	万吨	10000 tn	200	288	46695	62772
萤石(氟石)	Fluorite	万吨	10000 tn	37	34	8826	8307
天然硫酸钡(重晶石)	Barite	万吨	10000 tn	160	202	18559	20421
滑石	Talcum	万吨	10000 tn	76	70	18471	16295
氧化铝	Aluminium Oxide	吨	tn	105517	55737	6560	5633
煤及褐煤	Coal and Lignite	万吨	10000 tn	879	817	69836	110394
焦炭及半焦炭	Coke and Semi-coke	万吨	10000 tn	1012	809	143210	215953
原油	Crude Oil	万吨	10000 tn	294	486	94349	182237
成品油	Petroleum Products Refined	万吨	10000 tn	4831	5216	1939585	2539869
石蜡	Paraffin Wax	万吨	10000 tn	64	52	58801	51142
仲钨酸铵	Tungstate	吨	tn	3545	5427	5925	10646
氧化锌及过氧化锌	Zinc Oxide and Zinc Peroxide	吨	tn	15751	13405	2914	3493
合成有机染料	Synthetic Organic Dyestuffs	吨	tn	259114	257382	143937	139165
医药品	Medical and Pharmaceutical Products	吨	tn	945197	1012529	1360481	1508363
#中式成药	Medicaments of Chinese Type	吨	tn	11435	12330	22456	25004
医用敷料	Pharmaceutical Goods	吨	tn	185370	204198	129510	134650
洗衣粉	Detergent	吨	tn	534185	535383	33028	32917
烟花、爆竹	Fireworks and Firecrackers	吨	tn	313926	323410	73218	71996
松香及树脂酸	Resin and Resin Acids	吨	tn	59720	56609	10644	10088
新的充气橡胶轮胎	Rubber Tyres	万条	10000 pc.	46868	48351	1289551	1416302
纸及纸板(未切成形的)	Paper and Paperboard in Rolls	万吨	10000 tn	683	652	776688	745177
棉纱线	Cotton Yarn	吨	tn	355657	393512	155401	165496
丝织物	Silk and Satins					64497	61556
棉机织物	Cotton Cloth					1381244	1392890
亚麻及苎麻机织物	Flax or Ramie Cloth	万米	10000 m	24568	27275	75112	76429
合成短纤与棉混纺机织物	Polyester Cotton Cloth	万米	10000 m	195459	173908	258569	202047
地毯	Carpets	万平方米	10 000 sq.m	52442	58498	252299	270342

6-26 续表 2 Continued 2

单位：万美元

Unit: USD 10000

商　品	Commodities	单　位	Unit	数量 Quantity		金额 Value	
				2016	2017	2016	2017
塑料编织袋	Bags of PP or PE Strip	万条	10000 pc.	703791	656350	95113	97091
水泥及水泥熟料	Cement	万吨	10000 tn	1785	1286	69044	57793
平板玻璃	Plate Glass	万平方米	10000 sq.m	22661	21032	154684	145061
玻璃制品	Glass Products	万吨	10000tn	368	387	618790	639752
家用陶瓷器皿	Porcelain and Pottery Ware for Household Use	万吨	10000 tn	314	344	839792	1004751
生铁及镜铁	Pig Iron and Spiegel	万吨	10000 tn	13	9	2797	2263
钢坯及粗锻件	Billet and Crude Forgings	万吨	10000 tn	1	1	743	701
钢材	Rolled Steel	万吨	10000 tn	10853	7541	5448866	5450430
未锻轧铜及铜合金	Unwrought Copper an its Alloys	吨	tn	428520	338034	208076	205761
铜材	Rolled Copper	吨	tn	452313	477989	306576	370463
未锻轧铝及铝合金	Unwrought Aluminium and its Alloys	万吨	10000 tn	51	55	94142	106449
铝材	Rolled Aluminium	万吨	10000 tn	407	424	1143073	1202600
未锻轧的锌及锌合金	Zinc and Zinc Alloys	吨	tn	22642	16445	4730	4783
未锻轧的锡及锡合金	Tin and Tin Alloys	吨	tn	736	2181	1154	2054
未锻轧的锑、粉末及废碎料	Antimony	吨	tn	5817	2890	3570	1937
未锻轧的锰	Manganese	吨	tn	331115	435618	52841	78125
钢铁或铜制标准紧固件	Nails, Bolts,etc	万吨	10000 tn	276	292	463856	515784
手用或机用工具	Hand Tools and Tools for Machines	万吨	10000 tn	152	170	921430	1028643
电扇	Fans	万台	10000 sets	61584	69345	465896	501027
纺织机械及零件	Textile Machinery					298111	344813
缝纫机(包括工业用)	Sewing Machines (Including Industrial Use)	万台	10000 sets	1112	1089	124375	125483
金属加工机床	Machine Tools	万台	10000 sets	831	911	295122	328434
电子计算器	Electric calculator	万台	10000 sets	20639	20186	40701	37724
自动数据处理设备及其部件	Automatic Data Processing Machines and Components	万台	10000 sets	159189	154208	13736991	15824130
自动数据处理设备的零件	Parts for Auto Data Processing Equipment	万吨	10000 tn	52	51	2500897	3307654
轴承	Bearings	万套	10000 pc.	539651	595727	350791	386522
电动机及发电机	Electric Motors and Generators	万台	10000 sets	290624	278218	1045909	1079164
静止式变流器	Static Converters	万个	10000 pc.	516056	543586	1635275	1707272
原电池	Primary Cells and Batteries	百万个	million pc.	27855	29461	200384	204450
蓄电池	Electric Accumulators	万个	10000 pc.	227917	245965	994258	1125137
电话机	Telephone Sets	万台	10000 sets	136405	129498	11708244	12744483
收音设备(包括收录音组合机及整套散件)	Radio Sets(Including Sound Recording Apparatus)	万台	10000 sets	21869	22891	475990	444039

6–26 续表 3 Continued 3

单位：万美元
Unit: USD 10000

商 品	Commodities	单 位 Unit	数量 Quantity 2016	数量 Quantity 2017	金额 Value 2016	金额 Value 2017
彩色电视机	TV Sets	万台 10000 sets	8029	8151	1224574	1386746
电容器	Electrical Capacitors				391275	397501
通断保护电路装置及零件	Electrical apparatus for switching or protecting electrical circuits	吨 tn	23672656	25031508	2473457	2706524
二极管及类似半导体器件	Semi Conductors	百万个 million pc.	702567	595264	2425147	2415575
电线和电缆	Insulated Wire or Cable	万吨 10000 tn	224	241	1961758	2068073
集装箱	Containers	万个 10000 units	199	300	422856	838392
汽车	Motor Vehicles	万辆 10000 units	73	104	1068747	1327352
自行车	Bicycles	万辆 10000 units	5757	5640	309431	310989
照相机	Cameras	万架 10000 sets	3805	3760	248316	280586
医疗仪器及器械	Medical Instruments and Appliances				936286	1006220
手表	Wrist Watches	万只 10000 pc.	61148	68134	254354	238744
日用钟	Clocks	万只 10000 sets	28714	26482	92582	81457
家具及其零件	Furniture				4778219	4992232
非针织钩编织物服装	Garments (Excluding Knitwear and Crochet)				6476269	6641636
针织或钩编的服装	Garments, Knitted or Crocheted				6502509	6190262
皮面鞋	Leather Shoes	万双 10000 pairs	69039	68232	962176	930115
橡胶或塑料底纺织材料为面的鞋	Cloth Shoes With Outer of Rubber or Artificial Plastic Materials(including Gym Shoes)	万双 10000 pairs	266940	287561	1241048	1340033
塑料制品	Plastic Articles	万吨 10000 tn	1041	1168	3568771	3877201
玩具	Toys				1838261	2394188
足球、篮球、排球	Footballs、Basketballs and Volleyballs	万个 10000 pc.	23044	22607	48396	45578
伞	Umbrellas	万把 10000 pc.	43716	46292	245594	234776
竹编结品	Bamboo Products	吨 tn	25552	28853	14165	16664
藤编结品	Rattan Products	吨 tn	8261	8500	6219	5940
草编结品	Straw Products	吨 tn	16012	16561	11614	12430
柳编结品	Wickerwork	吨 tn	50474	51072	44469	44880
机电产品	**Mechanical and Electrical Products**				**120905590**	**132146261**
高新技术产品	**High and New-technology Products**				**60357347**	**66744367**

6–27 主要进口商品数量和金额
Major Import Commodities in Quantity and Value

单位：万美元
Unit: USD 10000

商　品	Commodities	单 位	Unit	数量 Quantity		金额 Value	
				2016	2017	2016	2017
谷物及谷物粉	Cereals and Cereals Flour	万吨	10000 tn	2199	2559	570524	648524
#玉米	Maize	万吨	10000 tn	317	283	63856	60337
小麦	Wheat	万吨	10000 tn	341	442	81585	108252
稻谷和大米	Rice	万吨	10000 tn	356	403	161428	186000
大豆	Soybean	万吨	10000 tn	8391	9553	3398115	3963765
食用植物油(含棕榈油)	Edible Vegetable Oil	万吨	10000 tn	553	577	416394	453056
食糖	Sugar	万吨	10000 tn	306	229	117056	107848
天然橡胶(包括胶乳)	Natural Rubber	万吨	10000 tn	250	279	335460	491702
合成橡胶(包括胶乳)	Synthetic Rubber	万吨	10000 tn	331	436	535603	847274
原木	Logs	万立方米	10000 cu.m	4873	5540	808519	992068
锯材	Wood Sawn	万立方米	10000 cu.m	3150	3739	813776	1006549
纸浆	Paper Pulp	万吨	10000 tn	2107	2372	1224071	1534167
羊毛及毛条	Wool and Wool Tops	万吨	10000 tn	32	35	238729	279948
棉花	Cotton, not Carded or Combed	万吨	10000 tn	90	116	157008	218977
纺织用合成纤维	Synthetic Fiber Suitable for Spinning	万吨	10000 tn	32	40	71628	89146
#聚酯纤维	Polyester Fiber	万吨	10000 tn	12	16	16896	23024
聚丙烯腈纤维	Polyacrylonitrile Fiber	万吨	10000 tn	14	15	30047	34378
铁矿砂及其精矿	Iron Ore	万吨	10000 tn	102395	107474	5803258	7627780
锰矿砂及其精矿	Manganese Ores	万吨	10000 tn	1705	2126	207464	400563
铜矿砂及其精矿	Copper Ores	万吨	10000 tn	1696	1735	2088805	2638571
铬矿砂及其精矿	Chromium Ores	万吨	10000 tn	1058	1385	161853	344181
氧化铝	Aluminium Oxide	万吨	10000 tn	303	287	87205	110096
煤及褐煤	Coal and Lignite	万吨	10000 tn	25543	27090	1415193	2263671
原油	Crude Oil	万吨	10000 tn	38101	41957	11666075	16232843
成品油	Petroleum Products Refined	万吨	10000 tn	2784	2964	1115737	1448563
乙二醇	Ethylene Glycol	万吨	10000 tn	752	872	485077	738983
对苯二甲酸	Terephthalic Acid	万吨	10000 tn	50	54	30243	35293
己内酰胺	CPL	万吨	10000 tn	22	24	27785	42946
医药品	Pharmaceutical Products	万吨	10000 tn	12	14	2209492	2679557
肥料	Fertilizer	万吨	10000 tn	832	918	240445	233967

6-27 续表 Continued

单位：万美元
Unit: USD 10000

商品	Commodities	单位	Unit	数量 Quantity 2016	数量 Quantity 2017	金额 Value 2016	金额 Value 2017
#尿素	Urea	吨	tn	65794	114655	1595	2989
氮、磷、钾复合肥	Compound Fertilizers of Nitrogen, Phosphor and Kalium	万吨	10000 tn	113	111	55426	46129
磷酸氢二胺	Diammonium Phosphate	万吨	10000 tn	3		1426	3
氯化钾	Potassium Chloride	万吨	10000 tn	682	753	172178	171426
初级形状的聚乙烯	Polyethylene in primary Forms	万吨	10000 tn	733	877	851159	1056508
初级形状的聚丙烯	Polypropylene in Primary Forms	万吨	10000 tn	302	318	352594	384386
初级形状的苯乙烯聚合物	Polystyrene in Primary Forms	万吨	10000 tn	291	314	463952	580104
#ABS树脂	A BS Copolymers	万吨	10000 tn	169	179	275733	350914
初级形状的聚氯乙烯	Polyvinyl Chloride in Primary Forms	万吨	10000 tn	87	100	86368	105273
聚酯切片	Slices or Chips of Polyethylene Terephthalate	万吨	10000 tn	18	20	27213	30700
杀虫剂、除草剂及类似品	Pesticides	吨	tn	84797	83544	67496	68136
纸及纸板(未切成形的)	Paper and Paperboard	万吨	10000 tn	297	475	328042	432210
钢材	Rolled Steel	万吨	10000 tn	1322	1330	1315312	1517011
未锻轧的铜及铜合金	Copper and Copper Alloys	万吨	10000 tn	439	411	2158474	2545870
铜材	Rolled Copper	万吨	10000 tn	56	58	481536	579969
未锻轧的铝及铝合金	Aluminium and Aluminium Alloys	万吨	10000 tn	26	19	48910	39685
铝材	Rolled Aluminium	万吨	10000 tn	39	40	242043	247150
蒸汽锅炉及过热水锅炉	Boilers	台	set	349	563	4148	5336
制冷设备用压缩机	Compressors for Refrigerating Equipment	万台	10000 sets	995	1031	91958	103740
金属加工机床	Machine Tools	台	set	69655	88656	751350	874189
阀门	Valves	万套	10000 sets	85923	106226	538817	610881
自动数据处理设备及其部件	Automatic Data Processing Machines	万台	10000 sets	55682	50588	2718247	2757804
电话机	Line Telephonic or Telegraphic Switching Apparatus	万台	10000 sets	1507	599	255487	77159
收音设备(包括收录音组合机及整套散件)	Sound Recording Apparatus	万台	10000 sets	161	163	25251	25848
彩色电视机	TV Sets	万台	10000 sets	12	6	4346	2449
汽车	Motor Vehicles and Chassis	万辆	10000 units	107	124	4448413	5053147
#小轿车	Cars	辆	unit	377370	473471	1350043	1722187
货车	Trucks	辆	unit	7743	9662	37680	48366
非公路用自卸车	Dump Trucks	辆	unit	27	17	761	630
装有引擎的汽车底盘	Chassis with Engines	台	unit	1888	1467	18428	12675
飞机及其他航空器	Aircraft	架	unit	7385	14266	2043250	2305314
医疗仪器及器械	Medical Instruments and Appliances					897957	970473
机电产品	**Mechanical and Electrical Products**					**77138530**	**85449641**
高新技术产品	**High and New-technology Products**					**52362058**	**58403359**

6-28 各地区进出口总额(按境内目的地、货源地分)

Import and Export Value by Region in Border According to Destination or Source of Goods

单位：万美元

Unit: USD 10000

地　区	Region	2016 出口 Exports	2016 进口 Imports	2017 出口 Exports	2017 进口 Imports
全　国	**Total**	**209763119**	**158792622**	**226337133**	**184379294**
北　京	Beijing	2545583	9686649	2648035	9513813
天　津	Tianjin	4165702	6531668	4264197	7905283
河　北	Hebei	4399827	3099319	4373347	3780198
山　西	Shanxi	1252731	631203	1385502	693256
内蒙古	Inner Mongolia	519570	802902	580940	1008402
辽　宁	Liaoning	4481363	5131461	4942669	6310715
吉　林	Jilin	490726	1433409	525775	1453518
黑龙江	Heilongjiang	491955	902214	527019	1143675
上　海	Shanghai	16638077	23823304	17412685	27322249
江　苏	Jiangsu	33095875	21617700	37497007	26152168
浙　江	Zhejiang	27344970	6999950	29239726	9157566
安　徽	Anhui	2596629	1500255	3000619	2098062
福　建	Fujian	8722975	4957393	9224366	6083380
江　西	Jiangxi	2414947	1121277	2480687	1211317
山　东	Shandong	14431326	12908296	15729541	15899167
河　南	Henan	4532273	2879110	5012190	3124704
湖　北	Hubei	2476326	1425218	2901100	1718973
湖　南	Hunan	1427500	887896	1766953	1233840
广　东	Guangdong	65413652	40598704	67631430	43734461
广　西	Guangxi	1262617	3127889	1439955	3819998
海　南	Hainan	346879	870564	430166	934869
重　庆	Chongqing	3355524	1829542	3782905	1874070
四　川	Sichuan	2620151	2185523	3516899	3144854
贵　州	Guizhou	399211	121194	550042	262013
云　南	Yunnan	885517	855885	965886	1172793
西　藏	Tibet	47183	12027	36925	24089
陕　西	Shaanxi	1580336	1366532	2380721	1674960
甘　肃	Gansu	191568	255392	169461	330599
青　海	Qinghai	35839	16208	28232	16793
宁　夏	Ningxia	205259	105082	267106	165813
新　疆	Xinjiang	1391030	1108857	1625048	1413699

6-29 各地区进出口总额(按经营单位所在地分)

Import and Export Value by Location of Importers and Exporters

单位：万美元

Unit: USD 10000

地区	Region	2016		2017	
		出口 Exports	进口 Imports	出口 Exports	进口 Imports
全国	**Total**	**209763119**	**158792622**	**226337133**	**184379294**
北京	Beijing	5202284	23032612	5856599	26545144
天津	Tianjin	4427869	5837725	4356105	6935811
河北	Hebei	3057554	1609984	3135740	1849814
山西	Shanxi	993219	672922	1019561	699126
内蒙古	Inner Mongolia	439599	724431	487796	899556
辽宁	Liaoning	4306277	4349413	4486592	5472917
吉林	Jilin	420201	1425088	441936	1412361
黑龙江	Heilongjiang	503553	1150365	520925	1374194
上海	Shanghai	18335213	25041606	19364290	28255375
江苏	Jiangsu	31905309	19024332	36302623	22775191
浙江	Zhejiang	26786375	6871216	28679328	9111420
安徽	Anhui	2844668	1596618	3059612	2342551
福建	Fujian	10367799	5314821	10491667	6610337
江西	Jiangxi	2979840	1023001	3248827	1185072
山东	Shandong	13709609	9725976	14703746	11751349
河南	Henan	4280551	2840759	4703096	3059913
湖北	Hubei	2603934	1334943	3048623	1585096
湖南	Hunan	1769254	855093	2317084	1286246
广东	Guangdong	59860199	35669602	62286837	38381001
广西	Guangxi	2292641	2470102	2809119	2978747
海南	Hainan	212580	922263	436591	600815
重庆	Chongqing	4065438	2209926	4259526	2400585
四川	Sichuan	2794762	2135863	3755343	3055263
贵州	Guizhou	474279	95683	579371	236860
云南	Yunnan	1149031	841205	1146651	1198460
西藏	Tibet	47173	31020	43329	43016
陕西	Shaanxi	1583756	1410966	2454381	1565899
甘肃	Gansu	406256	277042	170979	311655
青海	Qinghai	137006	15914	42417	23158
宁夏	Ningxia	248675	76574	365107	138845
新疆	Xinjiang	1558217	205558	1763334	293520

6-30 外商投资企业出口额

Exports of Foreign-funded Enterprises

单位：万美元

Unit: USD 10000

年 份 Year	合计 Total	中外合资经营企业 Equity Joint Venture	中外合作经营企业 Contractual Joint Venture	外商独资经营企业 Wholly Foreignowned Enterprises
1980	824	824		
1981	3235	3022		213
1982	5287	2925		2362
1983	33036	3815		29221
1984	6894	5994		900
1985	29670	21825		7845
1986	58203	47865		10338
1987	120809	103793		17016
1988	245642	215391		30251
1989	491320	343596	79470	68254
1990	781379	526405	132135	122839
1991	1204725	769116	188447	247162
1992	1735619	1046465	261462	427692
1993	2523717	1411653	387817	724247
1994	3471297	1807458	535529	1128310
1995	4687587	2268886	679095	1739606
1996	6150636	2975031	794900	2380705
1997	7489986	3468059	898836	3123091
1998	8096189	3557015	872930	3666244
1999	8862766	3712097	814642	4336027
2000	11944121	5031107	992921	5920093
2001	13321810	5407673	1017667	6896470
2002	16998509	6207651	1169507	9621351
2003	24030598	8101382	1324353	14604863
2004	33859184	10962004	1478119	21419061
2005	44418252	13598693	1566396	29253163
2006	56377905	16372461	1771238	38234206
2007	69537077	19875818	1811744	47849515
2008	79049270	22674411	1833782	54541078
2009	67207409	18232943	1458524	47515943
2010	86222882	23758160	1647020	60817702
2011	99522704	27301423	1766749	70454532
2012	102262008	28726066	1616005	71919937
2013	104372410	30049934	1568839	72753637
2014	107461992	30549336	1364473	75548183
2015	100461441	28244922	1138024	71078495
2016	91676690	25416625	985142	65274923
2017	97755948	26349914	933683	70472351

注：1989年以前中外合资数据包含了合作企业数据(下表同)。

Note: Figures of equity joint venture before 1989 include contractual joint ventures. The same applies to the table following.

6-31 外商投资企业进口额
Imports of Foreign-funded Enterprises

单位：万美元
Unit: USD 10000

年份 Year	合计 Total	中外合资经营企业 Equity Joint Venture	中外合作经营企业 Contractual Joint Venture	外商独资经营企业 Wholly Foreignowned Enterprises
1980	3441	3412		29
1981	11087	10089		998
1982	27642	23999		3643
1983	28801	6159		22642
1984	39921	11720		28201
1985	206410	188594		17816
1986	243031	223568		19463
1987	312218	289851		22367
1988	574671	534534		40137
1989	879617	653242	142478	83897
1990	1230633	885345	177366	167922
1991	1690700	1140857	245268	304575
1992	2637070	1720559	381398	535113
1993	4183320	2590434	703739	889147
1994	5293418	2988082	920002	1385334
1995	6294271	3481818	901023	1911430
1996	7560380	4109442	929004	2521934
1997	7772135	4019173	913914	2839048
1998	7671749	3744447	795342	3131960
1999	8588361	4112889	690888	3784584
2000	11727269	5433175	851674	5442420
2001	12584296	5635689	773729	6174878
2002	16025439	6079503	840325	9105611
2003	23186398	8081936	995078	14109384
2004	32444849	10914713	1072630	20457506
2005	38745612	11834619	958539	25952453
2006	47248045	13552683	992681	32702680
2007	55979304	15495775	885985	39597544
2008	61942848	18128172	880413	42934264
2009	54540486	15886071	663684	37990732
2010	75485663	20978710	2385128	52121824
2011	86467170	25581427	856855	60028888
2012	87150012	27493460	824107	58832446
2013	87459048	28406594	828521	58223933
2014	90893776	28557893	864891	61470992
2015	82886624	24507116	623416	57756092
2016	77076962	22385785	428756	54262421
2017	86157562	24513847	450497	61193217

6-32 各地区外商投资企业进出口额
Exports and Imports of Foreign-funded Enterprises by Region in Border

单位：万美元

Unit: USD 10000

地　区	Region	2016		2017	
		出口 Exports	进口 Imports	出口 Exports	进口 Imports
全　国	**Total**	**91676690**	**77076962**	**97755948**	**86157562**
北　京	Beijing	1233331	5204643	1237412	5350566
天　津	Tianjin	2655835	2992735	2715856	3275077
河　北	Hebei	605448	512401	565248	491735
山　西	Shanxi	650935	373442	615977	401306
内蒙古	Inner Mongolia	49104	51380	50898	53696
辽　宁	Liaoning	1792056	2083353	1847860	2402921
吉　林	Jilin	134240	799537	129169	872132
黑龙江	Heilongjiang	53190	55705	144999	106696
上　海	Shanghai	12359874	16266217	12929457	18806348
江　苏	Jiangsu	18653752	13942088	21144246	16535881
浙　江	Zhejiang	5038671	2489921	5067406	3018082
安　徽	Anhui	770892	546132	919664	778099
福　建	Fujian	3632614	2265597	3833620	2618537
江　西	Jiangxi	607474	556465	652159	638983
山　东	Shandong	5048387	3198060	5081870	3333257
河　南	Henan	2944128	2006974	3108816	2228579
湖　北	Hubei	601594	462904	657865	560356
湖　南	Hunan	327002	300702	403218	420576
广　东	Guangdong	28871961	18156491	28741496	18391769
广　西	Guangxi	429350	544601	558177	855885
海　南	Hainan	111261	611283	331625	348670
重　庆	Chongqing	2324298	1008972	2774228	1109735
四　川	Sichuan	1589845	1532928	2423400	2215288
贵　州	Guizhou	18211	12194	136016	122032
云　南	Yunnan	34959	13785	31053	12850
西　藏	Tibet	9	0.2		55
陕　西	Shaanxi	1100106	1059344	1608397	1171562
甘　肃	Gansu	1404	1161	1195	1942
青　海	Qinghai	267	148	1341	85
宁　夏	Ningxia	29765	14970	36328	27330
新　疆	Xinjiang	6726	12830	6951	7532

6–33 各地区中外合资企业进出口额

Exports and Imports of Equity Joint Ventures by Region in Border

单位：万美元

Unit: USD 10000

地 区	Region	2016		2017	
		出口 Exports	进口 Imports	出口 Exports	进口 Imports
全 国	**Total**	**25416625**	**22385785**	**26349914**	**24513847**
北 京	Beijing	452509	1065137	384318	966496
天 津	Tianjin	1207089	1351753	1226130	1469575
河 北	Hebei	286836	291968	266012	302811
山 西	Shanxi	638822	363518	604076	339932
内蒙古	Inner Mongolia	16397	38379	17466	41110
辽 宁	Liaoning	717115	1251069	709203	1440019
吉 林	Jilin	43236	703441	33133	763082
黑龙江	Heilongjiang	37217	25564	125119	75737
上 海	Shanghai	2025682	1992317	2037913	2304327
江 苏	Jiangsu	3775591	3127118	4187872	3535303
浙 江	Zhejiang	2435511	1116445	2374731	1368528
安 徽	Anhui	324404	390032	359557	493700
福 建	Fujian	895200	792083	940737	1042792
江 西	Jiangxi	125743	338167	143328	432150
山 东	Shandong	2277989	1444997	2135181	1488970
河 南	Henan	2807714	1950942	3011786	2188214
湖 北	Hubei	401713	357945	418117	426173
湖 南	Hunan	175472	222482	209606	293845
广 东	Guangdong	6044291	4052722	6259816	4009245
广 西	Guangxi	229694	345460	324067	602054
海 南	Hainan	81201	571023	128282	295442
重 庆	Chongqing	170955	304950	151734	265211
四 川	Sichuan	121175	138720	139106	203459
贵 州	Guizhou	8136	6639	7879	8510
云 南	Yunnan	13136	9620	12744	6713
西 藏	Tibet	6			53
陕 西	Shaanxi	78111	126254	108076	138931
甘 肃	Gansu	684	196	329	880
青 海	Qinghai	132	144	1136	84
宁 夏	Ningxia	20702	4349	28229	9883
新 疆	Xinjiang	4159	2353	4231	615

6-34 各地区中外合作企业进出口额

Exports and Imports of Contractual Joint Ventures by Region in Border

单位：万美元

Unit: USD 10000

地区	Region	2016 出口 Exports	2016 进口 Imports	2017 出口 Exports	2017 进口 Imports
全国	**Total**	**985142**	**428756**	**933683**	**450497**
北京	Beijing	3226	6068	1887	5686
天津	Tianjin	5414	18317	2955	18451
河北	Hebei	14351	7092	11184	8293
山西	Shanxi	1498	119	2198	177
内蒙古	Inner Mongolia	26		14	84
辽宁	Liaoning	26723	6315	27549	7374
吉林	Jilin	6017	3451	7301	3309
黑龙江	Heilongjiang	13		15	
上海	Shanghai	147050	81772	133340	100191
江苏	Jiangsu	118984	161506	165158	174938
浙江	Zhejiang	29009	14542	33511	10360
安徽	Anhui	4317	243	5062	748
福建	Fujian	14287	10671	17576	14751
江西	Jiangxi	3592	187	3959	171
山东	Shandong	36456	14304	39915	21645
河南	Henan	1276	361	538	2970
湖北	Hubei	1780	104	130	143
湖南	Hunan	115	597	109	171
广东	Guangdong	547806	92559	457363	71425
广西	Guangxi	1893	640	1264	414
海南	Hainan	9051	31	12586	78
重庆	Chongqing	6190	34	4356	46
四川	Sichuan	1378	3071	1858	3576
贵州	Guizhou	72	18		5
云南	Yunnan	4277	2039	3598	2881
西藏	Tibet				
陕西	Shaanxi	232	28	132	20
甘肃	Gansu				
青海	Qinghai	10	2	50	0.1
宁夏	Ningxia				
新疆	Xinjiang	97	4686	74	2594

6-35 各地区外商独资企业进出口额

Exports and Imports of Wholly Foreign-owned Enterprises by Region in Border

单位：万美元

Unit: USD 10000

地 区	Region	2016 出口 Exports	2016 进口 Imports	2017 出口 Exports	2017 进口 Imports
全 国	**Total**	**65274923**	**54262421**	**70472351**	**61193217**
北 京	Beijing	777596	4133439	851206	4378383
天 津	Tianjin	1443333	1622665	1486771	1787051
河 北	Hebei	304261	213340	288051	180631
山 西	Shanxi	10614	9805	9704	61197
内蒙古	Inner Mongolia	32681	13001	33418	12502
辽 宁	Liaoning	1048218	825969	1111109	955529
吉 林	Jilin	84986	92645	88735	105740
黑龙江	Heilongjiang	15960	30141	19864	30959
上 海	Shanghai	10187142	14192128	10758205	16401830
江 苏	Jiangsu	14759176	10653464	16791216	12825641
浙 江	Zhejiang	2574150	1358934	2659164	1639194
安 徽	Anhui	442171	155857	555045	283651
福 建	Fujian	2723127	1462843	2875307	1560993
江 西	Jiangxi	478139	218111	504872	206662
山 东	Shandong	2733942	1738758	2906774	1822643
河 南	Henan	135138	55672	96492	37394
湖 北	Hubei	198101	104854	239618	134040
湖 南	Hunan	151415	77624	193503	126561
广 东	Guangdong	22279863	14011210	22024317	14311100
广 西	Guangxi	197763	198502	232846	253417
海 南	Hainan	21008	40230	190757	53149
重 庆	Chongqing	2147153	703988	2618138	844478
四 川	Sichuan	1467292	1391137	2282436	2008254
贵 州	Guizhou	10003	5537	128138	113517
云 南	Yunnan	17546	2126	14710	3257
西 藏	Tibet	3	0.2		2
陕 西	Shaanxi	1021762	933063	1500188	1032611
甘 肃	Gansu	721	965	866	1061
青 海	Qinghai	125	2	155	0.1
宁 夏	Ningxia	9062	10622	8099	17448
新 疆	Xinjiang	2470	5791	2646	4322

6-36 经济特区中外合资企业进出口额

Exports and Imports of Equity Joint Ventures in Special Economic Zone

单位：万美元

Unit: USD 10000

地　区	Region	2016		2017	
		出口 Exports	进口 Imports	出口 Exports	进口 Imports
合　计	**Total**	**2651606**	**2363026**	**2655962**	**1964023**
深　圳	Shenzhen	1974852	1308255	1912283	1003626
珠　海	Zhuhai	126468	171034	125138	228767
汕　头	Shantou	53256	10501	52601	10240
厦　门	Xiamen	415830	302213	437658	425948
海　南	Hainan	81201	571023	128282	295442

6-37 经济特区中外合作企业进出口额

Exports and Imports of Contractual Joint Ventures in Special Economic Zone

单位：万美元

Unit: USD 10000

地　区	Region	2016		2017	
		出口 Exports	进口 Imports	出口 Exports	进口 Imports
合　计	**Total**	**313464**	**51911**	**257300**	**37465**
深　圳	Shenzhen	276787	36593	215950	19686
珠　海	Zhuhai	4294	2309	2226	724
汕　头	Shantou	12939	2784	12535	2653
厦　门	Xiamen	10392	10195	14002	14325
海　南	Hainan	9051	31	12586	78

6-38 经济特区外商独资企业进出口额

Exports and Imports of Wholly Foreign-owned Enterprises in Special Economic Zone

单位：万美元

Unit: USD 10000

地　区	Region	2016		2017	
		出口 Exports	进口 Imports	出口 Exports	进口 Imports
合　计	**Total**	**11087435**	**7608183**	**10974820**	**7786782**
深　圳	Shenzhen	8403320	6033411	8093675	6019163
珠　海	Zhuhai	1126687	511155	1036549	638446
汕　头	Shantou	67780	60920	60449	58503
厦　门	Xiamen	1468639	962467	1593389	1017521
海　南	Hainan	21008	40230	190757	53149

6-39 服务进出口分类金额(2017年)
Total Value of Imports and Exports of Services by Sector(2017)

单位：亿美元
Unit: USD 100 million

类　别	Classification	进出口 Imports and Exports	出口 Exports	进口 Imports
总额	**Total**	**6957**	**2281**	**4676**
运输	Transport	1300	371	929
旅行	Travel	2936	388	2548
建筑	Construction	325	239	86
保险服务	Insurance Services	145	40	104
金融服务	Financial Services	53	37	16
电信、计算机和信息服务	Telecommunications, Computer and Information Services	469	278	192
电信服务	Telecommunications Services	36	18	18
计算机和信息服务	Computer and Information Services	434	260	174
知识产权使用费	Charges For The Use of Intellectual Property	333	48	286
研发成果使用费	Charges For The Use of The Results of Research and Development	149	6	143
视听及相关产品许可费	Charges For Licenses of Audio-visual and Related Product	23	1	22
个人、文化和娱乐服务	Personal, Cultural, and Recreational Services	35	8	28
维护和维修服务	Maintenance and Repair Services	82	59	23
加工服务	Processing Services	182	181	2
其他商业服务	Other Business Services	1044	615	429
技术	Technology	264	149	115
专业和管理咨询服务	Professional and Management Consulting Services	473	311	162
研发成果转让费及委托研发	Charges For The Transfer of The Results of Research and Development and Commissioned Research and Development	137	80	57
政府服务	Government Services	52	17	35

注：本表按照国际货币基金组织《国际收支和国际头寸手册》(第六版)标准统计，下表同。
Note: Data in this table are compiled on Balance of Payments and International Investment Position Manual (6th edition) of IMF.The same applies to the table following.

6-40 服务进出口分类金额(2017年)
Total Value of Imports and Exports of Services by Sector(2017)

单位：亿元人民币
Unit: RMB 100 million

类　别	Classification	进出口 Imports and Exports	出口 Exports	进口 Imports
总额	**Total**	**46991**	**15407**	**31584**
运输	Transport	8784	2506	6278
旅行	Travel	19831	2621	17210
建筑	Construction	2195	1616	579
保险服务	Insurance Services	976	273	703
金融服务	Financial Services	359	250	109
电信、计算机和信息服务	Telecommunications, Computer and Information Services	3171	1876	1295
电信服务	Telecommunications Services	242	120	122
计算机和信息服务	Computer and Information Services	2929	1755	1174
知识产权使用费	Charges For The Use of Intellectual Property	2252	322	1930
研发成果使用费	Charges For The Use of The Results of Research and Development	1009	44	965
视听及相关产品许可费	Charges For Licenses of Audio-visual and Related Product	157	8	149
个人、文化和娱乐服务	Personal, Cultural, and Recreational Services	237	51	186
维护和维修服务	Maintenance and Repair Services	554	400	153
加工服务	Processing Services	1232	1220	12
其他商业服务	Other Business Services	7051	4157	2895
技术	Technology	1786	1008	778
专业和管理咨询服务	Professional and Management Consulting Services	3195	2102	1093
研发成果转让费及委托研发	Charges For The Transfer of The Results of Research and Development and Commissioned Research and Development	924	539	385
政府服务	Government Services	348	115	233

利用外资

UTILIZATION OF FOREIGN CAPITAL

第7篇

7-1 利用外资合同金额

Contractual Amount of Foreign Capital

单位：亿美元

Unit: USD 100 million

年 份 Year	总 计 Total		对外借款 Foreign Loans		外商直接投资 Direct Foreign Investment		外商其他投资 Other Foreign Investment
	项目(个) Number of Contracts (unit)	金 额 Amount	项目(个) Number of Contracts (unit)	金 额 Amount	项目(个) Number of Contracts (unit)	金 额 Amount	金 额 Amount
1979-1982	947	194.96	27	135.49	920	49.58	9.89
1983	690	36.15	52	15.13	638	19.17	1.85
1984	2204	50.15	38	19.16	2166	28.75	2.24
1985	3145	102.69	72	35.34	3073	63.33	4.02
1986	1551	122.33	53	84.07	1498	33.30	4.96
1987	2289	121.36	56	78.17	2233	37.09	6.10
1988	6063	160.04	118	98.13	5945	52.97	8.94
1989	5909	114.79	130	51.85	5779	56.00	6.94
1990	7371	120.86	98	50.99	7273	65.96	3.91
1991	13086	195.83	108	71.61	12978	119.77	4.45
1992	48858	694.39	94	107.03	48764	581.24	6.12
1993	83595	1232.73	158	113.06	83437	1114.36	5.31
1994	47646	937.56	97	106.68	47549	826.80	4.08
1995	37184	1032.05	173	112.88	37011	912.82	6.35
1996	24673	816.10	117	79.62	24556	732.76	3.71
1997	21138	610.58	137	58.72	21001	510.03	41.82
1998	19850	632.01	51	83.85	19799	521.02	27.14
1999	17022	520.09	104	83.60	16918	412.23	24.26
2000	22347	711.30			22347	623.80	87.50
2001	26140	719.76			26140	691.95	27.81
2002	34171	847.51			34171	827.68	19.82
2003	41081	1169.01			41081	1150.69	18.32
2004	43664	1565.88			43664	1534.79	31.09
2005	44001	1925.93			44001	1890.65	35.28
2006	41473	1982.16			41473	1937.27	44.89
2007	37871				37871		
2008	27514				27514		
2009	23435				23435		
2010	27406				27406		
2011	27712				27712		
2012	24925				24925		
2013	22773				22773		
2014	23778				23778		
2015	26575				26575		
2016	27900				27900		
2017	35652				35652		

注：本数据来自商务部，从2007年起商务部不公布合同外资金额。

Note: Ministry of Commerce did not issue the Relative Data since 2007.

7–2 实际利用外资额
Amount of Foreign Capital Used

单位：亿美元

Unit: USD 100 million

年 份 Year	总 计 Total	对外借款 Foreign Loans	外商直接投资 Foreign Direct Investment	外商其他投资 Other Foreign Investment
1979–2012	14814.35		12761.08	581.71
1979–1982	130.60	106.90	17.69	6.01
1983	22.61	10.65	9.16	2.80
1984	28.66	12.86	14.19	1.61
1985	47.60	25.06	19.56	2.98
1986	76.28	50.14	22.44	3.70
1987	84.52	58.05	23.14	3.33
1988	102.26	64.87	31.94	5.45
1989	100.60	62.86	33.92	3.81
1990	102.89	65.34	34.87	2.68
1991	115.54	68.88	43.66	3.00
1992	192.03	79.11	110.08	2.84
1993	389.60	111.89	275.15	2.56
1994	432.13	92.67	337.67	1.79
1995	481.33	103.27	375.21	2.85
1996	548.05	126.69	417.26	4.10
1997	644.08	120.21	452.57	71.30
1998	585.57	110.00	454.63	20.94
1999	526.59	102.12	403.19	21.28
2000	593.56	100.00	407.15	86.41
2001	496.72		468.78	27.94
2002	550.11		527.43	22.68
2003	561.40		535.05	26.35
2004	640.72		606.30	34.43
2005	638.05		603.25	34.80
2006	670.76		630.21	40.55
2007	783.39		747.68	35.72
2008	952.53		923.95	28.58
2009	918.04		900.33	17.71
2010	1088.21		1057.35	30.86
2011	1176.98		1160.11	16.87
2012	1132.94		1117.16	15.78
2013	1187.21		1175.86	11.34
2014	1197.05		1195.62	1.44
2015	1262.67		1262.67	
2016	1260.01		1260.01	
2017	1310.35		1310.35	

7-3 分方式外商投资

Foreign Direct and Other Investment by Form

单位：亿美元

Unit: USD 100 million

方式	Form	2015		2016		2017	
		项目(个) Nunber of Contracts (unit)	金额 Amount	项目(个) Nunber of Contracts (unit)	金额 Amount	项目(个) Nunber of Contracts (unit)	金额 Amount
总计	**Total**	**26575**	**1262.67**	**27900**	**1260.01**	**35652**	**1310.35**
一、外商直接投资	**Direct Foreign Investment**	**26575**	**1262.67**	**27900**	**1260.01**	**35652**	**1310.35**
合资经营	Equity Joint Venture	5989	258.85	6662	302.04	8364	297.41
合作经营	Contractual Joint Venture	110	18.45	126	8.30	124	8.05
独资经营	Wholly Foreign-owned Enterprise	20398	952.85	21024	861.26	27007	913.44
外商投资股份制企业	FDI Shareholding Inc.	78	32.51	86	88.42	125	64.75
合作开发	Joint Exploration					2	11.80
合伙企业	Partnership					30	14.90
其他	Other			2			
二、外商其他投资	**Other Foreign Investment**						
对外发行股票	Sale Share						
国际租赁	International Lease						
补偿贸易	Compensation Trade						
加工装配	Processing and Assembly						

7-4 外商直接投资行业分布(2017年)

Foreign Direct Investment by Sector(2017)

单位：万美元

Unit: USD 10000

行业	Sector	合同项目(个) Number of Contracts (unit)	实际使用金额 Actually Utilized Value
总计	**Total**	**35652**	**13103513**
农、林、牧、渔业	Agriculture,Forestry,Animal Husbandry and Fishing	706	107492
农业	Agriculture	451	35411
采矿业	Mining	26	130198
石油和天然气开采业	Petroleum and Natural Gas Mining	5	118402
制造业	Manufacturing	4986	3350619
纺织业	Textile	154	49023
化学原料及化学制品制造业	Chemistry Raw Material and Chemical Product Manufacturing	241	238425
医药制造业	Medicine Manufacturing	126	214165
通用设备制造业	General Purpose Equipment Manufacturing	574	288687
专用设备制造业	Special Purpose Equipment Manufacturing	524	244324
通信设备、计算机及其他电子设备制造业	Communication Facility, Computer and other Electronic Installation Manufacturing	576	589812
电力、燃气及水的生产和供应业	Production and Distribution of Electricity ,Gas and Water	372	352132
建筑业	Construction	633	261940
交通运输、仓储和邮政业	Transport, Storage and Post	517	558803
信息传输、计算机服务和软件业	Information Transmission, Computer Services and Software	3169	2091861
批发和零售业	Wholesale and Retail Trade	12283	1147808
住宿和餐饮业	Hotel and Restaurants	703	41914
旅游饭店	Traveling Hotel	107	13628
金融业	Financial Intermediation	1742	792119
房地产业	Real Estate	737	1685559
房地产开发经营	Property Development Management	409	1540006
租赁和商务服务业	Leasing and Business Services	5087	1673855
科学研究、技术服务和地质勘查业	Scientific Research, Technical Service and Geologic Prospecting	3391	684373
水利、环境和公共设施管理业	Management of Water Conservancy, Environment and Public Facilities	156	56951
居民服务和其他服务业	Services to Households and Other Services	349	56723
教育	Education	203	7747
卫生、社会保障和社会福利业	Health, Social Security and Social Welfare	114	30516
文化、体育和娱乐业	Culture, Sports and Entertainment	476	69846
公共管理和社会组织	Public Management and Social Organizations	2	3057

7-5 分国别(地区)外商直接投资

Foreign Direct Investment by Country or Region

单位：万美元

Unit: USD 10000

国别(地区)	Country/Region	2016		2017	
		外商直接投资合同项目(个) Number of FDI Contracts (unit)	外商直接投资 Foreign Direct Investment	外商直接投资合同项目(个) Number of FDI Contracts (unit)	外商直接投资 Foreign Direct Investment
总　计	**Total**	**27900**	**12600142**	**35652**	**13103513**
亚洲	**Asia**	**22106**	**9883103**	**27915**	**10919387**
阿富汗	Afghanistan	87	35	153	73
巴林	Bahrain	2		1	30
孟加拉国	Bangladesh	46	7	69	10
文莱	Brunei	12	6567	7	2573
缅甸	Myanmar	34	2	27	170
柬埔寨	Cambodia			5	1505
塞浦路斯	Cyprus	7	216	9	1192
朝鲜	Korea DPR	12		9	
中国香港	Hong Kong, China	12753	8146508	18066	9450901
印度	India	197	5181	281	15772
印度尼西亚	Indonesia	34	6399	51	4076
伊朗	Iran	159	382	222	
伊拉克	Iraq	64	223	163	182
以色列	Israel	42	5008	55	773
日本	Japan	576	309585	590	326100
约旦	Jordan	47	155	62	19
科威特	Kuwait	3	152	1	1474
老挝	LaoPDR	2		2	1082
黎巴嫩	Lebanon	29	160	21	19
中国澳门	Macao, China	676	81756	843	63738
马来西亚	Malaysia	242	22113	329	10836
马尔代夫	Maldives	2		2	
蒙古	Mongolia	11		10	308
尼泊尔	Nepal	10		33	1
阿曼	Oman	2	6	4	599
巴基斯坦	Pakistan	141	65	212	99
巴勒斯坦	Palestine	14	8	22	73
菲律宾	Philippines	33	7760	35	500
卡塔尔	Qatar	3		1	
沙特阿拉伯	Saudi Arabia	30	1345	35	1493
新加坡	Singapore	684	604668	706	476318
韩国	Korea	2018	475112	1627	367253
斯里兰卡	Sri Lanka	7	20	20	22
叙利亚	Syria	82	105	127	934
泰国	Thailand	74	5615	81	11023
土耳其	Turkey	109	3205	140	674
阿联酋	United Arab Emirates	30	3933	26	1357
也门共和国	Yemen Rep.	228	251	312	33
越南	Vietnam	27		18	353
中国台湾	Taiwan, China	3517	196280	3464	177247
哈萨克斯坦	Kazakhstan	26	275	30	561
吉尔吉斯斯坦	Kirghizia	8	3	4	12
塔吉克斯坦	Tadzhikistan	6		12	2
土库曼斯坦	Turkmenistan	3		5	
乌兹别克斯坦	Uzbekstan	16	3	23	
亚洲其他国家	Oth.Asia.nes	1			
非洲	**Africa**	**677**	**112720**	**899**	**65746**
阿尔及利亚	Algeria	15	3	13	3

单位：万美元
Unit: USD 10000

国别(地区)	Country/Region	2016 外商直接投资合同项目(个) Number of FDI Contracts (unit)	2016 外商直接投资 Foreign Direct Investment	2017 外商直接投资合同项目(个) Number of FDI Contracts (unit)	2017 外商直接投资 Foreign Direct Investment
安哥拉	Angola	2	359	10	120
贝宁	Benin	1		4	
博茨瓦纳	Botswana			2	
布隆迪	Burundi	3		3	
喀麦隆	Cameroon	28	4	40	
中非	Central Africa			1	
乍得	Chad	2		3	
科摩罗	Comoros			1	
刚果(布)	Congo	9		8	2
吉布提	Djibouti	1		5	
埃及	Egypt	60	269	68	75
埃塞俄比亚	Ethiopia	16	6	27	
冈比亚	Gambia	2	7	7	390
加纳	Ghana	43		66	950
几内亚	Guinea	10		25	2
几内亚比绍	Guinea-Bissau	1		2	103
科特迪瓦共和国	Cote d'Ivoire	3	2	12	2
肯尼亚	Kenya	14	6	22	309
利比里亚	Liberia	1	572	1	50
利比亚	Libya	22	18	18	38
马达加斯加	Madagascar	6		1	
马拉维	Malawi			1	
马里	Mali	56	4	68	8
毛里塔尼亚	Mauritania	2		13	
毛里求斯	Mauritius	15	86176	15	34368
摩洛哥	Morocco	9		15	
莫桑比克	Mozambique			3	1473
纳米比亚	Namibia			2	
尼日尔	Niger	7		12	
尼日利亚	Nigeria	56	87	56	625
卢旺达	Rwanda	3		3	
塞内加尔	Senegal	1		13	
塞舌尔	Seychelles	203	24593	183	20409
塞拉利昂	Sierra Leone	1		3	
索马里	Somalia	1	34	16	
南非	S. Africa	15	382	33	6518
苏丹	Sudan	16	50	29	
坦桑尼亚	Tanzania	8	112	11	51
多哥	Togo	3	-56	5	
突尼斯	Tunisia	10		12	80
乌干达	Uganda	11		31	
布基纳法索	Burkina Faso	3		2	
刚果(金)	Congo DR			24	
赞比亚	Zambia	4		3	
津巴布韦	Zimbabwe	10		6	150
厄立特里亚	Eritrea	2		1	
非洲其他国家	Oth. Afr. Nes	2	92		20
欧洲	**Europe**	**1987**	**943439**	**2250**	**883619**
比利时	Belgium	46	14765	34	14759
丹麦	Denmark	37	16281	57	81947
英国	United Kingdom	345	135368	393	100333
德国	Germany	392	271046	387	154163
法国	France	200	86975	209	79018
爱尔兰	Ireland	28	3308	38	14881
意大利	Italy	185	22317	201	19482
卢森堡	Luxembourg	24	138635	25	59587
荷兰	Netherlands	110	55586	122	217398
希腊	Greece	9	9	14	85
葡萄牙	Portugal	9	1042	12	1499

7-5 续表 2 Continued 2

单位：万美元

Unit: USD 10000

国别(地区)	Country/Region	2016 外商直接投资合同项目(个) Number of FDI Contracts (unit)	2016 外商直接投资 Foreign Direct Investment	2017 外商直接投资合同项目(个) Number of FDI Contracts (unit)	2017 外商直接投资 Foreign Direct Investment
西班牙	Spain	89	19815	100	14246
阿尔巴尼亚	Albania	2			
奥地利	Austria	34	4271	42	9488
保加利亚	Bulgaria	2	133	7	9
芬兰	Finland	32	25804	21	5385
直布罗陀	Gibraltar			1	
匈牙利	Hungary	12	325	14	148
冰岛	Iceland	1	58	1	734
列支敦士登	Liechtenstein				24
马耳他	Malta	5	5740	4	246
摩纳哥	Monaco	1	11		27
挪威	Norway	29	366	26	732
波兰	Poland	20	585	29	289
罗马尼亚	Romania	5	204	13	711
瑞典	Sweden	56	74697	42	50695
瑞士	Switzerland	71	54749	68	45961
爱沙尼亚	Estonia	4		3	
拉脱维亚	Latvia	3	10	6	
立陶宛	Lithuania	6	1554	5	2372
格鲁吉亚	Georgia	3		6	
亚美尼亚	Armenia	1		4	
阿塞拜疆	Azerbaijan	10	8	35	
白俄罗斯	Belarus	9	4	10	824
摩尔多瓦	Moldavia	2		5	
俄罗斯	Russia	150	7343	211	2384
乌克兰	Ukraine	30	172	56	2707
斯洛文尼亚	Slovenia	2	55	4	37
克罗地亚	Croatia	1	37	4	
捷克	Czech	10	1148	13	797
斯洛伐克	Slovak	7	66	9	44
马其顿	Macedonia	1		2	
波黑	Bosnia & Herzegovina			1	
塞尔维亚	Serbia			14	7
黑山	Montenegro			1	
欧洲其他国家	Oth. Eur. Nes	4	952	1	2600
拉丁美洲	**Latin America**	**557**	**1221618**	**615**	**636273**
安提瓜和巴布达	Antigua and Barbuda			1	2272
阿根廷	Argentina	7	3	9	
巴哈马	Bahamas	4	4271		
巴巴多斯	Barbados	3	17902		4103
伯利兹	Belize	11	1988	5	931
玻利维亚	Bolivia	3	64	3	
巴西	Brazil	35	4667	43	4228
开曼群岛	Cayman Is.	113	515133	105	217690
智利	Chile	8	300	16	516
哥伦比亚	Colombia	26	6	32	5
多米尼克	Dominica		4	2	
哥斯达黎加	Costa Rica	1		2	
古巴	Cuba	5	761	2	
多米尼加共和国	Dominica Rep.	1		2	
厄瓜多尔	Ecuador	4		5	
危地马拉	Guatemala	2		1	
洪都拉斯	Honduras			2	
牙买加	Jamaica	1		2	
墨西哥	Mexico	25	74	29	1204

7-5 续表 3 Continued 3

单位：万美元
Unit: USD 10000

国别(地区)	Country/Region	2016 外商直接投资合同项目(个) Number of FDI Contracts (unit)	2016 外商直接投资 Foreign Direct Investment	2017 外商直接投资合同项目(个) Number of FDI Contracts (unit)	2017 外商直接投资 Foreign Direct Investment
巴拿马	Panama	8	2427	8	2137
秘鲁	Peru	4	1	11	
萨尔瓦多	EI Salvador			3	
圣文森特和格林纳丁斯	SaintVincent & Grenadines		15		
苏里南	Surinam	1		2	
特立尼达和多巴哥	Trinidad and Tobago			1	
乌拉圭	Uruguay	2		2	4087
委内瑞拉	Venezuela	15	3	17	2
维尔京群岛	Virgin Is.	274	673957	309	399076
圣其茨——尼维斯	St. Kitts-Nevis	3	35		22
拉美洲其他国家	Oth. L. Amer. Nes	1	7	1	
北美洲	**North America**	**1635**	**310421**	**1817**	**428552**
加拿大	Canada	385	26240	459	29269
美国	United States	1238	238601	1346	264905
百慕大	Bermuda	11	45580	6	134213
北美洲其他国家	Oth. N. Amer. nes	1		6	165
大洋洲及太平洋岛屿	**Oceania and Pacific Is.**	**712**	**126794**	**675**	**160950**
澳大利亚	Australia	346	26264	343	27618
斐济	Fiji	1		2	
瓦努阿图	Vanuatu	1	2920	1	
新西兰	New Zealand	53	3182	67	2116
萨摩亚	Samoa	274	87248	250	122943
马绍尔群岛	Marshall Is.	17	4825	12	4863
大洋洲其他国家	Oth. Ocean. Nes	20	2355		3410
其他	**Others**	**1**	**2047**	**3**	**8986**
东南亚国家联盟	**Association of Southeast Asian Nations**	**1142**	**653124**	**1261**	**508436**
欧洲联盟	**European Union**	**1680**	**879992**	**1817**	**828811**

注：1．东南亚国家联盟包括：文莱、缅甸、柬埔寨、印度尼西亚、老挝、马来西亚、菲律宾、新加坡、泰国、越南。
2．欧洲联盟包括：比利时、丹麦、英国、德国、法国、爱尔兰、意大利、卢森堡、荷兰、希腊、葡萄牙、西班牙、奥地利、芬兰、瑞典塞浦路斯、匈牙利、马耳他、波兰、爱沙尼亚、拉脱维亚、立陶宛、斯洛文尼亚、捷克、斯洛伐克、保加利亚、罗马尼亚、克罗地亚。

Note: a) Association of Southeast Asian Nations include Brunei, Myanmar, Cambodia, Indonesia, Laos,Malaysia, Philippines, Singapore, Thailand, Vietnam.

b) European Union include Belgium,Denmark,United Kingdom,Germany,France,Ireland,Italy,Luxembourg,Netherlands,Greece,Portugal,Spain, Austria,Finland,Sweden,Cyprus,Hungary,Malta,Poland,Estonia,Latvia,Lithuania,Slovenia,Czech,Slovak,Croatia.

7–6　历年外商投资企业登记概况

Status of Registered Enterprises with Foreign Capital

年　份 Year	企业数 (户) Number of Enterprise (unit)	投资总额 (万美元) Total Investment (USD 10000)	注册资本(万美元) Registered Capital(USD 10000)	
			小　计 Subtotal	#外　方 Foreign Partner
1980	7	470	432	179
1981	82	13248	11411	6646
1982	330	65085	60697	44201
1983	616	176747	143037	89589
1984	1999	434644	325086	207109
1985	4912	1641154	834410	508846
1986	6524	2140438	1163741	582717
1987	8546	2641308	1466820	827307
1988	13747	3780628	2154354	1169072
1989	18968	4690829	2759003	1501813
1990	25389	5457370	3304208	1866511
1991	37215	7178332	4465808	2577358
1992	84371	17845550	11598693	6866484
1993	167507	38238877	24563127	15018236
1994	206096	49072446	31227534	19631486
1995	233564	63900854	39912302	25688422
1996	240447	71532202	44148483	28979610
1997	235681	75347010	45981372	30298675
1998	227807	77422942	46728674	31371224
1999	212436	77856752	46354938	31668255
2000	203208	82467505	48394975	33719912
2001	202306	87501079	50579271	35968275
2002	208056	98189328	55211904	40199985
2003	226373	111735062	62264052	46577863
2004	242284	131118108	72848575	55799291
2005	260000	146399267	81203319	63193522
2006	274863	170756477	94647381	74062533
2007	286232	210878940	115541864	92114807
2008	434937	232413047	130055348	103885057
2009	434248	249996531	140348130	113694532
2010	445244	270593108	157384290	125896928
2011	446487	299312402	172942962	138102850
2012	440609	326104777	188141484	149034975
2013	445962	351760847	202802980	160771193
2014	460699	379772862	218351038	174138864
2015	481179	453902025	266815811	207567406
2016	505151	512400783	312433576	239184522
2017	539345	689924356	371071855	282661856

注：本数据来源于国家市场监督管理总局，从2008年起企业户数包含分支机构。
Note: Data in this table are from State Administration for Industry & Commerce. The number of enterprise includes branch Since 2008.

7-7 年末登记外商投资企业行业分布情况(2017年)

Registered Foreign-funded Enterprises by Sector at the Year-end(2017)

行 业	Sector	企业数 (户) Number of Enterprises (unit)	投资额 (万美元) Total Investment (USD 10000)	注册资本 (万美元) Registered Capital (USD 10000)	
				小 计 Subtotal	#外 方 Foreign Partner
总 计	**Total**	**539345**	**689924356**	**371071855**	**282661856**
农、林、牧、渔业	Agriculture, Forestry, Animal Husbandry and Fishery	6832	91355651	7105270	5885939
采矿业	Mining	767	2145031	1230036	887519
制造业	Manufacturing	147547	215756440	114246146	89356354
电力、热力、燃气及水生产和供应业	Production and Supply of Electricity, Heat, Gas and Water	5156	29854416	13060068	7997633
建筑业	Construction	5791	12507067	7995574	4571317
批发和零售业	Wholesale and Retail Trades	141322	41404058	24049460	20083551
交通运输、仓储和邮政业	Transport, Storage and Post	12685	19712411	11472877	7270306
住宿和餐饮业	Hotels and Catering Services	32027	5491576	3688318	3192307
信息传输、软件和信息技术服务业	Information Transmission, Software and Information Technology	41940	21544556	12078438	11004474
金融业	Financial Intermediation	16638	32204296	30279451	18420543
房地产业	Real Estate	17777	79753410	46321928	38000450
租赁和商务服务业	Leasing and Business Services	64479	81122491	67013912	50197196
科学研究和技术服务业	Scientific Research and Technical Services	33558	42756317	24414425	19348785
水利、环境和公共设施管理业	Management of Water Conservancy, Environment and	1308	4809779	2469964	1811473
居民服务、修理和其他服务业	Service to Households, Repair and Other Services	5134	2438764	1422752	1171318
教育	Education	635	739621	279044	257948
卫生和社会工作	Health and Social Service	441	1918550	965875	731174
文化、体育和娱乐业	Culture, Sports and Entertainment	4929	4024224	2730946	2279663
其他	Others	379	385698	247370	193906

7-8 各地区年末登记的外商投资企业数及投资额
Number and Investment of Registered Enterprise with Foreign Capital by Region or Department at the Year-end

地　区	Region	企业数 (户) Number of Enterprise (unit)		投资总额 (万美元) Total Investment (USD 10000)	
		2016	2017	2016	2017
总　计	**Total**	**505151**	**539345**	**512400783**	**689924356**
北　京	Beijing	30401	31442	42737060	48640860
天　津	Tianjin	13339	13938	22259397	25482286
河　北	Hebei	7286	7956	8482129	9581812
山　西	Shanxi	3699	3437	4216327	4972449
内蒙古	Inner Mongolia	3362	3453	4108003	4597937
辽　宁	Liaoning	16949	16883	21327844	31585001
吉　林	Jilin	3853	4044	3560561	3887356
黑龙江	Heilongjiang	4227	4444	2828047	3366862
上　海	Shanghai	79410	84007	73424636	79823905
江　苏	Jiangsu	55938	58577	87986813	96581873
浙　江	Zhejiang	34442	37422	31986996	37341457
安　徽	Anhui	5549	6135	6725627	8664121
福　建	Fujian	28351	28264	22631550	26072064
江　西	Jiangxi	6918	6059	7773812	8079723
山　东	Shandong	28527	29512	25187374	30421775
河　南	Henan	8058	7827	8224876	10453774
湖　北	Hubei	8976	10962	9931627	11510270
湖　南	Hunan	6677	7733	5800000	16339193
广　东	Guangdong	119688	135869	78157078	176222731
广　西	Guangxi	4485	4872	4372025	5620020
海　南	Hainan	2660	2442	7603881	7608902
重　庆	Chongqing	5555	5739	8806512	9455839
四　川	Sichuan	10370	11462	9419264	11279723
贵　州	Guizhou	1511	1671	2371930	3125132
云　南	Yunnan	4087	4366	3300474	3738226
西　藏	Tibet	236	252	225927	303136
陕　西	Shaanxi	5953	5629	5608107	8003950
甘　肃	Gansu	2079	2061	752885	2019750
青　海	Qinghai	440	470	752735	769932
宁　夏	Ningxia	651	738	870693	3042021
新　疆	Xinjiang	1474	1679	966596	1332275

7-9 各地区外商投资企业年末注册资本
Registered Capital of Foreign-funded Enterprise by Region or Department at the Year-end

单位：万美元
Unit: USD 10000

地区	Region	注册资本 Registered Capital		外方注册资本 Registered Foreign Capital	
		2016	2017	2016	2017
总计	**Total**	**312433576**	**371071855**	**239184522**	**282661856**
北京	Beijing	27552182	31235958	18948732	21741836
天津	Tianjin	14847272	17625855	10923833	12764162
河北	Hebei	4265127	4674982	3198423	3537268
山西	Shanxi	2294048	2619918	1113534	1364775
内蒙古	Inner Mongolia	1969527	2072599	1258559	1328693
辽宁	Liaoning	13184825	17540697	10573889	13907612
吉林	Jilin	1206003	1420156	760775	881307
黑龙江	Heilongjiang	1491008	2003948	1103739	1482970
上海	Shanghai	50872845	54727717	39221134	41736671
江苏	Jiangsu	47182292	52261586	39522865	43637106
浙江	Zhejiang	19214008	22861676	15187618	17559826
安徽	Anhui	3457685	4890363	2551017	3522679
福建	Fujian	13212653	15026839	10509411	11614399
江西	Jiangxi	5506037	5660631	4387186	4239566
山东	Shandong	14761960	18197892	11524142	13807994
河南	Henan	4490041	5552909	3316329	4086877
湖北	Hubei	5440680	6106191	4199725	4611494
湖南	Hunan	3088770	6841640	2207904	5328261
广东	Guangdong	50858849	64318635	37280192	47916016
广西	Guangxi	2295495	2987481	1899674	2396003
海南	Hainan	6066839	6100225	5489813	5546292
重庆	Chongqing	5490078	6017893	4273466	4543629
四川	Sichuan	5528245	6582232	4110283	4480074
贵州	Guizhou	1312175	1670920	1000054	1348487
云南	Yunnan	1874265	2144859	1330662	1595014
西藏	Tibet	173567	211694	118661	148401
陕西	Shaanxi	3096965	4726904	2093928	3496407
甘肃	Gansu	319029	1599653	223548	1518559
青海	Qinghai	287375	295413	134599	147895
宁夏	Ningxia	530847	2285449	312116	1802195
新疆	Xinjiang	562887	808941	408712	569387

对外投资与经济合作

OVERSEAS DIRECT INVESTMENT AND ECONOMIC COOPERATION

第8篇

8-1 按主要国别(地区)分对外直接投资
Overseas Direct Investment by Countries or Regions

单位：万美元

Unit: USD 10000

国家（地区）	Country or Region	对外直接投资净额 Net Overseas Direct Investment		截至2017年对外直接投资存量 Overseas Direct Investment Stock at the End of 2017
		2016	2017	
合计	**Total**	**19614943**	**15828830**	**180903652**
亚洲	**Asia**	**13026769**	**11003986**	**113932379**
中国香港	Hong Kong, China	11423259	9115278	98126568
印度	India	9293	28998	474733
印度尼西亚	Indonesia	146088	168225	1053880
日本	Japan	34401	44405	319734
中国澳门	Macao, China	82150	-102447	968029
新加坡	Singapore	317186	631990	4456809
韩国	Republic of Korea	114837	66080	598347
泰国	Thailand	112169	105759	535847
越南	Vietnam	127904	76440	496536
非洲	**Africa**	**239873**	**410500**	**4329650**
阿尔及利亚	Algeria	-9989	-14053	183366
苏丹	Sudan	-68994	25487	120156
几内亚	Guinea	3667	623	7639
马达加斯加	Madagascar	-655	7120	76630
尼日利亚	Nigeria	10850	13795	286153
南非	South Africa	84322	31736	747277
欧洲	**Europe**	**1069323**	**1846319**	**11085468**
英国	United Kingdom	148039	206630	2031817
德国	Germany	238058	271585	1216320
法国	France	149957	95215	570271
俄罗斯	Russia	129307	154842	1387160
拉丁美洲	**Latin America**	**2722705**	**1407659**	**38689230**
巴西	Brazil	12477	42627	320554
开曼群岛	Cayman Islands	1352283	-660596	24968219
墨西哥	Mexico	21184	17133	89802
英属维尔京群岛	Virgin Is. (E)	1228849	1930117	12206075
北美洲	**North America**	**2035096**	**649827**	**8690597**
加拿大	Canada	287150	32083	1093686
美国	United States	1698081	642549	6738100
大洋洲	**Oceania**	**521177**	**510539**	**4176327**
澳大利亚	Australia	418688	424196	3617531
新西兰	New Zealand	90585	59661	249180

8-2 按行业分对外直接投资
Overseas Direct Investment by Sector

单位：万美元
Unit: USD 10000

行　　业	Sector	对外直接投资净额 Net Overseas Direct Investment		截至2017年对外直接投资存量 Overseas Direct Investment Stock at the End of 2017
		2016	2017	
总　　计	**Total**	**19614943**	**15828830**	**180903652**
农、林、牧、渔业	Agriculture, Forestry, Animal Husbandry and Fishery	328715	250769	1656194
采矿业	Mining	193020	-370152	15767026
制造业	Manufacturing	2904872	2950737	14030075
电力、热力、燃气及水生产和供应业	Production and Supply of Electricity, Heat, Gas and Water	353599	234401	2499090
建筑业	Construction	439248	652772	3770399
批发和零售业	Wholesale and Retail Trades	2089417	2631102	22642713
交通运输、仓储和邮政业	Transport, Storage and Post	167881	546792	5476795
住宿和餐饮业	Hotels and Catering Services	162549	-18509	351305
信息传输、软件和信息技术服务业	Information Transmission, Software and Information Technology	1866022	443024	21889737
金融业	Financial Intermediation	1491809	1878544	20279304
房地产业	Real Estate	1524674	679506	5375505
租赁和商务服务业	Leasing and Business Services	6578157	5427321	61577349
科学研究和技术服务业	Scientific Research and Technical Services	423806	239065	2168399
水利、环境和公共设施管理业	Management of Water Conservancy, Environment and Public Facilities	84705	21892	238996
居民服务、修理和其他服务业	Service to Households, Repair and Other Services	542429	186526	1901733
教育	Education	28452	13372	328616
卫生和社会工作	Health and Social Service	48719	35267	138880
文化、体育和娱乐业	Culture, Sports and Entertainment	386869	26401	811536
公共管理、社会保障和社会组织	Public Management, Social Security and Social Organization			

8-3 对外经济合作概况
Foreign Economic Cooperation

年 份 Year	对外承包工程 Foreign Engineering Projects				对外劳务合作 Foreign Labour Services	
	合同数（份） Contract Number (unit)	合同金额（亿美元） Contract Value (USD 100 million)	完成营业额（亿美元） Turnover (USD 100 million)	年末在外人数（万人） Persons Abroad by the End of Year (10000 persons)	派出劳务人数（万人） Dispatched Labor (10000 persons)	年末在外人数（万人） Persons Abroad by the End of Year (10000 persons)
1979	27	0.33	1.23 (1979–1981)			
1980	138	1.40				
1981	250	2.76				
1982	195	3.46	1.00			
1983	280	7.99	1.89			
1984	344	15.38	4.94	2.19		2.76
1985	465	11.16	6.63	3.06		2.49
1986	486	11.89	8.19	2.74		1.90
1987	616	16.48	11.14	3.13		3.19
1988	642	18.13	12.53	3.00		3.98
1989	776	17.81	14.84	2.40		4.31
1990	920	21.25	16.44	2.18		3.61
1991	1171	25.24	19.70	2.15		6.83
1992	1164	52.51	24.03	2.54		10.56
1993	1393	51.89	36.68	3.42		13.09
1994	1702	60.27	48.83	3.83		18.43
1995	1558	74.84	51.08	3.84		22.59
1996	1634	77.28	58.21	3.88		24.66
1997	2085	85.16	60.36	4.78		28.55
1998	2322	92.43	77.69	6.11		29.08
1999	2527	101.99	85.22	5.53		32.65
2000	2597	117.19	83.79	5.56		36.93
2001	5836	130.39	88.99	6.00		41.47
2002	4036	150.55	111.94	7.85		41.04
2003	3708	176.67	138.37	9.40		42.97
2004	6694	238.44	174.68	11.47	17.30	41.94
2005	9502	296.14	217.63	14.48	18.34	41.87
2006	12996	660.05	299.93	19.86	21.48	47.52
2007	6282	776.21	406.43	23.60	21.49	50.51
2008	5411	1045.62	566.12	27.16	22.49	46.71
2009	7280	1262.10	777.06	32.69	18.01	45.03
2010	9544	1343.67	921.70	37.65	18.68	47.01
2011	6381	1423.32	1034.24	32.40	20.91	48.84
2012	6710	1565.29	1165.97	34.46	27.84	50.56
2013	11578	1716.29	1371.43	37.01	25.57	48.26
2014	7740	1917.56	1424.11	40.89	29.26	59.69
2015	8662	2100.74	1540.74	40.86	27.68	61.83
2016	19157	2440.10	1594.17	37.29	26.40	59.60
2017	22774	2652.76	1685.87	37.68	30.02	60.23

注：自2011年起，商务部不再公布对外劳务合作项下合同数、合同金额以及完成营业额数据。

Note: Since 2011, Ministry of Commerce do not publish the number of projects contracted, contracted value and turnover fultilled data of Labor Services.

8-4 分国别(地区)对外承包工程合同数量及金额
Contracts Signed for Foreign Engineering Projects by Country or Region

国别(地区)	Country/Region	2016		2017	
		合同(份) Nunber of Contracts (unit)	金额(万美元) Contract Value (USD 10000)	合同(份) Nunber of Contracts (unit)	金额(万美元) Contract Value (USD 10000)
合　计	**Total**	**19157**	**24401009**	**22774**	**26527599**
亚 洲	**Asia**	**7668**	**12266711**	**7433**	**14366594**
阿富汗	Afghanistan	14	2721	12	35522
巴林	Bahrain	2	1553	2	1468
孟加拉国	Bangladesh	114	747852	201	1042051
文莱	Brunei	65	3717	52	141130
缅甸	Myanmar	157	280751	142	198901
柬埔寨	Cambodia	443	213348	109	330058
朝鲜	Korea DPR	1	8	1	2
中国香港	Hong Kong, China	171	792647	222	892373
印度	India	1154	223727	897	257606
印度尼西亚	Indonesia	856	1072546	1521	1720404
伊朗	Iran	162	861800	199	497130
伊拉克	Iran	211	552858	125	590619
以色列	Israel	14	85074	10	40004
日本	Japan	74	37867	43	33768
约旦	Jordan	5	933	15	207066
科威特	Kuwait	68	408281	33	360682
老挝	Laos	96	671193	159	521086
黎巴嫩	Lebanon	2	13	6	207
中国澳门	Macao, China	43	110068	71	214892
马来西亚	Malaysia	666	1123745	773	2485305
马尔代夫	Maldives	12	85097	21	124873
蒙古	Mongolia	83	359428	55	59571
尼泊尔	Nepal	39	29792	57	89893
阿曼	Oman	19	81895	25	115240
巴基斯坦	Pakistan	261	1158425	297	1075464
巴勒斯坦	Palestine	9	52	4	2553
菲律宾	Philippines	280	298259	177	368574
卡塔尔	Qatar	23	26799	13	43595
沙特阿拉伯	Saudi Arabia	139	502886	124	292833
新加坡	Singapore	381	246808	237	351710
韩国	Korea	223	77482	292	137237
斯里兰卡	Sri Lanka	68	249915	75	174738
叙利亚	Syria			1	310
泰国	Thailand	388	384303	435	372566
土耳其	Turkey	112	65524	70	82785
阿联酋	United Arab Emirates	567	504686	111	499300
也门共和国	Yemen Rep.	7	2319	11	965
越南	Vietnam	325	378870	246	609764
中国台湾	Taiwan, China	91	4265	196	6379
东帝汶	Timor Leste	6	29475	7	32450
哈萨克斯坦	Kazakhstan	151	341080	280	234843
吉尔吉斯斯坦	Kirghizia	43	46139	25	31700
塔吉克斯坦	Tadzhikistan	67	37541	30	35396
土库曼斯坦	Turkmenistan	27	45012	25	12431
乌兹别克斯坦	Uzbekistan	29	106385	26	41151
亚洲其他国家(地区)	Other Countries (Regions) in Asia		13572		

国别(地区)	Country/Region	2016 合同(份) Nunber of Contracts (unit)	2016 金额(万美元) Contract Value (USD 10000)	2017 合同(份) Nunber of Contracts (unit)	2017 金额(万美元) Contract Value (USD 10000)
非洲	**Africa**	**3969**	**7952015**	**2964**	**7650376**
阿尔及利亚	Algeria	212	584815	270	538949
安哥拉	Angola	215	855759	175	858220
贝宁	Benin	8	1763	7	17083
博茨瓦纳	Botswana	16	8860	39	25902
布隆迪	Burundi	2	1082	5	18341
喀麦隆	Cameroon	398	130896	307	115218
佛得角	Cape Verde	6	1162	9	5667
中非	Central African	5	46142	3	17239
乍得	Chad	76	167930	26	39807
科摩罗	Comoros	10	2511	5	21584
刚果(布)	Congo	50	357227	63	184503
吉布提	Djibouti	12	28431	46	35273
埃及	Egypt	31	802220	33	160510
赤道几内亚	Eq. Guinea	86	169220	57	123325
埃塞俄比亚	Ethiopia	206	835405	116	706366
加蓬	Gabon	21	163757	40	18778
冈比亚	Gambia	4	161	3	20205
加纳	Ghana	67	251069	81	290608
几内亚	Guinea	35	183716	48	143157
几内亚(比绍)	Guinea Bissau	2	2134	4	540
科特迪瓦	Cote d'Ivoire	18	150528	22	46309
肯尼亚	Kenya	110	424789	174	1007838
利比里亚	Liberia	63	58148	66	9033
利比亚	Libya	5	3643	2	3
马达加斯加	Madagascar	18	7373	28	32624
马拉维	Malawi	40	11886	44	13786
马里	Mali	18	33291	23	39386
毛里塔尼亚	Mauritania	9	12335	11	163249
毛里求斯	Mauritius	22	10582	24	15861
摩洛哥	Morocco	42	65383	44	82110
莫桑比克	Mozambique	66	40518	73	60172
纳米比亚	Namibia	47	53721	77	16047
尼日尔	Niger	98	28483	35	48497
尼日利亚	Nigeria	166	598971	154	1148032
卢旺达	Rwanda	15	40421	19	33089
圣多美和普林西比	Sao Tome and Principe	4	253	2	152
塞内加尔	Senegal	842	104114	43	74477
塞舌尔	Seychelles	5	863	13	2579
塞拉利昂	Sierra Leone	24	34894	22	12692
索马里	Somali	3	2800	4	2100
南非	S. Africa	109	54869	54	84663
苏丹	Sudan	230	170250	95	143545
坦桑尼亚	Tanzania	56	135713	83	109999
多哥	Togo	10	13477	26	13131
突尼斯	Tunisia	17	27923	28	18381
乌干达	Uganda	95	160573	83	95493
布基纳法索	Burkina Faso	1	12	1	1202
刚果(金)	Congo DR	129	94614	135	286961
赞比亚	Zambia	145	631253	175	486454
津巴布韦	Zimbabwe	45	217304	40	148153
莱索托	Lesotho	5	2340	3	829
斯威士兰	Swaziland	1	34		
厄立特里亚	Eritrea	16	1553	11	3199
南苏丹共和国	Republic of South Sudan	33	164845	13	109060

国别(地区)	Country/Region	2016		2017	
		合同(份) Nunber of Contracts (unit)	金额(万美元) Contract Value (USD 10000)	合同(份) Nunber of Contracts (unit)	金额(万美元) Contract Value (USD 10000)
欧洲	**Europe**	**4868**	**1011988**	**8044**	**1721542**
比利时	Belgium	7	1117	95	3523
丹麦	Denmark			2	2688
英国	United Kingdom	109	106401	38	56548
德国	Germany	86	63535	456	74234
法国	France	2396	156796	4312	166336
爱尔兰	Ireland			1	11
意大利	Italy	100	6860	302	7004
卢森堡	Luxembourg	5	677		
荷兰	Netherlands	963	24479	2096	25456
希腊	Greece	13	7618	15	7961
葡萄牙	Portugal	13	7463	15	36540
西班牙	Spain	77	33828	37	31692
阿尔巴尼亚	Albania	8	915		143
奥地利	Austria	14	6344	17	12141
保加利亚	Bulgaria	37	9440	12	3425
芬兰	Finland	1	357	11	86959
匈牙利	Hungary	11	3487	12	3742
冰岛	Iceland			1	1704
马耳他	Malta			2	213
摩纳哥	Monaco	1	47		
挪威	Norway	5	16907	2	140
波兰	Poland	19	6228	52	2593
罗马尼亚	Romania	528	25438	188	8347
瑞典	Sweden	13	8789	22	15934
瑞士	Switaerland	3	318	44	2530
爱沙尼亚	Estonia	16	1633		
拉脱维亚	Latvia	3	1002		
立陶宛	Lithuania	3	256	6	720
格鲁吉亚	Georgia	18	35624	14	39232
亚美尼亚	Armenia	5	48240	3	31345
阿塞拜疆	Azerbaijan	12	522	18	3885
白俄罗斯	Byelorussia	45	50774	80	24960
俄罗斯	Russia	255	265909	137	775229
乌克兰	Ukraine	32	53133	20	112508
斯洛文尼亚	Slovenia	9	174	3	78415
克罗地亚	Croatia	3	99	4	138
捷克	Czech Rep.	16	9162	11	8117
斯洛伐克	Slovak			2	627
马其顿	Macedonia			2	80
波黑	Bosnia and Hercegovina			2	38223
塞尔维亚	Serbia	41	57624	9	58182
黑山	Montenegro	1	791	1	15

国别(地区)	Country/Region	2016 合同(份) Nunber of Contracts (unit)	2016 金额(万美元) Contract Value (USD 10000)	2017 合同(份) Nunber of Contracts (unit)	2017 金额(万美元) Contract Value (USD 10000)
拉丁美洲	**Latin America**	**1079**	**1610050**	**1002**	**1585882**
安提瓜和巴布达	Antigua Barbuda	2	448		9
阿根廷	Argentina	50	159737	245	143278
阿鲁巴岛	Aruba			1	214
巴哈马	Bahamas		16618	5	3382
巴巴多斯	Barbados	2	702	2	20021
玻利维亚	Bolivia	16	84626	23	165854
巴西	Brazil	169	166656	102	174270
智利	Chile	41	13688	33	12121
哥伦比亚	Colombia	109	20228	104	17075
多米尼克	Dominica		346	4	9435
哥斯达黎加	CostaRica	25	13208	16	4139
古巴	Cuba	20	32213	22	66606
库腊索岛	Curacao			2	663
多米尼加共和国	Dominican Rep.	8	454	16	3181
厄瓜多尔	Ecuador	80	209362	67	88757
格林纳达	Grenada	2	205	3	6813
危地马拉	Guatemala	14		8	5012
圭亚那	Guyana		20	5	12040
海地	Haiti	3	274		
洪都拉斯	Honduras	9	6462	6	895
牙买加	Jamaica	13	143237	12	15322
墨西哥	Mexico	83	149543	45	76790
尼加拉瓜	Nicaragua	13	625	5	943
巴拿马	Panama	35	35242	42	20720
巴拉圭	Paraguay	3	671	2	423
秘鲁	Peru	113	48817	121	110876
萨尔瓦多	El Salvador	7		2	228
苏里南	Suriname	6	7340	2	22822
特立尼达和多巴哥	Trinidad & Tobago	1	1283	6	23388
乌拉圭	Uruguay	61	3504	4	919
委内瑞拉	Venezuela	193	493848	97	579687
圣基茨和尼维斯	St. Kitts-Nevis	1	695		
北美洲	**North America**	**1341**	**435005**	**2983**	**361245**
加拿大	Canada	20	8767	23	25423
美国	United States	1319	425738	2959	335797
格陵兰	Greenland			1	25
北美洲其他国家(地区)	Oth. N.Amer. nes	2	500		
大洋洲及太平洋岛屿	**Oceania and Pacific Is.**	**232**	**568562**	**348**	**841960**
澳大利亚	Australia	113	356707	120	497393
库克群岛	Cook Islands	1		2	1760
斐济	Fiji	13	10305	26	38728
新喀里多尼亚	New Caledonia (Fr)		1200		
瓦努阿图	Vanuatu	17	3356	20	15415
新西兰	New Zealand	16	47339	76	73746
巴布亚新几内亚	Papua New Guinea	58	143134	85	199090
所罗门群岛	Solomon Is.	1	911	2	1589
汤加	Tonga	8	4480	10	707
萨摩亚	Samoa	4	1007	2	10641
基里巴斯	Kiribati			1	866
图瓦卢	Tuvalu			1	1072
密克罗尼西亚联邦	Micronesia Commonwealth			1	917
帕劳共和国	Republic of Palau	1	92	2	35
东萨摩亚	American Samoa		31		
其他	**Others**		**556678**		

8-5 分国别(地区)对外承包工程营业额

Turnover of Foreign Engineering Projects by Country or Region

单位：万美元

Unit: USD 10000

国别(地区)	Country/Region	2014	2015	2016	2017
合　计	**Total**	**14241066**	**15407423**	**15941749**	**16858661**
亚洲	**Asia**	**6483818**	**6907010**	**7685147**	**8828857**
阿富汗	Afghanistan	1630	1133	4058	5073
巴林	Bahrain	265	27	814	2198
孟加拉国	Bangladesh	177854	175184	191623	314660
文莱	Brunei	3822	8653	54793	71016
缅甸	Myanmar	81856	189471	191713	161406
柬埔寨	Cambodia	96533	121396	165598	176373
塞浦路斯	Cyprus	8191	113	11400	6
朝鲜	Korea DPR	9049	1832	292	2
中国香港	Hong Kong, China	372760	402744	423313	554531
印度	India	253595	267458	182435	246496
印度尼西亚	Indonesia	458443	481528	408870	556185
伊朗	Iran	222979	159048	224689	205025
伊拉克	Iraq	489810	397661	345464	273809
以色列	Israel	9535	15238	23162	113073
日本	Japan	33406	44346	31249	32778
约旦	Jordan	1661	8459	3813	66940
科威特	Kuwait	140063	128114	151314	196352
老挝	Laos	232773	321606	294729	422894
黎巴嫩	Lebanon	935	721	13	6371
中国澳门	Macao, China	79792	147710	181538	278641
马来西亚	Malaysia	310112	356227	474809	814615
马尔代夫	Maldives	6866	14380	24705	41467
蒙古	Mongolia	114102	93484	74583	106814
尼泊尔	Nepal	27283	25302	22279	29860
阿曼	Oman	30408	44939	80646	82085
巴基斯坦	Pakistan	424619	516289	726809	1133799
巴勒斯坦	Palestine	2	527	74	542
菲律宾	Philippines	134928	204150	166180	188546
卡塔尔	Qatar	156402	136173	119875	103368
沙特阿拉伯	Saudi Arabia	594713	701812	948175	634381
新加坡	Singapore	337607	354079	375551	343707
韩国	Korea	39342	27393	33612	36759
斯里兰卡	Sri Lanka	219139	136871	147677	225245
叙利亚	Syria	941	1634	254	62
泰国	Thailand	183624	281007	293579	338380
土耳其	Turkey	180958	133887	214547	120443
阿联酋	United Arab Emirates	115007	153943	224637	249594
也门共和国	Yemen Rep.	10485	3354	1591	1457
越南	Vietnam	398439	352317	332394	287860
中国台湾	Taiwan, China	8702	3945	11935	4061
东帝汶	East Timor	2824	5315	23805	35519
哈萨克斯坦	Kazakhstan	235768	234700	275779	223838
吉尔吉斯斯坦	Kirghizia	58736	54857	55663	47998
塔吉克斯坦	Tadzhikistan	40931	64377	70787	19042
土库曼斯坦	Turkmenistan	124000	68921	31916	25264
乌兹别克斯坦	Uzbekistan	49772	61241	49111	50320
亚洲其他国家	Oth.Asia.nes	3154	3444	13297	

8-5 续表 1 Continued 1

单位：万美元
Unit: USD 10000

国别(地区)	Country/Region	2014	2015	2016	2017
非洲	**Africa**	**5297475**	**5478376**	**5146029**	**5118786**
阿尔及利亚	Algeria	633429	824061	843421	784898
安哥拉	Angola	639843	495275	433194	669326
贝宁	Benin	25616	9159	9291	8110
博茨瓦纳	Botswana	29025	31504	30017	25281
布隆迪	Burundi	6789	7146	6297	2704
喀麦隆	Cameroon	123886	141350	151751	189239
佛得角	Cape Verde	4424	2458	806	1694
中非	Central African	297	486	1073	1981
乍得	Chad	111247	71585	96547	62785
科摩罗	Comoros	3640	2225	1757	1457
刚果(布)	Congo	253189	297587	216928	74754
吉布提	Djibouti	36871	107188	84088	36605
埃及	Egypt	92402	201777	228114	154179
赤道几内亚	Eq.Guinea	207670	136854	118268	102500
埃塞俄比亚	Ethiopia	683203	589402	470603	552174
加蓬	Gabon	77985	56413	69496	47548
冈比亚	Gambia	496	734	519	1010
加纳	Ghana	153439	140598	114846	108511
几内亚	Guinea	60925	48642	38617	61500
几内亚(比绍)	Guinea Bissau	2326	3245	1631	669
科特迪瓦	Cote d'Ivoire	35319	63005	63977	97663
肯尼亚	Kenya	169556	384569	454772	372919
利比里亚	Liberia	20577	19873	24981	22136
利比亚	Libya	15616	17380	3205	5118
马达加斯加	Madagascar	13812	7484	5935	13270
马拉维	Malawi	9016	9232	8306	8771
马里	Mali	34099	23462	29981	38323
毛里塔尼亚	Mauritania	29174	28413	14098	22821
毛里求斯	Mauritius	15105	19824	11051	11720
摩洛哥	Morocco	60700	113109	76666	37649
莫桑比克	Mozambique	81471	118750	133231	110875
纳米比亚	Namibia	36489	76642	69828	69667
尼日尔	Niger	88152	63689	43483	17150
尼日利亚	Nigeria	453165	348142	261276	310383
卢旺达	Rwanda	23564	21251	15777	19627
圣多美和普林西比	Sao Tome & Principe	102	127	244	122
塞内加尔	Senegal	35526	50037	60022	94765
塞舌尔	Seychelles	7511	3517	2500	1044
塞拉利昂	Sierra Leone	17881	7928	12683	9193
索马里	Somalia	49	224	3003	1527
南非	S. Africa	39980	45177	42091	56880
苏丹	Sudan	181811	154873	146050	82125
坦桑尼亚	Tanzania	206965	141471	152409	102586
多哥	Togo	25395	21176	14424	25729
突尼斯	Tunisia	11717	11067	13586	21896
乌干达	Uganda	111751	155063	188990	217429
布基纳法索	Burkina Faso	2585	320	77	27
刚果(金)	Congo DR	144968	114388	117896	149954
赞比亚	Zambia	203020	178981	179045	230749
津巴布韦	Zimbabwe	30581	45789	44363	30591

单位：万美元
Unit: USD 10000

国别(地区)	Country/Region	2014	2015	2016	2017
莱索托	Lesotho	13011	12610	7579	1441
斯威士兰	Swaziland			34	
厄立特里亚	Eritrea	12010	12487	10191	12239
南苏丹	Republic of South Sudan	20052	36614	16015	35473
非洲其他国家(地区)	Other Countries (Regions) in Africa	44	4011	1000	
欧洲	**Europe**	**715057**	**878279**	**798582**	**931617**
比利时	Belgium	7002	3638	15389	14280
丹麦	Denmark	102	218	100	495
英国	United Kingdom	48281	84736	71896	108268
德国	Germany	38138	52252	59559	63631
法国	France	148177	184421	136049	144236
爱尔兰	Ireland	713			
意大利	Italy	6176	14498	20105	20105
卢森堡	Luxembourg		111	949	235
荷兰	Netherlands	23173	24584	17588	16163
希腊	Greece	3345	7632	29930	15973
葡萄牙	Portugal	5044	6561	5645	4939
西班牙	Spain	8902	18809	29689	27916
阿尔巴尼亚	Albania	616		896	182
奥地利	Austria	1895	3041	4469	7490
保加利亚	Bulgaria	20894	8537	7758	3997
芬兰	Finland		2613	357	1676
匈牙利	Hungary	3693	4650	3883	3390
冰岛	Iceland				1704
马耳他	Malta	105	3443	31	213
摩纳哥	Monaco		4032	47	
挪威	Norway	1432	6873	5797	20666
波兰	Poland	12952	5037	5814	966
罗马尼亚	Romania	16331	14794	18457	9322
瑞典	Sweden	9284	11506	10528	6057
瑞士	Switzerland	485	96	255	1112
拉脱维亚	Latvia	467	399		
爱沙尼亚	Estonia			497	
立陶宛	Lithuania			287	1063
格鲁吉亚	Georgia	19323	19049	10918	38840
亚美尼亚	Armenia	857		1750	5226
阿塞拜疆	Azerbaijan	12947	7592	1392	2363
白俄罗斯	Belorussia	117515	98955	109905	66747
摩尔多瓦	Moldavia	16			11
俄罗斯	Russia	115501	171440	148599	199234
乌克兰	Ukraine	16937	31375	28915	35320
斯洛文尼亚	Slovenia	76	194	688	826
克罗地亚	Croatia	85	213	471	138
捷克	Czech Rep.	4618	7754	5698	6003
斯洛伐克	Slovak				201
马其顿共和国	Macedonia,FYR	16515	36906	20958	14071
波黑	Bosnia & Herzegovina	29548	19410	1724	693
塞尔维亚	Serbia	23525	19801	17889	36897
黑山	Montenegro	385	3107	3696	50968
拉丁美洲	**Latin America**	**1318059**	**1640035**	**1453965**	**1291514**
安提瓜和巴布达	Antigua & Barbuda	11133	6320	1085	166
阿根廷	Argentina	50205	217332	112859	158003
阿鲁巴岛	Aruba	26			214

单位：万美元
Unit: USD 10000

国别(地区)	Country/Region	2014	2015	2016	2017
巴哈马	Bahamas	66672	29469	33519	48724
巴巴多斯	Barbados	46	7	456	4273
伯利兹	Belize	30			
玻利维亚	Bolivia	32950	26524	54937	46715
巴西	Brazil	150443	202023	196329	185365
智利	Chile	11219	19620	17941	16595
哥伦比亚	Colombia	30827	39564	37893	20473
多米尼克	Dominica	923	66	932	3483
哥斯达黎加	Costa Rica	5447	7070	7575	3560
古巴	Cuba	8667	9162	44691	25850
库腊索岛	Curacao				382
多米尼加共和国	Republic of Dominica	3272	4473	1673	3567
厄瓜多尔	Ecuador	240342	328837	286223	212748
格林纳达	Grenade	3065	1443	123	128
危地马拉	Guatemala	1374	1644	1569	1398
圭亚那	Guyana	11211	9147	17595	13979
海地	Haiti	142		242	
洪都拉斯	Honduras	401	3933	7068	12722
牙买加	Jamaica	46559	38860	29681	18884
墨西哥	Mexico	55670	90219	125078	74962
尼加拉瓜	Nicaragua	11508	3271	2443	409
巴拿马	Panama	6994	11141	9343	29929
巴拉圭	Paraguay	903	1596	671	423
秘鲁	Peru	41608	62566	56907	59341
圣文森特和格林纳丁斯	Saint Vincent & Grenadines	10			
萨尔瓦多	El Salvador	78		47	229
苏里南	Suriname	2755	2624	17461	3331
特立尼达和多巴哥	Trinidad & Tobago	16373	22525	11244	11622
乌拉圭	Uruguay	6458	6395	4246	1428
委内瑞拉	Venezuela	500509	494205	369534	332612
英属维尔京群岛	Virgin Is. (E)			4560	
圣其茨--尼维斯	St. Kitts-Nevis	240		41	
北美洲	**North America**	**201736**	**281411**	**231590**	**237285**
加拿大	Canada	12412	10663	8708	13859
美国	United States	188912	270429	222280	223413
格陵兰	Greenland		5		13
北美洲其他国家(地区)	Oth.N.Amer.nes	411	314	602	
大洋洲及太平洋岛屿	**Oceania and Pacific Is.**	**224761**	**222313**	**407936**	**450601**
澳大利亚	Australia	114742	121217	292578	337472
库克群岛	Cook Islands	837	1600	2150	1035
斐济	Fiji	12904	15380	14171	18441
新喀里多尼亚	New Caledonia	220	90		
瓦努阿图	Vanuatu	5387	4433	14005	13921
新西兰	New Zealand	14815	11749	20671	15816
巴布亚新几内亚	Papua New Guinea	70426	60010	54491	55698
所罗门群岛	Solomon Is.	32		482	1863
汤加	Tonga	1832	2177	4492	3311
萨摩亚	Samoa	1559	4165	3842	2167
基里巴斯	Kiribati		377	898	444
密克罗尼西亚	Micronesia	258	902		425
帕劳共和国	Republic of Palau			17	9
东萨摩亚	American Samoa	1725	211	139	
大洋洲其他国家（地区）	Other Countries (Regions) in Oceanic	26	2		
其他	**Others**	**160**		**218500**	

8-6 分国别(地区)年末在境外从事承包工程人员
Personnel Abroad for Engineering Projects Classified by Country or Region at the Year-end

单位：人
Unit: person

国别(地区)	Country/Region	2014	2015	2016	2017
合　计	**Total**	**408851**	**408565**	**372880**	**376827**
亚洲	**Asia**	**165571**	**168038**	**173780**	**193438**
阿富汗	Afghanistan	31	49	17	162
巴林	Bahrain	7	3	137	2
孟加拉国	Bangladesh	3799	3335	4936	7861
文莱	Brunei	124	202	400	3814
缅甸	Myanmar	4025	4548	3362	3651
柬埔寨	Cambodia	4763	5573	4732	3896
朝鲜	Korea DPR	666	721	80	
中国香港	Hongkong,China	690	783	759	641
印度	India	1873	1491	1289	1279
印度尼西亚	Indonesia	15468	12940	15433	16363
伊朗	Iran	1371	2030	1899	2149
伊拉克	Iraq	11586	10421	7822	9100
以色列	Israel	106	105	86	511
日本	Japan	65	521	519	510
约旦	Jordan	80	57	199	343
科威特	Kuwait	2833	2728	3253	6903
老挝	Laos	13664	10247	9428	16879
黎巴嫩	Lebanon	5			
中国澳门	Macao,China	1394	1581	1427	1345
马来西亚	Malaysia	10130	9351	12312	21214
马尔代夫	Maldives	185	252	342	724
蒙古	Mongolia	3791	3875	3589	2852
尼泊尔	Nepal	1883	711	1028	1439
阿曼	Oman	495	467	585	916
巴基斯坦	Pakistan	7481	9038	14582	20850
巴勒斯坦	Balestine				2
菲律宾	Philippines	1498	1474	1582	3564
卡塔尔	Qatar	2404	2807	2897	1855
沙特阿拉伯	Saudi Arabia	22960	27334	31633	22080
新加坡	Singapore	7615	5659	4075	3588
韩国	Korea	60	87	92	86
斯里兰卡	Sri Lanka	3043	3432	3775	3705
泰国	Thailand	3021	2787	2567	2542
土耳其	Turkey	3495	6709	7917	6330
阿联酋	United Arab Emirates	5461	5485	4682	4847
也门共和国	Yemen Rep.	503	162	139	21
越南	Vietnam	9132	8521	8966	7636
中国台湾	Taiwan,China	15	16	23	25
东帝汶	Timor Leste	167	332	908	843
哈萨克斯坦	Kazakhstan	8960	11129	7271	8065
吉尔吉斯斯坦	Kirghizia	2841	3505	2722	1650

8-6 续表 1 Continued 1

单位：人
Unit: person

国别(地区)	Country/Region	2014	2015	2016	2017
塔吉克斯坦	Tadzhikistan	1262	1633	1327	891
土库曼斯坦	Turkmenistan	1019	990	498	481
乌兹别克斯坦	Uzbekstan	2164	2904	2010	1823
亚洲其他国家	Oth.Asia.Nes	3436	2043	2480	
非洲	**Africa**	**197853**	**194848**	**165080**	**147093**
阿尔及利亚	Algeria	46266	59888	58630	44545
安哥拉	Angola	38427	31030	19398	16872
贝宁	Benin	482	172	221	164
博茨瓦纳	Botswana	1427	1218	567	458
布隆迪	Burundi	482	569	400	385
喀麦隆	Cameroon	3532	4185	3671	2596
佛得角	Cape Verde	459	404	307	352
中非	Central African	665	667	39	183
乍得	Chad	3060	3197	2393	2106
科摩罗	Comoros	226	235	303	121
刚果(布)	Congo	12288	8021	4921	3547
吉布提	Djibouti	154	965	1264	906
埃及	Egypt	185	2301	1545	1849
赤道几内亚	Eq. Guinea	10885	7942	4332	3615
埃塞俄比亚	Ethiopia	13325	9385	9044	8636
加蓬	Gabon	1251	2004	2421	1952
冈比亚	Gambia	53	38	68	303
加纳	Ghana	2377	2228	2094	3314
几内亚	Guinea	2126	1037	2074	3211
几内亚(比绍)	Guinea bissau	592	391	354	344
科特迪瓦	Cote d'Ivoire	541	715	583	1121
肯尼亚	Kenya	4816	7269	7937	8271
利比里亚	Liberia	462	749	813	1054
利比亚	Libya	77	128	221	87
马达加斯加	Madagascar	189	163	108	163
马拉维	Malawi	331	285	236	237
马里	Mali	845	771	658	480
毛里塔尼亚	Mauritania	1115	979	763	757
毛里求斯	Mauritius	1161	903	496	474
摩洛哥	Morocco	1042	1201	692	527
莫桑比克	Mozambique	2688	3281	3486	3325
纳米比亚	Namibia	1370	1450	1037	807
尼日尔	Niger	1748	1629	1016	771
尼日利亚	Nigeria	7044	6665	6037	6272
卢旺达	Rwanda	1143	474	466	687
圣多美和普林西比	Sao Tome & Principe	6	7	7	
塞内加尔	Senegal	1803	1809	1392	1798
塞舌尔	Seychelles	199	228	228	112

8-6 续表 2 Continued 2

单位：人
Unit: person

国别(地区)	Country/Region	2014	2015	2016	2017
塞拉利昂	Sierra Leone	721	778	766	605
索马里	Somalia			30	3
南非	S. Africa	3354	2106	280	400
苏丹	Sudan	8029	5993	4825	3760
坦桑尼亚	Tanzania	4924	5017	3698	2945
多哥	Togo	926	173	399	329
突尼斯	Tunisia	319	310	203	211
乌干达	Uganda	2506	3446	3247	3174
布基纳法索	Burkina Faso	36			3
刚果(金)	Congo DR	4522	4575	3935	5111
赞比亚	Zambia	5576	5430	5482	6728
津巴布韦	Zimbabwe	651	818	879	669
莱索托	Lesotho	442	327	275	130
厄立特里亚	Eritrea	394	463	497	278
南苏丹共和国	Republic of South Sudan	596	792	342	345
非洲其他国家(地区)	Other Countries (Regions) in Africa	15	37		
欧洲	**Europe**	**13713**	**13943**	**9244**	**9842**
比利时	Belgium	40			
英国	United Kingdom	28	32	67	69
德国	Germany	17	55	115	384
法国	France	26	26	59	63
意大利	Italy	28	71	82	76
卢森堡	Luxembourg		10	20	
荷兰	Netherlands	1	1	58	38
希腊	Greece	22	22	22	22
西班牙	Spain	1022	1022	29	19
阿尔巴尼亚	Albania	12		76	32
奥地利	Austria			36	101
保加利亚	Bulgaria	214	167	152	104
芬兰	Finland				16
冰岛	Iceland				1
马耳他	Malta	10	10	11	27
挪威	Norway	1	1		
波兰	Poland	97	89	100	28
罗马尼亚	Romania	67	67	54	54
瑞典	Sweden	4	4	4	4
瑞士	Switzerland			14	11
立陶宛	Lithuania				3
格鲁吉亚	Georgia	717	529	564	882
亚美尼亚	Armenia			69	240
阿塞拜疆	Azerbaijan	366	220	114	80
白俄罗斯	Byelorussia	1743	3510	2716	2109
俄罗斯	Russia	7858	6652	3624	3578
乌克兰	Ukraine	29	29	34	264
斯洛文尼亚	Slovenia		10	35	
克罗地亚	Croatia	18	28		
马其顿共和国	Macedonia, FYR	248	393	497	578
波黑	Bosnia & Hercegovina	578		60	39
塞尔维亚	Serbia	567	301	254	178
黑山	Montenegro		587	372	842
欧洲其他国家(地区)	Other Countries(Regions) in Europe		107	6	

8-6 续表 3 Continued 3

单位：人
Unit: person

国别(地区)	Country/Region	2014	2015	2016	2017
拉丁美洲	**Latin America**	**26564**	**26226**	**19115**	**18608**
安提瓜和巴布达	Antigua Barbuda	653	151	24	27
阿根廷	Argentina	1207	1753	1328	1434
巴哈马	Bahama	511	376	253	133
巴巴多斯	Barbados	11		19	26
玻利维亚	Bolivia	277	881	820	1172
巴西	Brazil	324	314	399	401
智利	Chile	36	54	112	79
哥伦比亚	Colombia	336	343	685	306
多米尼克	Dominica	85	76	140	26
哥斯达黎加	CostaRica	144	292	262	22
古巴	Cuba	246	256	247	175
库腊索岛	Curacao				5
多米尼加共和国	Dominica Rep.		50	12	13
厄瓜多尔	Ecuador	7150	7369	3939	3341
法属圭亚那	French Guyana				10
格林纳达	Grenade	152	23	21	19
危地马拉	Guatemala	101	66	65	51
圭亚那	Guyana	393	270	237	84
海地	Haiti	2	3		
洪都拉斯	Honduras		77	164	178
牙买加	Jamaica	543	546	349	334
墨西哥	Mexico	271	274	269	261
尼加拉瓜	Nicaragua	68	9	73	68
巴拿马	Panama	25	115	354	493
秘鲁	Peru	4605	4724	4959	6819
圣卢西亚	Saint Lucia	7			
苏里南	Suriname	327	176	153	139
特立尼达和多巴哥	Trinidad & Tobago	1851	1314	1102	883
乌拉圭	Uruguay	3	3	3	3
委内瑞拉	Venezuela	7236	6711	3111	2091
圣基茨和尼维斯	St. Kitts-Nevis			15	15
北美洲	**North America**	**1261**	**1579**	**1698**	**4828**
加拿大	Canada	49	77	91	101
美国	United States	1209	1502	1607	4727
格陵兰	Greenland	3			
大洋洲及太平洋岛屿	**Oceania and Pacific Is.**	**3885**	**3931**	**3963**	**3018**
澳大利亚	Australia	485	448	157	159
库克群岛	Cook Islands	40	6	3	96
斐济	Fiji	521	551	637	720
新喀里多尼亚	NewCaledonia	1171	1171	1131	
瓦努阿图	Vanuatu	160	214	511	507
新西兰	New Zealand	26	21	26	36
巴布亚新几内亚	Papua New Guinea	1101	1045	683	829
所罗门群岛	Solomon Is.	3	3	3	3
汤加	Tonga	209	223	431	323
萨摩亚	Samoa	62	69	309	276
基里巴斯	Kiribati		55	34	27
密克罗尼西亚	Micronesia				42
东萨摩亚	American Samoa	107	125	38	
其他	**Others**	**4**			

8-7 分国别(地区)年末在境外从事劳务合作人员
Personnel Abroad for Labour Services Classified by Country or Region at the Year-end

单位：人
Unit: person

国别(地区)	Country/Region	2014	2015	2016	2017
合　计	**Total**	**596881**	**618295**	**595976**	**602342**
亚洲	**Asia**	**469013**	**487077**	**469996**	**474146**
巴林	Bahrain	73	9	2	2
孟加拉国	Bangladesh	137	119	226	336
不丹	Bhutan	1			
文莱	Brunei				214
缅甸	Myanmar	632	787	1271	1031
柬埔寨	Cambodia	2345	2311	2012	1981
塞浦路斯	Cyprus	260	324	284	298
朝鲜	Korea DPR	38			
中国香港	Hong Kong, China	50850	52371	47066	58001
印度	India	149	149	139	165
印度尼西亚	Indonesia	867	835	1002	1371
伊朗	Iran		227	227	284
伊拉克	Iraq	183	163	326	339
以色列	Israel	243	231	299	712
日本	Japan	159384	154353	145488	143384
约旦	Jordan	1050	1040	246	106
科威特	Kuwait	2252	2285	2110	887
老挝	Laos	1151	1534	2060	2908
黎巴嫩	Lebanon	6			
中国澳门	Macao, China	113489	120414	121209	127302
马来西亚	Malaysia	3779	5267	6885	6705
马尔代夫	Maldives	21			123
蒙古	Mongolia	2169	657	593	822
尼泊尔	Nepal	158	366	366	284
阿曼	Oman	23	20	20	36
巴基斯坦	Pakistan	478	477	506	428
巴勒斯坦	Palestine			1	9
菲律宾	Philippines	65	183	207	208
卡塔尔	Qatar	1482	1463	1514	1220
沙特阿拉伯	Saudi Arabia	9548	10643	10436	7427
新加坡	Singapore	86020	96726	96537	91900
韩国	Korea	14465	13207	11029	11002
斯里兰卡	Sri Lanka	297	1678	586	603
泰国	Thailand	721	901	694	863
土耳其	Turkey	33	31	32	443
阿联酋	United Arab Emirates	6187	6177	5393	3886
也门共和国	Republic of Yemen		16	7	
越南	Vietnam	3308	3246	3452	2108
中国台湾	Taiwan, China	6273	7238	6462	4807
东帝汶	East Timor				13
哈萨克斯坦	Kazakhstan	345	1265	961	1614
吉尔吉斯斯坦	Kirghizia	271	228	205	218
塔吉克斯坦	Tadzhikistan	103	105	112	106
乌兹别克斯坦	Uzbekistan	114	31	30	
亚洲其他国家(地区)	Oth.Asia.nes	43		1	

8-7 续表 1 Continued 1

单位：人
Unit: person

国别(地区)	Country/Region	2014	2015	2016	2017
非洲	**Africa**	**61532**	**68848**	**67438**	**55596**
阿尔及利亚	Algeria	25276	31234	32966	16946
安哥拉	Angola	11804	13076	10030	8695
贝宁	Benin	151	147	159	166
博茨瓦纳	Botswana	31	29	29	29
布隆迪	Burundi	59	265	268	264
喀麦隆	Cameroon	104	118	104	81
佛得角	Cape Verde	183	135	114	74
中非	Central African				36
乍得	Chad	402	740	899	142
刚果(布)	Congo	2195	921	1372	1352
吉布提	Djibouti	24		206	355
埃及	Egypt		1	1	1
赤道几内亚	Eq. Guinea	1665	1623	1376	1069
埃塞俄比亚	Ethiopia	753	588	839	1027
加蓬	Gabon	309	300	265	329
冈比亚	Gambia		28	48	23
加纳	Ghana	974	1309	948	1585
几内亚	Guinea	252	463	467	554
几内亚(比绍)	Guinea bissau	1	1	1	1
科特迪瓦	Cote d' Ivoire	105	106	108	120
肯尼亚	Kenya	122	167	222	432
利比里亚	Liberia	3637	3215	2350	4885
利比亚	Libya	38	7	28	47
马达加斯加	Madagascar	366	383	394	438
马拉维	Malawi	21	26	49	44
马里	Mali	259	221	201	
毛里塔尼亚	Mauritania	454	457	721	829
毛里求斯	Mauritius	1203	1124	687	605
摩洛哥	Morocco	195	180	172	170
莫桑比克	Mozambique	526	665	710	740
纳米比亚	Namibia	101	143	167	73
尼日尔	Niger	110	114	118	119
尼日利亚	Nigeria	1633	1993	2882	3921
卢旺达	Rwanda	239	736	897	992
塞内加尔	Senegal	116	156	242	314
塞舌尔	Seychelles	192	214	73	27
塞拉利昂	Sierra Leone	588	548	610	772
南非	S. Africa	832			111
苏丹	Sudan	1779	1917	1377	1474
坦桑尼亚	Tanzania	695	779	736	746
多哥	Togo	131	129	255	397
突尼斯	Tunisia	4	2	2	78
乌干达	Uganda	311	1027	1181	1512
刚果(金)	Congo DR	633	1253	1176	1182

8-7 续表 2 Continued 2

单位：人
Unit: person

国别(地区)	Country/Region	2014	2015	2016	2017
布基纳法索	Burkina Faso	1			
赞比亚	Zambia	1913	1142	1098	2052
津巴布韦	Zimbabwe	42	146	62	80
莱索托	Lesotho	852	858	625	495
斯威士兰	Swaziland	3			
厄立特里亚	Eritrea	126	125	125	126
南苏丹共和国	Republic of South Sudan	122	37	78	86
欧洲	**Europe**	**20295**	**20970**	**19962**	**20142**
比利时	Belgium	1	2	2	32
丹麦	Denmark	69	56	62	76
英国	United Kingdom	961	989	785	1220
德国	Germany	3622	4181	5090	4905
法国	France	25	22	24	2
爱尔兰	Ireland	1			
意大利	Italy	630	661	650	1256
卢森堡	Luxembourg				1
荷兰	Netherlands	267	286	284	316
希腊	Greece	97	179	145	290
葡萄牙	Portugal		2	1	13
西班牙	Spain			7	7
芬兰	Finland	2	5	18	13
直布罗陀	Gibraltar	156	154	7	143
匈牙利	Hungary	4	4	4	4
冰岛	Iceland			1	9
马耳他	Malta	456	355	580	1012
摩纳哥	Monaco	5	8	24	20
挪威	Norway	550	534	548	521
波兰	Poland	20	24	23	51
瑞典	Sweden	31	37	50	16
瑞士	Switzerland	2		49	123
立陶宛	Lithuania	8	5	3	2
格鲁吉亚	Georgia	230	550	550	550
白俄罗斯	Belorussia	29	20	25	12
俄罗斯	Russia	13110	12781	10916	9433
乌克兰	Ukraine				2
斯洛文尼亚	Slovenia	4			
克罗地亚	Croatia	2	2	2	2
塞尔维亚	Serbia	13	12	12	11
黑山	Montenegro		101	100	100
拉丁美洲	**Latin America**	**34974**	**29867**	**26473**	**39066**
安提瓜和巴布达	Antigua & Barbuda	42	43	20	10
阿根廷	Argentina	215	94	112	147

8-7 续表 3　Continued 3

单位：人
Unit: person

国别(地区)	Country/Region	2014	2015	2016	2017
巴哈马	Bahamas	4576	2077	1608	5191
巴巴多斯	Barbados	74	122	137	62
伯利兹	Belize	1267	1219	1591	2004
玻利维亚	Bolivia	27	27	27	60
巴西	Brazil	160	160	157	157
开曼群岛	Cayman Is.	57	45	27	58
智利	Chile	508	261	369	344
哥伦比亚	Colombia	21	18	18	2
多米尼克	Dominica	22		3	29
哥斯达黎加	Costa Rica		72	72	72
多米尼加共和国	Dominica Rep.	2	2	7	50
厄瓜多尔	Ecuador	432	679	702	632
法属圭亚那	French Guyana	40	77	69	
圭亚那	Guyana				37
洪都拉斯	Honduras	16	5	9	55
牙买加	Jamaica	397	366	320	478
墨西哥	Mexico	14	119	31	31
尼加拉瓜	Nicaragua	7	7	6	6
巴拿马	Panama	24023	22194	19308	28239
秘鲁	Peru	242	411	410	410
圣文森特和格林纳丁斯	Saint Vincent & Grenadines	1079	1029	853	733
苏里南	Suriname	26			8
特立尼达和多巴哥	Trinidad & Tobago	844			46
委内瑞拉	Venezuela	805	761	502	125
英属维尔京群岛	Virgin Is.(E)	50	50	108	73
圣其茨-尼维斯	St. Kitts-Nevis	28	29	7	7
北美洲	**North America**	**2117**	**2161**	**2743**	**3494**
加拿大	Canada	877	945	965	890
美国	United States	1137	1215	1763	2582
百慕大群岛	Bermuda	103	1	15	22
大洋洲及太平洋岛屿	**Oceania and Pacific Is.**	**7830**	**8008**	**8461**	**9898**
澳大利亚	Australia	767	871	1040	1265
库克群岛	Cook Is.		6	16	27
斐济	Fiji	1467	1399	1395	477
新喀里多尼亚	New Caledonia	285	140	85	
瓦努阿图	Vanuatu	350	350	350	369
新西兰	New Zealand	59	62	73	188
巴布亚新几内亚	Papua New Guinea	49	38	386	503
汤加	Tonga		13	13	13
萨摩亚	Samoa	1037	1037	1037	1043
基里巴斯	Kiribati	927	955	950	796
图瓦卢	Tuvalu	138	153	200	460
密克罗尼西亚	Micronesia	59	29	259	235
马绍尔群岛	Marshall Is.	2664	2922	2551	4281
帕劳共和国	Republic of Palau	11	28	73	241
纽埃	Niue	17	5	33	
其他	**Others**	**1120**	**1364**	**903**	

8-8 分地区签订对外承包工程合同数量及金额
Contracts Signed for Foreign Engineering Projects by Region

地区	Region	2016 合同(份) Nunber of Contracts (unit)	2016 金额(万美元) Contract Value (USD 10000)	2017 合同(份) Nunber of Contracts (unit)	2017 金额(万美元) Contract Value (USD 10000)
总计	**Total**	**19157**	**24401009**	**22774**	**26527599**
一、中央企业	**Enterprises Managed by the Central Government**	**2146**	**11919683**	**1741**	**13212665**
二、地方企业	**Provincial Enterprises**	**17011**	**12481326**	**21033**	**13314935**
北京	Beijing	229	514151	272	905968
天津	Tianjin	78	264840	192	450524
河北	Hebei	130	467386	128	584589
山西	Shanxi	20	22266	18	104648
内蒙古	Inner Mongolia	4	1704		
辽宁	Liaoning	165	235243	206	172178
吉林	Jilin	20	37200	24	48425
黑龙江	Heilongjiang	101	324124	84	125164
上海	Shanghai	7341	1184459	14063	1085190
江苏	Jiangsu	1543	728708	548	1082087
浙江	Zhejiang	3377	542232	1593	506843
安徽	Anhui	63	307609	119	525384
福建	Fujian	36	58143	86	131113
江西	Jiangxi	198	289082	284	411064
山东	Shandong	306	1266500	417	1295541
河南	Henan	151	364720	232	314829
湖北	Hubei	159	1263523	438	1486979
湖南	Hunan	65	224244	88	183174
广东	Guangdong	1503	2198726	1151	2218294
广西	Guangxi	61	79521	47	93726
海南	Hainan				
重庆	Chongqing	448	186298	102	116813
四川	Sichuan	489	998205	320	791610
贵州	Guizhou	55	59614	35	32508
云南	Yunnan	48	191875	99	136260
西藏	Tibet				
陕西	Shaanxi	209	353156	283	370652
甘肃	Gansu	91	47215	69	19490
青海	Qinghai		20	2	320
宁夏	Ningxia	3	5085	2	1167
新疆	Xinjiang	98	207698	121	96905
新疆兵团	Xinjiang Bingtuan	20	57779	10	23490

8–9 分地区对外承包工程营业额
Turnover of Foreign Engineering Projects by Region

单位：万美元

Unit: USD 10000

地　区	Region	2014	2015	2016	2017
总　计	**Total**	**14241066**	**15407423**	**15941749**	**16858661**
一、中央企业	**Enterprises Managed by the Central Government**	**4972428**	**5033658**	**5889992**	**5937330**
二、地方企业	**Provincial Enterprises**	**9268638**	**10373765**	**10051757**	**10921331**
北　京	Beijing	357432	354900	249642	402944
天　津	Tianjin	403259	476260	629220	502007
河　北	Hebei	408696	359910	257649	294101
山　西	Shanxi	73542	73754	68641	71249
内蒙古	Inner Mongolia	1653	656	300	60
辽　宁	Liaoning	236557	243819	178127	146357
吉　林	Jiling	56481	36830	38257	38580
黑龙江	Heilongjiang	89805	253359	242900	240894
上　海	Shanghai	740168	745479	665611	993262
江　苏	Jiangsu	795426	876128	911122	952857
浙　江	Zhejiang	517582	618719	667262	713969
安　徽	Anhui	322693	269258	309408	348146
福　建	Fujian	71559	92656	95014	113202
江　西	Jiangxi	285147	351093	394256	426287
山　东	Shandong	925011	1017083	1093045	1175577
河　南	Henan	299691	280004	257122	294883
湖　北	Hubei	579636	523369	511109	707516
湖　南	Hunan	257945	311539	256535	267451
广　东	Guangdong	1241121	1987790	1816382	1809649
广　西	Guangxi	87736	93986	84764	68824
海　南	Hainan	100			
重　庆	Chongqing	103210	62835	96352	98431
四　川	Sichuan	706295	559590	409403	393093
贵　州	Guizhou	50129	68056	68133	86209
云　南	Yunnan	207036	234162	257525	170278
西　藏	Tibet				
陕　西	Shaanxi	178759	220429	242935	390921
甘　肃	Gansu	33939	29210	26870	23451
青　海	Qinghai	15477	12510	30931	39214
宁　夏	Ningxia	5243	1902	2435	1261
新　疆	Xingjiang	159077	158182	123886	82607
新疆兵团	Xinjiang Bingtuan	58232	60297	66921	68051

8-10 分地区年末在境外从事承包工程人数
Personnel Abroad for Foreign Engineering Projects Classified by Region at the Year-end

单位：人
Unit: person

地　区	Region	2014	2015	2016	2017
总　计	**Total**	**408851**	**408565**	**372880**	**376827**
一、中央企业	**Enterprises Managed by the Central Government**	**117207**	**111972**	**102511**	**97670**
二、地方企业	**Provincial Enterprises**	**291644**	**296593**	**270369**	**279157**
北　京	Beijing	21683	19287	13176	11806
天　津	Tianjin	11374	12428	13307	12958
河　北	Hebei	9049	8414	6277	8715
山　西	Shanxi	4220	4998	7575	5202
内蒙古	Inner Mongolia	592	206	163	52
辽　宁	Liaoning	8624	6993	6605	6330
吉　林	Jiling	3397	3284	2708	3427
黑龙江	Heilongjiang	5245	10339	10767	11406
上　海	Shanghai	12483	10565	12546	16959
江　苏	Jiangsu	36552	37907	32403	31944
浙　江	Zhejiang	24733	26008	27323	20701
安　徽	Anhui	13527	14082	11220	12461
福　建	Fujian	4074	3714	3967	4518
江　西	Jiangxi	8860	9072	6859	8905
山　东	Shandong	31832	31452	30546	35470
河　南	Henan	14258	16032	18151	14759
湖　北	Hubei	21386	22629	15429	20735
湖　南	Hunan	8555	7505	6827	5425
广　东	Guangdong	3405	3633	4350	6293
广　西	Guangxi	3527	3656	3843	4064
海　南	Hainan	42	10		
重　庆	Chongqing	1654	1712	1597	1557
四　川	Sichuan	11604	10968	8888	9717
贵　州	Guizhou	2677	4857	2068	2470
云　南	Yunnan	10995	8629	9351	7709
西　藏	Tibet				
陕　西	Shaanxi	7942	8488	7890	9423
甘　肃	Gansu	2028	2068	1080	1665
青　海	Qinghai	629	970	752	627
宁　夏	Ningxia	305	158	132	257
新　疆	Xingjiang	3377	2941	1485	1645
新疆兵团	Xinjiang Bingtuan	3015	3588	3084	1957

8-11 分地区年末在境外从事劳务合作人数

Personnel Abroad for Foreign Labour Services Classified by Region at the Year-end

单位：人

Unit: person

地　区	Region	2014	2015	2016	2017
总　计	**Total**	**596881**	**618295**	**595976**	**602342**
一、中央企业	**Enterprises Managed by the Central Government**	**50449**	**34193**	**30247**	**38003**
二、地方企业	**Provincial Enterprises**	**545780**	**584102**	**565729**	**564339**
北　京	Beijing	7774	14896	7260	12782
天　津	Tianjin	7029	6865	5507	6940
河　北	Hebei	2231	2340	3159	3554
山　西	Shanxi	12	12	12	12
内蒙古	Inner Mongolia	3554	1716	1251	591
辽　宁	Liaoning	38328	40213	38335	41690
吉　林	Jiling	31941	28275	27533	25383
黑龙江	Heilongjiang	6943	8609	8769	8427
上　海	Shanghai	23245	23002	21980	25524
江　苏	Jiangsu	59850	63911	55371	59506
浙　江	Zhejiang	6546	6226	6490	7172
安　徽	Anhui	11182	9609	7977	7588
福　建	Fujian	52125	55499	56392	71426
江　西	Jiangxi	6023	6188	5011	3082
山　东	Shandong	83496	84648	89109	94914
河　南	Henan	75305	85257	81404	46863
湖　北	Hubei	10864	10895	9345	10001
湖　南	Hunan	23705	29113	37262	36551
广　东	Guangdong	72788	81600	80468	79440
广　西	Guangxi	213	1295	751	401
海　南	Hainan				
重　庆	Chongqing	4001	3963	2473	2655
四　川	Sichuan	6810	7041	6797	6731
贵　州	Guizhou	60	63	48	35
云　南	Yunnan	1283	1831	3208	2956
西　藏	Tibet				
陕　西	Shaanxi	7003	5950	4930	5079
甘　肃	Gansu	2805	3702	4042	4403
青　海	Qinghai	83	71	40	22
宁　夏	Ningxia	318	576	749	611
新　疆	Xingjiang				
新疆兵团	Xinjiang Bingtuan	263	736	56	
三、其他	**Others**	**652**			

旅　游

TOURISM

第9篇

9-1 历年入境游客
Visitor Arrivals

单位:万人次

Unit: 10000 person-times

年 份 Year	合 计 Total	#入境过夜游客 Overnight Tourists	外国人 Foreigners	港澳台同胞* Compatriot*	#台湾同胞 Taiwan Province
1978	180.92	71.60	22.96	156.15	
1979	420.39	152.90	36.24	382.06	
1980	570.25	350.00	52.91	513.90	
1981	776.71	376.70	67.52	705.31	
1982	792.43	392.40	76.45	711.70	
1983	947.70	379.10	87.25	856.41	
1984	1285.22	514.10	113.43	1167.04	
1985	1783.31	713.30	137.05	1637.78	
1986	2281.95	900.10	148.23	2126.90	
1987	2690.23	1076.00	172.78	2508.74	
1988	3169.48	1236.10	184.22	2977.33	43.77
1989	2450.14	936.10	146.10	2297.19	54.10
1990	2746.18	1048.40	174.73	2562.34	94.80
1991	3334.98	1246.40	271.01	3050.62	94.66
1992	3811.49	1651.20	400.64	3394.34	131.78
1993	4152.69	1898.20	465.59	3670.49	152.70
1994	4368.45	2107.00	518.21	3838.72	139.02
1995	4638.65	2003.40	588.67	4038.40	153.23
1996	5112.75	2276.50	674.43	4422.86	173.39
1997	5758.79	2377.00	742.80	5006.09	211.76
1998	6347.84	2507.29	710.77	5625.00	217.46
1999	7279.56	2704.66	843.23	6425.52	258.46
2000	8344.39	3122.88	1016.04	7320.80	310.86
2001	8901.29	3316.67	1122.64	7778.65	344.20
2002	9790.83	3680.26	1343.95	8446.88	366.06
2003	9166.21	3297.05	1140.29	8025.92	273.19
2004	10903.82	4176.14	1693.25	9210.57	368.53
2005	12029.23	4680.90	2025.51	10003.71	410.92
2006	12494.21	4991.34	2221.03	10273.19	441.35
2007	13187.33	5471.98	2610.97	10576.36	462.79
2008	13002.74	5304.92	2432.53	10570.21	438.56
2009	12647.59	5087.52	2193.75	10453.84	448.40
2010	13376.22	5566.45	2612.69	10763.53	514.06
2011	13542.35	5758.07	2711.20	10831.15	526.30
2012	13240.53	5772.49	2719.16	10521.37	534.02
2013	12907.78	5568.59	2629.03	10278.75	516.25
2014	12849.83	5562.20	2636.08	10213.75	536.59
2015	13382.04	5688.57	2598.54	10783.50	549.86
2016	13844.38	5926.73	2815.12	11029.26	573.00
2017	13948.24	6073.84	2916.53	11031.71	587.13

注：港澳台同胞来自香港特别行政区、澳门特别行政区和台湾省(下同)。
Note: Compatriot From Hong Kong, Macao and Taiwan Province.(next the same)

9-2 历年入境游客增长速度
Growth Rates of Visitor Arrivals

单位：%
unit: %

年 份 Year	合 计 Total	#入境过夜游客 Overnight Tourists	外国人 Foreigners	港澳台同胞 Compatriot	#台湾同胞 Taiwan Province
1979	132.4	113.5	57.8	144.7	
1980	35.6	128.9	46.0	34.5	
1981	36.2	7.6	27.6	37.2	
1982	2.0	4.2	13.2	0.9	
1983	19.6	-3.4	14.1	20.3	
1984	35.6	35.6	30.0	36.3	
1985	38.8	38.7	20.8	40.3	
1986	28.0	26.2	8.2	29.9	
1987	17.9	19.5	16.6	18.0	
1988	17.8	14.9	6.6	18.7	
1989	-22.7	-24.3	-20.7	-22.8	23.6
1990	12.1	12.0	19.6	11.5	75.2
1991	21.4	18.9	55.1	19.1	-0.1
1992	14.3	32.5	47.8	11.3	39.2
1993	9.0	15.0	16.2	8.1	15.9
1994	5.2	11.0	11.3	4.6	-9.0
1995	6.2	-4.9	13.6	5.2	10.2
1996	10.2	13.6	14.6	9.5	13.2
1997	12.6	4.4	10.1	13.2	22.1
1998	10.2	5.5	-4.3	12.4	2.7
1999	14.7	7.9	18.6	14.2	18.9
2000	14.6	15.5	20.5	13.9	20.3
2001	6.7	6.2	10.5	6.3	10.7
2002	10.0	11.0	19.7	8.6	6.4
2003	-6.4	-10.4	-15.2	-5.0	-25.4
2004	19.0	26.7	48.5	14.8	34.9
2005	10.3	12.1	19.6	8.6	11.5
2006	3.9	6.6	9.7	2.7	7.4
2007	5.5	9.6	17.6	3.0	4.9
2008	-1.4	-3.1	-6.8	-0.1	-5.2
2009	-2.7	-4.1	-9.8	-1.1	2.2
2010	5.8	9.4	19.1	3.0	14.6
2011	1.2	3.4	3.8	0.6	2.4
2012	-2.2	0.3	0.3	-2.9	1.5
2013	-2.5	-3.5	-3.3	-2.3	-3.3
2014	-0.5	-0.1	0.3	-0.6	3.9
2015	4.1	2.3	-1.4	5.6	2.5
2016	3.5	4.2	8.3	2.3	4.2
2017	0.8	2.5	3.6	0.0	2.5

9-3 历年入境过夜游客和国际旅游收入
International Tourism Receipts and Tourist Arrivals

年份 Year	入境过夜游客(万人次) Tourist Arrivals (10000 person-times)	入境过夜游客增速(%) Growth Rates (%)	入境过夜游客居世界位次 Rank	国际旅游收入合计(亿美元) Tourism Receipts (USD 100 Million)	国际旅游收入增速(%) Growth Rates (%)	国际旅游收入居世界位次 Rank
1978	71.60			2.63		
1979	152.90	113.5		4.49	70.7	
1980	350.00	128.9	18	6.17	37.4	34
1981	376.70	7.6	17	7.85	27.2	34
1982	392.40	4.2	16	8.43	7.4	29
1983	379.10	-3.4	16	9.41	11.6	26
1984	514.10	35.6	14	11.31	20.2	21
1985	713.30	38.7	13	12.50	10.5	21
1986	900.10	26.2	12	15.31	22.5	22
1987	1076.00	19.5	12	18.62	21.6	26
1988	1236.10	14.9	10	22.47	20.7	26
1989	936.10	-24.3	12	18.60	-17.2	27
1990	1048.40	12.0	11	22.18	19.2	25
1991	1246.40	18.9	12	28.45	28.3	21
1992	1651.20	32.5	9	39.47	38.7	17
1993	1898.20	15.0	7	46.83	18.6	15
1994	2107.00	11.0	6	73.23	56.4	10
1995	2003.40	-4.9	8	87.33	19.3	10
1996	2276.50	13.6	6	102.00	16.8	9
1997	2377.00	4.4	6	120.74	18.4	8
1998	2507.29	5.5	6	126.02	4.4	7
1999	2704.66	7.9	5	140.99	11.9	7
2000	3122.88	15.5	5	162.24	15.1	7
2001	3316.67	6.2	5	177.92	9.7	5
2002	3680.26	11.0	5	203.85	14.6	5
2003	3297.05	-10.4	5	174.06	-14.6	7
2004	4176.14	26.7	4	257.39	47.9	7
2005	4680.90	12.1	4	292.96	13.8	6
2006	4991.34	6.6	4	339.49	15.9	5
2007	5471.98	9.6	4	419.19	23.5	5
2008	5304.92	-3.1	4	408.43	-2.6	5
2009	5087.52	-4.1	4	396.75	-2.9	5
2010	5566.45	9.4	3	458.14	15.5	4
2011	5758.07	3.4	3	484.64	5.8	4
2012	5772.49	0.3	3	500.28	3.2	4
2013	5568.59	-3.5	4	516.64	3.3	4
2014	5562.20	-0.1	4	569.13	10.2	4
2015	5688.57	2.3	4	1136.50	7.8	2
2016	5926.73	4.2	4	1200.00	5.6	2
2017	6073.84	2.5	4	1234.17	2.8	2

注：2015年以后"国际旅游收入"补充完善了停留时间为3-12个月的入境游客花费和游客在华短期旅居的花费，与以前年度不可比，以下表同此。

Note: After 2015,Tourism Receipts supplemented the cost of inbound tourists staying for 3-12 months and the short-term travel expenses in China, which is incomparable with previous years. The same applies to the following table.

9-4 入境外国游客分组构成

Foreign Visitor Arrivals by Sex, Age, Purpose and Mode of Transport

单位：万人次

Unit: 10000 person-times

项　目	Item	2016		2017	
		人次数 person-time	比 重 structure (%)	人次数 person-time	比 重 structure (%)
总　计	**Total**	**3148.38**	**100.0**	**4294.30**	**100.0**
按性别分	**By Sex**				
男	Male	1982.04	63.0	2607.98	60.7
女	Female	1166.33	37.0	1686.32	39.3
按年龄分	**By Age**				
14岁及以下	Under 14	114.73	3.6	134.75	3.1
15～24岁	15～24	303.32	9.6	568.82	13.2
25～44岁	25～44	1473.56	46.8	2143.34	49.9
45～64岁	46～64	1078.39	34.3	1256.03	29.2
65岁以上	Over 65	178.37	5.7	191.36	4.5
按事由分	**By Purpose**				
会议/商务	Meeting/Business	579.74	18.4	569.68	13.3
观光/休闲	Sightseeing/Leisure	1051.15	33.4	1593.04	37.1
探亲/访友	Visiting Relatives and Friends	96.19	3.1	110.28	2.6
服务员工	Work and Crew	471.75	15.0	633.91	14.8
其他	Others	949.55	30.1	1387.40	32.3
按入境方式分	**By Mode Of Transport**				
船舶	Sea	284.49	9.0	277.55	6.5
飞机	Air	1691.12	53.7	1717.09	40.0
火车	Rail	41.98	1.3	42.78	1.0
汽车	Motor	442.74	14.1	685.18	16.0
徒步	Foot	688.05	21.9	1571.70	36.6

注：2016年开始统计边民来华旅游人数。

Note: Since 2016, including international arrivals from the border areas to china.

9-5 按国籍分入境外国游客
Foreign Visitor Arrivals by Nationality

单位：人次

Unit: person-time

国　籍	Nationality	2014	2015	2016	2017
总　计	**Total**	**26360827**	**25985421**	**28151200**	**29165300**
亚洲	**Asia**	**16331289**	**16594709**	**17881795**	**18184676**
#阿富汗	Afghanistan	12569	11642	12290	14668
巴林	Bahrain	3534	3611	3288	3233
孟加拉国	Bangladesh	69776	80196	85037	91683
不丹	Bhutan	672	750	723	946
文莱	Brunei	9163	7024	7338	7604
缅甸	Myanmar	132787	144373	157650	9662152
柬埔寨	Cambodia	39285	42455	49916	61625
塞浦路斯	Cyprus	3040	2933	3429	3594
朝鲜	Korea DPR	184355	188337	181277	229757
印度	India	709896	730490	799310	821965
印度尼西亚	Indonesia	566859	544762	633671	683059
伊朗	Iran	113687	113164	128043	136840
伊拉克	Iraq	23795	23723	22024	23537
以色列	Israel	78520	76165	82991	91784
日本	Japan	2717621	2497657	2589869	2682999
约旦	Jordan	27668	26540	30893	29639
科威特	Kuwait	7895	6436	6039	6495
老挝	Laos	21697	26136	34325	235127
黎巴嫩	Lebanon	20923	19728	19351	19646
马来西亚	Malaysia	1129568	1075451	1165435	1233237
马尔代夫	Maldives	5534	6848	7785	5824
蒙古	Mongolia	1082729	1014102	1232643	1864519
尼泊尔	Nepal	53625	49954	68960	133203
阿曼	Oman	5001	5081	6156	8881
巴基斯坦	Pakistan	108856	113087	117428	127506
巴勒斯坦	Palestine	5829	5967	6427	6876
菲律宾	Philippines	967925	1004008	1135114	1168512
卡塔尔	Qatar	2655	2313	2568	2612
沙特阿拉伯	Saudi Arabia	36148	35300	37388	34579
新加坡	Singapore	971379	905269	924614	941210
韩国	Korea	4181714	4444389	4775332	3863847
斯里兰卡	Sri Lanka	50030	58059	60335	63130
叙利亚	Syria	17027	16835	10300	10748
泰国	Thailand	613081	641483	753456	776692
土耳其	Turkey	106163	99583	79134	75611
阿联酋	United Arab Emirates	7982	7788	7671	7786
也门共和国	Yemen Rep.	24601	21088	14108	14554
越南	Vietnam	1709437	2160756	2429654	6546874
哈萨克斯坦	Kazakhstan	343605	241478	225498	223067
吉尔吉斯斯坦	Kirghizia	50423	43733	44278	34295

9-5 续表 1 Continued 1

单位：人次
Unit: person-time

国　籍	Nationality	2014	2015	2016	2017
塔吉克斯坦	Tadzhikistan	33610	24961	21671	22474
土库曼斯坦	Turkmenistan	17030	14918	13806	14488
乌兹别克斯坦	Uzbekistan	63044	55398	52633	46360
非洲	**Africa**	**596877**	**580188**	**588816**	**629091**
#阿尔及利亚	Algeria	31670	26568	25738	26571
安哥拉	Angola	27331	17368	10894	15031
贝宁	Benin	6308	6082	5456	4405
博茨瓦纳	Botswana	1864	2271	1985	2215
布隆迪	Burundi	1589	1472	1631	1997
喀麦隆	Cameroon	8453	8608	8631	8227
佛得角	Cape Verde	639	679	676	841
中非	Central African	318	318	355	493
乍得	Chad	1128	1422	1484	1323
科摩罗	Comoros	1026	1229	1359	1640
刚果(布)	Congo(B)	5909	4787	4838	5035
吉布提	Djibouti	753	1219	1363	1402
埃及	Egypt	83925	86509	82859	83618
赤道几内亚	Eq.Guinea	1038	1251	1076	1326
埃塞俄比亚	Ethiopia	29921	31648	37751	45108
加蓬	Gabon	1292	1320	1445	1466
冈比亚	Gambia	2656	1794	1740	2199
加纳	Ghana	16777	18980	20533	22602
几内亚	Guinea	8136	5035	6379	7915
几内亚(比绍)	Guinea Bissau	905	683	520	630
科特迪瓦	Cote d'Ivoire	4402	4917	6376	7463
肯尼亚	Kenya	23277	25707	27400	27488
利比里亚	Liberia	1195	1256	2199	2834
利比亚	Libya	10712	6223	3444	2895
马达加斯加	Madagascar	10102	9517	9867	14157
马拉维	Malawi	1851	2256	2096	2820
马里	Mali	18650	17713	13003	6428
毛里塔尼亚	Mauritania	2038	1850	1948	2203
毛里求斯	Mauritius	18865	20571	24158	25276
摩洛哥	Morocco	15090	14643	17522	20350
莫桑比克	Mozambique	4886	5251	4480	5722
纳米比亚	Namibia	2302	2249	2654	2790
尼日尔	Niger	12023	10108	10044	8776
尼日利亚	Nigeria	54458	54149	52446	46254
卢旺达	Rwanda	2362	2753	3598	4308
圣多美和普林西比	Sao Tome & Principe	112	86	82	428
塞内加尔	Senegal	9976	10131	13005	14308

9-5 续表 2 Continued 2

单位：人次
Unit: person-time

国　籍	Nationality	2014	2015	2016	2017
塞舌尔	Seychelles	1559	1658	2652	1971
塞拉利昂	Sierra Leone	2239	1350	2624	3546
索马里	Somalia	1095	1150	1197	1232
南非	S.Africa	68230	65451	66807	75064
苏丹	Sudan	14585	15940	18429	20065
坦桑尼亚	Tanzania	23517	23040	21860	23827
多哥	Togo	3451	3632	3838	3994
突尼斯	Tunisia	10764	10650	8006	8115
乌干达	Uganda	15198	15127	16514	17711
布基纳法索	Burkina Faso	3725	4346	5016	6127
刚果(金)	Congo DR	12018	10583	11286	13445
赞比亚	Zambia	7095	7388	7491	9709
津巴布韦	Zimbabwe	6639	8071	8810	10924
莱索托	Lesotho	536	770	760	994
斯威士兰	Swaziland	390	438	447	518
厄立特里亚	Eritrea	840	836	716	838
欧洲	**Europe**	**5514300**	**4916735**	**5471548**	**5911652**
#比利时	Belgium	67375	65183	66736	68397
丹麦	Denmark	77556	70873	71638	70350
英国	United Kingdom	604657	579637	595038	591756
德国	Germany	662634	623374	624867	635474
法国	France	517038	486935	503840	494670
爱尔兰	Ireland	42046	41500	42396	42004
意大利	Italy	253128	246145	267285	280544
卢森堡	Luxembourg	2773	2830	2954	3139
荷兰	Netherlands	180439	181789	199618	194293
希腊	Greece	35719	36694	38593	42394
葡萄牙	Portugal	52287	53387	55040	56351
西班牙	Spain	141037	136333	149808	156040
阿尔巴尼亚	Albania	2631	2527	3198	3563
安道尔	Andorra	167	150	190	177
奥地利	Austria	64826	60758	66117	67729
保加利亚	Bulgaria	19037	19235	21156	21568
芬兰	Finland	60283	55110	57928	57889
匈牙利	Hungary	20789	19201	21499	22531
冰岛	Iceland	3555	3715	2841	2791
列支敦士登	Liechtenstein	354	309	372	382
马耳他	Malta	2013	1879	1987	2020
摩纳哥	Monaco	147	129	139	103
挪威	Norway	47860	41113	38270	39105

9-5 续表 3 Continued 3

单位：人次
Unit: person-time

国　籍	Nationality	2014	2015	2016	2017
波兰	Poland	76135	74823	84056	90744
罗马尼亚	Romania	40749	43589	47757	48891
圣马力诺	San Marino	164	134	186	162
瑞典	Sweden	141964	118362	115347	111870
瑞士	Switzerland	79539	72675	72628	72290
爱沙尼亚	Estonia	5056	5202	5777	5812
拉脱维亚	Latvia	6761	7087	8019	8326
立陶宛	Lithuania	8655	8614	9545	10835
格鲁吉亚	Georgia	8933	8496	9905	11327
亚美尼亚	Armenia	5437	4612	5325	6346
阿塞拜疆	Azerbaijan	18894	15126	13876	14366
白俄罗斯	Byelorussia	15575	13904	17262	19194
摩尔多瓦	Moldavia	3100	2970	3473	4020
俄罗斯	Russia	2045807	1582279	1976602	2356835
乌克兰	Ukraine	117262	141706	160439	172182
斯洛文尼亚	Slovenia	6121	6034	6263	7509
克罗地亚	Croatia	17270	18971	21647	23384
捷克	Czech	23123	24720	32698	34640
斯洛伐克	Slovak	10732	11778	13612	14251
波黑	Bosnia & Hercegovina	1902	2101	2933	3543
拉丁美洲	**Latin America**	**346211**	**349754**	**390402**	**426476**
#安提瓜和巴布达	Antigua & Barbuda	299	445	447	545
阿根廷	Argentina	24427	28407	32445	35208
巴哈马	Bahamas	788	1042	930	871
巴巴多斯	Barbados	481	505	484	592
伯利兹	Belize	3203	2995	2850	2786
玻利维亚	Bolivia	6477	6451	7554	7138
巴西	Brazil	94559	85487	93406	105372
开曼群岛	Cayman Is	24	34	21	35
智利	Chile	19096	19196	22973	23625
哥伦比亚	Colombia	37299	35955	37818	40094
哥斯达黎加	Costa Rica	5682	5790	7220	7409
古巴	Cuba	3486	4773	4870	4635
多米尼加共和国	Dominican Rep.	3373	3248	3848	4043
厄瓜多尔	Ecuador	8702	8698	9145	11523
格林纳达	Grenada	215	576	994	2088
危地马拉	Guatemala	2826	2768	3560	3655
圭亚那	Guyana	996	1150	1347	1455

9–5 续表 4 Continued 4

单位：人次

Unit: person-time

国　　籍	Nationality	2014	2015	2016	2017
海地	Haiti	444	512	548	652
洪都拉斯	Honduras	2856	4351	5840	6228
牙买加	Jamaica	5229	6072	6804	7269
墨西哥	Mexico	65762	68261	73364	82249
尼加拉瓜	Nicaragua	625	817	1158	1993
巴拿马	Panama	7728	8611	10691	12994
巴拉圭	Paraguay	1382	1187	1408	1383
秘鲁	Peru	14869	16465	20035	20821
波多黎各	Puerto Rico	5	5	3	4
圣卢西亚	Saint Lucia	260	146	274	1455
圣文森特和格林纳丁斯	S. Vinc. & Grenadines	419	414	763	811
萨尔瓦多	El Salvador	1160	1414	1614	1672
苏里南	Suriname	2946	3030	3289	3936
特立尼达和多巴哥	Trinidad & Tobago	2092	2422	2539	2882
乌拉圭	Uruguay	4074	3979	4437	4443
委内瑞拉	Venezuela	22678	22713	25795	24621
北美洲	**North America**	**2760296**	**2765595**	**2990937**	**3118996**
加拿大	Canada	667084	679775	741265	806043
美国	United States	2093153	2085788	2249629	2312929
百慕大	Bermuda	59	32	43	24
大洋洲及太平洋群岛	**Oceania and Pacific Islands**	**810058**	**776353**	**825549**	**892237**
#澳大利亚	Australia	672058	637315	675097	734337
斐济	Fiji	3620	4269	4609	4933
瑙鲁	Nauru	387	392	322	231
瓦努阿图	Vanuatu	493	526	539	855
新西兰	New Zealand	126593	125413	136206	143656
巴布亚新几内亚	Papua New Guinea	1588	1431	1484	1606
所罗门群岛	Solomon Is.	664	627	678	660
汤加	Tonga	1135	1012	1078	1248
萨摩亚	Samoa	867	1307	1834	1869
基里巴斯	Kiribati	1719	2828	2507	1903
图瓦卢	Tuvalu	289	472	454	204
密克罗尼西亚	Micronesia	149	199	201	262
马绍尔群岛	Marshall Is.	398	430	397	374
国际组织及其他人员	**Others**	**1796**	**2087**	**2153**	**2172**

9-6 国际旅游收入构成

Breakdown of International Tourism Receipts

单位：亿美元

Unit: USD 100 million

指　标	Item	2014	2015	2016	2017
总　计	**Total**	**569.13**	**1136.50**	**1200.00**	**1234.17**
一、商品收入	**Commodities**	**161.56**	**291.60**	**305.70**	**333.02**
1.商品销售	Shopping	113.28	209.00	209.50	229.95
2.餐饮	Food and Beverage	48.28	82.60	96.20	103.07
二、劳务收入	**Services**	**407.58**	**844.90**	**894.30**	**901.15**
1.长途交通	Long-Distance Transportation	195.95	448.50	446.50	449.46
民航	Air	145.79	294.80	290.60	304.87
铁路	Rail	20.90	43.20	53.20	49.52
汽车	Motor	15.68	32.50	31.60	29.43
轮船	Sea	13.59	78.00	71.00	65.65
2.游览	Sightseeing	32.54	44.80	67.10	65.04
3.住宿	Accommodation	69.50	132.90	116.30	122.08
4.娱乐	Entertainment	36.74	53.90	77.10	74.16
5.邮电通讯	Communication	11.04	23.90	28.90	27.57
6.市内交通	Local Transportation	16.04	22.40	40.40	39.20
7.其他服务	Others	45.77	118.60	118.00	123.64

9-7 各地区国际旅游收入
International Tourism Receipts by Locality

单位：亿美元

Unit: USD 100 million

地　区	Region	2014	2015	2016	2017
北　京	Beijing	46.08	46.05	50.70	51.30
天　津	Tianjin	29.92	32.98	35.57	37.51
河　北	Hebei	5.34	5.02	5.52	5.79
山　西	Shanxi	2.81	2.97	3.17	3.50
内蒙古	Inner Mongolia	10.03	9.62	11.39	12.46
辽　宁	Liaoning	16.18	16.37	18.24	17.78
吉　林	Jilin	5.84	7.24	7.91	7.66
黑龙江	Heilongjiang	5.64	3.95	4.58	4.80
上　海	Shanghai	56.02	58.60	64.19	66.99
江　苏	Jiangsu	30.33	35.27	38.04	41.95
浙　江	Zhejiang	57.53	67.88	31.28	35.86
安　徽	Anhui	18.40	22.63	25.42	28.81
福　建	Fujian	49.12	55.61	66.26	75.88
江　西	Jiangxi	5.57	5.67	5.85	6.30
山　东	Shandong	23.30	28.96	30.63	31.74
河　南	Henan	5.38	6.24	6.47	6.62
湖　北	Hubei	12.39	16.72	18.72	21.05
湖　南	Hunan	8.00	8.58	10.05	12.95
广　东	Guangdong	171.06	178.85	185.77	199.60
广　西	Guangxi	15.72	19.17	21.64	23.96
海　南	Hainan	2.69	2.49	3.50	6.81
重　庆	Chongqing	13.54	14.69	16.87	19.48
四　川	Sichuan	8.58	11.81	15.82	14.47
贵　州	Guizhou	1.89	2.31	2.53	2.83
云　南	Yunnan	24.21	28.76	30.75	35.50
西　藏	Tibet	1.45	1.77	1.94	1.98
陕　西	Shaanxi	17.69	20.00	23.39	27.04
甘　肃	Gansu	0.10	0.14	0.19	0.21
青　海	Qinghai	0.25	0.39	0.44	0.38
宁　夏	Ningxia	0.18	0.21	0.41	0.38
新　疆	Xinjiang	4.97	5.56	5.19	8.11

9-8 各地区接待入境过夜游客情况
International Tourists by Region

地区	Region	人数（万人次）Tourist Arrivals (10000 person-times)		#外国人 Foreigners		人天数（万人天）Tourist Arrivals Night (10000 person-night)		#外国人 Foreigners	
		2017	2016	2017	2016	2017	2016	2017	2016
北京	Beijing	392.56	416.53	332.00	354.76	1688.00	1791.09	1427.61	1525.48
天津	Tianjin	79.21	82.43	68.53	71.89	1524.93	1348.91	1253.08	1110.57
河北	Hebei	91.01	83.79	70.40	65.99	330.00	274.75	275.54	233.41
山西	Shanxi	67.00	62.98	43.47	40.42	174.76	162.35	116.39	103.49
内蒙古	Inner Mongolia	184.83	177.91	175.70	168.19	575.85	527.96	535.25	484.36
辽宁	Liaoning	278.85	273.67	217.05	212.21	802.22	768.91	621.68	605.21
吉林	Jilin	148.43	161.95	128.34	142.17	350.68	394.35	301.63	344.53
黑龙江	Heilongjiang	103.88	95.70	98.46	90.87	234.14	209.54	223.65	199.83
上海	Shanghai	719.33	690.43	589.48	572.57	2388.02	2216.62	1945.30	1794.58
江苏	Jiangsu	370.10	329.77	241.75	218.00	1388.87	1233.85	839.20	752.66
浙江	Zhejiang	589.06	525.59	430.13	387.30	1552.25	1332.13	1181.91	1016.01
安徽	Anhui	351.09	313.43	205.28	184.46	977.45	753.26	573.40	430.87
福建	Fujian	691.74	611.48	292.87	254.12	3529.83	2949.80	1669.91	1377.61
江西	Jiangxi	174.69	164.83	57.05	49.80	360.04	312.38	119.34	94.60
山东	Shandong	440.52	328.82	316.14	237.66	1344.54	1107.87	983.14	836.97
河南	Henan	155.89	149.93	99.69	95.81	307.68	313.97	204.35	209.64
湖北	Hubei	368.14	337.56	277.95	254.65	926.78	802.65	719.86	611.96
湖南	Hunan	322.28	240.81	155.48	127.41	625.78	471.11	313.19	265.52
广东	Guangdong	3654.52	3507.21	864.83	909.49	9206.86	9070.51	2507.35	2853.74
广西	Guangxi	512.44	482.52	255.38	251.98	1111.29	995.70	560.87	518.12
海南	Hainan	111.95	74.89	78.70	46.98	324.26	164.59	266.88	115.85
重庆	Chongqing	224.85	180.89	136.21	119.00	1045.55	958.70	633.38	630.70
四川	Sichuan	336.17	308.79	241.29	219.23	626.74	566.49	458.79	412.65
贵州	Guizhou	32.40	72.29	13.49	31.86	69.02	133.50	29.13	61.49
云南	Yunnan	667.69	600.38	507.52	450.69	1348.22	1171.59	1026.47	831.65
西藏	Tibet	34.35	32.19	26.88	21.12	97.74	99.37	72.86	63.56
陕西	Shaanxi	383.74	338.20	262.06	228.52	1316.21	1265.03	999.74	976.93
甘肃	Gansu	7.88	7.15	4.22	3.96	12.18	10.63	6.69	6.20
青海	Qinghai	7.02	7.01	5.70	5.03	22.83	24.77	19.36	17.62
宁夏	Ningxia	6.53	5.12	3.32	2.35	24.23	19.96	10.29	9.17
新疆	Xinjiang	77.41	58.21	67.15	51.56	361.27	228.98	313.14	201.39

9–9 各地区入境过夜游客人均天花费额

Average Daily Per Capita Expenditure of International Tourists by Region

单位：美元/人天
Unit: USD/night per capita

地区	Region	人均天花费 Average Expenditure		外国人 Foreigners		香港同胞 Hongkong SAR	
		2017	2016	2017	2016	2017	2016
北京	Beijing	274.76	264.42	276.95	265.52	234.83	250.03
天津	Tianjin	230.08	219.35	239.21	220.89	195.38	211.76
河北	Hebei	178.47	176.43	176.14	176.55	199.03	181.30
山西	Shanxi	195.60	185.94	198.55	187.34	193.57	186.67
内蒙古	Inner Mongolia	211.29	200.76	213.06	202.41	195.68	178.72
辽宁	Liaoning	214.97	212.63	214.15	214.95	215.61	197.96
吉林	Jilin	186.67	183.53	186.46	183.45	200.17	182.32
黑龙江	Heilongjiang	203.35	200.30	205.18	205.86	213.12	193.89
上海	Shanghai	280.77	274.35	281.58	271.92	283.99	296.24
江苏	Jiangsu	258.70	239.96	265.13	241.34	249.95	236.08
浙江	Zhejiang	225.29	222.87	223.75	224.24	241.15	225.78
安徽	Anhui	203.91	195.99	205.95	195.67	175.61	193.33
福建	Fujian	213.06	201.78	235.61	214.51	190.11	179.04
江西	Jiangxi	180.92	170.95	192.83	176.68	170.08	158.94
山东	Shandong	229.37	211.51	235.94	214.80	220.02	214.85
河南	Henan	176.59	166.23	175.52	166.67	174.13	162.81
湖北	Hubei	209.34	198.95	226.67	210.11	163.96	172.16
湖南	Hunan	210.49	198.48	217.90	198.62	191.50	197.10
广东	Guangdong	187.93	180.16	202.65	195.63	173.58	162.23
广西	Guangxi	202.86	193.94	207.80	190.85	189.57	197.66
海南	Hainan	202.28	189.59	201.12	189.82	200.11	184.50
重庆	Chongqing	209.28	196.16	218.72	198.61	188.93	172.43
四川	Sichuan	202.08	193.32	205.88	192.96	199.48	192.35
贵州	Guizhou	203.11	189.29	210.63	192.27	184.05	177.12
云南	Yunnan	225.10	206.76	231.14	210.21	188.66	189.34
西藏	Tibet	210.15	201.58	213.25	205.49	167.43	152.93
陕西	Shaanxi	206.78	195.17	206.92	195.01	198.34	199.21
甘肃	Gansu	173.39	165.74	184.71	175.18	159.86	144.61
青海	Qinghai	168.50	166.28	167.98	168.11	171.00	157.83
宁夏	Ningxia	186.69	173.21	190.17	176.14	135.89	127.71
新疆	Xinjiang	187.74	180.51	188.74	180.60	173.67	179.90

9-9 续表 Continued

单位：美元/人天

Unit: USD/night per capita

地区	Region	澳门同胞 Macao SAR		台湾同胞 Taiwan Province	
		2017	2016	2017	2016
北京	Beijing	298.31	272.62	255.79	253.22
天津	Tianjin	194.34	210.54	202.57	217.46
河北	Hebei	196.38	178.75	166.33	167.34
山西	Shanxi	186.72	169.79	176.24	186.20
内蒙古	Inner Mongolia	217.08	205.05	207.32	195.27
辽宁	Liaoning	214.34	202.37	211.09	193.06
吉林	Jilin	169.22	170.63	173.49	191.62
黑龙江	Heilongjiang	187.75	176.69	190.28	176.90
上海	Shanghai	268.65	291.96	270.77	286.33
江苏	Jiangsu	251.94	231.04	237.06	238.24
浙江	Zhejiang	237.31	224.50	204.01	209.61
安徽	Anhui	184.00	196.73	187.63	203.03
福建	Fujian	196.83	202.01	190.67	191.10
江西	Jiangxi	166.24	157.92	159.40	168.39
山东	Shandong	194.80	177.51	210.99	200.08
河南	Henan	160.84	148.28	190.90	175.83
湖北	Hubei	200.47	183.73	208.95	195.79
湖南	Hunan	190.35	193.71	200.65	201.43
广东	Guangdong	162.32	170.69	190.98	176.71
广西	Guangxi	190.83	193.75	196.08	207.38
海南	Hainan	213.47	194.38	211.18	192.83
重庆	Chongqing	184.41	174.16	216.29	197.55
四川	Sichuan	205.49	194.31	185.80	196.34
贵州	Guizhou	171.90	177.63	172.39	185.91
云南	Yunnan	201.34	187.11	204.73	198.83
西藏	Tibet	163.62	153.99	194.33	181.84
陕西	Shaanxi	215.37	200.72	195.65	217.09
甘肃	Gansu	164.20	154.91	151.14	158.87
青海	Qinghai	137.37	150.98	180.64	165.77
宁夏	Ningxia	153.00	141.09	148.00	133.89
新疆	Xinjiang	178.54	175.00	165.97	183.26

9–10 历年国内旅游情况
Major Statistics of Domestic Tourism

年 份	国内游客 (亿人次) Domestic Travelers (100 million person-times)	城镇居民 Urban Residents	农村居民 Rural Residents	旅游总花费 (亿元) Tourism Earnings (100 million yuan)	城镇居民 Urban Residents	农村居民 Rural Residents	人均花费 (元) Average Expenditure Per Capita (yuan)	城镇居民 Urban Residents	农村居民 Rural Residents
1994	5.24	2.05	3.19	1023.51	848.21	175.30	195.33	414.67	54.88
1995	6.29	2.46	3.83	1375.70	1140.10	235.60	218.71	464.02	61.47
1996	6.40	2.56	3.83	1638.38	1368.36	270.02	256.20	534.10	70.45
1997	6.44	2.59	3.85	2112.70	1515.10	560.87	328.06	599.80	145.68
1998	6.95	2.50	4.45	2391.18	1515.10	876.05	345.00	607.00	197.00
1999	7.19	2.84	4.35	2831.92	1748.23	1083.69	394.00	614.80	249.50
2000	7.44	3.29	4.15	3175.54	2235.30	940.28	426.60	678.60	226.60
2001	7.84	3.75	4.09	3522.40	2651.70	870.70	449.50	708.30	212.70
2002	8.78	3.85	4.93	3878.36	2848.09	1030.27	441.80	739.70	209.10
2003	8.70	3.51	5.19	3442.27	2404.08	1038.19	395.70	684.90	200.00
2004	11.02	4.59	6.43	4710.70	3359.00	1351.70	427.50	731.80	210.20
2005	12.12	4.96	7.16	5285.90	3656.10	1629.70	436.10	737.10	227.60
2006	13.94	5.76	8.18	6229.74	4414.74	1815.00	446.90	766.40	221.90
2007	16.10	6.12	9.98	7770.60	5550.40	2220.20	482.60	906.90	222.50
2008	17.12	7.03	10.09	8749.30	5971.75	2777.55	511.03	849.36	275.28
2009	19.02	9.03	9.99	10183.69	7233.79	2949.90	535.40	801.10	295.30
2010	21.03	10.65	10.38	12579.77	9403.81	3175.96	598.20	883.00	306.00
2011	26.41	16.87	9.54	19305.39	14808.61	4496.78	731.00	877.80	471.40
2012	29.57	19.33	10.24	22706.22	17678.03	5028.19	767.90	914.50	491.00
2013	32.62	21.86	10.76	26276.12	20692.59	5583.53	805.50	946.60	518.90
2014	36.11	24.83	11.28	30311.86	24219.76	6092.11	839.70	975.40	540.20
2015	39.90	28.02	11.88	34195.05	27610.90	6584.15	857.00	985.50	554.20
2016	44.35	31.95	12.40	39389.82	32241.95	7147.87	888.20	1009.10	576.40
2017	50.01	36.77	13.24	45660.77	37673.03	7987.74	913.00	1024.60	603.30

附　录

APPENDIX

附录Ⅰ　简要说明和主要统计指标解释

一、国内贸易部分

（一）主要内容

这一部分主要反映中国国内消费品市场、批发和零售业、住宿和餐饮业的发展变化情况。主要内容包括限额以上批发和零售业的基本情况、商品流转情况和财务状况，限额以上住宿和餐饮业的基本情况、经营情况和财务状况，社会消费品零售总额，商品交易市场成交情况，连锁零售业、餐饮业经营情况等。

（二）统计范围

1. 批发和零售业、住宿和餐饮业：限额以上批发和零售业、住宿和餐饮业法人企业和个体户。统计限额标准为：批发业，年主营业务收入2000万元及以上；零售业，年主营业务收入500万元及以上；住宿和餐饮业，年主营业务收入200万元及以上。

2. 社会消费品零售总额：从事商品零售活动或提供餐饮服务的法人企业、产业活动单位和个体户。

3. 商品交易市场：年商品成交额在亿元及以上的商品交易市场。

4. 连锁经营情况：零售业连锁总店（总部）、餐饮业连锁总店（总部）。

（三）资料来源

国家统计局贸易外经司根据《批发和零售业统计报表制度》、《住宿和餐饮业统计报表制度》进行搜集和加工整理而得。

（四）统计调查方法

限额以上批发和零售业、住宿和餐饮业单位（包括法人企业、产业活动单位和个体户，下同）、商品交易市场以及连锁总店（总部）采用全面调查方法，限额以下批发和零售业、住宿和餐饮业单位采用抽样调查方法。

（五）主要指标解释

1. 批发和零售业

批发业　指向其他批发或零售单位（含个体经营者）及其他企事业单位、机关团体等批量销售生活用品、生产资料的活动，以及从事进出口贸易和贸易经纪与代理的活动，包括拥有货物所有权，并以本单位(公司)的名义进行交易活动,也包括不拥有货物的所有权，收取佣金的商品代理、商品代售活动；本类还包括各类商品批发市场中固定摊位的批发活动，以及以销售为目的的收购活动。

零售业　指百货商店、超级市场、专门零售商店、品牌专卖店、售货摊等主要面向最终消费者（如居民等）的销售活动，以互联网、邮政、电话、售货机等方式的销售活动，还包括在同一地点，后面加工生产，前面销售的店铺（如面包房）；谷物、种子、饲料、牲畜、矿产品、生产用原料、化工原料、农用化工产品、机械设备（乘用车、计算机及通信设备除外）等生产资料的销售不作为零售活动；多数零售商对其销售的货物拥有所有权，但有些则是充当委托人的代理人，进行委托销售或以收取佣金的方式进行销售；零售业按销售渠道分为有店铺零售和无店铺零售，其中有店铺零售分为综合零售和专门零售。

商品购进额　指从本企业以外的单位和个人购进（包括从国外直接进口）作为转卖或加工后转卖的商品金额（含增值税）。本指标反映批发和零售业从国内外市场上购进商品的总价。

商品购进包括：（1）从工农业生产者、批发和零售业、住宿和餐饮业、出版社或报社的出版发行部门和其他服务业等企事业单位和个体经营户购进的商品；（2）从机关、社会团体购进的商品；（3）从海关、市场管理部门购进的缉私和没收的商品；（4）从居民收购的废旧商品等。

不包括：（1）企业为本单位自身经营用，不是作为转卖而购进的商品，如材料物资、包装物、低值易耗品、办公用品等；（2）未通过买卖行为而收入的商品，如接受其他部门移交的商品、借入的商品、收入代其他单位保管的商品、其他单位赠送的样品、加工回收的成品等；（3）经本单位介绍，由买卖双方直接结算，本单位只收取手续费的业务；（4）销售退回和买方拒付货款的商品；（5）商品溢余；（6）期货交易商品。

商品销售额 指对本单位以外的单位和个人出售的商品金额（包括售给本单位消费用的商品，含增值税），在批发和零售业中，本指标反映在国内市场上销售商品以及出口商品的总价。

商品销售包括：（1）售给个人和社会集团消费用的商品；（2）售给农业、工业、建筑业、服务业等国民经济各行业用于生产、经营用的商品，包括售予批发和零售业作为转卖或加工后转卖的商品；（3）对国（境）外直接出口的商品。

商品销售不包括：（1）未通过买卖行为付出的商品，如因机构变动移交给其他企业单位的商品、借出的商品、归还受其他单位委托代保管的商品、付出的加工原料和赠送给其他单位的样品等；（2）促销返券所销售的、不计入营业收入的商品；（3）经本单位介绍，由买卖双方直接结算，本单位只收取手续费的业务；（4）未发生所有权转移的商品预付卡销售，如加油卡；（5）汽车维修、电话卡销售等服务性经济活动；（6）购货退回的商品；（7）商品损耗和损失；（8）出售本单位自用的废旧物资；（9）期货交易商品；（10）自来水供应企业、电力企业、天然气供应企业提供的水、电、气。

商品库存额 对于批发和零售业法人单位和个体经营户，是指报告期末取得所有权的全部商品金额（含增值税）；对于批发和零售业产业活动单位，是指报告期末实际在库且归属法人具有所有权的全部商品金额（含增值税）。这个指标反映批发和零售业的商品库存情况，以及对市场商品供应的保证程度。

库存商品包括：（1）存放在本单位（如门市部、批发站、采购站、经营处）的仓库、货场、货柜和货架中的商品；（2）挑选、整理、包装中的商品；（3）已记入购进而尚未运到本单位的商品，即发货单或银行承兑凭证已到而货未到的商品；（4）寄放他处的商品，如因购货方拒绝付款而暂时存在购货方的商品；（5）委托其他单位代销（未作销售或调出）尚未售出的商品；（6）代其他单位购进尚未交付的商品。

库存商品不包括：（1）所有权不属于本单位的商品，如商品已作销售但买方尚未取走的商品，代替他人保管、运输、加工的商品，代其他单位销售（未做购进或调入）而未售出的商品；（2）委托外单位加工的商品（包括本单位所属加工厂和其他生产单位加工生产尚未收回成品的商品）；（3）外贸企业代理其他单位从国外进口，尚未付给订货单位的商品；（4）代国家储备部门保管的商品。

2.住宿和餐饮业

住宿业 指为旅行者提供短期留宿场所的活动，有些单位只提供住宿，也有些单位提供住宿、饮食、商务、娱乐一体的服务，本类不包括主要按月或按年长期出租房屋住所的活动。

餐饮业 指通过即时制作加工、商业销售和服务性劳动等，向消费者提供食品和消费场所及设施的服务。

营业额 指住宿和餐饮业单位在经营活动中因提供服务或销售商品等取得的全部收入（含增值税），收入主要来源于提供客房、餐费服务、商品销售和其他服务，如商务服务。不包括多产业法人企业附营的其他行业产业活动单位的餐费收入、商品销售收入等各项收入。

客房收入 指住宿和餐饮业单位在经营活动中因提供住宿服务取得的收入（含增值税）。不包括多产业法人企业附营的其他行业产业活动单位的客房收入。

餐费收入 指本单位为顾客提供就餐服务取得的收入（含增值税）。包括：经烹饪、调制加工后出售的各种食品，如主食、炒菜、凉拌菜等的收入。不包括多产业法人企业附营的其他行业产业活动单位的餐费收入。

3．商品交易市场

商品交易市场 指经有关部门和组织批准设立，有固定场所、设施，有经营管理部门和监管人员，若干市场经营者入内，常年或实际开业三个月以上，集中、公开、独立地进行生活消费品、生产资料等现货商品交易以及提供相关服务的交易场所，包括各类消费品市场、生产资料市场等。

商品交易市场成交额 指市场内所有摊位、写字间或门面的全年商品交易额之合计。

4．连锁经营

连锁总店（总部） 负责连锁企业资源（商号、商誉、经营模式、服务标准、管理模式等）的开发、配置、控制或使用等功能的企业核心管理机构。连锁经营是指经营同类商品或服务，使用统一商号的若干店铺，在同一总店（总部）的管理下，采取统一采购或特许经营等方式,实现规模效益的组织形式，包括直营连锁、特许连锁和自愿连锁三种形式。

直营连锁 指连锁店铺由连锁公司全资或控股开设，在总部的直接控制下，开展统一经营的连锁经营形式。

特许连锁 指拥有注册商标、企业标志、专利、专有技术等经营资源的企业（特许人），以合同形式将其拥有的经营资源许可其他经营者（被特许人）使用，被特许人按合同约定在统一的经营模式下开展经营，并向特许人支付特许经营费用的连锁经营形式。

自愿连锁 指若干个店铺或企业自愿组合起来，在不改变各自资产所有权关系的情况下，以同一个品牌形象面对消费者，以共同进货为纽带开展的连锁经营形式。

5．社会消费品零售总额

社会消费品零售总额 指企业（单位、个体户）通过交易直接售给个人、社会集团非生产、非经营用的实物商品金额，以及提供餐饮服务所取得的收入金额。个人包括城乡居民和入境人员，社会集团包括机关、社会团体、部队、学校、企事业单位、居委会或村委会等。

二、对外经济贸易和旅游部分

（一）货物贸易

1．主要内容：包括进出口货物的品种、数(重)量、金额、国别（地区）、收发货人所在地、境内目的地、境内货源地、贸易方式等项目。

2．统计范围：货物贸易统计范围是按照联合国国际商品（货物）贸易统计原则制定的，即凡是引起中华人民共和国关境内物质资源存量增加或减少的进出口货物（除制度另有规定者外）均列入该项统计。

3．资料来源：货物贸易统计资料来源于海关总署，调查方法是全面调查，统计原始资料是海关确认的《中华人民共和国海关进口货物报关单》、《中华人民共和国海关出口货物报关单》以及其他申报单证。

4．商品分类：进出口商品目录是在海关合作理事会（世界海关组织 WCO）制定的《商品名称和编码协调制度》（HS）的基础上，结合我国进出口实际情况制定的。历年出口商品分类金额和历年进口商品分类金额按照联合国《国际贸易标准分类》（SITC）进行统计。

5．货物进出口国家（地区）：进口货物统计原产国（地区），出口货物统计最终目的地国（地区）。原产国（地区）是指进口货物生产、开采或加工制造的国家（地区），对经过两个以上国家（地区）加工制造的进口货物，则以最后一个对货物进行经济上可以视为实质性加工的国家（地区）作为该货物的原产国，原产国确实不详时，按“国别不详”统计；最终目的地国（地区）是指出口货物已知的消费、使用或进一步加工制造国家（地区），包括直接使用或进行加工的国家（地区），最终目的地国（地区）不能确定时，按货物出口时尽可能预知的最后运往国（地区）统计。

6．主要指标解释

货物进出口总额 指实际进出我国关境的货物总金额。包括对外贸易实际进出口货物，来料加工装配进出口货物，国家间、联合国及国际组织无偿援助物资和赠送品，华侨、港澳台同胞和外籍华人捐赠品，租赁期满归承租人所有的租赁货物，进料加工进出口货物，边境地方贸易及边境地区小额贸易进出口货物，中外合资企业、中外合作经营企业、外商独资经营企业进出口货物和公用物品，到、离岸价格在规定限额以上的进出口货样和广告品（无商业价值、无使用价值和免费提供出口的除外），从保税仓库提取在中国境内销售的进口货物，以及其他进出口货物。该指标用以观察一个国家在对外贸易方面的总规模。我国规定出口货物按离岸价格统计，进口货物按到岸价格统计。

商品收发货人所在地进、出口额 指在所在地海关注册登记的有进出口经营权的企业实际进、出口额。

（二）服务进出口

1．资料来源：服务进出口按国际收支口径统计，资料来源于商务部。

2．主要指标解释

服务进出口 指常住单位与非常住单位之间相互提供的服务。包括运输，旅行，建筑，保险服务，金融服务，电信计算机和信息服务，知识产权使用费，个人、文化和娱乐服务，维护和维修服务，加工服务，其他商业服务，政府服务。

（三）利用外资

1．主要内容：包括外商直接投资和外商其他投资、外商投资企业登记注册情况。

2．统计范围：凡经工商行政管理机关核准登记，在中华人民共和国境内所有利用外资的单位和部门，经批准设立的中外合资经营企业、合作经营企业、外资企业、外商投资股份制企业、合作开发项目等具有法人资格的独立核算企业（包括港澳台地区投资企业），在境内从事经营活动的外国及港澳台地区企业及外国公司在中国境内设立的分支机构。

3．资料来源：利用外资统计资料来源于商务部，其中，外商投资企业的登记注册情况资料来源于国家工商行政管理总局，调查方法是全面调查。说明的是：利用外资统计 1985 年及以前为政府统计部门的调查汇总数，1986 年及以后全部来源于对外贸易经济合作部（现为商务部）。2000 年以后利用外资统计中不含对外借款数。

4．主要指标解释

外商投资 指我国政府、部门、企业和其它经济组织通过吸收外商直接投资以及其它方式筹措的境外现汇、技术、设备等。

批准企业（项目）个数 指外商直接投资管理部门批准设立的外商投资企业个数、批准的合作开发项目个数。

利用外资的国家（地区） 指外资来源或投资者的法人注册地所在的国家和地区。除政府贷款按贷款国家名称统计外，其它方式吸收的外资按外国公司、企业或其它经济组织以其法人的注册所在地国家（地区）统计。

实际使用外资金额 指批准的合同外资金额的实际执行数，外国投资者根据批准外商投资企业的合同（章程）的规定实际缴付的出资额和企业投资总额内外国投资者以自己的境外自有资金实际直接向企业提供的贷款。

（四）对外投资和经济合作

1．主要内容：包括对外直接投资、对外承包工程的合同数、合同金额、完成营业额，按国别、地区分的对外经济合作完成营业额和对外劳务合作派出劳务人数、期末在外人数等。

2．**统计范围**：对外直接投资、对外承包工程和对外劳务合作。该制度统计单位是经各级商务主管部门批准的从事对外承包和劳务合作业务并具有法人地位的对外承包劳务企业。

3．**资料来源**：对外投资和经济合作统计资料来源于商务部，调查方法是全面调查。需要说明的是，自2009年起，对外承包工程涵盖了对外设计咨询业务，对外设计咨询不再单独列出。

4．**主要指标解释**

对外直接投资 指我国企业、团体等（简称境内投资主体）在国外及港澳台地区的现金、实物、无形资产等方式投资，并以控制国（境）外企业的经营管理权为核心的经济活动。

对外承包工程 根据《对外承包工程管理条例》，对外承包工程是指中国的企业或者其他单位承包境外建设工程项目的活动。

对外劳务合作 指组织劳务人员赴其他国家或地区为国外的企业或机构工作的经营性活动。

完成营业额 指企业在报告期内完成的以货币形式表现的工作量。

派出人数 指企业在报告期内派往国（境）外执行对外承包工程和劳务合作项目的人数。

（五）旅游

1．**主要内容**：包括旅行社、星级饭店基本情况，入境、出境旅游人数、国内居民旅游人数，以及国际、国内旅游收入等。

2．**统计范围**：旅行社、星级饭店和游客。

3．**资料来源**：旅游业有关资料主要根据公安部、文化和旅游部的资料编制而成。旅游数据中的国际、国内旅游收入和国内出游人数等指标采取抽样调查方法，其余数据均为全面调查统计取得。

4．**指标解释**

游客 指任何为休闲、娱乐、观光、度假、探亲访友、就医疗养、购物、参加会议或从事经济、文化、体育、宗教活动，离开常住国（或常住地）到其他国家（或地方），其连续停留时间不超过12个月，并且在其他国家（或其他地方）的主要目的不是通过所从事的活动获取报酬的人。游客不包括因工作或学习在两地有规律往返的人，按出游时间分为旅游者（过夜游客）和一日游游客（不过夜游客）。

入境游客 指报告期内来中国（大陆）观光、度假、探亲访友、就医疗养、购物、参加会议或从事经济、文化、体育、宗教活动的外国人、港澳台同胞等游客（即入境旅游人数）。统计时，入境游客按每入境一次统计1人次。入境旅游人数包括入境（过夜）游客和入境一日游游客。

国内游客 指报告期内在中国（大陆)观光游览、度假、探亲访友、就医疗养、购物、参加会议或从事经济、文化、体育、宗教活动的中国（大陆）居民，其出游的目的不是通过所从事的活动谋取报酬。统计时，国内游客按每出游一次统计1人次。

出境人数（出境游客） 指中国（大陆）公民因公或因私出境前往其他国家、中国香港特别行政区、澳门特别行政区和台湾省观光、度假、探亲访友、就医疗养、购物、参加会议或从事经济、文化、体育、宗教活动的人数（即出境游客）。统计时，出境游客按每出境一次统计1人次。

旅游收入 指游客（入境游客和国内游客）在旅游过程中（由游客或游客的代表为游客）支付的一切旅游支出就是国家（省、区、市)的旅游收入。旅游支出应包括（过夜）旅游者和一日游游客在整个游程中行、游、住、食、购、娱，以及为亲友、家人购买纪念品、礼品等方面的旅游支出，不包括为商业目的购物、购买房、地、车、船等资本性或交易性的投资、馈赠亲友的现金及给公共机构的捐赠。旅游收入包括国际旅游收入和国内旅游收入。

（1）国际旅游收入指入境旅游者在中国（大陆）境内旅行、游览过程中用于交通、参观游览、住宿、餐饮、购物、娱乐等全部花费。

（2）国内旅游收入指国内旅游者在国内旅行、游览过程中用于交通、参观游览、住宿、餐饮、购物、娱乐等全部花费。

（六）其他

1．国际收支平衡表：由国家外汇管理局依据国际货币基金组织编写的《国际收支和国际投资头寸手册》（第六版）编制。

2．历年人民币对美元、日元、港币的年平均汇价：资料来源于国家外汇管理局。

3．黄金和国家外汇储备：资料来源于国家外汇管理局。

APPENDIX Ⅰ　Brief Introduction and Explanatory Notes on Main Statistical Indicators

Domestic Trade

Ⅰ　Main Content

Data reflect the development and change of China's domestic consumer goods market, wholesale and retail trades, hotels and catering services. Main contents include basic condition, circulation of commodities and financial status of wholesale and retail trades above designated size; basic condition, business and financial status of hotels and catering services above designated size; total retail sales of consumer goods; turnover of huge commodity exchange markets; development of chain stores of retail trades and catering service, etc.

Ⅱ　Coverage of Statistics

1. Wholesale and retail trades, hotels and catering services: corporation enterprises, establishments and getihus of wholesale and retail trades, hotels and catering services above the designated size.

The designated size of wholesale and retail trades, hotels and catering services is defined as follows: wholesale trade, with annual revenue from principal business over 20 million yuan; retail trade, with annual revenue from principle business over 5 million yuan; hotels and catering services, with annual revenue from principal business over 2 million yuan.

2. Total retail sales of consumer goods: corporation enterprises, establishments and getihus engaged in commodity retail activities or providing catering services.

3. Commodity exchange markets: the commodity markets with an annual transaction over 100 million.

4. Chain stores: Chain stores of retail trades and catering services.

Ⅲ　Sources of Data

Data are collected and processed in accordance with the statistical reporting scheme on wholesale and retail trades, hotels and catering services by the Department of Trade and External Economic Relations of the National Bureau of Statistics.

Ⅳ　Survey Methodology

Data of all enterprises of wholesale and retail trades, hotels and catering services above the designated size (Including corporation enterprises, establishments and getihus, the same below), commodity exchange markets and chain head stores (headquarter) are collected through comprehensive reporting systems. Data of enterprises below the designated size are according to sampling surveys.

Ⅴ　Explanatory Notes on Main Statistical Indicators

1. Wholesale and Retail Trades

Wholesale Trade refers to the activities of selling wholesale commodities for daily use and capital goods to enterprises of wholesale and retail trades (including self-employed individuals) and other enterprises, institutions and government organs and organizations, and the activities of engaging in import and export and acting as a trade agent. The wholesaler may have the ownership of commodities for wholesale and trade in the name of its own (a company), and the wholesaler can act as commission agent or commodity broker without the ownership of commodities. Also included are the wholesale activities at the fixed stalls in wholesale market and the acquisition for sales purpose.

Retail Trade refers to the activities of department store, supermarket, franchised store, brand store, retail stall and on-the-spot-making-selling store selling commodities to the final consumers (residents) by any means including internet, post, telephone, sales machine. It also includes shops with sales and production located in the same places (such as bakeries). Retail trade excludes the activities of sales of capital goods such as grain, seed, feed, livestock, mineral products, raw material for production, industrial chemicals, chemical products for agricultural use, machine and equipment (excluding vehicles, computers and communication equipment). Most retailers have the ownership of commodities to sell, but some are acting as agent or brokers to make transactions for a commission. According to the sales channels, retail trade can be divided into store retail and non-store retail, among which store retail is divided into comprehensive retail and special retail.

Total Purchases of Commodities refers to the total value of purchases of commodities by enterprises (establishments) from other establishments or individuals (including direct import from abroad) for the purpose of re-selling, either with or without further processing of the commodities purchased(including VAT).This indicator reflects the total value of goods purchased by the wholesale and retail industries from domestic and foreign markets.

The commodities include: (1) commodities purchased from agricultural and industrial producer, wholesaler, retailer, publishing house and other service business; (2) commodities purchased from institutions and government departments; (3) confiscated goods purchased from the customs authorities or market management agencies; (4) second-hand goods and wastes purchased from residents.

The commodities exclude: (1) commodities purchased by enterprises (establishments) for use in their own business operation, commodities obtained without buying or selling procedures such as materials, consumable goods of low value, office appliances, etc;(2) received goods without trading, such as goods handed over from others, borrowed goods, preserved goods for others, donated goods from others, processed and retrieved goods, etc;(3)goods of direct settlement between buyer and seller with handling fees introduced by others; (4)goods returned or refused to pay by the buyer;(5)excessive goods.(6) commodities of futures trading.

Total Sales of Commodities refers to the value of commodities sold by the establishments to other establishments and individuals (including goods sold for self consumption, including the value-added tax).In the wholesale and retail trades, this indicator is reflected the total value of the commodities sold in the domestic market and exported to abroad.

The commodities include: (1) commodities sold to individuals and social groups for their consumption; (2) commodities sold to establishments in all industries for their production and operation, including agriculture, industry, construction, transportation, post and telecommunications, catering services, and public utility including commodities sold to wholesale and retail establishments for re-selling, with or without further processing; (3) commodities for direct export to abroad.

The commodities exclude: (1) extended commodities without trading, such as goods handed over to other enterprises and institutions because of the change of organizations, lent goods, returned goods preserved for others, extended processing materials and samples donated to others; (2) goods sold by the promotion coupons that are not included in the operating income; (3) goods of direct settlement between buyer and seller with handling fees introduced by others; (4) sales of prepaid cards for goods that have not undergone ownership transfer, such as fuel cards; (5) service economic activities such as vehicle maintenance and telephone card sales; (6) goods returned after purchase; (7) damaged and spoiled goods; (8) waste and used goods of self use; (9) commodities of futures trading; (10) water, electricity and gas provided by water supply enterprises, power companies and natural gas supply enterprises.

Total Stock of Commodities For the legal entities and self-employed individuals engaged in wholesale and retail trade, it refers to total value (including VAT) of commodities possessed at the end of the reference period; and for wholesale and retail establishments, it refers to the value (including VAT) of all commodities actually in stock and owned by their legal person at the end of reference period. This indicator reflects the inventory of goods in the wholesale and retail industries, as well as the degree of assurance of the supply of goods in the market.

The stock commodities include: (1)commodities located in storage, garages, counters, and shelves of operating places (such as sale stores, wholesale centres, and operating offices); (2) commodities in the process of being selected, sorted, and packed; (3) commodities not arrived but recorded as purchase in the account, i.e. commodities not arrived but payment receipts for the commodities from the sellers or the banks arrived; (4)commodities deposited in other places rather than places mentioned above, for instance: commodities in the hold of purchasers temporarily due to the refusal of payment and commodities not taken back after going through the formalities; (5) commodities entrusted to other units to sell but not sold yet; (6) commodities purchased for other units but not delivered yet.

The commodities exclude: (1) commodities not owned by the enterprises (units), such as goods that have been sold but not taken by the buyer; commodities on commission for keeping, transporting, and processing; unsold commodities that sold for other units (not purchased or adjusted); (2) commodities processed by the commissioned external unit(including finished productions, processed by owned plants and other plants, that have not been delivered).(3) commodities purchased by agent of foreign trade enterprises that have not been delivered to the ordering unit; (4) commodities that are put in stock on behalf of the state material reserves units.

2. Hotel Services and Catering Services

Hotel Services refer to the short-term accommodation services provided to visitors. Some units may provide only accommodation while others provide a combination of accommodation, meals business services and/or recreational facilities. It excludes activities related to the provision of long-term primary residences in facilities such as apartments typically leased on a monthly or annual basis.

Catering Services refer to the activities of providing foods, serving locations and facilities to customers through instant processing, commercial sales and service-type labor.

Business Revenue refers to the total revenue (including VAT) of hotels and catering services received from providing services or selling commodities through operating activities, including income from hotels, from catering services, from selling of commodities and from other services, for example, business service. Excluded are the income from meals, merchandise sales and other items of the industrial activity unit affiliated to the multi-industry legal person enterprise.

Income from hotels refers to the income (including VAT) of enterprises and establishments engaged in hotel and catering services by providing lodging services. Excluding the income of other industrial activity units affiliated with multi-industry corporations.

Income from catering services refers to income (including VAT) of enterprises and establishments engaged in hotel and catering services by providing catering services. Including selling of cooked or prepared foods, such as staple food, cooked dishes, or cold dishes. Excluding the income of other industrial activity units affiliated with multi-industry corporations.

3. Commodity Exchange Markets

The commodity Exchange markets refers to the markets approved and managed by related departments, where there are fixed sites, facilities, managers and administration offices, where there are a certain number of traders to operate for three month and above or all the year, where the commodities including the articles for daily consumption and capital goods and services are traded in a centralized, independent and open way., Such market includes markets of daily goods and market of capital goods, etc.

Volume of Transaction in Commidity Trading Market refers to total annual commodity transaction volume of all stores and shops in the market.

4. Chain stores

Chain Head Stores (headquarter) refers to the core leading stores responsible for development, allocation, administration and unitization of resources (name of stores, goodwill, operation model, service standard, management way, ect.) of chain stores. Chain stores refers to the stores engaged in providing homogeneous commodities or services, with the central leadership of head store and guided by common policies, conduct centralized purchase and distributed selling of commodities, in order to gain better efficiency through standardized operation. The chain stores include regular chain stores, franchise chain stores and voluntary chain stores.

Regular Chain store refers to chain stores that are invested or controlled by the headquarters. They operate under direct and unified management from the headquarters.

Franchise chain store refers to the chain stores (franchisees) which are franchised with operation resources such as trade marks, names, patent and operation know-how by the franchisors in form of contract and pay the operation fees to the franchisors.

Voluntary chain store refers to the stores operate jointly on the voluntary bases while maintaining their status of independent legal entities with full ownership of their assets. They sell goods of same brand from same channel of resource to the consumers.

5. Total Retail Sales of Consumer Goods

Total retail sales of consumer goods refers to the revenue of non-productive, non-operating physical goods sold to individuals and social groups directly through transaction or the income of catering services provided by corporation enterprises (establishments, getihus). Individuals include urban and rural residents and persons entering the country. Social groups include government agencies, social organizations, army, schools, enterprises and institutions, neighborhood or village committee, etc.

Foreign Trade, External Economic Transaction and Tourism

I. Trade in Goods

1.Data on foreign trade include: varieties of imports and exports, amount (weight), value, countries (regions), consignee and shipper location, destination within territory, origin of goods within territory, mode of trade and so on.

2.The scope of trade in goods statistics: are designed according to United Nations' principles on international trade statistics, that is: all imports or exports that will lead to stock changes of material resources with the territory of People's Republic of China; excluding goods by escape clause.

3.Sources of data on trade in goods: are from the General Administration of Customs of the People's Republic of China through a comprehensive reporting system. Original data comes from *Customs Declaration for Import of the People's Republic of China*, *Customs Declaration for Export of the People's Republic of China*, and other declaration vouchers that are confirmed by customs.

4.Import and export commodity classification: the list of import and export commodities is compiled based on the *Harmonized Commodity Description and Coding System (HS)* stipulated by the Customs Cooperation Council (World Customs Organization) and China's reality of imports and exports. Customs statstics in value terms for both imports and exports are compiled according to the classifications of *UN Standard International Trade Classification (SITC).*

5. Trading partner: the country (region) of origin is recorded for imports while the country (region) of final destination for exports.

The country (region) of origin refers to the country or region where the import goods have been grown, mined or manufactured. If two or more countries (regions) were involved in the manufacture of the products, the place where the last substantial working or processing was carried out will be recorded as the country (region) of origin. However, commodities whose nature or states have not been substantially changed will not be considered as having been processed or remanufactured.

The country (region) of final destination refers to the country or region where the export goods are to be consumed, utilized or further processed or manufactured. In instance where the country of final destination can not be ascertained, the exports will be credited to the final country (region) dispatched to as known at the time of exportation.

6.Explanatory notes on main statistical indicators

Total Import and Export of Goods refer to the real value of commodities imported and exported across the border of China. They include the actual imports and exports through foreign trade, imported and exported goods under the processing and assembling trades and materials, supplies and gifts as aid given gratis between governments and by United Nations and other international organizations, and contributions donated by overseas

Chinese, compatriots in Hong Kong and Macao and Chinese with foreign citizenship, leasing commodities owned by tenant at the expiration of leasing period, the imported and exported commodities processed with imported materials, commodities trading in border areas, the imported and exported commodities and articles for public use of the Sino-foreign joint ventures, cooperative enterprises and ventures with sole foreign investment. Also included is import or export of samples and advertising goods for which CIF or FOB value are beyond the permitted ceiling (excluding goods of no trading or use value and free commodities for export), imported goods sold in china from bonded warehouses and other imported and exported goods. The indicator of the total imports and exports at customs can be used to observe the total size of external trade in a country. In accordance with the stipulation of the Chinese government, imports are calculated at CIF, while exports are calculated at FOB.

Import Export Value by Consignee and Shipper Location refers to actual value of imports and exports carried out by corporations which have been registered by the local Customs house and are vested with right to run import export business.

II. Imports and Exports in Services

1.Sources on imports and exports in services: statistics are compiles according to Balance of Payments (BOP) and from the Ministry of Commerce.

2. Explanatory notes on main statistical indicators

Imports and Exports in Services refers to services provided between resident and non-resident units, including transportation, travel, construction, insurance, finance, telecommunications, computer and informations, technology, professional and management consultancy, intellectual property fee, individual, culture and recreation, maintenance and repair, and other services, but excluding government service.

III. Foreign Capitals

1.Data on foreign capitals include: foreign direct investments and other foreign investments, and the basic condition of registration of foreign funded enterprises.

2.The scope of foreign capitals: all the units and departments which have utilized foreign capital and all the Sino-foreign joint ventures, Sino-foreign cooperative enterprises, ventures exclusively with foreign investment, foreign-funded stock companies, Sino-foreign cooperative development projects and other corporate enterprises (including the enterprises funded by the entrepreneurs from Hong Kong, Macao and Taiwan) with independent accounting system which have been approved by the Chinese government to set up in the boundary of the People's Republic of China.

3.Sources of data on foreign capitals: data on utilization of foreign capitals are from Ministry of Commerce, of which, data on basic condition of registration of foreign funded enterprises are from State Administration for Industry and Commerce through comprehensive reporting system. Special notice: data on utilization of foreign capitals before 1985 were survey results from governmental statistical agencies, since 1986 all data are from Ministry of Commerce (formerly MOFTEC). Data on utilization of foreign capitals since 2000 do not include foreign loans.

4.Explanatory notes on main statistical indicators

Utilization of foreign capital refers to direct foreign investments, commodity credits and other funds used by domestic institutions that are supplied from abroad and from Hong Kong, Macao and Taiwan.

Number of approval enterprises (projects) refers to the number of foreign-invested enterprises and cooperative development projects approved by the foreign direct investment management division.

Agreement number of utilization of foreign capital refers to the project numbers of the loans from the foreign governments and international monetary organization, the numbers of the enterprises with foreign investment and the contract numbers of the joint exploitation on offshore oil which are all approved according to law. The agreements of utilization of foreign capital, which are signed in other ways, are only collected into total amount without project numbers.

Country (region) of foreign capital refers to the country and region where the investor registers as a juridical Person and the foreign capital and investment comes. In the statistic classification, as the other ways in absorbing foreign investment, country (region) refers to the place where the foreign companies, enterprises and other economic organization register as juridical persons, except government loans just in terms of the name of the country.

Foreign capital actually used refers to the amount which has been actually used according to the agreements and contracts, including cash, materials and invisible capital such as labour service and technology which both parties agree to take as investment.

IV. Foreign Investment and Economic Cooperation

1.Data on foreign economic cooperation include: foreign direct investment, contracted projects, labour services cooperation, design and consultation services, contracted volume, complete business turnover, business turnover by countries (regions) and so on.

2.The scope of foreign economic cooperation: the statistics cover foreign direct investment, contracted projects, labour services cooperation and design & consultation service with foreign countries (regions). The statistical unit in the scheme is the corporate enterprise engaged in contracted projects and labour services cooperation with foreign countries and has been approved by the department of commerce at various levels.

3.Sources of data on foreign economic cooperation: data on foreign economic cooperation are from Ministry of Commerce through a comprehensive reporting system. Data on contracted projects include design & consultation service since 2009.

4.Explanatory notes on main statistical indicators

Foreign Direct Investment refers to foreign investment in China through the establishment of foreign invested enterprises, cooperative exploration and development of petroleum resources with domestic investors and the establishment of branch organizations of foreign enterprises. Foreign investment can be made in forms of cash, physical investment, intangible assets and equity, in addition with reinvestment of the foreign enterprises with the profits gained from the investment.

Overseas Contracted Projects refer to activities of contracting overseas construction projects by Chinese enterprises or any other units, which are stipulated in the *Regulations on Administration of Foreign Contracted Project.*

Overseas Labour Services refer to operational activities of organizing labour force to go abroad providing services to foreign enterprises or agencies.

Accomplished Turnover refers to the workload enterprises completed in the form of currency during the reporting period.

Dispatched Labor refers to the number of overseas labours in the overseas project contracting and labor cooperation businesses.

V. Tourism

1.Main Contents: the basic conditions of travel agencies and star-rated hotels; number of international tourists and Chinese residents going abroad, number of domestic tourists and income from international and domestic tourism.

2.Scope of Statistics: data in this chapter cover travel agencies, star-rated hotels and tourists.

3.Sources of Data: the data on tourism are from the Ministry of Public Security, the Ministry of Culture and Tourism. The data on tourism are from the comprehensive reporting form system except those on the earnings from international and domestic tourism and number of domestic tourists going abroad from sample surveys

4.Explanatory notes on main statistical indicators

Visitors refers to any person who travels to a country (or place) other than that of his or her residence for a period not exceeding 12 months for leisure, entertainment, sightseeing, holiday, visiting relatives or friends, medical care, shopping, meeting, or taking part in economic, cultural, sports or religious activities, where the main purpose of the travel is not for remuneration. A visitor does not refer to any person who commutes between two places regularly for career or education. According to the length of stay, visitors are classified as tourists (i.e., overnight visitors) and same day visitors (non overnight visitors).

International visitors (Inbound Visitor Arrivals) refer to foreigners or compatriots from Hong Kong, Macao and Taiwan who come to China within the reporting time frame for sightseeing, holiday, visiting friends and relatives, medical care, shopping, meeting, or taking part in economic, cultural, sports or religious activities. Each time of entry is recorded as one time of arrival, and the total sum makes up the inbound visitor arrivals. Inbound visitor arrivals (international visitors) include inbound (overnight) tourists and inbound same day visitors.

Domestic visitors refer to Chinese nationals who travel within the country within the reporting time frame for sightseeing, holiday, visiting friends and relatives, medical care, meeting, or taking part in economic, cultural, sports or religious activities. Their purposes of travel are not for remuneration from the activities afore mentioned. Each time of their travel is recorded as one person time. Domestic visitors include domestic (overnight) tourists and domestic same day visitors.

Outbound visitors refer to a Chinese (mainland) citizen who departs from China to a foreign country (or region) for leisure, entertainment, sightseeing, holiday, visiting relatives or friends, medical care, shopping, meeting, or taking part in economic, cultural, sports or religious activities. Each time of departure is recorded as one person time. Outbound visitors include outbound (overnight) tourists and outbound same day visitors.

Tourism receipts refer to all the expenditures made by visitors (inbound visitors and domestic visitors) or by representatives of the visitors in the course of their travel constitute the tourism receipts of a country (province, region, city). Tourism expenditures of visitors should include expenses made by (overnight) tourists and same day visitors throughout their travel on transport, tours, lodging, food, shopping, entertainment, and souvenirs and gifts for friends and relatives. Tourism expenditures do not include purchases of goods, real estate, house, motor vehicle, water vessel for commercial purposes, neither include capital nor transactional investments, cash given to friends and relatives, donations to public organizations. Tourism receipts include international tourism receipts and domestic tourism receipts.

1) International Tourism Receipts refer to the total expenditure made by inbound tourists within the territory of China (the mainland) in their course of travel on transport, tours and sightseeing, lodging, food and beverage, shopping, entertainment and etc.

2) Domestic Tourism Receipts refer to the total expenditure made by domestic tourists within the territory of China (the mainland) in their course of travel on transport, tours and sightseeing, lodging, food and beverage, shopping, entertainment and etc.

VI. Others

1.The Balance of Payments Table is compiled by the State Administration of Foreign Exchange in accordance with the 6th edition of the *Balance of Payments and International Investment Position. Manual (BPM6)* prepared by the International Monetary Fund.

2.The average exchange rates of RMB yuan to US dollar, Japanese yen and Hong Kong dollar over the years come from the State Administration of Foreign Exchange.

3. The data on gold and foreign exchange reserves are also from the State Administration of Foreign Exchange.

附录Ⅱ　英文缩略语及符号

APPENDIX Ⅱ　Abbreviations and Symbols in English

APEC	Asia-Pacific Economic Cooperation
ASEAN	Association of Southeast Asian Nations
Co, Ltd	Corporation Limited
Corp	Corporation
DPR	Democratic People's Republic
EU	European Union
FR	Federal Republic
IMF	International Monetary Fund
Is	Islands
No	Number of items
Prov	Province
RMB	Renminbi Yuan
SDR	Special Drawing Rights
USD	Dollar of United States of America
USSR	Union of Soviet Socialist Republics